Intervention Planning for Adults with Communication Problems: A Guide for Clinical Practicum and Professional Practice

Harriet B. Klein
New York University

Nelson Moses
Long Island University

Allyn and Bacon

Boston • London • Toronto • Sydney • Tokyo • Singapore

Vice president: Sean Wakely
Series editor: Steve Dragin
Marketing manager: Ellen Mann Dolberg/Brad Parkins
Composition and prepress buyer: Linda Cox
Manufacturing buyer: Dave Repetto
Cover administrator: Jenny Hart
Editorial-production service: Shepherd, Inc.
Electronic composition: Shepherd, Inc.

Copyright © 1999 by Allyn & Bacon
A Viacom Company
Needham Heights, MA 02194

Internet: www.abacon.com

Library of Congress Cataloging-in-Publication Data

Klein, Harriet B.
     Intervention planning for adults with communication problems : a
guide for clinical practicum and professional practice / Harriet B.
Klein, Nelson Moses.
         p.   cm.
     Includes bibliographical references and index.
     ISBN 0-205-17385-3
     1. Communicative disorders—Treatment.   2. Communicative
disorders—Patients—Rehabilitation.   3. Medical protocols.
I. Moses, Nelson.   II. Title.
     [DNLM: 1. Language Disorders—therapy.   2. Speech Disorders-
-therapy.   WL 340.2K64i 1999]
RC423.K57   1999
616.85'506—dc21
DNLM/DLC
for Library of Congress   98-34776
                                                           CIP

Printed in the United States of America

10 9 8 7 6 5 4 3 2 1   03 02 01 00 99 98

Dedication:
To my grandsons, Benjamin, Jonah, and David, who are my constant
reminders of the wonders of communication
—Harriet B. Klein

To my nieces, Joanna and Abigail, who know that when you put pennies
in milk you get "coin flakes," and to my wife and partner, Sandra
—Nelson Moses

CONTENTS

11   Intervention Planning for Second Language Phonology   348

PREFACE

We view this second volume on intervention planning in speech-language pathology as a natural and necessary companion to our first volume—*Intervention Planning for Children with Communication Disorders: A Guide to Clinical Practicum and Professional Practice*. Students completing coursework for certification by the American Speech-Language-Hearing Association are required to accrue practicum hours in assessment and intervention with adult clients.

As with our first volume, this book is directed at answering the question typically asked by our practicum students in speech-language pathology—"What should I do first?" Here too, we engage students in a problem-solving, decision-making process in selected areas of intervention: aphasia and related disorders, motor-speech disorders, language-learning disabilities in adults, fluency disorders, voice disorder, and bidialectal/bicultural phonological differences. We guide students in the derivation of intervention goals and procedures, moving from the development of long-term goals and procedural approaches to specific session goals and procedures.

In reviewing the literature we found little published material that addressed students' need for information about intervention planning for adults. We believe that our book fulfills this need. Clinical decision making for adult clients involves management of complex information. The current thinking is that speech and language disorders in children typically involve an interaction among semantic, syntactic, phonologic, and pragmatic components. This is also true for adults but it is not explicitly addressed in current texts on intervention planning. In addition, impaired speech and language performance may rest on the relationship between linguistic and nonlinguistic behavioral systems such as cognitive, sensorimotor, and psychosocial. This aspect, as well, is not addressed in any intervention-planning text. Thus, it is clear to us that there exists a need in the field of speech-language pathology for a book that deals with problem solving and decision making in intervention planning for adults. This book stresses the importance of understanding general principles underlying the formulation of an intervention plan. It includes information on how to make management decisions at three major points in the intervention process, regardless of speech-language disorder type and severity. To facilitate decision making with adult clients, this text provides a comprehensive body of information about normal communication performance throughout the various phases of adulthood. In addition, information is presented about cognitive, sensorimotor, and psychosocial functioning—areas that may contribute to communication problems in adults. With a view toward theory guiding practice, readers are introduced to theories of learning and rehabilitation that apply to the treatment of adult communication problems. This text is clinically and practically oriented, containing numerous examples of the application of our model of intervention planning to specific speech-language disorder types and levels of severity.

Chapters 1–6 present an overview of the intervention-planning process, including general sources of information that guide intervention planning. Chapters 1 and 2 introduce the three phases of intervention planning: (a) developing long-term goals and a general procedural approach, (b) identifying short-term goals and a delimited procedural approach, and (c) developing session goals and procedures. Issues that must be addressed at each phase of the process are specified. These include: clinician's conceptual framework, baseline data, factors maintaining communication disorders, and theories of learning and rehabilitation. Chapters 3 and 4 present an in-depth presentation of information on normal language functioning from early adulthood to the geriatric period of life. This information on language is presented within the framework of content, form, and use. The discussion of normal adult functioning is extended to the cognitive, sensorimotor, and psychosocial domains in Chapter 5. Chapter 6 introduces several theories of learning and rehabilitation that are used to guide goal setting and procedure planning at each phase of the intervention-planning process.

Chapters 7 through 11 may be seen as the second major unit of the book. Here, the model of intervention planning presented in chapters 1–6 is applied to adults with various types of communication problems, as well as second language learning. Chapters 7–10 deal with four types of communication problems that are typically encountered in adult clients: language-learning disabilities, aphasia and related disorders of language, voice disorders, and disorders of fluency. Chapter 11 addresses an area of intervention that is presently receiving much attention within the profession: bidialectal/bicultural phonological differences. Each of these five chapters is organized similarly to demonstrate how a fundamental decision-making process applies across various communication problems. Each chapter is divided into two sections. The first section details the sources of information that need to be referenced to make decisions at the three phases of intervention planning: (a) information about normal or expected performance in the specific area of communication under consideration, (b) a consideration of factors that may influence performance during treatment, and (c) principles from theories of learning and rehabilitation that apply to the specific area of communication. In the second section of these five chapters, a case study is presented. These case studies, based on actual clients, illustrate the intervention-planning process. We demonstrate the way an array of assessment data are used to derive long-term, short-term, and session goals and procedures. Two additional components of intervention planning—collaboration with allied professionals and family involvement—are addressed within these chapters.

Joining the primary authors of this text are three speech-language pathologists with extensive clinical, research, and teaching expertise in the treatment of adult communication problems. Celia Stewart illustrates the application the intervention-planning model to adults with aphasia. Stephen Cavallo applies the model to adults with voice disorders. David Shapiro demonstrates the usefulness of this approach to intervention planning with fluency disorders.

The book is intended to be used as a primary text in second- or third-term clinical practicum courses at upper undergraduate and graduate levels. It is designed to be a companion text to our first book: *Intervention Planning for Children with Communication Disorders: A Guide to Clinical Practicum and Professional Practice.* Both texts could be used by students across all practicum courses and may be used as guides throughout the clinician's professional career. The content of this book presumes some basic coursework in speech and language acquisition, communication disorders in adults, and diagnostics.

ACKNOWLEDGMENTS

We would like to thank the many people who have contributed to the writing of this book. First, we extend our thanks to the students from New York University and Long Island University who have been a major impetus for this writing. Our students continually asked questions about normal adult behavior and communication disorders in adults not covered in our first book targeting children, *Intervention Planning for Children with Communication Disorders: A Guide to Clinical Practicum and Professional Practice.* We also thank our students for their questions, comments, and suggestions about earlier drafts. Special thanks go those students who contributed research time and editorial assistence: from NYU, Angela Vitagliano, Ira Kittrell, May Liu, Jasodhara Paruchuru, Heidi Owen; from LIU, Bonnie Moss who provided invaluable insight into decontextualization and narratives. We also thank Brenda Lyons who was always ready to facilitate the technical preparation of the manuscript (student assistance and emergency computer repair).

We also thank our colleagues who have contributed essential chapters to this book: Stephen Cavallo for his extension of our model of intervention planning to voice disorders in adults; to David Shapiro for his chapter on planning intervention for individuals who stutter; and to Celia Stewart for her application of our model to planning intervention for patients with aphasia. We thank Laura Koenig for her help with the voice figures.

We appreciate the constant support and encouragement of our editor Steven Dragin and the careful critiques of the reviewers for Allyn & Baccon.

We are deeply grateful to our spouses and families for tolerating yet another energy- and time-consuming project.

Last, we would like to thank each other for a stimulating and enjoyable collaboration. Our collaboration represents an equal partnership, with the order of names merely alphabetical.

1 Introduction to the Intervention-Planning Process with Adults

CHAPTER OUTCOMES

The reader will:

1. identify the parameters of adulthood;
2. define goals and procedures;
3. identify the major sources of information used for the development of goals and procedures.

Planning interventions for communication problems is a challenging process, regardless of the age of the client. Klein and Moses (1999), writing about children with communication disorders, identified two reasons why intervention planning in speech-language pathology is so complex and challenging. First, clinical interactions are often unpredictable. One never knows exactly how a client will respond to session plans. Second, a great deal of information must be considered when developing treatment plans. Although these points were initially raised with reference to intervention planning for children, they apply to the adult population as well.

As clinical supervisors, we have found that unpredictability is especially disconcerting for novice clinicians. When beginning-practicum students are asked about their concerns in treating an adult client, their responses generally center around having enough to do during the session. You can always play another game with a child, but what can you do with an adult client (maybe one who is older than you) who finishes all you have prepared, 25 minutes before the end of the session? Another concern is the possibility of not being able to answer a client's question about treatment. Do you call on your supervisor for help?

The veritable mountain of information that must be considered when developing a treatment plan for a client with communication problems is also disconcerting to student clinicians. We can only glimpse this enormous amount of information when we try to answer three questions fundamental to intervention planning: (a) What are the linguistic components (semantics, syntax, phonology, pragmatics) and nonlinguistic behavioral systems (cognition, sensorimotor, psychosocial) that may be implicated in the communication problem; (b) what are the mechanisms underlying learning and rehabilitation that need to be addressed in treatment procedures; (c) what are the norms of adult communication that can be used to gauge the appropriateness of goals of intervention? Interestingly, speech-language clinicians often look to prefabricated cookbook therapies to circumvent uncertainty (and, perhaps, to avoid being overwhelmed by too much information). Experience teaches, however, that the more systematically one approaches the second challenge—addressing the variables implicated in a particular communication problem—the better one is equipped as a clinician to anticipate common problems that arise during a session and to resolve unexpected difficulties.

The process of intervention planning in speech-language pathology was originally examined in detail in the context of children with communication disorders (Klein & Moses, 1999). Intervention planning with adults raises issues unique to the characteristics of this population. These issues are explored here, first in general and then in the context of intervention planning for a representative set of communication problems that are typically encountered in adult clients: specifically, language-learning disabilities, aphasia, voice, fluency, and phonological patterns associated with second language (L2) learning. In this first chapter we define adulthood, intervention goals and procedures and the fundamental sources of information that contribute to the development of goals and procedures for treating communication problems in an adult population.

The Adult Client

Who Is an Adult?

According to Jewish law, a boy becomes a man at age 13 years 1 day, an event celebrated by the Bar Mitzvah. A girl becomes a woman at 12 years 1 day, and may also have a nice *Bas* Mitzvah. By way of contrast, when the males of the primitive Dieri of southeast Australia reached puberty, they were required to undergo a "ritual death" in order to "rise or be reborn as men" (Noss & Noss, 1984, p. 24). Within the secular domain, adulthood is ushered in at a later age.

According to *Webster's New World Dictionary* (1980), an adult is a "man or a woman who has reached an age set by law that qualifies him for full legal rights, in common law, generally 21 years" (p. 19). This definition does not identify a particular age as marking adulthood. The legal age of adulthood varies according to legislative province. Individuals are given the right to vote, to marry without parental consent, and, in many states, to purchase liquor at the age of 18. However, according to state and federal law, parents continue to be financially responsible for their dependent offspring until the age of 21 (C. Lackenbach, personal communication, February 4, 1994). Legislation designed to assure civil rights and educational funding for people with handicapping conditions (e.g.,

PL 94-142, PL 101-476, PL105-17) maintains funding for children through the age of 20; this is tantamount to the heralding of adulthood at 21.

Influenced by the literature on human development, we identify the age of 18 as marking the entrance into adulthood. The age of 18 is often cited as the end of the developmental period in intellectual functioning (e.g., American Psychiatric Association, 1980; Grossman, 1973). Many clinicians no longer view the onset of speech or language disorders after the age of 18 as developmental (e.g., Shriberg & Kwiatkowski, 1982).

We do not necessarily believe that development in all areas stops at age 18. However, treatment of speech and language disorders after the age of 18 raises questions that are not encountered in the treatment of developmental disorders of childhood. These questions are about (a) sources of information available for goal planning and sequencing goals, (b) theories of learning and rehabilitation that apply to the acquisition of language after the age of 18, and (c) the effects social and vocational environments have on language functioning. Consequently, although the boundary between childhood and adulthood should not be viewed as rigid, for the discussion in this book, adulthood is ushered in at 18.

Components of Intervention Planning for Adults

Goals and Procedures

In some ways decision making for adult clients is similar to the process of intervention planning we described for children. Developing a management plan involves the formulation of goals and procedures across three phases of decision making. An *intervention goal* is a potential achievement by an individual with a communication problem directed toward the improvement of functional communication. An *intervention procedure* is the clinician's plan of action in which linguistic and nonlinguistic contexts are designed to facilitate the achievement of functional communication (see Klein & Moses, 1999). These definitions indicate that a goal refers to the client's behavior whereas a procedure refers to the clinician's actions to facilitate goal achievement. These definitions indicate further that the focus of intervention goals is *functional communication,* and the focus of procedure planning is the design of the therapeutic context—specifically, the linguistic context (i.e., the clinician's communication with the client) and nonlinguistic context (i.e., materials and activities).

A fundamental tenet of the intervention-planning model is that a basic decision-making process applies across disorder types. In accordance with this precept, core sources of information must be referenced and certain essential decisions made whenever planning treatment, regardless of the communication problem. In planning goals and procedures clinicians draw from four major categories of knowledge. These are knowledge of (a) the nature of functional communication in adults; (b) behavioral systems that maintain communication problems; (c) performance demands; (d) principles of learning and rehabilitation that account for how adults acquire new behaviors or reestablish previously learned behaviors.

Categories of Knowledge Utilized in Intervention Planning

Functional Communication

The first category of knowledge is the conceptualization of functional communication. The clinician must be able to define and describe the entity that needs change or modification. The definition and description of functional communication adopted for this book derives from two sources: the Functional Assessment of Communication Skills for Adults (ASHA FACS, Frattali, Thompson, Holland, Wohl, & Ferketic, 1995) and Bloom and Lahey's (1978) content, form, and use model of language (see also Lahey, 1988).

ASHA FACS.   ASHA recently developed the FACS—a tool to highlight "functional communication" as the focus of assessment and intervention with adults. ASHA FACS specifically:

> recognizes the importance of communication in natural (as opposed to clinical) contexts; accepts wholly that functional communication can occur in various ways, including verbal and nonverbal, or using a device or system; and emphasizes independence as well as effectiveness of communication (Frattali et al., 1995, p. 42).

With reference to intervention planning, we adapt the ASHA FACS definition of functional communication as follows: the ability to [systematically] receive [and] convey messages regardless of the mode, to communicate effectively and independently in natural environments. We inserted "systematically" in this definition to signify that communication systems are organized and rule based (Bateson, 1980; Watzlawick, Beavin, & Jackson, 1967).

Reference to *receiving and conveying messages* indicates a two-way *exchange of ideas* between two sender-receivers (Martin, 1981; Seiler, 1996). The emphasis here is on the exchange of ideas. Exchange implies a social context—to many, the raison d'etre of adult communication (e.g., Seiler, 1996). To others, the construction and expression of ideas (or "wonderful ideas" in the words of Duckworth, 1972) is the central, motivating force for communication in children (Bloom, 1991; Duckworth, 1972) and adults (Fosnot, 1990; Granott, 1994). Highlighting both social interaction and the expression of ideas captures the dual thrust that is at the heart of functional communication in adults (Bayles & Kaszniak, 1987; Granott, 1993). Returning to the definition, the expression "sender-receiver" emphasizes that all participants in a communication interaction both create messages and interpret messages (Martin, 1981; Seiler, 1996). Communicating effectively and independently in natural environments indicates that the communication act is expressed for an adaptive purpose or intent. The proviso "regardless of mode" suggests that the communication system may be verbal or nonverbal (e.g., by sign, by augmentative device).

Language As a Primary Vehicle for Functional Communication.   The definition of functional communication presented above presumes that language (oral, written, technologically augmented, etc.) is the primary vehicle for functional communication in adults. Our concept of language in adults derives from the work in child language of Bloom and Lahey (1978) and Lahey (1988). Before we define language from this perspective, we need to contextualize it with reference to more traditional approaches to adult language.

Traditionally, speech-language pathologists have viewed the language of adults within models implicit in tests of aphasia (e.g., Porch, 1967; Schuell, 1973). On the basis of these test formats, we can assume that the authors view language as comprising two major modalities: receptive and expressive. Within these modalities language skills are generally viewed in terms of complexity of information processing. Lower level processes traditionally identified are sensation, discrimination, and retention in the receptive modality, and recall and sequencing in the expressive modality. Higher level processes involve comprehension and formulation of language (Chapey, 1994; Nation & Aram, 1984).

The Bloom and Lahey (1978) approach to language, which we follow in this text, represents an alternative framework. Within this framework, language comprises three interactive components: content, form, and use. *Content* refers to the ideas about the world expressed in language. *Form* refers to the "code" or symbol system used to express ideas. Form includes the systems of phonology, morphology, and syntax. *Use* refers to the adaptive functions and pragmatic conventions of language (Chapey, 1986).

There are several "assumptions" about speech and language intervention with children intrinsic to the Bloom and Lahey framework (Lahey, 1988). These assumptions are as follows:

1. Intervention is "three dimensional"; that is, content, form, and use will be considered.
2. Language performance is the basis for evaluating and facilitating progress in any plan for language intervention.
3. The formulation of intervention goals is based on what is known about normal language development.
4. Goals target the language *production* as opposed to language comprehension.

In adapting the Bloom and Lahey model for adults, we incorporate some of the assumptions that apply to children but make certain adjustments in several others.

We adopt without modification the first two assumptions that intervention planning for communication problems must be three dimensional and that the long-term goals of intervention must target functional language performance. We modify the third assumption to read that the formulation of intervention goals should be based on what is known about normal communication and language functioning across the entire life span, including changes associated with aging. We make the greatest modification to the fourth assumption—that goals should relate to language production as opposed to language comprehension. In adults, we allow that goals may relate to comprehension as well as production. We stipulate, however, that long-term goals of comprehension, like production, must be situated within a *functional communicative context.*

Developmental Milestones and Intervention Planning with Adults: Delimitations. In the companion volume to the present book (Klein & Moses, 1999), the formation of intervention plans for children is approached from a developmental perspective. Decisions about goal sequences are made with reference to hierarchies of skills or behaviors that are normally attained by children at specific ages. Decisions about procedures are made with reference to a set of theories about how children attain developmental milestones. This is consistent with the adoption of Bloom and Lahey's (1978) definition of language. When planning goals for adults, however, age cannot be referenced as a marker for the achievement of particular skills and behaviors. Adulthood by definition is the completion of age-related developmental mile-stones, including the achievement of linguistic competence. It is commonly accepted that adults present a mature level of competence in syntax (Chomsky, 1957; Ellis & Beattie, 1986; Pinker, 1994), semantics (Brownell & Joanette, 1993), and pragmatics (Rees, 1978), and may also lose information-processing efficiency with aging (e.g., Davis & Ball, 1989; Au, Obler & Albert, 1991).

With adults, therefore, clinicians cannot set goals for the achievement of developmen-tal milestones as is typical with children. Instead, developmental milestones derived from studies of child language can be used with adults as indexes of behavioral complexity; such indexes may be useful for prioritizing goals for adults. We will discuss the derivation of goals and procedures with reference to expected norms of performance in adults in Chapters 6–10.

Learning and Development in Adulthood.   Although developmental milestones associ-ated with child language are completed by adulthood, adults can acquire additional knowledge and skills in all areas of language, and they may lose efficiency with aging (e.g. Au et al., 1991; Davis & Ball, 1989; Obler & Albert, 1980). Speech-language developments in adulthood are associated primarily with the particular paths one's adult life has taken. Adulthood implies that individuals must learn the pragmatic skills necessary to adapt their speech-language behavior to accommodate to the specific demands of different communicative contexts (e.g., vocational, social, familial, etc.). Adults must learn a lexicon and speech style suitable to the occupational and social choices they have made. Furthermore, it has been suggested that there are develop-mental changes in adult cognition that reflect the challenges inherent in individual life experi-ences (Fischer, 1980; Karmiloff-Smith, 1986; Moses, 1994; Moses & Shapiro, 1996). The absence of such cognitive growth may maintain speech-language problems. Since individuals continue to learn and develop across the lifespan, goals can be set for adults during interven-tion that represent novel skills and increased competence. Developmental processes affecting functional communication in adults, as well as areas of degeneration, will be discussed at some length in Chapters 3 and 4.

Summary.   Having defined functional communication and language, we have specified the nature of the behavioral system that should always be the focus of intervention in speech-language pathology. Moreover, by adopting the Bloom and Lahey (1978) approach to language, we are continually reminded of the interactive nature of the three compo-nents—content, form, and use—in goal and procedure planning across disorder types.

Factors That Maintain Communication and Language Problems

We assume that intervention planning for adult communication problems needs to address behaviors other than language that may be interfering with communication. We refer to inter-fering nonlinguistic behaviors as maintaining factors. The clinician's knowledge of potential maintaining factors constitutes the second category of information necessary for intervention planning. We identify three non-linguistic behavioral systems as influencing communication performance in adults: cognitive, psychosocial, and sensorimotor. Consequently, we assume that intervention planning for adult communication problems will address these behavioral systems to facilitate the achievement of goals. In subsequent chapters we will discuss each of these behavioral systems at length (Chapter 5) and present examples of how maintaining factors are considered during intervention planning (Chapters 7–11).

Performance Demands

A third source of knowledge that guides intervention planning concerns the challenge speech-language clinicians present to clients. These challenges are inherent in the communication tasks that are set as goals for the clients. These challenges, which we call "performance demands," reflect the inherent complexity and difficulty of tasks. The complexity of a task is an objective determination; complexity is based on the linguistic organization demanded by that task (e.g., the number of syntactic transformations, the feature contrasts implicated in the processing of two discrete phonemes, etc.). For example, producing a phrase with a relative clause such as, "The man who painted the house fell on the lawn," reflects a greater degree of linguistic organization than the sentence, "The man is painting the house." The former is objectively more complex than the latter (e.g., van Riemsdijk & Williams, 1986). Reading sentences aloud demands more complex physiologic integration of the subsystems of speech production (i.e., respiration, phonation, resonation, articulation) than phonating /a:/ for 10 seconds (e.g., Andrews, 1986).

Degrees of *complexity* may be contrasted with perceptions of *difficulty*. Ease or difficulty of a task depends, in part, on the information-processing characteristics, skills, and attitudes of an individual. When the degree of complexity is kept consistent, a particular act may be more difficult for one person than for another. For example, the production of a three-constituent phrase may be more difficult for a client with aphasia and dysarthria than one with aphasia alone. The degree of performance demand is, therefore, manipulated systematically when planning goals—especially session goals for a particular client. The factors that add to performance demands in specific areas of communication are discussed in the chapters (6–10) that examine specific instances of intervention planning. Next, we will introduce an additional critical source of information that must be considered when planning interventions for communication problems in adults: theories of learning and rehabilitation.

Theories of Learning and Rehabilitation

How adults learn represents the fourth area of knowledge that must be considered during intervention planning. When clinicians plan treatment for children they presume to be facilitating a naturally occurring language-learning process. Can this notion be applied to adults? Critical language-learning periods have been identified in the literature (Lenneberg & Lenneberg, 1975; Pinker, 1994). According to Pinker, "acquisition of normal language is guaranteed for children up to the age of six, is steadily compromised from then until shortly after puberty, and is rare thereafter" (p. 293). This signifies that a normally achieving adult who has achieved mature syntactic and phonologic patterns is no longer actively involved in the process of learning language. There are adults, however, who must be engaged in the improvement of communication skills. These may be individuals who are learning impaired and have not achieved mature linguistic skills. Others may have suffered disease or trauma rendering them communicatively impaired.

There are at least two ways to view the process of facilitating improved communication performance in adults. The first is that the clinician is helping the client learn novel communication skills. This would be assumed if the client had never demonstrated the skills being taught (e.g., in cases of language-learning disabilities, Moses, Klein, & Altman, 1989). A second point of view is that the clinician is helping the client access skills that are presently inaccessible (e.g., due to a neurological insult such as stroke), but still maintained somewhere in the client's system (e.g., Duffy, 1986; Martin, 1981). A related point of view is that information processing functions that support language, such as attention span or short-term memory, have been rendered inefficient following cerebral insult and that the job of language intervention is to improve efficiency by exercising these processes (e.g., Duffy, 1986).

To address communication improvement in adults, therefore, it is necessary to consider how adults learn novel aspects of language, reaccess language abilities that have been rendered inaccessible, improve information-processing skills, or compensate for language disability. Thus, intervention planning for adults requires consideration of principles of human learning and rehabilitation.

In the volume on intervention planning with children (Klein & Moses, 1999), principles of language learning are derived from four major learning theories: behavioral, social-cognitive, constructivist-cognitive, and motor. These theories have been applied to skill development in adults. The most commonly applied learning theory is operant or behavioral (e.g., Hegde, 1985; Leith, 1984; Lovaas, 1977). In addition, principles derived from social-cognitive (Chapey, 1994; Reid, 1988) and constructivist-cognitive (Moses et al., 1990) learning theories have been applied to the habilitation and rehabilitation of communication problems in adults. We intend to apply principles from the theories of learning and rehabilitation identified above to intervention planning with adults. These theories provide useful guidelines for the formulation of intervention procedures. An in-depth discussion of adult learning and rehabilitation will be undertaken in Chapter 5.

Additional Sources of Information

Related to the four major sources of information reviewed above is the information collected from the assessment of a particular client. This information emanates from *baseline data* and the *client's past history.*

Baseline Data.   Baseline data refers to information about a client's current linguistic functioning and performance in areas that may be maintaining a communication problem. Baseline data may derive from results of formal and informal testing, and background information gathered about the client (e.g., from client, family, and related service providers). Baseline data may be available in speech-language evaluations that lead to a referral for intervention. If not, the clinician responsible for intervention planning will be responsible for conducting an evaluation and gathering baseline data. This information is used at each phase of intervention planning.

Client's Premorbid History.   Client's premorbid history refers to information about the client before the onset of the current communication problem. This includes information about the individual's past performance in speech and language and the three categories of maintaining factors. Information about past history provides data for both goal and procedure planning. This information bears upon the identification of severity of involvement as well as potential for achievement. Information about premorbid status is most apparently valuable for clients who have sustained neurological insult or traumatic injury (e.g., stroke, head trauma, laryngectomy). It would be unreasonable to expect more of an individual than was typical before the communication problem arose.

With reference to planning goals, consider two clients who have undergone laryngectomies. Each may demonstrate different rates of improvement because of different past experiences. P., a successful and highly motivated real estate agent, who relied on her speech skills professionally, suffered a crushed larynx. Determined to resume her career, she quickly and efficiently became an outstanding esophageal speaker. Another individual who displayed less motivation and whose professional and personal demands on vocal production was minimal never fully achieved good esophageal speech.

Procedural planning may also be affected by the client's past history. Most significant would be the skills the client has acquired through his or her social and vocational experiences. The clinician may wish to reenact positive and familiar routines using strengths that were retained from the pretrauma period (playing a musical instrument, computer programming, gardening, architectural planning).

Information from Performance During Treatment. Sometimes additional information and ideas relevant to the emerging management plan are discovered during treatment. The clinician learns more about a client as a result of observing the client's reactions to specific treatment approaches. An example of information discovered during treatment comes from the case of Bernie, an adult with a learning disability. As a result of the evaluation, it was determined that this client needed to work on narrative organization. Because the client was a professional writer, it was assumed that he did not require perceptual support to organize verbal expression. Early in treatment, however, it became apparent that he needed a tangible referent, such as an outline of events, to relate them coherently. This added knowledge helped in planning more appropriate procedures.

Summary

In this chapter we identified functional communication as the target of speech-language intervention with adults. We also defined functional communication in a way that is consistent with the Bloom and Lahey content/form/use model of language and with ASHA's definition of functional communication for adult intervention planning. We identified maintaining factors, performance demands, theories of learning and rehabilitation, baseline data, a client's past history, and information garnered during treatment as sources of information that guide decision making (see Figure 1.1). It will become apparent in the next chapter how this information contributes to intervention planning for adults.

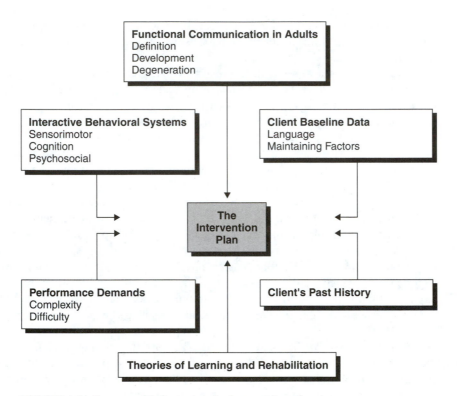

FIGURE 1.1   Sources of information for intervention planning.

REFERENCES

Andrews, M. (1986). *Voice therapy for children.* New York: Longman.

Au, R., Obler, L. K., & Albert, M. L. (1991). Language in aging and dementia. In M. Sarno, (Ed.), *Acquired aphasia* (2nd ed., pp. 405–423). New York: Academic Press.

Bateson, G. (1980). Mind and nature: A necessary unity. New York: Bantam.

Bayles, K. A., & Kaszniak, A. W. (1987). Communication and cognition in normal aging and dementia. Austin, TX: Pro-Ed.

Bloom, L. (1991). *Language development from two to three.* New York: Cambridge.

Bloom, L., & Lahey, M. (1978). Language development and language disorders. New York: Wiley.

Brownell, H. H., & Joanette, Y. (Eds.). (1993). Narrative discourse in neurologically impaired and normal aging adults. San Diego, CA: Singular.

Chapey, R. (Ed.). (1994). *Language intervention strategies in adult aphasia* (3rd ed.). Baltimore: Williams & Wilkins.

Chomsky, N. (1957). *Syntactic structures.* The Hague: Mouton.

Davis, G. A., & Ball, H. (1989). Effects of aging on comprehension of complex sentences in adulthood. *Journal of Speech and Hearing Research, 32,* 143–150.

Duckworth, E. (1972). The having of wonderful ideas. *Harvard Educational Review, 42,* 217–231.

Duffy, J. R. (1986). Schuell's stimulation approach to rehabilitation. In R. Chapey (Ed.), *Language intervention strategies in adult aphasia* (Vol. 2, pp. 187–214). Baltimore: Williams & Wilkins.

Ellis, A., & Beattie, G. (1986). *The psychology of language and communication.* NY: Guilford.

Fischer, K. W. (1980). A theory of cognitive development: The control and construction of hierarchies of skills. *Psychological Review, 87,* 477–531.

Fosnot, C. (1990). *Enquiring teachers, enquiring learners.* New York: Teachers College Press.

Frattali, C. M., Thompson, C. M., Holland, A. L. Wohl, C. B., & Ferketic, M. M. (1995). The FACS of life. *ASHA, 37,* 46.

Granott, N. I. (1993). Patterns of interaction in the co-construction of knowledge. In R. W. Wozniak & K. W. Fischer (Eds.), *Development in context: Acting and thinking in specific environments* (pp. 183–210). Hillsdale, NJ: Erlbaum.

Hegde, M. N. (1985). *Treatment procedures in communicative disorders.* Boston: Little, Brown.

Karmiloff-Smith, A. (1986). Stage/structure versus phase/process in modelling linguistic and cognitive development. In I. Levin (Ed.), *Stage and structure* (pp. 164–190). Norwood, NJ: Ablex.

Klein, H. B., & Moses, N. (1999). *Intervention planning for children with communication disorders.* (2nd ed.). Needham, MA: Allyn & Bacon.

Lahey, M. (1988). *Language disorders and language development.* New York: McGraw-Hill.

Leith, W., (1984). *Handbook of clinical methods in communication disorders.* San Diego: College Hill Press.

Lenneberg. E., & Lenneberg, E. (1975). *Foundations of language development: A multidisciplinary approach* (Vol. I–II). New York: Academic Press.

Lovaas, O. I. (1977). *The autistic child: Language development through behavior modification.* New York: Irvington Press.

Martin, A. D. (1981). An examination of Wepman's thought centered therapy. In R. Chapey (Ed.), *Language intervention strategies in adult aphasia* (pp. 141–154). Baltimore: Williams & Wilkins.

Moses, N. (1994). The development of procedural knowledge in adults engaged in a tractor-trailer task. *Cognitive Development, 9,* 103–130.

Moses, N., Klein, H. B., & Altman, E. K. (1990). An approach to assessing and facilitating causal language in learning disabled adults based on Piagetian theory. *Journal of Learning Disabilities, 23,* 220–229.

Moses, N., & Shapiro, D. A. (1996). A developmental conceptualization of clinical problem-solving. *Journal of Communication Disorders, 29,* 199–221.

Nation, J. & Aram, D. (1984). *Diagnosis of speech and language disorders* (2nd ed.). San Diego: College Hill Press.

Noss, D. S., & Noss, J. B. (1984). *Man's religions* (7th ed.). New York: Macmillan.

Obler, L. K., & Albert, M. L. (1980). Language and aging: A neurobehavioral analysis. In D. S. Beasley & G. A. Davis (Eds.), *Aging processes and disorders* (pp. 107–121). New York: Grune & Stratton.

Pinker, S. (1994). *The language instinct.* New York: William Morrow.

Porch, B. E. (1967). *The Porch index of communicative abilities.* Palo Alto, CA: Consulting Psychologists Press.

Rees, N. S. (1978). Pragmatics of language. In R. L. Schiefelbusch (Ed.), *Bases of language intervention.* Baltimore: University Park Press.

Reid, D. K. (1988). *Teaching the learning disabled: A cognitive developmental approach.* Needham, MA: Allyn & Bacon.

Schuell, H. (1973). *Differential diagnosis of aphasia with the Minnesota test.* Minneapolis: University of Minnesota Press.

Seiler, W. (1996). *Communication: Foundations, skills, and application* (3rd. Ed). New York: Harper Collins.

Shriberg, L. D., & Kwiatkowski, J., (1982). Phonological disorders I: A diagnostic classification system. *Journal of Speech and Hearing Disorders, 47,* 226–241.

van Riemdijk, H., & Williams, E. (1986). *Introduction to the theory of grammar.* Cambridge, MA: The MIT Press.

Watzlawick, P., Beavin, J. H., & Jackson, D. D. (1967). *Pragmatics of human communication: A study of interactional patterns, pathologies, and paradoxes.* New York: Norton.

Webster's New World Dictionary (2nd college ed.). (1980). New York: Simon.

2 The Phases of Intervention Planning

C H A P T E R O U T C O M E S

The reader will:

1. understand how intervention planning proceeds across three phases;
2. distinguish among long-term, short-term, and session goals;
3. identify procedural decisions made at each intervention-planning phase;
4. understand how various sources of information are used for decision making at each intervention-planning phase.

As described in the volume on intervention planning for children (Klein and Moses 1999), decision making for speech-language intervention proceeds across three phases: long term, short term, and session. The focus of decision making at each of these phases is the formulation of goals (long term, short term, and session) and related procedures. These goals and procedures guide both the initiation of treatment and the monitoring of progress during intervention.

Our conception of intervention planning as proceeding in phases is a function of the complexity inherent in the decision-making process. As illustrated in Chapter 1, the speech-language clinician must digest a great deal of information and make several decisions to plan treatment for a client. The clinician must give thought to current performance across the multiple behavioral systems that support functional communication: speech and language (syntax, semantics, phonology, morphology, fluency, phonation), cognition, psychosocial, and sensorimotor. The clinician must be knowledgeable about how these components of language and associated behavioral systems may interact, and about how adults are expected to perform in each of these areas. It is also important to understand what promotes learning and rehabilitation. Thus, many decisions about goals and procedures must be made with reference to this complex body of information.

Below we describe the planning process that begins with the assessment of a new client, proceeds through the three phases of intervention planning, and continues throughout the course of treatment as goals and procedures are reviewed and revised. We focus on the three phases of intervention planning. We identify the nature of the goals and procedures formulated at each phase and show how the sources of information identified above guide decision making.

The Long-Term Planning Phase

In the text on intervention planning with children we remarked upon an apparent paradox in planning speech-language interventions: The first set of decisions clinicians make concerns predicting the final outcome of therapy (also termed "functional outcomes," Krebs & Augustine, 1997). While this approach to planning appears paradoxical, it is in fact logical; on any journey, one needs a destination in order to plan the route. During the first phase of intervention planning, therefore, clinicians formulate long-term goals and the procedural approach. In the process of long-term planning clinicians reference their conceptualization of functional communication and the sources of information identified above (i.e., baseline data, the client's past history, maintaining factors). Ultimately, long-term planning ensures clinician accountability. Our discussion of this planning phase is organized as follows: First, we define the long-term goal, discuss clinician accountability, and describe the way long-term goals are derived; second, we define the procedural approach and illustrate its derivation.

The Long-Term Goal Defined

A *long-term goal* is in essence a prognosis. It is defined as "a general statement about the best performance that can be expected of an individual in one or more [functional] communication areas within a projected period of time" (Klein & Moses, 1999, p. 98).

Functional Communication. This definition of a long-term goal highlights the precept that *functional communication* is always the long-term goal of speech-language intervention with adults (as well as children), regardless of the communication problem being addressed (e.g., language, voice, fluency, phonology, etc.). With reference to our definition in Chapter 1, functional communication involves content/form/use interactions, and both manifests an intrinsic, systematic organization. The long-term goal, therefore, is a general statement about the parameters of content/form/use interactions governing the client's performance in functional communication contexts at the end of speech-language intervention. An example of a long-term goal in fluency is, "The client will maintain fluency while producing narratives for regulatory and discourse functions." The production of narratives for regulatory and discourse functions represents the communication context for the achievement of fluency in this long-term goal.

An Additional Emphasis on Functional Communication. Our emphasis on targeting functional communication may seem redundant. The idea that improved functional communication should be the outcome of speech-language intervention with adults seems self-evident. Often, however, it is not. Many adult clients enter therapy with a variety of serious problems in addition to impaired communication abilities that demand attention. Examples include compromised self-help skills, emotional stress, and sensorimotor difficulties. These problems sometimes overshadow communication in intervention planning. In other cases, information-processing skills are seen as the as the focus of intervention. Assuming these skills underlie effective communication, clinical exercises targeting these are often observed. Examples include recalling number sequences, identifying main ideas in reading passages, and practicing fluency techniques while imitating the clinician. Although it may be necessary to spend time and energy addressing noncommunicative adaptive abilities and information-processing skills, these behaviors are never the long-term goal of speech-language intervention. Functional communication is.

Best Performance and Time Frame.   The definition of a long-term goal also indicates it is a statement about the best communication performance that can be expected of a client within a delimited time. Although this statement is described in the definition as "general," it must specify a framework or set of guidelines for measuring "best communication performance." Compare the example of the long-term goal statement presented above (targeting fluency) with the following statement that typifies a lack of specificity in a long-term goal: "The client will improve fluency." The former goal statement provides a framework for describing characteristics of expected behaviors (fluent, narratives, serving regulatory and discourse functions). The second long-term goal statement is so unspecific that it is practically meaningless. Any behavior could be interpreted as an improvement of fluency.

The implicit requirement for specificity in the long-term goal statement relates to two additional functions of the long-term goal: guidance for planning short-term goals and specification of clinician accountability.

A Framework for Organizing Short-Term Goals.   The long-term goal statement provides a framework for specifying parameters of functional communication. Consequently, the clinician is establishing a basis for organizing goals at subsequent planning phases. Consider again the long-term goal presented above: "The client will maintain fluency while producing narratives for regulatory and discourse functions." This goal statement references parameters of content/form/use interactions (fluency, narratives for regulatory and discourse functions). As a result, one can envision sequencing *short-term goals* in terms of the progressive attainment and maintenance of fluency (i.e., efficient coordination of respiration, phonation, and articulation) in progressively more complex linguistic and communicative contexts. We elaborate on options for prioritizing goal sequences in the subsequent sections on short-term and long-term planning phases.

Clinician Accountability.   Specificity in the formulation of long-term goals also represents a statement of clinician accountability. By specifying in measurable terms the outcome of intervention, the clinician is making a commitment. He or she is providing a measurable standard by which the effectiveness of the intervention may be judged. Besides being an ethical responsibility of this profession, the specification of treatment outcomes is becoming an economically driven necessity in this age of managed care and shrinking health care resources (see also Klein & Moses, 1999).

The Formulation of Long-Term Goals

The two most useful sources of information for planning long-term goals are (a) the clinician's conceptual framework regarding the nature of functional communication and its primary vehicle—language—and (b) baseline data in language and language-related systems. This information aids in making two basic decisions: what aspects of communication performance to target and what level of performance is ultimately possible for the client (including the time frame).

Conceptual Framework. A conceptual framework directs the clinician to target certain linguistic structures and communicative functions rather than others as long-term goals. An example of a conceptual framework guiding goal planning for aphasics was presented by Chapey (1994). According to Chapey, content/form/use is a product of five mental operations: cognition, memory, convergent thinking, divergent thinking, and evaluative thinking. With a focus on remediating underlying mental operations, Chapey suggests general objectives (which correspond with our notion of long-term goals) that derive from Chapey's conceptualization of language function. Some of Chapey's objectives are as follows:

> To stimulate ability to fix new information in memory in order to improve communication;
> To stimulate ability to generate logical alternatives to given information, to produce a quantity and variety of responses during communication, and to be able to elaborate on ideas and plans during communication;
> To stimulate the integration of all cognitive operations through the use of problem solving, decision making, and planning tasks and through conversational discourse in order to communicate more effectively and efficiently. (p. 236)

By way of contrast, a clinician may focus on the client's language itself (current level of content/form/use interactions). Within this framework a clinician would likely target the remediation of impaired content/form/use performance. Long-term goals formulated for a client with severe aphasia in accordance with this orientation may look like the following:

1. John will produce two-word utterances coding existence, action, and state.
2. John will use language spontaneously to comment upon actions and regulate his environment (e.g., direct attention, protest, obtain object).
3. John will demonstrate conversational skills such as turn taking and presupposition.

Another example may be drawn from a client with a phonological problem due to learning English as a second language. A clinician who ascribes to a traditional sound-by-sound approach to articulation treatment may focus on remediating individual vowel productions based on intuition about ease of articulation or conspicuousness of misarticulations. This clinician, working with an Hispanic individual, might focus on differentiating /i/ from /I/ because this substitution is one of the prominent features of a Spanish accent. Another clinician, operating from a more phonological-process-oriented framework, might look for error patterns in several superficially disparate substitutions. Thus, productions of /i/ for /I/ and /u/ for /ʊ/ may be seen as the result of underlying difficulty with differentiating tense/lax features. As a result, the long-term goal would be directed toward the production of appropriate tense and lax features across vowels. The first approach highlights the production of individual phonemes; the second approach highlights the acquisition of a feature that underlies multiple error productions, yielding a long-term goal such as: "Sylvia will produce lax vowels in conversational contexts."

At the risk of being redundant, we emphasize again that in our definition and description of long-term goals our focus is on facilitating functional communication. We also reiterate the caution that with some adult clients, communication problems may be accompanied by other difficulties. Some clinicians may target improvement of these accompanying problems as long-term goals. For example, a client may exhibit cognitive problems; for cases such as this, long-term goals are frequently written in terms of improvement of attention, discrimination, and memory. Another client may exhibit sensorimotor problems such as dysarthria or "parietal and frontal neglect" (Myers, 1986). Long-term goals in these cases may be written in terms of improved tongue movement or attention to "neglected" sensory fields and spaces. This focus is not consistent with the central tenant of our model of intervention planning.

As speech-language pathologists, we are obligated to keep communication performance in sight. Thus, within our intervention-planning model we do not target improvement in nonlinguistic behavioral systems as a long-term goal. Neither do we disregard the need for improvement in these systems. Instead, we address these system deficits (maintaining factors) in a sequence of session goals leading to the achievement of the ultimate communication target. We will amplify this position later in this chapter and throughout the book (see also, Martin, 1981).

Knowledge of Parameters of Normal Communication and Language Functioning Across the Life Span.
In setting long-term goals, it is important to be knowledgeable about the parameters of normal communication and language functioning in adults. This is because communication and language performance do not remain static across the life span. Performance changes as adults' physical and psychosocial status evolves with the aging process. It is necessary, therefore, to adjust expectations to these changing parameters. It is especially important not to exceed what an adult can reasonably be expected to accomplish at a particular age. Parameters of normal adult performance in communication and language, as well as performance in behaviors that may maintain a communication problem, are presented in Chapters 3–5.

Baseline Data.
Baseline data contribute to decisions about communication or language goals and prognoses. Baseline data in speech and language describe the status of current communication performance organized within a selected conceptual framework, preferably the same one used for initial assessment (see discussion above, also Bloom & Lahey, 1978; Klein & Moses, 1999; Lahey, 1988). These data provide a starting point from which to generate long-term goals. Baseline data about both language and maintaining factors help in making decisions about how much can be expected of the client by the termination of treatment. The severity of the language problem, the number of maintaining factors, and the extent to which they are involved will determine (a) the ultimate level of performance realistically possible and (b) a time frame for the accomplishment of this level of performance. For example, an individual with aphasia who is using only single words and who

has severe sensorimotor involvement (dysarthria) and psychosocial stresses (no family support system) would be given a poorer prognosis than an individual producing syntax without the sensorimotor and psychosocial involvements.

Premorbid Interests and Experiences. As we noted above, knowledge of an individual's past performance level will influence ultimate expectations. At best, a client can only be expected to return to prior levels of performance.

Summary. In this section four categories of knowledge were identified that help define best communication performance—the performance that will be achieved by the client at the conclusion of the therapeutic process (see Box 2.1). These categories of knowledge are (a) the clinician's conceptual framework for defining what constitutes functional communication and language; (b) the clinician's knowledge about parameters of normal adult communication and language performance across the life span; (c) baseline data about the client's present functioning in communication, language, and behavioral systems that may maintain the communication problem; and (d) the client's premorbid behavioral characteristics and competencies. Next, we examine categories of knowledge that aid in establishing a procedural approach.

Procedural Approach Defined

Speech-language clinicians typically associate the selection of methods and materials (i.e., procedures) with session planning. The clinician, however, actually begins to make decisions about procedures at the long-term planning phase. This is when the clinician begins to think about (a) factors that are suspected of maintaining the communication problem, (b) principles of learning and rehabilitation that explain how adults learn or reaccess communication skills, and (c) the client's premorbid interests. To formulate a procedural

---

B O X **2.1**

Sources of Information for Long-Term Goal Planning

Sources of Information	Application in Goal Planning
1. The clinician's conceptual framework	▪ affects which goals are targeted ▪ affects the choice of framework for organizing and formulating goals
2. Knowledge about parameters of normal adult development	▪ guides in the selection of age-appropriate goals
3. Baseline data on current communication performance	▪ affect which goals are targeted
4. Baseline data on maintaining factors	▪ affect projection of ultimate outcome of treatment ▪ affect projection of treatment duration
5. Client's premorbid characteristics and competencies	▪ affect projection of ultimate outcome

approach, the clinician needs to identify the maintaining factors that will be addressed during treatment, the principles of learning that will guide treatment, and information about the client's premorbid status that bear on treatment procedures. Each component of the procedural approach derived at the long-term phase will guide more specific procedural planning.

The identification of maintaining factors provides a basis for selection of materials, activities, and clinician-client interactions. These components of the clinical environment are designed to reduce or compensate for the influence of maintaining factors on the communication problem. Envision, for example, a client who manifests right-sided hemiplegia following stroke. This client has compromised body stability, which in turn is affecting voice and articulation. Recognition of this sensorimotor maintaining factor might guide the clinician in subsequent planning phases. The clinician might, following the physical therapist's recommendations, plan to compensate for the problem by working with the client seated. The clinician might also plan to get the client to more actively compensate by engaging the client's right hand.

A clinician's beliefs about processes of adult learning and rehabilitation provide a second guidepost for the subsequent planning of specific treatment procedures. For example, imagine a clinician who believes in operant learning principles. That clinician, when planning session procedures for a client who suffered a stroke, might recommend stimulating communication behaviors through imitation. The clinician might then plan to reward behaviors with food or praise. In contrast, a clinician who believes in constructivist principles might hope to evoke communication through natural conversation while posing problems for the client to solve.

The client's premorbid interests and occupation are a third area that provides direction for the planning of more specific procedures. The clinician would try to incorporate familiar activities in therapy as a motivation and as a way to minimize the necessity of learning skills that were never part of the client's repertoire.

The specification of maintaining factors, principles of learning and rehabilitation, and premorbid interests and occupations constitute the *procedural approach* (see Box 2.2). The procedural approach anticipates the direction the clinician will take to facilitate achievement of the long-term goal (when developing session plans). Now, we will discuss the derivation of the procedural approach.

BOX **2.2**

Sources of Information for Planning a Procedural Approach

Sources of Information	Effect on Procedural Approach
1. Maintaining factors	■ alert the clinician to those factors that will require modification or compensation
2. Principles of learning and rehabilitation	■ guide the development of linguistic and non-linguistic contexts
3. Client's premorbid interests	■ guide the development of linguistic and non-linguistic contexts

Derivation of a Long-Term Procedural Approach

We now examine procedural approaches designed for two individuals in their midforties, Harold and Martha, who have sustained closed head injury. Harold was an architect before his accident and Martha was a musician. Because of linguistic impairment, the long-term goal is the same for both individuals: "The client will produce complex sentences for a variety of communicative functions." One of the first considerations in planning a procedural approach is the specification of maintaining factors that will be addressed by the procedures. Because of the nature of head trauma, the most obvious maintaining factor is cognitive (e.g., Ylvisaker & Szekeres, 1994). As is commonly seen with this condition, the clients demonstrate reduced attention span and diminished metacognitive skills related to problem solving (e.g., identifying goals and relevant information, weighing the merits of possible solutions, predicting consequences; Ylvisaker & Szekeres, 1994). The results of sensorimotor evaluations revealed that Harold engages in excess movements possibly related to proprioceptive and sensory integration difficulties. Martha exhibits mild dysarthria and weakness on the right side of her body. In addition, both clients exhibit frustration and anger and tend to withdraw from social contact. Consequently, we need to address all three maintaining factors in the formulation of a procedural approach: cognitive, sensorimotor, and psychosocial.

Next, we hypothesize about theories of learning and rehabilitation that guide us in designing procedural contexts. Klein and Moses (1999) presented a description of several frequently referenced theories of child-language learning. We apply principles derived from these theories as well as from theories of rehabilitation to procedural planning with adults. (These theories will be described in Chapter 6.) To illustrate a procedural approach at this point, however, we will apply selected principles from social-cognitive and motor theories generally associated with adult neurological problems. Principles such as the following will guide the specification of clinical interactions: Learning is facilitated by: efforts to match models presented by the clinician, the internalization of problem-solving strategies mediated by clinicians, and sensory stimulation from movement (Klein & Moses, 1999). Thus, these principles constitute an important component of the procedural approach for Harold and Martha because they provide the basis for planning clinical activities and interactions.

For the last component of our procedural approach, we consider information about past history that may guide procedure planning. Each client's unique social and vocational history will affect individualized procedural approaches. Harold's career as an architect gives him an advantage in the area of visual-spatial performance; conversely, Martha, a cellist before her head injury, excelled in the auditory-perceptual area. This knowledge will suggest tasks we can use in facilitating communication performance. Table 2.1 summarizes the procedural approach for Harold and Martha.

The Short-Term Planning Phase

The focus of the short-term planning phase is on identifying a set of accomplishments for a semester or several months (i.e., short-term goals) that will lead to the achievement of the long-term goal and on making more specific procedural decisions. As in phase 1, baseline data about language and factors maintaining communication difficulty serve as important sources of information.

TABLE 2.1 Procedural Approach for Harold and Martha

---

1. The achievement of all goals will be facilitated by modifying cognitive, sensorimotor, and linguistic maintaining factors.

2. The procedural approach has been influenced primarily by the following principles from social-cognitive and motor learning theory.

Learning is facilitated by:

—efforts to match models presented by the clinician;
—the internalization of problem-solving strategies mediated by clinicians;
—sensory stimulation from movement;
—interaction with materials and tasks commensurate with the individual's academic and vocational experiences.

3a. (for Harold) Procedures will incorporate materials and tasks that are visually-spatially oriented to capitalize on Harold's premorbid architectural skills.

3b. (for Martha) Procedures will incorporate materials and tasks that are auditory and musical to capitalize on Martha's premorbid musical talent.

Short-Term Goals Defined

A *short-term goal* is defined as "a linguistic and or communicative achievement that has been given priority within a hierarchy of achievements required for the realization of the long-term goal" (Klein & Moses, 1999, p. 132). This definition indicates that some *linguistic or communicative* achievement (or achievements) should be targeted as the short-term goal, and that the linguistic or communicative achievements targeted must lead to the achievement of the long-term goal.

Defining a short-term goal as a linguistic achievement acknowledges that organization intrinsic to communicative or linguistic behavior is always implicated in speech-language intervention. By organization, we mean the underlying rules of language and communication and systematic interactions among the components of the speech mechanism. Examples include the syntactic structure that defines a relative clause (e.g., van Reimsdijk & Williams, 1986); content/form/use interactions (Lahey, 1988); and coordinations of respiration, phonation, and articulation in fluency.

There are two ways a clinician may work with reference to organization. The first is to modify the organization intrinsic to a client's communication. For example, the clinician may target the production of sentences with relative clauses in a client who can only produce sentences with conjunctions. Alternatively, the clinician may set goals which are consistent with the client's present organizational system. Consider, for example, a client who has the capacity for producing three-constituent utterances (subject-verb-complement) but is only using a limited number of verbs. In this case, the expansion of verb use could be targeted within the constraints of three constituents.

Implicit in linguistic organization is the premise of hierarchies. More complex organizational states are assumed to emerge from less complex states. This idea first guided the specification of a framework for measuring achievements in the long-term goal statement. This framework provides direction for sequencing short-term goals in terms of the progressive attainment of higher levels of organization, or for selecting communication skills within a delimited linguistic parameter. An example of the first approach to goal sequencing in fluency might involve targeting the maintenance of fluency (i.e., efficient coordinations) in progressively more complex linguistic and communicative contexts. An example of the second is teaching an individual with aphasia to use an augmentative communication device (computer) to express language at a prescribed level of performance (i.e., content/form/use interactions) retained following stroke. The decision-making process leading to the formulation and ordering of short-term goals is further elaborated in the section on decision making at the short-term planning phase.

The Formulation of Short-Term Goals

The major task during the short-term planning phase is making prioritization decisions. How do clinicians decide which behaviors should be learned before others on the road to the designated long-term accomplishment? Systematic planning at the short-term phase involves the identification of an organizational framework that serves as a basis for sequencing goals. Two well-established considerations for sequencing goals are task difficulty and task complexity (e.g., Brookshire, 1992; Chapey, 1994; Schuell, Jenkins, & Jimenez-Pabon, 1964).

Complexity vs. Difficulty.   Earlier in this chapter we identified task complexity and difficulty as considerations in sequencing goals. The complexity of a task is an objective determination; complexity is based on a consideration of the linguistic organization demanded by that task (i.e., the number of syntactic transformations, the feature contrasts implicated in the processing of two discrete phonemes, etc.). For example, producing a phrase with a relative clause such as, "The man who painted the house fell on the lawn," reflects a greater degree of linguistic organization than the sentence, "The man is painting the house." The former is objectively more complex than the latter (e.g., van Riemsdijk & Williams, 1986). For a second example, consider two acts of expression: reading sentences aloud and phonating /a:/ for 10 seconds. The former task (reading) demands more complex physiologic integration of the subsystems of speech production (i.e., respiration, phonation, resonation, articulation) than the latter (phonating /a:/, e.g., Andrews, 1991).

Degrees of *complexity* may be contrasted with perceptions of *difficulty*. Ease or difficulty of a task depends, in part, on the information-processing characteristics, skills, and attitudes of an individual. Keeping the degree of complexity consistent, a particular act may be more difficult for one person than another. For example, the production of a phrase with a relative clause in it may be less difficult for a client with aphasia who searches for redundancy to extract meaning than a client with aphasia who does not use this strategy.

How Complexity Inherent in Content, Form, and Use May Affect Short-Term Goal Decisions.   When planning for children, prioritization decisions lean heavily upon developmental data. As we noted earlier, developmental data, in addition to reflecting the order in which children acquire certain behaviors, suggest hierarchies of behavioral complexity. The literature in language acquisition provides ample sources of developmental hierarchies (see Bloom, 1991; Bloom & Lahey, 1978; Lahey, 1988; Nelson, 1993). When planning for adults, developmental data continue to be useful as indexes of complexity for sequencing short-term goals. Developmental data may be used in making decisions about complexity of targeted achievements in short-term planning since the literature on adult language does not typically address the issue of complexity. For example, tests that are constructed to identify areas of difficulty in adult communication (i.e., aphasia tests) do not reference complexity hierarchies as a basis for making treatment decisions. "Easy" tasks appear to be differentiated from "hard" ones (e.g., Goodglass & Kaplan, 1983) frequently on the basis of utterance length and perceptual support. Often the basis for the sequence is intuitive and unsystematic. Developmental hierarchies of content/form interactions in children present, in a systematic manner, levels of complexity of the semantics and syntax of word combinations, sentences, and sequences of sentences (narratives).

The domain in which task complexity is ordered depends on the presenting disorder. For example, dysarthrias have been described as "a group of speech disorders resulting from disturbances in muscular control over the speech mechanism due to damage of the central or peripheral nervous system" (Darley, Aronson, & Brown, 1969, p. 246). Because of the nature of this disorder, we would sequence short-term goals according to the complexity of the motor act expected of the client. Task complexity would be approached differently in cases of linguistic disturbance (e.g., aphasia). Here, short-term goals might be sequenced according to the complexity of linguistic structures.

Alternative Considerations in Sequencing Short-Term Goals.   It is important to note that it is not a requirement to gradually complicate all aspects of linguistic and communicative organization when treating adults. The clinician may choose to maintain complexity in one aspect of language while manipulating difficulty or complexity in another. For example, in working with disfluent adults, Shapiro (Chapter 10 in this book) often targeted fluency in complex linguistic structures throughout therapy (spontaneous utterances produced during conversation). He did this while manipulating difficulty of communication function and topic (e.g, discussions of more or less familiar topics in more or less threatening exchanges).

Examples of Short-Term Goals.   The following are examples of short-term goals related to the long-term goals stated earlier for two clients with different communication problems. Long-term goals for a client with aphasia:

1. John will produce two-word utterances coding existence, action, and state.
2. John will use language spontaneously to comment upon actions and to regulate his environment (e.g., direct attention, protest, obtain object).

Short-term goals:

1. John will point to the appropriate picture to direct the clinician in a familiar routine (i.e., cooking, repairing).
2. John will direct the clinician by using single-word utterances representing objects or actions.

Long-term goals for a client with a phonological problem due to learning English as a second language:

1. Sylvia will produce lax vowels in conversational contexts.
2. Sylvia will reduce stress in unstressed syllables of polysyllabic words in conversational contexts.

Short-term goals:

1. Sylvia will differentially produce lax vowels /I/ and /ʊ/, and tense vowels /i/ and /u/ in single-word utterances.
2. Sylvia will produce unstressed syllables in three- and four-syllable, single-word productions within a variety of stress patterns.

Summary. In this discussion we considered how short-term goals are formulated and prioritized. These tasks are accomplished with reference to baseline data, information about maintaining factors, and task complexity and difficulty. Task complexity and difficulty can be evaluated with reference to developmental taxonomies and information about a client's social, cultural, and information-processing characteristics. These sources of information are summarized in Box 2.4 (on pg. 30).

Delimited Procedural Context Defined

At the short-term planning phase procedures are considered in terms of the contexts that will best facilitate the achievement of short-term goals. The term *context* refers to the therapeutic environment—everything surrounding and interacting with the client. We now make decisions about what would be the optimum linguistic and nonlinguistic contexts for learning. We describe the *linguistic context* (i.e., the language and other communication behaviors that the clinician will use during the session to stimulate learning or rehabilitation). We also describe the *nonlinguistic context* (i.e., the types of materials and activities, such as manipulable objects versus printed material) that will best promote learning or rehabilitation. These decisions follow from decisions about maintaining factors and learning principles identified in the procedural approach at the long-term planning phase. Sample descriptions of delineated procedural contexts and the decision-making process yielding these descriptions are presented in the section on decision making at the short-term planning phase.

Delineating the Procedural Context

To organize the clinical environment for a particular client, we turn to the sources of information specified in the long-term procedural approach: maintaining factors, principles from theories of learning and rehabilitation, and premorbid interests and experiences (e.g., employment, hobbies, major skills). This information indicates the specific linguistic and nonlinguistic contexts that will be most beneficial for a given client.

Considering Maintaining Factors.   Recall Harold and Martha above who sustained head injuries. They both presented with similar cognitive and psychosocial problems: reduced attention span, diminished metacognitive skills related to problem solving, and frustration and anger. They differed, however, in their sensorimotor impairments: Harold engages in excess movements possibly related to proprioceptive and sensory integration difficulties; Martha exhibits mild dysarthria and weakness on the right side of her body. The long-term goal for Harold and Martha was to produce complex sentences for various communicative functions. An associated short-term goal was to produce sentences coding additive and temporal semantic relations while planning an activity.

In addressing the *cognitive* factor we must envision activities that facilitate attention and engage the metacognitive skill of talking about planning. Principles of constructivist and social cognitive learning theories are useful for this purpose (see Chapter 6.) Initially, we would create activities that are perceptually salient and that may be enacted during the session (planning a party table setting, replacing batteries in a nonfunctioning remote control). A consideration of the *psychosocial* factor would lead to goals that could be achievable within a delimited time frame (so that frustration would be minimized).

The last maintaining factor is sensorimotor performance. With the client's specific impairments in mind, we would make an effort to engage Martha's right side and accept less than precise articulation. Harold's difficulty with excessive movement is expected to be diminished with increased attention to task and compensatory cognitive strategies (Ylvisaker & Szekeres, 1994).

Considering Premorbid Interests and Experiences.   To further describe these activities we must also consider each client's premorbid interests and experiences. Given their diverse backgrounds, the range of topics each would address would be different. Harold's topics might include the designing of architectural projects, while Martha's topics might include musical programs. In planning it is important to remember that both clients have a low tolerance for frustration and easily become angry (the psychosocial domain). The clinician must employ techniques for minimizing frustration and increasing persistence in problem solving. These include the use of praise and encouragement, acceptance of error (e.g., accept a wrong response as long as the client is using temporal sentence structure), and rephrasing of questions and directives.

Considering Principles of Learning and Rehabilitation.   In deriving a procedural approach for Harold and Martha at the long-term planning phase, we identified the following four principles of learning and rehabilitation. Learning is facilitated by:

1. efforts to match models presented by the clinician;
2. the internalization of problem-solving strategies mediated by clinicians;
3. sensory stimulation from movement;
4. interaction with materials and tasks commensurate with the individual's academic and vocational experiences.

At the short-term phase these principles provide direction about how to design and organize the linguistic and nonlinguistic contexts. For example, Principle 1 suggests the clinician will present models of target sentences (coding additive and temporal relations)

TABLE 2.2   Examples of Delineated Procedural Contexts for Harold and Martha

The nonlinguistic context will involve:
—activities that are perceptually salient and that may be enacted during the session;
—tasks that reflect Harold's vocational interests, such as the designing of architectural projects;
—tasks that reflect Martha's vocational history, such as planning musical programs.

The linguistic context will involve the clinician:
—modeling target utterances;
—encouraging imitation;
—instructing the client to use rehearsed problem-solving strategies;
—engaging client in speech-*production* activities;
—consulting with a physical and/or occupational therapist (for Harold).

---

for the client to imitate. Principle 2 suggests the clinician will instruct the client to use several rehearsed strategies to achieve the goal of sequencing steps in a procedure. Principle 3 suggests the client must be engaged in speech-production activities with the potential for sensory feedback. For Martha, sensory feedback addresses the inappropriate tension and positioning of articulators due to dysarthria. Harold, on the other hand, exhibits excessive movements possibly related to proprioceptive and sensory integration difficulties. In this case, Principle 3 indicates that the speech-language clinician should consult with a physical and/or occupational therapist in procedure planning. Principle 4 complements our consideration of premorbid interests and experiences. This principle suggests that activities be planned involving music and architecture, in line with the clients' vocational histories.

Table 2.2 summarizes the delineated procedural context for Harold and Martha. Box 2.3 summarizes the sources of information discussed above that guide decision making about a delineated procedural approach across disorder types. Now that we have formulated short-term goals and delineated a procedural approach, we are ready to plan session goals and procedures.

The Session-Planning Phase

Session Goals and Procedures Defined

The final set of decisions centers around the formulation of session goals and corresponding procedures. The *session goal* is defined as an observable behavior expressed in a specified context that represents an act of learning that will lead to the acquisition of functional communication behavior targeted as a short-term goal (Klein & Moses, 1999). This is a lengthy definition that includes several aspects that must be considered in the planning process.

An Act of Learning.   We view session goals as means to an end—behaviors that are evidence that the client is learning or reacquiring communication competencies targeted as short-term and long-term goals. Therefore, we define session goals as acts of learning.

BOX 2.3

Sources of Information for Planning a Delineated Procedural Approach

Sources of Information	Effect on Procedural Approach
1. Maintaining factors	■ guide in the selection of materials and compensatory devices ■ direct collaborations with allied professionals
2. Principles of learning and rehabilitation	■ direct interaction and communication style with client ■ guide the selection of therapeutic materials
3. Client's premorbid interests	■ guide the selection of materials and clinical tasks

Observable Behaviors. Learning takes place within the client. We cannot directly observe the act of learning. Accountability requires that we identify concrete evidence of learning. In defining session goals for adults, we are influenced by behavioral theory and conventions of goal writing for individualized educational plans for children. These conventions demand that we write session goals in terms of observable, measurable behaviors.

Thus, to formulate session goals decisions need to be made about what is an *observable* behavior that constitutes *an act of learning.* For example, we may decide that learning to discriminate between minimal word pairs and pictures is a necessary act of learning for an individual with aphasia to achieve the short-term goal of "using an augmentative communication device (boardmaker) to express actions." We cannot observe the process of discrimination directly. We may decide that an eye gaze directed at one of two pictures in response to a clinician's command is a sufficient response to indicate that the individual is learning to discriminate among named and pictured verbs. Thus, a session goal might read: "The client will gaze at one of two pictures depicting minimal-pair verbs (bump-jump, sip-dip) corresponding to the clinician's command." In this example, eye gaze is targeted as a session goal because it is observable.

In formulating the session goal, the clinician must consider targeting an observable behavior that must be achieved on route to the short-term goal. In the example mentioned above, "appropriate eye gaze" in a minimal-pairs exercise was believed to be a necessary step on route to operating an augmentative communication device to express actions (i.e., the short-term goal).

Context. A description of the context in which the target behavior is to be expressed is included as part of the session goal. As defined above, context refers to the surrounding linguistic and nonlinguistic environment. Consider the session goal introduced above: "The client will gaze at one of two pictures depicting minimal-pair verbs (bump-jump, sip-dip) that correspond to the clinician's command." The observable behavior of gazing at a picture takes place in context of "two Mayer-Johnson pictures" and "the clinician's command." The context is also described in the session procedure.

The Session Procedure.   The session procedure corresponds to the context component of the session goal in that it focuses on what the clinician must do to facilitate the client's response. The clinician must make decisions about how to arrange the clinical environment, what materials to provide, what to say to the client, and how to say it. The decision-making process surrounding the derivation of session goals and procedures is elaborated below, in the section on the session-planning phase.

Formulation of Session Goals and Procedures

Both session goals and procedures are influenced by answers to the following questions: (a) What constitutes an "act of learning" relevant to achievement of the short-term goal; (b) What are the contextual variables that increase or decrease performance demands (i.e., that affect the relative difficulty and complexity of a task); and (c) What are the criteria for achievement of goals? The answer to each of these questions will use several sources of information first considered in planning for the first two phases of intervention: maintaining factors, premorbid interests and experiences, and theories of learning and rehabilitation.

What Constitutes an Act of Learning?

When interacting with clients during the actual treatment sessions, clinicians are engaging in a process directed toward the ultimate speech and language outcomes. This process is demarcated by a series of steps or behaviors, each envisioned as enabling the client to get closer to the short-term goal. These steps or behaviors are viewed as acts of learning. These acts of learning in which the client will be expected to engage (i.e., the session goals) are observable manifestations of this process. To envision this process and in turn determine session goals, the clinician must ask the following question: How is the client going to acquire the linguistic/communicative competence targeted as the short-term goal? The answer to this question will be influenced primarily by (a) the clinician's knowledge of factors maintaining the particular communication problem and (b) the theory of learning or rehabilitation to which the clinician subscribes.

The Effect of Maintaining Factors.   Consider, for example, the client with a phonology problem resulting from the acquisition of a second language. The short-term goal for Sylvia is to produce /i/ and /ɪ/ and /ʊ/ and /u/ in single-word utterances in response to simple questions. To formulate a series of sessions goals directed toward this short-term goal, we address the question above: How is the client going to acquire this linguistic target? To answer this question we first consider maintaining factors. One of the major maintaining factors for this client, as with most clients learning a second language, is sensorimotor. Given that the client's first language, Spanish, has no tense/lax contrasts among vowels, it is likely that the client has had no experience in differentiating or producing these contrasts. As a consequence, we may assume the client has no sensorimotor representation for these contrasting vowels. Thus, our task is to eliminate this maintaining factor by engaging the client in activities leading to the construction of sensorimotor representations for tense/lax distinctions.

Effect of Principles of Learning and Rehabilitation. We also need to consider the principles of learning and rehabilitation that bear upon the acquisition of the distinctions noted above. Three principles were specified in a long-term procedural approach for Sylvia. These were that learning is facilitated by:

1. noticing similarities and distinctions among actions and events mediated by others;
2. making an effort to match models presented by the clinician;
3. experiencing sensory stimulation (i.e., sensory feedback) from movement, including movement involved in articulation.

Based on these principles, we anticipated in the delineated procedural approach (at the short-term planning phase) that we would create discrimination and production activities.

What Variables Influence Performance Demands?

The next step in specifying a series of session goals is to determine gradations of complexity and difficulty of the tasks the client is expected to perform. Recall, in the discussion of short-term planning we distinguished between complexity and difficulty. Task complexity involves demands inherent to the task regardless of who is performing it. In contrast, task difficulty involves the individual's skill or perception. The nature of the client's speech-language impairment and the client's evaluation of the task contribute to the task's ease or difficulty.

The complexity or difficulty of a task is measured according to several variables. Some of variables are: perceptual support (the extent of visual or auditory stimuli required), response mode (the type of response expected—receptive or expressive), linguistic complexity of response (degree of semantic/syntactic organization), phonetic/prosodic environment (stress of syllable and surrounding phonemes), and propositional content (the extent to which novel information must be transmitted). The factors we evaluate to control task difficulty are closely related to the individual's speech/language impairment and idiosyncratic combination of maintaining factors. For example, perceptual support would be a major consideration in designing tasks for an individual with aphasia or head trauma with information-retention problems. For an individual with a stuttering problem, a more relevant consideration might be the propositional content of the message. The overall context we create in the session is influenced by the client's social and vocational interests and experiences. The issue of performance demands will be developed further as session planning is considered in subsequent chapters dealing with specific clients and communication problems.

Sample Session Goals

Having discussed the various factors that need to be considered in sequencing session goals, we are prepared to generate sample session goals for Sylvia. We will present two goals: one likely to be written early in treatment and the other at the end of the short-term period. After formulating goals we will illustrate their derivation with reference to maintaining factors, principles of learning and rehabilitation, and performance demands.

Recall that the short-term goal for Sylvia is to produce /i/ and /I/ and /ʊ/ and /u/ in single-word utterances in responses to simple questions.

Early Session Goal: Sylvia will *place cards* containing *monosyllabic words* with /i/ and /I/ in appropriate piles after words are produced by the clinician.

Derivation:

> Maintaining factor addressed: sensorimotor
>
> Principles from theories of learning and rehabilitation:
>
>> Learning is facilitated by noticing similarities and distinctions among actions and events mediated by others.
>
> Performance demands controlled:
>
>> Response mode: discrimination before production
>>
>> Number of syllables: monosyllabic less complex than polysyllabic

Session Procedure: Clinician will:

- provide cards containing monosyllabic minimal pairs that contrast in their vowels;
- produce /i/, /I/ minimal pairs varying vowel order.

Later Session Goal: Sylvia will *read* lists of *word pairs* (containing contrasting vowels /i/-/I/, and /u/-/ʊ/).
Derivation:

> Maintaining factors addressed: sensorimotor
>
> Principles from theories of learning and rehabilitation:
>
>> Learning is facilitated by noticing similarities and distinctions among actions and events mediated by others;
>>
>> Learning is facilitated by sensory stimulation (i.e., sensory feedback) from movement, including movement involved in articulation.
>
> Performance demands controlled:
>
>> Perceptual support: responses to printed stimuli precede spontaneous productions
>>
>> Phonetic environment: productions of consecutive words with vowel constrasts after successive words with the same vowel

Session Procedure: Clinician will:

- provide lists of word pairs (containing contrasting vowels /i/-/I/ and /u/-/ʊ/).
- model correct response and request imitation if initial response is incorrect.

Criteria for Achievement of Goals

There is legislation that mandates the establishment of numerical criteria for determining goal achievement for children; clinicians typically indicate that the child will achieve some goals with a proscribed degree of accuracy (e.g., 80–100%). There is no such legislation that applies to adult treatment. We feel, however, that some objective measure of achievement is warranted. This is especially true in light of the recent proliferation of health maintenance organizations requiring quantitative indexes of improvement. One approach for adults could be the specification of a performance frequency within a delimited period, similar to one recommended for use with children in natural contexts (Bloom & Lahey, 1978). An example of this alternative method is, "The client will initiate conversation, three times in a one half-hour session."

Summary

In this chapter we defined phases of intervention planning for adults with communication problems. At each phase we described the derivation of goals and procedures with special attention to the sources of information that guided decision making. These sources include: baseline data, maintaining factors, principles from theories of learning and rehabilitation, and premorbid social/vocational history.

In intervention planning for adults as with children, our knowledge of normal speech and language functioning guides us in setting appropriate goals. Our knowledge of normal functioning of behavioral systems that may maintain a communication problem guides procedure planning, as do our beliefs concerning learning and rehabilitation. Chapters 3 and 4 present a summary of normal adult performance in speech and language. Chapter 5 examines normal adult performance and expected changes in performance with aging in the nonlinguistic behavioral systems. Chapter 6 reviews principles of learning and rehabilitation applicable to adults.

BOX **2.4**

Sources of Information for Planning Short-Term Goals

Sources of Information	Application to Goal Planning
1. The long-term goal(s)	▪ establishes the direction and framework (taxonomies) in which short-term goals are planned
2. Baseline data	▪ determine point of entry into intervention process
3. Task complexity and difficulty hierarchies	▪ guide the prioritization of targets

---

REFERENCES

American Psychiatric Association. (1980). *Diagnostic and statistical manual of mental disorders* (3rd ed.). Washington, DC: Author.

Andrews, M. L. (1991). Voice therapy for children. San Diego, CA: Singular.

Bayles, K. A., & Kaszniak, A. W. (1987). *Communication and cognition in normal aging and dementia.* Austin, TX: Pro-Ed.

Bloom, L. (1991). Language development from two to three. New York: Cambridge University Press.

Bloom, L., & Lahey, M. (1978). *Language development and language disorders.* New York: Wiley.

Braine, M. D. S. (1990). The "natural logic" approach to reasoning. In W. F. Overton (Ed.), *Reasoning, necessity, and logic: Developmental perspectives* (pp. 133–157). Hillsdale, NJ: Erlbaum.

Brookshire, R. H. (1992). *An introduction to neurogenic communication disorders* (4th ed.). St. Louis, MO: Mosby.

Brown, R. (1973). *A first language: The early stages.* Cambridge, MA: Harvard University Press.

Bruner, J. (1990). *Acts of meaning.* Cambridge, MA: Harvard University Press.

Byrnes, J. P. (1992). The conceptual basis of procedural learning. *Cognitive Development, 7,* 235–257.

Chapey, R. (Ed.). (1994). *Language intervention strategies in adult aphasia.* (3rd ed.). Baltimore, MD: Williams & Wilkins.

Chi, M. T. H., de Leeuw, N., Chiu, M-H, & LaVancher, C. (1994). Eliciting self-explanations improves understanding. *Cognitive Science, 8,* 439–477.

Cook, R. E., Tessier, A., & Klein, M. D. (1992). Adapting early childhood curriculum for children with special needs (3rd ed.). New York: Merrill.

Corrigan, R., & Stevenson, C. (1994). Children's causal attributions to states and events described by different verbs. *Cognitive Development, 9,* 235–256.

Darley, F. L., Aronson, A. E., & Brown, J. R. (1969). Clusters of deviant speech dimensions in the dysarthrias. *Journal of Speech and Hearing Research, 12,* 462–496.

Gentner, D., & Stevens, A. L. (Eds.). (1983). *Mental models.* Hillsdale, NJ: Erlbaum.

Goffman, E. (1967). *Interaction ritual: Essays on face-to-face behavior.* New York: Pantheon.

Goodglass, H., & Kaplan, E. (1983). Boston Diagnostic Aphasia Examination (2nd ed.). Philadelphia: Lea and Febiger.

Klein, H. B., & Moses, N. (1999). *Intervention planning for children with communication disorders* (2nd ed.). Needham, MA: Allyn & Bacon.

Kreb, R. A., & Augustine, R. M. (1997). Teaching and modeling—Current clinical practice: Infusing the concepts of managed care, outcomes, and costs across the curriculum. Workshop presented to the Council of Graduate Programs in Communication Sciences and Disorders. Charleston, IL: April 8.

Lahey, M. (1988). *Language disorders and language development.* New York: Macmillan.

Martin, A. D. (1981). An examination of Wepman's thought centered therapy. In R. Chapey, (Ed.), *Language intervention strategies in adult aphasia* (1st ed.). (pp. 141–154). Baltimore, MD: Williams & Wilkins.

Miyake, A., Carpenter, P. A., & Just, M. A. (1994). A capacity approach to syntactic comprehension disorders: Making normal adults perform like aphasic patients. *Cognitive Neuropsychology, 11,* 671–717.

Moshman, D. (1990). The development of metalogical understanding. In W. F. Overton (Ed.), *Reasoning, necessity, and logic: Developmental perspectives* (pp. 205–225). Hillsdale, NJ: Erlbaum.

Myers, P. (1986). Right hemisphere communication impairment. In R. Chapey,(Ed.), *Language intervention strategies in adult aphasia* (pp. 444–461). Baltimore: Williams & Wilkins.

Nelson, N. W. (1993). *Childhood language disorders in context: Infancy through adolescence.* Needham, MA: Allyn & Bacon.

Nippold, M. A. (1993). Developmental markers in adolescent language: Syntax, semantics, and pragmatics. *Language, Speech, and Hearing Services in Schools, 24,* 21–28.

Obler, L. K. (1985). Language through the lifespan. In J. B. Geason (Ed.), *The development of language* (pp. 277–306). New York: Academic Press.

Piaget, J. (1971). *Biology and knowledge.* Chicago: University of Chicago Press.

Rothstein, S. F. (1990). *Special education law.* New York: Longman.

Sankoff, D., & Lessard, R. (1975). Vocabulary richness: A sociolinguistic. *Science, 190,* 689–690.

Schuell, H., Jenkins, J. J., & Jimenez-Pabon, E. (1964). *Aphasia in adults.* New York: Harper & Row.

Searle, J. (1969). *Speech acts: An essay in the philosophy of language.* London: Cambridge University Press.

van Riemsdijk, H., & Williams, E. (1986). Introduction to the theory of grammar. Cambridge, MA: Massachusetts Institute of Technology Press.

Ylvisaker, M., & Szekeres, S. F. (1994). Communication disorders associated with closed head injury. In R. Chapey (Ed.), *Language intervention strategies in adult aphasia* (3rd ed., pp. 546–567). Baltimore: Williams & Wilkins.

3 Funds of Knowledge for Intervention Planning with Adults: Normal Communication and Discourse

CHAPTER OUTCOMES

The reader will:

1. differentiate between conversational and narrative discourse;
2. differentiate between micro and macro levels of discourse structure;
3. identify functional discourse as the ultimate outcome of intervention for all types of communication problems;
4. become familiar with normal conversational and narrative discourse in adults;
5. become aware of changes in adult discourse with aging.

Overview

This chapter begins an overview of typical adult communication performance. Knowledge about communicative functioning in normally achieving adults is essential to the establishment of realistic goals in intervention planning. Describing communicative functioning in adults, however, is a complicated task. This is because there are different linguistic expectations at different points in the life cycle. The life span picture of communication in normally achieving adults includes optimal functioning (the parental home, marriage, employment, child rearing, retirement, etc.) and deterioration in the system associated with aging. There is also substantial variability in linguistic performance at each stage of the life cycle. Those systems that interact with language (psychosocial, cognitive, and sensorimotor) may undergo change as well.

Consistent with our focus on functional communication as the ultimate outcome of speech-language intervention, we review research on normal parameters of adult language with reference to content, form, and use. This approach contrasts with much research on adult language and aging, which has traditionally focused on performance in standardized test formats (e.g., reading comprehension, receptive vocabulary tests, etc.). The traditional focus tends to be on information-processing skills, such as short-term memory, lexical recall, and such (e.g., Bayles & Kaszniak, 1987; Obler & Albert, 1981). These skills will be examined principally in Chapter 5, in a discussion of information-processing factors that can maintain communication problems.

We begin our overview of normal adult communication with language use; specifically, the discourse functions and conventions of communication and language. The ability to engage in discourse (i.e., extended communication sequences) represents the ultimate outcome of speech-language intervention with adults. This is the case when discourse itself is the focus of intervention or when discourse is the linguistic context in which other types of communication skills (e.g., articulation, fluency, voice) are finally achieved. Furthermore, discourse is most sensitive to the changing phases of adulthood.

The Discourse Functions and Conventions of Communication and Language

As adults leave school and their childhood home to enter marriage and the workplace, they are confronted with the demands of learning how to carry on conversations in various settings, adopting new and varied communication registers (e.g., as husband to wife, ex to ex, subordinate to authority, authority to subordinate, child to parent, parent to child, grandparent to grandchild). Successful adaptation to these multifaceted roles involves learning appropriate pragmatic skills for various communication contexts. These aspects of communication are commonly categorized as components of language use (e.g., Lahey, 1988). Language use, however, has been defined from several perspectives.

Within the Bloom and Lahey (1978; Lahey, 1988) content/form/use framework, language use refers to the communicative functions of language and the linguistic and nonlinguistic contexts in which they occur. These authors view use (more frequently referred to as "pragmatics") as integrated with content and form from the first word throughout adulthood. Other language professionals have a different focus—on the emergence of semantics, morphology, and syntax as a result of their functions in *discourse* (the functionalist view represented by, for example, Bates, Thal, & MacWhinney, 1991; Mentis, 1994; Mentis & Thompson, 1991).

Discourse defined in behavioral terms is the integration of sentences into coherent communication (Gordon, 1993). Defined structurally by Hough and Pierce (1994), discourse "is a series of connected sentences that convey a message" (p. 250). Hough and Pierce delineated four types of discourse that have been identified in the literature: "(a) conversation, in which speaker and listener take turns exchanging information; (b) expository, which centers on a particular topic; (c) procedural, which involves telling how something is done; and (d) narrative, which describes a happening expressed as a sequence of events or episodes" (p. 252). In children, the ability to engage in discourse emerges gradually, after the egocentric production of single words, single sentences that refer to single events, and complex sentences that refer to two or more events (Lahey, 1988). In adults, discourse is the context in which communication most typically and spontaneously takes place, and in which normative data on functional communication and language in adults have most often been collected (e.g, Brownell & Joanette, 1993; Bayles & Kaszniak, 1987). Furthermore, discourse may best represent what adults know about the language use and how language use relates to the other grammatical components. It is well known, too, that children and adults with language problems may evidence well-developed linguistic knowledge at the sentence level yet experience difficulty when engaged in discourse (e.g., Fey, 1986; Lahey, 1988; Mentis & Prutting, 1987, 1991; Mentis & Thompson, 1991; Nelson, 1993). Since discourse provides the context in which functional communication in adults most naturally occurs, discourse will frame our examination of normal communication functioning in adults.

In any examination of adult discourse, it is important to remember that conventions of discourse differ among cultures (e.g., Cheng, 1993, 1996; Roseberry-Mckibbins, 1997). As such, when judging normalcy of discourse the clinician must consider the client's cultural background.

The Microstructural and Macrostructural Levels of Discourse

Within the functionalist literature, discourse has been characterized within two structural levels: microstructural and macrostructural. The microstructural level is viewed as the "local level" of discourse and involves the construction of sentences and their relationship to one another (see also, Tannen, 1994, who termed this level "cohesion"). The way sentences are formulated and relate to one another involve certain linguistic devices that have been identified in the literature (e.g., Halliday & Hasan, 1976; Hough & Pierce, 1994; Lahey, 1988; Mentis, 1994; Mentis & Prutting, 1987; Prutting & Kirshner, 1983; Roth & Spekman, 1986). Some of these devices that are engaged in maintaining cohesion between and among sentences are reference, ellipsis, and conjunction. These will be illustrated later in the section on conversation.

The macrostructural level is viewed as the "global level" of discourse and involves overall comprehensibility as well as the style in which the discourse in organized. This level corresponds with Tannen's (1994) view of *topic coherence,* which is defined as "the underlying organizing structure making the words and sentences into a unified discourse that has cultural significance for those who create or comprehend it" (p. 14). Hough and Pierce (1994) suggested that macrostructure is reflected in theme, gist, topic, plan, main idea, or goal.

When working with adults the clinician must keep in mind the inextricable connection between the micro- and macrostructures of discourse. For example, if the overall goal for a client is to produce a well-organized, coherent conversation or narrative about the Superbowl (the macrostructure), it would be necessary to incorporate appropriate microstructural elements such as relevant connectives (e.g., because, if/then, so) and clear pronominal reference (e.g., it, they, his). Alternatively, if the focus is on the microstructural level (e.g., connectives, pronominal reference, etc.), it would be necessary to insure that the client could keep the overall topic of discourse in mind (e.g., the Superbowl).

To describe expected discourse performance in normally functioning adults, we highlight two discourse areas: conversation and narrative. These areas have been studied most frequently in normally developing adults and in adults with language disorders (e.g., see Mentis & Prutting, 1987, 1991). We view conversation as the area of discourse that focuses on the interchange between the participants in a communication exchange. Contrastively, narrative discourse is oriented more toward an individual who relates an event to a listener (e.g., explaining events, telling stories, etc.). We will address these two discourse types with reference to their macrostructural components (e.g., topic introduction, shading, maintenance), and microstructural components (linguistic and nonlinguistic devices necessary for their execution).

Production and Comprehension As Components of Discourse

As a social process, all participants in discourse are both senders and receivers of messages (Martin, 1981). In other words, discourse incorporates both language comprehension and production. This is clearly the case in a typical conversation, and when narratives are inserted into the conversation. In the following discussion of discourse, descriptions of conversational forms focus primarily on language production. Comprehension is addressed more specifically in the subsequent section on narratives.

Conversation

Orestrom (1983) characterizes conversation as "an informal speech event which is largely guided by the spontaneous wishes and interests of the participants and may occur for no other reason than to carry out a social interaction" (p. 23). There have been some recent attempts by ethnographic researchers to analyze conversations in English-speaking adults (e.g., Orestrom, 1983; Psathas, 1995). Psathas presented a set of transcription symbols for the study of "talk-in-interaction," his term for conversation. These symbols, which capture important aspects of conversation and are therefore relevant to its organization, include notations for silence, onset of speech, overlapped speech, turn transitions, and turn completions. Orestrom collected data on aspects of speaker/listener interaction in spontaneous everyday conversational interchanges. These included turn-taking behaviors, length of speaker turn, and simultaneous speech and interruption. Information about adult conversational patterns have also emanated from the literature on gender differences in communication (Arlis & Borisoff, 1993; Borisoff & Merrill, 1992; Cooper & Anderson-Inman, 1988; Tannen, 1994).

Within speech-language pathology there is little research in normal pragmatic development during and after adolescence; this paucity of information extends to conversational discourse (Stephens, 1988; Stover & Hanes, 1989). This may be because conversational competence develops through the life span and is affected to a great extent by the social context (Cooper & Anderson-Inman, 1988; Stephens, 1988). As a result, clinicians generally have based their expectations about successful adult conversation on what is known about conversational developments through adolescence (e.g., Nippold, 1993) and corroborated these expectations with findings of conversational differences between normally functioning adults and those with brain injury (e.g., Hough & Pierce, 1994; Mentis & Prutting, 1987, 1991). The following discussion on conversational skills is based on a consideration of information provided by the various disciplines noted above.

Topic Management

Topic management is perhaps one of the most important prerequisites for successful conversation. Topic management is a complex pragmatic skill dependent on underlying cognitive and linguistic knowledge (Mentis, 1994). According to Mentis, topic management involves mastery of two major components: topic introduction and topic maintenance. Each of these components is in turn supported by semantic/syntactic forms that undergo developmental changes during late childhood and into adulthood.

Topic Introduction and Change. Successful conversation demands that topics be initiated, shifted, or changed in such a way that the coherence and cohesion of the conversational interaction be maintained. It has been suggested that topic and subtopic introduction be described with reference to at least three parameters: (a) the extent to which the speaker initiates topics and subtopics, (b) the manner in which topics and subtopics are introduced, and (c) the types of topics and subtopics introduced (Mentis, 1994). Research suggests that adults center conversations around fewer topics than children and do not move as quickly from topic to topic (e.g., Brinton & Fujiki, 1984; Tannen, 1994). There are also some data to suggest that the manner in which topics are introduced (shifts and shading) continue to be mastered though adolescence (e.g., Tannen, 1994; Wanska & Bedrosian, 1985).

Types of topics also appear to be sensitive to developmental changes and gender influence. For example, it has been shown that with aging the tendency to reintroduce a previously discussed topic decreases (e.g., Brinton & Fujiki, 1984). Topic content would also be expected to reflect cumulative education and experience expected with development (Mentis, 1994; Nippold, 1988).

Patterns of topic choice have also been related to gender of speakers. Tannen (1994), who studied eight conversational dyads of second, sixth, tenth graders, and 25-year-old males and females found that patterns of topic introduction and types of topics differentiated the genders. She reported that girls' and women's talk was more tightly focused, while boys' and men's talk was more diffuse. Males used the physical space (the room) as a topic in contrast to the females who did not. There were occasional references in the males' talk to violence that was absent in the females; the females tended to be concerned with separation from significant others and avoidance of anger and disagreement.

In perhaps the only normative study on topic management in normal adults over a wide age range (30–90), Stover and Haynes (1989) investigated aspects of "topic manipulation." Five dyads within four age groups (30–41, 46–59, 65–75, 78–90) were audio tape recorded as they engaged in (as natural as possible) a conversation. The aspects of conversations analyzed with reference to topic introduction were the tendency to (a) introduce new topics, (b) reintroduce old topics, and (c) shade topics (i.e., elaborating upon relationships within a conversation). The results revealed no difference among age groups with reference to topic introduction. A similar number of topics was introduced by each group. Stover and Haynes were unable to analyze the reintroduction of topics because of the limited number of such cases across the dyads. With reference to topic shading, the oldest group (78–90) tended to shade topics less than younger groups (30–41, 46–59, 65–75). Stover and Haynes explained that this finding may be related to the older group's presupposition of much shared knowledge with the listener. This may contrast with the tendency of younger adults to use shading to explain or clarify. Other explanations offered were that older adults may avoid shading so as not to lose the main topic at hand, or that the process of shading may require manipulations too subtle or complex for these older subjects.

Linguistic Devices That Support Topic Introduction and Topic Shifts.   A number of linguistic devices have been identified that support the pragmatic function of topic introduction. These are discourse particles and phrases, questions, relative clauses (Mentis, 1994; Mentis & Thompson, 1991), and adverbial conjuncts (Nippold, Schwartz, & Undlin, 1992). Mentis has proposed that the following "discourse particles and phrases" have been used to perform the function of topic introduction: "by the way," "well," "anyway," "before I forget," "incidently," and "you know what?" These forms, along with topic-introducing questions (e.g., "So, where did you go on your vacation?"), and relative clauses (which identify relevant referents, "The man with the red hat painted the house") appear to be developing through adolescence (Mentis, 1994).

The introduction of new topics into a continuing conversation represents topic shifting. Adverbial conjuncts are "explicit cohesion devices that serve to join phrases, clauses, or sentences in spoken and written discourse" (Nippold et al., 1992, p. 108). They are used for topic shifting and shading (Mentis, 1994). Adverbial conjuncts, which have been studied developmentally, have been shown to develop past adolescence into adulthood.

Nippold et al. (1992) studied the comprehension and use of two types of adverbial conjuncts. The first type is *concordant,* comprising conjuncts such as "similarly," "moreover," and "consequently." The second type is *discordant,* represented by words such as "contrastively," "rather," and "nevertheless." The authors reported that their subjects (120 adolescents and adults, 12:9 to 23:8 years of age) demonstrated an increasing ability to use and understand these words in written material. In addition, they found that both groups of conjuncts were equally difficult, and that, although the young adults had mastered the comprehension of these words, they continued to display difficulty in using these words correctly. Table 3.1 presents a list of the adverbial conjuncts used in the Nippold et al. study in order of the accuracy of responses demonstrated on the reading and writing tasks.

Topic Maintenance.   Successful conversation also demands that utterances produced are related to the topic being discussed and contribute to its development. According to Mentis (1994), maintaining a topic "requires the ability to produce contingent responses and structure and organize new and old topic-related information across extended sequences of discourse" (p. 34). Several syntactic devices have been suggested to support efficient topic maintenance (e.g., Halliday & Hasan, 1976; Hough & Pierce, 1994; Lahey, 1988; Mentis, 1994; Mentis & Prutting, 1987). There are differences among professionals in the organization and description of these devices. Some of the most frequently addressed in research as tools for successful discourse are described below.

TABLE 3.1   Order of accuracy (most to least) of the 10 adverbial conjuncts for the two tasks, all subjects combined (*n* = 120).

Writing task		Reading task	
therefore (+)	.98	therefore (+)	.84
however (−)	.90	however (−)	.81
consequently (+)	.84	rather (−)	.80
rather (−)	.75	furthermore (+)	.76
nevertheless (−)	.62	contrastively (−)	.72
furthermore (+)	.57	consequently (+)	.71
moreover (+)	.53	similarly (+)	.70
conversely (−)	.47	moreover (+)	.67
contrastively (−)	.43	nevertheless (−)	.66
similarly (+)	.39	conversely (−)	.64
Overall mean	.65	Overall mean	.73

Note: (+) = concordant, (−) = discordant.

From Nippold, Schwartz and Undlin, 1992. Used with permission.

Linguistic Devices That Support Topic Maintenance.   As with topic introduction and shading, cohesive devices support topic maintenance. In describing cohesion, Halliday & Hasan (1976) wrote, "Cohesion occurs where the interpretation of some element in the discourse is dependent on that of another. The one presupposes the other, in the sense that it cannot be effectively decoded except by recourse to it" (p. 4). Mentis and Prutting (1987) studied the cohesive strategies of normally speaking adults and adults with closed head injury (CHI), using the five cohesion categories proposed by Halliday and Hasan: reference, substitution, ellipsis, conjunction, lexical. In addition, they added one category of their own—incomplete cohesive ties. See Table 3.2 for definitions and examples of each.

Among the results of their study, Mentis and Prutting (1987) found that adults with head injury used the three categories—incomplete, ellipsis, and lexical—more than the other group. The normally speaking group never used incomplete ties. The excessive use of ellipsis and lexical cohesion by the CHI group was interpreted as a compensatory device that enabled them to maintain conversation by using the conversational partner's statement or lexical item as a scaffold for the formulation of their own utterances.

Another aspect of the Stover and Haynes (1989) study noted above was an analysis of topic maintenance. The authors found that the oldest group of subjects (78–90) maintained significantly more topics than those aged 30–75. According to these investigators, the elderly speakers may have a great wealth of information to contribute to a subject and prefer to stay with a particular topic. They also suggested that elderly speakers may also feel more comfortable staying with a topic they know rather than changing or shading. Stover and Haynes made the point that the oldest category of speakers did not tend to ramble as the aged are often depicted.

Despite the finding that the oldest group of adults tended to maintain topics to a greater extent, Stover and Haynes found that as age increased individuals produced fewer cohesive ties (see Table 3.2 for examples of cohesive ties). Groups aged 65–75 and 78–90

TABLE 3.2   Definitions and Examples of the Five Cohesion Categories Delineated by Halliday and Hasan (1976).

Reference

Reference is a semantic relation whereby the information needed for the interpretation of some item is found elsewhere in the text and the information needed is the referential meaning or identity of the thing or class of things being referred to. Thus the cohesion lies in the continuity of reference, as the same thing is referred to more than once in the discourse. Reference is subdivided into three separate categories: pronominal, demonstrative, and comparative. The following are examples of referential cohesive ties.

Pronominal: *Mary* is a teacher. *She* teaches third grade.

Demonstrative: Tom is in the *office*. You can find him *there*.

Comparative: John wore his *red* shirt. His *other* shirts were dirty.

Substitution

In substitution, the cohesive bond is established by the use of a substitute item of the same grammatical class as the item necessary for interpretation. The substitute has the same structural function as that for which is substitutes. Substitution may be nominal, verbal or clausal. The following are examples of substitution ties.

Nominal: I need a bigger *cup*. I'll get *one*.

Clausal: *They've lost then?* I regret *so*.

Ellipsis

Ellipsis is "substitution by zero" and refers specifically to sentences or clauses whose structure is such as to presuppose some preceding item, which then serves as the source of the missing information. Ellipsis is divided into three categories: nominal, verbal, and clausal. The following are examples of elliptical ties.

Nominal: What kind of coffee do you want? Decaffeinated (coffee).

Verbal: Who's going. I am (going).

Clausal: Has she done her school work? She has (done her school work).

Conjunction

Conjunction expresses a logical relation between clauses by specifying how what is to follow in a text is systematically related to what has gone before. The cohesive bond is achieved through the expression of certain meanings that presuppose the presence of other components in the discourse. Conjunction is subdivided into five categories: additive, adversative, causal, temporal, and continuative. The following are examples of conjunction ties.

Additive: I fell. and everything came falling down on top of me.

Adversative: All the data was correct. Yet the conclusion seemed impossible.

Causal: I did not know. Otherwise, I would have come immediately.

Temporal: She opened the door. Then she switched on the light.

Continuative: You needn't apologize. After all, you did not know all the facts.

Lexical

Lexical cohesion is the cohesive effect achieved through vocabulary selection. Lexical cohesion may either take the form of reiteration (where both the cohesive item and that to which it refers have a common referent) or collocation (where cohesion is achieved through the association of lexical items that regularly co-occur). Within the category of reiteration, lexical cohesion may take the form of the same root, synonym, superordinate, or general item. The following are examples of lexical ties. Reiteration:

Same word: We went to the *house* on the hill. It was a round *house*.

Synonym: He's a fine *boy*. He's one of the brightest *lads* I know.

Superordinate: You can take some *peaches*. I have plenty of *fruit*.

General word: I gave *Mary* my book. The *idiot* lost it.

Collocation: I told her to call a *doctor*. She was very *ill*.

Incomplete Cohesive Ties

This category was an additional category included in the cohesion analysis. These ties referred to instances where a referring item was used and the item to which it referred was not specified or evident from the immediate context. The following are examples of incomplete ties.

Mary gave *it* to John

where the obligatory referent for *it* is neither supplied in the text nor evident from the context.

He gave me a book

where the obligatory referent for *he* is neither supplied in the text nor evident from the context.

From Mentis and Prutting (1987). Used with permission.

produced significantly more incomplete ties than the groups aged 30–41 and 46–59. Stover and Haynes suggested that inappropriate cohesive reference may be related to a type of egocentricity. They hypothesized that as a person ages there is a reduction in the ability to take another's perspective—"reduced awareness of the listener's need for clarification" (p. 147). Another speculation by Stover and Haynes was that some elderly speakers may forget to specify referents, believing they have already provided this information.

Conversational Protocol

In addition to the use of semantic/syntactic devices for the management of conversational topics, the adult must be aware of conversational style or protocol. Conversational protocol comprises at least the following categories of behavior: (a) turn-taking skills, (b) awareness of communication breakdown, (c) knowledge of polite forms, and (d) "face-saving" skills.

Turn Taking Skills. Turn taking has been described as "an example of a device that directs organization of the conversation" (Hough & Pierce, 1994, p. 255). Although turn-taking behavior is observed as early as infancy (e.g., Lahey, 1988; Stern, Jaffe, Beebe, & Bennett, 1975) it continues to be modified throughout an individual's life (Arlis & Borisoff, 1993; Borisoff & Merrill, 1992; Cooper & Anderson-Inman, 1988; Tannen, 1994), affected by an individual's cognitive/linguistic achievements (e.g., Klein, Moses, & Altman; 1988) and personality (e.g., Tannen, 1994). Two major turn-taking issues are turn durations and interruptions.

During conversation adults are expected to be aware of addressing the questions and statements proposed by another in a given turn ("to assert, respond, or react to what the listener has in turn, asserted or responded," Lahey, 1988, p. 17), be aware of turn durations (addressing a statement or question "to-the-point"), and attend to nonverbal cues that signal the end of turn (theirs or another's; e.g., head nod, head tilt, eye contact [or averting], eyebrow raising, and smiling). Based on 10 adult conversations with speakers ages 21–60, Orestrom (1983) found that the shift from one speaker to another occurred most frequently at the end of a (a) completed tone unit, (b) syntactically completed sequence, and (c) semantically fully rational sequence. Length of speaking turns was measured by the number of words produced. There was a great deal of variability among speakers with reference to the total number of turns and the number of words per turn. When words were divided into categories according to number of words per turn (1–10, 11–20, 21–30, etc.), the mean was 28 words. Very long turns (over 100 words) were infrequent. There were no differences related to sex or age of speaker.

There is some indication that individuals who have difficulty monitoring verbal output may not be aware of turn-taking signals or length of their own turns. Adults with learning disabilities have been observed to be frequently unaware of turn boundaries. Recorded conversations of adults with learning disabilities demonstrated that turns were continued with apparent lack of awareness of listener's failing attention or interest (e.g., Klein et al., 1988). Interestingly, this behavior differs from children with specific language impairment who frequently take shorter turns and do not use interruptions to gain a turn at speaking (Craig & Evans, 1989).

Entering the conversation before the ongoing speaker has finished is generally termed interruption. Others terms such as "unsmooth speaker-shift" (Orestrom, 1983) or "overlap" (Tannen, 1994) have also been used to refer to this phenomenon. Much of the literature on interruption behavior in conversation addresses gender differences. Interruption, which has traditionally been viewed as a sign of power, attributed primarily to males, has also been seen as being used by the powerless (Tannen, 1994). Tannen pointed out that this conversational strategy commonly is interpreted differently by different speakers. The interpretation of overlap depends for the most part on the setting, individuals' status, their relationship to each other, and culturally expected linguistic conventions. Some speakers consider talking along with another to be a sign of enthusiasm in the conversational dialogue; for example, within the African-American culture interruptions are expected and viewed as appropriate conversational conduct (e.g., Owens, 1996). Contrastively, others assume that only one voice should be heard at a time; for them, any sign of overlap is an interruption, a power play, and it causes them to become silent (Tannen, 1994). In a similar vein, the results of Orestrom's (1983) study indicated no differences in interruption patterns due to sex or age.

Awareness of Communication Breakdown.   Communication breakdown may occur when topics are not introduced clearly or not maintained efficiently, semantic relations are not processed, or lexical items are unfamiliar. Participants in conversational discourse must be able to identify breakdown caused by another speaker (i.e., become aware of a comprehension problem and request repair). They must also be able to repair breakdown caused by an aspect of their own utterances. Dollaghan and Kaston (1986) studied conversational breakdown due to inadequate comprehension monitoring in children. They found that it was possible to instruct their subjects in identifying instances of breakdown and requesting repair. Areas of breakdown included the following: signal inadequacies (too low, too fast, or in the presence of a competing noise); inadequate information (e.g., inexplicit, ambiguous); exceeded comprehension (containing unfamiliar lexical items, excessive length, excessive syntactic complexity). Researchers also studied communication breakdowns in children's conversations due to the speaker's self-monitoring (e.g., MacLachlan & Chapman, 1988). Such monitoring often results in filled pauses, self-initiated repairs, and abandoned utterances, which generally occur with greater frequency as length of communication unit is increased (e.g., MacLachlan & Chapman, 1988).

When normally functioning and aphasic adults were compared, both groups were found to revise communication breakdowns similarly. Both groups attempted to revise communication breakdowns, with any differences in aphasic adults apparently related to the extent of their linguistic impairments (Newhoff, Tonkovich, Schwartz, & Burgess,

1985). Hough & Pierce (1994) highlighted the conversational device of contingent query for the amelioration of breakdown episodes. Contingent queries, such as "What do you mean?" are often used in situations of unclear messages.

Breakdown in communication may also occur when the conversational participants "do not say the right thing at the right time in the right manner" (Cheng, 1996, p. 10) because of linguistic and cultural differences. Speakers of English as a second language may fail to understand the meaning of a conversation if they lack familiarity with culturally based proverbs and metaphors and are not familiar with multiple meanings of words. It is likely these speakers would be unaware of the source of such breakdowns.

Polite Forms and Prosocial Awareness. Conversational competence also requires knowledge of social skills. According to Hough and Pierce (1994) these include polite forms and prosocial awareness. Polite form use includes appropriate verbal forms (please, thank you, excuse me) and nonverbal manners such as eye contact, smiling, and body alignment. Prosocial awareness addresses how pragmatic skills are used in everyday communications, such as dealing with embarrassment, apologizing, asking personal questions, giving criticism, and dealing with accusation (Hough & Pierce, 1994). These forms were found to be subject to cultural differences (e.g., Cheng, 1993, 1996; Cooper, & Anderson-Inman, 1988; Owens, 1996; Tannen, 1994) as well as gender differences (Tannen, 1994). For example, Cheng (1996) described cultural differences in the polite form of greetings; these may be handled by "bowing (Japan), closing one's hands (Thailand), or hugging and kissing (Spain)" (p. 17). Roseberry-McKibbins (1997) presented examples of a type of prosocial awareness—personal questions. She reported Filipinos ask some personal questions that would probably startle an American clinician; these include questions about others' ages, marital status, cost of clothing, and annual salary. To establish rapport with clients from other cultures, clinicians must be aware of such cultural differences. More important, this area may become a source of goals for adults with communication problems.

Face-Saving Devices. Pragmatic skills are particularly challenged in situations that cause embarrassment and the "loss of face." Goffman (1967) defined face as "the positive social value a person effectively claims for himself by the line others assume he has taken during a particular contact" (p. 2). Most people have experienced the embarrassment or even humiliation of losing face when an attempt to maintain face fails. Each of the authors can point to a failed lecture as an example. Being shamefaced, flustered, disgraced, and chagrined are additional feelings associated with the loss of face; pride and self-respect are effects associated with the establishment and maintenance of face.

Different cultures have different ways of maintaining face personally, and helping others establish and avoid the loss of face. In the United States, individuals use several common strategies to avoid losing face themselves, or to help others save face during a face-to-face encounter. These include (a) avoiding or withdrawing from social contact in potentially embarrassing situations; (b) shifting the topic of conversation; (c) suppressing displays of emotion; (d) suppressing information that might embarrass self or others through omissions or circumlocutions; (e) using self-deprecating humor and a joking manner; and (f) tactful overlooking or nonobservance of behavior (such as pretending that a conversational partner's stomach is not audibly rumbling). When a loss of face does occur, individuals may employ strategies to minimize disgrace. In the United States, strategies to repair face may be an apology, such as "excuse me," or a sequence of steps including (a) a challenge by the parties who observed the misconduct; (b) an offering by the challenged party; (c) acceptance by the offended; and (d) thanks by the offending person. Offerings by the person losing face (step b) may be (a) a statement that the offense was meaningless, unintended, the consequence of overpowering factors such as alcohol or medication, or a joke; (b) self-deprecation; (c) provision of compensation to an injured party; (d) self-punishment; (e) indications of being renewed or transformed; and (f) explicit recognition of the feelings of others in response to the transgression. Only upon acceptance of an offering by the offended from one who has lost face is forgiveness given and the corrective process terminated. By way of contrast, Roseberry-Mckibbins (1997) reported some examples of face-saving devices among Filipinos who are averse to open disagreements. They may say "yes" when they mean "no" or they may use silence or anger to communicate dissatisfaction.

Summary.　　Elements of conversational competence in normally functioning adults and supporting linguistic devices were reviewed in the previous section. A summary of these aspects of conversational competence in adults appears in Box 3.1. This box contains illustrations of the way each component of conversational competence (e.g., topic introduction, topic maintenance, and conversation protocol) addressed above may be used for planning intervention goals at each of the three phases.

BOX 3.1

Aspects of Conversational Competence in Adults

Component of Conversation	Linguistic and Nonlinguistic Devices	Application to Intervention Planning
Topic introduction 1. Topic initiation, shifts, and shading continue to be mastered through adolescence and into early adulthood 2. Adults center conversations around fewer topics than children 3. Types of topics are sensitive to developmental changes, gender, cumulative education, and experience 4. Older adults tend to maintain topics to a greater extent than younger groups 5. Older adults shade topics less frequently than younger adults	1. Introductory words, phrases, and questions 2. Adverbial conjuncts (and disjunctives)	1. Topic introduction targeted as long-term goal 2. Linguistic devices targeted as short-term goals 3. Specific lexical items or phrases for topic introduction, shift, or shading targeted as session goals

Component of Conversation	Linguistic and Nonlinguistic Devices	Application to Intervention Planning
Topic maintenance 1. Utterances produced are related to the topic discussed and contribute to its maintenance 2. Older adults produce a greater number of incomplete and erroneous ties than younger groups 3. Erroneous and incomplete ties within the older groups are characterized by greater use of personal pronouns, possessive determiners, possessive pronouns, and demonstratives	1. Supported by cohesive devices: reference substitution ellipsis conjunction vocabulary selection incomplete ties relative and adverbial clauses	1. Topic maintenance targeted as a long-term goal 2. Cohesive devices targeted as short-term goals 3. Specific lexical items or phrases targeted as session goals
Conversational protocol 1. Turn-taking aspects continue to be modified throughout a person's lifetime: ■ length of turn ■ interruption	1. Average turn found to be approximately 28 words—long turns (over 100 words) are infrequent 2. Termination of turn signaled by: ■ completed tone unit ■ syntactically complete sequence ■ semantically fully rational sequence	1. Turn taking targeted as a long-term goal. 2. Topic duration and interruption targeted short-term goals 3. Specific turn-taking signals targeted as session goals
2. Recognizing conversational breakdown: in another in self	1. Monitor comprehension of another's utterances 2. Request further clarification 3. Repair unclear utterances in self	1. Comprehension monitoring targeted as long-term goal. 2. Categories of comprehension difficulties targeted as short term goals: signal inadequacies, inadequate information, unfamiliar or excessively complex material 3. Specific messages in each category targeted as session goals
3. Social skills polite forms prosocial awareness	1. Please, thank you, excuse me, etc. 2. Appropriate words for dealing with situations like apologizing, criticizing, defending, etc.	1. Conversational protocol targeted as long-term goal 2. Polite forms and proforms targeted as short-term goals 3. Specific forms in each category targeted as session goals
4. Face-saving devices	Appropriate pragmatic devices for dealing with situations that threaten self-esteem	Identification and management of specific types of face-saving devices targeted as short-term and session goals.

Implications for Intervention Planning.   Conversation may be addressed in goal planning, from both a pragmatic perspective and a semantic/syntactic perspective. If the target is the improvement of conversational competence, goals would be conversational components (e.g., topic management), linguistic devices (e.g., cohesion devices), and conversational protocol as long-term and short-term goals. If the target is conversation protocol, goals would be the achievement of those pragmatic skills that promote social interaction (e.g., turn-taking skills, repair of communication breakdown, polite forms, social awareness, and face-saving devices). If the target is the comprehension and production of semantic/syntactic structures, the goals would be set in a conversational context. Examples of long-term, short-term, and session goals targeting conversational aspects appear in Box 3.2.

Narratives

Another functionally significant type of discourse in adults is the production and comprehension of narratives. Narratives have been defined broadly as "the ways in which people link together the bits and pieces of language to create representations of events, objects, beliefs, personalities, and experiences" (Brownell & Joanette, 1993, p. vii). Narratives have also been referred to as stories (e.g., Brownell & Joanette, 1993) and defined as any effort to talk about more than one event—an event being defined as a single action represented by a single verb (Lahey, 1988). Bruner (1991b) defined narratives as a specific kind of story—an account of particular events occurring over time, involving the breach or violation of a script (i.e., the normal course of familiar events) From Bruner's point of view, narratives are stories about conflict, trouble, problem solving, and conflict resolution. Functionally, narratives decontextualize experience (Bruner, 1986). Narratives allow individuals to express how they or groups they belong to cope with frightening or challenging situations, and how individuals and their families view themselves (Bruner, 1990; Bruner & Feldman, in press). Events composing a narrative may be real or imagined; often the distinction between reality and imagination is not clear-cut. Bruner and Weiser (1991), for example, viewed autobiography, one's life story, as a reconstruction of or theory about actual experience.

Narratives comprise identifiable macrostructures and functions—some universal, some culture or family specific (Gordon, 1993; Mandler & Goodman, 1982; Rummelhart, 1975). These structures and functions are implicated in the production and comprehension of discourse (e.g., Gordon, 1993; Grosz & Sidner, 1986; Rummelhart, 1977). Given the important functions that narratives serve in adult language, these macrostructures and functions may be intervention targets or contexts for adults with communication problems.

Universal Narrative Structures

One aspect of narrative discourse that may require attention in intervention planning is the way an individual organizes a story. Lahey (1988) identified a developmental sequence of organization within narratives (i.e., story grammars), culminating in the production of "dramatic" narratives that involve problems and problem resolution. These are additive, temporal, and causal chains. Children manifest Lahey's sequence of narrative structures by

BOX **3.2**

Addressing Conversation in Goal Planning

Focus	Target		Examples of Goals
Expression	Conversational Competence	Long-term:	Client will manage conversational topics with a variety of conversational partners.
		Short-term:	Client will maintain topics using a variety of linguistic devices (e.g., reference, ellipsis, conjunction, relative and adverbial clauses).
		Session:	Client will use three adverbial conjuncts (therefore, moreover, and furthermore), in a five-minute conversation with clinician, about a selected current world issue.
	Syntactic Competence	Long-term:	Client will produce complex sentences coding causal and epistemic relations in conversational contexts.
		Short-term:	Client will produce complex sentences coding causal relations in recounting a recent event.
		Session:	Client will produce complex sentences coding causal relations while looking at pictures depicting problematic situations, five times during the session.
Comprehension	Conversational Competence		Long-term goals:

Long-term goals:

1. Client will indicate by eye gaze or gesture the meaning of three-constituent semantic relations produced by a conversational partner.
2. Client will appropriately carry out verbal requests of another in functional communication situations.
3. Client will identify instances of communication breakdown in conversation and request repair.

Short-term goals:

1. Client will indicate by eye gaze or gesture the meaning of two-word semantic relations relative to environmental functioning.
2. Client will appropriately carry out verbal requests of another regarding the completion of household chores.
3. Client will identify instances of communication breakdown when speaker uses unfamiliar lexical items or excessive syntactic complexity.

Session goals:

1. Client will gaze at the picture representing the agent/action relation expressed by the speaker in 8 of 10 presentations.
2. Client will appropriately carry out requests of his wife to bring her various items in specific rooms of their apartment during natural daily interactions.
3. Client will identify instances of communication breakdown during five short conversations as speaker introduces five new lexical items.

approximately six years of age. All three types of narrative structures continue to be manifested by adults, and causal chains continue to develop in complexity into adulthood.

Additive chains constitute the first type of narrative structure to appear developmentally. Additive chains are strings of events connected by conjunctions that have no dependent relationship. An example is: "My wife went to the store to get some bread and the dog just peed in the family room and these things happen all the time." The next type of narrative structure to develop is the temporal chain. Temporal chains comprise a series of events connected by conjunctions that have an explicit temporal relationship to one another. An example is: "I told my wife I was going to the store (knowing full well that I just had to get away for a while). Then I snuck over to Alan's house where I met this really sympathetic girl. So we went out for a drink and one thing lead to another, and, well, the rest is history."

The most advanced types of narratives in Lahey's (1988) scheme are causal chains. Causal chains may be more highly organized than stories with additive or temporal structures. In causal chains, events in the story often relate to one another as causes and effects. In goal-based causal chains, the story begins with a goal or destination, and then problems arise that may or may not get resolved. With the inclusion of problems, goal-based causal chain represents the first form of narrative, following Bruner's (1991b) definition, cited above. A more complex type of causal chain is the embedded causal chain. In such a story problems lead to additional complications that must be cleared up before the initial problem can be resolved. The popular television series "Murder She Wrote" typically follows this format.

Goal-based and embedded causal chains comprise constituent schema; story schema may include setting, complications, internal responses of characters (i.e., how the characters feel about the events), attempts to resolve problems and achieve goals, consequences that are the result of successful or unsuccessful attempts, and reactions precipitated by the complications (also see models of story schemas proposed by Mandler, 1984; Schank & Abelson, 1977).

In sum, individuals organize stories as they express relationships among the component events. These relationships that have been identified as additive, temporal, and causal may be addressed in the course of intervention planning. Universal narrative structures are summarized in Box 3.3 and may be used as a guide for goal planning.

Dramatic Structure of Narratives

Another way of viewing the organization within narratives is with reference to dramatic structure. Here the emphasis is on the distinction between (a) the characters' thoughts and feelings about events and (b) the expression of the events themselves. Bruner (1986, 1991) labeled these two primary components of dramatic structure: landscape of consciousness and landscape of action. The term *landscapes of consciousness* refers to how the world is felt or perceived by characters in the narrative. The storyteller uses internal state verbs to convey this information (e.g., thinks, feels, believes). Contrastively, *landscapes of action* refers to temporal sequences of actions. Interpretation of narratives comprising both types of landscapes requires sensitivity to both types of information. Developmentally, references to landscapes of consciousness increase significantly with the transition from childhood to adulthood.

This was shown by Feldman, Bruner, Kalmar, & Renderer (1993) who evaluated how three groups of subjects (10–12, 15–19, and 26–49 years of age) interpreted narratives. One narrative was about a young man who was pressured to become a priest by his mother but who became attracted to a young woman while on vacation with his mother. The narratives had no conclusion. Feldman et al. identified three systems of interpretation across the three age groups.

The interpretations of the youngest group were organized around categories that corresponded to functions of the plot (or the landscape of action). This group identified the protagonists and their main attributes (often describing characters as opposites of one another, e.g., good or bad, lame or cool, etc.). They also focused on action sequences. Teenagers used a more advanced interpretive system organized around a human plight—still more action oriented than dramatic. Narratives were time bound, with an emphasis on events reaching a point necessitating a decision to break away from habitual behavior. The oldest subjects' interpretations reflected increased focus on emotional substance. In the priest/girl story this shift was manifested in anticipations of conflict, as represented by the words "set" as in, "They were all set to do X"; "heading" and "toward" as in, "He was heading into a relationship with this girl." Sexual references were made to what was instrumental in creating trouble. The word "knowing" was often used to capture the landscape of consciousness ("He's trying to do the right thing without really knowing why he's doing it.").

Dramatic structure reviewed above represents a second potential area for intervention planning. The landscapes of consciousness and action may be targeted as goals in cases of language impairment. This area may be particularly applicable to an individual who demonstrates discrepancy in the ability to express feelings about events as compared with the ability to accurately relate events.

BOX 3.3

Universal Narrative Structures

Category	Structural Components
Additive Chains	Strings of events that have no dependent relation to one another and occur simultaneously
Temporal Chains	Series of events connected that have an explicit temporal relationship to one another
Causal Chains	Events in the story often relate to one another as causes and effects
Simple Causal Chains	No goal or destination is specified, and no solutions are offered for problems that arise
	The story begins with a goal or destination, and then problems arise that may or may not get resolved
Goal-Based Chains	The story begins with a goal, followed by problems that lead to additional complications that must be cleared up before the initial problem can be resolved
Embedded Causal Chains	May comprise a setting, complications, internal responses of characters, attempts to resolve problems and achieve goals, consequences of attempts, and reactions precipitated by complications

Four Narrative Genres

It is highly functional for adults to use several narrative type or genres. Five of the most useful types of narratives are the personal narrative or autobiography, fable, social drama, ritual, and expository. Facility with such narrative types enables an individual to maintain self-esteem, deal with problems, access information, participate in community events, and so forth. Consequently, the comprehension and production of various narrative types has significance for the development of goals and procedures with adult clients.

Personal Narrative.   The narrative type that is, perhaps, most central to the self-esteem of the individual, and therefore deserving of careful attention in communication problems in adults, is the personal narrative. Stern and Henderson (1993) distinguished the personal narrative from other narrative forms by its focus on site-specific events drawn from the speaker's own personal experiences. Stern and Henderson explained that the personal narrative is metalinguistic in nature: personal narratives reflect awareness on the part of the speaker that he or she is a speaker speaking to others.

Personal stories are often about frightening experiences that call into question the storyteller's assumptions about self and how self will react under pressure. As such, personal stories have referential and evaluative functions; they explicate the storyteller's evaluation of the personal experience. According to Stern and Henderson (1993), the speaker's telling of the story can be seen as a performance of themselves (who they are and how they function within special circumstances).

Often stories that start out as commentaries and reflections on self develop over time. They may eventually be told for different social and political ends beyond the immediate event and comment on self. Another interesting aspect of personal storytelling is that its telling is often a collective process. A personal story may be told by a husband and wife, family, or other cohesive social group. It may be difficult to distinguish between the originator and expander of a tale as a story is retold. The story's telling may even be intertextual; that is, it combines a number of voices expressing different cultural, regional, and historical orientations (see also Bruner & Feldman, in press).

The following is a personal story offered by one of the authors of this text who recently underwent open heart surgery. We present this story to illustrate the important adaptive functions that personal stories can serve for individuals who face challenging and often frightening experiences—people like those we treat for communication problems. Given the personal nature of this story, the author will speak for himself in presenting and discussing the story.

This experience was certainly frightening. It raised issues for me concerning how I would be able to cope with an imminent life-threatening situation. Unfortunately, I am not inherently brave. Telling this story and others like it helped me create a framework within which I could approach, interpret, and adapt to frightening situations as they arose. These narratives were expressions to myself and others of my ego strength and problem-solving strategies.

It is important to note that the story I am relating here was told less than one week after surgery, when I was relieved that I had made it through a major crisis but was concerned about emergent situations. (I was telling similar but different stories before surgery.) This story was told to friends who were supporting me. You will see that the following story is in no way extraordinary, except perhaps for the function it served for the storyteller. It is the kind of story that clients who have suffered trauma may tell. This story, about an emergency, was told as follows:

> I was sitting up, preparing to take a short walk, when I glanced at the heart monitor and I noticed that my heart rate was increasing from 90 to 100, 110, 120, 130 beats per minute. I felt my heart racing, and I also felt it becoming arrhythmic. I was in step-down—one level of care below intensive care—and there was supposed to be constant monitoring of patients, but at that moment there was no nurse in the room. I called to another patient for help. Finally, the nurse appeared and then a cardiac emergency team, who gave me a shot of the drug, Lopressor. The arrythmia continued for a couple of hours. I must say that I was really panicked during those two hours. I asked that my primary cardiologist or surgeon be informed of this problem, but was told they were not presently available. I really felt helpless, and like I said I was really nervous. Finally, after talking to my friend and colleague, David Shapiro, who just happened to call the hospital during this crisis, I decided to become proactive to get some control over the situation. I insisted that my cardiologist be paged and summoned to examine me. He arrived and suggested that I be given additional medication. Within a half hour the arrhythmia converted to a normal rhythm. I think that my attitude and the language I used to express myself helped as much as the medication to reverse the arrhythmia. Being proactive is extremely important. I now know that it is important to take control of emergency situations. It is important to make sure someone you trust is nearby to oversee decisions, especially decisions that may seem to some small in comparison to major surgery.

This story served important functions for this storyteller. It was a vehicle for dealing with a life-threatening situation. Through this and similar narratives, I could express to others and myself my view of my personal ego strength and problem-solving abilities. The message is that I had the emotional resources to take charge of an emergency, and to emerge successfully.

As noted in the introductory description of personal narratives, stories that are initially self-reflective in nature often evolve to express broader messages; they become social or political commentaries. This happened with a related story I told, for which several variations evolved. In one, I focused on the absence of a monitor when I needed one, and I referred to a second emergent situation (when I was unable to summon a nurse in intensive cardiac care). In these tellings, I made a broader political point about variation in quality of nursing service, even in intensive care. I criticized recent cutbacks in nursing staff and the 12-hour shifts that are standard in the institution in which I was hospitalized.

It should be noted that personal narratives may not simply be rote retellings of events. Bruner (1991b, 1993) emphasized that autobiographies—a type of personal narrative—are acts of interpretation. That is because the act of committing a life event to memory involves interpretations of real experiences.

Given the important functions that personal narratives serve for adults (e.g., maintenance of self-esteem, problem solving, definition of role within family), this narrative genre should be considered a potential intervention target. Consider a client with aphasia who was accustomed to entertaining his family with stories of personal accomplishments at the dinner table. The clinician may choose to work with the patient to facilitate the telling of personal stories; alternatively, the clinician may focus on the family to support communication by recounting the patient's stories or cuing the patient's attempts.

Fables.   Ulatowska, Sadowska, Kordys, & Kadzielawa (1993) suggested that fables (a second narrative type) can be especially useful for language intervention. Fables include a paradigmatic set of characters (often animals) who are clearly and unambiguously classified according to capabilities for performing specific actions. Characteristics are carefully assigned to specific animals to describe human characteristics, and the assignments are always carefully selected and allow a high predictability of outcome. The plot of a fable consists of the actions of a character ordered according to exposition, motivation to act, action itself, and an unexpected outcome. The primary purpose of a fable is to convey its main point, i.e., the lesson to be learned. Fables may be useful for adult language intervention because (a) the stories are generally familiar to adults, (b) the characters and event relations are concretely presented, and (c) the narrative contains both a concrete level of interpretation and a metaphoric lesson to be derived (Ulatowska et al., 1993). The clinician must be aware that fables may be culture specific in their familiarity to the client.

Social Drama and Ritual.   The third and fourth types of narrative structure that have relevance for intervention planning for adult communication disorders are the social drama and ritual. Social dramas and rituals are used by people to handle conflict and restore and maintain order.

Stern and Henderson (1993) noted that social dramas occur at all social levels, within families, communities, and countries. They arise out of conflict (between husbands and wives, parents and children, states). They progress in an organized manner through four stages: breach, crisis, redress, resolution or deteriorization. According to Stern and Henderson, ritual behavior may be seen as a rite of passage, usually marking periods of transition when an individual moves from one socially designated position to another. Based on their social utility it is clear that these narrative genres may also be targets during the intervention process.

Expository Text.   Expository text, compared with the narrative genres discussed above, have been more traditionally the focus of language interventions with adults. This narrative type is used by adults to describe, inform, explain, and direct.

Westby (1994) identified seven forms of expository text: (a) descriptions, i.e., text telling what something is; (b) collections, i.e., lists of things related to a common topic; (c) sequence, i.e., how to do something; (d) comparison-contrast, i.e., how things are the same or different; (e) cause-effect, i.e., why something happened; (f) problem-solution; i.e., states a problem and possible solutions; (g) argument-persuasion, i.e., taking and justifying a position on a subject. These forms of expository text are often the focus of intervention plans that target both listening comprehension and language production.

The five types of narratives reviewed above, including their structural components and functions served in adult language, are summarized in Box 3.4. This information may be used for goal planning.

BOX **3.4**

Types of Narratives, Structural Components, and Functions Served in Adult Language

Category	Structural Component	Functions Served in Adult Language
Personal narrative	Narratives about frightening experiences that call into question the storyteller's assumptions about self and how self will react under pressure. The storyteller's evaluation of the personal experience is detailed. The telling may be collective process, involving a husband and wife, other family members, or cohesive social group.	Maintain self-esteem Resolve problems Define and maintain role within family and other social groups Deal with trauma
Fable	A narrative that emerges in a specific time and place, but that is able to transform traditional values and become invested with new meanings reflective of the people who tell them and the broader social context. The fable "tells about something what has happened or been imagined from the perspective of a social community passing on its collective wisdom."	Represent social knowledge
Social drama and ritual	A narrative involving breach, crisis, redress, resolution, or deteriorization. Used by families and other social groups to handle conflict and restore and maintain order.	Solve problems Resolve conflicts Define self in relation to a social group
Expository text	A narrative that comprises descriptions, lists of related items, procedural and causal sequences, problems and solutions, and arguments.	Describe Inform Explain Direct

Culture and Narrative Structure

For intervention planning relevant to narrative storytelling and story comprehension, it is necessary to understand the influence of cultural diversity on narratives. Kamhi, Pollock, & Harris (1996) distinguished between oral and literate language styles (also Heath, 1986). The story grammars presented above represent the literate tradition. Meanings and relationships are stated explicitly and are decontextualized. That is, the listener is presumed not to have shared information with the storyteller. Consequently, settings, characters, temporal sequences, and causal relations are organized and stated explicitly.

In the oral tradition, contrastively, meaning and relations are not always expressed explicitly. Shared knowledge between speaker and listener is presumed. Stories, therefore, may not have strictly sequenced beginnings, middles, and ends; explicated settings; background information; explanations (i.e., the components of traditional story grammars—see Lahey, 1988, summarized above). Instead, the language style is contextualized. Meanings may be expressed in slang, gestures, and intonation patterns. Literate cohesion devices may not be used. Instead, topic-associating styles may be employed. The listener is expected to be an active participator, supplying personal knowledge of events.

With reference to the oral-literate framework, some cultures are viewed as more literate in style while other cultures are viewed as more oral. African-American cultures are viewed as oral in tradition, although Kamhi et al. (1996) showed significant variation in narrative structures across narrative tasks (e.g., retelling a story from a book versus a story from personal experience) and social contexts.

Also in the oral tradition, stories of Native Americans may not have clear beginnings and endings, and may provide incomplete information that must be derived from a knowledge of tribal traditions and cultures (Johnson, 1995). Linear time lines often are not followed. Native Americans, Japanese, and African Americans create stories by merging events that are topically related without regard or reference to when they actually occurred (Guttierez-Clellen & Quinn, 1993).

As mentioned above, many cultures engage in collaborative storytelling, in which members of the audience contribute (Guttierez-Clellen & Quinn, 1993; Johnson, 1995; Stern & Henderson, 1993), often on the basis of assertiveness (Heath, 1986). It is important to note in conclusion that there is diversity in storytelling within as well as across cultures. This diversity is often related to the perceived audience, as well as to the genre of the narrative being expressed.

The distinct cultural influence on narrative performance must be considered during goal and procedure planning. The clinician must recognize that narrative forms that are consistent with the client's cultural background and experiences would be appropriate as intervention targets. Any departure from the client's culturally based expectations may increase demands on communication.

Linguistic Devices That Support Narratives

The narrative structures and types represent macrostructural considerations for interventions. As discussed earlier in the section on conversation, microstructural aspects of discourse must also be considered. There are several linguistic devices that support coherence between sentences and propositions in narrative discourse. These devices, such as reference, substitution, ellipsis, and conjunction appearing in Table 3.2, apply to the production of narratives as well. For narrative we would like to add another cohesion category: parallel structure (Lahey, 1988). Lahey identified a developmental sequence of parallel structure types with an increase in use of structural parallelism. Structural parallelism involves the maintenance of consistent verb phrase structure. When applied to adults, consistency of tense is especially important.

Changes in Narrative Discourse Skills with Aging

In planning appropriate goals of intervention with adult clients, it is important to be cognizant of changes in narrative discourse skills that accompany aging. The majority of research on aging and narrative discourse has been concerned with comprehension. Studies of production are limited in number and scope. The following is a summary of research on the effects of aging on the production and comprehension of narrative discourse.

Aging and Production.   Glosser and Deser (1992) studied narrative discourse abilities as reflected in autobiographical stories of 14 normally achieving middle-aged adults (mean age 51.9) and 13 elderly adults (76.2). With reference to the microlinguistic components, elderly subjects scored lower (but not significantly lower) than middle-aged subjects on measures of syntax. The elderly manifested no apparent deficits in phonological or lexical performance (Glosser, 1993). Analysis of the macrolinguistic component of thematic coherency, however, revealed a specific deficit for the elderly subjects. Elderly subjects scored significantly poorer than middle-aged adults on ratings of global coherence. Furthermore, a significantly greater proportion of the elderly's verbalizations was wholly unrelated to the assigned topic of discourse.

Aging and Comprehension.   Most studies on aging and comprehension deal with the influence of reduced information-processing capacities. These are reviewed in Chapter 5. There have been several studies of linguistic factors in narrative comprehension, however, and these have yielded mixed and contradictory results. Most of these studies involved comprehension of written text, and most found that older people recall fewer propositions than younger and middle-aged adults (e.g., Kemper, 1988). Maintenance of propositional recall across the life span, however, has also been reported (e.g., Meyer & Rice, 1981). Several studies looked at the number of propositions adults recalled immediately after reading stories, and whether these were main ideas or supplemental information (e.g., Meyer & Rice, 1981; Zelinsky, Light, & Gilewski, 1984). Bayles and Kaszniak (1987) summarized contradictions among these studies. They pointed out that older adults as compared with young adults recalled less primary and supplemental information in some studies (e.g., Zelinski et al., 1984), less main information but more supplemental information in others (Dixon, Simon, Nowak, & Hultsch, 1982; Zelinski, Gilewski, & Thompson, 1980), and proportionally more supplemental information in still another study (Meyer & Rice, 1981). Differential educational backgrounds, expertise related to subjects discussed in narratives, verbal abilities, and cultural histories were cited to explain the apparently disparate findings (see Bayles & Kaszniak, 1987; also Hultsch, Hertzog, & Dixon, 1984; Meyer & Rice, 1981). Interestingly, differences in recall between young and older college graduates disappeared when Meyer & Rice (1981) had subjects practice outlining stories. Additional studies on the effect of time elapsed between reading and recall in the aged are summarized in the section on cognitive information-processing skills in Chapter 5.

Few studies on narrative comprehension have attempted to control for the narrative's inherent semantic type or syntactic organization. One exception in semantics was an examination of the ability of older adults to abstract implicit versus explicit information from stories (Ulatowska, Sadowska, Kordys, & Kadzielawa, 1993). When three groups of Catholic nuns (ages 27–55, 64–76, and greater than 76) were compared, the ability to recall information that required inferencing was significantly poorer in the two older groups than in the young adults.

In syntax, Kemper (1988) investigated how sentence embedding and subordination affect the ability of elderly individuals to recall topic and detail information. Kemper compared 12 elderly (mean age 80 years) and 12 middle-aged (mean age 50.2 years) adults with similar educational and professional histories (college educated, professional). Three versions of 12 prose paragraphs were presented to the subjects, with topic and detail sentences varied according to syntactic structure. Findings indicated that the elderly subjects were impaired in their ability to recall information from left-branching structures with a single level of subordination (e.g., relative clauses). These subjects recalled 22% of the left-branching or subordinate clauses, whereas they recalled 60% of the right-branching structures (the same number recalled by the middle-aged subjects). These findings in comprehension correspond to the kinds of syntax produced by adults in oral and written narratives (e.g., Kynette & Kemper, 1986; also see the section on syntax, below).

In sum, aging appears to be related to a reduction in the amount of information recalled, and changes in the ratio of main versus supplemental information remembered.

Implications for Intervention Planning

Goals.   It is likely that for most adults who experience communication problems following trauma, listening to or telling stories played a central role in their lives before the onset of the communication disorder. For these individuals, it may be useful, if not necessary, to tell personal stories about their ordeals. Telling about experiences such as coping with or recovering from a stroke or other injury can be palliative or even healing. The power to engage in social dramas and ritual storytelling can help to resolve conflicts as well as provide a sense of continuity, functionality, and even well being after the onset of a communication problem. It is also important to recognize the central role that expository narratives (i.e., narratives that contain instructions, explanations, directives, etc.) play in social, vocational, and academic contexts.

The comprehension and production of functional narrative forms and supportive linguistic devices may be targeted as goals at all levels of intervention planning with adults. It is important, however, for the clinician to be familiar with the narrative style of the client's culture. Premorbid experiences will influence narrative performance after a language problem arises. Background information, therefore, provides direction for intervention planning in this area.

Familiar narrative forms may also provide the linguistic context for working on more basic content/form interactions, or on other types of speech-language-communication goals. For example, one could target causal content/form interactions in context of a social drama or ritual aimed at resolving (or initiating) a family conflict. One could attack fluency

---

BOX 3.5

Examples of Goals Addressing the Narrative As a Target and As a Context

Goal type: Narrative as a target

Long-term goal:	Client will produce narratives in social and vocational contexts.
Short-term goal:	Client will produce personal narratives incorporating embedded causal chains.
Session goals:	Client will produce a narrative about a recent personal problem and its resolution, which includes one goal-based causal chain.

Goal type: Narrative as a context

Long-term goal:	Client will use pronouns with clear reference while producing a variety of narratives.
Short-term goals:	Client will reference pronouns while producing autobiographical narratives
Session goals:	Client will reference third-person pronouns while producing single autobiographical episodes

---

or voice in such a narrative context as well. Box 3.5 presents examples of goals addressing the narrative as a target and as a context.

Procedures.   Direction for the development of procedures that support goals targeting narratives comes from knowledge about the nature of stories and storytelling. As discussed above, stories are comments on self. Storytelling can be a collaborative effort. Stories are often embedded in familiar conflict and conflict resolution. Different cultures manifest different narrative conventions. Certain narrative genres, such as folk tales, tap fundamental emotional states. This information suggests linguistic and nonlinguistic contexts that could support the achievement of narrative goals. For example, the clinician could collaboratively create a story with a client or facilitate a collaborative effort between a client and a family member (i.e., a collaborative linguistic context). As noted above, specific narrative genres or content can be used as contexts to support the achievement of other types of speech-language-communication objectives (e.g., to facilitate fluency, Shapiro, Chapter 10 in this text).

Summary

In this chapter we began to consider normal communication functioning in adults. We presented research findings on conversation and narrative forms of discourse across the adult life span. The emphasis on discourse as a foundation for intervention planning is consonant with our focus on functional communication as the ultimate outcome of speech-language intervention across disorder types.

REFERENCES

Arlis, L. P., & Borisoff, D. J. (1993). *Women & men communicating.* New York: Harcourt Brace Jovanovich.

Bates, E., Thal, D., & MacWhinney, B. (1991). A functionalist approach to language and its implications for assessment and intervention. In T. M. Gallagher (Ed.), *Pragmatics of language: Clinical practice issues* pp. 133–161). San Diego, CA: Singular.

Bayles, K. A., & Kaszniak, A. W. (1987). *Communication and cognition in normal aging and dementia.* Austin, TX: Pro-Ed.

Bloom, L., & Lahey, M. (1978). *Language development and language disorders.* New York: Wiley.

Borisoff, D., & Merrill, L. (1992). *The power to communicate* (2nd ed.). Prospect Heights, IL: Waveland Press.

Brinton, B., & Fujiki, M. (1984). Development of topic manipulation skills in discourse. *Journal of Speech and Hearing Research, 27,* 350–358.

Brookshire, R., & Nicholas, L. (1984). Comprehension of directly and indirectly stated main ideas in discourse by brain damaged and non brain damaged listeners. *Brain and Language, 21,* 21–36.

Brownell, H. H., & Joanette, Y. (Eds.). (1993). *Narrative discourse in neurologically impaired and/normal aging adults.* San Diego, CA: Singular.

Bruner, J. (1986). *Actual minds, possible worlds.* Cambridge, MA: Harvard University Press.

Bruner, J. (1990). *Acts of meaning.* Cambridge, MA: Harvard University Press.

Bruner, J. (1991a). Self making and world making. *Journal of Aesthetic Education, 25,* 67–78.

Bruner, J. (1991b). The narrative construction of reality. *Critical Inquiry, 18,* 1–21.

Bruner, J. (1993). The autobiographical process. In R. Folkenflik (Ed.), *The culture of autobiography: Constructions of self-representation* (pp. 38–56). Stanford, CA: Stanford University Press..

Bruner, J., & Feldman, C. F. (in press). Group narrative as a cultural context of autobiography. In D. Rubin (Ed.), *Autobiographical memory: An update.* New York: Cambridge University Press.

Bruner, J., & Weiser, S. (1991). The invention of self: Autobiography and its forms. In D. R. Olson & N. Torrance (Eds.), *Literacy and orality.* New York: Cambridge University Press.

Cheng, L. R. L. (1993). Asian-American cultures. In D. E. Battle (Ed.), *Communication disorders in multicultural populations.* Stoneham, MA: Butterworth-Heinemann.

Cheng, L. R. L. (1996). Beyond bilingualism: A quest for communicative competence. *Topics in Language Disorders, 16,* 9–21.

Cooper, D. C., & Anderson-Inman, L. (1988). Language & socialization. In M. A. Nippold (Ed.), *Later language development: Ages 9 through 19* (pp. 225–245). Boston: Little, Brown.

Craig, H., & Evans, J. (1989). Turn exchange characteristics of SLI children's simultaneous and nonsimultaneous speech. *Journal of Speech and Hearing Disorders, 54,* 334–347.

Dixon, R. A., Simon, E. W., Nowak, C. A., & Hultsch, D. F. (1982). Text recall in adulthood as a function of level of information, input modality, and delay interval. *Journal of Gerontology, 37,* 358–364.

Dollaghan, C., & Kaston, N. (1986). A comprehension monitoring program for language-impaired children. *Journal of Speech and Hearing Disorders, 51,* 264–271.

Feldman, C. F., Bruner, J., Kalmar, D., & Renderer, B. (1993). Plot, plight, and dramatism: Interpretation at three ages. *Human Development, 36,* 327–342.

Fey, M. (1986). *Language intervention with young children.* San Diego, CA: College Hill Press.

Glosser, G. (1993). Discourse production patterns in neurologically impaired and aged populations. In H. H. Brownell and Y. Joanette (Eds.), *Narrative discourse in neurologically impaired and/normal aging adults.* San Diego, CA: Singular.

Glosser, G., & Deser, T. (1992). Aging changes in microlinguistic and macrolinguistic aspects of discourse production. *Journal of Gerontology, 47,* 266–272.

Goffman, E. (1967). *Interaction ritual: Essays on the face-to-face behavior.* New York: Pantheon Books.

Gordon, P. C. (1993). Computational and psychological models of discourse. In H. H. Brownell, & J. Yves (Eds.), *Narrative discourse in neurologically impaired and normal aging adults* (pp. 23–46). San Diego, CA: Singular.

Grosz, B. J., & Sidner, C. L. (1986). Attention, intentions, and the structure of discourse. *Computational Linguistics, 12,* 175–204.

Guttierez-Clellen, V., & Quinn, R. (1993). Assessing narratives of children from diverse cultural and linguistic groups. *Speech, Language, Hearing Services in Schools, 24,* 2–9.

Halliday, M. A. K., & Hasan, R. (1976). *Cohesion in English.* London: Longman.

Heath, S. B. (1986). Taking a cross-cultural look at narratives. *Topics in Language Disorders, 7,* 844.

Hough, S., & Pierce, M. (1994). Pragmatics and treatment. In R. Chapey (Ed.), *Language intervention strategies in adult aphasia* (3rd ed.). Baltimore, MD: Williams & Wilkins.

Hultsch, D. F., Hertzog, C., & Dixon, R. A. (1984). Text recall in adulthood: The role of intellectual abilities. *Developmental Psychology, 20,* 1192–1209.

Johnson, C. J. (1995). Expanding norms for narration. *Language, Speech, and Hearing Services in Schools, 26,* 326–341.

Kamhi, A. G., Pollock, K. E., & Harris, J. L. (1996). *Communication development and disorders in African-American children: Research, assessment, and intervention.* Baltimore, MD: Brookes.

Kemper, S. (1988). Geriatric psycholinguistics: Syntactic limitations of oral and written language. In L. Light & D. Burke (Eds.), *Language. Memory, and aging* (pp. 58–76). Cambridge, MA: Cambridge University Press.

Klein, H., Moses, N., & Altman, E. (1988). Communication of adults with learning disabilities: Self and others' perceptions. *Journal of Communication Disorders, 21,* 423–436.

Kynette, D., & Kemper, S. (1986). Aging and the loss of grammatical forms: A cross-sectional study of language performance. *Language and Communication, 6,* 65–72.

Lahey, M. (1988). *Language disorders and language development.* New York: MacMillan.

MacLachlan, B. G., & Chapman, R. S. (1988). Communications breakdowns in normal and language learning-disabled children's conversation and narration. *Journal of Speech and Hearing Disorders, 53,* 2–7.

Mandler, J. M. (1984). *Stories, scripts, and scenes: Aspects of schemata theory.* Hillsdale, NJ: Erlbaum.

Mandler, J. M., & Goodman, M. S. (1982). On the psychological validity of story structure. *Journal of Verbal Learning and Verbal Behavior, 21,* 507–523.

Martin, A. D. (1981). An examination of Wepman's thought centered therapy. In R. Chapey, (Ed.), *Language intervention strategies in adult aphasia.* (pp. 141–154). Baltimore, MD: Williams & Wilkins.

Mentis, M. (1994). Topic management in discourse: Assessment and intervention. *Topics in Language Disorders, 14,* 29–54.

Mentis, M., & Prutting, C. A. (1987). Cohesion in the discourse of normal and head-injured adults. *Journal of Speech and Hearing Research, 30,* 88–98.

Mentis, M., & Prutting, C. A. (1991). Analysis of topic as illustrated in a head-injured and a normal adult. *Journal of Speech and Hearing Research, 34,* 583–595.

Mentis, M., & Thompson, S. A. (1991). Discourse: A means for understanding normal and disordered language. In T. M. Gallagher (Ed.), *Pragmatics of language: Clinical practice issues* (pp. 199–227). San Diego, CA: Singular.

Meyer, B., & Rice, G. E. (1981). Information recall from prose by young, middle, and old adult readers. *Experimental Aging Research, 7,* 253–286.

Nelson, N. W. (1993). *Childhood language disorders in context: Infancy through adolescence.* New York: Macmillan.

Newhoff, M., Tonkovich, J. D., Schwartz, S. L., & Burgess, E. K. (1985). Revision strategies in aphasia. *Journal of Neurological Communication Disorders, 2,* 2–7.

Nippold, M. A. (Ed.) (1988). *Later language development: Ages 9–19.* Austin, TX: Pro-Ed.

Nippold, M. A. (1993). Developmental markers in adolescent language: Syntax, semantics, and pragmatics. *Language, Speech, and Hearing Services in Schools, 24,* 21–28.

Nippold, M. A., Schwartz, I. E., & Undlin, R. A. (1992). Use and understanding of adverbial conjuncts: A developmental study of adolescents and young adults. *Journal of Speech & Hearing Research, 35,* 108–118.

Obler, L. K., & Albert, M. L. (1981). Language and aging: A neurobehavioral analysis. In D. S. Beasley & G. A. Davis (Eds.), *Aging: Communication processes and disorders* (pp. 107–121). New York: Grune and Stratton.

Orestrom, B. (1983). *Turn-taking in English conversation.* Lund, Sweden: LiberForlag Lund.

Owens, R. E. (1996). *Language development: An introduction.* Boston: Allyn & Bacon.

Prutting, C. A., & Kirshner, D. M. (1983). Applied pragmatics. In T. Gallagher & C. A. Prutting (Eds.), *Pragmatic assessment and intervention issues in language.* San Diego, CA: College-Hill Press.

Psathas, G. (1995). *Conversation analysis: The study of talk-in-interaction.* Thousand Oaks: Sage.

Roseberry-McKibbins, C. (1997). Understanding Filipino families: A foundation for effective service delivery. *American Journal of Speech Language Pathology, 6,* 5–14.

Roth, F. P., & Spekman, N. J. (1986). Narrative discourse: Spontaneously generated stories of learning-disabled and normally achieving students. *Journal of Speech and Hearing Disorders, 51,* 8–23.

Rummelhart, D. E. (1975). Notes on a schema for stories. In D. G. Bobrow & A. Collins (Eds.), *Representation and understanding* (pp. 211–236). New York: Academic Press.

Rummelhart, D. E. (1977). Understanding and summarizing brief stories. In D. LaBerge, S. J. R. C. Schank, & R. P. Abelson (Eds.), *Scripts, plans, and goals, and understanding: An inquiry into human understanding.* Hillsdale, NJ: Erlbaum.

Stephens, M. I. (1988). Pragmatics. In M. A. Nippold (Ed.), *Later language development: Ages 9 through 19* (pp. 247–262). Boston: Little, Brown.

Stern, C. S., & Henderson, B. (1993). *Performance: Texts and contexts.* White Plains, New York: Longman.

Stern, D., Jaffe, J., Beebe, B., & Bennett, S. (1975). Vocalizing in unison and in alternation: Two modes of communication within the mother-infant dyad. In D. Aronson & R. Rieber (Eds.), *Developmental psycholinguistics and communication disorders. Annals of the New York Academy of Sciences, 263,* 89–100.

Stover, S. E., & Haynes, W. O. (1989). Topic manipulation and cohesive adequacy in conversations of normal adults between the ages of 30 and 90. *Clinical Linguistics and Phonetics, 3,* 137–149.

Tannen, D. (1994). *Gender and discourse.* New York: Oxford University Press.

Ulatowska, H. K., Sadowska, M., Kordys, J., & Kadzielawa, D. (1993). Selective aspects of narratives in Polish speaking aphasics as illustrated in Aesop's fables. In H. H. Brownell, & Y. Joanette (Eds.), *Narrative discourse in neurologically impaired and/normal aging adults* (pp. 171–190). San Diego, CA: Singular.

Wanska, S., & Bedrosian, J. (1985). Conversational structure and topic performance in mother-child interaction. *Journal of Speech and Hearing Research, 28,* 579–584.

Westby, C. E. (1994). The effects of genre, structure, and style of oral and written texts. In G. P. Wallach & K. G. Butler (Eds.), *Language learning disabilities in school-age children and adolescents.* New York: Merrill.

Zelinski, E. M., Gilewski, M. J., & Thompson, L. W. (1980). Do laboratory tests relate to self-assessment of memory ability in the young and old? In L. W. Poon, J. L. Fozard, L. S. Cermak, D. Arenberg, & L. W. Thompson (Eds.), *New directions in memory and aging: Proceedings of the George Talland Memorial Conference* (pp. 519–544). Hillsdale, NJ: Erlbaum.

Zelinski, E. M., Light, L. L., & Gilewski, M. J. (1984). Adult age differences in memory for prose: The question of sensitivity to passage structure. *Developmental Psychology, 20,* 1181–1192.

4 Funds of Knowledge for Intervention Planning with Adults: Language Content and Form

CHAPTER OUTCOMES

The reader will:

1. identify normal parameters of content/form interactions in adult language;
2. become aware of areas of lexical knowledge in adults;
3. become aware of components of syntax;
4. learn how to apply information about content/form interactions in adult language to intervention planning.

Overview

This chapter continues our examination of typical communication performance in adults. Here we will focus on the content and form of language—those components of communication that complement discourse. The performance of normally achieving adults in content and form represents an important source of knowledge for intervention planning. The expected achievements of normally functioning adults provide a guiding framework for goal planning. In addition, the content and form of messages represent factors that must be considered in designing contexts for the achievement of any speech-language target (e.g., articulation, voice, fluency).

Content

Overview of Normal Functioning in Adults

Broadly speaking, the content of language is meaning or semantics—the linguistic representation of what people know about objects, events, and relations. Language content refers to the type of meaning (or semantic) relationships that exist between parts of a sentence (e.g., between a subject and complement, two verb phrases, or multiple phrases or sentences in narratives). An example of language content is action reflected in the statement, "The dog bit the man." In this sentence, there is an action relation (bit) between the subject (dog) and complement (man). Another example of content is the relation between the two verb phrases in the following complex sentence: "I can't watch television because I don't have cable." Here, there is a causal relationship between "not being able to watch" and "not having."

Adults continue to represent the same meaning relations in discourse as children, albeit about more adult-like topics. Topic refers to the particular idea encoded in the message, such as a particular object (computer) or action (typing). According to Bloom and Lahey (1978),

> There . . . is a continuity of language content from earliest language to progressively later and eventually mature language: 2-year olds , 5-year olds, and adults all talk about the same content (i.e., they talk about objects, actions, and relations). But whereas the content of language is cumulative and continuous as it evolves in the course of development, the topics of language are variable, with respect to age as well as culture. Two year olds talk about bouncing balls, 5-year olds talk about baseballs, and adults talk about golf balls. (p. 13)

Figure 4.1 illustrates the ways Bloom and Lahey's distinction between content and topic may be applied to adults.

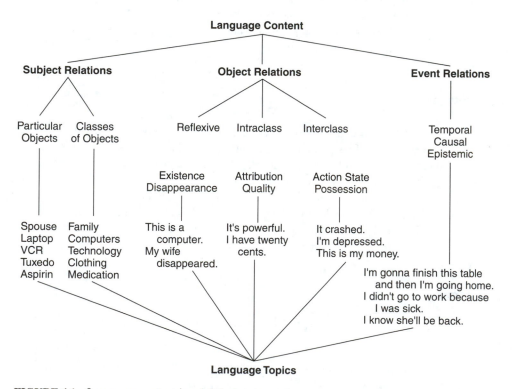

FIGURE 4.1 Language content in adult language.

Although there is much continuity in the meaning relations that adults and children represent linguistically, some research suggests that subtle changes in organization within complex content categories occur as reasoning abilities become more advanced. One category of meaning that has received some attention in adults is causality (e.g., Moses, in progress; Siegler, 1984). Causality is a meaning category that is relevant to adult vocational or academic pursuits; adults are frequently expected to explain or interpret other's explanations in work, school, or social settings. For example, it has been demonstrated that adult's reference in causal explanations changes with the development of expertise in a particular problem-solving situation (Moses, Klein, & Altman, 1990).

Moses et al. (1990) identified three types of causal semantic relations in explanations offered by normally achieving and learning-disabled adults concerning why boards with asymmetric weight distribution balance on a fulcrum (see Figure 4.2; see also Moses, in progress). These relations were contiguous, comparative, and compensatory. In a contiguous causal statement, an observable event, feature of the material, or attribute of behavior is referenced as causal; for example, "The board balanced because the block helped" or "If you see it's going to start to fall, move it around a little bit." In comparative causal statements, a comparative relation between parts of material is referenced; for example, "It balances because this side is longer" or "If I cut this off (one end of the board) and move it over here (on top of the newly cut side of the board) it would be a block like that." Notice that the second type of causal statement incorporates comparative language (i.e., "longer," "a block like that"). The last category, compensatory causal statements, is the most complex. In this case reference is made to intuited rather than observed variables (e.g., weight). Something is said about how one variable compensates for

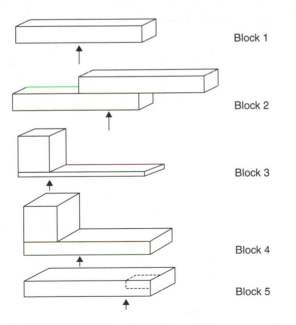

FIGURE 4.2   The board-balancing task.

From Moses, Klein, and Altman (1990). Used with permission.

another; for example, "Boards balance because the weight is the same on both sides" or "If I cut this off and put it on that side it would create a block that weighs just as much as that one." Notice that this third type of causal statement incorporates comparative and quantitative terms.

This board-balancing task may strike the reader as unusual but it was designed to permit a range of causal explanations representative of those encountered in common social and vocational contexts. Other tasks, perhaps more relevant to the client's interests and experiences, could also be designed to encourage the use of causal language. Further discussion of task development appears in the section on cognitive maintaining factors below and in chapters dealing with intervention planning for specific disabilities.

We know of no additional research that documented changes in proportion or type of semantic relations produced by adults across the life span (except, perhaps, those implicit in descriptions of adult storytelling, which we addressed in the section on language use earlier). As Bloom and Lahey (1978) suggested, it appears that content categories remain cumulative and continuous across the life cycle. Continuous signifies that the same content categories may be used to capture what adults talk about. In terms of adult language, cumulative may represent the addition of new topics to the adult's repertoire due to individual life experiences. Cumulative may also represent the increasingly complex organization reflective of developments within specific content categories.

Implications for Intervention Planning

Goal Planning.   Language content may be targeted at all three phases of intervention planning. Recall our intervention-planning principle that linguistic organization is targeted at the long- and short-term planning phases. Consequently, semantic relations (an aspect of linguistic organization) receive attention in long- and short-term goal statements. We suggest that Bloom and Lahey's (1978) content categories, augmented by research on semantic developments in adolescents and adults (e.g., Wallach & Butler, 1994; Moses et al., 1990), are useful resources for long-term and short-term goal setting with adults. At the session phase of goal planning, the focus may be on specific conversational topics that represent instances of semantic organization targeted at the long-term and short-term planning phases. Examples of goal statements targeting language content appear in Box 4.1.

Procedural Planning.   Planning procedures for goals that target language content also takes places at each of the three phases. Long-term procedural planning involves the selection of principles from learning theories that explain how adults achieve increasingly complex levels of semantic organization or learn about specific communication topics. Short-term procedural planning involves identifying general properties of nonlinguistic contexts (materials, layout of the therapy room, etc.) and linguistic contexts (clinician-client interactions and linguistic stimuli), consistent with learning principles identified at the long-term planning phase. The idea is to provide direction for the selection of materials and interactions that would facilitate achievement of the short-term objective. Session planning—conducted with reference to short-term procedural decisions—

B O X 4.1

Examples of Goal Statements Addressing Language Content

Long-term: Client will produce temporal and causal relations to explain procedures and causes in voca-
             tional settings.
Short-term: Client will produce contiguous and comparative causal relations with reference to the oper-
             ation of mechanical appliances at his place of employment.
Session: Client will explain why a dishwasher does not operate, in a role-playing situation involving
             a customer and himself, five times in a half-hour session.

---

involves designing specific interactions and selecting specific materials that will facilitate session achievements.

An important task for the clinician at the session phase is controlling "performance
demands"—factors that may complicate or simplify the performance of the session goal.
In language content, performance demands emanate from the processing of increasingly
complex ideas, and aspects of form and use that interact with the comprehension and
expression of these ideas. The status of behavioral systems related to language also affect
the demands on the expression of content. Thus, the clinician may start with the simplest
structures and move to the more complex. For example, the clinician may incorporate less
frequently used vocabulary when targeting simple semantic relations. Contrastively, the
clinician might incorporate more frequently used words when targeting complex meaning
relations. We discuss performance demands in Chapter 2 and in some detail in Chapter 5
on information-processing factors that may maintain a speech-language problem.

Content/Form Interactions: Lexicon

Bayles and Kaszniak (1987) remarked that "the study of vocabulary is the most researched
aspect of communicative competency [in adults]" (p. 134). In working with adults, vocabulary is frequently targeted in the course of intervention planning. For making a decision
about targeting vocabulary as an intervention goal, it is important to be familiar with normal patterns of vocabulary use throughout adulthood. This information would helpful in
determining whether the individual exhibits a vocabulary deficit. If it is determined that
vocabulary is a deficit area, it is useful to consider at least three aspects of vocabulary:
functionality of word for the client (usefulness of word in everyday life), content category
to which the word belongs (e.g., existence, action, attribute), how words may be used to
express more than one meaning (e.g., idiom, metaphor, humor).

Lexical Knowledge in Adults

Research has primarily provided information about adults' use of functional vocabulary.
The vocabulary in most research studies is drawn from standardized tests, in which items

are organized according to frequency of occurrence—a presumed index of functionality. An example of an early study taking this approach is Fox (1947) who examined comprehension of vocabulary from the Wechsler Adult Intelligence Scale (WAIS). Comprehension of vocabulary has typically been judged by quality of definitions produced or scores on picture vocabulary tests, in which the subject selects a picture named by the clinician. This line of research has produced conflicting results.

Fox (1947) investigated the ability of 40- and 70-year-olds to define words on the vocabulary subtest of the WAIS. He found no age effect for quality of definition. Botwinicke and Storandt (1974), however, found that young adults (17–20) produced qualitatively better definitions for the WAIS vocabulary items (superior synonyms) than elderly subjects (62–83). The elderly subjects produced more multiword descriptions and illustrations. Similarly, no age effect was found by Bayles, Tomoeda, and Boone (1985) for subjects ranging in age from 30 to 80 years on the Peabody Picture Vocabulary Test-Revised (a test of receptive vocabulary).

Many studies on the effects of aging on lexical knowledge examined retrieval and recognition of grapheme strings, which we view as information-processing skills. Some studies seemed to show that knowledge of vocabulary remains constant or improves with age (e.g., Fox, 1947; Guy & Boyd, 1990; Obler, 1985; Sankoff & Lessard, 1975), although the ability to retrieve words declines, especially in confrontational naming tasks (e.g., Obler & Albert, 1981). We examine life span trends in these areas more closely in Chapter 5.

The derivation of goals based solely on the functionality of words is inconsistent with the model of intervention planning espoused in this book. We argue that linguistic organization should also be considered in vocabulary selection. An example of such an approach would be the classification of lexical items produced by adults according to semantic categories, such as action, attribution, and location. At the present time there appears to be no studies of lexical knowledge in normally achieving adults conducted with reference to semantic organization or categorical knowledge of language content. Consequently, there is little normative data available for planning goals within a semantic organization framework. The use of such a framework is supported by reports on lexical deficits in adults with language disorders, such as aphasia and closed head injury (e.g., the speech of individuals with Broca's aphasia contains primarily nouns and verbs that code "existence" and "action" [Chapey, 1994; Goodglass & Kaplan, 1983]).

Figurative Language

Multiple Meanings.   One group of lexical forms that can pose difficulties for adults with communication problems is "nonliteral" lexical units; i.e., lexical structures that have multiple, ambiguous, and nonliteral meanings. Examples of nonliteral lexical forms are (a) ambiguity (e.g., "The elephant was ready to lift"—i.e., to lift something or be lifted, Wiig & Secord, 1987); (b) metaphor (i.e., "symbolic devices that are used to highlight the similarity between entities"; e.g., calling somebody a "little snake" [Milosky, 1994, p. 277]); (c) simile (i.e., a metaphor incorporating "like" or "as"; e.g., "This institution is like the titanic"]); and (d) allegory (a metaphor presented as a story that represents something other than the surface referent). An example offered by some is Wagner's Ring Cycle, which is seen as possibly a recoding of Aryan philosophies (Millington, 1987). Although many of these nonliteral forms comprise multiword phases, they are included in this section on lexicon because they are typically analyzed or learned in a unitary manner (Milosky, 1994).

Pollio and Pollio (1979) found that knowledge of metaphors continues to develop well into adolescence. Ortony, Turner, & Larson-Shapiro (1985) identified cultural differences in the use of metaphors (see also Cheng, 1996). The adroit use of metaphor and other forms of figurative language by African-American cultures is seen in rap music and in the practice of "sounding"—a ritualized trading of insults (Milosky, 1994; Ortony et al., 1985). An example is Eddie Murphy's sounding of the character Ritchie in the "The Nutty Professor," as Murphy produces a string of fat mother jokes including: "Your mother is so fat her blood type is rocky road. Your mother is so fat her belt size is the equator. Your mother is so fat the XXX gets her toenails painted at Earl Scheib."

Learning to comprehend figurative language forms is viewed by many researchers as a cognitive achievement (see the discussion of cognition in Chapter 5, especially Nippold, 1994). One developmental hierarchy of metaphor comprehension with a linguistic foundation was presented by Silberstein, Gardner, Phelps, and Winner (1982). In this hierarchy, metaphors based on comparisons of perceptual attributes (color, shape) develop first, followed by dynamic perceptual comparisons (sound, movement), conceptual comparisons (obstruction, impending danger), and finally metaphors based on multidimensional comparisons.

Nippold, Uhden, & Schwarz (1997) presented a developmental hierarchy for adults' comprehension of another type of figurative language that transmits social values—proverbs. Comprehension of concrete proverbs (e.g., "A good sailor likes a rough sea") preceded understanding of abstract proverbs (e.g., "A wonder lasts but nine days"). Comprehension of both types of proverbs increased across the life span until age 60, when comprehension of abstract proverbs declined.

Idioms represent yet another nonliteral language form. Idioms are commonly used expressions whose meanings are not derivable from the meanings of the constituent individual words (e.g., "out of touch"). Idioms, like metaphors, are often culturally specific (Milosky, 1994). Some factors that seem to affect comprehension of idioms are frequency of use in the language or culture (Milosky, 1994; Nippold & Rudzinsky, 1993), context (Milosky, 1994), transparency (ease with which the meaning can be deduced from the constituent words), and syntactic and semantic flexibility. Syntactic flexibility refers to the ability to transform the syntax of the idiom. Milosky explained that it is possible to transform "Joe cut Sue down to size" into "Sue was cut down to size by Joe." It is not, however, possible to transform "Joe jumped down Sue's throat." Gibbs and Gonzales (1985) found that adults processed inflexible (i.e., frozen) idioms more rapidly in story contexts than flexible ones, but remembered flexible ones better. Milosky (1994) also pointed out that the more meanings an idiom can have, the more quickly and accurately adults appear to comprehend it (see also Mueller & Gibbs, 1987). Idioms—especially opaque ones whose meanings are not related to their constituent lexicon—appear to be learned as single units or "giant words" (Milosky, 1994).

Humor.   Nonliteral language and idiomatic expressions play especially important roles in humor. The ability to use and comprehend humorous expressions represents an important social competency. According to Spector (1990), elements of humor may be classified according to phonological, morphological, or syntactic variables (see also Green & Pepicello, 1978; Pepicello & Weisberg, 1983). Box 4.2 summarizes and exemplifies phonological, morphological, and syntactic bases of humor (derived from Spector, 1990, pp. 534–535).

Spector examined humor comprehension in 12 normally achieving adolescents, 14–19 years of age, and 12 adolescents with learning disabilities. The subjects who had learning disabilities demonstrated significantly poorer humor comprehension than their normally achieving peers. Among the normally achieving subjects, humor based on metathesis, stress/juncture, phrase structure, and transformational ambiguity yielded the most errors of comprehension. It was apparent in this study that comprehension of humor continues to develop into adulthood. It was difficult, however, to draw conclusions about the precise nature of development because of the unequal number of stimulus items representative of each humor type presented to subjects.

Implications for Intervention Planning

The lexicon represents primarily an area of goal planning. Improvement of vocabulary and word retrieval are historically popular and functional goals for adolescents and adults with language disabilities (e.g., Chapey, 1994; Wallach & Butler, 1994). When deriving goals within the present model of intervention planning, several variables are considered: (a) the functionality of the lexical item for the specific client, (b) the syntactic role of the lexical item, and (c) the content category to which lexical item belongs (i.e., the underlying linguistic organization). Consideration is also given to the phonological characteristics of the item in light of the areas of impairment manifested by the client (Holland & Forbes, 1994). A consideration of these factors facilitates the prioritization and sequencing of goals.

The use and comprehension of nonliteral or figurative lexical forms (jokes, metaphors, etc.) also are viewed as potentially important targets with language-impaired populations (e.g., Larson & McKinley, 1995; Wallach & Butler, 1994). This is in recognition of the important social and discourse functions these language forms play in adult conversation.

Content/Form Interactions: Syntax

Overview of Mature Syntactic Competence

Syntax is, of course, a central component of the microstructure of discourse and can be a primary target of intervention with adults. The term *syntax* refers to the linguistic conventions for combining morphemes to create well-formed sentences (Osherson & Laznik, 1990). Chomsky and the generation of cognitive scientists he influenced (e.g., Pinker, 1994; van Riemsdijk & Williams, 1986) provided us with extensive descriptions of adult syntactic competence. The following is a synopsis of some fundamental syntactic competencies of the adult speaker of English. It is provided as a reference to help clinicians select

B O X **4.2**

Categories of Humor (Adapted from Spector, 1990)

Element	Bases of Humor	Definition and Examples
Phonological	Lexical items	Humor is based on the ambiguity of the word. Example: The first horse motel was opened to provide animals with a stable environment.
	Minimal pairs	The element involves the difference of one phoneme. Example: Men's briefs are manufactured in the West Undies.
	Metathesis	The element involves the difference of one phoneme. A knife that cuts four loaves of bread at the same time could be advertised as a four-loaf cleaver.
Morphological	Irregular morphology	Exploiting a misinterpretation of a grammatical form. Example: Customer—I'd like a can of talcum powder, please. Storekeeper: Would you like it scented? Customer: No thanks. I'll just take it with me.
	Morphological analysis	One morpheme is abstracted from a word and treated as if it were an independent word with which it is homophonous. Example: What do frogs sit on at mealtime? Toadstools.
	Exploitation of bound morphemes	A bound morpheme is deliberately confused with an independent word or is otherwise exploited. Example: A drama critic summed up his reaction to the opening of a Broadway play by saying: I was underwhelmed.
	Pseudomorphology	A phonologic sequence is deliberately confused with a phonologic sequence from another, larger word, but the sequence is really not a morpheme of the larger word. Example: What is the key to a good dinner? A turkey.
Syntactic elements	Phrase structure	A given surface sequence of words has more than one syntactic analysis. Example: When the first credit card was issued, the people got a charge out of it.
	Transformational ambiguity	Two different underlying structures have an identical surface form. Example: I can lift an elephant with one hand. Really? Sure. Get me an elephant with one hand and I'll show you.

one or more aspects of syntax to target when developing goals of intervention for adults with language problems. This synopsis is organized according to three major syntactic competencies: these are the ability to (a) transform basic sentence structure, (b) apply knowledge of case and theme assignment properties of verbs and prepositions to the construction of sentences, and (c) interpret pronouns with reference to government and binding properties of sentences. Although our focus is English, speakers of other languages manifest analogous skills, since a delimited set of parameters of syntactic functioning is thought to be universal—i.e., one aspect of the genetic endowment of our species (Piaterelli-Palmarini, 1980; Pinker, 1994).

The following overview of adult grammatic abilities presupposes that the fundamental syntactic skills described by Bloom and Lahey (1978) and Lahey (1988) in children at phases 8 and 8+ underlie mature language systems. Although syntactic functioning at Lahey phase 8+ can be attributed to a four-year-old child, these syntactic abilities continue across the life span and must be considered in assessment and management of impaired language functioning in adults. They include the ability to transform sentences; construct complex sentences (conjunction, relativization, complementation); and use tense, subject-verb agreement, articles, modifiers, modals, and anaphora.

Transforming Sentences and the Essence of Non-Transformed Sentences.   It is important for clinicians to recognize that some sentences that clients are expected to produce or comprehend may involve transformation, whereas other sentences may not. This recognition will aid in pinpointing goals for clients and in analyzing the complexity of expected behaviors. To understand what transformations are about, it is necessary to consider first what are the essential components of a nontransformed sentence.

What Is a Nontransformed Sentence?   The term nontransformed sentence refers to the basic organization of all sentences, according to Chomsky (1986). Based on Chomsky, it is presumed that all sentences will be produced (and interpreted) in this manner unless the speaker goes through extra "processing steps" to change that fundamental organization.

Again, based on Chomsky, it is presumed that sentences comprise component phrases, including noun phrases (NP), verb phrases (VP), prepositional phrases (PP), and so forth. All phrases (e.g., noun phrases, verb phrases, prepositional phrases) have similar architectures; all phrases have heads, determiners, and complements. The head is the word that belongs to the unit of grammar that the phrase is named for; thus, the NP, "The cat with the long whiskers," contains the noun head "cat." The determiner provides some extra information about the head; in the cat NP, the determiner is the article "the." A complement is a phrase or sentence that gives still more information about the head. In the cat NP, the complement is the PP, "with the long whiskers." The PP "with the long whiskers" has the preposition head "with" and the NP complement "long whiskers." The VP "quickly ate the cat food" has the head "ate," the determiner "quickly," and the NP complement "the cat food."

The VP itself is the complement of a broader "inflectional phrase (IP)," which is the sentence itself. In the IP (sentence), the NP subject of the sentence is the determiner, "inflection" (i.e., tense) is the head, and as noted above, the VP is the complement.

Nontransformed sentences (i.e., IPs) in English are produced in the order: NP subject, inflection (optionally realized as an auxiliary), tensed VP complement (with a tense

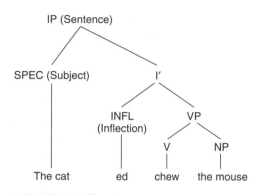

FIGURE 4.3   Simple sentence.

marker attached to the verb and a complement following the verb). An example of a simple nontransformed sentence—i.e., IP in the form described above (agreement between a NP and tensed VP containing a tensed verb with an appropriate object)—is "The cat chewed the mouse." "The cat" is the NP and "chewed the mouse" is the VP comprising the past-tensed verb "chewed" and its NP complement "the mouse." There is no auxiliary in the sentence, although one could have been produced just before the VP (e.g., "The cat did chew the mouse"). The underlying organization of a sentence like this before it under goes transformation was termed by Chomsky, "D-structure" (formerly deep structure). The presumption is that whether or not a person says such a sentence out loud, all sentences start out in the mind as an IP, with number agreement between the NP and VP (with the VP possibly requiring a specific, appropriate complement, Chomsky, 1986; Shapiro, 1997). Figure 4.3 illustrates the architecture of such a simple IP sentence.

The sentence structure just described is so fundamental to human language that such a string of words does not have to make sense to be judged grammatical (as Chomsky, 1957; Berko, 1958; and others [e.g., Carroll, 1871/1981, author of *Alice in Wonderland*] have shown.) Consider the following excerpt from *Alice in Wonderland,* cited by Pinker (1991):

> Twas brillig, and the slithy toves
> Did gyre and gimble in the wabe:
> All mimsy were the borogoves,
> And the mome raths outgrabe.

What Is a Transformed Sentence?   This fundamental organization may be transformed before the sentence comes out of the speaker's mouth. There are certain transformational rules that all mature speakers of any language are presumed to know. One such rule is to move *wh* complements of the sentence to into a complement phrase (CP). A CP is the superordinate phrase in which the IP sentence is embedded. Figure 4.4 illustrates the architecture of a CP.

The determiner of the CP and its head exist in front of an IP (sentence). It provides places for complements and auxiliaries to move into (e.g., when creating questions), or for complement pronouns (that, which) to move into when forming complex sentences (Chomsky, 1986; Shapiro, 1997).

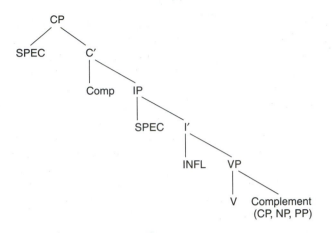

FIGURE 4.4   The organization of sentences, including the "CP" structure.

Consider the question, "What did the little boy know?" This sentence is presumed to have been created by transforming a sentence that started out in the mind of the speaker as, "The boy knew what?" To create the question, the NP complement "what" of the verb "knew" moved from its complement position to one of the "invisible" spaces (SPEC) before the subject of the sentence in an invisible CP presumed to embody the entire sentence (in the speaker-listener's mind). Tense (in the form of the auxiliary "did") moved from being attached to the verb to a slot (COMP) in the CP. Figure 4.5 illustrates a *wh* transformation.

Another example of a transformation involving NP movement involves the creation of passive forms. "The boy ate his spinach" becomes "The spinach was eaten by the boy." The passive form is created by moving the subject NP to the object position, and the object NP into a CP slot. (For further details, see van Riemsdijk & Williams, 1986; Pinker, 1994; Shapiro, 1997.)

Individuals with language disorders sometimes produce partial transformations. An example or such a syntactic error would be the question, "What he ate?" rather than "What did he eat?" In this case the complement was moved to the CP in front of the subject but tense remained attached to the verb instead of changing to an auxiliary (and moving from its original position in the IP to CP).

Implications for Intervention Planning.   All of this may appear to be highly abstract and theoretic to the clinician. However, it has important implications for intervention planning. First, knowing that there are nontransformed and transformed versions of sentences serves a basis for analyzing complexity for goal sequencing. We can presume that sentences in subject-verb-complement order are less complex than transformed questions. Second, knowing that phrase architecture, nontransformed sentence forms, and transformations are functions of the mind, and not evidence of memorized rules, has procedural implications. This knowledge leads the clinician to learning theories, such as social cognitive or constructivist theories, that would account for the development of organizational

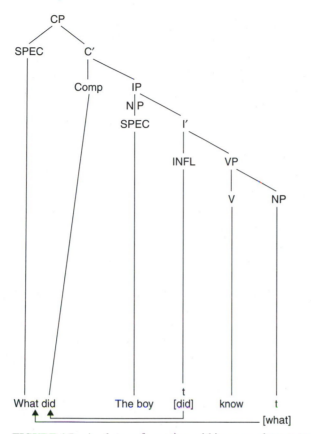

FIGURE 4.5　A wh transformation within a complex sentence.

capacities in the speaker. Such theories (reviewed in Chapter 6) suggest that teaching rules for creating and transforming sentences makes less sense than modeling and encouraging performance (see Pinker, 1994; Shapiro, 1997).

Chomsky (1995) has explained that moved items leave traces to facilitate processing. This gives us insight into what might make the processing of transformations difficult for some adults with language disorders. Adults who have suffered trauma, for instance, might experience an impaired ability to establish or use traces. Without a trace to refer to, the client might not know whether a moved complement such as "what" related to the subject (boy) or the verb (eat). This type of impairment might result in difficulties in comprehending and/or producing transformations. Thus, the processing of transformations has implications for goal and procedure planning; the reestablishment of traces might be a goal of language intervention. Knowledge of the neurologic nature of traces suggests appropriate learning theories that could guide procedure planning. One such paradigm, social cognitive theory, suggests modeling, and practicing transforming and untransforming structures.

Complex Sentences.   Another syntactic skill that is important for clinicians to be aware of for intervention planning is the formulation of complex sentences. A complex sentence is a sentence with a second sentence inside of it. An example of a complex sentence is, "The little boy knew that the cat ate the mouse." In this sentence, the VP ("knew that the cat ate the mouse") comprises the verb "knew" and a sentence complement ("the cat ate the mouse"). There are three types of complex sentence constructions.

Conjunction.   Conjunction is characterized by two complete sentences connected by a conjunction (e.g., "The cat jumped on the table and the bird flew away"). "The cat jumped on the table" is one sentence; "the bird flew away" is a second sentence; "and" is the conjunction.

Complementation.   In this structure, a sentence is the complement of the verb (the complex sentence presented above). An example is, "The little boy knew that the cat ate the mouse." The sentence complement is presumed to be created by placing a complementary pronoun (that, which) in the CP before the embedded complement sentence and placing the CP right after the verb as its complement.

Relativization.   Here a sentence is embedded in the NP of a larger sentence. An example is, "The little boy who was afraid of mice ran away." In this case the initial NP includes a whole sentence (i.e., "The little boy *who was afraid of mice*"; the sentence within the noun phrase is italicized). A relative clause is presumed to be created by deleting the subject of the embedded sentence (i.e., *the boy* was afraid of mice) and replacing it with a relative pronoun (e.g., who, that, which). The sentence is embedded as the complement of the subject (boy) of the primary sentence.

Being able to recognize complex sentences is important for clinicians planning interventions with adults. The formulation and comprehension of such sentences can be goals of intervention. Understanding how complex sentences are constructed (by the integration of more basic sentence forms) has implications for procedure planning as well.

Verb Knowledge.   Nouns have been the focus of our discussion of adult syntax so far. We turn our attention to verbs. Verbs, according to some syntactic theories, play a pivotal role in sentence construction (see Bloom, 1993; Bloom & Lahey, 1978; Pinker, 1989; van Riemsdijk & Williams, 1986). As such, an important source of knowledge for intervention planning directed at problems of syntax is knowing the full story of what it means to know a verb.

Case Assignment.   Verbs that have tense and that are not infinitival ("to eat") require "arguments." An argument is a subject or a complement. Different verbs have different argument requirements. The verb "eat" may have two arguments—a subject and a NP complement—to make a well-formed sentence (e.g., "The boy ate the cookie"). The verb "hiccough" can only have one argument—a subject. "The boy hiccoughed." It does not need a complement to make a sentence. Verbs assign "case" to NPs to establish them as arguments. In the sentence, "The boy ate the cookie," the verb "ate" assigns "nominative" case to the noun "boy" to establish it as the "subject," and "accusative" case to the noun "cookie" to establish it as the complement. If a verb (such as hiccough) cannot assign case directly to a noun, it cannot have a noun as its complement. Prepositions also assign case (oblique) to nouns, which explains why verbs such as "hiccough" are followed by prepositional phase complements (e.g., "The boy hiccoughed in the living room"; see van Riemsdijk & Williams, 1986; Pinker, 1994; Shapiro, 1997, for more detailed information).

Theme Assignment. Verbs also assign themes to their arguments. Theme signifies a semantic theme or function served by a particular word in a sentence. For example, the noun "nail" in the sentence, "The boy hit the nail with the hammer," is assigned the theme "recipient of an action." Prepositions also assign themes to complements. Thus, hammer is assigned the "instrumental" theme by the preposition "with." Each noun that serves as a subject or complement (i.e., argument) of a verb must be assigned an appropriate theme.

Knowledge of a verb, therefore, involves knowing what arguments it requires and the themes it can assign to its arguments. Moreover, mature speakers know that arguments must be close to their case and theme assigners. In the sentence, "The boy hit the nail with the hammer," "hit" assigns a theme (recipient of the action) to "nail," while the preposition "with" is required to assign a theme (instrument) to hammer. "The boy hit the nail hammer" is ungrammatical because the verb "hit" cannot take two arguments and cannot assign a theme to "hammer." The verb requires help. The noun "hammer" must receive case and theme from a preposition (with).

In sum, adults know many verbs and prepositions. Knowing signifies not only being aware of the basic meaning of the words, but also knowing their argument and theme-assignment properties, which play a central role in sentence formation. It is important for clinicians to recognize, too, that learning argument and theme-assignment properties of verbs may rely on the individual's making subtle semantic distinctions among words (Pinker, 1988).

Implications for Intervention Planning. For intervention planning with adults, it is important for clinicians to understand the full implication of what it means to know a verb. Sentence formulation or comprehension problems in native speakers and speakers of a second language can reflect incomplete or inaccurate verb knowledge (i.e., knowledge of argument and theme assignment properties of particular verbs). The implications for intervention planning are both goal oriented and procedural. Goals targeting particular aspects of verb knowledge can be formulated. Procedures can be developed that take into account the neurologic nature of verb knowledge (i.e., that the roles and functions of verbs are intrinsic to linguistic organization). Several alternative learning theories may be applicable to the development of linguistic organization (see Chapter 6).

Binding. Another important syntactic competence of mature speakers is the ability to interpret and keep track of anaphoric reference (making reference to other words in a sentence). There are two types of pronouns that refer to other words in sentence: bound anaphora (himself/herself) and free anaphora (him, her). According to Chomsky (1981), anaphoric reference is determined by the smallest domain of the subject. The term *domain of a subject* refers to the sentence that has a particular noun as its subject (i.e., governed by that noun). Chomsky proposed that mature speakers use the following rules of anaphoric reference:

1. A pronoun must be free in the smallest domain of a subject in which it occurs ("John likes him"). The term *free* means not referring to another word in the sentence. The pronoun "him" can not refer to John; it must refer to someone outside of the sentence.
2. A bound anaphor must be bound in the smallest domain of a subject in which it occurs (e.g., "John likes himself"). The term *bound* means to refer, by necessity, to another word in the sentence.
3. A lexical NP must be free in all domains ("John likes John"); i.e., a name can never refer to another name in a sentence, no matter what the subject of the sentence is.

Consider the more complex sentences in applying these rules. First, "John, whom Harry despises, loves himself." Upon reading this sentence we immediately know that "himself" refers to John even though there is another possible referent, Harry. How do we know this? Recall that a bound anaphor must refer to the subject of its smallest domain (the most immediate sentence to which it belongs). The anaphor "himself" is governed by the subject, "John." In other words, the smallest domain of the subject "John" is the sentence, "John loves himself." Therefore, we interpret "himself" as referring to John.

Now, consider how the reader's interpretation would change by modifying the pronoun: "John, whom Harry despises, loves him." In this case, we interpret "him" as possibly referring to Harry but not John. Because a pronoun such as him or her may not refer to the subject of the smallest domain in which it appears, it must refer to someone else (either Harry or someone not named in the sentence). Note that in the embedded sentence "whom Harry despises" two subjects may be identified: John and Harry. John is the subject of the complete sentence, "John whom Harry despises loves him," whereas, Harry is a subject of only the embedded sentence. John, however, is the only subject of the segment "John loves him." Therefore, the sentence "John loves him" is the smallest domain of the subject John; whereas, "whom Harry despises" is the smallest domain of the subject Harry.

Implications for Intervention Planning.   Knowing that the referential meaning of pronouns in sentences can have a syntactic foundation has important implications for intervention planning with adults. The ability to comprehend and produce anaphoric and other forms of pronoun references are possible goals of intervention with adults with language problems. Furthermore, the syntactic component of referential meaning again suggests that intervention procedures focus on sentence construction and not on the internalization of specific pronoun forms and their meanings separate from the sentential context in which they are embedded. Box 4.3 summarizes the important syntactic competencies of mature speakers of English.

Changes in Syntactic Competence with Aging

In a review of two longitudinal studies (in Montreal and Philadelphia) dealing with the effect of normal aging on the development of language, Labov and Auger (1993) reported "a steady continuation of language learning with advancing age" (p. 115). In the Montreal study, 60 of 120 adults originally interviewed in 1975 by Sankoff and Lessard (1975) were

BOX 4.3

Summary of Fundamental Adult-Syntactic Skills Related to Argument and Theme Assignment and Government and Binding.

Syntactic Skill	Definition	Example	
Knowledge of argument, case, and theme-assignment properties of verbs and prepositions:	Verbs must have appropriate complements to which they assign meaningful themes; all nouns must be assigned themes by governing verbs or prepositions.	Verb: ■ Eat	Examples: The boy eats the carrot.
			Possible arguments: Subject (agent) Noun phrase complement (recipient of act)
		■ Want	The girl wants the carrot to eat the carrot. Subject (agent) Noun phrase complement Infinitival complement
		■ Desire	Harry desires— Harry. Subject Noun phrase complement
The ability to interpret the referential meaning of nouns, pronouns, and anaphors with reference to the rules of binding:	A bound anaphor must be bound (i.e., must refer to the subject) in the smallest domain in which it occurs (i.e., the component sentence in which it occurs).	Ex. 1 Sentence containing anaphor John likes himself.	Possible referent(s) John Governing subject John
		Ex. 2 Sentence containing anaphor John knows that Jack likes himself.	Possible referent Jack Governing subject Jack
	A pronoun must be free (must not refer to the subject) in the smallest domain in which it occurs (i.e., the component sentence in which it occurs).	Ex. 1 Sentence containing anaphor John likes him.	Possible referent Anyone other than John. Governing subject John
		Ex. 2 Sentences containing anaphor John knows that Harry likes him.	Possible referent John or any other person Governing subject Harry
	A lexical noun phrase (person) must be free (must not refer to any other person in any sentence).	Ex.1 John likes John	Possible referent: Anyone other than John. Governing subject John
		Ex. 2 John knows that Harry likes John.	Possible referent: Anyone outside of sentence. Governing subject Harry

reinterviewed in the 1990s. In Philadelphia, 116 adults first interviewed in 1971 by Guy and Boyd (1990) were relocated and reinterviewed in 1989 by the same investigators. Conversational speech was examined in each study. In the Philadelphia study, subjects were encouraged to engage in dramatized narratives of personal experiences (Labov, 1984; Labov & Waletsky, 1967).

Results of the original studies (first interviews in the 1970s) indicated that vocabulary size increases with age. The second set of studies focused on syntactic complexity and the structure of narrative discourse (micro- and macrostructures). Changes in syntactic subordination and left branching were tracked in both studies. Subordination refers to the inclusion of a dependent clause within a sentence (e.g., "The boy who washed the car was a troublemaker"; the dependent clause in this sentence is "who washed the car"). Left branching refers to the placement of the dependent clause before the main verb (the example given above is left branching; the dependent clause comes before the verb "was").

Results of both the Montreal and Philadelphia studies demonstrated no relationship between age and syntactic complexity (actually, there was a slight but nonsignificant tendency favoring greater syntactic complexity with age across studies). Both studies reported variation in complexity across topics and social class of speaker. In the Montreal study, the subjects' discussions about the French language lead to the greatest proportion of subordination and left-branching structures. Retired professionals manifested greater syntactic complexity than retired blue-collar workers. Interestingly, the insertion in conversation of narratives that recounted actual events in the order that they originally occurred correlated with a decrease in syntactic complexity. These types of narratives comprised, primarily, a series of independent clauses. The investigators postulated that the simplification of syntax in such narratives by older adults is intentional; simplification may reflect a pragmatic device to aid the listener's processing of a temporal sequence of factual information.

In contrast to several findings of the Montreal study, Kynette and Kemper (1986) reported that elderly adults (older than 70) compared with younger adults use less complex syntax and manifest a greater frequency of errors. The older adults produced fewer left-branching constructions (relative clauses) or multiple embedded clauses. Older adults also more frequently manifested errors of past-tense agreement, subject-verb agreement, articles, and possessive markers. Kemper (1990) reported similar findings in a life span study of diary entries of adults born between 1820 and 1876. In a separate study, 16 elderly adults (70–89) compared with 16 middle-aged adults (30–40) had trouble imitating language constructions with embedded clauses. The authors postulated that memory demands made by this syntax on reduced short-term memory capacity in the elderly contributed to these results.

Implications for Intervention Planning.   Baseline data (from published tests or spontaneous conversation) may reveal some scattered errors (specific to past irregular tense or preposition use) or indicate a multiplicity of syntactic errors suggesting fundamental organizational deficits. Examples of organizational deficits include (a) executing transformations required to comprehend and produce questions, passives, and forms of specification, etc. (see Thompson, Shapiro, Ballard, Jacobs, Schneider, & Tait, 1997), and (b) producing direct and indirect objects appropriately indicating case and theme assignments of verbs.

Organizational parameters of syntax are targeted at the long- and short-term phases. Specific syntactic structures (or components of structures) representative of these organizational

BOX **4.4**

Goals Addressing Two Levels of Syntactic Difficulty

Client A. Adult with learning disabilities who has errors with subject-verb agreement and irregular past tense.

Long-term goals: 1. Client will produce simple, perfect, and pluperfect past tense forms of irregular verbs in conversational contexts.
2. Client will establish subject-verb agreement in conversational contexts.

Short-term goals: 1. Client will produce simple past-tense forms of irregular verbs in 3+ constituent utterances.
2. Client will establish subject-verb agreement for past-tense forms of "to be" and "to have" in 3+ constituent utterances.

Session objectives: 1. Client will use past tense forms of irregular verbs (where past tense is marked by changes in internal vowel and final consonant (e.g., creep, deal, feel) to produce 3+ constituent responses about the action of characters in a story read by the clinician with 80% accuracy.
2. Client will establish subject-verb agreement in 3+ constituent responses to a story read by the clinician involving simple past tense forms of "to be" with 80% accuracy.

Client B. Adult with aphasia who is unable to produce questions and passive forms

Long-term goals: 1. Client will produce sentences with question forms in conversation.
2. Client will comprehend and produce sentences with passive forms in conversation.

Short-term goals: 1. Client will produce questions with *wh* word and auxiliary in appropriate positions.
2. Client will comprehend sentences with passive forms in the context of manipulating objects.

Session objectives: 1. Client will formulate questions given declarative statements coding existence, action, and locative state, presented orally, accompanied by pictures, with 80% accuracy.

---

competencies are targeted at the session level. Bloom and Lahey (1978; also Lahey, 1988), augmented by accounts of mature syntactic competencies provided by current linguistic theory and research on aging reviewed above, may serve as sources of information for goal setting in syntax. Examples of goals addressing syntax appear in Box 4.4.

For intervention planning, it is also necessary to recognize that increasingly complex syntactic organization places increasingly greater performance demands on clients. As such, syntax also may influence other aspects of language form (i.e., voice, fluency) as well as linguistic content and pragmatics. Systematic efforts to control performance demands related to syntax are made at all levels of intervention planning.

Summary

In this chapter presented an overview of content/form interactions in normally achieving adults, paying special attention to lexical knowledge and syntactic performance. This information is a useful reference for planning appropriate goals in semantics and syntax for adults with language problems. We now turn to cognitive, psychosocial, and sensorimotor behavioral systems that interact with speech-language functioning and that may maintain a speech-language problem.

REFERENCES

Au, R., Obler, L. K., & Albert, M. L. (1991). Language in the elderly aphasic and in the dementing patient. In M. T. Sarno (Ed.), *Acquired Aphasia* (pp. 405–423). New York: Academic Press.

Bamberg, M., & Damrad-Frye, R. (1991). On the ability to provide evaluative comments: Further explorations of children's narrative competencies. *Journal of Child Language, 18,* 689–710.

Bayles, K. A., & Kaszniak, A. W. (1987). *Communication and cognition in normal aging and dementia.* Austin, TX: Pro-Ed.

Bayles, K. A., Tomoeda, C. K., & Boone, D. R.(1985). A view of age-related changes in language function. *Developmental Neuropsychology, 1,* 231–264.

Beasley G. A., & Davis, G. A. (Eds.). *Communication processes and disorders* (pp. 107–121). New York: Grune & Stratton.

Berko, J. (1958). The child's learning of English morphology. *Word, 14,* 150–177.

Bloom, L. (1993). *The transition from infancy to language: Acquiring the power of expression.* Cambridge, UK: Cambridge University Press.

Bloom, L., & Lahey, M. (1978). *Language development and language disorders.* New York: Wiley.

Botwinicke, J., & Storandt, M. (1974). Vocabulary ability in later life. *The Journal of Genetic Psychology, 125,* 303–308.

Braine, M. D. S. (1990). The "natural logic" approach to reasoning. In W. F. Overton (Ed.), *Reasoning, necessity, and logic: Developmental perspectives* (pp. 133–157). Hillsdale, NJ: Erlbaum.

Burke, K. (1945). *The grammar of motives.* New York: Prentice-Hall.

Carroll, L. (1871/1981). *Alice's adventures in wonderland and through the looking-glass.* New York: Bantam Books.

Chapey, R. (Ed.). (1994). *Language intervention strategies in adult aphasia.* (3rd ed.). Baltimore, MD: Williams and Wilkins.

Cheng, L-R, L. (1996). Enhancing communication: Toward optimal language learning for limited English proficient students. *Language, Speech, and Hearing Services in Schools, 27,* 347–356.

Chomsky, N. (1957). *Syntactic structures.* The Hague, The Netherlands: Mouton.

Chomsky, N. (1981). *Lectures on government and binding.* Paris: Dodrecht.

Chomsky, N. (1986). *Knowledge of language.* New York: Praeger.

Chomsky, N. (1995). *The minimalist program.* Cambridge, MA: MIT Press.

Fox, C. (1947). Vocabulary ability in later maturity. *Journal of Educational Psychology, 38,* 482–492.

Gibbs, R., & Gonzales, G. (1985). Syntactic frozenness in processing and remembering idioms. *Cognition, 20,* 243–249.

Goodglass, H., & Kaplan, E. (1983). The assessment of aphasia and related disorders. Philadelphia: Lea and Febiger.

Green, T. A., & Pepicello, W. J. (1978). Wit in riddling: A linguistic perspective. *Genre, 11,* 1–13.

Guy, G., & Boyd, S. (1990). The development of a morphological class. *Language Variation and Change, 2,* 1–18.

Halliday, M. A. K., & Hasan, R. (1976). *Cohesion in English.* London: Longman.

Holland, A. L., & Forbes, M. M. (Ed.). (1994). *Aphasia treatment: World perspectives.* San Diego, CA: Singular.

Kemper, S. (1990). Adults' diaries: Changes made to written narrative across the life span. *Discourse Processes, 13,* 207–223.

Kynette, D., & Kemper, S. (1986). Aging and the loss of grammatical forms: A cross-sectional study of language performance. *Language and Communication, 6,* 65–72.

Labov, W. (1984). Field methods of the project on linguistic change and variation. In J. Baugh & J. Sherzer (Eds.). *Language in use* (pp. 28–53). Englewood Cliffs, NJ: Prentice-Hall.

Labov, W., & Auger, J. (1993). The effect of normal aging on discourse: A sociolinguistic approach. In H. H. Brownell & Y. Joanette (Eds), *Narrative discourse in neurologically impaired and normal aging adults.* San Diego, CA: Singular.

Labov, W., & Waletsky, J. (1967). Narrative analysis. In J. Helm (Ed.) *Essays on verbal and visual arts* (pp. 12–44). Seattle: University of Washington Press.

Lahey, M. (1988). *Language disorders and language development.* New York: Macmillan.

Larson, V. L., & McKinley, N. (1995). *Language disorders in older students.* Eau Claire, WI: Thinking Publications.

Martin, A. D. (1981). An examination of Wepman's thought centered therapy. In Chapey, R. (Ed.), *Language intervention strategies in adult aphasia* (1st ed.), (pp. 141–154). Baltimore, MD: Williams and Wilkins.

Millington, B. (1987). *Wagner.* New York: Vintage Books.

Milosky, L. M. (1994). Nonliteral language abilities: Seeing the forest for the trees. In G. P. Wallach & K. G. Butler (Eds.), *Language learning disabilities in school-age children and adolescents* (pp. 275–303). New York: Merrill.

Moses, N. (in progress). Developmental relations between procedural and causal knowledge in adults engaged in a tractor-trailer task.

Moses, N., Klein, H. B., & Altman, E. (1990). An approach to assessing and facilitating causal language in learning disabled adults based on Piagetian theory. *Journal of Learning Disabilities, 23,* 220–229.

Mueller, R., & Gibbs, R. (1987). Processing idioms with multiple meanings. *Journal of Psycholinguistic Research, 16,* 63–81.

Nippold, M. A. (Ed.). (1994). *Later language development.* Austin, TX: Pro-Ed.

Nippold, M., & Rudzinsky, M. (1993). Familiarity and transparency in idiom explanation: A developmental study of children and adolescents. *Journal of Speech and Hearing Research, 36,* 728–737.

Nippold, M., Uhden, L. D., & Schwarz, I. (1997). Proverb explanation through the lifespan: A developmental study of adolescents and adults. *Journal of Speech, Language, and Hearing Research, 40,* 245–253.

Obler, L. K. (1985). Language through the lifespan. In J. Berko Gleason (Ed.). *The development of language* (pp. 277–306). New York: Academic Press.

Obler, L. K., & Albert, M. L. (1981). Language and aging: A neurobehavioral analysis. In D. S. Beasley & G. A. Davis (Eds.), *Aging: Communication processes and disorders* (pp. 107–112). New York: Grune and Stratton.

Ortony, A., Turner, T., & Larson-Shapiro, N. (1985). Cultural and instructional influences on figurative language comprehension by inner city children. *Research in the Teaching of English 19,* 25–36.

Osherson, D. N., & Laznik, H. (Eds.). (1990). *An invitation to cognitive Science: Language. Volume 1.* Cambridge, MA: MIT Press.

Pepicello, W. J., & Weisberg, R. W. (1983). In P. E. McGhee & J. H. Goldstein (Eds.). Handbook of humor research, (pp. 59–83). New York: Springer-Verlag.

Piatelli-Palmarini, M. (Ed.). (1980). *Language and learning.* Cambridge, MA: Harvard University Press.

Pinker, S. (1989). *Language learnibility.* Cambridge, MA: MIT Press.

Pinker, S. (1991). Rules of language. *Science, 253,* 530–535.

Pinker, S. (1994). *The language instinct.* New York: William Morrow.

Pollio, M. R., & Pollio, H. R. (1979). A test of metaphoric comprehension and some preliminary data. *Journal of Child Language, 6,* 111–120.

Reid, D. K. (1988). Teaching the learning disabled: A cognitive approach. Needham, MA: Allyn & Bacon.

Reid, D. K., & Hresko, W. P. (1981). A cognitive approach to learning disabilities. New York: McGraw Hill.

Samuels S. J. (Eds.). *Basic processes in reading: Perception and comprehension* (pp. 265–303). Hillsdale, NJ: Erlbaum.

Sankoff, D., & Lessard, R. (1975). Vocabulary richness: A sociolinguistic analysis. *Science, 190,* 689–690.

Shapiro, L. P. (1997). Tutorial: An introduction to syntax. *Journal of Speech, Language, and Hearing Research, 40,* 254–272.

Siegler, R. (1984). Mechanisms of cognitive growth: Variation and selection. In R. Sternberg (Ed.). *Mechanisms of cognitive development* (pp. 141–163). New York: Freeman.

Silberstein, L., Gardner, H., Phelps, E., & Winner, E. (1982). Autumn leaves and old photographs: The development of metaphor preferences. *Journal of Experimental Child Psychology, 34,* 135–150.

Spector, C. C. (1990). Linguistic humor comprehension of normal and language-impaired adolescents. *Journal of Speech and Hearing Disorders, 55,* 533–551.

Thompson, C. K., Shapiro, L. P., Ballard, K. J., Jacobs, B. J., Schneider, S. S., & Tait, M. E. (1997). Training and generalized production of wh- and NP- movement structures in agrammatic aphasia. *Journal of Speech, Language, and Hearing Research, 40,* 228–244.

Ulatowski, H. K., Hayashi, M. M., Cannito, M. P., & Fleming, S. G. (1986). Disruption of reference. *Brain and Language, 28,* 24–41.

van Riemsdijk, H., & Williams, E. (1986). *Introduction to the theory of grammar.* Cambridge, MA: MIT Press.

Wallach, G. P., & Butler, K. G. (Eds.). (1994). *Language learning disabilities in school-aged children and adolescents.* New York: Macmillan.

Wiig, E. M., & Secord, W. (1987). *The Test of Language Competence.* San Antonio, TX: Psychological Corporation.

5 Funds of Knowledge for Intervention Planning with Adults: Maintaining Factors

CHAPTER OUTCOMES

The reader will:

1. identify nonlinguistic factors that may contribute to communication problems;
2. become familiar with normative data on adult functioning in psychosocial, cognitive, and sensorimotor domains;
3. understand how information about maintaining factors may be used to guide intervention planning;
4. recognize changes with aging in psychosocial, cognitive, and sensorimotor areas.

In the previous two chapters (3 and 4), general parameters of normal adult communication performance were reviewed as a resource for setting appropriate intervention goals for language problems with a neurologic or cultural/linguistic basis. The ability to engage in discourse was identified as the ultimate outcome of speech-language interventions, across disorder types. Language content/form/use interactions were identified as potential goals of language intervention.

Intervention planning in speech-language pathology, however, extends beyond a description of content/form/use interactions. Planning effective interventions requires a consideration also of nonlinguistic behavioral systems that influence communication performance. Such a comprehensive focus allows clinicians to address a range of disorders including speech problems in areas such as voice or fluency. We identify three nonlinguistic behavioral systems as potential maintaining factors implicated in disorders of communication. These maintaining factors are psychosocial functioning, cognition, and sensorimotor behavior. The clinician is interested in how behavioral characteristics of normally achieving adults in each of these areas influences communication performance. This knowledge contributes to both goal and procedure planning.

Psychosocial Factors

One major factor influencing adult communication patterns is psychosocial functioning. Psychosocial functioning undergoes developmental changes throughout adulthood. Much has been written about changes in psychosocial (or socioemotional) patterns as individuals age. (See Santrock, 1995, for a review of this area.) Writing on adult phases in the life cycle, Dewald (1993) noted, "In Western society and culture there are a number of typical developmental and maturational tasks and crises to which the adult must adapt by using the psychological capacities and organizations which have evolved as the result of his previous life and experience" (p. 144). Dewald identified these "developmental tasks" or "milestones" as occupation or profession, marriage, parenthood, limitations and disappointments, illness and disability, retirement, aging, and death. She added that "the ideally healthy individual continues to develop, mature and evolve as life progresses" (p. 132). Among the life experiences that influence how the challenges cited above are experienced and met are cultural, cohort, and gender expectations.

For the speech-language pathologist a knowledge of an individual's psychosocial history will suggest the status of premorbid communication skill and or current expectations (e.g., language content, vocabulary, syntax, pragmatic style, etc.). In addition, the satisfaction with life's choices and outcomes at any point is likely to affect an individual's capacity and motivation for interpersonal communication.

Adult psychosocial development during the life cycle has traditionally been viewed within three primary stages (e.g., Levinson, 1978; Santrock, 1995): early adulthood (22–40), middle adulthood (40–65), and later adulthood (over 65). While many researchers agree that milestones of psychosocial development may be identified, they differ on the boundaries of the stages in which they occur and the precise nature of this development (as an example of divergent boundaries, compare Levinson (1978) with Sheehy (1995)). To provide a basis for understanding the psychosocial status of adult clients with speech-language disorders, we describe the expectations for normally developing adults at each of these age/stage periods.

Most of the early work on psychosocial development was based on the behavior of men (e.g., Levinson, 1978; Vaillant, 1977). Feminist writers only recently began to focus on women's experiences and development. Some authors stressed different accomplishments for women, highlighting female strengths, such as fostering others' emotional, social, and intellectual development and maintaining connectedness and sensitivity to others (e.g., Miller, 1986). Other authors emphasized the problems with focussing on the differences between the sexes, believing these are promoted by their expected roles in society (e.g., Tannen, 1990; Travis, 1992).

Early Adulthood

According to Levinson (1978), who studied 40 men between 35 and 45 years of age, early adulthood is the second era of the life cycle and "may be the most dramatic of all eras"

(p. 21). It is during the early part of this era that the young man makes his first major choices: marriage, occupation, residence, and style of living. He begins to contribute to society through having children and performing some labor. During this era men are seen as being more energetic, capable, and having greater potential than all subsequent periods. For Erikson (1950), a man is now in the sixth "age of life." At this "age" he must choose between intimacy and isolation. According to Erikson, he must find in himself "the capacity to commit himself to concrete affiliations and partnerships" (p. 263), or in Freud's terms, "lieben und arbeiten" (to love and to work). If this stage is not successfully accomplished the individual is left with feelings of isolation. As pointed out by Santrock (1995), gender issues and cultural trends also affect task expectations of this period.

Among contemporary cultural trends that may be affecting communication patterns of early adulthood are the later ages at which children leave home or marry. In addition, many marriages are not "forever after." The average duration of marriage in the United States is just over nine years. This trend is reflected by a major increase in people living alone, which took place between the 1970s and the 1980s (Santrock, 1995).

Middle Adulthood

As noted above, many stage theories of adult development that have described middle adulthood have a male bias (Santrock, 1995). Levinson (1978), focusing on men, described the middle years (40–65) from three perspectives: (a) changes in biological and psychological functioning, (b) changes from the prior and succeeding generation, and (c) the evolution of careers and enterprises. In his cohort of 40 men of 4 occupations, Levinson found a gradual biological decline occurring in the early 40s. With some loss of youthful vitality, some men experience these changes as a fundamental threat. A new change in generational status also occurs at this time. A man entering midlife is often surprised by being viewed as a parental figure rather than a buddy of people in their 20s. At this point in psychosocial development he begins to take stock of what he has done thus far with his life. He may begin to consider what value his life has been to society and to himself. He must deal with any disparity between his earlier goals and what he perceives as his accomplishments. Whether a man is pleased or disappointed with his present life appraisal, Levinson believed that in his early forties the man needs to "come to terms with the limitations and consider the next step in the journey" (p. 31).

This middle adulthood phase may be considered parallel to the seventh stage of psychosocial development according to Erikson's (1950) framework. Erikson viewed this time in life as one of "generativity vs. stagnation." He defined generativity as "primarily the concern in establishing and guiding the next generation" (p. 267). For Erikson, generativity is more than productivity and creativity and implies a type of immortality because one is leaving a legacy for the next generation. Contrastively, stagnation implies a sense of "personal impoverishment" and "self-indulgence" when individuals feel that they have not contributed to the next generation. Generativity is accomplished through work, as well as parenting (Santrock, 1995). Generative adults may promote and guide the next generation through encouraging, teaching, leading, or doing other things that benefit younger people.

Traditional stage theories of adult psychosocial development have not reflected the complex and varied paths women take in today's society (Santrock, 1995). The

emphasis has been essentially on career choice when many women place more importance on child bearing and child rearing. Moreover, those women who desire a career
must learn the complex balancing act of maintaining a career and family. The post-
ponement of a career to attend to family roles would put women out of sync with normative stage data on men. For one thing, many women may delay the beginning or completion of education or the commitment to a full-time job until after starting a family.
Some women may even wait until their children have begun school. Contrastively, other
women delay marriage and child bearing until establishing a career. This variability and
complexity in life styles make it difficult to describe a normative sequence of development for women (Santrock, 1995).

 Theories of adult development must also be viewed with reference to different social
expectations of the time (Neugarten, 1964, 1986; Sheehy, 1995). Neugarten believed that
the social environment of a particular age group can greatly influence the time table for
milestones expected during middle adulthood. Sheehy (1995) supported this notion with
her delineation of five cohort groups coexisting today. For example, she compared the
"World War II" (born between 1914 and 1929) and the "Silent" (1930–1945) generations
with the "baby boomers" ("The Vietnam" [1946–1955] and "Me" [1956–1965] generations) with reference to their achievement of adulthood. Sheehy, who divided the life cycle
into two major sections (first and second adulthoods), said that if one belongs to the former two generations, the first adulthood lasts roughly to age 45. Members of these generations chose careers, married, and had children as they were expected to. Members of the
later two cohorts had a more prolonged adolescence, with less predictable time frames for
attainment of the major milestones within the first adulthood. In view of Sheehy's (1995)
more recent data, the findings from Levinson's (1978) and Vaillant's (1977) studies of individuals born before and during the depression may not be appropriate reference models for
people born after World War II.

Late Adulthood

Once again, descriptions of psychosocial functioning in late adulthood focused on men.
For instance, one of the major contributors to this period, Levinson (1978) only observed
men who were 35–45 years of age. While he recognized that he was on "speculative
ground," he offered a "provisional" view of late adulthood to complete his model of the
life cycle.

 Levinson described this period as one in which certain mental and physical changes
intensify a man's experience of his own aging and mortality. While there is great variation
among men with reference to mental and physical health at this time, every man must deal
with the reduction or absence of some of his middle adult powers. Rather than focusing on
the youth he has lost, the man now needs to maintain youthfulness in a new form appropriate to late adulthood, being the creative, wise elder.

 In addition to experiencing growing physical and mental changes, a man becomes
more aware of the loss of power and authority both with the family and at work. Now in the
grandfather generation, he must allow more responsibility to his children as they approach
middle adulthood. With reference to his life's work, a man beyond 65 or 70 is not expected

to maintain a position of formal authority, but rather allow the succeeding generation to assume more responsibility. Levinson (1978) suggested that at this time there should be less distinction between work and play as in early years. A man may now devote himself to his true interests, continuing to use his youthfulness and creativity. Levinson believed that another developmental task is "to find a new balance of involvement with society and the self" (p. 36). This is becoming less interested in obtaining rewards offered by society and more interested in fostering one's own inner creative powers and capabilities.

This period of later adulthood corresponds with Erikson's (1950) age of "ego integrity vs. despair." Erikson's state of ego integration includes the ability to appraise one's life, accept it, and defend the dignity of it. When individuals look back on their life and feel it was well spent they will experience a sense of "ego integration" and be satisfied. According to Erikson the loss of accrued ego integration is represented by the fear of death and feelings of despair. Individuals will feel that life is too short now to attempt "to start another life and try out alternate roads to integrity" (p. 269).

Not all developmental theorists agree that late adulthood is a time for disengagement (a gradual withdrawal from work and societies affairs as proposed by Levinson, 1978). In fact, the opposite may be true, that "those adults who are active and involved will age less dramatically and lead more satisfying lives (Santrock, 1995). Peck (1968) reflected some of this activity in a modification of Erikson's (1950) final life stage. According to Peck, men and women have three developmental tasks when they become old. The first is "differentiation vs. role preoccupation." He believed that the older adult's task is to pursue areas of interests and activities in place of prior engagement with work or children. The second task is "body transcendence versus body preoccupation." This task is to go beyond a preoccupation with an aging body by maximizing activities that involve human relationships rather than physical strain. The third task is "ego transcendence versus ego preoccupation." This task requires adults to acknowledge the inevitability of death and still feel comfortable with the realization that they have contributed to the future through child rearing, vocational or ideational accomplishments.

Optimism about later adulthood was stressed even more in the writings of Friedan (1993) and Sheehy (1995). Friedan viewed the early studies of life stages (e.g., Levinson, 1978; Vaillant, 1977) as reflecting a gloomy and desperate clinging to youth. Through her interviews with men and woman throughout the country she found that a decline with aging was not always true. She argued that "deteriorization is not necessarily 'normal' or even usual, and probably not biologically programmed" (p. 128). Friedan suggested that "people from 60 to just before death are more different from each other than at any other time in life" (p. 114). Contrary to the findings from the studies of male development, she concluded from her interviews that the process of individuation, becoming more oneself, may occur much later than at age 45 (at 65, 70, and 80). Similarly, Sheehy (1995) shared great expectations for continued development and change within an individual during the later years. Sheehy marked age 45 as "the infancy of another life" (p. 6). Age 45 is viewed by the author as ushering in the beginning of the second adulthood, which lasts until 85 and beyond. According to Sheehy, the early part of this period (45–65—the "Age of Mastery") is the point at which one can control much of what happens in life rather than needing to prove oneself to others. It is a time during which there is the potential for following unlived passions and mastering new talents. Accomplishment at this phase sets the stage for the later part of second adulthood (65–85 and beyond). Sheehy saw this final phase as "the work of integration . . . being able to bring all the parts of one's life into harmony, as opposed to incongruity" (p. 355). In keeping with the traditional developmentalists cited above, this entails an emotional integration of all the different roles and identities that served individuals throughout earlier life phases. People who have met and mastered most of the passages and crises of life until this point now have the resilience to cope with any reduction of efficiency and/or loss.

An individual's cultural background contributes to feelings of optimism or depression in later life. For example, older African Americans have more contact with family, friends, and social institutions (e.g., church) than Caucasians (Payne-Johnson, 1992). These informal and formal support systems provide the older individuals with an extended family, often obviating potential feelings of despair. In a similar vein, Cheng (1993) described the feelings of depression experienced by older Asian immigrants in the United States when they do not receive the respect accorded elders in Asian cultures.

Box 5.1 summarizes the three major phases of the life cycle, with reference to developmental tasks, the result of not completing tasks, and the implications for speech language intervention.

BOX **5.1**

Psychosocial Achievements of Adulthood

Stage of Life Cycle	Developmental Tasks	Effect of Not Achieving Tasks	Effect on Communication
Early Adulthood[a]	1. To prepare for and begin a career; 2. To choose a significant other (to live with or marry); 3. To begin to have children; 4. To become a member of a professional or vocational community.	Feelings of isolation and lack of commitment.	1. Little interest in pursuing communicative interaction; 2. Reduced pragmatic skills; 3. Lexicon and speech style reflective of vocational preparation and experience.

Stage of Life Cycle	Developmental Tasks	Effect of Not Achieving Tasks	Effect on Communication
Middle Adulthood	1. To take stock of what has been done in life thus far; 2. To consider the disparities between original goals and actual achievements and plan for the next course; 3. To be generative, contribute to society in some way (through work or parenting)— Time frame must be modified for cultural and cohort differences: Women may begin careers later and need to balance career and family duties. People born within different decades may experience these life cycle expectations differently.	Feelings of "stagnation," confusion about the future.	Reduced interest in communication.
Late Adulthood	1. To pursue new areas of interest and activity in place of focus on work and children; 2. To engage in activities that minimize physical demands and promote human interactions; 3. To acknowledge the inevitability of death and still feel comfortable with the realization that one has contributed to the future through child rearing, vocational or ideational accomplishments; 4. To commit oneself to an active life; 5. To commit to the development of good coping skills in the face of reduction of efficiency and loss.	Feelings of deterioration and despair.	1. Lack of desire for communicative interactions; 2. Little improvement without adequate support systems.

Implications for Intervention

Speech-language pathologists are concerned with the psychosocial status of clients. An individual's socioemotional environment affects the content, form, and use of language. What individuals choose to talk about, their lexicon, and syntactic style will reflect their education, family background, social, cultural, and vocational milieu. Whether they wish to communicate at all may be a result of their psychosocial successes or failures. Moreover, whether the individuals or their families feel that treatment is even appropriate must be considered. (see Arambula, 1992 and Roseberry-McKibbin, 1997, for differing cultural values regarding treatment of speech/language disorders.) Consequently, information about a client's psychosocial history is essential in planning both goals and procedures of intervention.

Goals.   The formulation of goals at each phase of intervention planning is affected by the knowledge of the individual's education level, occupation, interests, and general adaptation patterns to changing demands over the life cycle. For example, preparation for and participation in a vocational area influences the nature and sophistication of one's vocabulary. At the long-term phase of planning such information would be essential in making prognostic decisions about the ultimate level of goal achievement in vocabulary.

It would be unwise to plan speech or language goals for an individual that are beyond the premorbid level of functioning. Expectation for attainment of a long-term goal may also be influenced by the individual's feelings of self-esteem and the existence of support systems (e.g., family, close friends). A depressed, isolated individual would be expected to be less motivated toward communicative interaction and improvement than an individual more satisfied with life's roles and status changes.

At the short-term goal phase, knowledge of an individual's area(s) of expertise and interests would be a basis for determining parameters for certain linguistic targets such as vocabulary, pragmatic skills, vocal characteristics, and precision of articulation. Finally, at the session-goal level an individual's overall history of meeting challenges and coping with stress, as well as the individual's present stage in life and relevant vocational and social goals and experiences, would help to determine performance expectations during a single session. For example, the content and use of narratives that might be targeted for a client during session planning would reflect the client's particular vocational experiences, social status (e.g., single, married, etc.), and goals (looking for a promotion, seeking a mate, etc.).

Procedures.   Approaches to the facilitation of intervention goals (i.e., intervention procedures) should also be based on a knowledge of an individual's premorbid social, educational, and vocational background and present place in the life cycle. These elements of the case history inform clinicians about differential areas of strength and weakness in their clients. At the long-term planning phase, we identified information about the client's past and present psychosocial status that would guide us in designing the nonlinguistic and linguistic therapeutic contexts (i.e., materials and clinician-client interactions). This information was summarized in the long-term procedural approach. Recall, for example, Harold (the architect) and Martha (the musician) from Chapter 2. We noted that, for Harold "procedures will incorporate materials and tasks that are visually-spatially oriented to capitalize on Harold's premorbid architectural skills." We noted for Martha that "procedures will incorporate materials and tasks that are auditory and musical to capitalize on Martha's premorbid musical talent" (see Table 2.1). At the short-term planning phase, recommendations are made about the design of nonlinguistic and linguistic contexts with reference to the psychosocial factors summarized in the long-term procedural approach. Thus, tasks for Harold might include designing architectural projects while those for Martha might include planning musical programs. Session planning involves the creation of specific activities with reference to these recommendations.

Cultural differences also influence procedural decisions. Potential conflicts among cultural norms need to be anticipated in procedural planning. For example, American-born clinicians, with the tendency to express friendliness through informality (calling clients by first name) may be perceived as disrespectful by an Asian elder. To insure a motivating clinical environment, clinicians should become knowledgeable about such cultural differences.

Cognition

Cognition represents a second behavioral system that may maintain communication problems in adults. As such, developing a management plan may require that the clinician address the specific aspect of cognition implicated in the communication disorder.

Four approaches to adult cognition have particular applicability for the treatment of speech/language disorders: traditional Piagetian stage theory (Inhelder & Piaget, 1958, Rice, 1983), neo-Piagetian "epigenetic" theory (e.g., Fischer, 1980; Grannott, 1993; Moses, 1994; Case, 1985), social-cognitive theory (Newell, 1981), and information-processing theory (Sternberg, 1984). These theoretic perspectives affect the definition of what constitutes cognition and how cognition influences speech-language behavior. The substance of these theories provide a basis for making decisions about the cognitive factors that may be addressed during speech-language intervention.

Traditional Piagetian Stage Theory

The Traditional Piagetian Perspective on Adult Cognition and the Strong Cognitive Hypothesis.   Cognition, from the perspective of traditional Piagetian stage theory, refers to awareness (of objects and event relations) and the mental operations that individuals apply to problem solving that lead to awareness, understanding, and adaptation (Piaget, 1971, 1985).

In the child development literature, assumptions about relations between cognition and language influenced by Piagetian theory have been identified on a continuum between strong and weak cognitive hypotheses (e.g., Rice & Kemper, 1984). The strong cognitive hypothesis presumes that cognitive achievements are prerequisite to the development of language content, form, and use. For example, among children, means-end behavior is viewed as prerequisite to intentional communication. Object permanence is seen as prerequisite to content categories and syntax.

The weak cognitive hypothesis recognizes some relations between cognition and language. This hypothesis does not, however, accept that all elements of language follow cognitive achievements. Thus, Tomasello and Farrar (1984) concluded that object permanence is not prerequisite to the use of simple content/form interactions in children, as long as the objects being labeled are in sight. They presumed that object permanence is necessary for more complex language structures about displaced objects and events.

Applying the strong cognitive hypothesis to adults, one would expect that specific cognitive achievements—concrete and formal operations, in particular—would be prerequisite to the generation of complex semantic relations. Such achievements have also been viewed as supporting the use of language for complex forms of reasoning and problem solving (e.g., Moses, Klein, & Altman, 1990). Concrete and formal operations are manifested in conservation and hypothetico-deductive reasoning.

Conservation involves making comparisons among features of events and inferring that something remains constant despite changes or differences in the observable features of events (Moses et al., 1990). At the concrete operational level, the individual needs objects to manipulate to arrive at conservation. In number conservation, individuals recognize that the number of objects in a group remains the same, even when the configuration changes, as long as they are given objects to manipulate. In quantity conservation, the amount of material in a container is understood to remain the same despite changes in the shape of the container. (It is likely that manufacturers and retailers take advantage of weaknesses in conservation ability when they manipulate the shape of coffee containers, cookie boxes, detergent bottles, etc.) From a strong cognitive perspective, concrete operations and conservation are viewed as underlying complex causal statements relevant to problem solving (e.g., "I can tell there is the same amount of coffee in the cheaper bag than in the more expensive can because the weight on the label is the same").

At the formal operational level, individuals can envision conservation without objects to manipulate. In addition, individuals can approach problems by engaging in hypothetico-deductive reasoning. Hypothetico-deductive reasoning involves generating "if-then" statements about procedures and causes (which may not be observable) and testing hypotheses systematically. The individual is capable of envisioning and manipulating combinations and permutations of interacting variables. One classic Piagetian test of formal operational reasoning concerns the discovery of which combinations of colorful chemicals produce a colorless liquid. In planning interventions in cases of language disorders, the clinician might consider engaging clients in tasks that evoke the requisite cognitive operations as a support for the attainment of complex language structures.

Performance on Piagetian Tasks and Aging.   It is important for the clinician to be aware of research findings concerning levels of cognitive performance manifested by normally achieving individuals across the adult age range. Such information is important for establishing appropriate performance expectations for adult clients. It is significant, therefore, that Piaget's assumption that all normally achieving adults attain conservation and formal operations has not been borne out by research. Many studies of adult cognition have revealed instances of nonconservation on the classic Piagetian tasks by normally achieving adults (e.g., McGillicuddy, Delisi, Delisi & Youniss, 1978; Murray & Armstrong, 1978). These findings were observed both with male and female subjects (typically college students); women, however, fared more poorly than men on spatial tasks, such as conservation of absolute horizontality.

A body of research has identified decrements in performance on Piagetian tasks with normal aging (Hooper & Sheehan, 1977). Papalia (1972), who studied 96 subjects from 6 through 65+ years of age, reported that variability in the oldest subjects' performance mirrored variability in conservation abilities of young children across Piagetian infralogical tasks (i.e., spatial, weight, volume, quantity). The majority of the elderly subjects (625) conserved substance, fewer (50%) conserved weight, and very few (6%) conserved volume. Interestingly, adults 54–64 years of age manifested the best performance of all subject groups in Papalia's study (see also Sanders, Laurendeau, & Bergeron, 1966; Papalia, Saverson, & True, 1973). In the study by Sanders et al. (1966), there was a decrement in functioning beyond the age of 39 (especially in area conservation, which was not investigated in all studies cited). Similarly, Papalia, Kennedy, & Sheehan (1973) reported low levels of area conservation in adults 50–70. In the other studies, performance either remained stable or improved until the age of 65.

Strategies that adults use to solve logical problems of the kind Piaget developed (classes, part-whole relations, probability, formal reasoning) also seem to change with age. Annett (1959), in a study of classification, found that adults above and below 40 years of age classify according to two criteria: similarity and complementation. Similarity criteria are perceptual or categorical in nature (e.g., screwdriver is analogous to awl), whereas complementation criteria involve a functional relation (e.g., screwdriver is analogous to screw). With increasing age there was an increase in the use of complementation criteria (as seen in young children) and a decrease in the number of similarity responses (see also Denney, 1974a). Denney (1974b), furthermore, identified an increase with age in the use of design and color of stimuli and a decrease in the use of shape and size as criteria for complementary relationships.

Elderly individuals (over 65) appear to manifest significantly poorer performance on tests of spatial egocentrism relative to younger adults (Looft & Charles, 1971; Bielby & Papalia, 1975; Rubin, 1974, 1976), with the best performance demonstrated by college-age students (Rubin, 1974). Notably, however, no significant differences between elderly and younger adults were found in studies of social egocentrism when the elderly were given additional time and social feedback (Looft; 1972; Looft & Charles, 1971).

Several studies of conservation in adults attempted to control for institutionalization and brain disease. As expected, performance levels declined with institutionalization and severity of pathology. Hooper & Sheehan (1977), and Rubin (1974) reported that institutionalized elderly performed significantly poorer on Piagetian reasoning tasks than elderly living in the community. Institutionalization, as well as age, appears to negatively affect performance of logical tasks (Denney & Cornelius, 1975). It is not clear from these studies, however, what role institutionalization versus brain disease played in the performance of elderly subjects, since these variables were generally confounded in the research design.

Findings of deterioration in cognitive functioning with age were not unequivocal. For example, Hooper and Sheehan (1977) reported a greater proportion of the elderly conserve when more adult-like materials are used in research. They also reported no age effect for conservation of length and weight, transitivity of length, and weight and class inclusion in life span studies in individuals 6–91.

Several studies of the effectiveness of training on the performance of the elderly on Piagetian tasks show significant improvement in performance. This suggests that environmental or "crystallized" intelligence factors (e.g., memorized information) rather than structural factors may influence the decline in performance with age (Hooper & Sheehan, 1977). Training studies focus on area and volume (Hornblum & Overton, 1976); logical reasoning (Vief & Gonda, 1976); and spatial egocentrism, space, and number (Schultz & Hoyer, 1976). Improvement was observed in community-based and institutionalized subjects.

Implications for Intervention Planning. The cognition-language relationship as viewed from the perspective of the strong cognitive hypothesis influences intervention planning primarily in the derivation of procedures and in the analysis of performance demands during session planning. The presumption of the strong cognitive hypothesis is that cognition influences language performance. There are several implications relevant to procedure planning.

One implication is that the type and level of reasoning stimulated by tasks presented to clients should correspond with content/form/use interactions targeted as goals. For example, the goal of intervention may be the use of a comparative causal statement (e.g., "They get the same amount of coffee in the smaller bag as in the bigger can because the coffee in the smaller bag is compressed"). A procedure developed for this task may involve experimentation with a scale, a bag and a can of coffee, and reasoning about weight and density.

The selection of tasks according to level of reasoning required to resolve the task relates to the issue of performance demands. Performance demands are information-processing demands made on the client as a function of the difficulty or complexity of the task being addressed. We try to control performance demands when planning session goals and procedures. The inherent level of reasoning required to achieve tasks represents an important performance demand that could be controlled when choosing tasks to present the client during session planning. The cognitive complexity could be increased or decreased depending upon the language output targeted and the client's ability to accommodate the problem.

The final implication of traditional Piagetian stage theory is that if cognitive functioning in adults could be improved, language competence might be improved. Procedures for improving cognitive functioning in adults are not made explicit in traditional Piagetian theory. Recent developments in cognitive theory along epigenetic lines, however, open up this possibility.

Developmental Achievements in Adults: Neo-Piagetian Theory

Although traditional Piagetian stage theory has for a long time been attractive to speech-language pathologists, its direct application to speech-language intervention has been limited by several factors. First, the idea of having individuals with language problems perform the traditional Piagetian tasks seems to have a limited and indirect connection to speech and language performance. Piagetian conservation tasks appear related only to talking about the subjects addressed by such tasks, such as equivalences of number, quantity, length, and weight. A second limiting factor is the seemingly immutable nature of a cognitive stage. Stage development has been traditionally seen as not affected by clinical intervention. Based on traditional Piagetian theory, clinicians would not consider promoting advances in cognitive achievement as a means of improving language performance. Piagetian theory might be viewed as more widely applicable to language intervention if (a) cognitive achievements were recognized in common, everyday, problem-solving tasks, and not just the traditional Piagetian Tests; and (b) the level of cognitive performance were changeable across the life span as a consequence of specific problem-solving experiences.

Consistent with the proposed change of focus, contemporary developmentalists influenced by Piaget have reconceptualized cognitive organization as sensitive to particular problem-solving situations. (see Case, 1985, 1992b; Fischer, Bullock, Rotenberg, & Raya, 1993; Karmiloff-Smith, 1986). From this point of view, aspects of cognitive organization originally identified in the traditional Piagetian tasks have been shown to be implicated in many kinds of problem-solving tasks (e.g., Piaget, 1985). The development of cognition, itself, is now seen as a life-long process, in which individuals may pass through a series of cognitive phases in a cyclic fashion each time they find themselves in complex, novel, problem-solving situations.

Fischer (1980), a prominent neo-Piagetian theorist, identified a "developmental range" within which individuals perform. This range represents the upper and lower limits of cognitive functioning that may be exhibited by an individual across all problem-solving contexts. This functional range becomes wider with age (Fischer, 1980). Cognitive development at any point in the life cycle will take place within this developmental range. Similar ideas were expressed by Vygotsky (Reiser & Carton, 1987) who labeled the area of cognition susceptible to developmental intervention "the zone of proximal development."

In adults, a major focus of these epigenetic theorists has been cognition as reflected in judgments about moral or intellectual concepts, and about procedures and causes intrinsic to problem solving. Reasoning about these subjects is central to an adult's use of language, especially in vocational and professional contexts. Procedural and causal knowledge contribute to metalinguistic knowledge, i.e., knowing how language works, including syntactic procedures and how language form may be varied with reference to pragmatic demands of various social interactions. Several theorists have proposed different versions of cognitive development. Some examples of these are presented below.

Fischer's Skill Theory. Fischer (1980) described four qualitatively different levels in the development of cognitive skills (i.e., mental representations about concepts, problem-solving procedures or causes). Fischer's model is applied to judgments about something familiar: intervention planning. The first skill level is characterized by one or more isolated ways of thinking about something (e.g., thinking of intervention planning as involving a uniform set of "cookbook procedures" for specific disorder categories). The second skill level is characterized by the abstraction of a modified concept based on earlier thinking and recognition that there may be more than one viewpoint about any issue (e.g., recognizing that there may be more than one way to approach intervention planning, and that one's view about language, language disorders, and language learning may affect one's conceptualization of the intervention-planning process). The third skill level involves conclusions drawn from reflection on prior thinking, consideration of different instances of the issue, and recognition of the need for justification of conclusions (e.g., recognizing that there are intervention-planning procedures that apply across disorder categories, and that intervention planning decisions must be justified with reference to baseline data and one's own beliefs about language and language learning). The fourth skill level, the highest level, involves the derivation of a system of abstract principles based upon earlier abstractions (e.g., recognition that intervention planning is a decision-making process. There are a set of intervention planning principles that apply across disorder categories. Within these uniform principles, however, is the recognition that intervention planning must be individualized; i.e., the same goals and procedures may make different "performance demands" on different individuals).

Fischer (1989) emphasized that relatively subtle changes in task conditions, such as a shift from verbal description to physical execution of procedures, can affect the performance level manifested by the individual. According to Fischer, individuals may pass through these phases across the life span, when they find themselves confronted by novel problem-solving contexts.

The most apparent application of Fischer's theory is to cases of impairment in language content, and to the formulation of intervention procedures. Fischer's theory suggests engaging clients in problem-solving tasks that allow the discovery of concepts relevant to communication performance targeted in intervention. Conceptual development could support improvements in language content.

Karmiloff-Smith's Modular Theory of Procedural Knowledge.   Karmiloff-Smith (1986) proposed a modular theory in which problem-solving procedures are represented initially within one of various distinct information-processing modalities (e.g., acoustic, kinesthetic, tactile, visual). Conscious knowledge develops as representations are *re-represented* within other modalities. Some types of knowledge, such as knowledge of syntactic procedures (i.e., rules for creating sentences), are resistant to re-representation and awareness according to Karmiloff-Smith. Karmiloff-Smith's theory applies primarily to procedure planning. This theory suggests that it may be easier to learn new language forms by producing them first and reflecting on one's own productions than by rule memorization (since the procedures by which individuals communicate is viewed as resistant to conscious knowledge). In language content, the theory again applies to learning about procedures (e.g., in this case, procedures about anything; e.g., how to work a computer program, how to run the New York Marathon, etc.). Again, the implication is that execution of the procedure (e.g., "how to") and reflection upon such action may be more efficacious to mental representation and language content than memorization or rules.

Moses' Theory of Procedural and Causal Knowledge.   Moses' (1994) model of cognitive development focuses on adults' knowledge of procedures ("how to") and causes ("why") and reinforces implications of Karmiloff-Smith's theory for intervention planning. In this model, adults manifest transformations in cognitive organization when conceptualizing procedures and causes while problem solving. These transformations are analogous to those seen in children. According to Moses, knowledge of procedures in adults develops before knowledge of causes.

While developing procedural knowledge, adults pass through three phases. During the first phase, conceptualizations about how to approach the task and actual procedures are holistic and nonreversible. This signifies that individuals overlook much pertinent information and execute a procedure that is not modified if it does not work. The procedure is simply repeated. For example, an individual tries to turn on a computer by flipping the switch on the main component but the computer does not activate. The person tries several times, jiggling the switch and perhaps checking the plug. But that individual does not recognize that there might be a preliminary switch, such as a surge protector.

During the second developmental phase, individuals differentiate their view of the task and their procedures. This signifies that individuals begin to notice overlooked information and try other procedures (including the opposite of the ineffective procedure just attempted). The individual may even anticipate that there could be a series of intermediate steps that will need to be executed before the task can be achieved. Individuals cannot yet, however, systematically envision the solution to the overall task. In the computer task, the individual may search for and discover the surge protector. He or she may then try it with the main computer component turned off and experience some confusion.

The third developmental phase is characterized by differentiated and reversible constructs. This signifies that the individual can envision intermediate task demands and procedures for solving the overall task. Furthermore, the individual can anticipate and avoid problems even when some aspect of the task changes (e.g., an IBM computer is substituted for an Apple). The individual can envision and execute procedures that are the reverse of earlier executed procedures.

Investigating adults' causal knowledge and related causal language, Moses et al. (1990) identified three developmental levels: preoperational, transitional preoperational, and concrete operational. This developmental pattern, described in Chapter 4, was identified in normally achieving adults and adults with learning disabilities engaged in a board-balancing task.

Implications of Neo-Piagetian Theories for Intervention Planning. One implication of neo-Piagetian research for intervention planning resides in the involvement of Piagetian forms of reasoning about causes and procedures in many daily activities. Such forms of reasoning are reflected in causal and procedural language (e.g., talking about why and how). Developments in cognition may lead to changes in the linguistic structure of adults' procedural and causal explanations. Such developments may be facilitated as adults engage in novel problem-solving tasks. It may be possible, therefore to devise intervention procedures aimed at modifying the individual's level of cognitive functioning within specific problem-solving contexts in order to influence language. A decision to address cognition would be stated in the long-term procedural approach, reflected in the design of short-term linguistic and nonlinguistic procedural contexts and in session goals and procedures.

Several additional implications of neo-Piagetian theories were presented above. One is that metalinguistic knowledge of language form, as reflected in syntax, fluency, and phonology, is primarily procedural in nature. Improvement of performance in these areas is more susceptible to action-oriented practice than conscious application of memorized procedural rules. A second implication is that conceptualization of procedures, in general, derives from reflection on the actual execution of procedures. We discuss implications of neo-Piagetian theory for procedural planning in greater detail in the section on principles of learning and rehabilitation in Chapter 6.

Developmental Achievements in Adults:
Reasoning and Logic

Propositional logic as well as inductive and deductive reasoning represent additional aspects of cognition associated with developmental theories such as Piaget's (e.g., Piaget & Garcia, 1991). Logic and deduction are components of verbal reasoning, and verbal reasoning represents an important function of adult language. Propositional logic is usually assessed through verbal deductive reasoning tasks. In these tasks, the individual must arrive at a conclusion (or make a decision about the veracity of a stated conclusion) given a set of premises. Inductive and deductive reasoning is usually evaluated through analogy and metaphor.

The ability to employ propositional logic to draw a reasonable conclusion based upon a set of stated premises represents a functionally significant adult competence. Adults are called upon to exercise such skills on a daily basis. For example, many advertisements present arguments that seduce consumers to make inferences automatically, without reflection: e.g., "People who smoke Brand A cigarettes (or drive Brand A automobiles) are cool and socially desirable. You smoke Brand A (or drive Brand A). Therefore, you are cool and socially desirable." One would have to have achieved a degree of sophistication in propositional reasoning to recognize that conclusions based on premises based on some questionable motivation is not the same as reasoning with an empirical basis. This sophistication would help individuals avoid untoward influence.

Kamhi (1988) emphasized that problem-solving tasks that employ inductive and deductive reasoning are especially pertinent to adult adaptive functioning. Determining the proportion of ingredients to use when it is necessary to triple the number of servings in a recipe invokes inductive reasoning. Deciding to have chocolate or strawberry but not both involves deductive reasoning. Solving a problem invokes induction if there is not enough information given to solve it; one must go to outside sources of information. Deductive reasoning is applied to problems that contain enough information to arrive at a solution.

Given the significant role that these forms of reasoning play in adult adaptive functioning and language use, the ability to discriminate among different types of reasoning skills and to address these skills during intervention planning represents important clinician competencies. The following is an overview of propositional, inductive, and deductive reasoning skills in adults.

Propositional Logic.   Braine (1990) identified inference schemas constituting natural propositional logic. Examples are presented in Table 5.1.

TABLE 5.1   Examples of Natural Propositional Logic

1. E.g., There is a cat; There is an apple/∴. There is a cat and an apple.
2. E.g., There is a chicken and a horse/∴. There is a chicken.
3. E.g., There is a grape, and there is a lemon or an egg/∴. There is a grape and a lemon, or there is a grape and an egg.
4. E.g., There is an orange; There is not an orange/INCOMPATIBLE.
5. E.g., There is a dog or a tiger; There is not a dog and there is not a tiger/INCOMPATIBLE.
6. E.g., It is false that there is not a banana/∴. There is a banana.
7. E.g., If there is either a cow or a goat, then there is a pear; There is a cow/∴. There is a pear.
8. E.g., There is a strawberry or a blackberry; There is not a strawberry/∴. There is a blackberry.
9. E.g., It is false that there is both a plum and a pineapple; There is a plum/∴. There is not a pineapple.
10. E.g., There is a fox or a wolf; If there is a fox, then there is a nut; If there is a wolf, then there is a nut/∴. There is a nut.
11. E.g., There is a duck or a goose; If there is a duck, then there is a plum; If there is a goose, then there is a cherry/∴. There is a plum or a cherry.
12. E.g., If there is a grapefruit, then there is an elephant; There is a grapefruit/∴. There is an elephant.

Adapted from Braine (1990). Used with permission.

Braine termed the forms of logic in Table 5.1 "inference schemas" because they are not conscious or learned and are available to children and adults for solving verbal and nonverbal problems; for example, for figuring out that if someone explains that it is not true that her name is not Mary (inference schema 6), that person can deduce that her name is Mary. Braine claimed that most, if not all, of the forms of propositional logic are available to children by school age and are reflected in the kinds of verbal and nonverbal problems that children can solve (see also Moshman, 1990; Piaget & Garcia, 1991).

Moshman (1990) suggested that Braine's (1990) forms of propositional logic may be developmental through age 5. Moshman proposed further that it is *metalogic* and its two components, *metalogical strategies* and *metalogical understanding,* which are developmental and which are most advanced in adults. Moshman defined metalogical strategies as "strategies of reasoning that go beyond simply assimilating premises to unconscious inference schemata. Metalogic involves an explicit distinction between premises and conclusions and a purposeful use of inference to deduce the latter from the former" (p. 208). Metalogical understanding, according to Moshman, "consists of conceptions about the nature of logic" (p. 209). Moshman identified the following four stages in the development of metalogic:

Stage 1: Explicit content-implicit inference (Preschooler). Given a problem like the example below, the individual simply solves the problem without thinking about how he or she is reasoning. Example: Sprognoids are either animals or plants. Sprognoids are not animals. Therefore, sprognoids are plants.

Stage 2: Explicit inference-implicit logic (6–10-year-old). Given a logically problematic conclusion (with reference to its premise) as in the example below, the child realizes there is a problem and may withhold judgment until he or she gets further information. Example: Sprognoids are animals or plants or machines. Sprognoids are not animals. Therefore, sprognoids are plants.

Stage 3. Explicit logic-implicit metalogic (12–13-year-old). The individual would not reject the premise in the problem below, which seems to contradict common sense, because the individual is explicitly aware of logical form and realizes that logical form is different from observable facts. Example: Elephants are either animals or plants. Elephants are not animals. Therefore, elephants are plants.

Stage 4. Explicit metalogic (Adults—perhaps a minority of undergraduate college students have reached this level). The individual can think about a formal logical system, as opposed to simply reasoning from the system or having a vague notion about the difference between the system and the problem thought about. Example: There is a system of logic offered by Moshman by which it is possible to draw conclusions about the truth or falsehood of verbal proposals.

Inductive and Deductive Reasoning.   As discussed above, inductive and deductive reasoning tasks, like tasks invoking propositional logic, are especially pertinent to adult adaptive functioning. A problem is inductive if there is not enough information given to solve it; one must go to outside sources of information. Deductive problems contain enough information to arrive at a solution.

Inductive reasoning tasks may be proportions (e.g., one package is to two cans as three packages are to _____ cans), analogies (e.g., bear is to cub as cow is to _____), series completions (June, August, October, ___), classifications (e.g., Which of the following does not go with the others? aunt, cousin, sister, friend), interpretations of metaphors (e.g., The house was a box with no lid.), and proverbs (e.g., The early bird catches the worm.). Deductive problems include solving syllogisms (e.g., All boxes are green. There is a box. Therefore, _____), probability problems (e.g., You toss a coin. It can land heads or tails. You toss it 100 times. How many times can you expect it to land heads?), and combinations (e.g., Here are three different shapes: a triangle, circle, and square. Show me all the different ways you can combine them.).

Nippold (1988) pointed out that age, intelligence, level of academic achievement, and problem-solving style affect verbal reasoning abilities in children. Children by the age of 12–14, as well as normally achieving adults, should be able to solve all of the inductive problem types exemplified above. There are factors, however, that can complicate the issue. Two general factors are semantic complexity and familiarity with lexicon. Another aspect that applies to analogies and syllogisms is the interaction between problem-solving strategies and structural complexity of analogies or syllogism.

With analogies, there is a developmental progression from the use of associative strategies to the application of analogical strategies. Thus, given the analogy "house is to cave as boy is to _____," young associative reasoners might respond "girl" without first reflecting on the relation between bear and cave. Impulsive reasoners persist in the use of associative reasoning strategies as compared with reflective reasoners (Achenbach, 1969).

The analogies presented above are first-order analogies. They require the individual to make comparisons within one set of data. Second- and third-order analogies may also be identified. These involve decisions about a second or third set of data with reference to an initial decision about an original set of data. An example of a third-order analogy is (sand is to beach as star is to _____(galaxy), as water is to ocean as air is to _____(sky). Adolescents often revert to associative reasoning strategies when presented with these more complex analogies, even though they are applying analogical reasoning strategies to first-order analogies. By adulthood, normally achieving individuals can apply second- and third-order analogies analogically (Sternberg & Downing, 1982).

Nippold (1988) reported that the intrinsic structure of an analogy affects verbal reasoning. Sternberg and Nigro (1982) found that functional and antonymous relationships appeared easier than synonymous, linear ordering, and superordinate-subordinate for subjects 9–18 years of age, when complexity of vocabulary has been controlled.

Structural factors affect deductive syllogistic reasoning, as well (Nippold, 1988). In a study involving children and young adults 7–19 years of age, Sternberg (1979) played a game in which he hid objects (e.g., a circle and/or a square) and gave children hints in the form of two premises of a syllogism. Five types of syllogisms were presented to the subjects: conjunctive (e.g., There is a circle in the box and there is a square in the box.), disjunctive (e.g., There is a circle in the box or there is a square in the box.), if-then conditional (e.g., If there is a circle in the box then there is a square in the box.), only-if conditional (e.g., There is a circle in the box only if there is a square in the box.), and biconditional (e.g., There is a circle in the box if and only if there is a square in the box, Nippold, 1988, p. 173.)

Subjects had to respond true, false, or maybe to the conclusion. In this study, conjunctive syllogism proved easiest, followed by exclusive disjunctive syllogisms, only-if conditionals, and if-then conditionals. In a study of if-then conditional syllogisms, denying the antecedent or affirming the consequent proved most difficult for subjects 9–17, whereas affirming the antecedent and denying the consequent were easier (Taplin, Staudenmeyer, & Taddonio, 1974). Sternberg (1979) suggested that linguistic competence is more important than logical competence in the development of syllogistic reasoning. Kuhn (1977) recommended providing subjects with verbal reasoning problems in more natural contexts to facilitate reasoning performance.

Implications for Intervention Planning

Reasoning skills may be addressed procedurally as maintaining factors in a language disability. Tasks involving propositional logic, analogies, metaphors, and such may be designed to facilitate content/form/use interactions or other linguistic goals. For example, comparative statements (sentences with "more than" and "like" may be facilitated in the context of analogies). In designing tasks that provoke reasoning skills, the clinician must recognize that solving logical problems presents performance demands that need to be controlled during session planning. In other words, the complexity of the problem presented to the client should be explicitly monitored and controlled.

Information Processing

Overview.   In developmental and social-learning approaches to cognition reviewed above, the focus is on continued intellectual development, learning, and improved adaptation across the life span. Especially in the Piagetian-influenced theories, this creative process is founded on organization intrinsic to the individual's behavior, which is applied to learning and controlling the environment. Contrastively, information-processing theories of cognition are more mechanical in nature and generally do not attend to organizational characteristics of behavior. They focus, instead, on processes by which information is noticed, absorbed from the environment, assigned meaning, stored, and retrieved. The processes that have attracted the greatest attention include sensory processes (hearing, vision, etc.), attention, perception, and memory. These processes are generally assessed in standardized, examiner-controlled contexts, where individuals must produce or evaluate linguistic units upon demand within time constraints, often in response to stimuli drawn from standardized tests (e.g., vocabulary subtests of the Wechsler Intelligence Test for Adults, or the Boston Naming Test). Since these processes are conceived as being mechanical in nature, it is not surprising that research with aging populations report a marked decline in information-processing skills associated with language comprehension and production (Au, Obler & Albert, 1991).

Language Comprehension.   Declines associated with language comprehension have been partially attributed to diminution in sensory acuity, especially impaired phoneme discrimination due to hearing loss in the elderly. These deficits are partially accounted for by decreases in pure tone acuity (affecting especially the high frequencies) and sensorineural losses (Obler & Albert, 1980).

Obler and Albert (1980) also attribute the degeneration of language comprehension skills to the following general neurologic concomitants of aging:

1. general slowing of neurologic response, as response time to tones increases gradually from young adulthood to the sixties, and then increases dramatically in the seventies;
2. increased reaction time as compared with middle-aged and young adults;
3. attenuation of subvocal processing time;
4. decreased ability to attend to competing stimuli, seen in impaired performance levels when two voices are presented to the same ear (older adults [59–81] perform as poorly as third- and fourth-grade children); performance improves (to a ninth-grade level) when voices are presented to separate ears (Maccoby, 1971)—this suggests that older adults either do not divide their attention as well as younger people or that self distraction (e.g., the act of reporting the first voice) interferes with memory (Obler & Albert, 1980);
5. difficulty comprehending messages that contain low redundancy, reflected in problems comprehending sentences such as, "He shows her bird the seed" (Scholes, 1978);
6. changes in monitoring strategies, manifested in impaired ability to identify word transformations (e.g., especially when a nonsense word repeatedly presented via a tape loop changes, (Clegg, 1971)—in such tasks, the elderly individuals appear to monitor speech input at a word-by-word level, whereas younger individuals analyze at the phonemic level;
7. degeneration of working (short-term) memory, reflected in findings of reduced comprehension performance in response to lengthy or complex stimuli (Au, Obler & Albert, 1991).

Five types of memory have been identified in the literature on information processing: sensory, primary, secondary, working short-term, and tertiary (Fozard, 1980). According to information-processing theory, when an individual first encounters a stimulus (either spontaneously or in an educational setting), the stimulus registers in sensory memory for a brief period. In a young adult, it is maintained for several thousandths of a second before it either fades or is processed further. Information processed at the level of sensory memory would be recognized as a fragmentary sound or sound in a word, feeling, taste, or so forth (Bayles & Kaszniak, 1987). If information in sensory memory is processed further, it is transferred to short-term memory (which Fozard, 1980, subdivided into primary, secondary, and working memory). Information is held in short-term memory for an additional 15–30 seconds before it is either processed further or fades (Bransford, Barclay & Franks, 1972). The recollection of digit sequences or groups of names are examples of information processing at the short-term memory level. Information may also be processed for longer-term storage in tertiary or long-term memory. Some information-processing theorists view information that is permanently accessible—for example, vocabulary—as "crystallized intelligence" in long-term memory (Horn & Cattell, 1967).

An important aspect of memory theory concerns how information is transferred into longer-term storage. Transfer is seen as involving repetitive attention, retrieval, and use of information (Craik & Lokhart, 1972; Craik & Tulving, 1975); the storage of information in multiple forms (Atkinson & Shifrin, 1971; Loftus, & Loftus, 1976); and the application of encoding strategies (e.g., Reiser, 1986; Shank & Abelson, 1977). More recently, the focus of learning research has been on the use of strategies and procedures for the retrieval of information from long-term memory (Reiser, 1986) and the use of knowledge structures in the transfer of information from short- to long-term memory. As explained in the text on intervention planning with children, knowledge structures are organized networks of ideas, associations, and scripts derived from past experiences (Galambos, Abelson, & Block, 1986; Nelson, 1986). In a related development, pharmacological approaches to long-term memory improvement in adults also are being evaluated. The focus of these treatments is the "CREB" genetic mechanism. This mechanism is seen as regulating the generation of proteins that in turn stimulate neurologic networking and the transfer of information from short-term to long-term store (Noble-Wilson, 1998).

As noted above, it is short-term or working memory that seems to be most affected by aging in the healthy adult. Short-term memory deficits seem to contribute to reduced ability of the elderly (60 years and older) to (a) answer questions that require recollection of explicitly presented information and (b) make inferences about orally presented sentences manipulated according to syntactic complexity or about paragraph-length material (e.g., Davis & Ball, 1989; Emery, 1986; Feier & Gerstman, 1980; Obler, Nicholas, Albert, & Woodward, 1985):

The information-processing picture in language comprehension is not entirely one of degeneration with advancing age. Given written material to analyze (which provides perceptual support and the ability to review information), elderly subjects make inferences as well as younger adults (further evidence that the problem with orally presented material resides in working memory according to Hasher & Zaks, 1988). Additionally, Au, Obler and Albert (1991) reported that the elderly compensate for decreased comprehension by developing strategies, such as lipreading, which facilitate visual synthesis (the identification of incomplete or partially obscured sentences or pictures).

Language Production. Aging also appears to have a deleterious effects on the processing of information related to language production. Consider the following:

1. Naming abilities deteriorate. On the Boston Naming Test (Kaplan, Goodglass, & Weintraub, 1976), the ability to label line drawings of objects (Borod, Goodglass, & Kaplan, 1980), and actions (Nicholas, Obler, Albert & Goodglass, 1985) decreases significantly after the age of 69. Au, Obler, Joung, & Albert (1990) found in a study of adults aged 30–75 that subjects demonstrated a slow, progressive decline in naming when presented the same set of pictures three times over seven years.
2. The ability to retrieve names of people and objects declines in middle age and then more dramatically in the older individual (60 years and older, Bowles & Poon, 1985; Nicholas et al., 1985). Correspondingly, tip-of-the-tongue phenomena (efforts to retrieve names following name blocks) increase in frequency with age (Cohen & Faulkner, 1986; Au, Obler, & Albert, 1991). Several types of research findings indicate that both young and old subjects can eventually recall names following the presentation of phonologic cues or given additional time for recall. These findings suggest that problems remembering involve retrieval of phonologic information as opposed to conceptual or representational data (Au, Obler & Albert, 1991).
3. The ability to retrieve lists of semantically or phonologically related words rapidly upon demand within a fixed time declines with age, although Au, Obler & Albert (1991) reported that the elderly perform as well as young adults given unlimited time for the task.

4. In a study of the spontaneous speech of middle-aged and elderly adults, subjects above 70 years produced a significantly reduced range of complex sentences than younger subjects (Kynette & Kemper, 1986), with fewer center-embedded and left-branching structures.

As with comprehension, all trends in information-processing skills with aging are not negative in direction. In an analysis of storytelling skills, Obler (1980) reported that the elderly produce stories with increased elaborateness because of more competent use of repetition, modifiers, and chunking of sentences as compared with younger adults. Similar findings were reported by Sandson, Obler and Albert (1987) who studied adults' descriptions of the pictured cookie theft story from the Boston Diagnostic Aphasia Examination (Goodglass & Kaplan, 1983). Older adults used more elaborate speech involving filler phrases, deictic references, comments, and modifiers as compared with middle-aged subjects.

Implications for Intervention Planning.   The idea that language functioning can be improved by practicing information-processing skills (e.g., recalling lists of digits, names, or picture sequences; completing visual cloze exercises; etc.) has been questioned for some time in the literature on language-learning disabilities in children (e.g., Lahey, 1988; Reid & Hresko, 1981; Reid, 1988). Research findings in language-learning disabilities have indicated that practice using linguistic structures in communicative contexts produces the best therapeutic results when content/form/use interactions are the target of intervention (see also Martin's [1981] comments on intervention planning for clients with aphasia).

With adolescents and adults who have sustained brain injury through head trauma, stroke, or the onset of dementia, information-processing theory continues to provide direction for much intervention (e.g., Chapey, 1994). For example, Duffy (1986) recommended tasks addressing the following information-processing skills consistent with Schuell's stimulation approach to rehabilitation with individuals with aphasia: response switching, verbal association, reception, and retention of auditory information.

We see the contribution of information-processing theory to intervention planning with adults as primarily prognostic and procedural in nature at all phases of intervention planning. In terms of long-term goal setting, the derivation of a reasonable prognosis and realistic long-term intervention goals depends, in part, on a consideration of the degree of sensorimotor and cognitive impairment affecting the reception, recollection, and production of language-relevant information and behavior. In addition, information-processing difficulties represent maintaining factors that place demands upon linguistic performance and, as such, must be controlled systematically in the derivation of session goals and in the design of procedures across planning phases.

Summary

In this section we discussed cognition as a maintaining factor for communication problems in adults. We presented four approaches to cognition: traditional Piagetian, neo-Piagetian, social cognitive, and information processing. Box 5.2 summarizes cognitive achievements in adults associated with each approach and implications for adult language.

BOX **5.2**

Four Perspectives on Cognition and Implications of Cognitive Achievements for Adult Language

Theoretical Perspective	Cognitive Achievement	Implications for Adult Language
Traditional Piagetian theory: Level of cognitive organization applied to reasoning will influence content/form/use interactions.	Preoperational reasoning	Causal statements comprise sequences of observable events.
	Concrete operational reasoning	More complex causal statements incorporate comparative, attributive-state relations and reference to nonobservable causal variables given perceptual support for reasoning.
	Formal operations	More complex causal statements incorporate attributive-state relations and reference to nonobservable causal variables without perceptual support for reasoning. Demonstrate ability to verbalize alternate possible solutions to problems, ability to describe/envision/ explain events from multiple/different perspectives.
Neo-Piagetian epigenetic/constructivist theory: Cognitive organization is sensitive to problem solving context. Cognitive organization intrinsic to procedural and causal knowledge is especially important in adult problem solving. It is possible to influence (modify) cognitive organization.	Holistic, undifferentiated organization	Descriptions of procedures omit intermediate variables and interactions among variables. Related causal statements focus on temporal sequences of observable events.
	Partially differentiated organization	Comments begin to incorporate intermediate steps and intermediate interactions among objects, often with much uncertainty and reversion to holistic procedural constructs. Descriptions of procedures often contradict actual procedures being executed.
	Differentiated organization	Causal statements incorporate intermediate steps and intermediate interactions among objects. Descriptions of procedures are consistent with procedures being executed. Reference is made to nonobservable causal variables, alternate possibilities and perspectives, and reciprocal interactions among causal variables in which some state is conserved. Use comparative terms.

(continued)

BOX **5.2** **Continued**

Theoretical Perspective	Cognitive Achievement	Implications for Adult Language
Social cognitive: Verbal, metacognitive problem-solving strategies facilitate the use of language for narrative and other forms of discourse comprehension, and for problem solving in general.	The acquisition and use of metacognitive problem-solving strategies	Facilitates all forms of discourse comprehension and the use of language for problem solving.
Information processing: Mechanistic processes that tend to deteriorate with age (memory, attention, rate of processing, discrimination) support language.	Attention to individual and competing stimuli.	Degeneration impairs conversational skills (topic maintenance) and comprehension.
	Short-term memory	Degeneration affects recall, comprehension, and inference-making ability to answer questions with reference to orally presented information (stories, names).
	Long-term memory	Degeneration impairs vocabulary retrieval, conversational skills, including topic initiation, and the ability to retain and use new information over time.
	Sensory acuity	Degeneration affects language comprehension and monitoring of language production.
	Speed of processing	Degeneration affects comprehension (vis-a-vis phoneme discrimination) and ability to complete tasks involving the recall or comprehension of orally presented material.

Sensorimotor

A third area in which change over the life cycle is documented is the sensorimotor system of behavior. With aging, there are physiological changes and their respective psychological consequences (Whitbourne, 1985). These changes have been documented in all of the bodily systems (i.e., cardiovascular, respiratory, excretory, endocrine, autonomic nervous, reproductive, central nervous, visual, somesthetic, vestibular, gustory, olfactory, and auditory, Whitbourne, 1985). Of these, the most significant to the speech-language pathologist are those that are foundational to voice and hearing. Thus, in this section we will focus on changes that occur with normal aging on the vocal and auditory mechanisms.

The Voice Mechanism

> The voice changes dynamically, minute by minute. But there are long-term changes that are associated with growth and decline in life. At the major stages of life, the uses of the voice are different, as are the demands placed upon it. The reasons for these differences are many and include biological maturation and the emotional and social changes that occur in the individual's life. (Colton & Casper, 1996, p. 3)

For intervention planning it is necessary to be aware of normal changes in voice production with aging. This knowledge provides a basis for setting realistic goals and for identifying maintaining factors that may be addressed during treatment.

It is also necessary to recognize that voice production involves complex interactions among behavioral subsystems. Dromey, Ramig, and Johnson (1995) put it more succinctly when they wrote that "phonatory adjustments, as those accompanying loud speech, reflect complex, goal oriented, systematic organizational changes in interactive behaviors" (pp. 751–752). As an example, Schulman (as cited by Dromey et al, 1995) discovered that loud speech elicited greater jaw openings, increased lip movement, and more complete lip closure than speech produced at a normal intensity level. For intervention planning, we are most interested in the perceptual characteristics of vocal changes with aging and the underlying neurophysiological correlates.

Adult Voice Onset.   One of the most salient features for the identification of adult-voice onset is change of pitch (i.e., fundamental frequency). Colton & Casper (1996) reported that between 14 and 19 years of age there is a significant drop in fundamental frequency of the voice, more so in males than in females. Concomitantly, the individual gains full control over a dynamic range of loudness, pitch levels, and voice quality. These vocal changes are a consequence of maturation of anatomical and physiological systems that support speech production. These achievements signal the onset of the adult voice.

Normal Changes in Vocal Parameters with Age.   While many aging individuals in good physical condition have been observed to maintain the voices of their prime (Colton & Casper, 1996; Ramig & Ringle, 1983), for others (generally dated in the literature at 65 years of age) there are changes in vocal parameters that reflect general physical decline.

Age-related changes in phonation are most readily recognized as changes in perceptual qualities of pitch, volume, and quality (Colton & Casper, 1996). These perceptual changes are more objectively measured in acoustic terms. Changes in pitch have been captured by acoustic measures of fundamental frequency (rate of vocal fold vibration), frequency perturbation or jitter (variation of fundamental frequency within a sustained tone, which is perceptually realized as vibrato), and maximum phonation range (the range of frequencies from the highest to the lowest that an individual can produce). Changes in volume have been described in terms of maximum intensity level, amplitude perturbation or shimmer (variation in amplitude within a sustained vocalization; variation in amplitude combined with frequency perturbation is recognized perceptually as tremor), and maximum phonation duration. A summary of findings concerning changes in these parameters with aging are presented in Appendix 5A, Tables A.1 through A.6 from Colton and Casper (1996).

In Appendix 5A, Table A.1 shows that (a) in males there is a marked decline in fundamental frequency between the ages of 14 and 19, stability until the age of 70, followed by an increase in fundamental frequency; (b) in females, there is a decline in fundamental frequency between 11 and 19 years of age (less marked than in males), a continuous graduate decline between 29 and 50, followed by a stable fundamental frequency beyond 60 (see also Russell, Penny, & Pemberton, 1995).

Table A.2 shows that jitter in males and females remains fairly stable across the adult life span, although small changes are noticeable during sustained phonation of specific vowels. Changes in maximum phonation range appear in Table A.3. As can be seen in this table, for males, the range is greatest between 17 and 26 years of age, with a significant drop after 35 years of age. For females, the range is similar between 18 and 26 years of age but tends to drop less than males with aging. Maximum intensity levels across the age range are in Table A.4. For males, mean maximum intensity levels are greatest between 45 and 65 with a drop after 68; for females, maximum intensity levels are greatest between 18 and 38 with a drop after 66. Amplitude perturbation or shimmer data appear in Table A.5. Here we can see that amplitude perturbation varies with vowel production and is generally greater for males than for females. Finally, as seen in Table A.6, maximum phonation duration reaches its peak at about 13 and declines after 65 for both males and females.

Anatomical and Physiological Changes with Aging.   Voice changes associated with aging reflect anatomical and physiological changes in the subsystems involved in speech production such as respiratory, laryngeal, and articulatory (e.g., Colton & Casper, 1996; Homes, Leeper, & Nicholson, 1994). The following is a brief overview of these changes.

Respiration.   With reference to respiration, Homes et al. (1994) described changes that may cause reduced driving force for voice production. These changes include "deterioration of lung tissue, with corresponding increases in residual volume, and decreases in elastic recoil, vital capacity, maximum expiratory flow, and forced expiratory volume" (p. 789). Major changes in respiratory function appear to be related to tissue changes in costal cartilages and increase in rate of force of respiratory muscle contractions for rest and speech breathing.

According to Hoit and Hixon (1987), older individuals operate within a more limited range of volumes for speech production. This appears to be a consequence of changes in vital capacity and residual volume, with vital capacity becoming progressively smaller and residual capacity becoming progressively larger. Total lung capacity, inspiratory capacity, and functional residual capacity appear to change little with aging.

Hoit and Hixon (1987) suggested that when an aged individual is compared with a young adult, the former will breathe for speech production with generally "(a) higher lung volume and rib cage volume initiations, (b) larger lung volume and rib cage volume excursions, (c) fewer syllables per breath group, and (d) greater average lung volume expended per syllable" (p. 364). The authors explained that some components of lung volume tend to remain constant across the adult life span, and others evidence change.

Laryngeal Changes.   Changes in laryngeal functioning have been described with reference to changes in (a) vocal fold structure, (b) atrophy of intrinsic and extrinsic laryngeal muscles, (c) ossification and calcification of the laryngeal cartilages, and (d) loosening of the cricoarytenoid joints (Homes et al., 1994). Changes in these structures have been found to affect the shape of the glottal opening and the vibratory patterns of vocal fold activity during phonation.

According to Gray, Hirano, & Sato (1993) there are great individual differences in the geriatric population regarding the changes in the laryngeal structures. In general, there are changes in three levels of the vocal folds: The outer layers of the folds experience edema and thickening; the elastic fibers of the intermediate layers become looser and atrophied and thinner, which may alter the contour of this layer; and the deepest layer of vocal fold tissue has collagenous fibers that become thicker and denser, thereby adding thickness to the fold. Changes in all three levels occur more frequently in males than in females. In addition, the vocalis muscle tends to become atrophied with age; atrophy of the intrinsic laryngeal musculature affects glottal configurations (Linville, 1992). Linville demonstrated that there was more change in glottal configuration across phonatory conditions for the elderly than for young speakers. Anterior gap was the single most common type of gap in the elderly. These laryngeal changes contribute to perceptions of an aging voice.

Honjo and Isshiki (1980) described some perceptual changes and accompanying laryngeal characteristics of aging. These investigators obtained measurements of roughness, breathiness, asthenia, and hoarseness in 20 men and 20 women, between the ages of 69 and 85. The results of this perceptual analysis corresponded with laryngoscopic examinations and two acoustic measures (i.e., fundamental frequency and frequency perturbation). The laryngeal analysis showed discoloration and edema of the vocal folds. The aging women exhibited vocal fold edema and slight hoarseness, while aging men exhibited vocal fold atrophy and edema with increases in fundamental frequency. These findings supported the role of a change in vocal fold mass (caused by atrophy or edema) in observed perceptual characteristics of slight hoarseness and changes in fundamental frequency.

As indicated earlier, changes in laryngeal structures have also been believed to affect the valving efficiency of the laryngeal mechanism (aerodynamic characteristics of voice production such as translaryngeal airflow and air pressure, Homes et al., 1994). Holmes et al. studied laryngeal airway resistance in 10 healthy male and female subjects in each of three age groups: 55:0–64:11; 65:0–74:11; 75:0+. They used a noninvasive procedure to investigate laryngeal airway resistance (RLAW) at four vocal sound pressure levels (SPL): normal 25th, 50th, 75th percentiles of the SPL range and comfortable voice level (CV). RLAW values for the oldest group of females were found to be higher at each SPL percentile than those of the two younger age groups. The oldest group of males differed from the youngest group in RLAW values only at the 75th percentile level of SPL. Laryngeal airway resistance values were higher for females than for males. Homes et al. speculated that increased resistance reflected a strategy for maintaining proscribed levels of intensity to compensate for reduced efficiency of air flow. The authors stressed the importance of different RLAW values in evaluating different ages for each gender.

In support of these findings, Sapienza and Dutka (1996), in a recent article on glottal airflow characteristics in women's voice production, found that physiologic changes in the larynx with aging in healthy women may not be significant enough to produce noticeable changes in phonation. According to the authors, these results may be explained partially by the ability of healthy women to compensate for any anatomic changes.

Implications for Intervention Planning. Normal parameters of adult vocal functioning are summarized in Box 5.3. Information about adult vocal functioning has implications primarily for intervention goals. This information will help in establishing goals for

BOX **5.3**

Vocal Characteristics of Adulthood

Phases of Adulthood	Implications for Intervention Planning
Transition to adulthood 1. Between 14 and 19 drop in fundamental frequency; 2. Full control over dynamic range of loudness and pitch levels and voice quality; 3. Maximum phonation range at ages 17–26; 4. Maximum phonation range peaks at age 13; 5. Maximum intensity level between 18 and 38 for females—males do not achieve maximum levels until age 45.	Long-term goals may target peak levels and ranges of vocal performance.
Changes with aging 1. Increase in fundamental frequency beyond 70 (in males); 2. Gradual decline in fundamental frequency (in females) between 29 and 50, with stability past 60; 3. Decline in phonation range after 35; 4. Decline in intensity level between ages 66 and 68; 5. Phonation duration declines after age 65; 6. Slight hoarseness in women aged 69–85 due to vocal fold edema.	Long-term goals may be delimited with reference to age-related respiratory and laryngeal changes.

age-appropriate optimal performance in the individual. Long-term objectives for healthy young adults could target peak level and range of vocal behavior; long-term objectives for aging individuals may reflect delimited expectations in vocal performance due to age-related respiratory and laryngeal changes.

The Hearing Mechanism

Optimal Functioning.   Newby and Popelka (1992) defined the normal ear as "the ear of a young adult (from eighteen to twenty-two years of age) who has had no known auditory disorder—no history of physical ear disorders nor hearing disorders of any kind" (p. 65). It is interesting that these authors designate the age of 22 as the upper boundary of normal. This seems to indicate that there is probably some deteriorization of hearing sensitivity that begins during early adulthood. While it has been reported that the loss of hearing sensitivity may begin as early as the twenties and become more noticeable with each decade (Newby & Popelka, 1992), deterioration of hearing sensitivity is generally identified at beyond approximately 50 years (Bess & Humes, 1995). This progressive change in hearing sensitivity is typically more rapid for men than for woman. Figure 5.1 illustrates the changes in hearing acuity with aging for men and woman. As illustrated in this figure, aging is most commonly associated with a high-frequency hearing loss that becomes more pronounced with advancing years.

Changes with Aging. It has been reported that hearing loss is prevalent in the aging population. Approximately 30% of noninstitutionalized persons over 65 have some degree of hearing loss and about 70–80% of residents of nursing homes suffer from auditory dysfunction.[1] Weinstein (1994), in a comprehensive chapter on presbycusis, described the following trends evolving from audiometric-based studies on hearing loss associated with aging:

1. Age is a significant risk factor for hearing loss with mean hearing loss levels increasing as a function of age.
2. Hearing levels in men are slightly poorer than those of women, especially in the high frequencies.
3. The prevalence of hearing loss is somewhat higher in nursing facilities most likely because of the mean age of residents (p. 569).

The Committee on Hearing, Bioacoustics, and Biomechanics (CHABA, 1988) defined presbycusis as "the sum of hearing losses that results from several varieties of physiological degeneration" (p. 861). This degeneration has been associated with exposure to noise, ototoxic agents, and medical disorders and treatments. A genetically determined predisposition to presbycusis is also possible (e.g., CHABA, 1988; Miller, 1963).

Presbycusis. Schuknecht (1964) identified four major types of presbycusis (see also CHABA, 1988; Weinstein, 1994, and Whitbourne, 1985, for reviews). These types are differentiated on the basis of structural origin within the inner ear and functional effects as represented on audiograms.

1. "*Sensory* presbycusis is characterized by atrophy of the organ of corti and auditory nerve in the basal end of the cochlea and is manifested by abrupt high-tone hearing loss" (Schuknecht, 1964, p. 369). Changes such as these may begin in middle age and progress slowly. The audiogram in cases of sensory presbycusis shows a steeply sloping, high-frequency hearing loss; word recognition is reduced relative to this loss.

---

[1]Shine (1995) offered another point of view regarding the relationship between aging and hearing loss. He argued that the correlation between hearing loss and aging presented in the literature should not imply a causal relation. According to Shine, it is more likely that hearing loss observed with age may be due to "cumulative insults" to the auditory mechanism incurred over a lifetime. Traumas to the auditory system such as infections, ototoxic drugs, and noise exposure cause destruction of CNS tissue that can be regenerated. This position stresses the benefits of hearing loss prevention.

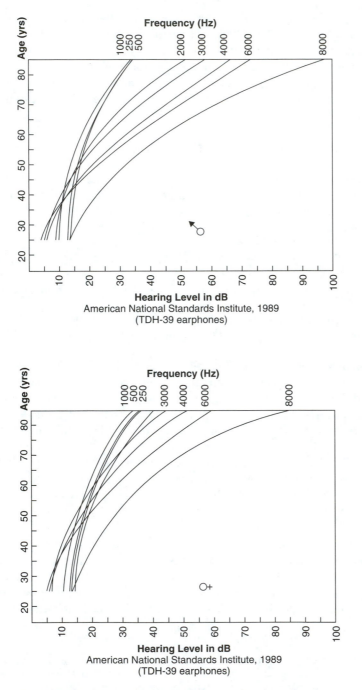

FIGURE 5.1 Hearing loss progression as a function of age in women (*left*) and men (*right*). (Adapted from Lebo, C. P., Redell, R. C.: The presbycusis component in occupational hearing loss. *Laryngoscope* 82: 1399–1409, 1972.)

From BCSS and Hume, 1995. Printed with permission.

2. "*Neural* presbycusis is due to a loss of neurons in the auditory pathways and cochlea" (Schuknecht, 1964, p. 370). This type of presbycusis usually occurs late in life. One outstanding feature of neural presbycusis is the unexpected level of impairment in speech recognition given the hearing loss for pure tones (Weinstein, 1994).

3. *Strial or metabolic* presbycusis is associated with the atrophy of the stria vascularis (Schuknecht, 1964). This type of presbycusis is described as a slowly progressing atrophy that may begin in the 20s, and by the 50s to 60s the effects of this degenerative process become apparent (Whitbourne, 1985). Audiometric findings associated with strial (or metabolic) presbycusis is equal hearing loss across frequencies. Contrasting with the neural type, strial presbycusis generally presents with intact speech-understanding ability despite the hearing loss.

4. *Mechanical* or cochlear-conductive presbycusis involves "stiffening of the basilar membrane or some other mechanical disorder" (Schuknecht, 1964, p. 382). Like the audiogram of an individual with a sensory loss, the audiogram in these cases shows hearing loss at high frequencies. Differing, however, from the audiogram of a sensory presbycusis, the audiogram in mechanical presbycusis reveals a gradually descending curve moving from low to high frequencies (Whitbourne, 1985).

Often, more than one of these presbycusis subtypes exist. Although there is seldom only one type, one type can predominate (M. H. Miller, personal communication, March 11, 1996).

Although presbycusis is the type of hearing loss most commonly associated with the aging process, hearing problems may also result from other degenerative processes. These include changes in the structures of the outer and middle ears (Weinstein, 1994).

Outer Ear.   Some structural changes in the outer ear include cracking or bleeding of the skin lining the external auditory meatus. These conditions often cause the hearing-aid wearer discomfort and interfere with the wearing of an aid, which promotes the hearing loss (Weinstein, 1994). Another outer ear problem is associated with the ceruminal glands located in the external auditory canal. With aging, atrophy of these glands and resulting decreased activity may cause accumulation of cerumen in the ear, contributing to reduced auditory acuity.

Middle Ear.   Structures of the middle ear also undergo age-related changes. These include stiffening of the tympanic membrane, progressive degeneration of the incudomalleal and incudostapedial joints of the ossicles, and atrophy of the tensor tympani and stapedius muscle. It is believed that although the impedance characteristics of the middle ear may be affected by these changes, hearing sensitivity is not compromised (Weinstein, 1994, p. 570).

Noise Induced Hearing Loss.   The audiometric pattern associated with hearing loss induced by noise exposure is often difficult to differentiate from that caused by aging. This is because the audiogram of an individual exposed to excessive noise may reveal a loss in the frequencies ranging from 3000 to 6000 Hz or present as a steeply sloping high-frequency hearing loss. Both produce hearing losses of the sensorineural type, are bilateral, and are usually symmetrical. The amount of hearing loss in the elderly caused by excessive noise is yet undeterminable from the audiogram (Weinstein, 1994).

Ototoxicity.   Excessive drug intake may also contribute to hearing loss as one of the many possible drug reactions. Some of the drugs implicated are antimicrobials, such as amino-glycosides that include gentamycin, streptomycin, and tobramycin; diuretics (furosemides); analgesics (aspirin); antiarrhythmics (quinidine); and antihypertensives (reserpine) (Weinstein, 1994). A high-frequency sensory neural hearing loss is characteristic of ototoxicity. It is often difficult, however, to specify audiometically the contribution of the ototoxicity as compared with other factors inducing geriatric hearing loss (Weinstein, 1994).

Tinnitus.   Tinnitus is described as "a sensation of sound in the head which may be localized in one or both ears or perceived in the cranial region; perceived as a throbbing, hissing, whistling, booming, clicking, buzzing, roaring or high pitched tone or noise" (Nicolosi, Harryman, & Kresheck, 1996, p. 280). Although tinnitus is not a hearing loss it may be associated with a hearing loss anywhere along the auditory pathway (Miller, Crane & Fox, 1995). The speech-language pathologist should be aware of the sometimes devastating effects of this condition in their adult clients. Some individuals suffer symptoms so severe that they are driven to commit suicide (Miller et al., 1995). According to Miller et al., patients with severe tinnitus should be referred to the appropriate mental health professional as soon as severe emotional problems are suspected. They also caution against surgical treatments that are not proven procedures.

Effects of Hearing Loss.   The effects of hearing loss with aging have been studied widely. In general, the effects of aging and hearing loss varies with the complexity of the task (Weinstein, 1994). Several studies demonstrated that the aging factor without any notable hearing loss may affect speech perception. Helfer & Wilber (1990) studied the age and the amount of pure-tone hearing loss contributing to changes in the ability to understand noisy, reverberant speech. They found that pure-tone threshold and age were correlated negatively with performance in reverberation plus noise. Age and pure-tone hearing loss were not correlated with each other. In fact, many older adults with very little reduction in peripheral hearing had difficulty understanding distorted consonants. Similarly, Helfer (1992) found that even a small amount of hearing loss in the over-60 population limited the perception of distorted consonants. Perceptual cues for the identification of durational differences in pure tones and silent intervals (Fitzgibbons & Gordon-Salant, 1994) and in vowel quality has also been shown to be age related even in normal-hearing adults (Fox, Wall, & Gokcen, 1992). Some difficulties in speech-sound discrimination of the elderly have been hypothesized to be related to a reduced ability to localize sounds (Cranford, Boose, & Moore 1990) or process interaural difference cues (Grose, Roth, & Peters, 1994). It has also been suggested that there are changes in certain aspects of auditory processing, such as duration discrimination, frequency discrimination, and upward spread of masking with aging. These changes have been believed to affect the integrity of speech recognition (Hargus, 1995). Aging has also been associated with a reduced ability to process rapid fluctuations in the waveform (Gordon-Salant & Fitzgibbons, 1995). Gordon-Salant & Fitzgibbons found that aging was a major factor in the recognition of speech that had been distorted by time compression. This finding was viewed as another symptom of the slowing process associated with aging.

Implications for Intervention Planning.   Hearing characteristics of adulthood are summarized in Box 5.4. The greater the auditory processing deficit, the poorer the

BOX **5.4**

Hearing Characteristics of Adulthood

Phases of Adulthood	Implications for Intervention Planning
Optimal functioning early adulthood	Maintains optimal speech language performance.
Changes with aging	
Hearing levels of men are slightly poorer than women, especially in the high frequencies.	
Sensorineural hearing impairment affecting discrimination of speech sounds is most common and associated with:	Affects level and duration of long-term goals.
■ different types of presbycusis; ■ drug-induced ototoxicity; ■ excessive noise.	Affects maintaining factors that should be considered in procedure planning.
Atrophy of ceruminal glands cause increased cerumen, resulting in discomfort to the aging individual.	Affects maintaining factors that should be considered in procedure planning.
Stiffening of tympanic membrane, degeneration of ossicular joints, and atrophy of the tensor tympani and stapedius muscle affect impedance characteristics.	No significant affect on hearing.
Tinnitus may cause client extreme psychological disturbance without necessarily a hearing loss, although tinnitus is almost always associated with a hearing loss.	A maintaining factor that should be considered in procedure planning.
Reduced ability to localize sounds or process interaural difference cues, resulting in reduced perceptual/ discrimination ability (i.e., perception of distorted consonants, discrimination of duration and frequency, and rapid fluctuations in the waveform).	Will affect session-goal planning in two possible ways. 1. Clinician may target discrimination and localization of stimuli (e.g., phonemes, words). 2. Clinician must consider the possibility of difficulties in perception and discrimination of stimuli due to the aging process in controlling performance demands.

patient's prognosis will be as a candidate for amplification; consequently, there will be a greater need for intensive audiologic rehabilitation. All candidates for speech and language intervention should have a complete audiological evaluation, have their amplification needs assessed, and be fitted with appropriate high-quality binaural hearing aids. The speech-language pathologist must be certain before each treatment session that the patient's hearing aids are in good working order. Attention should also be directed to the use of assistive listening devices. The patient should be carefully supervised on an ongoing basis by a highly skilled audiologist with expertise in working with geriatric patients (M. H. Miller, personal communication, March 11, 1996).

Knowledge about an adult's auditory processing will affect session-goal planning in two ways. First, the clinician may target the modification of maintaining factors such as problems with discrimination and localization of stimuli (e.g., phonemes, words) as session goals. Improvement in these areas is likely to facilitate short-term and long-term goals directed at improvement in communication performance. Second, the clinician must consider the possibility of difficulties in perception and discrimination of stimuli due to the aging process in controlling performance demands. The formulation of session goals should be guided by a consideration of potential processing complexity of given stimuli and the unique processing difficulties of individual clients. Such considerations will be useful in sequencing session goals.

Summary

In Chapter 5 normative data were reviewed that describe adult functioning in three areas of behavior that may maintain communication problems: psychosocial, cognitive, and sensorimotor. The review of each area included a consideration of how that area affects communication performance in adults. Each review concluded with implications for intervention planning. Implications were made primarily for procedure planning, since goals of intervention in speech-language pathology always focus on communication and language.

REFERENCES

Achenbach, T. M. (1969). Cue learning, associative, responding, and school performance in children. *Developmental Psychology, 1,* 717–725.

Alpiner, J. G., & Garstecki, D. C. (1996). Audiologic rehabilitation of adults: Assessment and management. In R. L. Schow & M. A. Nerbonne (Eds.), *Audiologic rehabilitation* (3rd ed.). Needham Heights, MA: Allyn & Bacon.

Annett, M. (1959). The classification of instances of four common class concepts by children and adults. *British Journal of Educational Psychology, 29,* 223.

Arambula, G. (1992). Acquired neurological disabilities in Hispanic adults. In H. W. Langdon & L. L. Cheng (Eds.), *Hispanic children and adults with communication disorders: Assessment and intervention.* Gaithersburg, MD: Aspen.

Atkinson, R. C., & Shiffrin, R. M. (1971). The control of short-term memory. *Scientific American, 225,* 82–90.

Au, R., Obler, L. K., Joung, P., & Albert, M. L. (1990). Naming in normal aging: Age-related differences or age-related changes? *Journal of Clinical and Experimental Neuropsychology, 12,* 30.

Au, R., Obler, L. K., & Albert, M. L. (1991). Language and aging in dementia. In M. Sarno (Ed.), *Acquired Aphasia* (2nd ed.). NY: Academic Press.

Baken, R. J. (1987). *Clinical measurement of speech and voice.* Austin, TX: Pro-Ed.

Bates, E., Thal, D., & MacWhinney, B. (1991). A functionalist approach to language and its implications for assessment and intervention. In T. M. Gallagher (Ed.), *Pragmatics of language: Clinical practice issues* (pp. 133–161). San Diego, CA: Singular.

Bayles, K. A., & Kaszniak, A. W. (1987). *Communication and cognition in normal aging and dementia.* Austin, TX: Pro-Ed.

Bess, F., & Humes, L. (1995). *Audiology: The fundamentals.* Philadelphia, PA: Williams & Wilkins.

Bielby, D., & Papalia, D. (1975). Moral development and perceptual role-taking egocentrism: Their development and relationship across the life span. *International Journal of Aging and Human Development, 6,* 293.

Borod, J., Goodglass, H., & Kaplan, E. (1980). Normative data on the Boston Diagnostic Aphasia Examination, Parietal Lobe Battery, and the Boston Naming Test. *Journal of Clinical Neuropsychology, 2,* 209–215.

Bowles, N. L., & Poon, L. W. (1981). Aging and retrieval of words in semantic memory. *Journal of Gerontology, 40,* 71–77.

Braine, M. D. S. (1990). The "natural logic" approach to reasoning. In W. F. Overton (Ed.), *Reasoning, necessity, and logic: Developmental perspectives* (pp. 133–157). Hillsdale, NJ: Erlbaum.

Bransford, J., Barclay, J., & Franks, J. (1972). Sentence memory: A constructive versus interpretive approach. *Cognitive Psychology, 3,* 193–209.

Busch, C. R., Brookshire, R. H., & Nicholas, L. E. (1988). Referential communication by aphasic and nonaphasic adults. *Journal of Speech and Hearing Disorders, 53,* 475–482.

Case, R. (1985). *Intellectual development from birth to adulthood.* Orlando, FL: Academic.

Chapey, R. (Ed.). (1994). *Language intervention strategies in adult aphasia.* (3rd ed.). Baltimore, MD: Williams & Wilkins.

Cheng, L-R. L. (1993). Asian-American cultures. In D. E. Battle (Ed.), *Communication disorders in multicultural populations.* Stoneham, MA: Butterworth-Heinemann.

Clegg, J. (1971). Verbal transformations on repeated listening to some English consonants. *British Journal of Psychology, 62,* 303–309.

Cohen, G., & Faulkner, D. (1986). Memory for proper names: Age differences in retrieval. *British Journal of Developmental Psychology, 4,* 187–197.

Colton, R. H., & Casper, J. K. (1996). *Understanding voice problems.* Baltimore, MD: Williams & Wilkins.

Committee on Hearing, Bioacoustics, and Biomechanics (CHABA). Working Group on Speech Understanding and Aging. (1988). Speech understanding and aging. *Journal of the Acoustical Society of America, 83,* 859–895.

Craik, F. I. M., & Lokhart, R. S. (1972). Levels of processing: A framework for memory research. *Journal of Verbal Learning and Verbal Behavior, 11,* 671–684.

Craik, F. I. M., & Tulving, E. (1975). Depth of processing and retention of words in episodic memory. *Journal of Experimental Psychology, 104,* 268–294.

Cranford, J. L., Boose, M. M., & Moore, C. A. (1990). Effects of aging on the precedence effect in sound localization. *Journal of Speech and Hearing Research, 33,* 645–659.

Davis, G. A., & Ball, H. (1989). Effects of age on comprehension of complex sentences in adulthood. *Journal of Speech and Hearing Research, 32,* 143–150.

Denney, N. (1974a). Evidence for developmental changes in classification criteria in children and adults. *Human Development, 7,* 41.

Denney, N. (1974b). Classification abilities in the elderly. *Journal of Gerontology, 29,* 309.

Denney, N., & Cornelius, S. (1975). Class inclusion and multiple classification in middle and old age. *Developmental Psychology, 11,* 521.

Denney, N., & Denney, D. (1974). Modeling effects on the questioning strategies of the elderly. *Developmental Psychology, 10,* 458.

Dennis, W. (1953). Animistic thinking among college students. *Science Monthly, 76,* 247.

Dewald, P. A. (1993). In G. H. Pollack & S. I. Greenspan (Eds.), *The course of life.* Madison, CT: International Universities Press.

Dromey, C., Ramig, L. O., & Johnson, A. B. (1995). Phonatory and articulatory changes associated with increased vocal intensity associated with Parkinson disease. *Journal of Speech and Hearing Research, 38,* 751–754.

Duffy, J. R. (1986). Schuell's stimulation approach to rehabilitation. In R. Chapey (Ed.), *Language intervention strategies in adult aphasia 2nd ed.* (pp. 187–214). Baltimore, MD: Williams & Wilkins.

Emery, O. (1986). Linguistic decrement in normal aging. *Language and Communication, 6,* 467–64.

Erikson, E. H. (1950). *Childhood and society.* New York: Norton.

Feier, C. D., & Gerstman, L. J. (1980). Sentence comprehension abilities throughout the adult lifespan. *Journal of Gerontology, 35,* 722–728.

Fischer, K. W. (1980). A theory of cognitive development: The control and construction of hierarchies of skills. Psychological Review, 87, 477–531.

Fischer, K. W. (1989, June). *The failure of competence: How context contributes directly to skill.* Paper presented at the nineteenth Annual Symposium of the Jean Piaget Society, Philadelphia, PA.

Fischer, K. W., Bullock, D., Rotenberg, E. J., & Raya, P. (1993). The dynamics of competence: How context contributes directly to skill. In R. W. Wozniak & K. W. Fisher. *Development in context: Acting and thinking in specific environments.* Hillsdale, NJ: Erlbaum.

Fitzgibbons, P. J. & Gordon-Salant, S. (1994). Age effects and measures of auditory duration discrimination. *Journal of Speech and Hearing Research, 37,* 662–670.

Fox, R. A., Wall, L. G., & Gokcen, J. (1992). Age-related differences in processing dynamic information to identify vowel quality. *Journal of Speech nd Hearing Research, 35,* 892–902.

Fozard, J. L. (1980). The time for remembering. In L. W. Poon (Ed.), *Aging in the 1980's: Psychological issues.* (pp. 273–290). Washington, DC: American Psychological Association.

Friedan, B. (1993). *The fountain of age.* New York: Simon & Schuster.

Galambos, J. A., Abelson, R. P., & Black, J. B. (Eds.). (1986). *Knowledge structures.* Hillsdale, NJ: Erlbaum.

Goodglass, H., & Kaplan, E. (1983). *Boston Diagnostic Aphasia Examination* (2nd ed.). Philadelphia, PA: Lea and Febiger.

Gordon-Salant, S., & Fitzgibbons, P. J. (1995). Recognition of multiply degraded speech by young and elderly listeners. *Journal of Speech and Hearing Research, 38,* 1150–1156.

Granott, N. I. (1993). Patterns of interaction in the co-construction of knowledge: Separate minds, joint efforts, and weird creatures. In R. W. Wozniak & K. W. Fischer (Eds.). *Development in context: Acting and thinking in specific environments* (pp. 183–210). Hillsdale, NJ: Erlbaum.

Gray, S. T., Hirano, M., & Sato, K. (1993). Molecular and cellular structure of vocal fold tissue (1–35). In I. R. Titze (Ed.), *Vocal fold physiology.* San Diego, CA: Singular.

Grose, J. H., Roth, E. A., Peters, R. W. (1994). Masking level differences for tones and speech in elderly listeners with relatively normal audiograms. *Journal of Speech and Hearing Research. 37,* 422–428.

Hargus, S. E. (1995). Accuracy of speech intelligibility index predictions for noise-masked young listeners with normal hearing and for elderly listeners with hearing impairment. *Journal of Speech and Hearing Research, 38,* 234–243.

Hasher, L., & Zaks, R. T. (1988). Working memory, comprehension, and aging: A review and a new view. In G. Bauer (Ed.), *The psychology of learning and motivation: Advances in research and theory* (Vol. 22, pp. 193–225). San Diego, CA: Academic Press.

Helfer, K. S. (1992). Aging and the binaural advantage in reverberation and noise. *Journal of Speech and Hearing Research, 35,* 1394–1401.

Helfer, K. S., & Wilber, L. A. (1990). Hearing loss, aging, and speech perception in reverberation and noise. *Journal of Speech and Hearing Research, 33,* 149–155.

Higgens, M. B., & Saxman, J. H. (1991). A comparison of selected phonatory behaviors of healthy aged and young adults. *Journal of Speech and Hearing Research, 34,* 1000–1010.

Hoit, J. D., & Hixon, T. J. (1987). Age and speech-breathing. *Journal of Speech and Hearing Research, 30,* 351–366.

Hoit, J. D., Watson, P. J., Hixon, K. E., McMahon, P., & Johnson, C. L. (1994). Age in velopharyngeal function during speech production. *Journal of Speech and Hearing Research, 37,* 295–302.

Homes, L. C., Leeper, H. A., & Nicholson, I. R. (1994). Laryngeal airway resistance of older men and woman as a function of vocal sound pressure. *Journal of Speech and Hearing Research, 37,* 789–799.

Honjo, I., & Isshiki, N. (1980). Laryngoscopic and voice characteristics of aged persons. *Archives of Otolaryngology, 106,* 149–150.

Hooper, F. H., Fitzgerald, J., & Papalia, D. (1971). Piagetian theory and the aging process: Extensions and speculations. *Aging & Human Development, 2,* 3.

Hooper, F. H., & Sheehan, N. W. (1977). Logical concept attainment during the aging years. In W. F. Overton & J. M. Gallagher. *Knowledge and development volume 1: Advances in research and development.* New York: Plenum.

Horn, J. L., & Cattell, R. B. (1967). Age differences in fluid and crystallized intelligence. *Acta Psychologica, 26,* 107–129.

Hornblum, J., & Overton, W. F. (1976). Area and volume conservation among the elderly. *Developmental Psychology, 12,* 68.

Inhelder, B., & Piaget, J. (1958). *The growth of logical thinking.* New York: Basic Books.

Kamhi, A. G., & Lee, R. F. (1988). Cognition. In M. A. Nippold (Ed.), *Later language development.* Austin, TX: Pro-Ed.

Kaplan, E., Goodglass, H., & Weintraub, S. (1976). *The Boston Naming Test.* Boston: Aphasia Research Center.

Karmiloff-Smith, A. (1986). *Stage/structure versus phase/process in modelling linguistic and cognitive development.* Norwood, NJ: Ablex.

Kuhn, D. (1977). Conditional reasoning in children. *Developmental Psychology, 13,* 342–353.

Kynette, D., & Kemper, S. (1986). Aging and the loss of grammatical forms: A cross-sectional study of language performance. *Language and Communications, 6,* 65–72.

Lahey, M. (1988). *Language disorders and language development.* New York: Macmillan.

Levinson, D. J. (1978). *The seasons of a man's life.* New York: Ballantine Books.

Linville, S. E. (1992). Glottal gap configurations in two age groups of women. *Journal of Speech and Hearing Research, 34,* 1209–1215.

Loftus, G. R., & Loftus, E. F. (1976). *Human memory: The processing of information.* Hillsdale, NJ: Erlbaum.

Looft, W. R. (1972). Egocentrism and social interaction across the lifespan. *Psychological Bulletin, 78,* 73–92.

Looft, W., & Charles D. (1971). Egocentrism and social interaction in young and old adults. *Aging and Human Development, 2,* 21–28.

McGillicuddy-Delisi, A. V., Delisi R., & Youniss, J. (1978). Representation of the horizontal coordinate with and without liquid. *Merrill-Palmer Quarterly, 24,* 199–210.

Maccoby, E. (1971). Age changes in the selective perception of verbal materials. In D. Horton & J. Jenkins (Eds.), *The perception of language.* Columbus, OH: Merrill.

Martin, A. D. (1981). An examination of Wepman's thought centered therapy. In R. Chapey, (Ed.). (1994). *Language intervention strategies in adult aphasia* (1st ed.) (pp. 141–154). Baltimore, MD: Williams & Wilkins.

Meisami, E. (1994). Aging of the sensory systems. In P. S. Timiras (Ed.), *Physiological basis of aging and geriatrics.* Ann Arbor, MI: CRC Press.

Miller, J. G. (1986). *Toward a new psychology of woman* (2nd ed.). Boston, MA: Beacon Press.

Miller, M. H. (1963). Audiological rehabilitation of the geriatric patient. *Maico audiological library series* (vol. 2). Eden Prairie, MN: Maico Inc.

Miller, M. H., Crane, M. A., & Fox, J. (1995). Intractable tinnitus: Managing the psychological component. *American Auditory Society Bulletin, 20,* 19–21.

Moses, N. (1994). The development of procedural knowledge in adults engaged in a "tractor-trailer" task. *Cognitive Development, 9,* 103–130.

Moses, N., Klein, H. B., & Altman, E. (1990). An approach to assessing and facilitating causal language in learning disabled adults based on Piagetian Theory. *Journal of Learning Disabilities, 23,* 220–229.

Moshman, D. (1990). The development of metalogical understanding. In W. F. Overton (Ed.), *Reasoning, necessity, logic* (pp. 205–226). Hillsdale, NJ: Erlbaum.

Murray, F. B., & Armstrong, S. L. (1978). Adult non-conservation of numerical equivalence. *Merrill-Palmer Quarterly, 24,* 255–263.

Nelson, K. (1986). *Event knowledge: Structure and function in development.* Hillsdale, NJ: Erlbaum.

Newell, A. (1981). Reasoning, problem solving, and decision processes: The problem space as a fundamental category. In R. S. Nickerson (Ed.), *Attention and performance* (Vol. 8, pp. 693–718). Hillsdale, NJ: Erlbaum.

Nicholas, M., Obler, L. K., Albert, M. L., & Helms-Estabrooks, N. (1985). Empty speech in Alzheimer's disease, healthy aging, and aphasia. *Journal of Speech and Hearing Research, 28,* 405–410.

Nicholas, M., Obler, L. K., Albert, M. L., & Goodglass, H. (1985). Lexical retrieval in healthy aging. *Cortex, 21,* 595–606.

Nippold, M. A. (Ed.) (1988). *Later language development: Ages 9–19.* Austin, TX: Pro-Ed.

Neugarten, B. L. (1964). *Personality in middle and late life.* New York: Atherton Press.

Neugarten, B. L. (1986). The aging society. In A. Pifer & L. Bronte (Eds.), *Our aging society: Paradox and promise.* New York: Norton.

Newby, H. & Popelka, G. (1992). *Audiology.* Englewood Cliffs, NJ: Prentice-Hall.

Nicolosi, L., Harryman, E., & Krescheck, J., (1996). (4th Ed.), *Terminology of communication disorders.* Baltimore, MD: Williams & Wilkins.

Noble-Wilson, J. (1998, February 10). Memory. *The New York Times,* pp. C1, 12–13.

Obler, L. K. (1980). Narrative discourse style in the elderly. In L. K. Obler and M. L. Albert (Eds.), *Language and communication in the elderly: Clinical, therapeutic, and experimental issues.* Lexington, MA: D. C. Heath.

Obler, L. K., & Albert, M. L. (1980). In D. S. Bezeley & G. Albyn Davis (Eds.), *Aging Communication processes and disorders* (pp. 107–121). New York: Grune & Stratton.

Obler, L. K., Nicholas, M., Albert, M. L., & Woodward, S. (1985). On comprehension across the adult lifespan. *Cortex, 21,* 273–280.

Papalia, D. (1972). The status of several conservation abilities across the lifespan. *Human Development, 15,* 229.

Papalia, D., & Bielby, D. (1974). Cognitive functioning in middle and old age adult: A review of research based on Piaget's theory. *Human development, 17,* 424.

Papalia, D., Kennedy, E., & Sheehan, N. W. (1973). Conservation of space in noninstitutionalized old people. *Journal of Psychology, 84,* 75.

Papalia, D., Salverson, S., & True, M. (1973). An valuation of quantity conservation performance during old age. *Aging and Human Development, 4,* 103.

Payne-Johnson, J. (1992). Communications in aging: A case for understanding African Americans who are elderly. *ASHA, 34,* 41–44.

Peck, R. C. (1968). Psychological developments in the second half of life. In B. L. Neugarten (Ed.), *Middle age and aging.* Chicago: University of Chicago Press.

Piaget, J. (1971). *Biology and knowledge.* Chicago: University of Chicago Press.

Piaget, J. (1985). *The equilibrium of cognitive structures.* Chicago: University of Chicago Press.

Piaget, J., & Garcia, R. (1991). *Toward a logic of meanings.* Hillsdale, NJ: Erlbaum.

Ramig, L., & Ringel, R. (1983). Effects of physiological aging on selected acoustic characteristics of voice. *Journal of Speech and Hearing Research, 26,* 22–30.

Reiser, B. J. (1986). The encoding and retrieval of memories of real world experiences. In J. A. Galambos, R. P. Abelson, & J. B. Black (Eds.), *Knowledge structures* (pp. 71–100). Hillsdale, NJ: Erlbaum.

Reiser, R. W. and Carton, A. S. (Eds.), *The collected works of L. S. Vygotsky.* New York: Plenum.

Reid, D. K. (1988). *Teaching the learning disabled: A cognitive developmental approach.* Needham, MA: Allyn & Bacon.

Reid, D. K. & Hresko, W. P. (1981). A cognitive approach to learning disabilities. New York: McGraw-Hill.

Rice, M. L., & Kemper, S. (1984). *Child language and cognition.* Baltimore: University Park Press.

Rice, M. L. (1983). Contemporary accounts of the cognition/language relationship: Implications for speech-language clinicians. *Journal of Speech and Hearing Disorders, 48,* 347–359.

Riegel, K., & Riegel, R. (1972). Development, drop, & death. *Developmental Psychology, 6,* 306.

Roseberry-McKibbin, C. (1997). Understanding Filipino families: A foundation for effective service delivery. *American Journal of Speech-Language Pathology, 6,* 5–14.

Roth, F. & Spekman, N. (1984). Assessing the pragmatic abilities of children: Part I: Organizational framework and assessment parameters. *Journal of Speech and Hearing Disorders, 49,* 2–11.

Rubin, K. (1974). The relationship between spatial and communicative egocentrism in children, young, and old adults. *Journal of Genetic Psychology, 125,* 295.

Rubin, K. (1976). Extinction of conservation: A lifespan investigation. *Developmental Psychology, 12,* 51.

Russell, A., Penny, L., & Pemberton, C. (1995). Speaking fundamental frequency changes over time in women. *Journal of Speech and Hearing Research, 38,* 101–109.

Sanders, S., Laurendeau, M., & Bergeron, J. (1966). Aging and the concept of space: The conservation of surfaces. *Journal of Gerontology, 21,* 281–285.

Sandson, J., Obler, L. K., & Albert, M. L. (1987). Language changes in healthy aging and dementia. In S. Rosenberg (Ed.), *Advances in applied psycholinguistics.* (Vol. 1). New York: Cambridge University Press.

Santrock, J. W. (1995). *Life span development.* Madison, WI: Brown & Benchmark.

Sapienza, C. N., & Dutka, J. (1996). Glottal airflow characteristics of women's voice production along an aging continuum. *Journal of Speech and Hearing Research, 39,* 322–328.

Schank, R. C., & Abelson, R. P. (1977). *Scripts, plans, goals, and understanding.* Hillsdale, NJ: Erlbaum.

Scholes, R. (1978). Syntactic and lexical components of sentence comprehension. In A. Camarazza & E. Surif (Eds.), *Language acquisition and language breakdown.* Baltimore: Johns Hopkins University Press.

Schuell, H. (1953). Auditory impairment in aphasia: Significance and retraining techniques. *Journal of Speech and Hearing Disorders, 18,* 14–21.

Schuknecht, H. F. (1964). Further observations on the pathology of presbycusis. *Archives of Otolaryngology, 80,* 369–382.

Schultz, N., & Hoyer, W. (1976). Feedback effects of spatial egocentrism in old age. *Journal of Gerontology, 31,* 72.

Shapiro, P. (1997). Tutorial: An introduction to syntax. *Journal of Speech-Language-Hearing Research, 40,* 254–271.

Sheehy, G. (1995). *New passages.* New York: Random House.

Shine, J. D. (1995). Guest editorial: Teaching old dogs. *Journal of Rehabilitation Research and Development. 32,* 7–8.

Sternberg, R. (Ed.). (1984). *Mechanisms of cognitive development.* New York: Freeman.

Sternberg, R. J. (1979). Developmental patterns in the encoding of and combination of logical connectives. *Journal of Experimental Child Psychology, 28,* 469–498.

Sternberg, R. J., & Downing, C. J. (1982). Reasoning, problem solving, and intelligence. In R. J. Sternberg (Ed.), *Handbook of human intelligence* (pp. 225–307). Cambridge, UK: Cambridge University Press.

Sternberg, R. J., & Nigro, G. (1982). Developmental patterns in the solution of verbal analogies. *Child Development, 51,* 27–38.

Tannen, D. (1990). *You just don't understand.* New York: Ballantine.

Taplin, J. E., Staudenmeyer, H., & Taddonio, J. L. (1974). Developmental changes in conditional reasoning. *Journal of Experimental Child Psychology, 17,* 360–373.

Thompson, C. T., Shapiro, L. P., Ballard, K. L., Jacobs, B. J., Schneider, S. S., & Tait, M. E. (1997). Training and generalization of wh and NP-movement structures in agrammatic aphasia. *Journal of Speech, Language, and Hearing Research, 40,* 228–244.

Tomasello, M., & Farrar, M. (1984). Cognitive bases of lexical development: Object performance and relational words. *Journal of Child Language, 11,* 477–493.

Trabasso, T., & van den Broek, P. (1985). Causal thinking and the representation of narrative events. *Journal of Memory and Language, 24,* 612–630.

Travis, C. (1992). *The mismeasure of women.* New York: Simon & Schuster.

Vaillant, G. E. (1977). *Adaptation to life.* Boston, MA: Little, Brown.

Vief, G., & Gonda, J. (1976). Cognitive strategy training and intellectual performance in the elderly. *Journal of Gerontology, 31,* 327.

Wanska, S. K., & Bedrosian, J. L. (1985). Conversational structure and topic performance in mother-child interaction. *Journal of Speech and Hearing Research, 28,* 579–584.

Weinstein, B. E. (1994). Presbycusis. In J. Katz (Ed.), *Handbook of clinical audiology* (pp. 568–584). Baltimore, MD: Williams & Wilkins.

West, C., & Zimmerman, D. H. (1983). Small insults: A study of interruption in cross-sex conversations between unacquainted persons. In B. Thorne, C. Kramarae, & N. Henley (Eds.), *Language, gender and society* (pp. 103–117). Rowley, MA: Newbury House.

Whitbourne, S. K. (1985). *The aging body.* New York: Springer-Verlag.

APPENDIX 5A

TABLE A.1 Fundamental Frequencies

Age Range	Mean F_O	Standard Deviation[a]	Range	Reference[b]
		Males Reading		
7	294	2.2		1
8	297	2.0		1
10	270	2.4		1
11	227	1.5	192–268	2
14	242	3.4		1
19	117	2.1	85–155	3
Adult	132	3.3		4
20–29	120			5
30–39	112			5
40–49	107			5
50–59	118			5
60–69	112			5
70–79	132			5
80–89	146			5
		Females Reading		
7	281	2.0		6
8	288	2.8		6
11	238	1.51	89–271	2
19	217	1.71	65–255	3
20–29	224	3.8	192–275	7
30–40	196	2.5	171–222	8
40–50	189	2.8	168–208	8
60–69	200	4.3	143–235	7
70+	202	4.7	170–249	7
80–94	200	2.7	183–225	9

[a]Standard deviation (SD) is expressed in semitones.

[b]Reference key:
1. Fairbanks, Wiley, and Lassman, 1949.
2. Horii, 1983.
3. Fitch and Holbrook, 1970.
4. Snidecor, 1943.

5. Hollien and Shipp, 1972; Shipp and Hollien, 1969.
6. Fairbanks, Herbert, and Hammond, 1949.
7. Stoicheff, 1981.
8. Saxman and Burk, 1967.
9. McGlone and Hollien, 1963.

TABLE A.2 Frequency Perturbation Data

Age Range	Measure	Jitter Factor /ee/	Jitter Factor /oo/	Directional Perturbation Factor /ee/	Directional Perturbation Factor /oo/	Pitch Perturbation Quotient /ee/	Pitch Perturbation Quotient /oo/
				Males			
20–29	Mean	0.78	0.72	70.73	6,948	0.65	0.57
	SD	0.4	0.36	11.25	14.87	0.3	0.26
40–49	Mean	0.99	0.87	74.37	72.49	0.77	0.7
	SD	0.61	0.51	10.86	14.84	0.38	0.32
60–69	Mean	0.91	0.87	67.77	69.43	0.77	0.74
	SD	0.63	0.56	15.46	14.55	0.5	0.43
				Females			
20–29	Mean	0.55	0.56	46.3	47.83	0.56	0.57
	SD	0.41	0.41	19.67	19.68	0.39	0.37
40–49	Mean	0.63	0.61	53.06	51.67	0.65	0.61
	SD	0.4	0.42	16.57	19.76	0.41	0.4
60–69	Mean	0.66	0.7	49.91	48.88	0.65	0.69
	SD	0.52	0.59	19.1	18.64	0.49	0.56

TABLE A.3 Maximum Phonational Range

Age Range	Low Frequency	High Frequency	Range	Reference[a]
		Males		
17–26	80	764	39.06	1
18–36	80	675	36.92	2
35–75	80	260	20.4	3
40–65	83	443	28.99	5
68–89	85	394	26.55	4
		Females		
18–38	140	1,122	36.03	2
66–93	134	571	25.09	4
35–70	136	803	30.75	5

[a]Reference key:
1. Hollien and Jackson, 1973.
2. Hollien, Dew, and Phillips, 1971.
3. Canter, 1965.
4. Ptacek, Sander, Maloney, and Jackson, 1966.
5. Colton and Hollien, 1972.

TABLE A.4   Maximum Intensity Levels

Age	Mean	SD	Range	Reference[a]
		Males		
18–39	106	5.1	92–116	1
45–65	110	7.1	99–129	2
68–89	101	5.9	88–110	1
		Females		
18–38	106	3	99–112	1
40–70	101	18.2	93–115	2
66–93	99	4.5	90–104	1

[a]Reference key:
1. Ptacek, Sander, Maloney, and Jackson, 1966.
2. Colton, Reed, Sagerman, and Chung, 1982.

TABLE A.5   Amplitude Perturbation Data

Vowel	Mean	SD
	Males	
/ah/	0.47	0.34
/ee/	0.37	0.28
/oo/	0.33	0.31
Mean	0.33	0.31
	Females	
/ah/	0.33	0.22
/ee/	0.23	0.08
/oo/	0.19	0.04
Mean	0.25	0.11

TABLE A.6 Maximum Phonation Duration

Group	Ages	Mean (sec)	SD
	Males		
Young children	3–4	8.95	2.16
Children	5–12	17.74	4.14
Adults	13–65	25.89	7.41
Aged	65+	14.68	6.25
	Females		
Young children	3–4	7.5	1.8
Children	5–12	14.97	3.87
Adults	13–65	21.34	5.66
Aged	65+	13.55	5.7

6 Funds of Knowledge for Intervention Planning with Adults: Theories of Adult Language Learning and Rehabilitation

CHAPTER OUTCOMES

The reader will:

1. become familiar with six alternative theories of adult learning and rehabilitation;
2. identify principles derived from each theory;
3. understand how principles of learning and rehabilitation apply to procedure planning.

Ask any clinician—novice or seasoned professional—how people acquire new skills or relearn old ones, and, explicitly or implicitly, that clinician will express some theoretic belief. The clinician might articulate this theory by saying, for example, that individuals learn through imitation. A particular belief may also become apparent from the clinician's insistence on the client's immediate imitations of his grammatical models. It is important to recognize that what a clinician believes about how clients learn novel language skills or recover lost abilities will influence procedural planning. Beliefs will affect what kinds of materials are used in treatment, how a therapy room is designed, and how the clinician interacts with the client. For example, if one believes that practical experience facilitates rehabilitation of lexical retrieval in adults with aphasia, concrete objects of daily living would likely be the type of material used in session, and natural conversation would be the type of clinician-client interaction. A natural context, such as the client's kitchen, might be the treatment location of choice. Alternatively, if one believes that repetitive practice, rewards, and punishments facilitate rehabilitation, pictures might be used as stimuli in treatment. Clinical interactions might involve commands and questions directed at the client in a therapy room devoid of material other than the items introduced by the clinician. The clinician might also focus on selecting rewards and setting reinforcement schedules.

If beliefs about how individuals learn invariably influence intervention planning, why devote a chapter to the systematic review of particular theories? The reason is that it is important for clinicians to be aware of their beliefs and to recognize that there are alternative theoretic orientations to learning and rehabilitation. This awareness permits clinicians to approach intervention planning systematically. That is, their planning will not be based on intuition but rather guided by principles derived from theories of learning and rehabilitation. A principle is a generalizable rule about a causal or procedural mechanism of learning or rehabilitation. It is the ability to conceptualize such principles that guides speech-language clinicians in the selection of appropriate materials and the design of clinical interactions.

Before turning to theories of learning and rehabilitation, consider a question that is typically asked by experienced as well as novice clinicians: Which theory is correct? The answer to that question, we believe, is that each of the theories accounts for some, but not all, aspects of language learning. So, the next question would be, "When do I apply a particular theory?" To be able to apply a theory appropriately it is necessary to know the assumptions about the behavior the theory endeavors to explain. For example, behavioral theory assumes that language comprises observable behaviors, such as production of sounds, vocal pitch, fluent utterances, and such (e.g., Skinner, 1957). The domain of this theory, therefore, is performance that may be observed. Principles derived from this theory focus on how such observable behaviors are acquired. By way of contrast, constructivist theory assumes that language comprises an intrinsic organization. This organization is not directly observable; it must be inferred. It is represented by linguists as semantic, syntactic, and phonologic behavioral categories (e.g., Bloom, 1970; van Riemsdijk & Williams, 1986). The domain of constructivist theories is internal organization underlying behavior. Principles derived from this theory focus on how this organization is established or transformed. The clinician's skill at explicating principles from alternate theories allows the clinician to use a single theoretic approach to plan intervention or "mix and match" when appropriate.

Theories of learning and rehabilitation apply to intervention planning for both children and adults. Language learning in adults, however, differs presumably from language learning in children. Children are at an age where natural developmental processes (i.e., processes affecting the fundamental organization of linguistic behavior) apply to language acquisition, even if these processes seem to have gone awry. With adults, we may presume that language development is complete and the optimal age for learning language has passed (Lenneberg & Lenneberg, 1975; Pinker, 1994). Language development has been observed to continue in adults to at least age 35 only in cases of mental retardation, autism, and other forms of severe and profound developmental disability.

Although we assume that adults have reached a stage where the fundamental organization of linguistic behavior is complete, learning novel language structures or recovering lost abilities is still possible. As speech-language pathologists we require knowledge about learning and rehabilitation as a basis of procedural planning. We are especially interested in theories that allow for the learning of novel communication skills across the life span, the rehabilitation of language skills rendered inaccessible by neurological insult, or the possible developmental changes in linguistic organization in adults.

A number of theories of learning and rehabilitation guide intervention planning in the chapters that examine specific communication problems. The following is a review of six theoretical orientations relevant to learning and rehabilitation in adults: operant, constructivist cognitive, social cognitive, functional communication, narrative comprehension, and motor. These are highlighted because of their broad applicability to intervention planning with adults across disorder categories. In the discussion that follows we present (a) an overview of these theories of learning and rehabilitation, (b) a summary of assumptions and principles derived from the theory, (c) a description of the domain of applicability, and (d) applications to intervention planning.

Behaviorism/Operant Theory

Overview

The goal of behaviorism is the "prediction and control of [observable] behavior" (Watson, 1919/1994, p. 248). Behaviorism embodies a theoretic stance aimed at explaining the acquisition of observable behaviors that can be measured directly. Sets of observable behaviors that serve adaptive functions are termed *operants*. They are called operants because they are the means by which individuals operate in their environment (Skinner, 1957). For example, reaching, grasping, turning, and pushing represent components of a door-opening operant.

Operant theory presumes that operants, which include verbal behaviors, are shaped, strengthened, or weakened, and ultimately evoked by their consequences; behavioral consequences are environmental events that occur after the behavior has been expressed (Goldfarb, 1981; Hayes & Hayes, 1992; Hedge & Davis, 1995; Skinner, 1957). Thus, a door opening serves to reinforce the door-opening operant. Consequences that increase the probability that a behavior will be expressed again are termed *reinforcers*. Positive reinforcers involve the provision of something tangible whereas negative reinforcers involve the removal of something noxious or uncomfortable following the expression of an operant. Consequences that decrease the subsequent rate of a behavior's expression are termed *extinguishers* or *punishments*.

Verbal behaviors, which include speech and other forms of communication, are considered a special set of operants. They are special because reinforcement is mediated by other people (Skinner, 1957). Thus, for the word "cookie" to be reinforced, a person must provide the cookie. Alternatively, reaching, grasping, and pulling may serve as a nonverbal operant, leading to a similar outcome, if those behaviors lead directly to the apprehension of a cookie from a bag taken out of the kitchen pantry.

Assumptions and Principles of Learning and Rehabilitation

Assumption.   Language is composed of observable behaviors that serve adaptive functions.

Principles.   The learning of observable behaviors is facilitated by:

1. events following a behavior (consequences, contingencies), which can reinforce (strengthen) or extinguish (weaken) a behavior;
2. the ability to discriminate and attend to stimuli associated with the target behavior.

Domain of Applicability

As noted above, behaviorism is associated primarily with the observable form of behavior and its adaptive functions. Ideas (i.e., language content) or metalinguistics (ideas about language) have no place in behaviorist theory, which can "dispense with consciousness in the psychological sense" (Watson, 1919/1994, p. 253). Behaviorists take no position on optimal ages for learning language. As such, behavioral principles may be applied to learning across the life span (e.g., see Goldfarb, 1981, with reference to aphasia; Shames & Florance, 1980, with reference to stuttering). Also, operant theory does not address linguistic organization. Behavioral principles apply to the establishment of new behaviors or the strengthening of behaviors already in the individual's repertoire. As such, behavioral principles apply to both habilitation and rehabilitation.

Application to Intervention Planning

Goal Planning.   Although learning principles have their most direct effect upon procedural planning, they may influence goal planning as well. One implication of operant theory is that the **function** of a behavior as opposed to its **intrinsic organization** is the most critical aspect to consider when selecting intervention targets (e.g., Hedge & Davis, 1995). Furthermore, breaking complex skills into smaller functional components (i.e., conducting a "common sense" task analysis) is the way to determine steps to the achievement of longer term objectives (e.g., Goldfarb, 1981; Hedge & Davis, 1995). The following is an example of goal selection and task analysis related to the acquisition of speech sounds by an Asian individual learning English as a second language. This individual presents with r/l, t/θ, and d/ð substitutions in all positions, and a variety of sounds deleted in the final position. Assume that the long-term goal for this client is the Standard American English production of all consonants. Consistent with the behaviorist approach, the short-term goal would likely be the production of a particular sound. The prioritization of the target might be based on either the client's ability to produce a sound in some contexts or the client's stimulabilty for a sound. It is likely that the Asian adult will be able to produce most consonants that are typically omitted from syllable-final position. Therefore, a sound-by-sound approach to the production of sounds in final position would be adopted. The derivation of a session goal would be the product of a task analysis such as the following: (a) identification of a phoneme in the final position within a sequence of consonant-vowel-consonant (CVC) words presented, (b) production of nonsense syllables with a target sound in final position following a model, (c) production of the sound in final position of a bisyllabic word after a model, (d) production of the sound in the final position of a CVC while identifying a picture.

This type of task analysis most closely resembles our analysis of performance demands that we conduct in deriving session goals. Within session goals we also target observable, measurable, and functional behaviors in specified contexts. Note, however, that this theoretic orientation is not consistent with our approach to deriving long- and short-term goals. We believe that behavioral organization as well as function must be considered in deriving goals within the first two planning phases. Thus, with reference to the example presented above, a long-term goal would target the phonologic reorganization necessary in producing final consonants (e.g., the construction of the underlying prosodic representation of the second consonant in a sequence (C2) of a CVC, or elimination of final consonant deletion).

Behavioral theory also influences the way goals of comprehension are conceptualized and written. Behavioral theory focuses on action. As such, it is easily applied to goals targeting the production of speech and language forms. Comprehension can only be inferred from the action exhibited by the individual in response to a stimuli. Comprehension objectives must be written, therefore, in terms of actions in response to stimuli; for example, "The adult will point to a pencil following the clinician's command, 'point to the pencil.' "

Procedure Planning.   In our procedure planning format, the clinician is directed to identify principles that will be used to guide the creation of therapeutic contexts, including the selection of materials and the format of clinician-client interactions.

If the clinician favors an operant approach, an important task of procedure planning will be the identification of an effective reward system. Consequences may be tangible and external to the client (e.g., the provision or removal or food, tokens, praise, etc.) or intrinsic to the client (the achievement of a personally set goal). A related task involves scheduling the provision of consequences (e.g., at regular, periodic intervals; random intervals; etc.); the nature of that schedule can affect the rate of expression of an operant (Hedge & Davis, 1995). The types of reinforcements and the reinforcement schedule are identified in the delineated procedural context (at the short-term planning phase).

Another focus of procedure planning guided by operant principles is the selection of an antecedent event. This event will be paired with the reinforcing consequence so that it will eventually serve as the stimulus for the target behavior (Goldfarb, 1981; Shriberg & Kwiatkowski, 1982). Clinician-client interactions and environmental design will be affected by the stimulus chosen to elicit the target behavior (i.e., the antecedent event). Antecedent events are typically pictures, clinician queries, models, and directives. These are usually presented to the client in a clinician-directed context (Goldfarb, 1981). For a more complete discussion of behavioral techniques, such as chaining and successive approximation, see Goldfarb (1981) and Hedge and Davis (1995).

Another way that behavioral principles influence intervention planning is vis-a-vis programmed instruction. These are instructional programs that are used by the client. These programs may be presented in the form of a workbook or computer program. An example is "Multicue," a word-finding program for aphasics (Visch-Brink et al., 1993). The selection and use of such instructional programs is a matter for session planning and should be based on sound principles of overall management planning.

We do not believe that long-term goals for a client should be established on the basis of prepackaged instructional programs. The selection of procedures should be consistent with goals that have been set with reference to baseline data, maintaining factors that need to be addressed in therapy, performance demands made on the client, and the clinician's belief about language and communication and how individuals learn or relearn targeted behaviors.

Constructivist Cognitive Theory

Overview

In contradistinction to behavioral theories, constructivist-cognitive theories are concerned with how organizational parameters of behavior are acquired or transformed. As explained in Chapters 1–4, content categories, rules of syntax, phonologic processes, and such reflect organizational parameters of language. Several constructivist-cognitive theorists (i.e., those with a neo-Piagetian orientation) maintain that in specific problem-solving contexts, organizational parameters of cognition can undergo developmental changes across the life span (e.g., Fischer, 1980; Moses, 1994; also, see the discussion of cognition as a maintaining factor in Chapter 5). Insofar as cognition may affect linguistic knowledge and behavior, processes that affect adults' cognitive functioning are of interest in intervention planning.

Constructivist learning theorists accept the nativist position that the mind of the learner comes equipped with a delimited set of possible organizational parameters (e.g., Piaget, 1971; Piatelli-Palmarini, 1980; Pinker, 1994). Some constructivists believe that transformations in organizational parameters of cognition may occur as individuals proceed through a problem-solving process. Constructive problem solving generally comprises goal-directed behavior, error, reflection on behavior, and correction for error (Gallagher & Reid, 1981; Inhelder, Sinclair, & Bovet, 1974; Moses, 1994, Moses, Klein, & Altman, 1990). Also central to constructivist theories as applied to adults are the concepts that (a) the individual's ideas about the object and social world are foundational to language acquisition and (b) constructive manipulations of concrete objects support cognitive development (Moses, 1994; Shapiro & Moses, 1989) and language acquisition (e.g., Bloom & Lahey, 1978; Lahey, 1988; Moses et al., 1990).

Assumptions and Principles of Learning and Rehabilitation

Assumption. Communicative competence in specific problem-solving contexts is based upon organization intrinsic to cognition and language.

Principles. Transformations in this organization are facilitated by:

1. tasks that are both accessible to individuals based on their current developmental level and sufficiently complex to pose developmental challenges;
2. the execution of sensorimotor procedures to achieve tasks or solve problems;
3. the act of reflecting, specifically on task demands (intermediate goals that need to be achieved to resolve the overall task), problems, problem-solving procedures, and causal mechanisms underlying problems or successes;
4. interpersonal interactions in which conversation reflects the learner's thoughts, provokes disequilibrium and conflict, and models solutions following disequilibrium.

Domain of Applicability

We take the position that with adults, constructivist principles may be applied to provoke organizational changes in language relevant to specific problem-solving contexts. Because of their focus on organization intrinsic to cognition and language, neo-Piagetian constructivist principles may be most directly applicable to cases of adult language disorders, such as those that are a consequence of learning disabilities, aphasia, and closed head injury.

Neo-Piagetian theories presume uneven performance across contexts; in other words, higher levels of cognitive organization may be present in certain problem-solving situations but not in others. Consequently, constructivist principles may be applied in novel problem-solving contexts to provoke a level of cognitive performance seen in familiar contexts. Such an application may be seen as rehabilitative as well as habilitative.

Application to Intervention Planning

Goal Setting.   Constructivist theories acknowledge the influence of organizational parameters of behavior on performance. Constructivist theories also allow for the development of organizational parameters of behavior throughout life. As a consequence, constructivist theories support consideration of linguistic organization in goal setting. Goals are formulated to target changes in organizational patterns (e.g., phonological classes, complex sentence structures, fluency patterns, vocal registers, etc.).

In terms of writing goals of expression or reception, constructivist theories, like behavioral theories, most naturally focus on action (the difference being that constructivist theories focus on organization intrinsic to behavior, whereas behaviorism focuses exclusively on the observable behavior). As with behavioral theory, constructivist theories usually are applied to performance goals (e.g., the client will code action or the client will produce a particular phonologic feature). However, goals that target comprehension can be written within a constructivist framework; such goals would reference the linguistic category of the utterance to be comprehended (e.g., "The client will identify *actions* in a story presented by the clinician").

Procedure Planning.   The principles of learning and rehabilitation cited above may guide procedure planning. Based on those principles, procedure planning focuses on four foundational activities presumed to facilitate understanding and expression: (a) the creation of tasks that are appropriate to the individual's developmental level but sufficiently complex and challenging to provoke developmental changes; (b) the creation of tasks that involve concrete experiences and the execution of sensorimotor procedures to achieve the task or solve the problem; (c) the provoking the act of reflecting, specifically on task demands, problems, problem-solving procedures, and causal mechanisms underlying problems or successes; and (d) the design of interpersonal interactions in which conversation reflects the learner's thoughts, provokes disequilibrium and conflict, or models solutions following disequilibrium. The following is a brief overview of these activities.

Tasks.   As discussed in Chapter 5, problem-solving tasks differ in complexity. As a consequence, different tasks may demand different levels of reasoning and, in turn, would require different levels of linguistic complexity to express that reasoning. Consider a practical daily task of making decisions about which brand of coffee would be most economical. Two cans of coffee are of identical size, identical price, but different weight; a third bag of coffee costs less than either can but weighs as much as one of these cans. Which is the bargain? Awareness of this dilemma may involve *concrete-operational* (making comparisons among features of concrete, manipulable objects and inferring that something remains constant despite changes in the observable features). Another task we often encounter in our daily lives is monthly budgeting of bills and expenditures within a given amount of income. In this case one must envision possibilities for partial payments as well as full payments without running out of funds. Successfully navigating this challenge may engage *formal operations* ("if-then" reasoning about imagined or possible events; see Chapter 4 for further discussion).

Advanced levels of reasoning about procedures involve cognizance of intermediate steps in the achievement of a task (task demands) and intermediate interactions among objects. Advanced levels of causal reasoning involve reference to nonobservable causal variables, alternate possibilities and perspectives, and reciprocal interactions among causal variables in which some state is conserved. To provoke such reasoning requires tasks of appropriate complexity and design. Guidelines for creating Piagetian tasks may be found in several articles and books on the application of Piagetian principles to developmental intervention with children and adults (e.g., Grannott, 1993; Moses, 1994; Moses et al., 1989; Inhelder & Piaget, 1958). Variables in addition to complexity should be considered when formulating Piagetian tasks. Tasks should be appropriate to the adult client's maturational level, social-vocational interests, needs, and experiences (see Moses et al., 1989).

Sensorimotor Action. Traditional Piagetian theory seems to imply that adults are capable of reasoning about conceptual as well as concrete events. Nevertheless, it has been shown that adults' reasoning about both abstract and concrete events is often inaccurate and that sensorimotor action executed on manipulables remains the basis for organizational changes in adult thinking and language used to express the results of that thinking. Consequently, neo-Piagetian constructivist theory indicates that adults be presented concrete practical problems to manipulate and reason about at early phases of intervention. Concrete problems may be gamelike, as in the use of board balancing to facilitate causal or procedural language (see Chapters 4 and 5). Some problems such as computer programming or intervention planning may be more related to the individual's vocation. Reasoning about imagined events presents greater performance demands and, thus, is a more advanced developmental achievement.

Reflection. Thoughtful reflection, or as Gallagher and Reid (1981) put it, "action between the ears," is necessary to facilitate cognitive and linguistic transformations. A principal of developmental intervention with adults, therefore, is to stimulate reflection on goal-directed behavior in specific problem-solving contexts (Grannott, 1993; Moses et al., 1990; Shapiro & Moses, 1989). Although success sometimes leads to reflection on how success was achieved, problems (failure, errors, unexpected events, feelings of conflict) are especially provocative of thoughtful reflection. In goal-directed tasks, problems often arise from unforseen task demands (intermediate achievements necessary to accomplish the overall task) and the use of wrong procedures. Thus, constructivist theory does not advocate avoiding or punishing error. Instead, constructivist theory suggest that errors can be functional if they lead to reflection on procedures and causal mechanisms, and if they are followed by behavioral change. Errors in everyday life motivate an individual to seek causes of these errors and modify behavior. You may recall the times you put film in a camera incorrectly, batteries upside down, or inserted the wrong disk in a computer. In each of these cases astute observers eventually see the source of error and discover something they may have overlooked before.

Interpersonal Interactions.   Developmental achievements take place in social as well as material contexts (Fischer & Bidell, 1993; Grannott, 1993). This signifies that learners pay attention to what their peers and teachers do, and that the teacher plays an active role in provoking development. Moses et al., (1990) identified a set of intervention procedures designed to provoke cognitive and linguistic developments in adults with learning disabilities in specific, problem-solving contexts. These are summarized in Box 6.1.

Box 6.1 illustrates that social interactions that facilitate developmental changes in adults target linguistic structures in appropriate problem-solving contexts. Such interactions involve conversation that (a) mirrors the learner's thoughts; (b) provokes disequilibrium and conflict; (c) encourages the creation of alternate procedures, anticipation of outcomes, and reflection on causal mechanisms; and (d) models solutions following disequilibrium. We also indicate in Box 6.1 that collaborative problem-solving interactions with peers can be developmentally advantageous (see also, Grannott, 1993; Wansart, 1990). The kinds of interactions described in Box 6.1 that support development tend to occur naturally when groups of adults focus on accomplishing a common task or solving a common problem. The implications of collaboration for intervention planning are elaborated below in the discussion of social-cognitive theories.

If constructivist learning principles are selected as guidelines for procedure planning, they are cited in the procedural approach statement at the long-term planning phase. General descriptions of materials and client-clinician interactions are developed at the short-term planning phase. Specific activities are planned at the session phase.

Social-Cognitive Learning Theories

Whereas constructivist learning theories traditionally have focused on the individual's role in development, social-cognitive theories focus on social influences on cognition. Certain aspects of social interactions, such as modeling and the provision of verbal directions, have always dominated common sense versions of how people learn. There are, in fact, social components in all formal theories of language learning, including nativist conceptualizations. Social-cognitive learning theories, however, go beyond common sense notions by identifying cognitive processes that are active in problem solving and trace the effect of human interaction on those processes (e.g., Wertch, Minick, & Arns, 1984). Social-cognitive theories identify scaffolding as the primary instructional interaction. The concept of scaffolding was articulated by Bruner in his studies of infant-caregiver interactions and game playing (e.g., Bruner, 1983; Ratner & Bruner, 1978). Applied to adults, scaffolding refers to a mentoring type of relation between an expert and a novice. In scaffolding, experts initially take the lead in problem solving by directing the novice's attention to important information, modeling procedures, and offering verbal explanations (e.g., Grannott, 1993). The expert gradually turns the lead over to the student as the student gains expertise, allowing the student to become increasingly self-directive.

BOX **6.1**

Constructivist Intervention Procedures

1. Engage client in concrete problem-solving tasks creating situations in which targeted semantic relations are obligatory or expected.
2. Interact with client to stimulate reasoning about problem-solving procedures and causes for outcomes
   - as the client is engaged in a problem-solving task describe the client's procedures using target semantic relations;
   - rephrase client's explanations using target semantic relations;
   - encourage the client to rephrase his or her own initial attempts.

3. Allow client to make errors and provoke reflection on errors.
4. Suggest alternative problem-solving procedures (a "how to" plan):
   - ask client to anticipate what will happen given the new procedure;
   - encourage the client to test and evaluate alternative procedures.

There are two schools of social-cognitive theories: (a) those that focus on executive processes of cognition; guide goal setting and problem solving and include attention to specific stimuli, the assignment of meaning to stimuli, and conscious self-monitoring (the conscious use of internalized problem-solving procedures and other forms of mental imagery); executive processes; and (b) those that focus on subordinate processes such as perception and memory.

A progenitor of social-cognitive theories was Vygotsky (who died in 1934). A second line of social-cognitive theories may be traced to the work of Jackson and Head during World War I.

Social-Cognitive Theories That Focus on Executive Functions

From the perspective of social cognitive theory, executive cognitive processes are implicated in the intentional setting and achievement of goals and the resolution of related problems (e.g., Wertch, 1979). Most important among these executive processes is the conscious self-monitoring of problem-solving behavior. The process of self-monitoring is conceived as the conscious use of verbal rules, procedures, and other mental images to guide problem solving. These guiding rules, procedures, and images are seen as deriving from social interaction.

With reference to such executive cognitive processes, Vygotsky coined the term "zone of proximal development" (Reiser & Carton, 1987). This term signifies that there is a window of opportunity in which it is possible to facilitate development. The requirement is that tasks presented to individuals be within their grasp given their present developmental level, and that teachers offer useful strategies for learners to capitalize on information relevant to accomplishing the task (e.g., Wertch, 1979). Two prevalent types of strategies are problem-reframing and metalinguistic procedures.

One influential problem-reframing paradigm is problem space theory (Newell, 1981; Newell & Simon, 1972). A central principle of this paradigm is that the way one conceptualizes or frames a problem can significantly affect learning and problem solving. For example, failure to provide background references for pronouns can be viewed either as a failure to learn a pragmatic rule of language or a reflection of a preoperational level of cognition in perspective taking (e.g., the client, when speaking, does not think about the listener's perspective; see also Schiff-Myers' [1983] discussion of role reversal). Helping the client to shift attention to the listener's perspective may promote more accurate pronoun use.

Metalinguistic procedures proposed by active learning theorists involve the teaching of instructions and strategies that individuals can dictate to themselves to successfully navigate a problem-solving situation. Such strategies often are taught to adolescents with learning disabilities and closed head injury to facilitate language-based problem-solving skills (e.g., Reid, 1988; Ylvisaker & Szekeres, 1986). Wong (1993) for example, taught learning-disabled students a set of tasks to perform while reading a passage to facilitate comprehension. These involved (a) underlining the main idea, (b) thinking of a question about that idea, (c) answering the question, and (d) reviewing. Similarly, Ylvisaker and Szekeres (1986) encouraged clients with closed head injury to approach problems with an internalized problem-solving guide; this guide includes asking oneself (a) "What is the problem?", (b) "What kind of problem is this?", (c) What will you gain by solving this?", (d) What do you need to know to solve this problem?", (e) What could you do to solve this problem?", (f) "What is good or bad about each of these solutions?" (p. 486). Metalinguistic strategies are taught through a process of scaffolding, in which the teacher describes the strategy, models it, allows the student to practice and then to take over its use.

Social-Cognitive Theories That Focus on Subordinate Processes

As noted above, we include under the rubric of social-cognitive theories those that focus on the facilitation of information-processing skills for rehabilitation. These dominate conceptualizations of language loss and language intervention in the treatment of language disorders whose onset is not considered developmental (e.g., aphasia, closed head injury, and degenerative neurological diseases of the elderly). The idea is that language skills are not obliterated in such cases. Instead, language skills are viewed as retained but access to information relevant to these skills is lost. This may be due to a general reduction in efficiency of the central nervous system (Martin, 1981) or blockage of neurological pathways.

Interventions focus on the rehabilitation of subordinate processes involved in accessing already acquired information. Subordinate processes that support language, according to Ylvisaker and Szekeres (1986), include attention, perception, and memory; component systems include working memory (storage of information presently being used) and long-term memory (highly organized permanent information—episodic or semantic in nature). These processes work in concert with the executive processes discussed above. Efforts are made to improve such information-processing skills through practice or metalinguistic strategy training.

An example of using repetitive practice to improve information processing abilities is seen in procedures for improving verbal and auditory reception and retention by Duffy (1986). These procedures are based on Schuell's (1953) stimulation approaches to therapy with individuals with aphasia. Duffy recommended repeating spoken words, then phrases, then series of items, then stereotypical phrases, and finally sentences. As in other types of social-cognitive theories, strategy training involves teaching the client mental procedures that can be used intentionally and consciously to facilitate information access and use. To facilitate memory and word retrieval in indivduals with closed head injury, Ylvisaker and Szekeres (1986) suggested strategies such as rehearsal, circumlocution, organization, and mnemonics.

Collaboration

An important line of social-cognitive thinking incorporates collaboration as a facilitating condition for learning (e.g., Grannott, 1993; Wansart, 1990). Grannott (1993) investigated collaboration in a study of adult problem solving with a set of Lego robots. Groups of college students worked together to figure out how the robots worked. By studying spontaneous interactions (and avoidances of interactions) among individuals in the group, Grannott identified developmental patterns of adult collaboration along two dimensions: degree of collaboration and relative expertise of participants.

With respect to degree of collaboration, Grannott identified collaborative, moderately collaborative, less collaborative, and disruptive interactions. In *collaborative interactions,* partners shared the activity, situation, observations, and hypotheses about procedures and causes. Knowledge was coconstructed; that is, meanings of events were shared by participants and knowledge was generated as a function of an interaction. No individual dominated interactions. Even though degree of knowledge among individuals may have been asymmetric (experts interacting with novices), all participants were concerned with the construction of their own knowledge. Individuals provided support for one another by scaffolding. In scaffolding, the guiding partner subtly directed the other partner while accommodating to that partner's wishes and ability.

Moderately collaborative interactions were characterized by a limited degree of shared meaning. The points of view of participants were more disparate, and, as a consequence, single individuals dominated aspects of the problem-solving activity. When the degree of knowledge among participants was asymmetric, the focus of the expert partner was on the novice's construction of knowledge via guidance and apprenticeship, not on personal knowing. Conflicts arose during problem solving, as would be predicted by Piagetian-based constructivist theories.

In *less collaborative interactions,* much activity was independent. Others provided ideas, examples, and models for novices, either explicitly or in a process resembling parallel play in children. Imitation was a major learning strategy. Knowledge construction occurred independently. In *disruptive interactions* participants interfered with one another either in attempts to collaborate or in more independent contexts.

Interestingly, individuals manifested different types of collaboration styles with different partners. In addition, styles of collaboration evolved over the course of a problem-solving experience. Grannott (1993) concluded that "there is no 'right' type of interaction that promotes cognitive change in one way, but rather many types that affect cognitive change in various positive and negative ways" (p. 203). Furthermore, personality, culture, gender, race, and prior experience conspired to affect learning styles in group problem-solving contexts.

Assumptions and Principles of Learning and Rehabilitation

Assumptions.   Comprehension and production may be facilitated by:

1. the internalization of verbal problem-solving strategies and other mental images that may be used to consciously monitor problem solving;
2. the appropriate conceptualization (framing) of tasks and problems and the ability to shift frames when one does not work out;
3. the efficient use of subordinate processes including discrimination, memory, etc;
4. collaborative problem solving.

Principles.   Learning and rehabilitation of processes relevant to language comprehension and production are facilitated through:

1. noticing similarities and distinctions among actions and events mediated by adults;
2. parallel problem solving (analogous to parallel play in children) in which ideas, examples, and models are provided for novices;
3. imitation;
4. practice.

Domain of Applicability

The two major strands of social-cognitive learning theory are rehabilitative in nature since they endeavor to access skills presumed to have been in the client's premorbid repertoire. Metalinguistic strategy training with the aim of improving efficiency of executive cognitive functions and subordinate information processes is used extensively with individuals with closed head injury and aphasia (e.g., Ylvisaker & Szekeres, 1986) and learning disabilities (Reid, 1988). Metacognitive strategy training is also applied to fluency (e.g., Shapiro, Chapter 10 of this book). The technique of helping clients frame problems has application primarily to adult language disorders, such as learning disabilities, closed head injury, aphasia, and neurological disorders of the aged. Scaffolding as an instructional technique is used across treatments and disorder types.

In sum, social cognitive theories focus on accessing appropriate approaches to problem solving from within the client's repertoire. This represents the primary aim of both metalinguistic strategy training and the practice of information-processing skills. Thus, intervention based on social-cognitive theory is rehabilitative in nature. It is important to recognize, however, that the acquisition of metalinguistic strategies also involves novel learning. New strategies are being acquired, even though these strategies will be used to access already learned material. The acquisition of novel metalinguistic strategies is, therefore, habilitative. Scaffolding is the primary instructional technique in social-cognitive approaches to intervention. Scaffolding, therefore, may apply both to habilitation and rehabilitation, depending on degree of novelty of the skills or information being presented to the learner.

Application to Intervention Planning

Goals.   Goals that target executive problem-solving procedures or information-processing strategies are set at the session-planning phase. That is because these skills facilitate functional communication behavior, the focus of long-term and short-term goals.

Procedures.   Social-cognitive learning principles yield procedures that support goals of comprehension and production. These principles suggest that the linguistic context of intervention be designed so that the clinician may effectively scaffold (i.e., demonstrate, direct, and model problem-solving procedures and strategies). This may be accomplished within a variety of types of interactions in a variety of nonlinguistic contexts. One could establish an apprentice-like relationship with a client in concrete and practical social and vocational non-linguistic contexts (e.g., while housekeeping, working on a work-related task, etc.). Physical and verbal guidance would be provided by the clinician in such contexts in a natural manner, analogous to play with children. One could also teach problem-solving strategies in a linguistically based context and in a more directive manner. An example would be the provision of guidelines to facilitate story comprehension given in written and oral stories.

In preparing intervention plans, guiding principles would be cited in the long-term procedural approach. General descriptions of clinician-client interactions that promote scaffolding and other social-cognitive techniques are presented as part of the delimited procedural context. Descriptions of actual interactions and materials guided by social-cognitive principles are created for the session procedure.

Functional Communication Theory

Based on a "thought-centered" approach to intervention for aphasia developed by Wepman (1972), Martin (1981) proposed that the act of functional communication, itself, facilitates communication skills. Wepman's approach emerged as a reaction to aphasia treatments that focused on information-processing skills to the exclusion of communication for transmitting ideas to a listener. Wepman wrote, "By changing therapy from the specifics of naming—the struggle for accuracy in word finding—to the realm of ideas, one hopes to increase the possibility of effecting change in what may be the basic discrepancy, the apparent limitation in the use of ideas" (1972, p. 205).

Martin (1981), like Wepman, emphasized the connection between thought and language, and the importance of supporting the individual in his or her expression of an intended message, even if that expression involves the use of impaired language. In proposing a communication-oriented approach to therapy, Martin declared that "as speech pathologists we are primarily interested in communication" (p. 150). Martin explained further that "the communication interaction does not depend on the successful transfer of a particular intended message, but rather on the assumption of the appropriate role to effect such transfer" (p. 150). In other words, a communication interaction depends on all parties assuming the role of listener and facilitator of message transference. Martin observed, however, that speech-language clinicians typically act as speakers and their clients as listeners. Martin proposed that clinicians adopt the role of facilitator and receiver of the client's intended message. As such, he redefined normal language functioning, disorder, and therapy as follows:

Normal functioning can now be defined as the maintenance, with maximum efficiency, of appropriate receiver-sender roles in a conversational exchange.

The disorder can then be viewed as the disruption of the interaction in which one of the participants is an aphasic through the failure of either or both participants as a receiver-sender in the exchange. Therapy would then become the attempt to maximize and improve performance as receiver-senders by both participants in the same situation. (Martin, 1981, p. 151)

Assumptions and Principles of Learning and Rehabilitation

Assumption.   The focus of language intervention should be the client's transmission of messages and assumption of a message sender-receiver role in communication.

Principles.   Rehabilitation may be facilitated when:

1. the clinician assumes a message receiver role;
2. the clinician facilitates the client's effort to transmit messages.

Domain of Applicability

Martin's (1981) communication-oriented theory of rehabilitation, like Wepman's (1972, 1976) thought-centered approach from which it derives, was designed for individuals with aphasia. In our estimation, it is applicable to all cases of language disorders and may be extended to all types of disorders including fluency (see Shapiro, Chapter 10 of this text) and voice. The theory is primarily rehabilitative in nature.

Application to Intervention Planning

Goals.   Consistent with a principle of our intervention model, the communication-oriented theory of rehabilitation targets communication acts as the primary focus of intervention. The facilitation of specific information-processing skills are subordinated to the act of communication. Furthermore, functional communication theory encourages writing session goals for family members in which they learn to use strategies that enhance the client's ability to successfully engage in the message sender's role. For example, a family member would encourage the client to request what he or she wants for dinner, acknowledge his or her efforts, and make every effort to understand the client despite the client's unintelligibility.

Procedures.   Martin (1981) recommended that clinicians improve their own ability to comprehend their patients. He directed that suggestion even to clinicians who work with patients who produce jargon. Although difficult to understand, it is possible to learn to decode messages from such individuals, and, according to Martin, once comprehension is possible, "nothing succeeds like success" (p. 152).

Given the idea that successful communication acts beget improved communication skills, Martin (1981) advocated various techniques to heighten the assumption of communicator roles by both clinicians and clients. He stressed the use of appropriate nonverbal gestures and signals by clinicians (head nods, rhythmic motions, etc.) to indicate to clients that they are being listened to, and to pace clients. Martin also suggested that gestural use by clients be encouraged. With improved comprehension, more direct therapy techniques such as modeling correct form may be used most effectively.

Within the context of the present intervention-planning model, communication-oriented principles of rehabilitation influence the design of the linguistic context at the short-term and session phases. The description of delimited procedural context (short-term planning phase) should emphasize techniques that heighten the clinician's role as listener and activities that encourage the client to attempt to communicate functional messages. Similar procedures may be developed for family members. There should be follow-through in the selection of activities used in actual therapy sessions.

Motor Theory

A category of learning theories focuses on the acquisition of patterns of behavior (i.e., sensorimotor representations as seen in the areas of phonology, voice, and fluency), not conscious ideas or cognitive processes. Processes identified in these "motor learning" theories as central to the acquisition of behavior patterns include the exercise of motor patterns; self-correction in response to problematic feedback; and the differentiation, integration, and coordination of different and often conflicting behavioral patterns (Klein & Moses, 1999).

Motor representations incorporate the use of various types of peripheral feedback (e.g., auditory, tactile, proprioceptive/kinesthetic from joints, tendons, muscles, air- and bone-conducted pressure changes) and central feedback (from the brain) as part of the control mechanism for self-regulation of behavioral patterns. Two types of feedback loops have been implicated in the process of self-regulation: open and closed (Leather & James, 1991; see also Locke & Pearson, 1992). Open-loop control involves preplanning and is more frequently used than closed-loop feedback (peripheral, for moment-to-moment control). Open-loop feedback relies on matching a current production with a known motor plan, and therefore is not as active in the learning of new motor patterns as closed-loops. Open-loops may, however, be more implicated in rehabilitation, where the emphasis is on the reactivation of previously acquired skills.

Domain of Applicability

Motor learning theories apply to both the learning of new skills and the rehabilitation of previously known behaviors.

Assumption. The acquisition or rehabilitation of a sensorimotor behavioral pattern (motor representation) involves the development of a motor pattern under the control of associated open and closed feedback loops.

Principles. The acquisition or rehabilitation of motor representations is facilitated by:

1. producing the motor pattern (i.e., producing sounds, syllables, words, sentences, etc., imitatively or spontaneously);
2. practicing the motor pattern;
3. making self-adjustments when experiencing problems through selected (single, multiple) sensory-feedback channels.

Theories of Discourse Comprehension

The principles of learning and rehabilitation that have been reviewed thus far have applied both to the facilitation of various components of language comprehension and production (linguistic, self-directed problem solving, etc.). There are several theories beyond those that have already been discussed that endeavor to explain the acquisition of a specific aspect of language. One such set of theories comprises those that endeavor to explain language comprehension in the context of discourse; these address how discourse in general and narratives in particular are deconstructed and analyzed by adults for comprehension (e.g., see Bayles & Kaszniak, 1987; Fayol & Lemaire, 1993, for summaries). We discuss this set of theories because of all of the work with adults with language disorders that is conducted in comprehension. These theories comprise elements of both constructivist and social-cognitive paradigms; they are, however, presented separately because of their specific application to narrative comprehension.

Script-Based Theories

A popular line of thought that endeavors to explain comprehension of narratives may be termed script based. Script-based theories suggest that listeners rely on scripts and other stores of situational knowledge when making inferences and otherwise interpreting stories (e.g., Schank & Abelson, 1977). Scripts comprise overlearned knowledge structures about familiar events (e.g., going to a fast-food restaurant, going to school, etc.). Knowledge structures that constitute scripts may comprise action sequences and related actors, vehicles, instruments, and such (e.g., the script "going to work for a rural school teacher" may comprise (a) the children's arrival at school involving the bus, guards, teachers, and the school building; (b) the settling down in homeroom; (c) the teaching of the subject; (d) the routine in the lunchroom, etc., Brownell & Joanette, 1993). A teacher would rely on such knowledge structures to comprehend discourse about teaching.

Causal Network

A second set of theories focuses on causal networks that have been viewed by some as representing the intrinsic organization of narratives (e.g., Schank & Abelson, 1977; Trabasso & van den Broek, 1985). From this point of view, stories can be analyzed according to causal relations that have been constructed within. Two types of causal relations are: (a) plan structures, which are procedures executed to achieve a goal; and (b) state or event sequences (i.e., motivations, physical and mental acts, etc.), which map out real-time causal connections (see Brownell & Joanette, 1993). Individual events may be related to one or more other events. Understanding a narrative involves parsing the narrative's causal network into constituent plans and state or event sequences, and mapping out relations. When events after a particular event are more related along a causal chain, they tend to be recalled better (Trebasso & van den Broek, 1985).

Intentional Structure

Another component of discourse comprehension, according to Grosz and Sidner (1986), involves analysis of the intentional structure of discourse. The term *intentional structure* refers to the purposes of discourse and the way purposes are related (Brownell & Joanette, 1993). The pragmatics of discourse involve expressions, prosody and intonation, and segment organization that cue intention. Some common expressions include "next, by the way, in any case, first, and last," (Brownell & Joanette, 1993). Part of the task of comprehension involves decoding the dominant and subordinate intentions of the speaker for the listener.

Micro- and Macrostructure

Perhaps the most comprehensive theory of comprehension relates story processing to the analysis of both micro and macro text structures. Deconstruction and analysis seem to be with reference to linguistic cues that constitute the text's microstructure (morphology and syntax of individual sentences and coherence devices relating sentences) as well as a number of interrelated aspects of story structure (i.e., the macrostructure, Grzybeck, 1993). The macrostructure includes type and organization of story grammar (e.g., Kintch & van Dijk, 1978; Schank & Abelson, 1977), components of story schema (Schank & Abelson, 1977), real-world knowledge of events which stories are about (Schallert, 1982), causal understanding capacity, and how networks of constituent propositions relate to one another (Kintch & van Dijk, 1978; Trabasso & van den Broek, 1985).

Propositions are the predicates and arguments of sentences that constitute a story. Propositions are seen as organized hierarchically, with the topical proposition seen as the highest node to which all other propositions relate (Fayol & Lemaire, 1993). Individuals are seen as parsing stories into propositions as the story is heard or read and constructing networks of propositions by comparing new propositions with those already encountered and held in working (i.e., short-term) memory. Overlaps lead to the development of a single network (a basis for recall). Lack of overlap may lead to the construction of new networks, which may require searching long-term memory for an informational base for recognition and inferencing to establish a linking proposition. If construction is not possible, the information will likely be lost. In making an effort at comprehension, the analysis of single sentences is termed *microprocessing*. The analysis of connected discourse is termed *macroprocessing* (Brownell & Joanette, 1993; Kintsch & van Dijk, 1978; see also Chapter 3 for discussion of macrostructure and microstructure in context of discourse).

Assumptions and Principles of Learning and Rehabilitation

We are going to treat the theories reviewed above collectively in summarizing principles of learning and rehabilitation relevant to discourse comprehension. That is because we view all of these theories as based in common social- and constructivist-cognitive principles and as collectively offering a coherent approach to the facilitation of comprehension.

Assumption.   Comprehension of discourse depends on analysis of both the macro- and microstructure of the discourse.

Principles.   The comprehension of discourse is facilitated by:

1. scripts and other types of knowledge structures derived from real-life experiences that compare to experiences communicated in discourse;
2. attention to cues that signal the intentions of the speaker and the speaker's intention for the listener;
3. identification of the causal connections within narratives;
4. analysis of predicates and arguments of sentences that constitute narratives.

Domain of Applicability

Theories of discourse comprehension are most applicable to language intervention in cases of learning disability, head trauma, and aphasia.

Application to Intervention Planning

Goal Planning.   Theories of discourse comprehension support procedural planning for goals of discourse and narrative comprehension.

Procedure Planning.   Principles of discourse comprehension lead to specific suggestions for procedure planning. These include modifying performance demands by (a) selecting discourse topics (including narrative topics) with reference to the client's familiar, real-life experiences and (b) selecting narratives with reference to the relation among propositions within the narratives. Narratives with single themes and related propositions should present fewer performance demands than narratives with multiple themes and many unclearly related propositions. Principles of discourse comprehension also suggest (a) training the client to recognize communicative behaviors that signal the intentions of the speaker and the speaker's intention for the listener (e.g., sarcasm signaled by prosody); and (b) practice identifying causal connections within narratives.

Summary

In this chapter we have introduced six theories of learning and rehabilitation that have broad application to intervention planning for adults with communication problems. The use of these theories, as well as other paradigms that may be more specific to particular communication problems, is illustrated in the following chapters. Box 6.2 summarizes principles from the six theories reviewed above.

B O X **6.2**

Principles of Language Learning and Rehabilitation

Theories of Learning and Rehabilitation	Derived Principles	Implications for Goals and Procedures
Operant (O)	Stimulus-response associations and operant behaviors are facilitated by: 1. the ability to discriminate and attend to stimuli associated with the target behavior; 2. events following a behavior that can reinforce or extinguish the behavior	Applies to all domains of communication: ■ target individual components of more complex skills; ■ identify an effective reward system.
Constructivist cognitive (CC)	Transformations in linguistic organization are facilitated by: 1. tasks that are accessible to the individual based on current developmental level and sufficiently complex to pose developmental challenges; 2. the use of action-oriented procedures to solve problems; 3. the act of reflecting on task demands, procedures, and causal mechanisms; 4. conversations that promote disequilibrium and conflict resolution.	Generally applied to rule-governed linguistic systems such as syntax, semantic, phonology): ■ target functional communication and linguistic organization; ■ work on communication goals in the context of goals set by clients; ■ allow clients to experience problems as well as successes; ■ help client reflect on problem-solving procedures.
Social cognitive (SC)	Learning and rehabilitation of strategies and processes relevant to language comprehension and production are facilitated by: 1. noticing similarities and distinctions among actions and events mediated by experts; 2. parallel problem solving (analogous to parallel play in children) in which ideas, examples, and models are provided for novices; 3. imitation; 4. practice.	Applies to all domains of communication: ■ target problem-solving strategies that may be used to consciously monitor communication behavior; ■ facilitate the efficient use of subordinate processes, including discrimination, memory, etc.; ■ stimulate collaborative problem solving; ■ use scaffolding techniques (e.g., modeling, cuing).

BOX **6.2**   **Continued**

Theories of Learning and Rehabilitation	Derived Principles	Implications for Goals and Procedures
Functional communication (FC)	Rehabilitation of communication skills may be facilitated when: 1. the clinician assumes a message receiver role; 2. the clinician facilitates the client's efforts to transmit message.	Generally applied to adult language disorders (e.g., aphasia and closed head injury): ■ language use is primary focus of intervention; ■ encourage client to communicate; ■ attempt to interpret client's communication intent.
Motor (M)	Learning and rehabilitation of sensorimotor patterns are facilitated by: 1. producing the motor pattern; 2. practicing the motor pattern; 3. making self-adjustments when experiencing problems through selected feedback channels.	Generally applies to motor acts such as the production of speech sounds, voice, and fluency patterns: ■ target speech production; ■ encourage practice and self-correction.
Theories of narrative comprehension (NC)	Narrative comprehension may be facilitated by: 1. the use of scripts and other types of knowledge structures derived from real life experiences; 2. the identification of causal relations within narratives; 3. the analysis of predicates and arguments of sentences that constitute narratives.	Generally applied to adult language disorders (e.g., learning disability, close head injury): ■ use narrative tasks related to client's premorbid and current life experiences; ■ facilitate inference making about causal relations within narrative; ■ focus on relations among events (episodes) within narratives; ■ encourage clients to comment on their own reactions to stories and characters, emotions, motivations, and internal states.

REFERENCES

Bloom, L. (1970). *Language development: Form and function in emerging grammars.* Cambridge, MA: MIT Press.

Bloom, L., & Lahey, M. (1978). *Language development and language disorders.* New York: Wiley.

Bayles, K. A., & Kaszniak, A. W. (1987). *Communication and cognition in normal aging and dementia.* Austin, TX: Pro-Ed.

Brownell, H. H., & Joanette, Y. (Eds.). (1993). Narrative discourse in neurologically impaired and normal aging adults. San Diego, CA: Singular.

Bruner, J. (1983). *Child talk.* New York: Norton.

Duffy, J. R. (1986). Schuell's stimulation approach to rehabilitation. In R. Chapey (Ed.), *Language intervention strategies in adult aphasia 2nd ed.* (pp. 187–214). Baltimore, MD: Williams & Wilkins.

Fayol, M., & Lemaire, P. (1993). Levels of approach to discourse. In H. H. Brownell, & Y. Joanette (Eds.), *Narrative discourse in neurologically impaired and normal aging adults* (pp. 3–22). San Diego, CA: Singular.

Fischer, K. W. (1980). A theory of cognitive development: The control and construction of a hierarchy of skills. *Psychological Review, 87,* 477–531.

Gallagher, J., & Reid, D. K. (1981). *The learning theory of Piaget and Inhelder.* Austin, TX: Pro-Ed.

Galambos, J. A., Abelson, R. P., & Black, J. B. (Eds.) (1986). *Knowledge Structures.* Hillsdale, NJ: Erlbaum.

Goldfarb, R. (1981). Operant conditioning and programmed instruction in aphasia rehabilitation. In R. Chapey (Ed), *Language intervention in adult aphasia* (pp. 249–264). Baltimore, OH: Williams & Wilkins.

Granott, N. I. (1993). Patterns of interaction in the co-construction of knowledge: Separate minds, joint efforts, and weird creatures. In R. W. Wozniak and K. W. Fischer (Eds.) *Development in context: Acting and thinking in specific environments* (pp. 183–210). Hillsdale, NJ: Erlbaum.

Hayes, S. C., & Hayes, L. J. (1992). Verbal relations and the evolution of behavior analysis. *American Psychologist, 47,* 1383–1395.

Hedge, M. N., & Davis, D, (1995). *Clinical methods and practicum in speech-language pathology.* San Diego, CA: Singular.

Inhelder, B., & Piaget, J. (1958). *The growth of logical thinking.* New York: Basic Books.

Inhelder, B., Sinclair, H., and Bovet, M. (1974). *Learning and the development of cognition.* Cambridge, MA: Harvard University Press.

Kintsch, W., & van Dijk, T. A. (1978). Toward a model of text comprehension and text production. *Psychological Review, 85,* 363–394.

Klein, H., & Moses, N. (1999). *Intervention planning for children with communication disorders: A guide for clinical practicum and professional practice* (2nd Ed.). Needham, MA: Allyn & Bacon.

Lahey, M. (1988). Language disorders and language development. New York: Macmillan.

Leather, J., & James, A. (1991) The acquisition of second language speech. *Studies in Second Language Acquisition, 13,* 305–341.

Lenneberg, E., & Lenneberg, E. (1975). *Foundations of language development: A multidisciplinary approach* (Vols. 1 & 2). New York: Academic Press.

Locke, J. L., & Pearson, D. M (1992). Vocal learning and emergence of phonological capacity. In C. A. Ferguson, L. Menn, & C. S. Stoel-Gammon (Eds.), *Phonological development: Models, research, implication. Phonological development, models, research, implications* (pp. 91–129). Timonium, MD: York Press.

Martin, A. D. (1981). An examination of Wepman's thought centered therapy. In R. Chapey (Ed), *Language intervention in adult aphasia* (pp. 141–154). Baltimore, OH: Williams & Wilkins.

Moses, N. (1994). The development of procedural knowledge in adults engaged in a tractor-trailer task. *Cognitive Development, 9,* 103–130.

Moses, N., Klein, H. B., & Altman, E. (1990). An approach to assessing and facilitating causal language in learning disabled adults based on Piagetian Theory. *Journal of Learning Disabilities, 23,* 220–229.

Moses, N., & Shapiro, D. A. (1996). A developmental conceptualization of clinical problem solving. *Journal of Communication Disorders, 20,* 19–27.

Newell, A. (1981). Reasoning, problem solving, and decision processes: The problem space as a fundamental category. In R. S. Nickerson (Ed.), *Attention and performance* (Vol. 8, pp. 693–718). Hillsdale, NJ: Erlbaum.

Newell, A., & Simon, H. A. (1972). *Human problem solving.* Englewood Cliffs, NJ: Prentice-Hall.

Piaget, J. (1971). *Biology and knowledge.* Chicago: University of Chicago Press.

Piatelli-Palmarini, M. (Ed.). (1980). *Language and learning.* Cambridge, MA: Harvard University Press.

Pinker, S. (1994). *The language instinct: How the mind creates language.* New York: Morrow.

Ratner, N., & Bruner, J. (1978). Games, social exchange, and the acquisition of language. *Journal of Child Language, 5,* 391–402.

Reid, D. K. (1988). *Teaching the learning disabled: A cognitive developmental approach.* Needham, MA: Allyn & Bacon.

Reiser, R. W., & Carton, A. S. (Eds.). (1987). *The collected works to L. S. Vygotsky.* New York: Plenum.

Schallert, D. L. (1982). The significance of knowledge: A synthesis of research related to schema theory. In O. Wayne and S. White (Eds.), *Reading expository material* (pp. 13–48). New York: Academic Press.

Schiff-Myers, N. (1983). From pronoun reversals to correct pronoun usage: A case study of a normally developing child. *Journal of Speech and Hearing Disorders, 48,* 394–402.

Schuell, H. (1953). Auditory impairment in aphasia: Significance and retraining techniques. *Journal of Speech and Hearing Disorders, 18,* 14–21.

Shames, G. H., & Florance, C. L. (1980). *Stutter-free speech: A goal for therapy.* Columbus, OH: Merrill.

Shank, R. C., & Abelson, R. P. (1977). *Scripts, plans, and goals: An inquiry into human understanding.* Hillsdale, NJ: Erlbaum.

Shapiro, D. A., & Moses, N. (1989). Creative problem solving in public school supervision. *Language, Speech, and Hearing Services in Schools, 20,* 320–332.

Shriberg, L., & Kwiatkowski, J. (1982). Phonological disorders II: A conceptual framework for management. *Journal of Speech and Hearing Disorders, 47,* 256–270.

Skinner, B. F. (1957). *Verbal behavior.* New York: Appleton-Century-Crofts.

Trabasso, T., & van den Broek, P. (1985). Causal thinking and the representation of narrative events. *Journal of Memory and Language, 24,* 612–630.

van Riemsdijk, H., & Williams, E. (1986). *Introduction to the theory of grammar.* Cambridge, MA: MIT Press.

Visch-Brink, E. G., van Hars Kamp, F., van Amerongen, N. M., Wielart, S. M., & vandeSandt-Koendermen, M. E. (1993). A multidisciplinary approach to aphasia therapy. In A. L. Holland and M. M. Forbes, *Aphasia treatment: World perspectives.* San Diego, CA: Singular.

Wansart, L. (1990). Learning to solve a problem: A microanalysis of the solution strategies of children with learning disabilities. *Journal of Learning Disabilities, 23,* 1634–170.

Watson, J. B. (1919/1994). Psychology as the behaviorist views it. *Psychological Review, 101,* 248 253.

Wepman, J. Aphasia therapy: A new look. *Journal of Speech and Hearing Disorders, 37,* 203–214.

Wertsch, J. V. (1979). From social interaction to higher psychological processes: A clarification and application of Vygotskian Theory. *Human Development, 22,* 1–22.

Wertsch, J. V., Minick, N., & Arns, F. (1984). The creation of context in joint problem solving. In B. Rogoff & J. Lave (Eds.), *Everyday cognition: Its development in social context* (pp. 151–171). Cambridge, MA: Harvard University Press.

Wong, B. Y. A. (1993). Pursuing an elusive goal: Molding strategic teachers and learners. *Journal of Learning Disabilities, 26,* 354–357.

Ylvisaker, M., & Szekeres, S. (1986). Management of the patient with closed head injury. In R. Chapey (Ed.). (1994). *Language intervention strategies in adult aphasia* 2nd ed. pp. 474–490. Baltimore, MD: Williams & Wilkins.

7 Intervention Planning for Adults with Language-Learning Disabilities

CHAPTER OUTCOMES

The reader will:

1. identify characteristics of language functioning in adults with language-learning disabilities;

2. identify factors that may maintain communication problems in adults with language-learning disabilities;

3. become familiar with approaches to the remediation of communication problems in adults with language-learning disabilities;

4. follow the derivation of a management plan for an adult with a language-learning disability.

The first application of our model of intervention planning will be with an adult with language-learning disabilities. Language-learning disabilities in adults have not received the same amount of attention as learning disabilities in children. This is despite research indicating that "a learning disability is a life-long disability. . . that . . . persists throughout the entire stage of adulthood" (Gerber, 1994, p. 6). The lack of attention to learning disabilities in adults was recognized as a problem by the National Joint Council on Learning Disabilities (1987) in its "call to action" to study and facilitate the transition of adults with learning disabilities from the school to the workplace (Huffman et al., 1987). This call to action was consistent with several legislative initiatives, namely: (a) section 503 of PL 93-112 (1973), which denied federal financial assistance to any program that excludes participation by individuals with handicaps; and (b) section 504 of PL 94-142 (1975) and the Americans with Disabilities Act (PL 101-336, 1989), which further prohibited discrimination from access to employment or any public service facility for any individual (adult or child) with disabilities (Gajar, 1992). Adding to the perceived need to address learning disabilities beyond childhood is the fact that adults with learning disabilities represent the largest group of individuals with disabilities who plan to and actually attend college (Jarrow, 1987; Morris & Leuenberger, 1990; White, Alley, Deshler, Schumaker, Warner, & Clark, 1982).

Research findings indicate that language-learning disabilities in adults are characterized by the same symptoms as learning disabilities in children (e.g., Aram, Ekelman, & Nation, 1984; Gajar, 1992; Gerber, 1994; Klein, Moses, & Altman, 1989; Seidenberg, 1988). Box 7.1 summarizes those symptoms of learning disabilities that have been identified in children.

Box 7.1 illustrates that language-learning disabilities in children are associated with various linguistic and metalinguistic processing deficits, including deficits in the production and comprehension of content/form/use interactions in oral and written language. Problems also are manifested in all of the nonlinguistic behavioral systems (i.e., psychosocial, cognitive, and sensorimotor) that can maintain communication and language-learning problems.

It has been the trend in recent years to focus on metacognitive and metalinguistic deficits in the treatment of language-learning disabilities in children (e.g., Reid, 1988; Wallach & Butler, 1994). The emphasis has been on characterizing children with learning disabilities as passive learners. Passive learning refers to the failure to develop efficient strategies for planning and problem solving, and the inefficient monitoring of personal behavior and others' perspectives. Ancillary problems include deficits in the comprehension and use of narratives and figurative language. Next, we examine research that has traced these difficulties as they extend into adulthood. This research will provide direction for goal planning for adults with language learning-disabilities.

Characteristics of Speech, Language, and Communication Functioning in Adults with Language-Learning Disabilities

Standardized Assessments of Content/Form/Use Interactions

Historically, most studies that have described behavioral characteristics of adults with learning disabilities report performance deficits on standardized tests of language functioning: for example, the Illinois Test of Psycholinguistic Abilities (Wiig & Semel, 1974), the Test of Adolescent Language (Gajar, 1992; Morris & Leuenberger 1990), the Verbal Subtest of the WISC-R, and the Boston Aphasia Test (Morris & Leuenberger, 1990; Wiig & Semel, 1973; Wiig, LaPointe, & Semel, 1977). These tests generally emphasize information-processing skills (which we treat as belonging to the domain of cognition). When language content/form interactions are assessed, the focus is usually on performance on formal, academically oriented tasks such as vocabulary definitions and sentence construction.

A series of seminal studies of academic and information-processing skills were conducted in the mid-1970s by Wiig and Semel (1974, 1975) and colleagues (Wiig, LaPointe, & Semel, 1977). Two types of disorders were described within adolescents and young adults with learning disabilities (13–18 years of age): cognitive-linguistic processing and dysnomia (Wiig, LaPointe, & Semel, 1977). Cognitive-linguistic processing deficit was characterized primarily by reductions in morphology and syntax. Dysnomia

B O X **7.1**

Difficulties Associated with Learning Disabilities in Children in Language and in Areas Maintaining Speech-Language Disorders

Area Relevant to Intervention Planning	Characteristic Deficit(s) in:
Content/form/use interactions[a]	■ Formulating and comprehending complex syntactic constructions, especially narratives; ■ Processing aural-oral and visual linguistic stimuli; ■ Interpreting and producing pragmatic conventions of language (e.g., those that reflect the perspective of others, such as elipsis, pronoun referencing, deixis, topic organization, conversational repairs): ■ Identifying multiple meanings for individual words and, relatedly, interpreting metaphor and humor; ■ Word finding; ■ Phonological perception and production; ■ Reading.
Cognition[b]	■ Word finding and retrieval; ■ Attending (especially to oral presentations); ■ Planning and organizing time, workspaces, notes, etc.; ■ Academic performance related to reading, writing, artithmetic; ■ Passive versus active learning (not able to engage in self-directed problem solving; ■ Metalinguistic and metacognitive deficits (i.e., thinking about language and thinking about thinking and problem solving); ■ Processing rapid speech signals.
Psychosocial[c]	■ Social skills; ■ Self-concepts.
Sensorimotor[d]	■ Sensory integration; ■ Proprioception; ■ Processing rapid speech signals and other rapid sensorimotor acts.

Sources: [a]Kamhi & Catts, 1986; Milosky, 1994; Roth & Spekman, 1986, 1989; Wiig & Secord, 1987; Wiig & Semel, 1975.

[b]Elliot-Faust, & Miller, 1985; Pressley, Forest-Pressley, Reid, 1988; Tallal & Piercy, 1978; Wallach & Butler, 1994.

[c]Lewandowski & Arcangelo, 1994.

[d]Ayres, 1968; Prinz & Sanders, 1984.

was reflected in verbal paraphasias and in word-retrieval difficulties. In another study on productive language abilities in adolescents with learning disabilities, Wiig and Semel (1975) identified deficits in accuracy and speed of naming objects and opposites, defining words, and in grammatical and other sentence production demands. Additional studies along this line are reviewed in the section on information-processing deficits that can maintain learning disabilities.

More recently, Wiig and colleagues reoriented their approach to learning disabilities, focusing on metalinguistic abilities as reflected in the comprehension of nonliteral aspects of language. In normative studies for the Test of Language Competence (Wiig & Secord, 1985) and the Clinical Evaluation of Language Functions-Revised (Wiig & Semel, 1984), deficits were identified in comprehension by adolescents and adults of such nonliteral forms as metaphors, idioms, similes, and the like (see Chapter 2 for a discussion of these forms). Difficulties were also identified in the ability to use context to make inferences about information not explicitly presented verbally or in written text. In another area of figurative language, Spector (1990) identified deficits in comprehension and production of humor in children with learning disabilities. It is likely that such difficulties extend to adulthood.

Nonstandard Assessments of Content/Form/Use Interactions

To reiterate, the bulk of research on communication problems in adolescents and adults with learning disabilities has focused on performance on standardized tests. There is little information about content/form/use interactions in context of more natural discourse. Two areas of discourse that have been addressed in at least a preliminary fashion are narrative expression and causal language. Within these areas, passive learning seems to be a common pattern related to language difficulties. Passive learning signifies difficulties adults may have monitoring and modifying their own problem-solving behavior, and using language for problem solving.

Narrative Comprehension and Production in Adults with Language-Learning Disabilities.   Among the few publications on narrative production in adults with learning disabilities is a study of story production and comprehension by Latino adolescents by Goldstein, Harris, & Klein (1993). Results revealed deficits in the spontaneous production of story grammar (e.g., gaps in structural complexity) as well as in the ability of young adults to use knowledge of story grammars to comprehend narratives (see also Gurney, Gersten, Domino, & Carnine, 1990).

In two experiments, Worden, Malmgren, and Gabourie (1982) evaluated memory for stories in adults with learning disabilities. In the first study, story recall of 12 adults with learning disabilities was compared with recall by normally achieving adults and third graders. The number and quality of five story node types (beginnings, reactions, goals, attempts, outcomes, endings) included in retold stories were analyzed. Results indicated that the adults with learning disabilities and third graders performed similarly; both groups recalled significantly fewer node types than the normally achieving adults. The outcome nodes were recalled the best, and the reaction/goal node, the poorest.

In the second experiment, two approaches for improving recall in the learning disabled population were evaluated: rote drill (repetitive readings of the passage) and training in the use of node categories as an information-retrieval strategy. Information recall improved only in the repetitive reading condition.

In a related study, Worden and Nakamura (1982) proposed that difficulties with recall might be a consequence of difficulties that adults with learning disabilities have in evaluating the relative significance of information encountered in reading comprehension tasks. These authors proposed that recall ability is facilitated by two factors: (a) the ability to rate the importance of information before engaging in a comprehension task and (b) the ability to learn from the task the kinds of information that facilitate recall. Comparing 24 college students with learning disabilities and 24 normally achieving peers, the learning disabled subjects (a) manifested poorer recall overall and (b) failed to modify their importance ratings, even when information initially regarded as important proved not to be helpful. Results of the two studies by Worden and Nakamura suggest that inadequate problem-solving skills play a role in difficulties that adults with learning disabilities manifest in the production and comprehension of narratives.

Narrative Production and Comprehension in Children with Learning Disabilities. At this point there is little research on the production of narratives in adults with learning disabilities. Since the research that does exist suggests deficits in narrative production, it is worthwhile to review research on storytelling in children with learning disabilities. Along these lines, Roth and Spekman (1986) compared spontaneously generated make-believe stories told by normally achieving children and children with learning disabilities, 8–13 years of age. Stories were analyzed according to the number of propositions (i.e., clauses) included and the functions that propositions served in the story grammar. The story-grammar analysis was conducted according to Stein and Glenn's (1979) story schema: the setting (major and minor statements) and initiating event; the character's response, plan, and attempt; the direct consequence of the attempt; and the character's reaction to the consequence. In addition, Roth and Spekman (1986) evaluated the types of relations among episodes (then, cause, and, embedded). Finally, the use of beginning and ending story markers was noted.

Results revealed that compared with their normally achieving peers, children with learning disabilities produced significantly fewer (a) propositions (see also Westby, 1985); (b) complete episodes (i.e., episodes with an initiating event or response, direct consequences and attempts); (c) embeddings; (d) minor setting statements; (e) middle parts of stories (i.e., cognitive planning, actions, and attitudes of the protagonist); and (f) causal relations. Interestingly, the children with learning disabilities also produced significantly fewer "and" connections among episodes coding simultaneity of events. Roth and Spekman (1986) attributed results to impaired information-processing skills and subjects' inability to properly consider the listener's perspective (necessary to provide adequate information about actions and attitudes of characters).

Some of the characteristics of narrative production and comprehension identified in children with learning disabilities seem to appear in narratives told by adults (e.g, Goldstein, Harris, & Klein, 1993). Unfortunately, not all characteristics have been examined in adults. Based on clinical experience, Myers (1993) recommended that three components of narratives be assessed in adults with neurologic impairments: informative content (i.e., concepts that convey information about a scene), efficiency (i.e., the absence of trivial, tangential, and information unrelated to the central themes of the narrative), and macrostructural integrity (the reduction of the narrative content to its essential message; i.e., topic statement). We suggest that an additional area intrinsic to narrative production be assessed: the use of cohesion devices with reference to the listener's need for information (see Chapter 3).

In sum, the above research suggests that adults with language-learning disabilities manifest deficits in narrative comprehension and production. These deficits include (a) impaired recall of information, (b) restricted production of narrative structure and detail (e.g., fewer prepositions and embeddings), and (c) tendency to include trivial or unrelated information in narratives. Underlying these deficits may be difficulties in developing metalinguistic strategies for managing linguistic information and interpersonal communication.

Causal Language.   The use of language for planning and problem solving has been identified as a major weakness in children with learning disabilities. The ability to comprehend and talk about causal relations (i.e., why things happen) is an important competence that supports these language functions. Causality also represents a distinct content category within complex sentence types (Bloom, 1993). As discussed in Chapter 4, the use of causal language is common in adult social, academic, and vocational settings. All in all, facility with causal language represents an important linguistic and communicative competence in adults.

The research on narrative production and comprehension in children and adults with learning disabilities reviewed above suggests weaknesses in the linguistic expression of causal relations. Moses, Klein, and Altman (1990) examined content/form interactions within causal language of young adults with learning disabilities engaged in a concrete problem-solving task (board balancing, see Chapter 5). Three levels of complexity of causal content/form interactions were identified and shown to correspond to Piagetian preoperational and operational levels of cognitive functioning (see Chapter 5). These findings suggest that causal language is variable among adults with learning disabilities, and that cognition is a maintaining factor in the use of causal language.

Summary and Application to Intervention Planning

Knowledge of communication problems in adults with learning disabilities orients the clinician in goal planning. Adults with learning disabilities appear to manifest problems on both the linguistic and metalinguistic planes. The linguistic components that appear to be compromised involve the production and processing of complex oral and written content/form interactions. Especially challenging are narratives, procedural (how), and causal (why) constructions, and low frequency and nonliteral vocabulary. Metalinguistic problems are seen in pragmatic abilities related to the use of language for planning and problem solving. Relatedly, making adjustments in language form (e.g., cohesion devices, pronoun reference) by considering the listener's background knowledge and point of view may pose additional problems for adults These areas of difficulty are aspects of speech and language that can be targeted in speech-language intervention (see Chapters 3 and 4 for examples of these linguistic components).

Baseline data concerning communication problems contribute primarily to goal planning. Procedure planning is influenced by knowledge of the nonlinguistic factors that may accompany and maintain communication problems. Maintaining factors associated with communication problems in adults with learning disabilities are examined next.

Maintaining Factors

Given that communication problems associated with learning disabilities in children often extend into adulthood, it is not surprising that cognitive, psychosocial, and sensorimotor difficulties associated with learning disabilities also continue into adulthood. As noted above, knowledge of the persistence of factors that maintain communication problems has particular relevance for procedure planning. The following is an overview of research findings identified factors that can maintain communication problems in adults with learning disabilities.

Cognition

Standardized Assessments.   As in the area of language, the bulk of research on cognition in individuals with learning disabilities has reported results on standardized tests of academic achievement, intelligence, or information-processing skills. Childhood deficits in performance on these standardized tests seem to persist into adulthood. For example, in a review of the literature on adults with learning disabilities, Gajar (1992) identified problems in reading, behavior, self-concept, arithmetic, written expression, handwriting, social-emotional functioning , vocational skills, short-term memory, and factor structure on intelligence tests. In a related report by Morris and Leuenberger (1990), 74 college students with learning disabilities compared with their normally achieving peers obtained significantly higher performance than verbal scores on intelligence tests. The students with learning disabilities also manifested significantly poorer reading, writing, and speaking skills as measured by the Woodcock-Johnson Test of Academic Achievement and the Test of Adolescent Language.

Nonstandard Assessments of Cognition.   In nonstandard assessments of problem solving, young adults with learning disabilities appear to maintain the same ineffective approaches to planning and problem solving observed in children; these behaviors implicate persistent metacognitive and metalinguistic deficits (e.g., Bursuck & Jayanthi, 1993; Butler, 1995; Klein et al., 1988). Metacognitive deficits are reflected in difficulties with tasks such as devising and maintaining schedules, organizing written material, and devising problem-solving strategies. Relatedly, these adults may also have difficulties identifying ineffective problem solving procedures and devising efficient alternative strategies. Metalinguistic deficits interfere with the processing of nonliteral language forms and the formulation of inferences when information is not explicated in text. These difficulties are discussed at greater length below in the discussion of cognitive approaches to intervention.

As discussed above and in Chapters 4 and 5, adults with severe learning disabilities expressed causal explanations indicative of preoperational reasoning on a spatial task requiring operational reasoning for success (Moses et al., 1989). Over time in the course of problem solving, some subjects eventually manifested operational reasoning. It is notable that deficits in spatial cognition have also been identified in children with learning disabilities (e.g., Reid & Hresko, 1981) as well as normally achieving college students (Delisi & Staudt, 1980; Fischer, 1980; Moses, 1994).

Psychosocial

Saracoglu, Minden, & Wilcheski (1989) reported that post-secondary students with learning disabilities who experience academic problems in college also experience stresses in self-esteem and personal-emotional adjustment. Not all research, however, has supported the notion that social-emotional problems associated with learning disabilities in children universally persist into adulthood. Lewandowski and Arcangelo (1994) sent questionnaires (The Social Adjustment Scale-Self Report, Weissman & Bothwell, 1976) to 40 young adults with learning disabilities (high school graduates, mean age 21.7 years) and 21 nondisabled young adults. The scale surveyed social functioning in (a) role as worker, (b) social and leisure time, (c) relationships with extended family, (d) marital relationships, (e) role as parent, and (f) role in family. In addition, perceived self-concept was evaluated. Contrary to expectations, no significant differences were found in the survey of the self-perceptions of social adjustment and self-concept.

The results from Lewandowski and Arcangelo (1994) may be compared with findings of Klein et al. (1988), who investigated self-perceptions of communication performance of 31 young adults with severe learning disabilities. These adults were enrolled in a vocational education program designed to prepare them to be paraprofessionals in educational settings. These adults and their teachers rated performance in four areas of communication seen as important for vocational success: problem solving, comprehension, verbal expression, and social communication. Although there were similarities in ratings between the groups (both students and their teachers rated problem solving as most problematic), the students rated themselves higher than did others. It is possible that self-perceptions of learning disabilities are not accurate. It is also possible that educators familiar with learning disabilities tend to underestimate skills of their students.

Sensorimotor

The literature on adults suggests that speech-related problems associated with sensorimotor involvement also continue to be problematic for some adults. These include phonological (segmental and suprasegmental) and voice (Nation & Aram, 1977). Such problems implicate sensorimotor processes as maintaining factors. In children with language-learning disabilities, problems were identified with the integration of multiple sources of sensory information (Ayres, 1975), perceptual problems affecting sound discrimination and rapid processing of aural and visual stimuli (Tallal & Percy, 1978), processing of proprioceptive and tactile feedback (Clark, Mailloux, & Parham & Primeau 1989), and apraxia (Crary, 1993). The persistence of such sensorimotor deficits in adults is further suggested by a profile of neurophysiologic characteristics of adults with learning disabilities (summarized by Bigler, 1992). Sensorimotor deficits can interfere with the comprehension, production, and learning of language, and they need to be considered during intervention planning, especially in the derivation of procedures.

Summary and Application to Intervention Planning

Knowledge of the nonlinguistic factors that can maintain communication problems in adults with learning disabilities provides direction for the derivation of procedures that can address these factors. In the area of cognition, adults with learning disabilities manifest problems in planning and problem solving. Factors that may be involved are impaired information-processing skills (especially related to working memory) and academic skills (especially reading and math). The implication is that problem-solving tasks relevant to the client's social and vocational experiences should be designed with information processing and academic demands in mind. Also implicated in problem-solving deficits are inefficient problem-solving strategies and associated metalinguistic and metacognitive skills. Therefore, consideration needs to be given to the use of strategy-training techniques. Performance on Piagetian tests of cognition relevant to procedural and causal knowledge appears to be variable among adults with learning disabilities (preoperational to operational). These aspects of cognitive functioning bear upon the types and complexity of problem solving tasks employed in therapy. Persistent social-emotional and sensorimotor problems also need to be addressed in the design of therapeutic tasks.

Box 7.2 summarizes the maintaining factors that influence intervention planning for adults with learning disabilities, and those aspects of planning affected. This summary is followed by an examination of contemporary approaches to language intervention for individuals with learning disabilities. These approaches are organized with reference to theories of learning and rehabilitation and are helpful in guiding procedure planning.

Theories of Learning and Rehabilitation

In Chapter 4, six theoretic approaches to language intervention were reviewed: neo-Piagetian constructivist, behavioral, social cognitive, functional communication, discourse comprehension, and motor. Principles from these theories have been applied to communication related interventions with adults. Language intervention programs incorporating these principles are reviewed next.

Social Cognitive

Perhaps the most prevalent intervention programs for adolescents and adults with learning disabilities are driven by social-cognitive principles (e.g., Reid, 1988). These programs typically advocate teaching metacognitive problem-solving strategies through scaffolding, i.e., presentation of models and direct verbal instruction to be internalized by the learner. The purpose generally is to improve academic or vocational performance or literacy skills. Specifically, reading comprehension, report writing, and vocabulary—especially metaphors and idiomatic expressions—are usually addressed in such programs (e.g., Blachowicz, 1994; Silliman &

BOX **7.2**

The Roles of Linguistic/Communicative and Maintaining
Factors in Goal and Procedure Planning

Factors	Role in Goal Planning	Role in Procedure Planning
Linguistic/Communicative		
Use of language for planning and problem solving	May be the basis of long-term, short-term, session goals Complexity and familiarity of planning or problem-solving tasks must be considered as performance demands, and such considerations may be used as a basis for sequencing short-term and session goals	Suggestive of planning or problem-solving tasks
Discourse functions of language (other than planning and problem solving)	May be the basis of long-term, short-term, session goals	Suggestive of linguistic/communicative procedural context
Narratives and other complex content/form interactions	May be the basis of long-term, short-term, session goals Complexity of content/form interactions and narrative structure (number and types of prepositions and interactions among prepositions) and difficulty (familiarity of content and other factors related to client's knowledge base and information-processing characteristics) must be considered as performance demands and used as a basis for sequencing short-term and session goals	May be context for addressing other goals Suggestive of tasks for addressing narrative goals
Cohesion devices in discourse	May be the basis of long-term, short-term, session goals	Suggestive of linguistic/communicative context for addressing cohesion
Nonliteral language forms	May be the basis of long-term, short-term, session goals	Suggestive of tasks for addressing nonliteral forms

B O X 7.2   Continued

Cognitive

Information-processing skills, including working memory/information retrieval and maintenance, discrimination and comparison of information	The demands that therapeutic tasks (linguistic and nonlinguistic contexts) make on the client may be used as a basis for sequencing session goals	Tasks' demands on the client's information-processing skills must be considered in designing therapeutic tasks
Type and level of reasoning required to address a therapeutic task (metacognitive, metalinguistic, Piagetian stage, type of logic)	The demands that therapeutic tasks (linguistic and nonlinguistic contexts) make on the client's reasoning abilities may be used as a basis for sequencing session goals	Tasks' demands on the client's reasoning abilities must be considered in designing therapeutic tasks The relation of a task's demands on reasoning and the content/form interaction targeted as a goal should be considered in designing therapeutic tasks
Psychosocial		Client's social-vocational experiences and emotional status can be considered in the design of the linguistic/communicative context of therapy

Wilkinson, 1994). The techniques employed typically involve teaching individuals how to talk themselves through problems. In some programs, general problem-solving strategies are taught that can be applied across tasks. For example, Blachowicz (1994, p. 306) advocated teaching the following steps to facilitate text and vocabulary comprehension:

1. Assess what you already know and think.
2. Set a purpose (i.e, goal, prediction, something to be verified, question to be answered).
3. Monitor as you read (by asking yourself if you understand and using "fix-up" strategies when you do not).
4. Make a final evaluation and use what you read (i.e., evaluate and pull together your thoughts and respond in some way, even if only to say you have understood well enough to stop reading).

Additional examples of clinician-client interactions are in the session-planning phase, later in this chapter.

Several social-cognitive programs incorporate neo-Piagetian constructivist principles. These programs teach students strategies that facilitate self-regulation of problem solving.

Self-regulation was defined by Butler (1995) as being able to "approach tasks in a problem-solving manner and flexibly select, implement, evaluate, and adapt task appropriate strategies as required" (p. 170). For example, in the Strategic Content Learning Program (Butler, 1995) the instructor engaged in discourse with the learner while addressing a problem-solving task. Within that discourse, the instructor collaborated with students to define goals relevant to the task and provoked students to think about (a) defining procedures for achieving goals, (b) abstracting principles from procedures, (c) monitoring success, and (d) modifying goals or procedures to resolve remaining problems. Butler applied her program to tasks such as writing essays for first-year college courses, learning statistics, and reading textbooks.

Neo-Piagetian Constructivist

Moses and Papish (1985) offered a critique of strategy-training programs. Recall that these programs typically teach individuals with language-learning disabilities to rely on verbal problem-solving procedures modeled by others and to engage in continuous self-monitoring while problem solving. Moses and Papish pointed out that expressive language and metalinguistics represent primary problem areas in many individuals with learning disabilities. Consequently, directing individuals with learning disabilities to memorize verbally encoded problem-solving procedures and then to talk to themselves while problem solving could present problems because these individuals would have to rely on their deficit area—expressive language and metalinguistics—to succeed. The research by Worden et al. (1982) reviewed above seems to support this position. These authors attempted to train adults with learning disabilities to use their knowledge of story-grammar categories to facilitate recall. Despite this training, the only effective procedure identified was repetitive readings of passages.

With reference to the facilitation of causal and procedural language, Moses and colleagues proposed a set of procedures derived from constructivist-cognitive theory (e.g., Moses, 1981; Moses et al., 1990; Moses & Papish, 1985). These procedures were summarized in Box 6.1. A different kind of constructivist program designed to facilitate comprehension of nonliteral meanings (e.g., metaphor, idiom, simile) was proposed by Milosky (1994). Milosky emphasized the use of context to support vocabulary interpretation by individuals with learning disabilities. An example would involve using pictures as perceptual cues to aid in the creation and interpretation of metaphors (e.g., showing a curled ocean wave to support the simile, "A wave in the ocean is a curl of hair," derived from Silberstein, Gardner, Phelps, & Winner, 1982).

Discourse Comprehension

Comprehension of oral and printed discourse—especially stories—has long been a focus of language interventions for individuals with learning disabilities (e.g., see Wallach & Butler, 1994, and Reid, 1988, for reviews of that literature). Comprehension programs have incorporated principles derived from the prevalent discourse-processing theory of the day. Presently, comprehension programs are incorporated into broader literacy facilitation efforts (e.g., Wallach & Butler, 1994). A narrow definition of literacy is the ability to "read and write the words of one's own language" (Wallach & Butler, 1994, p. 27). Literacy, however, has a much wider scope. According to Wallach and Miller (1988), literacy represents the ability to exist in hypothetical world s described by language. This definition encompasses print literacy (reading) as well as being knowledgeable about the events of one's culture.

Print literacy and writing share much with oral language, particularly the use and expression of a common syntax and cultural knowledge (Wallach & Butler, 1994). Distinctions between print and oral language are also recognized. Learning to read and write may implicate metalinguistic skills more so than learning to speak (i.e., learning to read and write involves cognizance of syntactic and phonologic segments, style, vocabulary, and meaning, whereas learning to speak and comprehend the language may involve a lesser level of linguistic awareness (Olson, 1996). Comprehension programs for adults must address the entire panoply of factors implicated in literacy. Wallach and Butler summarized several principles of literacy intervention. Three of these principles relevant to facilitating narrative comprehension are:

- the availability of two-way interactions along many language domains (e.g., spoken language facilitating written language and vice-versa, content knowledge influencing structure knowledge and vice-versa, etc.);
- practice of and familiarity with metacognitive comprehension strategies;
- having background knowledge of the topic of a narrative.

Gurney et al. (1990) developed an instructional strategy for teaching literature comprehension to adults with learning disabilities, which focuses on story grammar. By story grammar, Gurney et al. referred to "articulation of the main character's goals, a delineation of the sequence of his or her attempts to achieve these goals (which involves resolving problems encountered along the way), and an analysis of how major characters react to a deeper understanding of the story" (p. 336). The approach involves teaching components of story grammar and questions to ask oneself about story grammar. Blachowicz (1994) proposed similar procedures for facilitating expository comprehension, making connections among components of a story across a text, improving vocabulary, and making predictions about the content of stories by referencing story grammar.

Summary and Application to Intervention Planning

Intervention programs for adults with learning disabilities offer principles of learning that can be referenced in designing materials and clinician-client interactions. Principles and areas of application from the approaches to treatment reviewed above are summarized in Box 7.3.

Also, see Chapter 6 for a more thorough discussion of theories of learning and rehabilitation.

Performance Demands

Whereas principles of learning and rehabilitation guide the design of appropriate intervention contexts, an analysis of performance demands facilitates the sequencing of behavioral challenges presented to clients within and across sessions. As discussed in

BOX **7.3**

Summary of Approaches to Language Intervention for Adults with Learning Disabilities, Central Tenets, and Aspects of Speech-Language-Communication Addressed

Approaches to Language Intervention for Adults with Learning Disabilities	Central Tenets	Aspect of Speech-Language-Communication Addressed
Social cognitive (Reid, 1988; Wallach & Butler, 1994)	1. Teach individuals how to talk themselves through problems (teach problem-solving strategies); 2. Teach strategies by scaffolding (model, instruct, eventually allow student to use strategies independently).	Metacognitive problem-solving strategies (including the use of language for problem solving); literacy skills (including narrative production and comprehension) report writing, and vocabulary, especially metaphors and idiomatic expressions
Neo-Piagetian constructivism (e.g., Moses, 1981; Moses, Klein & Altman, 1990; Reid & Hresko, 1981)	1. Engage students in concrete tasks that provoke reasoning in the area and at the level necessary to achieve the language goal; 2. Interact with students in a conversational manner to facilitate identification of problems and to provoke reflection on problems and possible solutions; 3. Allow students to make errors—do not punish wrong answers; instead, provoke further reflection and provoke the student to test and evaluate alternative methods and ideas.	Complex content/form/use interactions, especially to express procedural and causal knowledge; pragmatic discourse skills that reflect consideration of the listener's perspective; comprehension of nonliteral lexicon
Discourse Comprehension	1. Encourage relations among multiple language domains (e.g., spoken language facilitating written language and vice-versa, content knowledge influencing structure knowledge and vice-versa, etc.); 2. Teach (through scaffolding) metacognitive comprehension strategies; 3. Ensure that the client has background knowledge of the topic of a narrative.	Literacy, production and comprehension of narratives

Chapter 2, we use the term *performance demands* to refer to the relative complexity and difficulty of a task. Recall that complexity is based on universal aspects of organization or information processing embedded within the task. Developmental or structural taxonomies are useful guides to the inherent complexity of communicative targets. Difficulty derives from information-processing and other functional characteristics of a particular client that make a task relatively easy or hard to achieve. Difficulty can be anticipated by referring to baseline data concerning communicative deficits and maintaining factors associated with a particular client. For example, knowing that a client manifests a deficit in spatial cognition signals to the clinician that spatial tasks will pose particular challenges. The following discussion addresses how to evaluate the inherent complexity and difficulty of goals are that characteristically addressed in the treatment of adults with language-learning disabilities.

Narrative Discourse

Production and comprehension of narratives represent one area of communication typically targeted in cases of language-learning disabilities. The structural complexity of stories represents a primary source of performance demands. The greater the structural complexity of a story to be processed by a client, the greater is the performance demand. Variables that bear upon structural complexity of a story include the following:

- story grammar (causal narratives with embedded problems and resolutions are more complex than additive and temporal narrative, Lahey, 1988);
- the inclusion of evaluative comments in narratives (i.e., landscapes of consciousness) appears developmentally more advanced than complex goal-based and embedded causal chains (Bruner, 1990; Baumberg & Damrad-Frye, 1991; Lahey, 1988);
- the number and organization of prepositions within the story (Mandler, 1984; Schank & Abelson, 1977);
- the number of different subcategories of information (e.g., initiating events, settings, attempts, internal responses, etc.);
- the listener's relative familiarity or ignorance of the content (requirements for perspective taking and explication of information increase complexity);
- explicitness of information presented (increasing the degree of inference making required for comprehension increases complexity, Wiig & Secord, 1987);
- the use of relative clauses and topic-subtopic organization of subordinate propositions as cohesion devices (these structures appear to be more complex than conjunction and complementation, Nippold, Schwartz, & Undlin, 1992).

Although general influences on complexity are cited in the listing presented above, several factors weigh differently in comprehension tasks compared with production tasks. For narrative comprehension, performance demands would be intensified by (a) the number of prepositions and embeddings and (b) reductions in explicitness of information. For narrative production, performance demands would be increased by (a) the number, type, and organization of propositions and (b) the need to attend to listener orientation (e.g., by providing adequate background information, organization of story components, cohesive devices). Several factors have the potential to have multiple effects on performance demands. One such factor is the nature and number of subcategories of information to be processed. Demands on memory are increased by an increase in numbers of subcategories of information (e.g., initiating events, settings, attempts, internal responses). Performance demands, however, might be reduced if these subcategories provide explicit details to the listener or reader. Another factor that may increase or reduce performance demands is sentence complexity. For example, performance demands may be increased by the syntactic processing of a relative clause. Demands may be reduced, however, by the semantic redundancy provided by the supportive clause.

Additional factors that may influence task *difficulty* (the client-specific aspect of performance demands) include (a) the information-processing load placed on working memory to keep track of information as compared with characteristics of the client's working memory, (b) the vocabulary included in the story compared with the client's lexical knowledge, and (c) the content of the narrative as it compares with the client's past educational, vocational, and social experiences.

Procedural and Causal Language

As discussed above, complex content/form/use interactions relevant to expressing procedural (how to) and causal (why) knowledge are potential goals for intervention with adults. Research conducted along both traditional Piagetian and neo-Piagetian lines (reviewed in Chapters 5 and 6) provides direction for analyzing performance demands associated with such goals.

Procedural knowledge is viewed as foundational to causal knowledge in specific problem-solving contexts (Moses, 1990, 1994). Therefore, language representing procedural knowledge poses less of a performance demand than language representing causal relations. Within the area of causal language, levels of reasoning provide a framework for projecting performance demands. Structures that code preoperational levels of reasoning (temporal and comparative content categories) are less complex than those supporting the expression of operational reasoning (comparative-compensatory categories, Moses, et al., 1990). Taxonomies of logic (e.g., Braine, 1990; Nippold, 1994; Chapter 5 in this book) offer an alternative approach to anticipating performance demands related to causal language. The linguistic expression of both procedural and causal knowledge is enhanced by manipulating concrete objects. Thus, the absence of manipulables increases performance demands (Moses, 1994).

Figurative Language

The use of lexical items with multiple meanings (e.g., metaphors, idioms, and humor) represents a third goal area for adults (e.g., Lahey, 1988; Wallach & Butler, 1994). Metaphors and humorous expressions based on the manipulation of semantic processing (lexical ambiguity) are viewed as less complex than metaphors based on the manipulation of syntax, morphology, and phonology (Nippold, 1994; Spector, 1990; Wiig & Secord, 1987). In adults, familial and cultural experiences with specific idiomatic, metaphoric, and humorous expressions are an additional critical variable that should be considered in evaluating the relative difficulty of particular expressions.

Additional Factors Affecting Performance Demands

Syntactic Complexity.   There are several factors intrinsic to communicative and linguistic targets that bear upon performance demands in treating language-learning disabilities. One is syntactic complexity. With adults, the syntactic complexity intrinsic to verbs and anaphors affects linguistic performance. As discussed in Chapter 4, verbs play a large part in dictating the grammar of sentences by allowing certain complement structures and disallowing others. Particular verbs assign specific types of case and particular themes. Some verbs allow a greater variety of complement structures than others (e.g., compare want, persuade, know, and eat). Although no systematic taxonomy is available that depicts verb complexity, Bloom & Lahey's (1978) developmental taxonomy of content/form/use interactions suggests that verbs that allow a greater variety of complement types may be more complex than transitive verbs that restrict complement structure such as "eat."

Anaphors represent another source of syntactic complexity because they derive referential meaning from an analysis of the organization of the sentence (i.e. identification of the governing subject). To complicate matters, sentences with relative clauses present multiple subjects to analyze in the processing of anaphors. Infinitival complements, moreover, present hidden referents.

Perceptual Support.   A final variable influencing task complexity is perceptual support. As with children, the presence of perceptual support relevant to the targeted goal (e.g., modeling, concrete objects to reference) decreases complexity, whereas the absence of perceptual support increases performance demands.

The primary focus of this discussion of performance demands has been sources of information that reveal the complexity of intervention goals. We conclude this discussion with a reminder that a client's information processing and experiential profile also need to be considered in evaluating task difficulty. Psychosocial and cultural experiences, sensorimotor characteristics, and academic strengths and weaknesses are all variables that bear upon the potential difficulty of tasks.

Implications for Intervention Planning

Analyses of task complexity and difficulty contribute primarily to the sequencing of goals, especially at the short-term and session-planning phases. Recall that short-term and session-planning phases involve envisioning goal sequences; short-term sequences lead to the long-term goal while session sequences lead to the short-term goal. The prioritization of short-term goal sequences is typically based upon analysis of the complexity of the intrinsic linguistic structure. Such analyses are generally made with reference to developmentally or organizationally based taxonomies. The sequencing of session goals is based both on such structural analyses and on considerations of task difficulty related to a particular client. Analyses of task difficulty lead to the design of a context in which the targeted communication act takes place. Context descriptions constitute an integral part of the session goal statement. Therapeutic contexts are designed to address maintaining factors that must be considered in projecting task difficulty.

Consider the following two session goals written for a client who becomes distressed when talking in front of a group: (a) The client will produce a procedural narrative to instruct the clinician to access the Internet; (b) The client will produce a procedural narrative to instruct a group of coworkers to access the Internet. For this particular client, the second task is more difficult than the first because of the context in which the communication takes place. The context shift from the first to the second goal (from talking to one person to a group) addresses a psychosocial maintaining factor.

Summary

This first part of Chapter 7 presented an overview of learning disabilities in adults, with reference to communication functioning, factors that may maintain communication problems, and variables that can influence the performance demands of particular intervention goals. Throughout the remainder of this chapter, we will illustrate the derivation of goals and procedures in adult language-learning disabilities as we develop intervention plans for a specific client, Barry.

Case Study: Baseline Data

Background Information

Barry, a 23-year-old man, was referred for a speech-language evaluation by his parents on the recommendation of a psychologist. Barry and his family were considering options for higher education or vocational training programs. At the time of testing, Barry was employed as an inventory and stock clerk at an electronics store near his home. Barry reported that he had been successfully working at that job for about a month.

Barry, who lives with his parents, was accompanied by them for the examination sessions. Barry appeared disheveled. Barry has one older brother, 26 years of age, who works in electronics. A second brother, who was described as hyperactive, died in an automobile accident. Barry earned a high school diploma. He was placed in classes for children with neurological impairments and learning disabilities throughout his school career. His parents reported that Barry tends to be socially immature and has few friends. He has difficulty planning and following daily schedules, cannot manage his earnings (or allowance), and has problems with his checking account. Barry has a driver's license and drives his car to and from work. His parents are especially interested in facilitating Barry's independence and social competence.

As a child, Barry was described by psychologists as hyperactive, excitable, and easily discouraged. He has taken Ritalin for his hyperactivity. Barry does not now behave in a hyperactive or inattentive manner. Prenatal history and birth were unremarkable. Barry, however, was delayed in all areas of development. No evidence of a genetic factor was found in testing for "Fragile X" syndrome. Recent opthamalogical reports indicated that visual acuity is good, although as a child Barry exhibited exophoria/tropia, an eye-muscle imbalance. He has received orthotropic therapy for the disorder.

Barry has undergone intelligence testing several times. He has consistently performed at the low average intelligence level (most recently on the Wechsler Adult Intelligence Scale [WAIS]). The psychologist who evaluated Barry most recently indicated that "difficulty integrating abstract material, particularly on a visual motor basis" contributed to depressed intellectual potential. Barry consistently performed below grade level in all areas (math, reading, spelling, visual motor skills) on achievement tests given when he was of school age (Wide Range Achievement Test [WRAT], KeyMath, Peabody Picture Vocabulary Test [PPVT], Beery Developmental Test of Visual-Motor Integration). The results on these standardized tests revealed no definitive relation between deficits in intelligence or scholastic skills and language. Findings regarding visual motor skills and weakness in abstract problem solving, however, suggest a spatial cognitive deficit that may be related to problems in language content and use; spatial cognition may be evaluated in greater depth on Piagetian-type tasks.

Boxes 7.4 summarizes the standard and nonstandard assessments of speech and language and potential maintaining factors presented to Barry in the current round of testing and the reasons for each evaluation. Box 7.5 summarizes results of these tests.

Summary of Results

Barry manifests significant difficulties in metalinguistic skills and several related aspects of discourse. These difficulties are most pronounced in lexical knowledge and figurative language narrative production and comprehension, and the use of cohesive devices.

With reference to lexical knowledge and figurative language, Barry manifests problems making inferences about ambiguous sentences and interpreting metaphors. He also has difficulty comprehending low-frequency vocabulary. With reference to oral narratives, Barry experiences difficulties planning and creating stories. He does not appear to produce more complex causal chain narratives, does not mark endings of stories, and does not offer evaluative comments. His stories are brief and devoid of elaborations and supporting detail. To maintain cohesion, Barry can produce certain complex syntactic forms (i.e., conjunction, complementation), although he does not produce relative clauses. He manifests problems producing complex syntax in written language.

In the cognitive domain, daily scheduling and financial planning pose problems. These types of difficulties may be symptomatic of more general deficits in the use of temporal and causal language and related cognitive skills. Barry is able to recall and execute a temporal sequence of commands when engaged in familiar tasks at work and in less familiar tasks, such as operating a computer graphics program. He uses preoperational strategies when reasoning about spatial problems, procedures, and causes on Piagetian tasks. He conserves number and continuous quantity. He does not systematically compare and contrast attributes of objects when reasoning verbally.

BOX **7.4**

Areas of Assessment for Intervention Planning

Necessary Information	Source	Utility of Procedure
I. Language and speech A. Content-form	Spontaneous language sample (Lahey, 1988)	To obtain most representative measure of developmental and functional status of content/form interactions and discourse skills
	Test of Language Competence (Wiig & Secord, 1989)	To assess metalinguistic knowledge (metaphors, multiple word meanings, figurative aspects of language, inferencing, sentence construction)
	Test of Written Language (Hammill & Larson, 1996)	To assess comprehension of narratives (by reading)
B. Use	Lahey (1988) coding system for language use in a conversational context	To obtain the most representative measure of the developmental status of language function and the influence of context
C. Phonology 1. Phonetic	None	Collecting an inventory of phonemes and phonetic ability on a standard test of articulation was not warranted based on the client's age and phonetic ability apparent during collection of background information
2. Phonological	Continuous speech sample	To obtain a measure of the phonologic status of the client's speech and language production in continuous speech
D. Fluency	Language sample	To obtain a sample of fluency in continuous speech
E. Voice	Language sample	To obtain a sample of vocal parameters in continuous speech
II. Maintaining factors A. Cognition	Piagetian tests of conservation of number and spatial reasoning, and spatial perspective Informal assessment of problem solving related to operating a computer Wechsler Adult Intelligence Scales (1955)	To obtain a measure of the client's developmental status in cognition relevant to vocational and social problem solving To obtain a comparative measure of intelligence in verbal and performance areas

B. Sensorimotor
    1. Peripheral speech mechanism
    2. Body stability
	Oral Speech Mechanism Screening Examination (St. Louis & Ruscello, 1978)
	Informal evaluation of sitting, standing, gait, and movement
		To determine the structural and functional adequacy of the articulators and other points of valving
		To obtain a measure of the developmental and functional status of the client's sensorimotor functioning

C. Psychosocial	Case history Observation of interactions with mother, father, and examiners	To determine the nature of psychosocial behavior

BOX **7.5**

Results of Assessment for Intervention Planning

I. Language
   A. Content-form:
      Results of standardized testing were as follows:

Test of Language Competence (TLC)
   The TLC evaluates metalinguistic knowledge (knowledge about language) and problem-solving abilities as they relate to the comprehension and use of verbal language. It tests the ability to make inferences about ambiguous sentences and listening comprehension, to process metaphors and other forms of figurative language, and to construct sentences. The following results indicate significant difficulties in these aspects of metalinguistic knowledge:
      Ambiguous sentences—standard score: 6
      Listening comprehension: making Inferences
                        —standard score: 4
      Oral expression: recreating sentences—standard score: 3
      Figurative language—standard score: 3
      Composite standard score: 65
      Standard deviation: -3
      Stanine: 1

Test of Written Language (TOWL)
   The TOWL evaluates vocabulary usage and thematic maturity when writing a narrative. The TOWL also assesses knowledge of punctuation and handwriting. The following results indicate significant difficulty in creating written narratives:

	Standard score	Percentile
Vocabulary:	7	10
Thematic maturity:	8	5
Spelling:	5	5
Style:	6	9
Handwriting:	7	16
Sum of standard scores:	33	
Written language quotient:	70	

   The complexity of narratives produced by Barry improved markedly when standardized test administration was broken and Barry was prompted to write a more complex story.

Lahey Content-Form Analysis of Language Sample:
   Achieved: Content/form interactions through Lahey Phase 8+

Moses, Klein, Altman Analysis of Causal Language
   Causal explanations are preoperational

Use

Lahey Narrative Assessment
   An evaluation of the story structure of the spontaneous narrative Barry created about the stimulus pictures on the TOWL revealed a goal-based causal chain with an obstacle. The story comprised complex sentences with conjunction and complementation.
   Barry also produced narratives about actual historical events, such as the job at the electronics store and school experiences. He told expository narratives about how to activate the computer and use the graphics program.

(continued)

B O X **7.5** **Continued**

I. Overall level
    A. Achieved:
        Goal-based causal chain with an obstacle
        Expository temporal sequences
    B. Not achieved: Multiple causal chains (conjoined, embedded)

II. Subcategories of causal chains and expository narratives
    A. Achieved: Included in the narrative:
    Initiating event and complication
        Setting
        Attempts
        Consequences
    B. Not achieved: Not included in narratives:
        Internal responses
        Ending: No formal ending or summary
        Evaluations: (i.e., statements of personal feelings by the narrator)
        Suspense mechanisms

IV. Cohesion (oral language)
    A. Not productive:
        Cohesion by use of hierarchic topic organization and transitions
    B. Productive: (inconsistent)
        Pronoun referencing
        Anaphoric and exophoric references
        Ellipsis
    C. Achieved:
        Variety of appropriate, high-frequency additive, temporal, causal conjunctions
        Cohesion established by repetitious references to principle characters in the story (either by name or pronoun substitution) and repetitious use of particular verbs
        Parallel structure (use of past [simple or progressive] tense)

V. Additional aspects of language use
        Initiated and changed topics in conversational contexts
        Used language for expository, response, and protest functions when speaking to parents and the examiner
        Reportedly (by parents) manifests problems with social functions of language with peers, the opposite sex

Reference errors that include unreferenced use of personal pronouns, possessive determiners, possessive pronouns, and demonstratives
Did not demonstrate use of the following syntactic cohesion and topic shading or elaborating devices:
relative clauses, prepositional phrases, adverbial clauses, and infinitives (for the functions of elaborating details about the noun, expressing personal attitudes) or the modal auxiliary (to signal contrasts in mood, e.g., would, will, might)

    A. Piagetian tasks:
        Conserved number and continuous mass when asked about reconfigured groupings of objects, and transformed object shapes
        Demonstrated preoperational reasoning on several spatial tasks:
        In the first, Barry was asked to predict how an axle with two unequal sized wheels would descend along an incline (it swerves in the direction of the smaller wheel). He also was asked to use that mechanism to strike targets and to explain why the mechanism behaved the way it did. Barry predicted verbally that the axle would descend straight down (after he had observed it swerving). After several trials he physically compensated for the swerve in order to successfully strike a target. Barry did not offer an explanation for why the axle moved the way it did.

B O X **7.5**   **Continued**

In response to a second spatial problem, Barry had to represent in a drawing how a set of objects appeared to the evaluator who was viewing the objects from another spatial perspective. The evaluator and Barry were sitting across from one another, and the objects were placed in between. Barry produced two identical drawings of the object configuration. However, he added a picture of the evaluator facing the objects in the second picture.

This indicates that Barry was aware that there was a difference in perspective. However, he did not attempt to represent that difference by transforming the positioning of the objects in a drawing.

Socially, Barry is struggling with the demands of living independently. Barry has few friends. His problems with scheduling and financial planning may have social-emotional components.

Long-Term Planning Phase

At the long-term planning phase, one or more long-term goals are written in terms of functional communication behaviors that will be achieved at the end of the contracted therapy period (recall our definition of a long-term goal as "a general statement about the best performance that can be expected of an individual in one or more [functional] communication areas within a projected period," Chapter 2). A procedural approach is also formulated. The procedural approach identifies the maintaining factors and principles of learning and rehabilitation that will guide the development of an appropriate linguistic and nonlinguistic therapeutic context. Below we identify the long-term goal and components of the procedural approach written for Barry. Following the goal and procedure statements, we explicate the derivation of each component of the intervention plan.

Long-Term Goals

Barry will:

1. use lexical items with multiple meaning (e.g., metaphors, idioms, and humor) in conversational speech;
2. produce multiple and embedded causal chain narratives in discourse;
3. Use topic-subtopic organization and relative clauses to establish and maintain cohesion in discourse;
4. include evaluative comments in narratives;
5. coordinate procedural (how to) sequences, comparatives, preoperational and operational causal explanations while planning and solving problems in vocational and social contexts;
6. extend a topic of conversation introduced by a partner by mirroring temporal procedural sequences, and responding to procedural and causal questions.

Procedural Approach

Maintaining factors: Cognitive, psychosocial

Principles of learning and rehabilitation (see Chapter 6, Box 6.2):

>   Constructivist-cognitive principles 1-4 (re: long-term goals 1, 2, 4).

>   Social-cognitive principle 2 (re: long-term goal 4):

>   Discourse comprehension principles 1-3 (re: long-term goals 2, 4)

Derivation of Goals

Four sources of information were used to derive the long-term goals identified above. These sources of information are:

1. the clinician's point of view on how to define functional communication and linguistic behavior;
2. baseline data about the present status of communication performance and maintaining factors (including current functioning and the potential for modification);
3. background information;
4. research findings that report age-appropriate, culturally acceptable, physiologically efficient communication behavior.

The derivation of the long-term goals is discussed with reference to these information sources.

Clinician's Point of View about Functional Communication, Speech, and Language.   It is our point of view that language comprises content/form/use interactions, that linguistic behavior manifests an intrinsic organization that accounts for the surface form of language, and that adults use language most typically to engage in discourse in social-vocational contexts. This point of view about language and functional communication in adults leads us to formulate long-term goals as the achievement of specific content/form interactions that serve specific discourse functions in specific social and vocational contexts.

As discussed in Chapter 1, our natural tendency is to focus on expressive over receptive language. There are several reasons. The achievement of measurable behavioral change, which is the aim of intervention planning, favors expression over reception, since expression is most easily and directly measured. Expression is also a core component of *functional communication.*

This focus on expression is not to deny the significance of receptive abilities. Receptive skills may be particularly important to address in adults with learning disabilities like Barry who may be working at jobs where following instructions is a critical vocational requirement, such as stock clerk and paraeducator.

Reception can be addressed in concert with expression by recognizing that receptive skills facilitate cohesion in discourse. Adequate receptive skills are necessary, for example, for extending a topic introduced by a partner or affirming that a message has been received and understood. We approach reception in this manner by targeting cohesion in discourse.

Baseline Data and Background Information.   Guided by our view of what constitutes speech, language, and functional communication, we turn to baseline data to discover what areas of communication to target. Furthermore, it is also our point of view that language interacts with sensorimotor, cognitive, and psychosocial behavioral systems, and that problems in these areas may maintain communication problems in adults. As such, we examine baseline data relevant to these potential maintaining factors to determine a prognosis; i.e., to predict how much the client can be expected to achieve within a specified period of intervention. We also address maintaining factors when planning procedures.

Language.   Barry does not use language to plan procedures that would facilitate independence (e.g., he does not plan and follow daily schedules efficiently and has problems budgeting). This is consistent with Barry's difficulties using complex content/form interactions. He does not produce complex temporal sequences or causal explanations, and he does not use comparatives for planning or when engaged in complex problem-solving situations. The use of such complex content/form interactions for planning and problem solving could facilitate social and vocational success, especially in unskilled physical work environments. As such, the production of temporal procedural sequences and causal language relevant to planning and problem solving is under consideration as long-term goals of intervention.

In the important area of narrative discourse, Barry is most challenged by the production and comprehension of complex causal narratives. In terms of production, Barry manifests difficulty embedding problems and resolutions in stories, providing commentaries, maintaining cohesion through hierarchical topic organization, using of relative clauses and transitions, and systematic referencing of pronouns, and elipsis. Since narratives are central to social and vocational competence in adults, narratives including the microstructural aspect of cohesion represent leading candidates for targeting as a long-term goal.

Deficits that Barry manifests in figurative language and other metalinguistic skills also have important implications for achieving social vocational success and independence. For example, social misunderstandings may arise as a consequence of difficulties Barry has interpreting humor or other kinds of comments that have double meanings. Thus, figurative language (in particular, comprehension and production of metaphors, idioms, and humor) and inference making about incomplete information presented in discourse are additional candidates for long-term goals.

Maintaining Factors and Establishing a Prognosis.   In setting long-term goals, we need to establish a realistic level of performance and a time frame for the achievement of the targeted objectives. Baseline data indicating level of language functioning and number and severity of factors that may be maintaining the communication problem provide direction for making this prognosis.

For Barry, intellectual functioning is in the low normal range. In the area of cognition, Barry can conserve number and actively problem solve (e.g., recognize problems and attempt trial-and-error solutions) with concrete, manipulable objects (e.g., a computer, tokens). However, he reasons about spatial problems at a preoperational level and has difficulties with adaptive living skills, such as planning personal finances. His ability to conserve number and solve concrete problems suggests that a long-term goal involving the production of complex, causal language for problem-solving functions could be achievable.

In terms of arriving at a time frame for achieving long range goals, there does not appear to be significant sensorimotor involvement. Psychosocial functioning is problematic in establishing and maintaining friendships and independent living skills (e.g., managing finances, scheduling, etc.). These problems indicate mild to moderate cognitive and psychosocial deficits, which, if addressed during intervention, should not impede achievement of language targets. Barry presently manifests simpler causal narratives and some degree of cohesion in narrative discourse. In sum, this information suggests that Barry should be able to achieve more complex narrative and metalinguistic competencies within a delimited time frame (one year) given regular intervention (two times weekly, one-hour sessions). This information helped establish the long-term goals listed above.

Derivation of Procedural Approach

The groundwork for deriving procedures is laid at the long-term planning phase. This is accomplished by identifying maintaining factors that will be addressed in the design of the therapeutic environment. Additionally, principles from theories of learning and rehabilitation are identified. These principles will provide guidance in the creation of therapeutic tasks and clinician-client interactions.

Identification of Maintaining Factors. As noted above, social-emotional functioning is perceived as a problem area by Barry and his parents. In addition, weak academic skills and difficulties with verbal problem solving represent difficulties in the cognitive domain. Procedures will be developed with these difficulties in mind.

Theories of Learning and Rehabilitation. The second major component of the procedural approach involves specification of assumptions and principles of learning and rehabilitation that can guide procedure planning. These principles will be abstracted primarily with reference to the literature on treatment of learning disabilities and this clinician's personal belief system about how behaviors targeted as long-term goals are acquired. The long-term goals established for Barry focus on the development of more complex lexical knowledge, narrative forms, and semantic relations relevant to problem solving. Current trends in the treatment of learning disabilities as well as our own beliefs about language learning in adults lead us to three theories: neo-Piagetian constructivist, social-cognitive, and discourse comprehension. Assumptions about what aspect of language learning or rehabilitation each theory explains and principles from these theories were derived in Chapter 6. The selected assumptions and principles that compose the procedural approach and the long-term goals to which they relate were presented above.

Short-Term Planning Phase

At the short-term planning phase, one or more short-term goals are written in terms of functional communication behaviors that will be achieved at the end of the contracted therapy period (recall our definition of a short-term goal in Chapter 2 as "a linguistic and or communicative achievement that has been given priority within a hierarchy of achievements required for the realization of the long-term goal"). The clinician also delimits the linguistic and nonlinguistic procedural context at the short-term planning phase. Recall that *context* refers to the therapeutic environment-everything surrounding and interacting with the client. Following the format established in the long-term planning section for Barry, we will identify short-term goals and the delimited procedural context first. Then, we will explicate the derivation of each of these components of the intervention plan.

Short-Term Goals

Barry will:

1. tell jokes based on lexical ambiguity in conversational speech;
2. explain to the clinician lexical ambiguity in jokes using causal semantic relations (reason for the humor);
3. produce narratives containing one goal-based embedded causal chain (problem and problem resolution);
4. respond with evaluative comments to requests for information about a character's reaction to a problem embedded in a story;
5. coordinate temporal sequences and causal explanations to justify procedures when manipulating concrete objects;
6. use comparatives when explaining reasons for the resolution of problems involving the manipulation of concrete objects.

Delimited Procedural Context

Nonlinguistic Context. Concrete problem-solving tasks related to Barry's work in a store (e.g., involving computers, spatial organization of materials in a warehouse or store display, etc.) and independent living experiences (e.g., furnishing and cleaning an apartment, balancing a checkbook) will be presented to support procedural and causal explanations. Videotapes of popular movies, books of fables and jokes based on lexical ambiguity, and familiar and humerous stories with redundant and highly interconnected prepositional structure will be presented in written and oral form. These materials will address the production and comprehension of narratives and humor. A computer will be used for writing and illustrating stories.

Linguistic Context. The clinician will use the techniques of narration (commenting on the client's actions), expansion (expanding on client's comments), requesting, and scaffolding (modeling and direct instruction faded as the client develops expertise) while engaged with Barry in concrete problem-solving tasks. The focus will be on the generation of procedural plans.

The clinician will tell jokes and relate fables and other highly structured, familiar stories. The clinician will model strategies for identifying problems and problem resolutions, and for identifying humor related to multiple meanings of vocabulary words. The clinician will encourage Barry to comment on his personal feelings about selected problem-solving experiences and story components.

Derivation of Short-Term Goals

As discussed in Chapter 1, deriving short-term goals involves making several prioritization decisions. These decisions concern which behaviors should be learned before others on the road toward the designated long-term accomplishment. The first decision involves determining which of the six long-term goals established for Barry to target first. Recall that these involve: (a) the use of lexical items with multiple meaning (e.g., metaphors, idioms, and humor) in conversational speech; (b) the production and comprehension of embedded causal chain narratives including evaluative comments and cohesion devices; and (c) the production of operational causal explanations, comparatives, and procedural sequences while solving problems in vocational contexts. The next decision is to prioritize a hierarchy of functional acts of communication that could be achieved within short-term periods that will lead to the achievement of the targeted long-term goal(s). To facilitate decision making, we will identify sources of information that can serve as a basis for gauging the relative complexity and difficulty of communication behaviors related to the long-term goals.

Decision 1.   The first decision involves determining which of the six long-term goals established for Barry to target first. Some questions that bear upon this decision are (a) Are any of these goals foundational to the achievement of any other; (b) Do the target behaviors interact in such a way that they can be worked on simultaneously; and (c) Is the achievement of any goal functionally more significant to the client's educational, social, or vocational well being than any other (Klein & Moses, 1999)?

Answering the First Question.   The first question (whether the achievement of any long-term goal is foundational to the achievement of any other) can be approached from two perspectives: developmental and behavioral. The following considerations influence decision making from a developmental perspective:

- In general, metalinguistic knowledge related to the use of nonliteral language, complex language relevant to narratives, and procedural and causal knowledge emerge contemporaneously throughout school age and adolescence (e.g. Lahey, 1988; Nippold, 1988; Wallach & Butler, 1994).
- Evaluative comments (characters' feelings about events) in narratives appear to emerge after complex goal-based and embedded causal chains (Bruner, 1990; Lahey, 1988); the content category internal state (talking about feelings), however, is an early developmental achievement related to evaluative comments.

- Relative clauses and topic-subtopic organization of propositions are used as cohesion devices; these competencies emerge late in adolescence and even into adulthood.
- Procedural knowledge is viewed as foundational to causal knowledge in specific problem- solving contexts.
- Talking about procedures and causes while manipulating concrete objects is developmentally less advanced than such expressions without the aid of manipulables (Moses, 1994).

From a behavioral perspective we ask whether any long-term goal incorporates skills that can be taught in a sequence to achieve the overall target (e.g., Hedge, 1995). The narrative goals lend themselves to such an analysis. The production of causal constructions in narratives could be taught first, followed by evaluative comments about the causal content. Coincidentally, this is the same order projected by the developmental analysis.

At this point, we are ready to answer the first question. Developmental and task analyses lead us to select long-term goals 5 and 6 as our first targets. These goals involve the production of procedural and causal constructions in concrete problem-solving tasks, causal narratives, and evaluative comments about characters in narratives. We will address cohesion later.

Answering the Second Question. The second question (whether the target behaviors interact in such a way that they can be worked on simultaneously) may be answered with reference to research on normal language use by adults, again augmented by the literature on child development. The skills and competencies embedded in all of the long-term targets are used by children and adults in discourse (including narrative discourse). These skills are presumably learned during a period following the acquisition of complex content/form/use interactions (e.g., after Lahey Phase 8). Acquisition is presumably supported by interactions with individuals who model complex language structures. Thus, all targets may interact and could be addressed during the same short-term goal period.

Answering the Third Question. The third question (whether the achievement of any long-term goal is functionally more relevant than any other) may be answered with reference to background information and baseline data in the psychosocial domain. Barry is employed as an inventory and stock clerk at a electronics store. Barry has few friends. A major concern of the family is that Barry be able to live independently, equipped with such self-help skills as managing money. Each long-term goal (related to lexical and narrative discourse skills and problem solving) bears upon vocational and social endeavors.

An Additional Question. There is one additional question that can help prioritize short-term goals: Is Barry capable of achieving multiple objectives during the same period? Baseline data relevant to the severity of the communication problem and the maintaining factors will help answer that question. Barry is already producing complex language structures. Consequently, his communication problem may be classified as mild to moderate. The primary maintaining factors appear to be social and cognitive, and Barry appears to be experiencing mild to moderate problems in these areas. In the social area, Barry is working successfully (as an unskilled laborer). He is, however, having some trouble with friendships and self-help skills relevant to independent living. In terms of cognition, Barry is functioning primarily at a preoperational level, although he is capable of operational performance (number conservation) and independent problem solving (given a concrete, developmentally appropriate task). The indication is that Barry could accomplish more than one short-term target, assuming that multiple short-term goals are appropriately delimited in complexity and relate to one another .

We are now prepared to arrive at the first major decision relevant to setting short-term goals: five of the long-term goals will be addressed during one short-term period (long-term goal 3 will be addressed later).

Decision 2.   Given that we decided to write short-term goals for five of the six long-term goals, the next decision to be made concerns prioritizing a hierarchy of behaviors that will lead to the achievement of the long-term goal(s). Before considering the sources of information that will help determine such a hierarchy, it is important to recognize that we are prioritizing *functional acts of communication*. This is consistent with our definition of a short- term goal as *a linguistic and/or communicative achievement.* This definition reflects our position that acts of communication as opposed to therapeutic exercises are the ultimate goals of speech-language intervention. As discussed in Chapter 2, we turn to developmental hierarchies, analyses of performance demands, and considerations relevant to the interaction between context and communication to make these decisions.

Developing Short-Term Goals That Address Long-Term Goal 1. The first long-term goal involves the use in conversational speech of nonliteral lexical items with multiple meanings (e.g., metaphors, idioms, and humor). Is there any basis upon which we can project a hierarchy or sequence nonliteral lexical forms to work on? There are several sources of developmental hierarchies that bear upon this achievement.

Spector (1992) offered some compelling reasons to consider humor as an early nonliteral target, as well as a framework for prioritizing goals that target humor. According to Spector (1992), language-based humor is founded on the identification and resolution of linguistic incongruity and ambiguity, and on an appreciation of multiple possible meanings. Spector identified humor elements within lexical, phonological, morphological, and syntactic components of language. The lexical element–word-meaning ambiguity-(e.g.,"janitors" union calls for sweeping reforms)–is a basic element of humor and is related to an aspect of figurative language that is problematic for Barry: identification of multiple word meanings. Because lexical-based humor may be motivational for Barry, addresses a linguistic weakness, and relates functionally to social success, we decided to target the production and comprehension of jokes based on lexical ambiguity as an early short-term goal.

Developing Short-Term Goals That Address Long-Term Goals 2 and 4.   Two long-term goals involve the production of narratives. The following considerations contribute to the derivation of related short-term goals:

- Barry is already producing simple goal-based causal chains with an obstacle (see baseline data); embedded causal chains (narratives containing one embedded problem and problem resolution) represents one of the next developmental achievements in children (Lahey, 1988).

- Barry omits comments about his own internal responses to events in a story, as well as those of other characters (baseline data).
- The inclusion of references to internal states of characters (emotions, frames of mind) follows, developmentally, inclusion of information about the actions (see the discussion of landscapes of consciousness and landscapes of action in Chapter 3).

In light of the information cited above, one short-term goal is to respond to a request for information about an internal response to a problem and solution in a narrative. This short-term goal actually addresses three long-term goals (producing more complex causal structures, including evaluative components in narratives, and maintaining conversational topics).

With reference to controlling performance demands, asking Barry to make one comment about one character's response to a problem should be easier than including multiple internal responses to multiple events in a story or commenting on responses from multiple characters. Discussing multiple responses to subordinate problems and resolutions could be future objectives.

Developing Short-Term Goals That Address Long-Term Goal 5. The final long-term goal to be considered involves the production of operational causal explanations, comparatives, and procedural sequences while solving problems in vocational contexts. The following information leads to the prioritization of relevant short-term goals.

- Baseline data indicate that Barry is capable of producing temporal sequences for expository functions, preoperational causal statements in response to requests, and causal relations in narrative contexts. However, Barry does not make comparisons in his causal statements and has difficulty processing procedural and causal information.
- Procedural explanations or plan structures involving temporal semantic relations develop before state or event sequences (i.e., motivations, physical and mental acts, interactions etc.), which map out real-time causal connections (see Chapter 4, and Brownell & Joanette, 1993).

The above information suggests having Barry reason about procedural sequences before focusing on more abstract causal explanations.

- Preoperational explanations that do not involve making comparisons precede explanations that involve comparisons. Comparatives, in turn, precede operational explanations.
- Explanations conducted in context of the concrete material being referenced pose fewer performance demands than explanations distanced in time and space from the activity being discussed.

Based on these hierarchies and Barry's present level of performance, we targeted the use of comparatives when explaining reasons for the resolution of problems involving the manipulation of concrete objects. Subsequently, we will target the use of causal and procedural structures that reflect operational reasoning. Box 7.6 summarizes these goals and their derivation.

BOX **7.6**

Short-Term Goals and Derivation

Short-Term Goals	Related Long-Term Goal	Prioritization Source
Barry will:		
1. tell jokes based on lexical ambiguity in conversational speech;	1	Spector (1992)
2. explain to the clinician semantic incongruities in jokes using causal semantic relations;	1,5	Klein, Moses, & Altman (1990)
3. produce narratives containing one goal-based embedded causal chain (problem and problem resolution);	2	Lahey (1988)
4. respond with evaluative comments to requests for information about a character's reaction to a problem embedded in a story;	4	Bamberg & Damrad-Frye (1991)
5. coordinate temporal sequences and causal explanations to justify procedures when manipulating concrete objects;	5	Brownell & Joanette, 1993 Moses, Klein, & Altman (1990)
6. use comparatives when explaining reasons for the resolution of problems involving the manipulation of concrete objects.	5	Moses, et al., (1990)

Derivation of the Delimited Procedural Context

The delimited procedural context represents the type of nonlinguistic environment (materials, tasks, organization of the clinical environment) and communication (the nature of the clinician-client interaction) that will be created in therapy. The primary sources of information that will facilitate the creation of an appropriate clinical environment are (a) the short-term goals that have been set, (b) principles of learning and rehabilitation that correspond to the clinician's belief system, and (c) the maintaining factors identified in the long-term procedural approach.

Without intending to belabor the obvious, the first source of information that guides the delimitation of a procedural context is the short-term goal established for the client; that is because the procedural context is designed to facilitate that behavior. With reference to the short-term goal(s), the second information source-principles of learning and rehabilitation–suggests materials and interactions appropriate for facilitating the achievement of each goal. The third information source is based on knowledge of the maintaining factors (i.e., the nonlinguistic behaviors that influence the client's communication), which leads us to identify the kinds of materials and interactions that might allow these factors to be addressed. Background information about the client's social and vocational status and needs suggests materials and interactions that are familiar, functional, meaningful, and motivational for the client. Below, we trace the delimitation of the nonlinguistic and linguistic contexts that will be created for Barry.

Delimitation of the Nonlinguistic Context. Background information reveals that Barry is 21 years old, works as a stock clerk in a computer store, and lives alone in an apartment. It makes sense, then, to present Barry with materials related to these experiences.

Short-term goals 5 and 6 involve making procedural plans and using comparatives in problem-solving contexts. Constructivist learning principles suggest engaging Barry in concrete, functional problem-solving tasks that provoke the generation of physical procedures to achieve concrete goals and, in the process, make comparisons. Thus, we plan to present problem-solving tasks involving comparisons among objects related to Barry's work in a store (e.g., involving computers, spatial organization of materials in a warehouse or store display, etc.) and his independent living experiences (e.g., furnishing and cleaning an apartment, balancing a checkbook).

Short-term goal 1 involves telling and interpreting jokes based on lexical ambiguity. This goal in itself suggests what material to present Barry (jokes based on lexical ambiguity). Short-term goal 3 involves producing narratives containing one emdedded causal chain (problem and problem resolution) and an evaluative comment about the problem. Two learning principles are relevant here. The first, a constructivist principle, suggests that the use of concrete material supports more complex language. This leads us to plan to use videotapes and books (concrete materials) relevant to storytelling in adults. The second principle, drawn from theories of narrative comprehension, suggests that story schema characterized by transparent, redundant relations among constituent prepositions facilitates comprehension, which involves analysis of the prepositional structure of stories. Thus, fables and other stories with obvious, redundant relations among prepositions will be used to support storytelling and the production of evaluative comments.

Linguistic Context. Referring to short-term goal 2, again (the use of comparatives in problem-solving contexts), constructivist and social-cognitive learning principles suggest client-clinician interactions. These principles (Box 4.1, constructivist principles 1 and 3 and social-cognitive principle 2) suggest the clinician should pose problems, collaborate on problem solutions, and engage in conversations about problem solving. In these conversations, the clinician should comment on the learner's actions and model strategies appropriate to solving problems (e.g., direct the client to the objects and attributes that are to be compared). In these conversations, the clinician also should encourage Barry to reflect on task demands (the intermediate goals that need to be addressed to resolve the overall problem).

Let us refer again to short-term goals 2 and 3 (telling and interpreting jokes based on lexical ambiguity and producing narratives containing one embedded causal chain and an evaluative comment). Theories of discourse comprehension (Box 6.2, discourse comprehension principles 1-3) indicate the clinician should teach the client how to produce such narratives through scaffolding techniques (i.e., modeling and explaining procedures). The clinician could also teach the client how to attend to cues that signal the intentions of the speaker. Thus, the clinician will tell jokes, fables, and other highly structured, familiar stories. The clinician will model strategies for identifying problems and problem resolutions, and for identifying lexical bases of humor.

Box 7.7 summarizes the delimited procedural context and its derivation.

B O X **7.7**

Delimited Procedural Context and Derivation

Delimited Procedural Context	Short-term Goal	Guiding Principles of Learning and Rehabilitation	Maintaining Factor(s) Addressed
Nonlinguistic Clinician will present:			
problem-solving tasks involving comparisons among objects related to Barry's work in a store;	5,6	Neo-Piagetian constructivist 1, 3	Cognition
videotapes and books (concrete materials) relevant to storytelling in adults;	1,3	Neo-Piagetian constructivist 1, 2	Cognition
fables and other types of strories with transparent propositional structure.		Narrative comprehension 3	Cognition
Linguistic Clinician will:			
pose problems, collaborate on problem solutions, comment on the learner's actions and model strategies appropriate to solving problems, encourage Barry to reflect on task demands;	2	Neo-Piagetian constructivist 1–4 Social learning 1–3	Cognition
use scaffolding techniques (i.e., modeling and explaining procedures for creating narratives and identifying and solving problems); teach the client how to attend to cues that signal the intentions of the speaker; tell jokes, fables, and other highly structured, familiar stories.	3	Discourse comprehension 1–3	Cognition

Session Planning Phase

At last we are in a position to decide what to do in an actual clinical session. We are ready to plan session goals and procedures. The first decision involves determining in what order to address short-term goals. We will then derive a series of session goals leading to the eventual achievement of the short-term goal being addressed. Recall our definition of a session goal in chapter 2 as "an observable behavior expressed in a specified context that represents an act of learning or rehabilitation that will lead to the acquisition of functional communication behavior targeted as a short-term goal." Thus, derivation of session goals will involve an analysis of (a) what constitutes an act of learning relevant to achievement of the short-term goal, (b) what are the contextual variables that increase or decrease performance demands (i.e., that affect the relative difficulty and complexity of a task), and (c) what are the criteria for achievement of goals. As discussed in Chapters 1 and 2, the answers to each of the questions will use the sources of information first considered in planning for the first two phases of intervention: maintaining factors, premorbid interests and experiences, and theories of learning and rehabilitation.

In this section we depart from the convention of first listing goals and procedures and then tracing their derivation, which we followed when discussing the derivation of long-term and short-term goals. Instead, we will prioritize the short-term goals, projecting which will be addressed first and which later throughout the designated short-term period. We will then derive two session goals and related procedures for each short-term goal: an early session goal and procedure and a later session goal and procedure (closer to the achievement of the short-term goal). The short-term goal is, incidentally, the last session goal targeted during the short-term period.

Deciding on What Order to Target Short-Term Goal(s)

Having established six short-term goals for the first six months of intervention, the first two decisions to be made at the session-planning phase are (a) how many to target at once and (b) if some are to be sequenced, in what order to address them. In our text on intervention planning for children (Klein & Moses, 1999), we posed a series of questions and identified sources of information that will guide these decisions. We have modified those questions and sources of information to make them applicable to adults; this resource appears in Box 7.8.

With reference to the questions in Box 7.8, let us review the six short-term goals. Barry will:

1. tell jokes in conversational speech based on lexical ambiguity;
2. explain to the clinician semantic incongruities in jokes using causal semantic relations;
3. produce narratives containing one embedded causal chain (problem and problem resolution) and an evaluative comment relevant to the problem and/or problem resolution;
4. respond to requests for information about a character's reaction to a problem embedded in a story with evaluative comments;
5. coordinate temporal procedural sequences and causal explanations to justify proce-

BOX **7.8**

Questions and Sources of Information for Deciding How to Sequence Short-Term Goals

Questions	Sources of Information	Relevant Decision
1. Can the short-term goals be ordered according to a maturational or developmental hierarchy?	Scales and taxonomies from the literature on child and adult development	If yes, consider sequencing session goals according to this developmental hierarchy
2. Is the client already producing the target structure in some contexts?	Baseline data in speech and language	If yes, consider targeting the short-term goal during initial sessions
3. Are there separate skills that could be addressed in initial sessions that are foundational to the achievement of multiple short-term goals?		If yes, consider targeting those short-term goals facilitated by similar skills during the same time
4. Does the client manifest any information-processing characteristic or background experience that makes one short-term objective more easily achievable than others?	Baseline data in speech and language	If yes, consider targeting the easier-to-achieve short-term goal first

dural sequences that direct the manipulation of concrete objects;
6. use comparatives when explaining reasons for the resolution of problems involving the manipulation of concrete objects.

Question 1: Can the Short-Term Goals Be Ordered According to a Maturational or Developmental Hierarchy?   As discussed in the derivation of short-term goals, each area targeted (identification of lexical ambiguity, storytelling, and causal and procedural language related to problem solving) appears to develop in a parallel manner in children and adolescents. A careful examination of the goals, however, yields some leads for proposing a developmental hierarchy.

The strongest evidence concerning developmental relations among short-term targets relates to goals 5 and 6 (coordinating procedural [how-to] sequences and causal explanations about concrete tasks and using comparatives when explaining reasons for solutions). As discussed above, procedural knowledge appears to be foundational to causal knowledge (Fischer, 1980; Karmiloff-Smith, 1986; Moses, 1994). This seems to argue for addressing short-term goal 5 before short-term goal 6. A case can also be made, however, for addressing both goals simultaneously. It could be argued that although procedural knowledge develops in advance of causal knowledge, individuals can reflect on both procedural and causal issues during the same problem-solving episodes, and this might facilitate development of knowledge in both areas (e.g., see Piaget, 1976, 1978, 1985). These two goals will be adressed simultaneously.

Taking context into consideration, it could be reasoned that the production of language about a concrete task (goals 5 and 6) might be less complex and easier to accomplish than thinking about language to compose stories and jokes about events distant in time and space (goals 1-4). The complex language produced while problem solving might even be foundational to metalinguistic skills relevant to goals 1-4, since metalinguistic reasoning may be viewed as causal reasoning (about language), expressed without perceptual support. Barry, however, is an adult who has experienced humor and who is capable of generating narratives. Although developmental considerations may provide some basis for prioritizing one target over another, there is no convincing argument that would mitigate against working on narratives and humor simultaneously.

Similarly, short-term goals 3 and 4 (production of an embedded causal chain narrative and identifying a character's internal response to a problem in such a narrative) represent a developmental sequence in the literature on child language (e.g., Bruner, 1986). A better basis for sequencing these short-term goals for adult client might, however, be functional significance. Embedding would improve story organization, which might facilitate communicative success. Referencing a character's internal state would certainly make stories more interesting, but it probably not would have the same effect on Barry's communicative competence as improving the intrinsic organization of narratives. Thus, we will target goal 4 before goal 5, although there will be an overlap; i.e., a period in which both goals will be addressed during the same time.

Question 2: Is the Client Already Producing the Target Structure in Some Contexts? It is presumed that Barry produces all target structures infrequently, except embedded causal chains. Consequently, all short-term goals will be potential early targets.

Question 3: Are There Skills That Could Be Addressed in Initial Sessions That Are Foundational to the Achievement of Multiple Short-Term Goals? One can conceive of specific skills that are foundational to several targeted behaviors. The ability to make comparisons and reason about procedures and causes is explicit in short-term goals 5 and 6. This ability also may be foundational to the narrative goals (3 and 4) and the goals involving lexical ambiguity (1 and 2); these goals implicate metalinguistic reasoning. There is, therefore, additional information supporting the prioritization of short-term goals 5 and 6.

Question # 4: Does the Client Manifest Any Information-Processing Characteristic or Background Experience That Makes One Short-Term Objective Easier to Achieve Than Others?   All short-term goals seem to make comparable demands on such information-processing skills as working memory. Each goal addresses a weak aspect of linguistic organization (e.g., story grammar, lexical knowledge). All short-term goals are related to Barry's social and vocational experiences. Therefore, each short-term goal poses a challenge for Barry.

Summary.   Taking all of the above information into consideration, we will prioritize goals 5 and 6 (involving causal and procedural language about problem-solving tasks) before beginning work on storytelling objectives (3 and 4). Decoding lexical ambiguity (goals 1 and 2) will be addressed last.

Derivation of Session Goals and Procedures

Having prioritized short-term goals, we will now present early and more advanced session objectives for each short-term goal, and we will explain how they were derived. The reader will note that selected parts of each goal and procedure statement are italicized. These are the main components that are justified in the subsequent derivation. Session goals are presented in the order in which we plan to address them.

As noted above and in Chapter 1, envisioning a sequence of session goals and related procedures involves making three major decisions: (a) what constitutes an act of learning relevant to achievement of the short-term goal, (b) what are the contextual variables that increase or decrease performance demands (i.e., that affect the relative difficulty and complexity of a task), and (c) what are the criteria for achievement of goals. We will discuss the derivation of session goals with reference to each of these decisions.

Table 7.1 presents session goals and procedures that address each short-term goal developed for Barry. The following discussion of their derivation refers to this table.

Derivation of Session Goals for Short-Term Goals 5 and 6.   Short-term goals 5 and 6 involve coordinating the use of causal and procedural explanations about concrete problem-solving tasks and producing comparatives when producing such explanations.

What Constitutes an Act of Learning Relevant to Achievement of the Short-Term Goal?   The answer to this first question relates to the principles of learning and rehabilitation first considered in the procedural approach. Given the personal theoretic orientation of the authors, constructivist-cognitive learning principles (2-4) will be referenced. According to these principles, acts of learning will involve:

- the execution of sensorimotor procedures to achieve tasks or solve problems;
- the act of reflecting, specifically on task demands (intermediate goals that need to be achieved to resolve the overall task), problems, problem-solving procedures, and causal mechanisms underlying problems or successes;
- interpersonal interactions in which conversation reflects the learner's thoughts, provokes disequilibrium and conflict, and models solutions following disequilibrium.

TABLE 7.1   Summary of Barry's Session Goals and Procedures and Derivation Factors

---

Short-Term Goal(s) Addressed: **Barry will:**

5. coordinate temporal procedural sequences and causal explanations to justify procedural sequences that direct the manipulation of concrete objects;
6. produce comparatives when explaining reasons for the resolution of problems involving the manipulation of concrete objects.

Early session goals:

  After *creating and disassembling* a *display for two appliances* (which would fall apart if too heavy an appliance were placed on one end without a *counterbalance* on the other), Barry will *tell the clinician* where to position one appliance and *explain the reason* for the arrangement *using a causal construction involving the conjunction "so"* (e.g., put the light toaster on the end so it doesn't tip over), five times in a half-hour session.

  After creating and disassembling a display for two appliances (which would fall apart if too heavy an appliance were placed on one end without a counterbalance on the other) the client will *prohibit the clinician* from positioning an appliance in a dangerous place and explain the reason for the arrangement using a *conditional-causal construction* (if-then) (e.g., "If you put the light toaster on that end it will tip over"), five times in a half-hour session.

Derivation:

  Maintaining factors addressed: cognition, psychosocial
  Principles from learning theories: constructivist-cognitive learning principles: 2, 3, 4 (Box 6.1)

  Performance demands controlled:
- level of cognitive organization inherent in the reasoning necessary to achieve the task: procedural knowledge supports causal knowledge in a novel problem-solving context and preoperational reasoning before operational reasoning (Inhelder & Piaget, 1988; Moses, 1994; Moses, Klein, & Altman, 1989);
- perceptual support and working memory capacity: the presence of perceptual support before removal of perceptual support (Moses, 1994; Moses et al., 1989);
- the organization inherent in the content/form interactions employed to describe procedures and causes: contiguous semantic relation before comparative or compensatory (Moses et al., 1989);
- lexicon: use familiar vocabulary before novel lexical items;
- task content: familiar task relevant to vocational experience before novel task.

Session *procedure:* The clinician will:

- *present a display* made of boards and several appliances (irons, toasters, telephones); the display will be constructed so that appliances will need to be distributed appropriately with reference to weight so that the *boards balance;*
- join Barry experimenting with arrangements;
- *model* "so" and "if-then" causal constructions to *explain* where and where not to place objects.

Additional derivation factors:

Principles from learning theories: constructivist-cognitive, 5 (Box 6.1)

  Early session goal (for short-term goal 6): Barry will *produce a comparative* to *direct the clinician* to *create an advertisement using a computer graphics program,* five times in a half-hour session.

(continued)

TABLE 7.1 Continued

Additional derivation factors:

Performance demands controlled:
- complexity of content/form interaction generated: produce comparatives in 3+ constituent utterances before complex semantic relations, such as causal statements involving conjunctions.

  Procedure. The clinician will *demonstrate* a *computer graphics program* for Barry. The *clinician will then present an idea* for an advertisement *comparing a large-screen TV with a small-screen TV.* The clinician will *encourage Barry to produce drawings* of the two TVs on different-sized stands or in different-sized rooms to emphasize the comparative sizes of the two TVs. The clinician will *model comparatives* in describing a display that he draws. Then he will model comparatives to *describe procedures* Barry uses as he draws the ad. Then he will *ask Barry to direct him* in drawing a display and will *encourage Barry to produce comparatives* when describing procedures (e.g., draw that line longer than that line).

  Later session goal (for short-term goal 6). Given a bank balance and purchases within or exceeding that balance, Barry will *produce a comparative to explain* why a check for the purchase either cleared or bounced, five times in a half-hour session.

Derivation:
  Maintaining factors addressed: cognition, psychosocial
  Principles from learning theories: constructivist-cognitive learning principles: 2, 3, 4 (Box 6.1)

  Performance demands controlled:
- level of cognitive organization inherent in the reasoning necessary to achieve the task: increase performance demands by expressing causal knowledge while making a comparison without first manipulating materials or referring to procedures;
- perceptual support and working memory capacity: reduce performance demands by the presence of perceptual support (checkbook) before removal of perceptual support (Moses, 1994; Moses et al., 1990);
- the organization inherent in the content/form interactions employed to describe procedures and causes: increase performance demands by requesting a comparative in context of a causal utterance after first producing a comparative in context of a 3+ constituent utterance (Moses et al., 1990);
- task content: reduce demands with familiar task relevant to social experience before novel task; increase demands with numerical/arithmetic task.

  Procedure. The clinician will *present Barry ads* for several items, including the prices of the items. The clinician will also *present an enlarged checkbook* (checks and balance sheet with balance and other payments that will be charged against the balance (e.g., rent, utilities) already entered). The clinician will *direct Barry* to choose a purchase, make out a check for it, and then compare it with his balance. The clinician will *direct Barry to predict* whether the check will clear or bounce and *to explain why* by comparing the amount of the check(s) to the balance in the checkbook (e.g., $375.00 for the suit and $800.00 for rent is more than $600.00 in the bank).

***Short-Term Goal(s) Addressed:* Barry will:**

3: Produce narratives containing one embedded causal chain (problem and problem resolution)

TABLE 7.1 Continued

Early session goals:

Given a videotape segment from the movie *Goldeneye* and the *clinician's verbal recounting* of James Bond's *goal, a problem* that arises to block the goal and the *problem resolution, Barry will identify* upon clinician request (a) Bond's original *goal,* (b) the *problem* that arises, and (c) *Bond's reaction* to the problem.

Derivation

Maintaining factors addressed: cognitive, psychosocial

Principles of learning and rehabilitation: Social cognitive principle 1 (following assumption 1), and narrative comprehension principle 3

Performance demands controlled:

- number of propositions and embeddings: present a segment relating to one superordinate proposition (main goal), one problem, and one response;
- subcategories of information (e.g., initiating events, settings, attempts, internal responses) and explicitness of events: focus on explicit main goal and problem, editing additional subcategories of information, and avoiding demands for inference making;
- perceptual support: identify content and scheme structure of observable movie before creating stories.

Session procedure:

Clinician will *verbally identify* Bond's main objective (to stop the badguys from _____) and *make verbal comments* about problems that arise and Bond's reactions. The clinician will then rerun a short segment containing a problem and Bond's reaction. The clinician will *ask Barry to identify* Bond's main goal, the problem, and Bond's response.

Additional derivation factors:

Principles of learning and rehabilitation: Social cognitive principle 3 (modeling)

Intermediate session goal;

Given a *videotape segment* of the movie *The Last Action Hero, following clinician's model,* Barry will *retell the story* identifying Scwartzenegger's *goal,* the *problem* that arises to block the goal, and the *problem resolution using the story form,* "Schwartzenegger wanted to (first goal) but (embedded problem description) so (problem resolution) and then he (resolution of original goal).

Later session goal: Barry will *tell the clinician an autobiographical story* about an *incident at work* in which he had a *goal,* encountered a *problem, resolved the problem,* and achieved his goal.

Maintaining factors addressed: cognitive, psychosocial

Principles of learning and rehabilitation: Social cognitive principle 1 (following assumption 1), and discourse comprehension principle 3

Performance demands controlled:

- number of prepositions and embeddings in the story analyzed or told/working memory: present a segment relating to one superordinate preposition (main goal), one problem, and two resolutions; request a story involving one main goal, one problem, and two resolutions;
- subcategories of information/working memory (e.g., initiating events, settings, attempts, internal responses) and explicitness of events: focus on explicit main goal and problem, editing additional subcategories of information and avoiding demands for inference making;

(continued)

TABLE 7.1   Continued

■ perceptual support: reduce performance demands by identifying content and scheme structure of observable movie before creating stories and increase performance demands by applying identified schema to create a story without perceptual support (based on memory).

Session procedure.
    Clinician will first identify a goal, problem, problem resolution, and goal resolution *after watching a segment* of *Last Action Hero* (modeling the story form, Arnold wanted to (first goal) but (embedded problem description) so (problem resolution) and then he (resolution of original goal).
    Clinician will then present another segment and *prompt* Barry to identify the goal, problem, and resolutions using the modeled format. The *clinician will expand on Barry's efforts,* modeling the form further if Barry runs into problems.
Additional derivation factors: Same as applied to goals

Short-Term Goal(s) Addressed: Barry will:

4. respond to requests for information about a character's reaction to a problem embedded in a story with evaluative comments.

Early session goal:
    Given an episode in the story *Top Gun,* Barry will *imagine "Maverick's emotional reaction to "Goose's" death* and his subsequent physical response.
Derivation factors:
    Maintaining factors addressed: Cognitive, psychosocial
    Principles of learning and rehabilitation: Neo-Piagetian constructivist

Performance demands controlled:
■ subcategories of information/working memory (e.g., initiating events, settings, attempts, internal responses) and explicitness of events: focus on three categories of information: relation between two characters, death of one character, and internal response, editing additional subcategories of information; increase performance demand by requesting that Barry make an inference (about a character's emotions);
■ perceptual support: reduce performance demands by asking Barry to comment on a familiar videotaped story.

    Session procedure: The clinician will *rerun a segment* from *Top Gun.* The clinician will *ask Barry to describe* Maverick's feelings about Goose's death. If Barry does not respond, the clinician will *model possibilities by commenting,* "If I worked with someone who was my friend and she got killed, I would probably feel sad, angry, depressed." Then the clinican will *prompt a response* from Barry.
    Later session goal: After Barry tells the clinician an embedded causal chain autobiographical story about an incident at work, Barry will *retell the story* including the *goal,* the *problem encountered,* his *feeling about the problem,* his *resolution* of the problem, his *achievement of the original goal,* and his *feeling about the problem's resolution.*

Derivation factors:
    Maintaining factors addressed: Cognitive, psychosocial
    Principles of learning and rehabilitation: Social cognitive assumption 1

(continued)

TABLE 7.1   Continued

- subcategories of information/working memory (e.g., initiating events, settings, attempts, internal responses) and explicitness of events: increase performance demands by asking Barry to include main and embedded prepositions, and internal responses;
- familiarity of information: reduce performance demands by asking for a familiar autobiographical story (already told, based on personal experience);
- perceptual support: increase performance demands by asking Barry to comment on a past event.

Session procedure. The clinician will first *model an autobiographical story* (already told) including the components identified above. The clinician will then *remind Barry of an autobiographical story he told earlier in the term* and will *request that Barry retell it,* commenting on his feelings when the problem arose and was resolved. If Barry does not remember the story, the *clinician will recall it.* If Barry tells it but omits personal reactions, the clinician will *ask "How did you feel about that?"* at the appropriate juncture (after Barry has told about the problem and then again the problem resolution).

These activities will take place in the context of tasks that are both accessible to the individual based on his current developmental level and sufficiently complex to pose developmental challenges (principle 1).

In terms of procedure planning, we make several decisions based on neo-Piagetian learning principles when delimiting a procedural approach (short-term planning phase). We will present problem-solving tasks requiring Barry to make comparisons among objects related to work in a store (e.g., involving spatial organization of materials in a warehouse or store display, etc.) and independent living experiences (e.g., furnishing and cleaning an apartment, balancing a checkbook). We will have the clinician use the techniques of narration (commenting on the client's actions), expansion (expanding on client's comments), requesting, and scaffolding (modeling and direct instruction fade as the client develops expertise) while engaged with Barry in concrete problem-solving tasks. These problem-solving tasks will focus on the generation of procedural plans.

What Are the Contextual Variables That Increase or Decrease Performance Demands?   Having identified acts of learning relevant to short-term goals 5 and 6, we identify factors that may influence the relative complexity and difficulty of the task that will be presented to Barry. We then plan a sequence of session goals and procedures by modulating these factors.

In the first part of this chapter we presented factors that could influence performance demands inherent in tasks relevant to the treatment of language-learning disabilities. With reference to those factors as they relate to baseline data from assessments of Barry, the following variables will be controlled: (a) complexity of reasoning and academic skill level inherent in tasks; (b) presence or absence of perceptual support for reasoning; (c) demands tasks make on such information-processing skills as working memory, and comparing information; (d) interpersonal interactions; and (e) relative familiarity and social/vocational functionality.

With reference to (a) and (c), tasks will be created that facilitate manipulation of the level of reasoning and amount and type of information processing required of Barry: One task will involve balancing appliances on a display; another will involve balancing a checkbook with reference to purchases made. Initially, Barry will justify procedures using simple effect-cause explanations. Later session goals will require conditional causal explanations (if-then), which requires more explicit comparative reasoning and a focus on more task components. With reference to (b), all tasks will involve the manipulation of concrete objects or graphic representations (e.g., computer, enlarged checkbook, newspaper ads providing perceptual support). With reference to (d), interactions will involve directions and prohibitions communicated to the clinician. With reference to (e), all tasks will be related to Barry's social and vocational experiences.

Derivation of Session Goals and Procedures for Short-Term Goals 3 and 4.   The second set of short-term goals to be addressed involve the production of embedded causal chain narratives and the production of evaluative comments in response to inquiries about such narratives. We prioritize the production of such narratives (short-term goal 3) as a prerequisite to making evaluative comments about components of such narratives (short-term goal 4).

What Constitutes an Act of Learning Relevant to Achievement of the Short-Term Goal?   With reference to the goal of producing causal chain narratives, we again ask, "What constitutes an act of learning relevant to achievement of this goal?" We can conceive of two answers to that question based on two learning theories. The first, based on constructivist-cognitive principles, is that the client should be provoked to create the structure without explicit instructions. Two early session goals incorporating this approach might have the client observe a videotape of a story with an embedded problem and resolution. The client would then (a) create a sequence of steps for producing a story with an embedded problem and resolution and (b) use that sequence to devise a story. A different answer, following social-cognitive learning principles, is that the client should learn a strategy for producing such a story. One strategy would be to explicitly follow a blueprint of the scheme structure presented by the clinician. A session goal following this approach might involve the use of this blueprint to identify embedded problems and problem resolutions in stories presented by the clinician. We prefer strategy training. Thus, the client will first identify embedded problems and problem resolutions in stories presented by the clinician. Later, the client will produce such stories.

What Are the Contextual Variables That Increase or Decrease Performance Demands?   With reference to the general discussion earlier in this chapter, the following variables are seen as performance demands that will be manipulated in developing session procedures relevant to the production of embedded causal chain narratives and emotional reactions to events in narratives: (a) the number and organization of propositions within the story, (b) the number of different subcategories of information (e.g., initiating events, settings, attempts, internal responses, etc.), (c) Barry's relative familiarity or ignorance of the content, and (d) the presence of perceptual support.

With reference to (a) and (b), Barry will initially produce stories with one goal, one interfering problem, and one resolution. With reference to (c), a popular movie (*Last*

Action Hero) and Barry's personal experiences (an incident at work) will provide familiar content for stories. With reference to (d), a videotaped segment from a movie and models provided by the clinician will provide perceptual support for the retelling of stories. Subsequently, Barry will recollect a past personal event without the aid of perceptual support.

Summary

In this chapter, the model of intervention planning developed over the first six chapters was applied to an adult with a language-learning disabilty. Five primary sources of information guided the development of a systematic management plan: (a) the nature of language-learning disabilities, (b) the clinician's beliefs about language and language-learning, (c) baseline data concerning the client's presenting communication characteristics, (d) non-linguistic factors contributing to the communication problem, and (e) the clinician's knowledge of normal language functioning in adults. The derivation of goals and procedures this chapter illustrate the way this information is used in the complex decision-making process that underlies intervention planning.

R E F E R E N C E S

Aram, D. M., Ekelman, B. L., & Nation, J. E. (1984). Preschoolers with language disorders. *Journal of Speech and Hearing Disorders, 27*, 232–244.

Ayres, A. J. (1975). Sensorimotor foundations of academic abilities. In W.M. Cruickshank & D.P. Hallahan (Eds.) *Perceptual and learning disabilities in children (Vol.2).* Research and theory (pp. 137–162). Syracuse, New York: Syracuse University Press.

Bamberg, M., & Damrad-Frye, R. (1991). On the ability to provide evaluative comments: Further explorations of children's narrative competencies. *Journal of Child Language,18*, 689–710.

Bigler, E. D. (1992). The neurobiology and neuropsychology of adult learning disorders. *Journal of Learning Disabilities,8*, 488–506.

Blachowicz, C. L. (1994). Problem-solving strategies for academic success. In G. P. Wallach & K. G. Butler (Eds.), Language learning disabilities in school-age children and adolescents. *Some principles and applications* (pp. 304–322). New York: Merrill.

Bloom, L., & Lahey, M. (1978). *Language development and language disorders.* New York: Wiley.

Braine, M.D.S. (1990). The "natural logic" approach to reasoning. In W.F. Overton (Ed.). *Reasoning, necessity, and logic: Developmental perspectives* (pp. 133–157). Hillsdale, New Jersey: Lawrence Erlbaum.

Brownell, H. H., & Joanette, Y. (Eds.). (1993). *Narrative discourse in neurologically impaired and normal aging adults.* San Diego, CA: Singular.

Bruner, J. (1990). *Acts of Meaning.* Cambridge, MA: Harvard University Press.

Bursuck, W. D., & Jayanthi, M. (1993). Strategy instruction: Programming for independent skill usage. In S. A. Vogel & P. B. Adelman (Eds.), *Success for college students with learning disabilities* (pp. 177-205). New York: Springer-Verlag.

Butler, D. L. (1995). Promoting strategic learning by postsecondary students with learning disabilities. *Journal of Learning Disabilities, 28* , 170–190.

Clark, F., Mailloux, Z., Parham, L. D., & Primeau, CA. (1989). Occupational therapy provision for children with learning disabilities or other mild-moderate perceptual motor deficits. *American Journal of Occupational Therapy, 45,* 1069–1074.

Crary, M. A. (1993). *Developmental speech disorders.* San Diego, CA: Singular

Crary, M. A., (1993). Clinical evaluation of developmental motor disorders. *Seminars in Speech and Language, 16,* 110–124.

Delisi, R. & Staudt, J. (1980). Individual differences in college students' performance on formal operational tasks. *Journal of Applied Developmental: Psychology, 1*, 201–208.

Fischer, K.W. (1980). A theory of cognitive development: The control and construction of a hierarchy of skills. *Psychological Review, 87*, 477–531.

Gajar, A. (1992). Adults with learning disabilities: Current and future research priorities. *Journal of Learning Disabilities, 25,* 507–519.

Gerber, P. J. (1994). Researching adults with learning disabilities. *Journal of Learning Disabilities, 27,* 6–9.

Goldstein, B. C., Harris, K. C., & Klein, M. D. (1993). Assessment of oral storytelling abilities of Latino junior high school students with learning handicaps. *Journal of Learning Disabilities, 26,* 138–143.

Gurney, D., Gersten, R., Domino, J., & Carnine, D. (1990). Story grammar: Effective literature instruction for high school students with learning disabilities. *Journal of Learning Disabilities, 23,* 335–348.

Hammill, D. D., Brown, V. L., Larsen, S. C., & Wiederholt, J. L. (1987). *Test of adolescent language.* Austin, TX: Pro-Ed.

Hammill, D. D., Leigh, J. E., McNutt, G., & Larsen, S. C. (1981). A new definition of learning disabilities. *Learning Disabilities Quarterly, 4,* 336–342.

Hegde, M. N. (1995). *Treatment procedures in communicative disorders.* San Diego, CA: Singular.

Hoffman, J., Sheldon, K. L., Minskoff, S. J., Sauter, E. W., Steidle, E. F., Baker, D. P., Brady, M. B., Echols, C. D. (1987). Needs of learning disabled adults. *Journal of Learning Disabilities, 20,* 43–52.

Inhelder, B., & Piaget, J. (1958). *The growth of logical thinking.* New York: Basic Books.

Jarrow, J. (1987). Integration of individuals with disabilities in higher education: A review of the literature. *Journal of Postsecondary Education and Disability, 5,* 38–57.

Kamhi, A., & Catts, H. (1986). Toward an understanding of developmental language and reading disorders, *Journal of Speech and hearing Disorders, 51,* 337–347.

Karmiloff-Smith, A. (1986). *Stage/structure versus phase/process in modeling linguistic and cognitive development.* Norwood, NJ: Ablex.

Klein, H. B., Moses, N. (1999). *Intervention planning for children with communication disorders.* Needham, MA: Allyn & Bacon.

Klein, H. B., Moses, N., & Altman, E. (1988). Communication of adults with learning disabilities: Self and others' perceptions. *Journal of Communication Disorders, 21,* 423-436.

Lahey, M. (1988) *Language disorders and language development. NY: MacMillan.*

Lenneberg, E., & Lenneberg, E. *(1975).* Foundations of language development: a multidisciplinary approach. (Vols I and II). New York: Academic Press.

Lewandowski, L. & Arcangelo, K. (1994). The social adjustment and self concept of adults with learning disabilities. *Journal of Learning Disabilities, 27,* 598–605.

Mandler, J. M. (1984). *Stories, scripts, and scenes: aspects of schemata theory,* Hillsdale, NJ: Erlbaum.

Martin, A. D. (1981). An examination of Wepman's thought centered therapy. In R. Chapey (Ed.).. *Language intervention strategies in adult aphasia. 1st ed. (pp. 141–154). Baltimore, MD: Williams and Wilkins.*

Milosky, L. M. (1994) Nonliteral language abilities: Seeing the forest for the trees. In G. P. Wallach & K. G. Butler (Eds.), Language learning disabilities in school-age children and adolescents: Some principles and applications (pp. 275–303). New York: Merrill.

Morris, M., & Leuenberger, J. (1990). A report of cognitive, academic, and linguistic profiles for college students with and without learning disabilities. *Journal of Learning Disabilities, 23,* 355–361.

Moses, N. (1981). Applying Piagetian Principles to the education of children with learning disabilities. *Topics in Learning and Learning Disabilities, 1,* 11–20.

Moses, N. (1990, June). *The relation between causal and procedural knowledge in adults engaged in a tractor-trailer task.* Paper presented at the Twentieth Annual Symposium of the Jean Piaget Society, Philadelphia, PA.

Moses, N. (1994). The development of procedural knowledge in adults engaged in a tractor-trailer task. *Cognitive Development, 9,* 103–130.

Moses, N., Klein, H. B., & Altman, E. K. (1990). An approach to assessing and facilitating causal language in learning disabled adults based on Piagetian theory. *Journal of Learning Disabilities, 23.* 220–229.

Moses, N., & Papish, M. (1985). Mainstreaming from a cognitive perspectives. *Learning Disabilities Quarterly,* 211–220.

Myers, P. S. (1993). Narrative expressive deficits associated with right hemisphere damage. In H.H. Brownell & Yves Joanette. Narrative discourse in neurologically impaired and normal aging adults. (pp. 279–298). San Diego; Singular.

Nation, J. E., & Aram, D. M. (1977). *Diagnosis of speech and language disorders.* St. Louis, MO: C. V. Mosby.

Nippold, M. A. (1988). *Later language development.* Austin TX: Pro Ed.

Olson, D. R. (1996). Towards a psychology of literacy: On the relations between speech and writing. *Cognition, 60,* 83–104.

Pinker, S. (1994). *The language instinct.* New York: Morrow.

Pressley, M., Forrest-Pressley, D. L., Eliot-Fausat, D., & Miller, G. (1985). Children's use of cognitive strategies, how to teach strategies, and what to do if they can't be taught. In M. Pressley & C. J. Brainerd (eds.). *Cognitive learning and memory research: Progress in cognitive developmental research* (pp. 1–48). New York: Springer-Verlag.

Prinz. W., & Saunders, A. P. (Eds.) (1986). *Cognition and motor processes.* NY: Springer-Verlag.

Reid, D. K. (1988). *Teaching the learning disabled: A cognitive developmental approach.* Needham, MA: Allyn & Bacon.

Reid, D. K., & Hresko, W. P. (1981). *A cognitive approach to learning disabilities.* NY: McGraw Hill.

Roth, F. P., & Spekman, N. J. (1986). Narrative discourse: Spontaneously generated stories of learning-disabled and normally achieving students. *Journal of Speech and Hearing disorders, 51,* 8–23.

Saracoglu, B., Minden, H., & Wilchesky, M. (1989). The adjustment of students with learning disabilities in university and its relationship to self-esteem and self-efficacy. *Journal of Learning Disabilities, 22,* 590–592.

Schank, R. C., & Abelson, R. P. 91977). *Scripts, plans, and goals: An inquiry into human understanding.* Hillsdale, NJ: Lawrence Erlbaum.

Scott, C. M. (1994). A discourse continuum for school-age students. In G. P. Wallach & K. G. Butler (Eds.). *Language learning disabilities in school-age children and adolescents: Some principles and applications* (pp. 219-252). New York: Merrill.

Seidenberg, P. (1988). Cognitive and academic instructional intervention for learning disabled adolescents. *Topics in Language Disorders, 8,* 56–71.

Shafrir, U., & Siegel, L. S. (1994). Subtypes of learning disabilities in adolescents and adults. *Journal of Learning Disabilities, 27,* 123–134.

Siegel, L. S., & Linder, B. A. (1984). Short-term memory processes in children with reading and arithmetic learning disabilities. *Developmental Psychology, 20,* 200–207.

Siegel, L. S., & Ryan, E. B. (1988). Development of grammatical sensitivity, phonological, and short-term memory skills in normally achieving and learning disabled children. *Developmental Psychology, 24,* 28–37.

Siegel, L. S., & Ryan, E. B. (1989). The development of working memory in normally achieving and subtypes of learning disabled children. *Child Development, 60,* 973–990.

Silberstein, L., Gardner, H., Phelps, E., & Winner, E. (1982). Autumn leaves and old photographs: The development of metaphor preferences. *Journal of Experimental Child Psychology, 34,* 135150.

Silliman, E. R., & Wilkinson, L. C. (1994). Discourse scaffolds for classroom intervention. In G. P. Wallach & K. G. Butler (Eds.), *Language learning disabilities in school-age children and adolescents: Some principles and applications* (pp. 27–49). New York: Merrill.

Skinner, B. F. (1957). *Verbal behavior.* New York: Appleton-Century-Crofts.

Van Riemsdijk, H., & Williams, E. (1986). *Introduction to the theory of grammar.* Cambridge, MA: MIT Press.

Spector, C. C. (1990). Linguistic humor comprehension of normal and language-impaired adolescents. *Journal of Speech and Hearing Disorders, 55,* 533–551.

Spector, C. C. (1992). Remediating humor comprehension of normal and language impaired adolescents. *Language, Speech, and hearing Services in School, 23,* 20–27.

St. Louis, K. O., & Ruscello, D. M. (1987). *Oral speech mechanism screening examination—Revised (OSMSE-R).* Austin, TX: Pro-Ed.

Stein, N. L., & Glenn, C. G. (1979). An analysis of story comprehension in elementary school children. In R. O. Freedle. (Ed.). *Advances in discourse processing, Vol. 2. New directions in discourse processing* (pp. 255–282). Norwood, NJ: Ablex.

Tallal, P., & Piercy, M. (1978). Deficits of auditory perception in children with developmental dysphasia. In M. Wyke (Ed.). *Developmental dysphasia* (pp. 63–84). London: Academic Press.

Van Kleeck, A. (1994). Metalinguistic development. In G. P. Wallach & K. G. Butler (Eds.), *Language learning disabilities in school-age children and adolescents: Some principles and applications* (pp. 53–98). New York: Merrill.

Wallach, G. P., & Butler, K. G. (1994). *Language learning disabilities in school-age children and adolescents: Some principles and applications.* New York: Merrill.

Wallach, G. P., & Miller, L. (1988). *Language intervention and academic success.* Austin, TX: Pro-Ed.

Wechsler, D. (1955). *Wechsler adult intelligence scale.* New York: The Psychological Corp.

Westby, C. E. (1985). Learning to talk—Talking to learn: Oral-literate language differences. In C. Simon (Ed.). *Communication skills and classroom success: Therapy methodologies for language-learning disabled students* (pp. 181–213). San Diego, CA: College-Hill.

White, W., Alley, G., Deshler, D., Schumaker, J., Warner, M., & Clark, F. (1982). Are there learning disabilities after high school? *Exceptional Children, 49,* 273–274.

Wiig, E. H., LaPointe, C., & Semel, E. M. (1977). Relationships among language processing and production abilities of learning disabled adolescents. Productive language abilities in learning disabled adolescents. *Journal of Learning Disabilities, 10,* 38–45.

Wiig, E. H., & Semel, E. M. (1974). Logico-garmmatical sentence comprehension by adolescents with learning disabilities. *Perceptual and Motor Skills, 38,* 1331–1334.

Wiig, E. H., & Semel, E. M. (1975). Productive language abilities in learning disabled adolescents. *Journal of Learning Disabilities, 8,* 578–586.

Wiig, E. M. & Secord, W. (1987). *The Test of Language Competence.* San Antonio, TX: Psychological Corporation.

Worden, P., & Nakamura, G. (1982). Story comprehension and recall in learning disabled versus normal college students. *Journal of Educational psychology, 74,* 633–641.

Worden, P., Malmgren, I., & Gabourie, P. (1982). Memory for stories on learning disabled adults. *Journal of Learning Disabilities, 15,* 145–152.

8

Intervention Planning for Adult Aphasia

CELIA F. STEWART

The Department of Speech-Language Pathology and Audiology, New York University and The Department of Neurology, Mount Sinai School of Medicine and Mount Sinai Hospital

CHAPTER OUTCOMES

The reader will:

1. become familiar with the various categories of aphasia and associated communication characteristics;
2. gain an understanding of the models of aphasia rehabilitation and their application to intervention planning;
3. identify factors maintaining communication problems in adults with aphasia;
4. be able to formulate a management plan about a specific client with reference to various sources of information (baseline data about language functioning and maintaining factors, and models of aphasia rehabilitation).

Introduction

Working with adults who have acquired aphasia is challenging and rewarding. It is challenging when patients' communicative performance fluctuates during sessions or between sessions; it is rewarding when patients make progress in treatment and communicate more easily. "The goals of treatment are (a) to assist people to regain as much communication as their brain damage allows and their needs drive them to, (b) to help them learn how to compensate for residual deficits, and (c) to help them learn to live in harmony with the differences between the way they were and the way they are" (Rosenbek, LaPointe, & Wertz, 1989, p. 131). This chapter examines the intervention-planning process as applied to adults with aphasia. It considers the sources of information used for this process and applies this information over three phases of intervention planning for a client with aphasia.

Patients who have acquired aphasia are different from patients who have a developmental language disorder. Individuals with a developmental disorder have always had trouble communicating. They never developed an intact communicative structure or experienced efficient communication. On the other hand, patients with aphasia had talked for most of their lives without difficulty. They had communicated when and how they wanted, tempered by the needs of the speaking situation. Accordingly, they had ordered food in restaurants, had read books, and had told their families they loved them. Unexpectedly, a medical event occurred and changed their lives by making communication effortful. Language is no longer automatic. They have difficulty understanding and producing language, and listeners often misunderstand their message. Their concentration must be split between the meaning of their speech and the way they are saying it. Individuals can be painfully aware of this change in their communicative ability and embarrassed by their awkward attempts to interact with others. In addition, they can be cognizant of the pain, frustration, and concern that their families have for their well being.

Categories of Aphasia

Aphasia is an acquired organic communicative disorder that affects comprehension and production of spoken and written communication. We can group the breakdowns into two general patterns of language loss: fluent and nonfluent. "These terms are used to distinguish features and clusters of features for the major forms of aphasia. . . . The fluency-nonfluency dichotomy, if not taken too literally, directs attention to the overlapping deficits for both encoding and decoding in aphasic patients" (Eisenson, 1984, p. 103). Most patients with aphasia have deficits in both encoding and decoding, but one deficit usually predominates.

Fluent Aphasia

Lesions in the posterior portions of the left hemisphere result in fluent aphasia. These lesions can occur in the temporal, parietal, or occipital lobes and result in Wernicke's aphasia, anomic aphasia, transcortical sensory aphasia, and conduction aphasia. Patients with fluent aphasia produce relatively fluent utterances but communicate little information. They generate words that are unrelated to the topic or that have little meaning. As a result, their speech is made up of low-content words and is empty or vague. Each type of aphasia has specific characteristics. Patients with *Wernicke's aphasia* speak fluently but their speech lacks content and can be incomprehensible. In addition, they have difficulty understanding the speech of others, their own speech, and written material. Their greatest communicative breakdown is in comprehension. *Anomic aphasia* and Wernicke's aphasia "do not have a sharp boundary, although the classic forms of each of these 'fluent aphasias' are unmistakably distinct" (Goodglass & Kaplan, 1983, p. 82). Anomic aphasia has a predominance of word-retrieval difficulties in fluent speech, and patients usually have good auditory comprehension. Individuals with *transcortical sensory aphasia* have symptoms that are similar to Wernicke's aphasia except that their ability to listen and to repeat information is not impaired (Goodglass & Kaplan, 1983). Nevertheless, they have poor comprehension. Patients with *conduction aphasia* also have fluent aphasia but their speech intelligibility is impaired because they use inappropriate words. They have severe difficulty repeating speech but can repeat numbers from a model. Patients with conduction aphasia have good comprehension and are aware of their errors.

Nonfluent Aphasia

Lesions to the anterior or frontal lobes of the left hemisphere produce two types of non-fluent aphasia: Broca's aphasia and transcortical motor aphasia. Patients with nonfluent aphasia have interruptions in their speech and produce few words and shorten and simplify their grammatical units. Their speech is sparse and contains only high-content words such as nouns and verbs. *Broca's aphasia* results in a decreased flow of speech, difficulty initiating speech, and problems "finding and sequencing of articulatory movements, and producing grammatical sequences" (Goodglass & Kaplan, 1983, p. 75). "Its essential characteristics are awkward articulation, restricted vocabulary, restriction of grammar to the simplest, most over learned forms, and relative preservation of auditory comprehension" (Goodglass & Kaplan, 1983, p. 75). Comprehension for both speech and writing are more intact than production of speech or writing. *Transcortical motor aphasia* is the second type of nonfluent aphasia and is characterized by limited speech with a preserved ability to repeat. Patients have difficulty initiating speech and responding to questions. As with Broca's aphasia, these patients have mildly impaired comprehension.

Global Aphasia and Mixed Aphasia

Some patients have serious problems with both comprehension and production of language and do not fit easily into the fluent or nonfluent categories. *Global aphasia* occurs when all aspects of language are so severely impaired that there is no longer a distinctive pattern of preserved versus impaired components" (Goodglass & Kaplan, 1983, p. 97). Some patients with global aphasia can answer "yes" or "no" appropriately to questions about themselves or their family but have difficulty understanding more complex utterances. In addition, their speech is limited to a few words or stereotypic utterances that consist of real or nonsense words. Their intonation can be preserved. *Mixed aphasia* describes a combination of Broca's aphasia and global aphasia. Patients with partially recovered global aphasia fall into this category. These patients have "the sparse output of Broca's aphasia, but . . . [their] . . . auditory comprehension is too impaired for them to be assigned comfortably to the Broca's category" (Goodglass & Kaplan, 1983, p. 97).

Models of Aphasia Rehabilitation

Aphasia models offer theoretical systems that influence observations and perceptions of patients who have aphasia (Martin, 1979). Models act as filters that focus attention on certain behaviors and away from others. Models offer guidance in describing a disorder and in planning treatment. Clinicians use theoretical models to assess efficacy of treatment and they use the responses to treatment to assess the validity of their models

(Horner & Loverso, 1991; Martin, 1981). Six models of aphasia rehabilitation used to guide aphasia treatment: will be described in this chapter: there are linguistic, stimulation-facilitation, modality, processing, minor-hemisphere mediation, and functional communication (Horner & Loverso, 1991; Horner, Loverso, & Rothi, 1994). These models are summarized in Table 8.1. As noted above, these models incorporate principles that guide both description of aphasic symptoms and the planning of rehabilitation. These models compliment the theories of learning and rehabilitation presented in Chapter 6. It is important to note that more than one model can be used in combination to plan rehabilitation for a patient.

Linguistic Model

The *linguistic model* is a relatively recent development in aphasia. Historically, we have defined language as a "socially shared code or conventional system for representing concepts through the use of arbitrary symbols and rule-governed combinations of these symbols" (Owens, 1994, p. 45). Accordingly, the linguistic model involves a disruption in lexical, semantic, and/or phonological rules (Horner & Loverso, 1991). Bloom and Lahey's (1978) definition of language is consistent with this view (see also Lahey, 1988).

In Chapter 1 of this book, Bloom and Lahey's (1978) definition of language was adopted to guide intervention planning with adults. Bloom and Lahey described three functional categories of language as content, form, and use. Content encompasses the semantics or meaning of language; form includes phonology, morphology, and syntax; and use describes the pragmatics of language. Interactions of content, form, and use govern the comprehension and expression of language. This model now influences the way aphasia is described and treated. The following are common disruptions in the processing of content/form interactions, organized according to comprehension and production.

Breakdowns in Content/Form Interactions. Aphasia causes patients to have difficulty understanding language and to communicate less information by producing significantly fewer words or fewer words with meaning, and by simplifying grammatical units (Brenneise-Sarshad, Nicholas, & Bookshire, 1991).

Comprehension. All patients with aphasia have some difficulty understanding spoken language (auditory comprehension) and written language (visual comprehension). The type of aphasia determines the severity of the comprehension deficit. Patients with fluent aphasia have greater problems understanding language, while patients with nonfluent aphasia have milder deficits with comprehension. However, one unifying characteristic of all patients with aphasia is that they have some difficulty understanding the content/form interactions of language (Chapey, 1994).

1. Auditory Comprehension. Aphasic patients have difficulty understanding both relational words, such as prepositions, conjunctions, and articles, and substantive words, such as nouns, verbs, and pronouns. Individuals with aphasia may also misunderstand the relationships of words to objects, persons, ideas, and actions, and the rules of phonology, morphol-

TABLE 8.1   From Horner and Lorerso, 1991

Stimulation-Facilitation Model

Premise: "Language is an integrative activity that is linked to sensory and motor modalities but cannot be considered bound to them" *(Duffy, 1986;* Schuell, Jenkins & Jimeniz-Pabon, 1964).
Aphasia: "A multimodality disturbance which is unidimensional in nature. . . all modalities tend to be impaired in aphasia. . . in the same manner and to about the same degree. . . . Auditory processes are at the apex of these interacting systems which aid in the acquisition, processing, and control of language" (Duffy, 1986; Schuell et al., 1964).
Treatment: Intensive auditory stimulation; meaningful material; abundant and varied material; repetitive sensory stimulation; a response for each stimulus; elicited rather than forced responses; stimulation rather than correction; stimulus is made adequate *(LaPointe, 1978;* Schuell et al., 1964).
Proponents: Duffy (1986): Schuell et al (1964); Wepman (1951, 1953).
Representative Clinical Aphasiology Research:
Cueing hierarchies and work retrieval: A therapy program *(Linebaugh & Lehner, 1997).*
Extended comprehension training reconsidered *(Marshall & Neuburger, 1984).*

Modality Model

Premise: Inner language is modality bound.
Aphasia: Aphasia can be modality specific and may be characterized as a uni- or multimodality performance deficit.
Treatment: Remediate input and output modalities, singly or in combination; reorganize modalities through selective intrasystemic or intersystemic stimulation; systematically pair weak with strong modalities to "deblock" impaired performances.
Proponents: Luria (1973); Rosenbek (1979a); Weigl and Bierwisch (1970).
Representative Clinical Aphasiology Research:
Gesture as a deblocking modality in a severe aphasic patient (Rao & Horner, 1978).
Gestural sign (Amer-Ind) as a facilitator of verbalization in patients with aphasia (Kearns, Simmons, & Sisterhen, 1982).

Linguistic Model

Premise: Language is a specialized, abstract, rule-governed cognitive activity.
Aphasia: Disrupted lexical-semantic, syntactic and/or phonological performance.
Treatment: Restore language performance by organizing stimuli according to linguistic system and linguistic system and linguistic complexity.
Proponents: Goodglass and Blumstein (1973); Jakobson (1971); Lesser (1979).
Representative Clinical Aphasiology Research:
Application of verbing strategies to aphasia treatment *(Loverso, Selinger, & Prescott, 1979).*
Generative use of locatives in multiword utterances in agrammatism: A matrix training approach *(Thompson, McReynolds, & Vance, 1982).*

Processing Model

Premise: Language reflects the operation of semiautonomous "faculties" or "modules" that carry out complex processes. The modules are highly discrete, and the relational processes are highly specific. A "central executive" governs the interaction of modules, which are probably stimulus, modality, and/or task specific.

(continued)

TABLE 8.1   Continued

Aphasia: Modular and relational processing deficits.
Treatment: Restore or compensate for language-specific and language-related processing deficits.
Proponents: Chapey (1986); Fodor (1983); Gardner (1985); Martin (1975); Porch (1986).
Representative Clinical Aphasiology Research:
Model-driven remediation of dysgraphia *Hillis & Caramazza 1987).*
A short-term memory treatment approach to the repetition deficit in conduction aphasia *(Peach, 1987).*

Minor-Hemisphere Mediation Model

Premise: The minor hemisphere has rudimentary linguistic, visual-spatial-holistic, affective-prosodic, and paralinguistic cognitive (organizational interpretive) abilities.
Aphasia: A manifestation of impaired dominant-hemisphere language and spared minor-hemisphere language.
Treatment: Use minor-hemisphere abilities to mediate (facilitate) communication through the use of imagery, drawing, melody, contextually rich stimuli, novel stimuli, and humor.
Proponents: Glass, Gazzaniga, and Premack (1973); Horner and Fedor (1983); Myers and Linebaugh (1984); Sparks, Helm and Albert (1976).
Representative Clinical Aphasiology Research:
Effects of hypnosis and imagery training on naming in aphasias *(Thompson, Hall, & Sison, 1985).*
Back to the drawing board: A treatment program for nonverbal aphasic patients *(Morgan & Helm-Estabrooks, 1987).*

Functional Communication Model

Premise: Communication reflects the application of pragmatic rules, unconstrained by modality, linguistic, or neurolinguistic considerations.
Aphasia: Ineffective or inefficient language use in natural communication contexts.
Treatment: Facilitate more normal communication by emphasizing pragmatic function over linguistic form and enhancing intermodality flexibility; establish strategies for circumventing and/or repairing communication breakdowns.
Proponents: Aten (1986); Davis and Wilcox (1981); *Holland (1980); Marshall (1983).*
Representative Clinical Aphasiology Research:
Communicative use of signs in aphasia: Is acquisition enough? *(Coehlo & Duffy, 1985).*
Treatment of aphasia through family member training *(Simmons, Kearns, & Potechin, 1978).*

ogy, and syntax. Breakdowns in auditory comprehension can occur in context of discourse, as evidenced by inappropriate responses to conversation (Chapey, 1994a). Patients show comprehension of content/form by pointing to the picture that best represents a word or sentence, answering "yes" or "no" questions, following commands, arranging cards to construct a sequenced story, and sequencing written words to form a sentence (Chapey, 1994b).

Individuals with aphasia often develop strategies to mask or compensate for comprehension breakdowns. Two common strategies are echolalia and requests for repetition of stimuli. When aphasic persons produce *echolalia,* their comprehension is impaired (Eisenson, 1984). Echolalia occurs when patients hear an utterance and reproduce it without apparent meaning.

To plan intervention for individuals with comprehension deficits, it is important to assess the accuracy, responsiveness, completeness, promptness, and efficiency of patients' responses to stimuli (Porch, 1967). Responses to stimuli can be totally correct, partially correct, or incorrect. Determining the level of correctness of the response is called *accuracy.* Some patients respond easily and others require prompts or use effort. *Responsiveness* characterizes "the ease with which the response is elicited, especially in terms of how much information the patient requires to complete the task" (Porch, 1967, p. 11). Clinicians assess *completeness* by determining "the degree to which the patient carries out the task in its entirety" (Porch, 1967, p.11). Patients can respond immediately or they can delay their responses. *Promptness* of response effects ability to communicate. Response delay interferes with the flow of conversation. Patients can have motor problems that interfere with the *efficiency* of motor responses (Porch, 1967). When clinicians assess the severity of breakdowns and describe their effect on communication, they consider these characteristics together. Obviously, if patients have difficulty with more than one area, their communication will be more severely impaired.

The consistency of errors affects recovery. During assessment clinicians manipulate the context to identify variation in the accuracy and speed of responses. When patients have inconsistency in their errors and responses, they are believed to have the potential to improve their performance on the language task. Patients who respond well to cues and have inconsistent errors have a good prognosis. In contrast, patients who do not respond to cues and show little variation in their responses have a poor prognosis.

2. Visual Comprehension. Visual comprehension impairments interfere with the association of pictures, objects, gestures, pantomime, and written stimuli with meaning (Shewan & Bandur, 1994). Patients can manifest visual comprehension deficits on picture identification, matching, picture sequencing, pantomime, and writing tasks (Glosser, Wiener, & Kaplan, 1986). These visual breakdowns can result from decreased vision, agnosia, or language impairment (Benson & Ardila, 1996).

Alexia denotes an impairment in the comprehension of written words and symbols. Some people with alexia "can read aloud but have little or no comprehension of what they are reading; others commit errors of sound and word substitution when reading aloud but have surprisingly good comprehension of the content (a disassociation between what is heard and what is seen)" (Eisenson, 1984). Patients with alexia also have difficulty recognizing words spelled orally. Alexia can occur on letters, words, sentences, paragraphs, or stories. Usually, patients with alexia make errors on the longer more complex words, and do better on the small words. Conversely, a small group make errors on the small functor words (Marshall & Newcombe, 1973). Alexia results if breakdowns occur either on association of a written word with the visual word in lexicon memory and association of meaning or on transformation of the written word into a spoken word following a graphophonemic set of rules and then association of meaning (Benson & Ardila, 1996).

Production. In addition to comprehension deficits, all patients with aphasia have difficulty with language production. Patients with nonfluent aphasia have greater difficulty with language production than patients with fluent aphasia. Production deficits affect oral, graphic, and gestural responses.

1. Oral Responses.   Patients with aphasia also produce significantly fewer words when they are talking or produce words that have little meaning or are unrelated to the topic. If they produce fewer words, they are classified as nonfluent aphasics. Conversely, if they produce words that are meaningless or are unrelated to the topic, they are classified as fluent aphasics. Breakdowns in the production of content/form interactions can be understood as involving word retrieval or agrammatism (Chapey, 1994b; Shewan & Bandur, 1994).

Anomia is one of the most frequently occurring linguistic deficits and refers to the inability to retrieve an appropriate word. Word-retrieval problems are most commonly associated with high-content words such as nouns and verbs (Kohn, Lorch, & Pearson, 1989; Miceli, Silveri, Villa, & Caramazza, 1984; Zingeser & Berndt, 1990). Anomia results in five types of verbal responses: vague imprecise words, paraphasias, neologisms, stereotypic utterances, and jargon. Anomic errors can be specific to one modality or semantic category and can respond to cues. The five types of verbal responses resulting from anomia are summarized in Table 8.2.

Anomia can be generalized to all speech or limited to one modality or semantic category. Modality-specific anomia affects one modality, such as vision, hearing, or touch. Patients with visual anomia have difficulty recalling the name of an item when seeing it. However, when they touch the object or hear a sound from it they will recall its name. For example, patients might not recall the word "watch" until they hold one in their hand and listen to it tick. A category-specific anomia occurs in only one semantic category such as proper names, occupational jargon, colors, foods, or body parts. One patient, with a category-specific aphasia for body parts, frequently calls his feet "shoes."

The second major category of production deficit affecting content/form interactions is *agrammatism.* Agrammatism results when patients produce syntactic errors, drop words out of sentences, and become hesitant with their speech (Caramazza & Zurif, 1976; Heilman & Scholes, 1976). The words most commonly omitted are function words including articles, prepositions, and conjunctions (Chapey, 1994b). Patients who have agrammatism are classified as nonfluent aphasics because their speech is hesitant and punctuated with unexpected pauses. Patients with agrammatism are usually aware of their errors and distressed by them. In oral language, agrammatism can result in telegraphic speech made up of short phrases and high-content words. Language production deficits are also observable in graphic and gestural responses.

*2. Graphic Responses.   "*Agraphic aphasia is a disorder in the retrieval of language in written form" (Eisenson, 1984, p. 221). Patients with agraphia have difficulty recalling the appropriate words, spelling, or sequence of letters for words and make written grammatical errors. Nonlinguistic deficits including motor weakness or apraxia can accompany the language deficit. Persons with agraphia can also have difficulty copying shapes, letters, words, or sentences from a model; writing their own signature and address; writing from dictation; and spontaneously writing numbers, letters of the alphabet, and a narrative about a picture (Benson & Ardila, 1996). Patients with apraxia (discussed below) can also have difficulty using gestures (Kaplan, 1991).

*3. Gestural Responses.   *Gestures include eye contact, facial expression, pantomime, hand signals, signs, and systematic codes (Shewan & Bandur, 1994). Gestural responses are usually less impaired than oral or graphic responses. Consequently, gestural

---

TABLE 8.2   Five Response Types Resulting from Anomia

---

1. *Imprecise words.*This term refers to the use of *vague or imprecise words. General terms* (such as "thing"), object functions, or other types of circumlocutions are substituted for target words (Chapey, 1994b). For example, the word "dog" might be replaced by the phrase "you know, the little guy at home." Aphasic patients who fail to retrieve the name for a pictured object commonly succeed in finding the full name-word when prompted with the initial sound (Wingfield, Goodglass, & Smith, 1990). One type of anomia, the "tip of the tongue phenomena," occurs when patients search for a word but it remains just beyond their reach (Kremin, 1993).

2. *Paraphasias.* Anomia can result in *paraphasias* where the speaker says a related word rather than the intended one. We observe two types of paraphasia: verbal and literal. Verbal paraphasic errors occur when a patient unintentionally uses a word similar to the intended word such as "chair" for "table." One of our patients called all of the female doctors and nurses "sister" and all of the male doctors and nurses "brother." The staff had puzzled over these titles until we learned that this patient was a priest. Literal paraphasias occur when an individual "produces syllables in the wrong order or distorts his sounds with unintended sounds" (Goodglass & Kaplan, 1983, p.8). When the distortions are mild, the target word remains recognizable. If the distortions become severe, however, neologisms result.

3. *Neolgisms. Neologisms* occur when patients unintentionally invent new words. On closer examination, neologisms often involve the introduction of extraneous phonemes or the transposition of phonemes "so that less than half the intended word is discernible" (Goodglass and Kaplan, 1983, p. 36). Patients can produce baffling neologisms such as "hoedoe."

4. *Sterotypic utterances.* Another result of anomia is the use of *stereotypic utterances;* i.e., recurrent syllables or words used in response to all stimuli. Stereotypic utterances include jargon, profanity, and words or phrases used without their intended meaning. Frequently patients are unaware of their stereotypic responses.

5. *Jargon.* Anomia can also result in *jargon* that is a generally free-flowing, unintelligible speech made up of neologisms and real words. Albert, Goodglass, Helm, Rubens, and Alexander (1981) described jargon as speech containing a combination of phonemic and semantic errors. We classify jargon as a symptom of fluent aphasia. Often, patients who are using jargon are unaware that listeners do not understand their speech. Patients who use jargon frequently act as though the listener should pay better attention. When the listener repeats some jargon-filled speech, sometimes the patient continues talking as though the speech were intelligible and sometimes the patient reacts as though it is unintelligible. Two types of jargon occur: *semantic* and *neologistic.* Semantic jargon contains a predominance of paraphasic errors on high-content words, while neologistic jargon contains a predominance of neologistic words.

---

language production is used frequently to compensate for difficulty with the production of oral language (Hadar, 1991; Porch, 1967). Many patients use gestures in various ways: to substitute for oral communication, to supplement oral speech, or to cue retrieval of oral language (Shewan & Bandur, 1994). These patients have elaborate gestures to communicate ideas. They use a combination of facial expressions, conventional gestures, and gestures they have developed on their own or learned in treatment including the Amer-Ind sign system (Skelly, 1979).

Breakdowns in Use.   The use of language refers to the way speakers apply the guide-lines that determine how and what they choose to say based on the environment, intent, pragmatic rules, and propositionality of the utterance (Chapey, 1994b; Craig, 1983; Prutting & Kirchner, 1983; Rice, 1984). Patients with aphasia have difficulty modifying their speech to adapt to the linguistic and nonlinguistic contexts of the language interaction (Muma, 1975). Individuals with nonfluent aphasia are aware of environmental changes but are restricted in the words and syntactic structures available, and they manifest increased effort when speaking. Consequently, they do not modify their language to adapt to a changing environment and so they have a rigid use of language. In contrast, patients with fluent aphasia are often unaware of their speaking environment or the listener's intent and so do not attempt to modify their language to match the environment. Therefore, patients with both fluent and nonfluent aphasia have a limited ability to adapt language.

Environmental Factors.   Crystal (1988) described seven factors that cause speakers to modify their language to meet the changing requirements of the *environment:* personal, regional, social, setting, mode, task, and audience. Skillful speakers modify their language production based on these factors. Each of these factors describes a characteristic of the speaking environment that changes the way the words are chosen or the reason for the interaction. When individuals do not modify their speech in response to these cues, the efficiency of communication suffers.

Almost half the environmental factors are internal to the speaker. These include per-sonal, regional, and social variables. *Personal* refers to using language that is appropriate to the speaker's age and sex. For instance, if adults talk like children, their communication will be impaired. Persons who modify their dialect to meet the speaking situation are mak-ing *regional* modifications. They want to use appropriate dialects for situations including speed of utterance, accent, and personal space. Speakers make *social* adjustments so their speech is appropriate to their occupation and social status.

Some environmental factors that are external to the speaker affect the type of lan-guage used including setting, mode, task, and audience. Speakers respond to the *setting* by using speech that is appropriate to the location. They use language differently at home and in a hospital. The use of slang, however, might be common to both settings, although slang would be inappropriate in a formal presentation. Adults typically adapt to the sophistica-tion of the environment. They order food in an elegant restaurant by saying the name of the dish not by holding up two fingers and calling out "number two."

Mode describes the method of communication such as speaking, listening, writing, reading, or gesturing matched it to the appropriate task and audience. The *task* describes the type of speech applied to the situation such as conversation or narration. In formal lec-tures at school, individuals use narration, but in conversation they would sound boring if they spoke mainly in narration. *Audience* describes the speaking partner (Crystal, 1988). For instance, different types of language are used when individuals talk with their boss and with their children. Skilled speakers adjust to all these factors, but when individuals have aphasia, they can no longer make these adjustments.

Intent.   The intent of the speaker affects language use. Individuals use language to interact socially with others, to regulate other people's behavior, to protest or argue, to fulfill the speaker's needs, and to get help (Chapey, 1994b; Dore, 1974; Searle, 1969). Competent speakers plan their language production to obtain their desired goals. People communicate differently based on their intent and their beliefs about the best way to reach their goal.

People modify their language production based on purpose. When they want to have *social interaction with others,* they use greetings and respond to others' speech with interest (Dore, 1974; Searle, 1969). They *regulate others' behavior* by making requests, asking questions, and giving advice or warnings (Dore, 1974; Searle, 1969). Speakers will protest or argue when they complain or attempt to persuade others to embrace their ideas by expressing their opposing thoughts. In addition, they *fulfill their needs* by requesting help or telling someone about their desires (Chapey, 1994b; Schlesinger, 1971). It is difficult for patients with aphasia to modify their language to match the intent of their communication. Patients with nonfluent aphasia have difficulty adjusting their interactions because of their limited word-retrieval skills and rigid language use. Conversely, patients with fluent aphasia can adapt to their own internal changes but they cannot adapt to change in others because they are oblivious to other people's changes in intent. When people have aphasia, they have limited ability to modify their language to match their intent and so they can be perceived as pushy, demanding, or inappropriate.

Topic Management Skills.   Four aspects of topic management are topic introduction, topic maintenance, topic shift, and topic repair. *Topic introduction* refers to the initiation of speech and topics that are appropriate for the conversation. "Usually, the communication act should contain new, relevant, and what is judged to be sincerely wanted information" (Chapey, 1994b, p. 231). *Topic maintenance* includes comprehending the topic, making appropriate responses to the topic, and staying on the topic for an appropriate period. The speaker and listener switch rolls when the listener responds to the speaker's message (Chapey, 1994b). Topic maintenance requires that each message share the same topic and that each following message add information to the prior communication act (Chapey, 1994b). For patients to *shift topics,* they must be aware that the topic has shifted and recognize the need to move onto the new topic. Breakdowns occur when patients make responses that are only tangentially related to the topic or when they change the topic abruptly. Patients with fluent aphasia have difficulty with topic shifts and will continue a topic after it has changed.

Pragmatic rules also guide the *repair* of communicative breakdowns. To recognize that breakdown has occurred, speakers must recognize that listeners did not understand the intent of the message (Chapey, 1994b). When breakdowns occur speakers reword or restate their message or tell listeners about the misunderstanding. If listeners are aware that they did not understand, they might ask speakers to repeat their message. Some patients are aware of communicative breakdowns and others are not (Rezania, Hambrecht, & Quist, 1989). When aphasics are aware of their breakdowns, they will try to reword their initial messages. However, linguistic difficulties such as word-retrieval problems, grammatical errors, and maintaining factors including short-term memory and inductive and deductive thinking limit their ability to restate their message (Rezania et al., 1989). Conversely, patients with fluent aphasia are unaware of their errors and they will not attempt to repair communication breakdown.

Propositionality.   The final aspect of language use to be discussed is *propositionality* of the message. Highly propositional language is important and meaningful, whereas nonpropositional language is linguistically unimportant and is repeated with little awareness or meaning. "Propositional utterances call for a creative formulation of words with specific and appropriate regard to the situation and do not come 'ready made' or prefomulated by the speaker" (Eisenson, 1984, p. 6). The propositional level of speech is related to the nature and significance of the way the utterance is used (Jackson, 1879). "Thus, 'You go to hell' produced by a speaker who is angry or irritated has a different significance from the same sequence of words spoken by a fundamentalist minister in response to the question, 'Reverend, that will happen to me if I continue to be a sinner?'" (Eisenson, 1984, p. 6). Profanities produced when someone is angry or irritated have low propositional value.

Implications for Intervention Planning.   The linguistic model is applicable to both goal and procedure planning. A consideration of the breakdown in content/form/use interactions provides a basis for goal planning, especially at the long- and short-term planning phases. The linguistic model, particularly the use aspect, also has implications for procedure planning. Since patients communicate best in familiar contexts, identifying the environment that is most conducive to communication is important. During assessment, clinicians identify the environmental factors that help a specific patient and apply them in rehabilitation. For example, if a patient has always used nonstandard English, the clinician plans language stimulation in nonstandard English. When a patient is bilingual, the clinician speaks in the patient's dominant language but accepts responses in either language. On the other hand, if the patient has severe aphasia and communicates by using a combination of gestures and speech, the clinician assesses the effectiveness of the gestures along with the patient's verbal communication. Role playing is an effective way to assess communication skills in different environments and to assess language use (Armus, Bookshire, & Nicholas, 1989).

Stimulation-Facilitation Model

Overview.   The linguistic model reviewed above guides the clinician in planning goals. That is because the linguistic model identifies aspects or components of communication that need to be targeted during treatment. Contrastively, the models presented next contribute primarily to procedure planning. These models identify the factors that may be maintaining the disorder as well as the process of rehabilitation. The first of these approaches to be reviewed is the *stimulation-facilitation model.* This widely used model derives from the work of Wepman (1951) and Schuell, Jenkins, and Jimenez-Pabon (1964). This model regards aphasia as an obstacle to language processing that results from injury to the brain. The focus is on stimulating disrupted language processes rather than reeducating or correcting language. This model does not facilitate new learning or new vocabulary (Darley, 1972; Wepman, 1951). The role of the clinician is to "communicate with the patient and to stimulate disrupted processes to function maximally" (Schuell et al., 1964, p. 338). "Clinical time should be spent in stimulation and in eliciting language, not in forcing patients to struggle for responses or in correcting erroneous ones" (Schuell et al.,1964, p. 342).

Schuell et al. (1964) defined "aphasia as a general language deficit that crosses all language modalities and may or may not be complicated by other sequelae of brain damage" (p. 133). The language modalities referred to are comprehension of spoken and written language and production of speech and writing. The language deficit is characterized as a "reduction in available vocabulary, impaired verbal retention span, and impaired perception and production of messages, perhaps secondary to impairment of the first two dimensions" (Schuell et al., 1964, p. 113).

Implications for Intervention Planning. The stimulation approach "employs strong, controlled, and intensive auditory stimulation of the impaired symbol system as the primary tool to facilitate and maximize the patient's recognition and recovery of language" (Duffy, 1994, p. 148). Thus, this approach has primarily procedural implications. It promotes sensory stimulation as the method for "making complex events happen in the brain" (Schuell et al., 1964, p. 338). One principle of this model is that stimulation must be adequate to reach the brain. Carefully controlling length, speed, loudness, familiarity, meaningfulness, and repetitiveness can strengthen stimuli (Darley, 1972; Wepman, 1976). Using combined auditory and visual stimulation also strengthens stimuli.

This model is effective with patients who have mild and moderate aphasia. On the other hand, severe aphasia "may sharply limit the use of the stimulation approach and reduce treatment to a short-term program aimed at improvement of comprehension, counseling of the patient and family, and the prevention of withdrawal and depression" (Duffy, 1994, p. 149).

Modality Model

Overview. The *modality model* "assumes that a seriously impaired function cannot be restored through direct stimulation of the defective modality. Resumption of function can be accomplished more effectively by bypassing defective systems and establishing 'new circuitry'" (Eisenson, 1984, p. 171). Luria (1966) described a primary function of the nervous system as receiving and processing incoming "information within channels or systems that are specific to the type of energy picked up from the environment. . . . Each modality consists of a sense organ peripherally, a sensory nerve or projection pathway, a primary cortex, and an associated secondary cortex" (Kagan & Saling, 1988, p. 7). Sensation and perception occur along modality-specific channels and breakdowns in a channel can result in communicative breakdowns (Luria, 1970). This model maintains that functional reorganization of language areas in the brain occurs during the recovery from aphasia (Benson & Ardila, 1996; Luria, 1963).

The modality model is most effective with patients who have mild to severe aphasia and have some defective modality-processing components and some well-preserved components (Seron & de Partz, 1993). Patients can use the preserved modalities to compensate for the impaired modalities and can rely on functional reorganization that occurs when patients develop new strategies to compensate for language deficits (Benson & Ardila, 1996). "The term functional reorganization implies that more or less the same behavior can be produced by recruiting other processing mechanisms. Functional reestablishment refers to reteaching the defective processes or representations" (Seron & de Partz, 1993). For instance, "patients with phonemic discrimination deficits learn to rely on proprioception and visual information to compensate for their deficits; patients with difficulties in expository language rely on automatized and emotional language" (Benson & Ardila, 1996, p. 346).

Implications for Intervention Planning. The modality model also focuses primarily on procedural applications. This model describes the clinician's roles during intervention. The stage of the disorder differentiates these roles (Rosenbek, 1978). During the acute stage the clinician has two roles: *facilitator* and *prophylactic.* "As facilitator, he systematically elicits and reinforces speech, using whatever stimuli, modes, and methods are most effective" (Rosenbek, 1978, p. 194). The clinician establishes the communicative conditions so that "an intact or nearly intact phonologic system is deblocked" (Rosenbek, 1978, p. 194). The prophylactic portions of treatment focus on improving the patient's attitude toward his communicative deficit to prevent the patient from forming bad habits that include using an effortful struggle during communication or reverting to silence rather than talking (Rosenbek, 1978).

During the chronic stage, treatment focuses on functional reorganization (Luria, 1970). Functional reorganization can result in using a different modality or simplifying the response in the same modality. Therefore, intact modalities are used to facilitate or deblock the modalities that are functioning at less than optimum levels (LaPointe, 1977). For example, in nonfluent aphasia, producing conversational speech is difficult for patients, but automatic sequences are produced more easily. Consequently, automatic speech can be used to facilitate speech for patients with nonfluent aphasia (Sarno, 1991). An example of a simpler level in the same modality involves using a primitive, reflexive response to elicit a response and then shifting "from the reflex level to one which the patient is able to control" (Kagan & Saling, 1988, p. 66).

Processing Model

Overview. The *processing model* includes cognition as part of communication. Normal communication is the "efficient action and interaction of the cognitive processes which support language behavior within and by the organism" (Martin, 1979, p. 157). Aphasia results from a reduction of the efficiency and interaction of these processes that support language behavior including executive function, problem solving, and memory skills (Brown, 1972; Chapey, 1994; Martin, 1979).

Processing breakdowns in naming can be explained by identifying disruptions in several levels of the cognitive processes (Hillis, 1994). For example, at the association level, breakdowns can result because the specific picture, at this angle, in this size, or with this type material such as wood or plastic does not trigger a memory or recognition of the object (Hillis, 1994). Another source of word-retrieval deficits can result from difficulty in associating multiple components of words (semantic, phonological, or motor) in response to pictures or objects (Hillis, 1994). Once the underlying deficit is identified, treatment is directed at the process where the breakdown occurs. This cognitive model defines treatment as an "attempt to manipulate and to excite the action and interaction of the cognitive processes which support language behavior within and by the organism so as to maximize their effective usage" (Martin, 1979, pp. 157-158). Patients who are medically stable and have variety in the accuracy of their responses benefit from this type of treatment (Porch, 1994).

Implications for Intervention Planning.   The processing model has implications for both goal and procedure planning. To plan treatment with this model, the processing problems that remain intact and those that are impaired need to be identified. The underlying cognitive deficit can be worked on to enhance language. According to the model of intervention planning presented in this book, goals that address information-processing skills are formulated during the session phase of intervention (see Chapters 1, 2, and 6). Hillis (1994) criticized treatment that focuses on improving a single cognitive mechanism of a complex language task. According to Hillis, "improved functioning of the single targeted aspect of language will not always improve use of language in everyday situations" (1994, p. 216). However, if additional treatment is targeted at the other cognitive processes, communication will be improved.

Minor-Hemisphere Mediation Model

Overview.   The *minor-hemisphere mediation model* rests upon two fundamental assumptions. The first assumption is "that the right hemisphere processes certain kinds of cognitive material in a relatively superior way, and that for aphasic individuals with damage limited to the left hemisphere, the right hemisphere can be used to *compensate* for the lost language functions" (Code, 1994, p. 380). A second assumption is that, "following damage to the left, the right hemisphere can be encouraged to restore lost functions" (Code, 1994, p. 380). The right hemisphere has the ability to process precise sequencing in space and timing for gesturing, speaking, and writing (Stein, 1988). In addition, the right hemisphere can process affirmatives, negatives, concrete nouns, and adjective phrases (Code, 1994). The right brain "has a vocabulary roughly equivalent to a 13-year-old child, but its syntactic competence is around the 5-year-old level. . . . [It] appears to possess little or no facility for processing phonological and phonetic information" (Code, 1994, p. 381). The right brain also processes the suprasegmental features of prosody and emotional language (Stein, 1988).

Implications for Intervention Planning.   Rehabilitation guided by the minor-hemisphere model employs a set of associated procedures. These focus on visual-spatial processing, prosody, and the rudimentary language abilities of the right hemisphere to compensate for deficits in the left hemisphere. Patients who have a wide range of disabilities can benefit from stimulation of the minor-hemisphere. Rehabilitation techniques associated with the minor-hemisphere mediation model include songs, recitation, melodic intonation therapy (Sparks & Holland, 1976), and humor. These techniques can be used to compensate for the aphasia or to restore function by retraining the right hemisphere to assume more functions of language (Code, 1994).

Functional Communication Model

Overview.   The *functional communication model* concentrates on improving the patient's "abilities rather than their linguistic accuracy or language functions per se, and uses a variety of approaches that encourage and reinforce conversational exchange of information in natural contexts" (Sasanuma, 1993, p. 185). This model offers a pragmatic perspective on *how* language is used in communication (Wilcox, 1983). "This is in direct contrast to a linguistic analysis which focuses on *what* language is used in communication" (Wilcox, 1983, p. 36). "In actual life 'functional communication' must be individually defined for each patient and must consider the severity of the communicative disturbance, the premorbid and present self-chosen lifestyle of the patient, and the setting in which that person will ultimately reside" (Aten, 1994, p. 292). For example, patients with severe aphasia can be in nursing homes and only communicate basic needs such as hunger or thirst, while patients with mild aphasia can return to work and communicate elaborate ideas (Aten, 1994; Chapey, 1994).

Implications for Intervention Planning. Functional treatment has implications for goal and procedure planning. At all phases of intervention planning, goals can target communication in social contexts and everyday activities (Aten, 1994). Stimulating communication through verbal and nonverbal means can facilitate pragmatic goals including gestures, writing, and pantomime, while less emphasis is placed on linguistic accuracy (Davis & Wilcox, 1981). Since patients rarely recover to their premorbid level, but many have preserved discourse and pragmatic abilities, functional stimulation is appropriate for patients with a large range of severity of impairment (Sasanuma, 1993).

Summary

Six models of aphasia rehabilitation have been discussed. These models contribute to goal and procedure planning at each phase of the planning process. With reference to procedure planning, these models suggest materials and client-clinician interactions. Rather than creating original material, the clinician can select published procedures such as computer applications, Amer-Ind Code (Skelly, 1979), melodic intonation therapy, Helm Elicited Language Program for Syntax Stimulation (Helm-Estabrooks, 1981), Promoting Aphasic's Communication Effectiveness (Davis & Wilcox, 1981), and visual action therapy (Helm-Estabrooks & Albert, 1991). These procedures have specific programmed steps and are designed to be used with patients who have distinctive types of deficits.

The rehabilitation models discussed above were described separately; however, they complement each other and can be used together in the planning process. Some of the rehabilitation models specify factors that may maintain communication problems. A more explicit discussion of factors possibly maintaining a communication disorder follows.

Maintaining Factors

Another information source for planning intervention comprises those factors maintaining the disorder. Injury to the brain that causes linguistic deficits can also cause health problems, sensorimotor deficits, decreased cognitive skills, and psychosocial changes. These nonlinguistic impairments, along with the patient's premorbid status, can affect communication and can impede rehabilitation of the communicative disorder. Maintaining factors interfere directly by making it more difficult for the patient to communicate and indirectly by decreasing motivation. As a result, the maintaining factors must be understood and their effects must be considered when planning goals and procedures.

Health Factors

Health problems can limit a patient's ability to participate in and benefit from treatment. Health problems can be a result of the brain damage that causes the aphasia or a chronic preexisting problem that is independent of the injury to the brain. Whatever the cause of the health problem, the speech-language pathologist needs to understand the effect of the medical problem on the patient's ability to communicate and recover from the aphasia.

Chronic Preexisting Medical Conditions.   Chronic preexisting medical conditions can interfere with a patient's ability to attend treatment and benefit from stimulation. When patients have conditions such as diabetes, chronic obstructive pulmonary disease, or arthritis, they might experience fatigue, have trouble walking, or have frequent appointments with other professionals. They can find it burdensome to schedule language rehabilitation or to practice homework. For rehabilitation to be effective, patients, and clinicians need to plan treatment to minimize these problems.

Medical Conditions from Brain Injury.   Brain injury results from cerebrovascular accidents (embolisms, thrombolisms, aneurysms, and hemorrhages) including tumors, infectious diseases, degenerative diseases, and trauma. Of these medical conditions, the cerebrovascular accidents are the most common (Davis, 1993; Eisenson, 1984). Adults who have language disorders that result from tumors, infectious diseases, degenerative diseases, and trauma have a better prognosis for language recovery than those with cardiovascular accidents (Butfield & Zangwill, 1946; Keenan & Brassell, 1974; Kertesz, Harlock, & Coates, 1979; Kertesz & McCabe, 1977). Despite their cause, health problems interfere with recovery from aphasia. Clinicians must be aware of the medical problems and plan treatment so that the medical problems have a minimum effect on language recovery.

When a patient has an acute illness such as a stroke, the initial concern is for survival. When the patient is stable and survival is no longer the issue, communicative rehabilitation begins. However, the residual health problems can complicate intervention planning and make communicative disorders appear more serious. Therefore, clinicians must be cautious not to diagnose problems that result from health issues as language disorders.

The location and size of the damage to the brain influence the prognosis. Usually, the larger the lesion, the worse the prognosis (Sands, Sarno, & Levita, 1971). There are exceptions to this rule, however. For example, a small lesion in Wernicke's area "is more disruptive for language than a larger lesion in the frontal lobes" (Basso, 1992, p. 341). Nevertheless, a lesion in Wernicke's area is often associated with good spontaneous recovery. Therefore, the overall recovery of language can be good for patients with Wernicke's aphasia although the initial disruption to language is great (Basso, 1992, p. 342).

Spontaneous Recovery.   Patients with aphasia have a period of spontaneous recovery following brain injury. The greatest amount of spontaneous recovery occurs during the first months after the onset of aphasia (Dordain & Norman, 1981; Hagen, 1973; Sarno & Levita, 1971; Vignolo, 1964). Spontaneous recovery continues at a slower rate for many months or years (Sands, Sarno, & Shankweiler, 1969; Sarno, Silverman, & Sands, 1970). During early recovery, greater improvement occurs in comprehension than in language production (Kenin & Swisher, 1972). Since patients with comprehension deficits make more progress than patients with anomia, anomia is one of the most frequently observed residual deficits after rehabilitation.

Adults with acquired aphasia seldom recover fully because their nervous systems are damaged. The severity of the initial aphasia affects the outcome of treatment. Individuals who start intervention with severe aphasia probably have more severe residual disorders than those who begin with mild aphasia. In addition, adults with milder disorders have a greater chance for recovery because the damage is milder (Basso, Capitani, & Vignolo, 1979; Sands et al., 1969; Schuell, 1955).

Implications for Intervention Planning.   Health factors affect both goal and procedure planning. The patient's prognosis (i.e., expectations for long-term changes) is affected by health conditions. Information about a patient's health also has implications for procedure planning. For example, assessment and treatment of an inpatient would involve shorter tests, the screening of several areas in a short time, and shorter treatment sessions. The clinician's schedule must also be modified to accommodate the effect of the medication on communcation skills.

Sensorimotor Deficits

Sensorimotor deficits are the second type of maintaining factor. These deficits impair the patient's ability to receive the stimuli, recognize it, and produce precise motor responses. Sensorimotor deficits include decreased reception of sensation, paralysis or paresis, dysarthria, and apraxia. Impairment to the sensorimotor functions can mimic aphasia. Consequently, clinicians must be careful during assessment to differentiate language breakdowns that result from a linguistic problem and breakdowns that result from senso-rimotor deficits. Not only can sensorimotor deficits impair communication, they can also impede rehabilitation.

Decreased Reception of Sensation.   As patients age, changes can occur in their sensory systems that cause *decreased reception of sensation.* The way patients hear, see, feel, smell, and taste stimuli are altered by sensory changes. The two sensory changes that have the great-est effect on communication are decreased hearing and vision. *Hearing impairments* inter-fere with communication directly. If patients cannot hear, they will have difficulty under-standing auditory stimuli and cues. Therefore, differentiating language problems from hearing problems is important. Hearing problems can occur as part of aging or from injury to the brain. Clinicians should evaluate patients who have hearing losses when they are wear-ing their hearing aids or when using an amplifier to limit the effect of the sensory deficit.

The second sensory loss, *decreased vision,* interferes with communication by cutting down on visual cues such as facial expression and gestures and by making it difficult to read and find objects. Some common causes of decreased vision are nearsightedness, farsight-edness, and cataracts. In addition, patients with aphasia can have a visual field cut. Near-sightedness, farsightedness, and cataracts cause a general loss of visual acuity, whereas visual field cuts cause a loss of part of a visual field. Some patients are aware of their blind areas and others are unaware. During assessment clinicians must learn whether errors of comprehension are due to linguistic problems or to auditory and visual deficits. Therefore, patients with vision problems must wear glasses during assessment or stimuli must be large enough for them to see. For patients with visual field cuts, stimuli must be placed in a location where they can be seen. During treatment clinicians must plan goals and procedures so that the patient's sensory losses will not interfere with rehabilitation.

Paralysis or Paresis. Another type of sensorimotor deficit called *paralysis or paresis* interferes with muscle power or function. Paralysis is a loss of movement and paresis is a partial loss of movement. Patients with paralysis are unable to perform voluntary, automatic, or reflexive movements because of muscle weakness or loss of muscle function; patients with paresis have decreased strength, precision, speed, and accuracy (Darley, Aronson, & Brown, 1975).

If the muscles of speech and swallowing are weakened or paralyzed, the precision of speech, facial expression, and swallowing will be impaired (Darley et al., 1975). Therefore, clinicians evaluate the structure and function of the respiratory, phonatory, articulatory, chewing, and swallowing muscles. Weakness in the muscles of respiration decreases the loudness of the speech and shortens the length of utterances (Darley et al., 1975). Deficiency in the muscles of phonation results in a breathy vocal quality, decreased loudness, short phrases, and a weak cough (Darley et al., 1975). Impairment to the muscles of articulation and mastication cause imprecise articulation and difficulty with chewing and manipulating food. Injury to the swallowing muscles causes saliva to pool in the mouth and pharynx and causes aspiration of food and liquids into the lungs. When saliva pools in the mouth, it is more difficult to speak. If any of these motor-speech and swallowing disorders occur simultaneously, their combined effect is worse than if they occurred alone (Darley et al., 1975).

Impaired facial expression decreases nonlinguistic cues and impairs the individual's ability to express feelings such as sarcasm, friendliness, or interest in the topic. Aphasic patients frequently increase their use of gestures or facial expressions to compensate for disorders of content, form, and use. As a result, clinicians must assess whether patients can use facial expressions to compensate for the communicative breakdown.

Decreased general body stability and motor control reduces patients' ability to maintain upright posture and adequate respiration, use gestures, and write. Poor body stability and balance impair patients' ability to support the chest wall adequately to maintain sufficient respiration for speech. Patients who have a weakened or paralyzed arm will make fewer gestures and have difficulty writing. When patients gesture infrequently, they have reduced effectiveness and completeness of communication and they have more difficulty expressing their messages. In addition, some patients use gestures and writing to supplement their impaired communicative skills. Consequently, paralysis of an arm hinders these compensatory techniques.

Dysarthria. *Dysarthria* is a motor-speech disorder caused by muscle weakness, slowness, or incoordination resulting in changes in respiration, phonation, resonation, and prosody (Darley et al., 1975). Dysarthria results from damage to the central or peripheral nervous system. Patients with dysarthria have impairment in the control of the muscles for both spontaneous and volitional movements, and both types of movements have the same amount of imprecision. In addition, when patients have dysarthria their speech breakdowns are consistent from one production to the next.

Voice, articulation, fluency, and intelligibility can be impaired because of dysarthria. Impairment in phonation results in altered vocal intensity, fundamental frequency, vocal quality, timing, position of the vocal folds during phonation, and resistance to aerodynamic pressures (Yorkston, Beukelman, & Bell, 1988). Articulatory disorders result in changes in the rate and precision of production of phonemes (Yorkston et al., 1988). Decreased fluency following injury to the brain, is associated with nonfluent aphasia (Helm-Estabrooks, 1986). The overall intelligibility of speech results from a combination of the efficiency of the production of voice, articulation, and fluency.

Dysarthria is a motor-speech deficit that can impair intelligibility. Patients with unclear speech might simplify the content/form of their speech to improve intelligibility. Therefore, clinicians must manipulate communication in the assessment to evaluate the effects of intelligibility on language function. Some patients begin to use more complex language structures when the intelligibility of their speech improves.

Apraxia.   *Apraxia* is another type of motor-speech disorder that results from a sensori-motor deficit. An impairment in planning motor activity causes apraxia (Darley et. al, 1975). Patients with apraxia do not have paralysis, paresis, or weakness. They spontaneously move their body in desired ways, but they do not perform these same movements on command. In other words, they chew and swallow spontaneously when eating; however, they do not chew in imitation or on command. Therefore, spontaneous movements are preserved and volitional movements are impaired. In addition, the pattern of apraxic breakdowns is inconsistent and varies from one production to the next.

Three types of apraxia have been recognized: oral apraxia, speech apraxia, and limb apraxia. The term *oral apraxia* describes an impairment in the planning of nonspeech oral movements. Patients with oral apraxia smile spontaneously and pucker up for kisses but do not do these same movements volitionally. Patients with oral apraxia may or may not have difficulty making speech movements. Apraxia that interferes with temporal and spatial programming of speech sounds is termed *speech apraxia.* Patients with speech apraxia say words spontaneously but do not say the same words on command or in imitation. They grope around and try to find the articulatory positions for the word. As a result, Articulatory patterns are highly variable. *Limb apraxia* is an impairment in the planning of volitional movements of the arms and legs. Patients with limb apraxia frequently have difficulty with writing and can use silverware to eat but do not do the same movements on command. Their spontaneous gestures may be appropriate, but they will not make the same gestures volitionally. Apraxia does not cause weakness or paralysis; it affects the planning of volitional movement.

Speech apraxia resembles word-retrieval difficulties because patients grope for words. Determining if the groping is due to apraxia or to word-retrieval deficits can be difficult. Some patients compensate for speech apraxia by saying words that are easier for them to articulate. As a result, their language might appear stilted or unusual. Patients frequently use gestures and facial expression to compensate for linguistic deficits. If they have limb apraxia or oral apraxia, individuals can find it difficult to use gestures or facial expression to compensate for their speech apraxia.

Dysphagia.   Problems associated with *dysphagia* include difficulty containing, controlling, and masticating food in the mouth, difficulty initiating a swallow, retention of food and saliva in the mouth after swallowing, coughing, aspiration of food into the airway, aspiration pneumonia, compromised nutritional status, and dehydration (Logemann, 1983). Dysphagia interferes directly with communication when saliva pools in the oral and pharyngeal areas and interferes with articulation. It interferes indirectly when patients develop aspiration pneumonia and are too ill to participate in rehabilitation.

Implications for Intervention Planning.   Knowledge of sensorimotor deficits influences goal and procedure planning. With reference to goal planning, severity and type of sensorimotor impairments influence prognosis, communicative modality (oral, gestural, written, or augmentative system), and target areas (e.g., language, motor speech, or dysphagia). When patients have decreased sensorimotor functions, collaborations with allied professionals may be necessary. For example, patients will benefit from appropriate compensatory devices such as glasses, hearing aids, and adaptive seating devices. Speech-language materials must also be designed to compensate for compromised sensorimotor functions (e.g., books with large print, placing stimuli in the field of vision, and using more than one sensory modality at a time).

Cognitive Impairment

Cognition involves the act of knowing through perception and leads to the accumulation of knowledge and judgment. Several approaches to the definition of cognition were presented in Chapters 3 and 4. Two of these involved information processing (subsumed under social cognition) and Piagetian processes. The information-processing model attempted to describe human thought and reasoning by comparing the mind's ability to acquire, process, store, and use information like a sophisticated computer system. The second approach, based on Piaget's model, viewed cognition as a process of assimilation and accommodation. An information-processing model is used in this chapter. The processing model includes cognition as part of communication and focuses rehabilitation on the cognitive processes underlying language.

Patients with brain damage typically experience cognitive deficits. Some cognitive functions that are frequently impaired when patients have aphasia and maintain communicative problems are: executive function, problem solving, awareness of the deficit, memory, orientation, recognition of information, attention, and arousal. Therefore, clinicians must identify these deficits and plan intervention to reduce their effects.

Executive Function.   The executive function of cognition refers to problem solving and goal-setting behavior (Helm-Estabrooks & Albert, 1991). Executive function skills are seen as responsible for processing and interpreting situations so that individuals can set their personal goals and adjust their goals to changes by creatively planning, initiating, monitoring, and evaluating behavior (Baddeley, 1992; Lezak, 1982). Acting as a supervisor, the executive function organizes activity, allocates resources, and controls impulses, agitation, and frustration (Baddeley, 1992).

Patients who have closed head trauma frequently have difficulty with executive function skills (Lezak, 1982; Ylvisaker, 1992). Decreased executive function limits planning, initiation and follow-through of behavior, awareness of deficits, and task-shifting behavior. Problems with executive functions are not readily observable in an assessment environment that is highly structured and controlled by clinicians. As a result, patients have little need to use their executive function skills, and their impairment might not be readily noticeable. Therefore, clinicians need to manipulate the level of structure in the testing environment to reveal these problems (Lezak, 1982; Ylvisaker, 1992).

Decreased executive function skills interfere with rehabilitation by preventing patients from planning, initiating, monitoring, and evaluating their communicative interactions (Helm-Estabrooks & Albert, 1991). Patients with executive function problems can have difficulty attending treatment because they do not plan their day so that they can arrive at treatment at an appointed time. They can also have difficulty following through and practicing homework.

Problem Solving and Thinking Skills. Problem solving and thinking skills are high-level cognitive functions. Adults frequently use their judgment to make decisions that affect their safety and security, such as whether to change jobs, make investments, or buy a new car (Okkema, 1993). Problem solving involves the use of knowledge to make appraisals, comparisons, and assessments about "known specifications or criterion, such as correctness, completeness, identity, relevance, adequacy, utility, safety, consistency, logical feasibility, practical feasibility, or social custom" (Chapey, 1994a, p. 223). Individuals use such information to arrive at solutions to problems.

Individuals whose problem solving and thinking skills are impaired might expose themselves to potentially dangerous situations such as forgetting to lock the wheels on a wheelchair or pulling the medical tubes out of their body (Chapey, 1994a; Okkema, 1993). In addition, such individuals can display poor judgment in communication; for instance, using vulgar language in treatment or saying hurtful things without censoring themselves. Some patients use poor problem-solving skills when answering hypothetical "what if" questions. If a patient who is confined to a wheelchair says that he would run down a flight of stairs to get out of a burning building, he is using poor judgment by not incorporating all information into his decision (Chapey, 1994a).

Awareness of Deficit. People who are aware of their mistakes can learn and change their behavior. Conversely, people who do not know about their mistakes cannot change. Patients who are aware of their deficits and attempt to compensate for them make better progress in treatment. An extreme case of lack of awareness is *anosognosia,* which is a denial of illness. When anosognosia occurs, providing treatment is difficult. Patients with anosognosia do not understand why clinicians are asking them to perform communicative tasks and they might refuse to do them. One of our patients, who denied having had a stroke, said that he had trouble talking because his dentures were loose. Motivating him to come to treatment was difficult because he did not believe he had a problem.

Memory.   Memory deals with retention and retrieval of experiences and allows people to learn, think, and reason (Helm-Estabrooks & Albert, 1991). Memory is not haphazard and uncensored but directed and well integrated. Individuals' ability to identify, organize, and remember is related to their interests and areas of knowledge and the vividness of their memories. Their levels of education and hobbies shape their responses to incoming information and help them select items that will be retained. The more knowledge individuals have, the more easily they retain new information.

Memory is described as a flow of information through different storage modules: immediate sensory memory, short-term memory, and long-term memory (Atkinson & Shiffren, 1968, 1971). The first module holds sensory memory for less than a second. If the information is selected as important, it is moved to *short-term memory.* Information in short-term memory is encoded in acoustic or phonemic forms and retained for up to 20 seconds. Some of these memories are selected and moved to *long-term memory* to store them in a semantic form (Atkinson & Shiffren, 1971). Obviously, if information is not recorded in immediate sensory memory, it will not be recorded in short-term memory. Consequently, the information will not be recorded in long-term memory and learning will not occur (Atkinson & Shiffren, 1968).

Working memory is used to retain information actively and associate it with new ideas. New information is held in *working memory,* it is associated with information in long-term memory, and a response is formulated (Baddeley, 1992). This moment-to-moment processing in working memory allows people to have conversations and to create new ideas or identify relationships between ideas (Baddeley, 1992). Working memory can be decreased when the other memory functions seem intact.

Breakdowns in memory can take several forms. In assessment, clinicians need to determine whether the deficit identified as aphasia is a language disorder or a memory disorder. If working memory is decreased, individuals have difficulty recalling linguistic information including the topic of conversation, what they were planning to say, instructions, or descriptions. Patients can also forget nonlinguistic information such as mailing letters, locking the wheels on their wheelchairs, and brushing their teeth. Sometimes patients forget episodes in their lives and do not remember whether they ate lunch or had any visitors (Demitrack, Szostak, & Weingartner, 1992). When patients have decreased memory skills, they become unsure of themselves and hesitate to challenge other people's memories of an episode. Some aspects of memory are idiosyncratic. One idiosyncratic aspect is vividness. Many people remember everything in great detail while others remember only vague generalities.

Patients can score within normal limits on a memory test and complain of memory loss. Clinicians must recognize that these patients may be suffering from some decline in memory. To find out whether patients have experienced a change in their memory, clinicians identify how well their memory was functioning before they developed aphasia and learn how long they have been worried about changes in their memory. Thus, although scores on memory tests may be within normal limits, memory might have been superior before the injury and the decreased function can be problematic. In contrast, some patients have had poor memories all their lives.

Orientation.   Orientation can be described as "a skill that requires integration of attention, memory, and perception" (Okkema, 1993, p. 31). When passing through an international border, travelers identify themselves, their homes, and their places of birth. During the day, people have a general idea of time and can determine when to eat and when to sleep without checking a clock. These activities occur because individuals are oriented to themselves, to their environment, and to time.

Orientation can become distorted in individuals with aphasia (Okkema, 1993). Patients' responses to questions and activities show their awareness of their surroundings, their understanding of people in the environment, and their appreciation of time (Okkema, 1993). Individuals who become disoriented cannot state demographic information, including name, age, address, and current president.

Some patients are confused about their location. One of our patients was convinced that she was on an ocean liner cruise instead of in the hospital. She held onto her belief even when she touched her bed rails, was shown the nurses' station, and received injections. She believed that all of the people on the hospital staff were employees of the ocean liner or members of her family. Another patient, a high-level executive, believed that he was in his office and that his clinician was a temporary secretary. He thought that the speech-language pathologist was insubordinate when she tried to test his language skills. When she did not take dictation, he fired her. A patient who is disoriented cannot cooperate or follow-through in treatment.

Agnosia.   A cognitive impairment can also be represented by the inability to recognize information. Such an impairment is termed *agnosia.* Freud (1891/1953) used the term agnosia to describe the perception of a stimulus without recognition of its significance. Five types of agnosia can interfere with communication: auditory, acoustic, amusia, visual, and tactile. These are summarized and organized according to modality in Table 8.3.

Attention.   Attention describes the ability to respond to stimuli (Demitrack et al., 1992). A continuum of attention can be identified, beginning with sustained attention, going on to selective attention, and culminating with alternating attention (Okkema, 1993). People sustain attention when they maintain constant responses to continuous activity in a quiet environment for at least one minute (Lezak, 1983). People have selective attention when they do one task and screen out another such as doing homework while having fan noise in the background (Okkema, 1993). Alternating attention requires flexibility between different tasks. An example of alternating attention occurs in class when students listen to a lecture and take notes or when a student is writing a paper and helping her children practice their music.

Decreased attention span often accompanies aphasia (Helm-Estabrooks & Albert, 1991). Attention deficits interfere with communication and treatment. Diminished attention causes patients to lose the topic of conversation, to make tangentially related remarks, and to appear disinterested in topics. As a result, reduced attention makes language impairment appear worse. When clinicians are assessing patients and providing treatment, they need to learn the cause of the decreased attention span so that they can help the patients compensate.

Arousal.   Arousal is "a state of readiness to receive information from the environment" (Okkema, 1993, p. 23). Arousal is associated with levels of consciousness. Decreased arousal can be experienced when being awakened from a deep sleep (as by a telephone call). Conversely, increased arousal can be experienced being in a potentially dangerous situation, such as a robbery or near miss in a car accident. People can remember minute details of the dangerous situation clearly for years.

Clinicians can detect arousal by administering the Rancho Los Amigos Scale of Cognitive Levels (Hagen & Malkamus, 1979) or the Glasgow Coma Scale (Teasdale & Jennett, 1976). Decreased arousal can impede communication and rehabilitation. Patients in acute care are often difficult to awaken for treatment. They might *fatigue* and fall asleep in the middle of activities or have cognitive problems including decreased alertness, attention, and concentration. If they become more alert, their communicative skills can appear to improve. However, these improvements are due to changes in cognition, not changes in language function.

Arousal influences recovery from aphasia. "For a patient with cognitive or perceptual problems that make even a simple task difficult, all of his attention may be required to focus on a simple repetitive task such as eating. For a less involved patient, sustained attention

---

TABLE 8.3   Five Types of Agnosia Organized According To Modality

Auditory

1. *Auditory agnosia* is a general deficit that affects the recognition of environmental sounds and speech sounds. Patients with auditory agnosia cannot identify important sounds because all sounds are equally meaningful. As a result, patients with auditory agnosia might attend evenly to the hum of a fan and to speech.
2. *Acoustic agnosia* represents difficult distinguishing between phonemes (Luria, 1966). Phonemes that have many features in common are more difficult to distinguish than those with fewer like features (Luria). The extreme form of acoustic agnosia *pure word deafness,* is characterized by the inability to understand spoken words (Albert, Goodglass, Helm, Rubens, & Alexander, 1981).
3. *Amusia* is an inability to recognize familiar melodies. Amusia does not directly affect communication.

Visual and Tactile

1. *Visual agnosia* is a general failure to attach meaning to visual stimuli. Visual agnosia can be specific to categories such as objects, shapes, colors, and letters or can be general to all visual stimuli. When visual agnosia is severe, patients can write their name and then be unable to read their own signature.
2. *Tactile agnosia* is a disturbance in the ability to recognize objects by touch. For example, a patient might search through his or her pockets and be unable to distinguish between keys and coins when touching the items. However, when the patient sees the coins, he or she immediately recognizes them. Agnosia can cause breakdowns in language that mimic word-retrieval deficits. When assessing patients, we must be aware of the agnosia and modify the speaking environment to learn when the agnosia has the greatest and the least effect. We can help patients compensate for agnosia by combining two sensory modalities, such as seeing and feeling.

may be challenged during a higher-level repetitive task such as balancing a checkbook, reading, or counting stitches in a needlework project" (Okkema, 1993).

Implications for Intervention Planning.   Decreased cognitive skills interfere with a patient's ability to communicate and benefit from treatment. Box 8.1 presents implications for goals and procedure planning that derive from each area of cognitive deficit discussed above.

Besides health problems, sensorimotor deficits, and decreased cognitive skills, patients can have psychosocial changes that impede communication and rehabilitation.

Psychosocial Changes

Before the onset of aphasia, the person had talked freely and had certain roles in his home, work, and social life. Friends, family, and co-workers had valued him for the roles he had fulfilled. In return, the roles had given him self-esteem. When that person no longer fulfills his roles, his feelings of self-worth change. If he cannot do simple math, he must stop managing the checkbook; if he cannot speak, he will stop making telephone calls. He might be concerned that this family will value him less if he cannot fulfill these roles. Consequently, his independence and feelings of self-worth are reduced. An individual who cannot feed and clean himself loses his privacy when others feed and clean him. In addition, if he drools, he may feel unattractive and fear others will not find him attractive. As a result, the patient can feel shame (Benson, 1980).

The family, too, can be expected to respond to the changes in their loved one. "The sudden loss of the ability to communicate affects all aspects of the lives of the person and their family" (Boisclair-Papillon, 1993, p. 175). When family members are faced with assuming the aphasic patient's duties and responsibilities, they may feel crushed or elated (Boisclair-Papillon, 1993). "The healthy spouse not only becomes the sole breadwinner, but also must raise the children and attend to the management and upkeep of the house. Furthermore, the spouse with aphasia often requires particular care and attention. In cases where the person with aphasia was the sole source of income for the family, the disruption is even more drastic" (Boisclair-Papillon, 1993, p. 176). Because of these changes the family can feel guilt, have unrealistic expectations of the patient, be overprotective, and reduce their social activities (Boisclair-Papillon, 1993). When the family is active in the rehabilitation process, patients make better progress. Therefore, including the family and educating them about aphasia is important to recovery.

When working with a patient who has aphasia, clinicians must remember that the person's basic nature has not changed. They need to treat him with dignity and plan treatment goals and procedures that are appropriate. It is imperative that they do not infantilize the patient.

> A person who has had a stroke has not reverted to a state of childhood. He is emotionally adult. But he is a man without the ability to communicate. He has lessened powers of concentration. He probably has poor memory. His confidence may have been shattered and he is in danger of losing his self-respect through no fault of his own. So never talk down to him. He is not odd or "touched," and he is most certainly not insane. He is you or me hit by trouble and in need of help (Griffith, 1970, p. 8).

BOX **8.1**

Implications for Goal and Procedure Planning that Derive from Areas of Cognitive Deficit

Area of Cognitive Deficit	Implications for Goal Planning	Implications for Procedure Planning
Executive function	Target the development of metalinguistic strategies for planning, initiating, and evaluating communicative interactions.	Manipulate the level of structure of the therapeutic context to promote the use of executive functions.
Problem solving and thinking skills	Target the use of language for adaptive problem solving and reasoning (e.g., making appraisals, comparisons, assessments) or for higher level decision making about criteria such as correctness, relevance, and logical feasibility.	Linguistic and nonlinguistic therapeutic contexts would be designed to promote appropriate levels of problem solving and reasoning; e.g., the linguistic context might include what-if questions, such as, "What would you do if you fell and could not get to the telephone to call for help."
Memory	Target improved memory skills (session phase) and/or the use of strategies such as schedules and diaries to compensate for memory loss (session phase).	Design methods and materials to compensate for or support rehabilitation of memory deficits.
Orientation	Target orienting the patient toward self, time, date, and location.	Use of materials, such as calendars, pictures, and clocks, which are orienting in time and space.
Agnosia	Target the use of language to identify information presented through various sensory modalities and to differentiate stimuli presented through a single sensory modality.	Procedures may promote the use of two or more sensory modalities in combination or the differentiation of stimuli presented through one modality.
Attention	Target using language to improve attention.	Plan procedures about topics of interest to the patient; design therapeutic environment to be free of background noise and visual distractions.
Arousal	Target using language to increase arousal.	Work collaboratively with other health professionals to present intervention during a patient's highest levels of arousal, or to promote heightened arousal.

Most patients with aphasia do not experience personality changes and have a normal range of emotions (Gainotti, 1972). Those patients who do may manifest a lack of inhibition, euphoria, depression, frustration, agitation, emotional lability, and flat affect. When patients develop a lack of inhibition, they use inappropriate language or actions. They begin telling off-color stories and using obscene words. One of our inpatients, who likes to eat, had asked us to go out and get her some pizza during the assessment. Euphoric patients deny having medical or communicative problems and can refuse medical care. Depressed patients have increased anxiety, low motivation, and lowered frustration levels (Benson, 1980; Horenstein, 1970). These changes can lead to emotional outbursts. Patients can become agitated and strike out at the medical staff or their family (Ritchie, 1961).

Some patients have changes in emotional responses that are not associated with strong feelings. Emotional lability occurs when patients laugh or cry inappropriately and uncontrollably in response to mild emotion. Sometimes they express the opposite emotion to the one that they are feeling such as laughing uncontrollably at funerals. When patients have emotional lability, they are surprised and embarrassed by their emotional outbursts. They can be afraid to attend treatment because of their altered emotions. Clinicians help patients understand their lability by discussing the first emotional outburst. Once they reassure patients that their laughing or crying does not distress them, the patients are better able to focus on intervention and ignore their own lability.

When patients do not smile or use other facial expression, they are described as having a flat affect. Both psychosocial and sensorimotor disorders cause flat affect. Patients who are depressed can have a mask-like face. The depression can be a response to the changes in the patient's life because of the aphasia. Patients who have motor disorders such as Parkinson's disease may be unable to make changes in facial expression because of decreased muscle movement. A flat affect interferes with communication because listeners frequently interpret the lack of facial expression as depression, anger, or disinterested behavior. Clinicians must learn the cause of the decreased facial expression. If patients have psychosocial disorders, they will be referred for psychological help. If they have motor problems, the clinician will help them compensate for the paralysis or paresis.

Implications for Intervention Planning.   Severe emotional problems reduce the expectations or treatment outcomes. Beyond the prognosis, knowledge of psychosocial involvement affects procedural planning. Psychosocial involvement may require collaboration with family, social workers, physicians, psychologists and psychiatrists.

Summary

All of the maintaining factors impinge upon rehabilitation addressing language deficits associated with aphasia. The factors combine with the language deficit to make the language deficit appear worse than if the maintaining factors did not exist. Furthermore, maintaining factors impede rehabilitation by making it difficult for patients to attend, remember, focus, follow-through, perceive, and practice at home. Clinicians need to identify the maintaining factors and to refer patients for assistance with the factors that can be alleviated and to plan intervention around factors that cannot be modified.

Performance Demands

Performance demands represent an additional source of information for intervention planning for adults with aphasia. As noted in Chapter 2, performance demands are those factors that contribute to the difficulty or complexity of the behavior expected of the client. The literature in aphasia rehabilitation suggests that several variables can influence performance demands for comprehension and production tasks.

The Semantic Category of Words. The semantic category of words influences language performance. Many tests for aphasia assess specific categories to find breakdowns in comprehension and production (Goodglass & Kaplan, 1983; Kertesz, 1982; Schuell, 1965). A category-specific deficit can occur in only one semantic category or it can occur in several categories. Table 8.4 presents a hierarchy for specific semantic category difficulties according to types of aphasia (Shewan & Bandur, 1994).

Frequency of Occurrence of Words. The frequency of occurrence of words influences comprehension and production. When going from high-frequency to low-frequency words, the complexity of content/form interactions increases (Howes, 1964; Schuell et al., 1964; Schuell, Jenkins, & Landis, 1961; Wepman, Bock, Jones, & Van Pelt, 1956). Commonly occurring words are easier for aphasics to recall than infrequently occurring words (Gardner, 1973; Siegel, 1959). Schuell et al. (1961) also found that patients made greater gains in treatment when using words that occur frequently.

Syntactic Complexity. Another way to modify linguistic complexity is to alter syntactic complexity. Tasks that employ simple grammar and syntax are easier to comprehend and produce than those that incorporate more complex structures. As the syntactic complexity of stimuli increases, the speed, completeness, and accuracy of patients' communication decrease (Holland & Levy, 1971). Shewan and Bandur (1994) constructed a hierarchy for sentence types ordered according to difficulty of language processing and expression from easiest to most difficult for sentences. This hierarchy can be used to detect the sentence type that will be most effective for a patient within any model of rehabilitation.

Chapey (1994b) developed a hierarchy of difficulty of syntactic constructions for comprehension and production of language, which is reproduced in Appendix 8A. She described

TABLE 8.4   Shewan and Bandur, 1994.

	Broca's	**Wernicke's**	**Anomic**
Easy	Body parts	Body parts	Body parts
	Actions	Actions	Objects
	Objects	Objects	Actions
	Numbers	Numbers	Numbers
	Colors	Letters	Colors
	Letters	Colors	Letters
Difficult	Geometric forms	Forms	Forms

TABLE 8.5   Shewan and Bandur, 1994. Difficulty Hierarchy for Sentence Types According to Difficulty.

Sentence Type	Example
Simple active affirmative	The dog is chasing the cat.
Declarative	
Negative	The dog is not chasing the cat.
Passive	
Nonreversible	The ball is being caught by the dog.
Reversible	The cat is being chased by the dog.
Negative-passive	The cat is not being chased by the dog.
Center-embedded	
Nonreversible	The cat that the dog is chasing is meowing.
Reversible	The cat that the dog is chasing is black.

Adapted from Shewan, C. M., and Bandur, D.L. (1986). *Treatment of aphasia: A language-oriented approach* (p. 47). Austin, TX: Pro-Ed.

five levels of difficulty. The simplest level involves two-word utterances. The second level adds morphological inflections, and the third level includes phrase structure rules. Chapey's fourth level incorporates transformations, and the fifth level comprises "complex sentences in which two or more constructions are joined in one sentence" (Chapey, 1994b, p. A13).

Word Order.   The order of words affects linguistic complexity and comprehension. Comprehension is best when words are presented in the canonical order of subject followed by logical object (Ansell & Flowers, 1982; Caplan, Baker, & Dehaut, 1985). Moving the verb to the final position in the sentence decreases the accuracy of comprehension for Wernicke's aphasics but not for Broca's aphasics (Friederici & Frazier, 1992). Broca's aphasics can identify inflectional morphology in single words but have breakdowns in sentences, whereas Wernicke's aphasics have breakdowns in both single words and sentences (Friederici, Wessels, Emmorey, & Bellugi, 1992). Comprehension improves when canonical order is used.

Adults with all types of aphasia have been shown to respond with greater accuracy to long, simple sentences than to short, complex ones (Goodglass, Blumstein, Gleason, Hyde, Green, & Statlender, 1979). This increased comprehension is associated with the redundancy of the longer sentences (Butler-Hinz, Caplan, & Waters, 1990; Clark & Flowers, 1987; Goodglass et al., 1979; Pierce, 1982). Patients respond more accurately to two simple sentences than to sentences with embedded clauses (Goodglass et al., 1979). Similar patterns of accuracy are found for language production: aphasics produce simple automatic responses more accurately than complex responses (Boller & Green, 1972; Green & Boller, 1974).

Patients manifest better understanding and production of written and spoken sentences that are active, positive, and declarative as compared with sentences that are passive and negative or complex (Lasky, Weidner, & Johnson, 1976; Shewan & Canter, 1971). Many aphasic patients have difficulty understanding passive, negative, and complex utterances or meaning inferred by tense and plurality. When clinicians simplify the form of language by using active structures, all types of aphasic patients manifest improved comprehension.

Prosody.   Auditory comprehension is influenced by intonational contours that differentiate among questions, statements, and commands and that express emotions such as concern, sarcasm, and anger (Shewan & Bandur, 1994). Aphasic patients sometimes understand the tone of the speech when they do not understand the specific meaning. They use these cues to help decode the overall meaning of the utterance.

Propositionality.   Propositionality also affects language comprehension and production in aphasic patients. Bacon, Potter, and Seikel (1992) described a hierarchy of difficulty in the auditory comprehension of verbal "yes-no" questions. They found that patients responded best to personal questions about themselves, next best to questions about the environment, and least well to questions about the general relationships between persons and objects. In this hierarchy, the difficulty increases as propositionality increases.

Propositionality in the speaking situation affects language comprehension and production. Clinicians can manipulate communicative situations to have low or high propositional value. Language comprehension tasks with low propositionality include asking the patient to point to items when the clinician names them and to follow directions. Language production tasks with low propositional value include swearing, serial speech, social speech, memorized passages, automatic serial naming, sentence completion, and repetition of words (Chapey, 1994b). Situations with high propositionality for both language comprehension and production include social speech, narratives, conversation, and role playing. Some patients do better with low propositionality and others do better with high propositionality. Adults spend most of their time communicating in high-propositional situations. Therefore, patients' performance on tasks with high propositionality usually corresponds to the overall severity of their communicative deficit. Discovering the individual's pattern of response is important so that the clinician can plan effective goals and procedures.

Low-propositional utterances usually remain intact for most aphasic patients. Tasks that are more automatic are usually easier than those that are less automatic. Therefore, clinicians plan short-term goals to progress from speech with low-propositional value to those with high value. Producing verbal series, social speech, and memorized speech represent low steps in the hierarchy. Descriptions of familiar pictures represent middle steps, and giving directions or expressing a logical argument about a controversial topic represents high steps in the hierarchy. Box 8.2 presents a hierarchy of propositionality for patients with aphasia. This hierarchy is applied to the case study that is discussed in the second part of this chapter.

Implications for Intervention Planning.   Performance demands are a source of information for intervention planning used primarily as a basis for projecting the hierarchy of goals. Goal sequences are generally projected at the short-term and session phases of rehabilitation planning and are based upon the performance demands that affect the patient's performance. Therefore, goals and procedures must be developed with reference to a combination of aphasia models, maintaining factors, and performance demands.

BOX **8.2**

**Difficulty Hierarchy for Propositionality of Speech Ordered
from Least to Most Difficult for a Patient
with Severe Nonfluent Aphasia**

Type	Example
Serial speech	Counting, saying the alphabet, saying the days of the week, and saying the months of the years.
Singing	"You are my Sunshine," "Happy Birthday"
Social greetings	Say: "Hello, How are you, Fine, Bye"
Phonemic cues	"MMM" to cue the patient to say "movie."
Automatic completion	"Pass the salt and _____." "The colors of the American flag are red, white, and _____."
Antonyms	"Yes and _____." "Hot and _____." "Up and _____."
Repetition	Say "word."
Open-ended completion	"Last night I _____." "I ate _____."
Embedded sentences	"You use a _____ for cutting." "I _____ the floor with a mop."

Summary

In the first section of this chapter an overview view of adult aphasia was presented. This overview highlighted sources of information relevant to intervention planning for individuals with aphasia. Sources of information reviewed included types of aphasia, models of aphasia rehabilitation, factors maintaining communication problems associated with aphasia, and variables affecting performance demands. The remainder of this chapter follows the course of intervention planning for an adult with aphasia, Mr. B.

Case Study

Mr. B, a 45-year-old, trilingual, maitre'd, was referred for speech-language assessment by himself and his neurologist. Mr. B has a family history of coronary disease, high cholesterol, exertional angina, and heavy smoking. A coronary angiogram had shown stenosis and occlusion of the aorta. He had suffered recurrent angina when walking only one block and had episodes of angina at work. As a result, he had undergone a coronary bypass. He had progressed well and he had been discharged from the hospital.

Seven days later in his sleep he had an embolic stroke and a sudden onset of aphasia with right hemiparesis. During the night, he awoke to use the bathroom, collapsed, and did not move or speak until his wife found him. On admission to the hospital, the neurologist described him as globally aphasic with total expressive aphasia, severe receptive aphasia, and moderate right hemiparesis. Computed tomography (CT) scan revealed a new, large lesion in the territory of the left middle cerebral artery and an old, smaller lesion in the left posterior cerebral artery. Mr. B was discharged two weeks after hospitalization with severe mixed aphasia and mild right hemiplegia affecting his face and arm more than his leg. He is presently taking Coumadin to prevent further strokes and has qualified for total disability because of his aphasia.

Mr. B lives at home with his wife and two teenage daughters whom he hopes to send to college. His hobbies include jogging, music, food, and his family. Before the stroke, he had worked as a maitre'd in a popular restaurant frequented by Broadway stars. He had enjoyed joking with his customers and had been a beloved personality at the restaurant. He had greeted many patrons by name and had made them feel comfortable by remembering their favorite table and drinks.

Mr. B came for the speech and language assessment one and one-half months after his stroke. The drastic reduction in his ability to talk concerned Mr. B and his family. He had a gregarious personality and never considered anyone he met to be a stranger. Now he is facing periods of depression because of his inability to communicate. He continues to attempt to talk but becomes frustrated when people do not understand what he is trying to say. Mr. B has begun to avoid speaking to friends. His speech is sparse and consists of one- and two-word utterances. He gets his message across by using a combination of speech, written words, and gestures. In order for his family to understand his speech, they interpret his words and gestures and say back to him what they think he said. He smiles and nods when they make the correct interpretations and shakes his head when they guess incorrectly.

Mr. B's wife reports that he understands most of what is said to him. However, he gestures or says "again" when asking her to repeat words and watches her mouth very closely when she repeats. He confuses phrases that sound similar such as "How are you?" and "How old are you?" and points to body parts inconsistently. He does not follow one-step commands, and when he goes shopping, he gets one or two items but forgets the rest. He does not identify words spelled aloud and he does not write words to dictation. He has difficulty with temporal sequencing of tasks and comprehension of words such as "tomorrow" and "next week." Based on his history and communicative difficulty, assessment is directed at the areas summarized in Box 8.3. A summary of Mr. B's baseline data is presented in Box 8.4.

We plan the long-term, short-term, and session goals for Mr. B based on the language deficits and maintaining factors identified during his assessment and our knowledge of aphasia. The planning process includes identifying the communicative areas that we can facilitate by the time we discharge Mr. B from treatment and determining the best course for reaching those goals based on the rehabilitation models. We will now review Mr. B's baseline data to plan long-term goals.

Long-Term Planning Phase

The long-term planning process involves using three bodies of information: baseline data on communication performance, maintaining factors, and models of rehabilitation. Consideration of these sources enables us to identify the severity of the disorder and to learn if the client will benefit from therapy. If we decide that he is a candidate for treatment, we will use the rehabilitation models to select the framework for rehabilitation. Then we will identify the areas that will respond to treatment. Finally, we will predict the amount and type of progress and estimate the time it will take him to reach his goals. This planning process enables us to analyze the data systematically and to plan goals and procedures based on both the assessment data and the rehabilitation models.

Baseline Data on Maintaining Factors.   The long-term planning phase begins by reviewing the maintaining factors to learn if Mr. B is a candidate for treatment at this time. We must classify his maintaining factors into three groups: those that can be treated by a speech-language pathologist, those that will respond to treatment from another professional, and those that will not respond to treatment. Several maintaining factors were uncovered during the evaluation, including health problems, sensorimotor deficits, decreased cognitive skills, and psychosocial changes. On the other hand, Mr. B has a premorbid personality that is friendly and outgoing and he is determined to improve his communicative ability. All these factors affect his recovery and must be considered when predicting if he will benefit from therapy at this time.

Health Problems.   Mr. B has medical problems associated with his stroke and has been experiencing spontaneous recovery. He is an outpatient who is young and in good general health, so he can tolerate treatment. Recall that Mr. B. has a history of heart disease and stenosis of the aorta. His embolic stroke occurred in his sleep after a coronary bypass. CT revealed a new large lesion in the territory of the left middle cerebral artery and an old smaller lesion in the left posterior cerebral artery. The history of two strokes suggests he could have another one.

The greatest amount of spontaneous recovery occurs during the first few months after a stroke. According to Mr. B's wife, he had made rapid progress during the first two weeks, but since then his rate of recovery has decreased mildly. At the time of the evaluation, it has been one and one-half months since his stroke. These medical factors suggest he has a good overall prognosis because of his spontaneous recovery and good health; these factors, however, are counterbalanced by his large lesion in Wernicke's area and his fatigue.

Furthermore, we know that patients who start intervention with severe language disorders will probably have more severe residual disorders than those who start with mild disorders. The greatest amount of spontaneous recovery for communication occurs in comprehension. Mr. B has difficulty with both comprehension and production. Therefore, we believe he has a good opportunity to make strong gains in his comprehension skills and milder gains in his production skills.

Sensorimotor Deficits.   During the planning phase we must consider the effect of sensorimotor problems including sensation, apraxia of speech, oral apraxia, and hemiparesis. Mr. B does not have visual or hearing problems. He has normal visual acuity and normal visual fields. In addition, he passed a bilateral hearing screening at 25 dB. His intact vision and hearing will help recovery.

Mr. B is suffering from a moderate to severe speech apraxia that impairs his articulation, fluency, and voice. His production of vowels is more precise than his articulation of consonants, and his articulatory precision is better in connected speech than on confrontation

BOX **8.3**

Areas of Assessment for Intervention Planning

Name_____   Age: _____   Primary Disorder: <u>Language</u>

Necessary Information	Source	Rationale
I. Language		
A. Content Form	■ Language sample; ■ Boston Diagnostic Aphasia Exam (BDAE); ■ Boston Naming Test.	To obtain a representative sample of the status of content-form interactions for all modalities.
	■ BDAE (Word discrimination, body part identification, commands; ■ Language sample (use of gestures).	To obtain a representative sample of nonverbal communication.
B. Use	■ Language sample; ■ BDAE (conversational and expository speech and oral sentence reading); ■ Role playing.	To obtain a representative measure of status of language function and the influence of context: environmental (personal, regional, social setting, mode, task, and audience), intent (for social interaction to regulate behavior, to protest or argue, to fulfill the speakers' needs, and to get help), pragmatic rules (topic maintenance, and repair), and propositionality (high and low).
II. Speech		
A. Phonology		
1. Phonetic	■ Frenchay dysarthria assessment; ■ BDAE (repetition of words, word reading, Response naming, visual confrontation naming, animal naming).	To obtain a representative measure of phonemes and an estimate of phonetic ability in single-word productions. To diagnose dysarthria or apraxia.

(continued)

8.3   Continued

A. Phonology

2. Phonological	■ BDAE (verbal agility, Automated sequences; recitation, singing, and rhythm; repeating phrases); ■ Frenchay Dysarthria Assessment; ■ Speech sample	To obtain a representative measure of speech intelligibility in connected speech. To diagnose dysarthria or apraxia.
B. Fluency	■ Speech sample; ■ BDAE (conversational and expository speech).	To obtain a sample of verbal fluency in connected speech.
C. Voice	■ Speech sample; ■ BDAE (Recitation, singing, and rhythm).	To obtain a sample of voice production in connected speech.
D. Intelligibility	■ BDAE (verbal agility; automated sequences; recitation, singing, and rhythm; repeating phrases); ■ Frenchay dysathria assessment; ■ Speech sample.	To assess the overall speech intelligibility.

III. Maintaining Factors

A. Health	■ Medical reports; ■ Case history form; ■ Interview; ■ Observation of patient.	To identify chronic preexisting medical conditions and medical conditions that result from the brain injury. To learn the current medical status of the patient and determine the prognosis. To evaluate spontaneous recovery.

B. Sensorimotor

1. Decreased reception of sensation

Hearing acuity	■ Audiological evaluation ■ Observation of patient.	To determine hearing acuity and to assess for agnosia.
Visual function	■ Ophthalmologist report.	To assess visual acuity. To assess visual field cuts.

3. Paralysis or paresis

Speech and swallowing motor mechanism	■ Frenchay dysarthria assessment; ■ Observation of patient.	To determine the structural and functional adequacy of the resonatory, phonatory, and respiratory systems. To assess for paralysis and paresis, and facial expression.
Body stability and motor control	■ Physical therapist report; ■ Observation of patient.	To determine status of balance, locomotion, and body stability and gestural skills. To learn structural and functional adequacy of head, trunk, hands, arms, and legs in eye contact, gestures, writing, and facial affect.
4. Dysarthria	■ See speech assessment.	
5. Apraxia	■ See speech assessment.	
6. Dysphagia	■ Clinical assessment of dysphagia.	To obtain a representative sample of swallowing function.
C. Cognition	■ Medical reports; ■ Neuropsychological reports; ■ Observation of patient	To obtain a representative sample of executive function skills, problem-solving skills, awareness of the deficit, orientation, agnosia, attention, and arousal.
D. Psychosocial	■ Medical report; ■ Case history; ■ Observations of interactions with family.	To obtain information about communicative environment and its effect on the prognosis. To obtain a representative sample of emotions including lack of inhibition, euphoria, depression, agitation, emotional lability, and affect.

BOX **8.4**

Summary of Baseline Data for Intervention Planning

Name: <u>Mr.B</u>   Age: <u>45</u>   Primary Disorder: <u>Language</u>

Area Assessed	Source	Results
I. Language		Results suggest problems of phonology, morphology, syntax, semantics, and pragmatics.
A. Content/Form	–Language sample.	Description of Cookie Theft Picture: "Boy...co..co..co. cookie...ga.ga.girl...ma..mama... water...ssinkie...window...nice...co.co... no...water..no..sinkie..eee... why..........ok.......I sorry." In conversation he uses a mixture of English, Spanish, and Italian words, gestures, writing, and drawing. In conversation he speaks in one- and two-word utterances coding existence. He produces the words with pauses between them making them appear as separate utterances. When asked, "what do you do with a razor?" he said, "....all the time." When cued with "sh" he said, "....sh...shave." When asked, "What do you do with soap?" he said, "........wa.wa..water." When asked, "what do you do with a pencil?" he said, "........sssometimes" but said "write" after the phonemic cue "r."
	-Boston Naming Test;	Severity level 1 10 to 20 second latencies on 25 of 60 pictures. Phonemic cues helped 50% of the time.

	-BDAE.		
		Word discrimination	30%
		Body part identification	20%
		Commands	0
		Complex ideational Material	0
		Response naming	0
		Confrontation naming	0
		Animal naming	0
		Word reading	80%
		Oral sentence reading	0
		Repetition of words	15%
		Repetition of high probability sentences	0
		Repetition of low probability sentences	0
		Automatic sequences	20%
		Reciting	0
		Symbol discrimination	40%
		Word recognition	40%
		Comprehension of oral spelling	0
		Word picture matching	80%
		Reading sentences and paragraphs	0

Area Assessed	Source	Results

		Writing mechanics	60%
		Serial writing	20%
		Primmer-level dictation	20%
		Spelling to dictation	0
		Written comprehension naming	0
		Sentences to dictation	0
		Narrative writing	0
		Singing	40%
		Rhythm	20%

Environment

B. Use — -BDAE;
-Language sample;
-Role playing.

Personal- Mr. B stated his name but wrote the first letter or number of his age, sex, address, and telephone number.

Regional- Mr. B's native language is Spanish. He now mixes Spanish, Italian, and English words in the same sentence.

Social- Mr. B has retired because of his communicative deficit.

Setting- Mr. B is eager to talk. Mr. B's wife has reported that he uses the same type of speech and mixture of Spanish, Italian, and English at home.

Mode- Mr. B communicates by using a combination of Spanish, Italian, and English words, jargon, gestures, written words, and drawing. He does not repeat words from a model and has produced some short phrases when using melodic intonation therapy (Sparks & Holland, 1976).

Task- Mr. B uses the same content/from for all speaking tasks.

Audience- Mr. B uses the same content/form when speaking in all situations.

Intent

Social Interaction- Mr. B uses speech and gestures to comment and direct attention to himself.

Regulate Others' Behavior- Mr. B makes requests and gives warnings by using gestures and speech.

Protest or Argue- Mr. B's communication becomes less coherent when he argues. He tells his daughters not to go out by using emphatic speech and gestures.

Fulfill Speaker's Needs- Mr. B obtains information, gives information, and requests items.

Get Help- Mr. B gets help by using a combination of words and gestures.

Pragmatic Rules

Topic Introduction- Mr. B initiates conversation and topics. He has exhibited planning and goal-directed behavior by scheduling the following treatment appointment by bringing out his calendar and pointing to the days and times he could come to treatment.

Topic Maintenance- Mr. B's utterances and gestures are related to the topics.

(continued)

8.4   Continued

Area Assessed	Source	Results
III. Maintaining Factors		
A. Health	-Medical chart; -Case history form; -Interview.	Mr. B is an outpatient. He has a history of heart disease and stenosis of the aorta. He had a coronary bypass and than seven days later had an embolic stroke is his sleep. CT has revealed a new large lesion in the the territory of the left middle cerebral artery and an old, smaller one in the left posterior cerebral artery. He takes Coumadin to prevent further strokes. He has a normal level of consciousness and fatigues quickly. He is alert but his attention and concentration are decreased when he fatigues.
B. Sensorimotor		
1. Decreased reception of sensation		
Hearing acuity	-Audiological examination; -Observation of patient.	Mr. B passed a bilateral hearing screening at 25 dB. He has frequently confuse words that sounded similar When asked, "How are you?" he replied "45." He confuses "card" and "car" and letter "t" and the word "key."
Visual function	-Medical chart	Mr. B has normal vision and does not have a visual field cut.
2. Paralysis or paresis	-Observation of patient.	
Speech and swallowing motor mechanism	-Frenchay dysarthria assessment; -Observation of patient.	Mr. B's articulators are mildly asymmetrical and quiet at rest. His respiration is rhythmical and appropriate during rest, speech, and swallowing. His spontaneous lip seal, smile, and pucker are appropriate at rest and during eating, but awkward and inaccurate when produced volitionally. He has attempted to move his mouth on command and has shaken his head. Spontaneous and volitional movements of the jaw and soft palate are normal. His tongue is normal at rest but he does not protrude, lateralize, or elevate his tongue on command. When asked to perform diadochokinesis, he has shaken his head, has laughed, and has said, "no." Mr. B has not sustained a vowel, changed vocal loudness, or sung a scale on command. He exhibits normal movements or his articulators during eating. During speech, he makes moderately slow, labored movements. His spontaneous cough is normal but he does not cough on command. He swallows his saliva and food spontaneously but does not swallow on command.

Area Assessed	Source	Results
		Topic Shift- Mr. B has mild to moderate difficulty changing topics when topics are similar or if the change is abrupt. His difficulty shifting topics is related to auditory comprehension.
		Topic Repair- Mr. B attempts to repair language breakdowns by using gestures, writing, and drawing.
		Propositionality- Mr. B did best on items with low propositionality. The hierarchy in Box 8.2 was designed for him.
II. Speech		
A. Phonetic	-BDAE; -Frenchay dysarthria assessment; -Speech sample.	Mr. B has apraxia of speech resulting in irregular arictulatory breakdowns, distorted consonants and vowels, literal and verbal paraphasic errors, and neologisms. He makes groping movements with his articulators to find the correct articulatory positions and sequences and some movements appear random. He occasionally adds sounds to words. The articulation of vowels is more precise than the articulation of consonants, and his articulation is more precise in connected speech than I isolation. Nevertheless, some single words are articulated precisely.
B. Fluency	-BDAE; -Speech sample.	Mr. B's speech is irregular, slow, and disfluent. His utterances are one- to two-words long with irregular pauses between sounds, syllables, and words. He matches rhythms when humming and produces fluent humming when engaged in melodic intonation therapy (Sparks & Holland, 1976). His singing is mildly impaired for familiar songs.
C. Voice	-BDAE; -Speech sample.	His pitch, loudness, and quality are appropriate. Prosodic features are distorted because of the short, slow speech and irregular pauses. He has monopitch and monoloudness with excess and equal stress on syllables. Nevertheless, he matches melodies when humming and singing.
D. Intelligibility	-BDAE; -Frenchay dysarthria assessment; -Speech sample.	Mr. B rarely says more than one word at a time. His speech is intelligibility for single words and two-word combinations is moderately imprecise. His speech is better in conversation than on confrontation naming. His apraxic articulation, disfluent speech, and impaired language skills interact to decrease his intelligibility.

(continued)

8.4   Continued

Area Assessed	Source	Results
Body stability and motor control	-Medical chart; -Observation of patient.	Mr. B has a mild right hemiparesis affecting his face and arm more than his leg. His eye contact is normal to excessive. At times he studies the face of the speaker very carefully. His gestures and facial expressions are eloquent and his shaping of letters and numbers is slightly distorted. He does not pucker or smile on command but performs both activities spontaneously. All volitonal movements are expressed slowly. Mr.B walks briskly and sits upright without aid.
3. Dysarthria	-See speech assessment.	
4. Apraxia	-See speech assessment.	
5. Dysphagia	-Clinical assessment of dysphagia; -observation of patient.	During his hospitalization Mr. B did not eat by mouth. His nutritional status was poor and he lost more than 20 pounds. Before discharge from the hospital, he began eating better. Since the time of the assessment he has been eating a regular diet. During the assessment, he drank water and ate a sandwich. He chewed the food and swallowed without difficulty. He did not cough nor dribble food, and his voice quality was normal during and after eating.
C. Cognition	-Medical chart; -Observation of patient.	Mr. B exhibited symptoms of acoustic agnosia when he indicated that some words sounded similar to him. His auditory short-term memory is impaired. He follows simple one-step commands but not two-step commands. At times he is unaware of his errors in comprehension but he frequently tries to self-correct his errors in production. Mr. B initiates conversation and topics. He plans by scheduling treatment appointments. He is impulsive and stands up to act out ideas that he cannot say. He is enthusiastic about testing and responds to failures by attempting to communicate through gestures, acting out scenes, writing and drawing. He does not exhibit emotional lability or persverative behavior.
D. Psychosocial	-Medical chart; -Case history; -Observations of interactions with family.	Mr. B is on long-term disability following the stroke. He lives at home with his wife and two teenage daughters. His family is supportive of his speech and is usually successful in understanding his communicative attempts. His wife has accompanied him to the assessment. He is highly motivated to go back to work to that he can help his two daughters go to college. In addition, he is highly motivated to communicate. When he does not say a word, he gestures, writes, or draws pictures. He works hard to be understood. His facial affect is appropriate.

naming. During repetition from a model, he makes groping movements with his articulators to find the correct articulatory positions and sequences. Furthermore, some movements are random and he occasionally adds sounds to words. Mr. B's speech rate is irregular, slow, and disfluent. His utterances contain irregular pauses between sounds, syllables, and words. However, his apraxia subsides when he matches rhythms, hums, and engages in melodic intonation therapy (Sparks & Holland, 1976). The disfluences also disappear when he sings familiar tunes in unison. Mr. B's pitch, loudness, and quality are appropriate in singing. However, his speech is monopitch and monoloud with excess and equal stress on syllables. His prosodic features are distorted because of his short phrases, slow speech, and irregular pauses. His apraxia impairs his speech intelligibility for single words and connected speech. Nevertheless, some isolated words are intermittently articulated precisely. Apraxia will also limit rehabilitation of his language since it is more difficult for him to produce speech. Conversely, when he is talking, Mr. B cannot focus only on the idea he wants to say, but must also focus on the language structure and motor programming. Thus, his attention is split and communication becomes complicated and effortful. As a result, we plan some of his treatment around simplifying his motor-speech production.

In addition to his moderate to severe speech apraxia, Mr. B has a moderate to severe oral apraxia and mild facial hemiparesis. Due to his oral apraxia, Mr. B's volitional motor control is decreased, and due to his hemiparesis, his face is mildly asymmetrical at rest. Nevertheless, his spontaneous facial expression is eloquent. Spontaneous lip seals, smiles, and puckers are normal but volitional productions of the same movements are awkward and overflow from one structure to another. When he attempts to move his lips on command, Mr. B starts, stops, and he shakes his head. In addition, Mr. B has a normal tongue at rest, but he does not protrude, lateralize, or elevate it on command. Furthermore, his tongue movements during speech are moderately slow and labored. When he was asked to perform diadochokinetic tasks, he shook his head, laughed, and said, "no." Mr. B did not sustain vowels, change vocal loudness, or sing a scale on command. Conversely, spontaneous and volitional movements of the jaw, soft palate, and respiration are normal. During eating he swallows his saliva and food spontaneously but he does not swallow on command. His spontaneous cough is normal but when asked to cough on command, he put his fist to his mouth and paused. He then shook his head, cleared his throat, and shook his head again. The combination of oral apraxia, speech apraxia, and right hemiparesis will hinder rehabilitation by making volitional compensation more difficult.

Additionally, Mr. B has a mild right hemiplegia that affects his arm more than his leg. Nevertheless, he walks briskly, sits upright without aid, and gestures elaborately. Because of the hemiplegia he holds his pencil in an awkward position and slightly distorts the shape of letters and numbers when writing. Since Mr. B's hemiplegia is mild, its effect on his progress in aphasia rehabilitation will be limited.

Decreased Cognitive Skills.   Mr. B displays several symptoms of cognitive involvement: auditory agnosia, decreased short-term memory, decreased concentration, increased impulsiveness, and overestimation of his comprehension skills. He has moderate acoustic agnosia that interferes with his ability to decode language. Mr. B frequently confuses similar-sounding items such as "card" and "car," the letter "t" and the word "key," and similar-sounding questions (e.g., When asked, "How are you?" he replied, "45.") He attempts to compensate by carefully studying the face of the speaker and asking the speaker to repeat.

Mr. B has mildly to moderately decreased short-term memory and attention and mildly to moderately increased impulsiveness. He follows simple one-step commands but not two-step commands. This problem with increased utterance length can result from decreased memory, reduced attention, or increased impulsiveness. To compensate for his deficits, Mr. B works hard when he is communicating. He watches the lips of the speaker and uses animated speech. In addition, he is impulsive and responds before he hears all the instructions. He jumps up to act out ideas when he cannot say them. As a result he fatigues. Unfortunately, when he fatigues, his memory skills and attention decrease and his impulsiveness increases, so the effectiveness of his communication suffers. Consequently, we must plan rehabilitation to minimize his impulsiveness, fatigue, and impaired short-term memory.

Both Mr. B and his wife overestimate his comprehension skills. His wife says that he understands most of what she says to him, but Mr. B asks for repetition on only some of the discourse that he does not understand. Intermittently, he misses shifts in topics, responds tangentially to questions, and is unaware of his language breakdowns. When he is aware of his breakdown, he asks for clarification of speech through gestures, facial expression, or by saying "again." He also compensates for his difficulty by carefully watching people's mouths when they are talking. Nevertheless, at times he is unaware of his errors in comprehension. His sporadic lack of awareness will make it difficult for him to monitor his speech and to compensate for his breakdowns.

Mr. B has retained many cognitive skills that can facilitate recovery. He is willing to use compensatory strategies and has developed some on his own. His executive function and problem-solving skills are intact and he responds to failures by attempting to communicate through gestures, pantomime, writing, and drawing. He exhibits planning and goal-directed behavior by using his calendar to point to the days and times he can come to treatment.

Psychosocial Factors.   Psychosocial factors represent another maintaining factor. Mr. B's desire to return to work and outgoing personality can aid his recovery while depression can impede it. Mr. B has qualified for total disability because of his aphasia, but he wants to return to work. However, we anticipate that because of the severity of his aphasia, he probably will not return to his previous job because it requires extensive verbal skills including recall of proper names.

Mr. B's wife reports that his personality has not changed since the stroke. He continues to attempt to talk but becomes frustrated when people do not understand what he is trying to say. His family is supportive and is usually successful in understanding his communicative attempts. Therefore, his strong desire to communicate will help him reach his goals, but his increased frustration will make his treatment more difficult. If we incorporate his goals into treatment it may help him reduce his frustration because he will feel he has control of his rehabilitation.

Summary.   Based on an evaluation of maintaining factors, Mr. B will need to compensate for health problems, sensorimotor deficits, decreased cognitive skills, and psychosocial changes. We will refer him to his medical doctor for his health problems, and for a psychological evaluation and treatment of his depression. Since Mr. B is concerned about working, we will refer him to the Office of Vocational Rehabilitation for assessment. As speech-language pathologists, we will be guided by the maintaining factors in goal and procedure planning.

Analyzing Baseline Data on Communication Performance Using Models of Rehabilitation.   We will now analyze Mr. B's communicative performance within the framework of the five models of rehabilitation described in Table 8.1. The linguistic model organizes baseline data according to content/form/use. This permits us to establish goals relevant to language content, form, and use and to regulate the linguistic aspects of stimuli. The linguistic model also allows us to prioritize goals according to hierarchies of complexity or difficulty. Shewan and Bandur's (1994) semantic and syntactic hierarchies in Tables 8.4 and 8.5 and Chapey's (1994b) syntactic hierarchy in Appendix 8A are examples of taxonomies that can be used to develop a linguistic plan for rehabilitation (see also Chapter 2 for a discussion of complexity and difficulty). The stimulation-facilitation model is used to control the type of stimulus used in the development of procedures. The modality model allows us to establish goals and procedures aimed at deblocking communication. The processing model is used for the improvement of memory and topic-shifting behavior. The minor-hemisphere model uses melody and writing to cue communication. Last, the functional communication model applies to the formulation of goals and procedures that target increased communication in natural communication contexts. Together, these models are used to generate hierarchies that can be used to plan the short-term goals and session goals.

Linguistic Model.   The linguistic model is useful for organizing information about communication based on the interactions of content, form, and use. The baseline data show that Mr. B has severe mixed aphasia and that his comprehension is better than his production of language. He recognizes common objects promptly but identifies terms within specific categories (e.g., actions, colors, letters, numbers, body parts) inconsistently and with delay. He also has difficulty decoding temporal terms such as *tomorrow, after, when,* and *next week.* Mr. B makes inconsistent errors processing three- and four-constituent utterances coding existence, action, locative state, or attribution. Moreover, he responds more accurately to short, simple sentences in the canonical order of subject followed by object than to more complex structures. His performance also improves when the linguistic environment is simplified by putting items in context such as "Show me the first letter of your name," rather than "Point to B." His receptive language level is at step one of Shewan and Bandur's (1994) hierarchy (Table 8.5) and level three of Chapey's (1994b) hierarchy (Appendix 8A).

Mr. B's language production is sparse and is restricted to one- and two-constituent utterances produced in a mixture of real words in English, Spanish, Italian, and jargon. When telling a narrative about pictures and during conversation, he names items rather than producing sentences. He omits verbs, adjectives, and adverbs. When describing the *Cookie Theft Picture* he said "............Boy....co..co..co. cookie...ga.ga.girl.... ma..mama... water.... sssinkie...window...nice...co.co...... no...water..no.....sinkie..eee ...why............ok.....I sorry." In conversation he speaks in one- and two-word utterances coding existence. He produces words with pauses between them, making them appear as separate utterances. He has latencies before responding and frequently makes gestural or drawing responses to questions rather than verbal ones. Mr. B's wife reports that he uses the same type of speech at home and at church. His performance is below level one of Chapey's hierarchy as described in Appendix 8A. Therefore, our long-term goals are guided by hierarchies reflective of a linguistic model.

These linguistic data suggest that language use is more intact than form/content interactions. Mr. B communicates better than we would expect for a person with this level of language disorder. He uses language to comment, direct attention to himself, obtain information, give information, and shape his environment. Although his language is severely limited, he usually communicates his basic wants and needs. He initiates and maintains conversation and topics (although there are problems comprehending topic shifts). Furthermore, he exhibits planning and goal-directed behavior as reflected in the completion of daily living tasks such as scheduling treatment appointments.

The Functional Model.   The functional model relates closely to the pragmatics of language (or Bloom and Lahey's [1978] use component). This model focuses on improving overall communication rather than specific linguistic (content/form) accuracy. The functional model is used to develop a natural communicative environment and focus on encouraging communication with decreased emphasis on precision of speech and language coding. Thus, this model is applicable to both goal and procedure planing. Mr. B has a severe communicative disorder, and we will plan goals that use the functional model to help him fulfill his basic needs. We will plan goals that Mr. B can carry-over into everyday conversations so that he will practice more often and will make more progress.

Given Mr. B's gregarious nature, he is embarrassed by his difficulty in producing social greetings and is starting to avoid his friends. He told us that he misses having conversations. It follows that one of the most powerful linguistic environments will be using structured conversation. Consequently, we will use role playing to aid production of social greetings and conversation. Because of Mr. B's severe communicative limitations, he needs to have the conversation structured around known topics with contextual cues. Therefore, we will create conversations around his family, work, hobbies, and current events. Structuring the topic allows us to understand Mr. B's communicative intent and helps Mr. B recognize his communicative breakdowns and repair them in an unobtrusive way. In addition, contextual cues such as pictures will be used to strengthen the topic and reinforce it.

Mr. B's language production is sparse and consists of one- and two-word utterances containing a mixture of English, Spanish, Italian, and jargon. He communicates best in familiar contexts and has begun to develop some compensatory strategies including gesturing, writing, and drawing. We will plan stimuli in his dominant language. However, since he is trilingual, we will accept responses in any of his languages. When moving up the hierarchy, we will increase the complexity of his responses by gradually reinforcing only single-language responses. In addition, we will encourage the use of gestures, writing, and drawing to facilitate communication. We will start by using simple gestures, writing, and drawing and gradually increase the complexity of his responses and use Amer-Ind (Skelly, 1979).

Furthermore, we will work with Mr. B and his family to help them develop reasonable expectations for his communication and to teach his family cues that will assist communication at home. As the family participates in his rehabilitation, they will accept his communicative limitations and use the techniques at home to enhance communication. By targeting communication rather than language production, we should be able to alleviate the patient's frustration level, resulting in greater communication efforts.

Stimulation-Facilitation Model.   When linguistic goals are identified, the stimulation-facilitation model helps us design the context for facilitating achievement of these goals.

One application focuses on controlling the strength of the stimuli in light of Mr. B's acoustic agnosia. The agnosia is revealed when Mr. B confuses phrases that have similar construction and sound similar such as "How are you?" and "How old are you?" The effects of the acoustic agnosia are reduced by adding information. He answered correctly when the questions are more redundant such as, "When were you born. How old are you?" He also compensates by watching the speaker's mouth carefully.

We will use the stimulation-facilitation model to increase Mr. B's comprehension by reducing the length and speed of the utterances, repeating or simplifying the stimuli, decreasing background noise, and adding visual cues. We plan intervention to move from stimuli that sound dissimilar to stimuli that sound similar so that he can redevelop discriminatory skills to perceive the small differences in auditory stimuli. In addition, we will construct a therapeutic environment that is free of background noise and visual distraction so that it is easier for Mr. B to focus on the auditory and visual stimuli. To aid comprehension, we will pair visual cues with auditory stimuli to reinforce the message. As Mr. B's ability to decode improves, we will gradually increase the background noise and reduce or remove the visual cues.

Modality Model.   The modality model is applied to develop procedures for using intact modalities to deblock or bypass defective processes. Overall, Mr. B's speech is sparse, but he successfully produces some material that has low propositionality. He sings "Happy Birthday" and counts to five in Spanish with only mild difficulty initiating speech. When asked, "What do you do with soap?" he said, ".......wa.wa..water." When asked, "What do you do with a pencil?" he replied, "ssssometimes" but said "write" after the phonemic cue "r." In addition, he intermittently substitutes "yes" for "no." When he recognizes his errors, he says, "no."

With reference to the modality model we will focus on the use of gestures, drawing, writing, phonemic cues, melody and nonpropositional speech to cue propositional responses. Since Mr. B spontaneously supplements his verbal output with gestures, drawing, and writing the first letter of words, we will encourage him to refine his gestures and use them to deblock his verbal coding. Additionally, when we give him phonemic cues, he frequently produces the intended words. Since he responds well to phonemic cues, they will also be used to deblock his coding skills. Additionally, he responded well to a trial period of *melodic intonation therapy* and intoned three-word sentences (Sparks & Holland, 1976). Melodic intonation therapy will be used to make the speech more fluent. Furthermore, we will have Mr. B use serial counting to produce numeric responses. We will increase propositionality by going from serial speech, singing, and phonemic cues to automatic sentence-completion tasks such as "salt and _____" and use these responses to answer propositional questions.

Processing Model.   The processing model focuses on rehabilitating the underlying cognitive processes to aid recovery of communication; as such, this model is applicable to goal and procedure planning. Mr. B has difficulty shifting topics when the topics are similar, when communication is unstructured, and when the change is abrupt. His difficulty in shifting topics results from his decreased auditory comprehension. He shifts topics better when we rephrase information to a simpler form or blatantly signal topic changes by saying "This is a new topic." Mr. B's comprehension also improves when we reinforce the message with gesture and pictures and change them when we introduce a new topic. He is intermittently unaware of his communicative breakdowns, but when he notices them he asks for clarification and watches the speaker's mouth for cues to the new topic. The processing model directs us to techniques such as *rapid alternating questions* for initiating and shifting topics (Martin, 1974).

Some of Mr. B's breakdowns in decoding interact with his memory deficits. He has greater difficulty as sentences get longer or the number of commands increases. He follows one-step commands but not two-step commands. Additionally, when he goes shopping, he buys one or two items but forgets the others. The processing model suggests targeting memory using, for example, the *eight-step model* (Harrell, Parente, Bellingrath, & Lisicia, 1992).

Minor-Hemisphere Model. As with other models listed above, the minor-hemisphere model guides us in the formulation of procedures. This model focuses on using cognitive functions in the right hemisphere to compensate for impaired functions in the left hemisphere. Mr. B's baseline data show that his verbal output is sparse. He talks hesitantly and inconsistently in one- and two-constituent utterances, supplemented with written letters, words, and drawings. When we ask him to name as many animals as possible, he names none. He is highly aware of these errors and struggles to correct them. Mr. B responded well to a trial period of melodic intonation therapy and has begun to use drawing to facilitate word retrieval and initiation of speech (Sparks & Holland, 1976). Consequently, we will use the minor-hemisphere model to aid communication through melodies, writing, and drawing. As his coding improves, Mr. B will be better able to manipulate his environment.

Predicted Recovery, Goals, and Time Frame. Having reviewed the baseline data about maintaining factors and communication performance, we are now prepared to establish long-term goals and predict a time frame. We will also summarize the procedural approach discussed above. The baseline data suggest that there are factors that will both aid and hinder recovery. Those that will aid recovery include his good health, continuing spontaneous recovery, high motivation, self-development of compensatory techniques, and supportive family. He also responds well to cues and often copies the cues and incorporates them into his utterances. Additionally, although he has deficits in language comprehension, early recovery is usually greatest for this area.

Contrastively, there are maintaining factors and communicative breakdowns that will interfere with recovery. The maintaining factors include speech apraxia, oral apraxia, dysarthria, auditory agnosia, decreased short-term memory, increased fatigue, impulsive behavior, intermittent lack of awareness of communicative breakdowns, depression, and frustration. Consequently, we believe that Mr. B will make good progress in treatment but will be left with a moderate residual communicative disorder. Table 8.6 presents a summary of the long-term phase of the management plan.

Short-Term Planning Phase

At the second phase of intervention planning we make three major decisions: establish treatment hierarchies, consider the time duration for this phase, and further delimit the rehabilitation procedures. Each short-term goal represents a step toward the long-term

---

TABLE 8.6   Long-Term Goals and Expected Duration

---

1. Mr. B will follow two-part commands (e.g., additive and temporal sequences).
2. Mr. B will maintain topics in conversational speech that contains transformations or passive voice (Chapey, 1994b, Appendix A, level four) and (Shewan & Bandur, 1994, Table 6.5).
3. Mr. B will produce various two- and three-constituent utterances (agent-action-object relations) with words and gestures in conversational speech (Chapey, 1994b, Appendix A level one).

Expected duration: Two years
Rationales concerning:
   Baseline data:
   1. makes inconsistent errors when decoding three-and four-constituent utterances coding existence, action, locative state, or attribution;
   2. responds more accurately to short, simple sentences in the canonical order of subject followed by object than to more complex structures.
   3. restricts language production to one-and two-constituent utterances produced in a mixture of real words in English, Spanish, Italian, and jargon;
   4. names items rather than produces sentences when asked to produce a narrative.
Procedural approach:
Models of Rehabilitation: functional , stimulation-facilitation, modality, processing, and minor-hemisphere.
Maintaining factors addressed: cognitive, sensorimotor, psychosocial.

---

goals. Therefore, we plan to increase the difficulty and complexity of goals systematically according to the hierarchies identified.

Time Frame.   The first decision made in short-term planning is determining the length of the short-term period and, relatedly, the frequency and length of sessions. Four factors influence the frequency of sessions: the patient's ability to tolerate the sessions, the ease with which he can come to treatment, the clinician's schedule, and the billing structure. Recall that Mr. B had a stroke one and one-half months ago, is young, and is in good general health. He will be treated as an outpatient at a medical center five blocks from his apartment. He can walk to treatment and has mentioned that he likes to walk and looks forward to treatment. Finally, Mr. B is on total disability and his insurance will cover the cost of three treatment sessions per week. Therefore, treatment will be scheduled three times per week.

The length of his sessions will be influenced by his sensorimotor, medical, cognitive, and psychosocial functions discussed above; the interaction of these maintaining factors leads to fatigue. The length of the sessions, therefore, will be limited to 30 minutes. Mr. B's continuing spontaneous recovery and good response to cues and treatment procedures are additional factors that contribute to a decision about short-term duration. Furthermore, both his insurance company and the medical facility require an update on his progress every three months. Therefore, Mr. B's short-term goals will cover a three-month period.

Deriving Short-Term Goals.   The second step in planning short-term goals for Mr. B is designing his treatment hierarchies based on the models of rehabilitation and derived hierarchies of relative complexity and difficulty. Short-term goals will be based primarily on linguistic hierarchies and functional hierarchies as they relate to baseline data in language.

Linguistic Considerations.   As noted earlier, Mr. B's comprehension is better for active, positive, and declarative sentences than for passive or negative sentences. In addition, Mr. B manifests decreased skills for coding the content, form, and use of language. His word-retrieval skills are slow and ineffective and his language production is sparse and limited to one- and two-constituent utterances. Mr. B's coding skills are slightly below those described by Chapey's level one. Consequently we estimate that Mr. B's language skills for coding will progress from inconsistent production of one- and two-word constructions to consistent production two-word constructions (Chapey, 1994b, Appendix A, level one). Table 8.7 presents the linguistic component of the short-term goals and derivation sources.

Considerations Based on Alternative Models of Rehabilitation.   We will now elaborate on the short-term linguistically oriented goals by specifying the context in which they will be targeted. These contexts derive from the other models of rehabilitation described in Table 8.1. These models suggest hierarchies of complexity and difficulty (summarized in Box 8.5, below, and propositionality of speech Box 8.2, above).

   1. Stimulation-Facilitation Model Hierarchy.   The stimulation-facilitation model emphasizes controlling the strength of stimuli to improve communication. Mr. B's comprehension is more impaired when there is background noise, when sentences are long, when sound is similar, and when the stimuli are not accompanied with visual cues. Therefore, we use stimulation-facilitation hierarchies, Box 8.5, to control the strength of stim-

---

TABLE 8.7   Linguistic Component of the Short-Term Goals

Linguistic Component of the Short-Term Goal

Mr. B will (accurately, responsively, completely, promptly, and efficiently):	Long-Term Goal Addressed	Prioritization Source: Chapey, 1994b:
1. follow commands (decode noun phrases);	1	Level three
2. follow commands (decode verb phrases);	1	Level three
3. show uses of objects through gesture;	1,3	Level one
4. switch topics given an agent-action-object phrase;	2,3	Level three
5. produce two-word constructions (e.g., agent +action, attribute+agent);	2,3	Level two
6. express social greetings.	3	Level one

uli. We control the general environment of the treatment room by starting with an environment that is free of both visual and auditory background noise that can interfere with Mr. B's ability to decode the language stimuli. As his ability to focus on speech improves, we will gradually introduce competing stimuli so that the therapeutic environment will be similar to his natural environments where several people talk at once and televisions and radios are playing in the background.

We will structure Mr. B's sessions so that we can facilitate his comprehension by controlling the similarity of tasks, number of repetitions, type of cues, and length and speed of stimuli. *Similarity* describes the resemblance of one stimuli to another. It is easier for Mr. B to distinguish between "Count to ten" and "Who is Marilyn Monroe" than "Touch your nose" and "Touch your neck." We control the similarity of the stimuli by starting with items that are dissimilar and gradually increasing the similarity of the stimulation as Mr. B's decoding improves. In addition, we will also control the number of *repetitions* that we use with Mr. B.

He responds better when he knows the routine and can predict the upcoming activities. Consequently, when we start treatment we will use frequent repetitions of stimuli to improve his comprehension and gradually increase the variety of topics and tasks. Another way to improve the strength of the stimuli is to pair visual stimuli with auditory stimuli. Mr. B decodes better when he has *visual cues.* As a result, we will begin rehabilitation with elaborate visual cues and gradually fade them out until he is primarily depending on auditory cues. Likewise, Mr. B decodes best when sentences are limited to four or five words. To adapt to his needs, we will control the *length of the stimuli* by using short sentences and gradually increasing their length as his comprehension improves. Moreover, he decodes best when the speaker uses a slow pace. Consequently, the hierarchy will go from speaking at a *slow pace* to gradually speaking at a faster pace. All these dimensions that control the stimuli will be increased commensurate with his accuracy of response.

The final dimension of the stimulation-facilitation model hierarchy that will be used with Mr. B focuses on his coding skills. Mr. B's verbal output is limited to one- or two-word phrases. The hierarchy will start with having Mr. B *produce single words* and progress to producing short phrases and then longer phrases. The phrases will be functional and focus on high-content words.

2. Modality Model Hierarchy. The modality model stresses the use of intact modalities to deblock or bypass defective processes. This model has four dimensions that apply to Mr. B's rehabilitation: gestures, propositionality, phonemic cues, and number of modalities. Mr. B has spontaneously begun using *gestures* to cue his speech. This compensatory strategy will be enhanced by practicing the gestures and by using *Ameri-Ind* (Universal Indian Hand Talk, Skelly, 1979). In addition, Mr. B will be shown how to use *nonpropositional* speech to cue social speech and answer questions. We will begin by enhancing his production of nonpropositional speech such as series, songs, and poetry and then teach him to use these utterances to answer questions. Mr. B can learn to use serial speech to identify numeric responses such as hours or quantities. Furthermore, Mr. B responds well to *phonemic cues* and can usually say the word when he is given the first sound. Consequently, we will work toward having him cue himself by either saying the sound or writing it. Finally, he responds well to having simultaneous *sensory stimulation* from several modalities such as seeing the object, holding it, reading its name, writing its name, and hearing its name. The sensory stimulation will be reduced as his performance improves. All four dimensions will help Mr. B communicate more effectively.

3. Processing Model Hierarchy. The processing model focuses on improving communication by enhancing the cognitive processes that underlie language. Mr. B's ability to switch topics and his memory are impaired. Mr. B does not always recognize when the topic has changed and becomes confused in conversations. His ability to switch topics will be enhanced by practicing rapid alternating questions (Martin, 1974). The procedure will start with dissimilar questions, and as his performance improves, the stimulation will move toward more similar questions. His *memory skills* are impaired when sentences are long. He also has difficulty remembering both items and actions. Therefore, treatment will focus on enhancing his ability to recall items and commands. The short-term hierarchy will start with recalling one to two simple items and increase to recalling three items.

4. Minor-Hemisphere Model Hierarchy. The minor-hemisphere model focuses on using melodies, writing, and drawing to facilitate communication. Mr. B has begun to use these techniques on his own and has responded well to suggestions during the evaluation. He occasionally produces a word when he writes the first letter and his listeners can guess his intent when he draws a picture. *Melodic intonation therapy* will be used to enhance the melody of communication and increase the spontaneity of his language (Skelly, 1979). In addition, writing and drawing will be used to cue his verbalizations. We will start by writing the first letters from words.

5. Functional Model Hierarchy. Following the functional model, intervention will be directed toward enhancing Mr. B's overall communication and helping him accept his residual communicative deficits. This model focuses on improving communication by using contextual cues and allowing Mr. B to "mix" languages (he is multilingual). Another problem that arises is that Mr. B does not recognize some of his communicative breakdowns; this often leads to greater communication failure. Therefore, we will begin treatment by providing many cues following breakdowns then fade them over time. Since Mr. B used several languages (his first language is Spanish), responses early in treatment will be accepted in any language; as his communication improves he will be encouraged to use one language. Mr. B communicates best when he talks about nonpropositional topics and about topics with which he is familiar. As a result, the overall hierarchy of treatment will move from nonpropositional to propositional and from familiar to unknown. Box 8.5 presents the alternative rehabilitation models and derived hierarchies for planning the context for linguistic goals.

Procedural Context. In planning short-term goals, we began to consider the context in which linguistic targets could best be facilitated. These contexts, determined with reference to the hierarchies derived from rehabilitation models (Box 8.5), were incorporated within the goal statements (Table 8.8) with reference to maintaining factors. We make further contextual decisions about Mr. B's maintaining factors. These decisions involve designing a therapeutic environment that will help Mr. B compensate for his maintaining factors. Box 8.6 lists maintaining factors and corresponding procedural hierarchies designed to compensate for these factors.

Session-Planning Phase

We are now prepared to plan a specific session for Mr. B. This involves formulating goals that are observable and measurable and designing corresponding procedures. Two dimensions of goal and procedure planning will be illustrated in the remainder of this chapter: (a) development of a sample session format and (b) derivation of session goals and procedures addressing each short-term goal. We begin with preliminary considerations concerning the number and length of sessions for the patient and the format for writing session goals.

Preliminary Considerations.

Number and Length of Sessions.   Based on a consideration of the maintaining factors described above, Mr. B will attend treatment sessions three times a week for 30 minutes. The combination of these disorders leads to fatigue. Therefore, we must change procedures every 8–10 minutes so that he will not lose concentration or interest.

Measuring Progress.   To plan the progressive steps in rehabilitation, Mr. B's performance on session goals will be measured along the dimensions of accuracy, responsiveness, completeness, promptness, and efficiency (Porch, 1967). We will use the accuracy of his responses to guide his progress in treatment. By measuring his responses, we will know when to simplify, to retain, or to increase the complexity of the goals.

Planning the Session Format.   We have adapted the format before the treatment session suggested by Porch (1994) in Table 8.9 to design individual sessions. To identify the number of goals that should be addressed in a session, we need to identify the format of the treatment session. The format summarized in Table 8.9 is widely used in aphasia rehabilitation. This format generally begins with, "a period of conversation, in which the clinician and the patient talk about what has happened since their last meeting, and the clinician deals with any problems that the patient might communicate (the hello segment)" (Brookshire, 1992, p. 132). This gives the patient a brief period to adjust to the treatment session "and to tell the clinician about any special occurrences problems, or questions that may have arisen since the last session" (Porch, 1994, p. 180). The patient has an opportunity to try out some communication skills he is developing in treatment (Porch, 1994). In addition, the clinician has an opportunity to assess the patient's overall level of communicative function and to assess how the patient appears as compared with previous sessions. The clinician can also evaluate the generalization of the communicative behaviors addressed in treatment and the effect of the maintaining factors on the patient's communication (Brookshire, 1992; Porch, 1994).

BOX 8.5

Hierarchies Derived from Model of Rehabilitation to be Used with Mr. B

Model	Hierarchies to be Used with Mr. B
Stimulation-facilitation model	- Start with an environment that is free of background visual and auditory noise and slowly increase the noise; - Start with stimuli that sound dissimilar and gradually go to ones that sound similar; - Start with frequent repetitions of stimuli to facilitate decoding and gradually decrease the repetitions; - Start with elaborate visual and tactile cues to facilitate decoding and fade them out gradually; - Start with decoding of four- to five-word utterances and gradually increase the length of stimuli; - Start with decoding slow speech and gradually increase speed of stimuli; - Start with producing single words, go to short phrases, and then to longer phrases.
Modality model	- Start with using gestures to evoke desired words and gradually fade the gestures; - Start with producing nonpropositional speech and gradually use it to say social greeting and answer questions; - Start with using long phonemic cues during coding and gradually shorten the cues; - Start with using several modalities to cue the coding of a word (see an object, hold it, read the name, write the name, hear the name) and gradually decrease stimulation from modalities.
Processing model	- Start with pairing shifting topics with direct cues and move toward conversational cues; - Start with remembering one or two items and move toward remembering three or four items; - Start with following one-step commands and move toward following two- and three-step ones; - Start with producing nonpropositional speech and move toward completing open-ended phrases.
Minor-hemisphere model Functional model	- Start with using speech melodies to cue production of speech and then fade the melodies; - Start with writing single letters and move toward phrases to facilitate communication; - Start with drawing simple shapes and move toward more complex shapes to facilitate communication. -Using a natural communicative environment; - Train family to facilitate communication; - Focus on nonlinguistic communication rather than linguistic communication; - Start with decoding stimuli in context and slowly decrease the contextual cues;

- Start with recognizing communicative breakdowns when given cues and gradually fade cues;
- Start with coding in a combination of English, Spanish, and Italian and then go to coding in one language;
- Start with simple gestures and move toward more complex gestures to facilitate communication;
- Start with conversation about family, work, and hobbies and go to less familiar topics;
- Start with nonpropositional social utterances and go to propositional utterances.

Sources: The hierarchies on this table are adapted from Aten, 1994; Benson & Ardila, 1996; Bloom & Lahey, 1978; Brown, 1972; Chapey, 1994; b. Code, 1994; Darley, 1972; Davis & Wilcox, 1981; Duffy, 1994; Eisenson, 1984; Hillis, 1994; Kagan & Saling, 1988; LaPointe, 1977; Luria, 1963, 1970; Martin, 1979; Owens, 1994; Porch, 1994; Rosenbek, 1978; Sarno, 1991; Sasanuma, 1993; Schuell, Jenkins, & Jimenez-Pabon, 1964; Seron & de Partz, 1993; Shewan & Bandur, 1994; Sparks & Holland, 1976; Stein, 1988; Wepman, 1951, 1976; Wilcox, 1983.

TABLE 8.8 Short-Term Goals Extended to Include Contexts Derived from Rehabilitation Models

Linguistic Component of Short-Term Goal	Long-term Goal addressed	Prioritization Source: Chapey, 1994b:	Rehab Model
Mr. B will (accurately, responsively, completely, promptly, and efficiently):			
1. follow commands (decode noun phrases) in structured situations when the stimuli are presented slowly with both auditory and visual cues;	1	Level Three	M, SF
2. follow commands (decode verb phrases) in structured situations when the stimuli are presented slowly with both auditory and visual cues;	1	Level Three	M,SF
3. show uses of objects through gesture in structured situations when the stimuli are presented slowly with both auditory and visual cues;	1, 3	Level One	M,SF
4. switch topics given an agent-action-object phrase;	2, 3	Level Three	L
5. produce two-word constructions (e.g., agent + action, attribute + agent) in structured dialogue using either non-propositional speech or melodic intonation as a cue;	2,3	Level Two	MI,M
6. express social greetings.	3	Level One	F

Key: SF = stimulation-facilitation model; M = modality model; MI = minor-hemisphere model; F = functional model; L = linguistic model.

BOX **8.6**

**Procedural Hierarchies Designed to Compensate
for Maintaining Factors**

Client: Mr. B	Clinician:
Supervisor:	Semester:

Maintaining Factors	Procedural Hierarchies
Mild fatigue	- Start with short sessions and gradually increase the length of the session.
Residual deficits	- Refer Mr. B to Office of Vocational Rehabilitation for job counseling; - Focus on communication rather than coding of language.
Moderate to severe apraxia of speech	- Start with automatic responses and move to propositional responses; - Develop acceptance and tolerance for some speech imprecision; - Use hierarchy for melodic intonation therapy (Sparks & Holland, 1976); - Use hierarchy for Amer-Ind (Skelly, 1979).
Moderate to severe oral apraxia	- Start with automatic responses and move to volitional ones; - Use vibrotactile stimulation on face.
Mild Facial hemiparesis	-Use Vibrotactile stimulation on face; - Start with simple facial and oral exercises and go to more complex ones.
Mild right hemiparesis	- Refer Mr. B for physical therapy; - Start with simple gestures and go to complex ones; - Use hierarchy for Amer-Ind code (Skelly, 1979).
Moderate acoustic agnosia	- Start with sounds and words that are dissimilar and go to ones that are more similar; - Start with an environment that is free of background visual and auditory noise and slowly increase the noise; - Start with visual and tactile cues to facilitate decoding and fade them out gradually.
Mild to moderate short-term memory deficit	- Use the eight-step model (Harrell, Parente, Bellingrath, & Lisicia, 1992); - Start with immediate answers and gradually insert longer delays before the response.
Mild decreased attention	- Start with familiar topics and move toward less familiar topics; - Start with topics of high interest and move to topics with lower interest.

Mild to moderate impulsiveness	- Start with signaling when to respond and gradually reduce the cues before the response; - Start with an established routine and gradually change the sequence of events; - Start with a room free of distractions and gradually introduce distractions.
Mild overstimation of comprehension/skills	- Gently make Mr. B aware of communicative breakdowns; - Pose rapid alternating questions (Martin, 1974).
Mild depression	- Refer Mr. B for evaluation of depression.
Moderate frustration	- Focus on communication rather than coding of language; - Develop acceptance and tolerance for some imprecision of speech.

TABLE 8.9   Porch, 1994

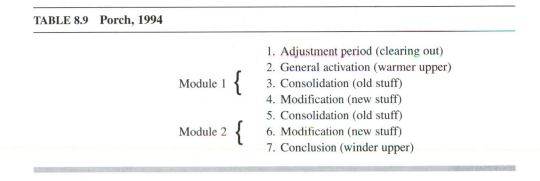

Module 1 {
1. Adjustment period (clearing out)
2. General activation (warmer upper)
3. Consolidation (old stuff)
4. Modification (new stuff)

Module 2 {
5. Consolidation (old stuff)
6. Modification (new stuff)
7. Conclusion (winder upper)

The second segments is a short period of easy tasks "for activating the patient's communicative systems and warming them up and furnishing the patient with a gradual transition into the more difficult tasks" (Porch, 1994, p. 180). This period is used to help generalize communicative abilities practiced on previous sessions. On a first session, warming-up activities are ones the clinician believes the patient can probably do easily. When the patient is responding effortlessly to the simple tasks it is time to move onto the next segment of the session.

The third segment of treatment focuses on reviewing difficult tasks worked on in previous sessions and improving the accuracy of responses. These tasks are more difficult than those practiced in the warm-up segment and are "those with which the patient has some difficulty, but in which most responses are correct, delayed, or self-corrected" (Brookshire, 1992, p. 132).

New material is introduced in the fourth segment. The new material can be an extension of the old material. "For instance, if, on an auditory task that requires the patient to point to one of four pictures after the clinician says the noun, the task might be modified by using six pictures, or by not allowing the patient to see the pictures while the clinician is saying the noun" (Porch, 1994, p. 180). These tasks may be accomplished with less accuracy than the tasks in the earlier sections.

The session ends with work on simple goals and procedures so that the patient can relax and leave the treatment session feeling productive and optimistic because he was successful on the tasks. These tasks are similar to the easy ones that followed the conversation at the start of the session. There can also be another short period of conversation at the end of the session to discuss the patient's progress and plan the next treatment session.

With reference to Porch's (1994) sequence, six session goals will be planned for each session. These goals will address conversation, warm-up, old stuff, new stuff, cool down, and conversation. This format is illustrated in Table 8.10 with sample goals from the first session with Mr. B.

Derivation of Sample Session Goals. The derivation of the sample goals for the first session will now be briefly discussed. This discussion will be followed by a presentation of early and later session goals directed toward the achievement of each short-term goal.

Session Goals 1 and 6. Because of his limited verbal output, Mr. B is self-conscious and is concerned that he is making others feel uncomfortable. Short-term goals 4a and 4b focus on improving production of social greetings including references to internal state (e.g., "hi," "fine," "better"). By improving his ability to produce social greetings we will help him become less self-conscious, be less isolated, and sustain his high level of motivation. Accordingly, our first and sixth session goals are to have Mr. B produce the social greetings "hi," "better," and "bye" during role playing 85% accuracy.

TABLE 8.10   Session Goals for First Thirty-Minute Session, Adapted from Porch, 1994.

Time	Classification	Session Goal
3 minutes	Conversation	Mr. B will code the social greetings "hi" and "better" during role playing with 85% accuracy.
4 minutes	Warm-up	Mr. B will sing familiar songs and count to 6 with 90% accuracy.
8 minutes	Old stuff	Mr. B will use melodic intonation therapy to code existence when describing pictures of movie stars with 85% accuracy (Sparks & Holland, 1976).
8 minutes	New stuff	Mr. B will gesture the use of objects with 85% accuracy at the first level of Promoting Aphasic's Communicative Effectiveness (PACE) (Davis & Wilcox, 1981).
4 minutes	Cool-down	Mr. B answer highly unrelated rapid alternating questions with 90% accuracy (Martin, 1974).
3 minutes	Conversation	Mr. B will code the social farewell "bye" and schedule the following session during role playing with 85% accuracy.

Session Goal 2.   In an assessment of automatic speech, Mr. B sang "Happy Birthday" and counted to five in Spanish after he was prompted. However, he continues to produce neologistic and paraphasic substitutions when reciting the alphabet and naming the days of the week and months of the year. When Mr. B has improved production of songs and serial speech, he can use the nonpropositional speech to deblock and cue propositional responses. Short-term goal 5 focuses on using serial speech, singing, and phonemic cues to code propositional responses in structured conversation. Therefore, Mr. B's second session goal is to sing familiar songs and to count to six with 90% accuracy.

Session Goal 3.   Mr. B's verbal output is sparse, hesitant, inconsistent, and limited to one- and two-word utterances coding existence. In conversation, he omits verbs, adjectives, adverbs, and all other word forms. He verbalizes more efficiently when he supplements his speech with gestures. In addition, he shifts from one language to another during a sentence and expresses frustration when we do not understand him. When he codes existence and action consistently, he will express his thoughts and manipulate his environment more effectively. He responded well to a trial period of melodic intonation therapy (Sparks & Holland, 1976). Consequently, our third session goal is to have Mr. B use melodic intonation therapy to code existence with 85% accuracy when describing pictures he collected of movie stars.

Sessions Goal 4.   The baseline data show that Mr. B becomes confused during conversations. He compensates by gesturing and asking people to repeat themselves. He watches speakers carefully for nonverbal cues about the topic and reads their lips. His comprehension is best when sentences are short and in expected order of subject followed by object and at Chapey level three (Appendix 8A). He also responds best to frequently occurring vocabulary, to known topics of conversation, and to visual cues. Conversely, his comprehension decreases when speech is rapid, there is more than one speaker, and complex linguistic structures are used. Accordingly, our fourth session goal for Mr. B is to gesture the use of objects with 85% accuracy after the clinician describes it using two-constituent utterances containing existence using the Promoting Aphasic's Communicative Effectiveness (PACE) program (Davis & Wilcox, 1981).

Session Goal 5.   Mr. B misses topic shifts in conversation and has trouble shifting tasks. He asks for clarification when he is aware of his breakdowns, but is not always aware of his breakdowns. When he requests that the speaker repeat, Mr. B watches the speaker's mouth closely for cues to the new topic. This reflects a "reduction in the efficiency of the cognitive processes which support language" (Martin, 1974, p. 68). His ability to shift topics can be enhanced by focusing on changing topics and by practicing switching behavior. Thus, Mr. B's fifth goal is to answer highly unrelated rapid alternating questions (Martin, 1974) with 90% accuracy.

Session Procedures

Our knowledge of the complexity of utterances helps us determine the complexity of communicative tasks for Mr. B. Subtle change in the appropriateness of the procedures can affect his linguistic performance and trigger success or failure of communication. With this awareness in mind, we plan a communicative environment that allows Mr. B to use his current level of communicative competence to help him reestablish his impaired communicative patterns. We describe the general environment that is compatible with Mr. B's interests and level of communicative function and then identify the specific procedures for each goal.

General Communicative Environment.   Mr. B's communicative skills fluctuate during and between sessions. Variability in his communicative deficit, sensorimotor skills, cognitive, and psychosocial well-being causes these fluctuations. We will identify these fluctuations during the conversation at the start of the session. In response to these fluctuations, we will plan strategies to cope with them. Mr. B has sensorimotor deficits including moderate to severe speech apraxia, moderate to severe oral apraxia, mild facial hemiparesis, and mild right hemiparesis. We will adapt to fluctuations in his sensory deficits by moving up and down the hierarchy of compensation described in Box 8.6. Changes in Mr. B's sensorimotor functions can interfere with his ability to understand communication. When his apraxia is more severe, we will use stimuli that are easily produced. We plan to facilitate his apraxia by using automatic responses, melodic intonation therapy, and Amer-Ind at their most basic levels to cue motor-speech programming (Skelly, 1979; Sparks & Holland, 1976). In addition, we will encourage simple gestures and slowly increase their complexity.

Mr. B has vacillations in his cognitive functions including auditory agnosia, impulsiveness, decreased short-term memory, decreased attention, and overestimation of his comprehension skills. These maintaining factors can interfere with his ability to relearn communicative strategies. When his acoustic agnosia is more severe, we will use stimuli that are dissimilar, make sure the environment is free of background distractions, and use visual cues to reinforce the verbal message so that Mr. B will decode communication more effectively. Then, when his acoustic agnosia is milder, we will move up the hierarchy and use stimuli that are similar. We will also establish a routine in the session where we start with a familiar procedure, move to an unfamiliar procedure and then back to a familiar procedure. By using a routine and starting with the familiar, he will remember the routine, will be less impulsive, and will be more likely to complete the task successfully. As his impulsiveness decreases, we will start to alter the routine. Additionally, to adapt to changes in his memory skills, we will follow the hierarchy of the eight-step model (Harrell et al., 1992), use immediate responses, and increase delays as his memory improves. We will compensate for changes in his attention and comprehension skills by using familiar topics of high interest when he has decreased attention and progressing to less familiar topics when his attention is improved.

Psychosocial issues must also be considered. Overall, procedures must be appropriate to Mr. B's age and sex. We choose procedures that are of interest to him because they will increase his focus. Since Mr. B has intimate knowledge of the entertainment business and likes to talk about it, we will focus treatment tasks around restaurants, stars, movies, plays, food, wine, and politics. When he experiences oscillations in psychosocial status, we will help to reduce his general frustration by focusing him on the success of his communication rather than the specifics of his speech production. As he builds an acceptance of his communicative changes, his overall communicative success will improve.

Fluctuations will also occur during the session when Mr. B fatigues. The promptness and accuracy of his responses decrease when he fatigues. Consequently, we plan rehabilitation to minimize his fatigue by limiting the sessions to 30 minutes, switching treatment goals every 8–10 minutes, and focusing on topics of interest. If we notice that he is fatigued, we will modify the stimuli and responses by moving toward less propositional and more frequently occurring speech. In addition, we will help Mr. B become aware of his own fatigue by asking him if he feels tired and by telling him about the changes we observe. As he becomes more aware of his fatigue, he can compensate by scheduling rest periods and work periods.

Having considered the range of issues bearing upon the planning of session procedures, we now return to the session goals in Table 8.10. The derivation of procedures specific to the goals in this table is discussed next.

Procedures for Specific Goals.

The *first* and *sixth session procedures* stipulate that Mr. B will produce the social greetings "hi," "better," and "bye" during role playing with 85% accuracy. We will use the functional model to develop a natural communicative environment and focus on producing communication. We will use role playing to develop the setting for production of social greetings to different people and in different locations. We will discuss specific stimuli and responses before the role playing begins. The scripts will be simple and straightforward so we can preserve the spontaneity of the conversational situation. We will pretend that we talk to each other in various locations, on the street, in stores, and on the telephone. We will take turns with Mr. B initiating the greeting in the role playing environment. He will be encouraged to use gestures to cue his responses. Since social gestures are an integral part of communication, they will transfer to his home environment.

The *second session goal* specifies that Mr. B will sing familiar songs and count to six with 90% accuracy. During the first session, the clinician will sing "Happy Birthday," "You Are My Sunshine," and "Row, Row, Row Your Boat" and count to six. We will start by singing the first line of the song and then ask Mr. B to join in, by saying "join me" and gesturing to "come along." When he starts singing, we will sing in unison. When working on counting, we will count to six and stop. We will then ask Mr. B to join in counting again. Then, we will count in unison. Cues during counting include using a slow, even rhythm and tapping the table in unison with the numbers.

Mr. B's *third session goal* is to use melodic intonation therapy to code existence when describing pictures of movie stars (Sparks & Holland, 1976). Mr. B is fond of stars and worked with them in a restaurant for more than 25 years. When he brought his pictures to the initial evaluation and coded existence, his responses were delayed and self-corrected. During a trial period of melodic intonation therapy his performance improved in both promptness and accuracy. We will start at the first level of melodic intonation therapy and follow its hierarchy. The first level involves humming the melody pattern for the phrase; the second level is intoning the phrase; the third level is having the patient answer questions; and the fourth level involves using *sprecgeshang,* which is a combination of intonation and speech. The fifth and final level includes transferring and maintaining the skills. This hierarchy will be used with Mr. B over the next several sessions.

The *fourth session goal* states that the patient will participate in PACE therapy to establish an environment for structured conversation (Davis & Wilcox, 1981). Procedures derived from PACE are based on four principles. The first is that both the clinician and patient participate as encoders and decoders of messages and the second is that the clinician and patient exchange novel information. The third is that the speaker is free to choose the modality to convey the message. For example, the speaker could speak, gesture, draw a picture, or pantomime the information (Davis & Wilcox, 1981). The fourth is that the adequacy of the speaker's message is evaluated based on the listener's response. For example, when the listener understands the speaker, the message was successful. These procedural components are found in conversational speech and, therefore, will transfer easily to the patient's home environment.

The *fifth session goal* stipulates that Mr. B will answer highly unrelated rapid alternating questions (Martin, 1974) with 90% accuracy. This goal is based on the assumption that some of Mr. B's decoding errors result from an impairment in his ability to switch behavior. Procedures for this goal increase ease of switching behavior by having Mr. B respond to questions where the topic changes for each successive question and no two adjacent questions are related. The purpose of this task is to encourage Mr. B to switch responses and to respond to questions but not to provide additional knowledge (Martin, 1974). A sample of rapid alternating questions includes these items: "What day comes after Tuesday?" In what season does it snow? Name one thing you can eat with bacon. Where do people wear bracelets?" (Martin, 1974, p. 69).

Tables 8.11 through 8.15 summarize the derivation of session goals and procedures discussed above. In addition, these tables present examples of later session goals for each short-term goal projected for Mr. B.

The goals and procedures described for Mr. B represent only one possible treatment plan. Many different plans could have been selected. The planning process for long-term, short-term, and session goals must be guided by theory and by the patient's performance. However, within this framework, we are free to help people maximize their recovery, to teach them to compensate for their residual deficits, and to help them learn to accept their communicative changes (Rosenbek et al., 1989).

TABLE 8.11   Session Goals and Procedures 1 and 6

Client: Mr. B   Clinician

Supervisor: Semester:

Short-Term Goal:

Mr. B will code social greetings and state using speech with low propositionality to cue utterances (Sparks & Holland, 1976). He will code accurately, responsively, completely, promptly, and efficiently.

First Session Goal:

Mr. B will code social greetings "hi," "better," and "bye," during role playing with 85% accuracy.

Derivation:

Maintaining factors addressed:

Psychosocial: Mr. B is a friendly individual who knows many people in his neighborhood. Whenever he goes out, his neighbors say hello and ask him how he is doing. He is embarrassed that he cannot talk to them and feels that he is being rude when he does not respond to their questions. This goal is directed at easing his social tension by helping him respond to their greetings.

(continued)

TABLE 8.11   Continued

Hierarchy: These responses are low on the difficulty and complexity hierarchy. Spontaneous use of one-word automatic greetings has little meaning. The role-playing context will give additional cues for the responses.

Short-Term Goal:

Mr. B will code social greetings and state using speech with low propostionality to cue utterances (Sparks & Holland, 1976). He will code accurately, responsively, completely, promptly, and efficiently.

Session Procedures:

The clinician will:

+ briefly explain the goal;
+ describe the role playing scenario;
+ role play the exchange by waving and saying "How are you?";
+ ask him "How are you feeling?";
+ take turns initiating the social interaction in the role-playing environment;
+ reinforce with social praise.

Later Session Goal:

Mr. B will respond appropriately to social greetings by responding "hi," "better," and "bye" when the clinician, the receptionist, and other members of the staff greet him.

TABLE 8.12   Session Goals and Procedures 2

Client: Mr. B	Clinician:
Supervisor:	Semester:

Short-Term Goal Addressed:

Mr. B will use serial speech, singing, and phonemic cues to code propositional responses in structured conversation. He will code accurately, responsively, completely, promptly, and efficiently.

First Session Goal:

Mr. B will sing familiar songs and to count to six with 90% accuracy.

Derivation:

Maintaining Factors:

Sensorimotor : Mr. B has moderate-to-severe apraxia of speech that affects his articulation, fluency, and voice. His production is better in connected speech that on confrontation naming. He counts and sings spontatneously. The spontaneous production will be used to deblock his production.

(continued)

TABLE 8.12   Continued

Psychosocial : Mr. B can use this technique to increase his communication skills and this will help decrease his frustration.

Performance Demands:

Perceptual support : Rhythm and inflection will facilitate production of serial speech and singing. Mr. B has begun to use low propostional speech to cue his coding of language. He learned the activity quickly and was enthusiastic about using it to communicate.

Short-Term Goal Addressed:

Mr. B will use serial speech, singing, and phonemic cues to code propositional responses in structured conversation. He will code accurately, responsively, completely, promptly, and efficiently.

Session Procedures:

The clinician will:

+ briefly explain the task and goals;
+ sing the songs and count;
+ signal Mr. B to join in singing and counting after the first model;
+ continue to sing or count in unison when Mr. B joins in;
+ fade out after several words and come back in if he starts to fade;
+ reinforce with social praise.

Later session goal:

Mr. B will code numbers, days, and months using series to cue propositional speech in response to questions with 90% accuracy.

TABLE 8.13   Session Goals and Procedures 3

| Client: Mr. B | Clinician: |
| Supervisor: | Semester: |

Short-Term Goal Addressed:

Mr. B will code two-word constructions in structured conversation using melodic intonation therapy (Sparks & Holland, 1976). He will code accurately, responsively, completely, promptly, and efficiently (Chapey's level one).

First Session Goal:

Mr. B will use melodic intonation therapy to code existance while humming and hand tapping when naming pictures he has collected of movie stars who came to his restaurant with 85% accuracy (Sparks & Holland, 1976).

(continued)

TABLE 8.13   **Continued**

Derivation:

Maintaining Factors:

Cognition : At times he is unaware of his errors in comprehension but he tries to self-correct when he is aware of the errors.

Personality/Emotions: Mr. B is highly motivated to communicate. When he did not say a word, he gestured, wrote, or drew pictures. His facial affect is appropriate. He is fond of movie stars and enjoys naming them. Many of them had come into his restaurant and he had taken pride in remembering the drinks or the table they liked.

Performance Demands:

Perceptual support: The use of structured linguistic environments with familiar pictures will facilitate comprehension. Mr. B has collected these pictures over many years. Mr. B had done well during a trial period of melodic intonation therapy. He had learned the activity quickly and appeared to enjoy the task.

Short-Term Goal Addressed:

Mr. B will code two-word constructions in structured conversation using melodic intonation therapy (Sparks & Holland, 1976). He will code the accurately, responsively, completely, promptly, and efficiently (Chapey's level one).

Session Procedures:

The clinician will:

+ briefly explain the task and goals;
+ select five pictures each of five stars;
+ put a pile of pictures in the center of the table face down;
+ take the first picture off the top of the pile and look at the picture;
+ hold the patients hand and intone the name of the star and tap the melody with their hands-this will be done twice;
+ signal the patient to join the humming after the two models and hum in unison;
+ fade vocal participation but continue hand tapping;
+ reinforce with social praise.

Later session goal:

Mr. B will us melodic intonation therapy to code existence while intoning the names and using hand tapping when naming pictures he collected of movie stars who came to his restaurant with 85% accuracy (Sparks & Holland, 1976).

TABLE 8.14   Session Goals and Procedures 4

Client: Mr. B   Clinician:

Supervisor: Semester:

Short-Term Goal Addressed:

Mr. B will follow commands or gesture uses of objects in response to noun phrases in structured situations when the stimuli are presented slowly with both auditory and visual cues. He will follow them accurately, responsively, completely, promptly, and efficiently (Chapey's level three).

First Session Goal: (1)

Mr. B will respond appropriately to morphological inflections using Promoting Aphasic's Communicative Effectiveness (PACE) therapy with 85% accuracy by gesturing the use of the object or by naming it after the clinician describes it (Davis & Wilcox, 1981).

Derivation:

Maintaining Factors:

Cognition: Mr. B's short-term memory is impaired. He follows simple one-step commands but does not follow two-step commands. At times he is unaware of his errors in comprehension but he frequently tries to self-correct.

Personality/emotions: Mr. B is highly motivated to communicate. When he does not say a word, he gestures, writes, or draws pictures. His facial affect is appropriate.

Performance Demands:

Perceptual support: The use of structured linguistic environment with modeling and pictures will facilitate comprehension.

Short-Term Goal Addressed:

Mr. B will follow commands or gesture uses of objects in response to noun phrases in structured situations when the stimuli are presented slowly with both auditory and visual cues. He will follow them accurately, responsively, completely, promptly, and efficiently (Chapey's level three).

Session Procedures:

The clinician will:

+ briefly explain the task and goals;
+ put a pile of action pictures in the center of the table face down;
+ take the first picture off the top of the pile and look at the picture;
+ gesture the activity and then describe it in three- to four-constituent utterances for example, if it is a picture of someone drinking water, the clinician will gesture taking a drink and then say, "Someone is thirsty";
+ show the picture to Mr. B when he identifies the action;
+ have Mr. B take a turn and the clinician guesses;
+ reinforce with social praise.

Later session goal:

Mr. B will respond appropriately to three- and four-constituent utterances containing action and existence in PACE therapy with 90% accuracy (Davis & Wilcox, 1981).

TABLE 8.15   Session Goals and Procedures 5

Client: Mr. B   Clinician:

Supervisor: Semester:

Short-Term Goal Addressed:

Mr. B will switch topics in structured conversation that contains verb phrases. He will switch accurately, responsively, completely, promptly, and efficiently (Chapey's level three).

First Session Goal:

Mr. B's will answer highly unrelated rapid alternating questions with 90% accuracy.

Deriviation:

Maintaining Factors:

Cognition: At times Mr. B is unaware of his errors in comprehension but he tries to self-correct when he is aware of the errors. This task will help him increase his ability to shift from task to task or topic to topic and decrease errors in comprehension.

Personality/emotions: Mr. B is highly motivated to communicate but he is also frustrated with communicative breakdowns. By increasing his ability to shift behavior, he will have fewer communicative breakdowns.

Performance Demands:

Perceptual support: Mr. B will be reminded that every question is different so that he will be ready to shift topics.

Short-Term Goal Addressed:

Mr. B will switch topics in structured conversation that contains verb phrases. He will switch accurately, responsively, completely, promptly, and efficiently (Chapey's level three).

Session Procedures:

The clinician will:

+ briefly explain the task and goals;
+ select the rapid questions from Martin, 1974;
+ tell Mr. B that each question will be different;
+ ask the questions in a slow pace;
+ encourage Mr. B to respond;
+ reinforce all responses whether they are correct or not because the goal is to increase his responses and switching behavior;
+ reinforce with social praise.

Later session goal:

Mr. B will answer more similar rapid alternating questions with 85% accuracy.

REFERENCES

Albert, M. L., Goodglass, H., Helm, N. A., Rubens, A. B., & Alexander, M. P. (1981). *Clinical aspects of dysphasia.* New York: Springer-Verlag.

Ansell, J. B., & Flowers, C. R. (1982). Aphasic adults' understanding of complex adverbial sentences. *Brain and Language, 15,* 82–91.

Armus, S. R., Brookshire, R. H., & Nicholas, L. E. (1989). Aphasic and non-damaged adult's knowledge of scripts for common situations. *Brain & Language, 36,* 518–528.

Aten, J. L. (1994). Functional communication treatment. In R. Chapey (Ed.), *Language intervention strategies in adult aphasia* (3rd ed.) (pp. 292–303). Baltimore: Williams & Wilkins.

Atkinson, R. C., & Shiffren, R. M. (1968). Human memory: A proposed system and its control processes. In K. W. Spence & J. T. Spence (Eds). *The psychology of learning and motivation: Advances in research and theory.* Volume 2. (pp. 89–195).

Atkinson, R. C., & Shiffren, R. M. (1971). The control of short-term memory. *Scientific American, 225,* 82–90.

Baddeley, A. D. (1992). Working memory. *Science, 255,* 556–559.

Bacon, G. M., Potter, R. E., & Seikel, A. (1992). Auditory comprehension of "yes-no" questions by adult aphasics. *Journal of Communication Disorders, 24,* 23–29.

Basso, A. (1992). Prognostic factors in aphasia. *Aphasiology, 6,* 337–348.

Basso, A., Capitani, E., & Vignolo, L. A. (1979). Influence of rehabilitation on language skills in aphasic patients. *Archives of Neurology, 36,* 190–196.

Benson, D. F. (1980). Psychiatric problems in aphasia. In M. T. Sarno & O. Hook (Eds.), *Aphasia: Assessment and treatment.* New York: Masson (pp. 192–201).

Benson, D. F., & Ardila, A. (1996). *Aphasia: A clinical perspective.* New York: Oxford University Press.

Bloom, L., & Lahey, M. (1978). *Language development and language disorders.* New York: Wiley.

Boisclair-Papillon, R. (1993). The family of the person with aphasia. In D. LaFond, Y. Joanette, J. Ponzio, R. DeGiovani, & M. Taylor-Sarno (Eds.), *Living with aphasia: Psychological issues.* San Diego, CA: Singular.

Boller, F., & Green, E. (1972). Comprehension in severe aphasia. *Cortex, 8,* 382–394.

Brenneise-Sarshad, R., Nicholas, L. E., & Brookshire, R. H. (1991). Effects of apparent listener knowledge and picture stimuli on aphasic and non-brain-damaged speaker's narrative discourse. *Journal of Speech and Hearing Research, 34,* 168–176.

Brookshire, R. H. (1972). Effects of task difficulty on naming performance of aphasic subjects. *Journal of Speech and Hearing Research, 15,* 551–558.

Brookshire, R. H. (1976). Effects of task difficulty on sentence completion performance of aphasic subjects. *Journal of Communication Disorders,* 167–173.

Brookshire, R. H. (1992). *An introduction to neurogenic communication disorders* (4th ed.). St. Louis, MO: Mosby.

Brown, J. (1972). *Aphasia, apraxia, agnosia: Clinical and theoretical aspects.* Springfield, IL: Thomas.

Butfield, E., & Zangwill, D. L. (1946). Reeducation in aphasia: A review of 70 cases. *Journal of Neurology, Neurosurgery, and Psychiatry, 9,* 2, 75–79.

Butler-Hinz, S., Caplan, D., & Waters, G. (1990). Characteristics of syntactic and semantic comprehension defects following closed head injury versus left cerebrovascular accident. *Journal of Speech and Hearing Research, 33,* 269–280.

Caplan, D., Baker, C., & Dehaut, F. (1985). Syntactic determinants of sentence comprehension in aphasia. *Cognition, 21,* 117–175.

Caramazza, A., & Zurif, E. (1976). Dissociation of algorithmic and heuristic processes in language comprehension: Evidence from aphasia. *Brain and Language, 3,* 572–582.

Chapey, R. (1994a). Cognitive intervention: Stimulation of cognition, memory, convergent thinking, divergent thinking, and evaluative thinking. In R. Chapey (Ed.), *Language Intervention Strategies in Adult Aphasia* (3rd ed.). Baltimore: Williams & Wilkins.

Chapey, R. (1994b). Assessment of language disorders in adults. In R. Chapey (Ed.), *Language Intervention Strategies in Adult Aphasia* (3rd ed.). Baltimore: Williams & Wilkins.

Clark, A. E., & Flowers, C. R. (1987). The effect of semantic redundancy on auditory comprehension in aphasia. In R. H. Brookshire (Ed.), *Clinical Aphasiology* (Vol. 17, pp. 174–179). St. Louis: Mosby.

Code, C. (1994). Role of the right hemisphere in the treatment of aphasia. In R. Chapey (Ed.), *Language intervention strategies in adult aphasia* (3rd ed.). Baltimore: Williams & Wilkins.

Craig, H. (1983). Applications of pragmatic language models for intervention. In T. M. Gallagher and C. A. Prutting (Eds.), *Pragmatic assessment and intervention issues in language.* San Diego, CA: College Hill Press (pp. 101–127).

Crystal, D. (1988). Linguistic levels in aphasia. In C. Rose, R. Whurr, & M. Wyke (Eds.), *Aphasia.* London: Whurr (pp. 23–46).

Darley, F. L. (1972). The efficacy of language rehabilitation in aphasia. *Journal of Speech and Hearing Disorders, 37,* 3–21.

Darley, F. L. (1982). *Aphasia.* Philadelphia: Saunders.

Darley, F. L., Aronson, A. E., & Brown, J. R. (1975). *Motor speech disorders.* Philadelphia: Saunders.

Davis, G. A. (1993). *A survey of adult aphasia and related disorders* (2nd ed.). Englewood Cliffs, NJ: Prentice-Hall.

Davis, G., & Wilcox, M. (1981). Incorporating parameters of natural conversation in aphasia treatment. In R. Chapey (Ed.), *Language intervention strategies in adult aphasia* (3rd ed.). Baltimore: Williams & Wilkins.

Demitrack, M. A., Szostak, C., & Weingartner, H. (1992). Cognitive dysfunctions in eating disorders: A clinical psychobiological perspective. In D. I. Margolin (Ed.), *Cognitive neuropsychology in clinical practice.* New York: Oxford University Press (pp. 96–127).

Dordain, M., & Norman, B. (1981). Comparative study of the oral language of aphasics with and without treatment. *Folia Phoniatrica, 33,* 6, 369–377.

Dore, J. (1974). A pragmatic description of early language development. *Journal of Psycholinguistic Research, 3,* 343–350.

Duffy, J. R. (1994). Schuell's stimulation approach to rehabilitation. In R. Chapey (Ed.), *Language intervention strategies in adult aphasia.* Baltimore: Williams & Wilkins.

Eisenson, J. (1984). *Adult aphasia* (2nd ed.). Englewood Cliffs, NJ: Prentice-Hall.

Friederici, A. D., & Frazier, L. (1992). Thematic analysis in agrammatic comprehension: Syntactic structures and task demands. *Brain and Language, 42,* 1–29.

Friederici, A. D., Wessels, J. M. I., Emmorey, K., & Bellugi, U. (1992). Sensitivity to inflectional morphology in aphasia: A real-time processing perspective. *Brain and Language, 43,* 747–763.

Freud, S. (1953). Zur Auffasung der aphasien. In E. Stengel Ed. and Trans. *Freud on aphasia* New York: International University Press. (Original work published in 1891.)

Gainotti, G. (1972). Emotional behavior and hemispheric side of lesion. *Cortex, 8,* 41–55.

Gardner, H. (1973). The contribution of operativity to naming capacity in aphasic patients. *Neuropsychologia, 11,* 213–220.

Glosser, G., Wiener, M., & Kaplan, E. (1986). Communicative gestures in aphasia. *Brain and Language, 27,* 345–359.

Goodglass, H., Blumstein, S. E., Gleason, J. B., Hyde, M. R., Green, E., & Statlender, S. (1979). The effect of syntactic coding on sentence comprehension in aphasia. *Brain and Language, 7,* 201–209.

Goodglass, H., & Kaplan, E. (1983). *The assessment of aphasia and related disorders.* Philadelphia: Lea and Febiger.

Green, E., & Boller, F. (1974). Features of auditory comprehension in severely impaired aphasics. *Cortex, 10,* 133–145.

Griffith, V. E. (1970). *A stroke in the family: A manual of home therapy.* New York: Delacorte Press.

Hadar, U. (1991). Speech-related body movement in aphasia: Period analysis of upper arms and head movement. *Brain and Language, 41,* 339–366.

Hagen, C. (1973). Communication abilities in hemiplegia: Effect of speech therapy. *Archives of Physical Medicine and Rehabilitation, 54,* 454–463.

Hagen, C. & Malkamus, D. (1979). *Interaction strategies for language disorders secondary to head trauma.* Paper presented at the American Speech-Language-Hearing Association, Atlanta, GA.

Harrell, M., Parente, F., Bellingrath, E. G., & Lisicia, K. A. (1992). *Cognitive Rehabilitation of Memory.* Gaithersberg, MD: Aspen Publication.

Heilman, K., & Scholes, R. (1976). The nature of comprehension in Broca's, conduction, and Wernicke's aphasia. *Cortex, 12,* 258–265.

Helm-Estabrooks, N. (1981). *Helm elicited language program for syntax stimulation.* Austin, TX: Exceptional Resources.

Helm-Estabrooks, N. (1986). Diagnosis and management of neurogenic stuttering in adults. In K. St. Louis (Ed.), *The atypical stutterer.* San Diego, CA: Academic Press.

Helm-Estabrooks, N., & Albert, M. L. (1991). *Manual of aphasia therapy.* Austin, TX: Pro-Ed.

Helm-Estabrooks, N., Fitzpatrick, P., & Barresi, B. (1982). Visual action therapy for global aphasia. *Journal of Speech and Hearing Disorders, 44,* 385–389.

Hillis, A. E. (1994). Contributions from cognitive analysis. In R. Chapey (Ed.), *Language intervention strategies in adult aphasia* (3rd ed.). Baltimore: Williams & Wilkins.

Holland, A. L., and Levy, C. B. (1971). Syntactic generalization in aphasics as a function of relearning an active sentence. *Acta Symbolica, 2,* 34–41.

Horenstein, S. (1970). Effects of cerebrovascular disease on personality and emotionality. In A. L. Benton (Ed.), *Behavioral change in cerebrovascular disease* (pp. 171–201). New York: Harper.

Horner, J., & Loverso, F. L. (1991). Models of aphasia treatment in clinical aphasiology 1972–1988. In T. E. Prescott (Ed.), *Clinical aphasiology* (Vol, 20, pp. 61–75). Austin, TX: Pro-Ed.

Horner, J., Loverso, F. L., & Rothi, L. G. (1994). Models of aphasia treatment. In R. Chapey (Ed.), *Language intervention strategies in adult aphasia* (3rd ed.). Baltimore: Williams & Wilkins.

Howes, D. (1964). Application of the word-fluency concept to aphasia. In A. deReuck & M. O'Connor (Eds.) (pp. 47–78). *Disorders of language.* London: Churchill.

Jackson, J. H. (1879). On affections of speech from disease of the brain. *Brain, 1,* 304–330.

Kagan, A., & Saling, M. M. (1988). *An introduction to Luria's Aphasiology: Theory and application.* Baltimore: Brookes.

Kaplan, E. (1991). Aphasia related disorders. In M. T. Sarno (Ed.), *Acquired aphasia.* San Diego, CA: Academic Press (pp. 313–338).

Keenan, J., & Brassell, E. (1974). A study of factors related to prognosis for individual aphasic patients. *Journal of Speech and Hearing Disorders, 39,* 257–269.

Kenin, M., & Swisher, L. (1972). A study of patterns of recovery in aphasia. *Cortex, 8,* 56–68.

Kertesz, A. (1982). *Western aphasia battery.* New York: Grune and Stratton.

Kertesz, A., Harlock, W., & Coates, R. (1979). Computer tomographic location, lesion size, and prognosis in aphasia an non-verbal impairment. *Brain & Language, 8,* 34–50.

Kertesz, A., & McCabe, P. (1977). Recovery patterns and prognosis in aphasia. *Brain, 100,* 1–18.

Klein, H. B., & Moses N. (1999). *Intervention planning for children with communication disorders.* Englewood Cliffs, NJ: Prentice-Hall.

Kohn, S. E., Lorch, M. P., & Pearson, D. M. (1989). Verb finding in aphasia. *Cortex, 25,* 57–69.

Kremin, H. (1993). Therapeutic approaches to naming disorders. In M. Paradis (Ed.), *Foundations of aphasia rehabilitation* (pp. 261–292). Oxford: Pergamon Press.

LaPointe, L. L. (1977). Base-10 programmed stimulation: Task specification scoring and plotting performance in aphasia therapy. *Journal of Speech and Hearing Disorders, 42,* 90–105.

Lasky, E. Z., Weidner, W. E., & Johnson, J. P. (1976). Influence of linguistic complexity, rate of presentation, and interphase pause time on auditory-verbal comprehension of adult aphasic patients. *Brain and Language, 3,* 386–895.

Lezak, M. D. (1982). The problem of assessing executive functions. *International Journal of Psychology, 17,* 281–297.

Lezak, M. D. (1983). *Neurological assessment.* (2nd ed.). New York: Oxford University Press.

Liles, B. Z., & Brookshire, R. H. (1975). The effects of pause time on auditory comprehension of aphasic subjects. *Journal of Communication Disorders, 8,* 221–235.

Logemann, J. (1983). *Evaluation and treatment of swallowing disorders.* San Diego, CA: College Hill Press.

Luria, A. R. (1963). *Restoration of functions after brain injury.* New York: Macmillian.

Luria, A. R. (1966). *Human brain and psychological processes.* New York: Harper & Row.

Luria, A. R. (1970). *Traumatic aphasia: Its syndromes, physiology and treatment.* The Hague: Mouton.

Marshall, R. C., & Newcombe, R. (1973). Patterns of paralexia: A psycholinguistic approach. *Journal of Psycholinguistic Research, 2,* 175–199.

Martin, A. D. (1974). A proposed rationale for aphasic therapy. In B. Porch (Ed.), *Clinical aphasiology: Conference Procedings* (pp. 60–70). Minneapolis, MN: BRK Publishers.

Martin, A. D. (1979). Levels of reference for aphasia therapy. In R. Brookshire (Ed.), *Clinical aphasiology: Conference Procedings* (pp. 154–162). Minneapolis, MN: BRK Publishers.

Martin, A. D. (1981). The role of theory in therapy: A rational. *Topics in Language Disorders, 63–72.*

Miceli, G., Silveri, M. M., Villa, G., & Caramazza, A. (1984). On the basis for grammatic's difficulty in producing verbs. *Cortex, 20,* 207–220.

Muma, J. (1975). The communication game: Dump and play. *Journal of Speech and Hearing Disorders, 40,* 296–309.

Okkema, K. (1993). *Cognition and reception in the stroke patient.* Gaithersburg, MD: Aspen Publication.

Owens, R. E. (1994). *Development of communication, language, and speech. Human communication disorders: An introduction* (4th ed.). New York: Merrill Macmillian International.

Pierce, R. S. (1982). Facilitating the comprehension of syntax in aphasia. *Journal of Speech and Hearing Research, 25,* 408–413.

Porch, B. (1967). *Porch index of communicative ability.* Chicago: Riverside Publishing Company.

Porch, B. (1994). Treatment of aphasia subsequent to the Porch Index of Communicative Ability (PICA). In R. Chapey (Ed.), *Language intervention strategies in adult aphasia* (3rd ed.). Baltimore: Williams & Wilkins.

Prutting, C. A., & Kirchner, D. (1983). Applied pragmatics. In T. M. Gallagher and C. A. Prutting (Eds.), *Pragmatic assessment and intervention issues in language* (pp. 29–64). San Diego, CA: College Hill Press.

Rezania, K., Hambrecht, G., & Quist, R. (1989). How do aphasic and normal speaking subjects restate a message in response to feedback? *Communication Disorders, 22,* 13–21.

Rice, M. (1984). Cognitive aspects of communicative development. In R. Schiefelbusch & J. Pickar (Eds.), *The acquisition of communicative competence* (pp. 141–189). Baltimore: University Park Press.

Ritchie, D. (1961). *Stroke: A study of recovery.* Garden City, NY: Doubleday.

Rosenbek, J. C. (1978). Treating apraxia of speech. In D. F. Johns (Ed.), *Clinical management of neurogenic communicative disorders* (pp. 191–241). Boston, MA: Little, Brown.

Rosenbek, J. C., LaPointe, L. L., & Wertz, R. T. (1989). *Aphasia: A clinical approach.* Boston: College Hill Press.

Sands, E., Sarno, M. T., & Levita, E. (1971). Evaluating language improvement after complete stroke. *Archives of Physical Medicine and Rehabilitation, 52,* 1, 73–78.

Sands, E., Sarno, M. T. & Shankweiler, D. (1969). Long-term assessment of language function in aphasia due to stroke. *Archives of Physical Medicine and Rehabilitation, 50,* 202–222.

Sarno, M. T. (1991). Recovery and rehabilitation in aphasia. In M. T. Sarno (Ed.), *Acquired aphasia* (pp. 521–582). San Diego, CA: Academic Press.

Sarno, M. T., & Levita, E. (1971). Recovery in treated aphasia in the first year post-stroke. *Stroke, 10,* 6, 663–670.

Sarno, M. T., Silverman, M., & Sands, E. (1970). Speech therapy and language recovery in severe aphasia. *Journal of Speech and Hearing Research, 13,* 607–623.

Sasanuma, S. (1993). Aphasia treatment in Japan. In A. Holland & M. M. Forbes (Eds.), *Aphasia treatment: World perspectives* (pp. 175–198). San Diego, CA: Singular.

Schlesinger, I. (1971). Production of utterances and language acquisition. In D. Slobin (Ed.), *The ontogenesis of grammar* (pp. 63–101). New York: Academic Press.

Schuell, H. M. (1955). Diagnosis and prognosis in aphasia. *Archives of Neurology and Psychiatry, 74,* 308–315.

Schuell, H. M. (1965). *The Minnesota Test for Differential Diagnosis of Aphasia.* Minneapolis, MN: University of Minnesota Press.

Schuell, H. M., Jenkins, J. J., & Jimenez-Pabon, E. (1964). *Aphasia in adults.* New York: Harper & Row.

Schuell, H. M., Jenkins, J. J., & Landis, L. (1961). Relationship between auditory comprehension and word fluency in aphasia. *Journal of Speech and Hearing Research, 4,* 30–36.

Searle, J. (169). *Speech acts.* London: Cambridge University Press.

Seron, X., & de Partz, M. (1993). The reeducation of aphasics: Between theory and practice. In A. L. Holland & M. M. Forbes (Eds.), *Aphasia treatment: Word perspectives* (pp. 131–144). San Diego, CA: Singular.

Shewan, C. M. & Bandur, D. L. (1986). Treatment of aphasia: A language-oriented approach. Austin, TX: Pro-Ed.

Shewan, C. M., & Bandur, D. L. (1994). Language-oriented treatment: A psycholinguistic approach to aphasia. In R. Chapey (Ed.), *Language Intervention Strategies in Adult Aphasia* (3rd ed.) (pp. 184–206). Baltimore: Williams & Wilkins.

Shewan, C. M., & Canter, G. J. (1971). Effects of vocabulary, syntax, and sentence length on auditory comprehension in aphasic patients. *Cortex, 7,* 209–226.

Siegel, G. M. (1959). Dysphasic speech responses to visual word stimuli. *Journal of Speech and Hearing Research, 2,* 152–160.

Skelly, M. (1979). *Ameri-Ind Gestural Code based on Universal American Indian Hand Talk.* New York: Elsevier.

Sparks, R., & Holland, A. (1976). Method: Melodic intonation therapy. *Journal of Speech and Hearing Disorders, 41,* 287–297.

Stein, J. F. (1988). Psychological differences between left and right. In R. Whurr & M. A. Wyke (Eds.), *Aphasia* (pp. 131–169). London: Whurr.

Teasdale, G., & Jennett, B. (1976). Assessment and progress of coma after head injury. *Acta Neurochir (Wien) 34,* 45–55.

Vignolo, L. A. (1964). Evolution of aphasia and language rehabilitation: A retrospective explorative study. *Cortex, 1,* 334–367.

Waller, M. R., & Darley, F. L. (1978). The influence of context on the auditory comprehension of paragraph in aphasic subjects. *Journal of Speech and Hearing Research, 21,* 732–748.

Wepman, J. M. (1951). *Recovery from aphasia.* New York: Ronald Press.

Wepman, J. (1976). Aphasia: Language without thought or thought without language? *Journal of the American Speech-Language-Hearing Association, 18,* 131–136.

Wepman, J., Bock, R., Jones, L., & Van Pelt, D. (1956). Psycholinguistic study of aphasia: A revision of the concept of anomia. *Journal of Speech and Hearing Disorders, 21,* 468–477.

Wilcox, M. J. (1983). Aphasia: Pragmatic considerations. *Topics in Language Disorders, 3,* 35–48.

Wingfield, A., Goodglass, H., & Smith, K. L. (1990). Effect of word-onset cuing on pictured naming in aphasia: A reconsideration. *Brain and Language, 39,* 373–390.

Ylvisaker, M. (1992). Communicative outcome following traumatic brain injury. *Seminars in Speech and Language, 13,* 239–250.

Yorkston, K. M., Beukelman, D. R., & Bell, K. R. (1988). *Clinical management of dysarthric speakers.* Austin, TX: Pro-Ed.

Zingeser, L., & Berndt, R. S. (1990). Retrieval of nouns and verbs in agrammatism and anomia. *Brain and Language, 39,* 14–32.

Suggested Hierarchy of Difficulty for Syntactic Constructions by Persons with Aphasia

LEVEL ONE—COMPREHENSION AND PRODUCTION OF TWO-WORD CONSTRUCTIONS

Level one is the comprehension and production of two-word constructions. These may include structures such as:

Agent + Action	John eat
Action + Object	Eat lunch
Agent + Object	John pipe
Attribution + Object	Dirty table

LEVEL TWO—COMPREHENSION AND PRODUCTION OF MORPHOLOGICAL INFLECTIONS

Level two involves comprehension and production of morphological inflections for nouns, verbs, and adjectives. According to Goodglass and Berko (1960), the order of production difficulty for aphasic patients is based on grammatical function rather than the phonological similarity. The order is as follows:

1. plural (-z) and (-s)
2. comparative (-r)
3. superlative (-st)
4. present (-s) and (-z)
5. past (-d)
6. past (-t) and (-z)
7. possessive (-s) and (-z)

LEVEL THREE—COMPREHENSION AND PRODUCTION OF PHRASE STRUCTURE RULES

Level three involves the comprehension and production of phrase structure rules. There are two basic types of phrase structure rules. There are two basic types of phrase structure rules: noun phrases (NP) and verb phrases (VP). Noun phrases contain an article plus a noun (NP→ Art + N) such as "the man." Verb phrases contain a verb and a noun phrase such as "ate the lunch." Thus a sentence can be rewritten as a noun phrase plus a verb phrase (S → NP + VP). Subject noun phrases, object noun phrases, and verbs are produced and processed at this level.

Other constructions at this stage are:

Agent + Action + Object	Girl eating the sandwich
Attribute (Modifier)+Agent +Action	Happy lady walking
Object + Relation + Object	Rain over the house
Agent + Conj + Agent + Action	John and Joe eating
Object + Prep + Object	Hat under the coat

LEVEL FOUR—COMPREHENSION AND PRODUCTION OF TRANSFORMATIONS

Ability to comprehend and produce transformed sentences characterizes level four. Transforming sentences involves rearranging parts of sentences. In order to question the statement "John can dance." for example, the auxiliary verb and the subject must be rearranged or inverted. The sentence is transformed or rearranged to 'Can John dance?' Examples of some transformations are as follows:

a. *Question transformation.* A question transformation involves the inversion of auxiliary verb and subject. For example, John can dance. → Can John dance?

b. *Do transformation.* A do transformation supplies "do" in a question transformation when there is no auxiliary verb. For example, John dances. → Does John dance?

c. *Negation transformation.* In a negation transformation, the negative element is incorporated into the sentence and is attached to the auxiliary verb. For example, John can dance. → John can't dance.

d. *Passive transformation.* A passive sentence is one in which the action denoted by the verb precedes the subject. For example, John ate lunch. → The lunch was eaten by John.

e. *Addition transformation.* The process of adding structures to an existing sentence is called an addition transformation. For example, John can read. → John can read and write.

f. *Deletion transformation.* A deletion transformation eliminates a component of a sentence that is expressed in a previous sentence or a previous part of the same sentence, or is thought to be understood by the listener. For example, John can fix the painting. → John can.

LEVEL FIVE—COMPREHENSION AND PRODUCTION OF COMPLEX SENTENCES IN WHICH TWO OR MORE CONSTRUCTIONS ARE JOINED INTO ONE SENTENCE

Level-five constructions include complex sentences in which two or more constructions are joined into one sentence. There are several types such as:

a. *Tag questions.* A tag question is a declarative sentence marked either by inflection or by an external marker (Muma, 1978); for example, It's raining outside, isn't it?

b. *Conjoined sentences.* Conjoined sentences involve the grouping of two sentences with a conjunction: for example, He ran a mile and then he ate his dinner.

c. *Relative clauses.* A relative clause is a sentence that modifies a noun phrase: for example, The man who came to dinner, stayed late.

d. *Object noun phrase complements.* An object noun phrase complement is a full sentence that takes the place of the object of a verb. It would be a noun phrase in a simple sentence: for example, I see you sit down.

e. *Wh clauses.* The *wh* clause is a very general mechanism permitting one sentence to serve virtually any role (such as subject, verb, and so forth) in another sentence: for example, Whoever did this, will pay for it.

f. *Right recursiveness.* Recursiveness means to apply a rule again and again (Muma, 1978). Right recursiveness is the production of a complex object noun phrase: for example, Fido ate a can of liver chunks and a can of spaghetti.

g. *Left recursiveness.* Left recursiveness is the production of a complex subject noun phrase: for example, The young slim and short freshman ran.

h. *Embedded sentences.* An embedded sentence is a sentence that modifies part of another sentence and is structurally within the other sentence: for example, The man who has the red and white scarf on stole the cake.

9 Intervention Planning for Adults with Voice Disorders

STEPHEN A. CAVALLO, PH.D.
Adelphi University

CHAPTER OUTCOMES

The reader will:

1. identify the characteristics constituting a voice disorder;
2. classify a variety of voice disorder types;
3. become familiar with factors that may maintain voice disorders;
4. recognize the way in which principles of learning affect treatment planning;
5. become aware of a variety of specialized treatment approaches;
6. be able to apply information from a variety of sources to planning treatment for an adult who has a voice problem.

Introduction

The purpose of this chapter is to examine the nature of problem solving and decision making in planning intervention for adults with voice problems. Voice presents its own unique set of challenges for intervention planning.

The Contribution of Voice to Language Form and Content

Vocal fold vibration, the foundation of voice production, is an important speech sound source. It provides the acoustic energy for all American English vowels, diphthongs, liquids, glides, and nasal sounds. In addition, vocal fold vibration is combined with noise generated within the oral cavity to produce the voiced fricative and affricate sounds. Thus, the voice makes an important contribution at the segmental level of language form. In other words, the human voice is responsible for producing many of the individual sound segments of speech.

In addition to creating many speech sounds, the voice is largely responsible for the suprasegmental features of speech, which, in turn, interact with language content. For example, variations in the amplitude and the fundamental frequency (f_o) of vocal fold vibration (which accompany changes in intonation and stress) are accomplished at the level of the larynx (Atkinson, 1978). Consider the phrase, "Ben and Jerry love ice cream," which a speaker produces with a rising intonation pattern, and again with a rising-falling intonation pattern. These two productions are identical at the segmental level of speech. That is, they have the same phonemic content. Yet, by varying the pattern of f_o change, the speaker can alter meaning. The phrase produced with a rising intonation pattern (increasing f_o level) signals a closed-ended question. The speaker's use of a rising-falling intonation pattern (rising f_o level followed by a falling f_o level) reveals a declarative statement. Similarly, as described by Atkinson (1978), the content of an identical phrase can be altered by systematically varying word stress. Consider three productions of the following simple phrase, in which the underlined word receives primary stress.

1. *Ben* loves Jerry.
2. Ben *loves* Jerry.
3. Ben loves *Jerry*.

In the first example, it is Ben (not Edy or Steve) who loves Jerry. In the second example, Ben doesn't merely like Jerry, he loves him. Finally, in the third example, Ben loves Jerry (not someone else). Atkinson (1978) discussed the different mechanisms of laryngeal control used by speakers to alter the suprasegmental features of stress and intonation.

The Contribution of Voice to Language Use

The voice is an acoustic signal that carries the meaning of the linguistic code. The voice should not interfere with or detract from this primary function. If the voice interferes with the speaker's intended message, it will compromise the speaker's ability to communicate effectively. A voice disorder secondary to vocal tract dysfunction can interfere with both language form and content. For example, a patient with significant velopharyngeal dysfunction will present with what is often classified as a resonance-based voice disorder. Such a speaker has difficulty achieving adequate velopharyngeal closure at the appropriate moment within the flow of speech. To appreciate the importance of the velopharyngeal valve to normal speech production, consider a simple consonant-vowel-consonant (CVC) syllable construct, e.g., "mom." To produce an acoustically acceptable "mom," the speaker must maintain an open velopharyngeal valve during the initial /m/ production. The velopharyngeal mechanism must then achieve significant closure for the vowel /a/ and then must open again for the final /m/ sound. If the speaker cannot effect adequate opening and closing of this articulatory valve at the appropriate moment, an imbalance of oropharyngeal-nasal resonance will occur. The voice will sound hypernasal, and, if velopharyngeal dysfunction is severe enough, audible nasal airflow may be perceived during speech production. In addition, as a consequence of a grossly incompetent velopharyngeal valve, a speaker will have difficulty producing consonant sounds that require high levels of intraoral pressure (specifically, the stop, fricative, and affricate sounds). The unusual vocal quality and imprecise articulation that will result are likely to interfere significantly with speech intelligibility. A voice disorder, then, may constitute a substantial barrier to effective communication and can interfere with language use as it interacts with content and form.

What Constitutes a Voice Disorder

Traditionally, a voice disorder is identified and defined by the perceived alteration in vocal quality that accompanies it. A principle source of voice disorders is the larynx. Within the larynx are two small shelves of tissue known as the vocal folds. When a speaker sets the vocal folds into vibration, sound is produced. This process of setting the vocal folds into vibration to produce sound is called phonation. The acoustic product of vocal fold oscillation is a complex quasiperiodic signal.

A complex periodic signal consists of multiple frequencies of vibration. That is, it consists of a set of sinusoidal waveforms, each having a different period or frequency of vibration. In addition, the pattern of the complex periodic waveform almost repeats itself exactly. Figure 9.1 shows a few cycles of the waveform /a/. Note that the pattern of vibration appears to repeat itself, but not exactly. Slight differences in cycle-to-cycle fundamental period and amplitude exist. Hence, it is considered a quasiperiodic signal instead of a periodic signal. The average fundamental period of this waveform is 5.8 ms. Consequently, the mean fundamental frequency (f_o) of this vowel is 172 Hz. Figure 9.2 reveals the three lowest frequency sinusoidal waveforms of a larger set of sinusoidal waveforms that, when added together, constitute the complex quasiperiodic waveform shown in Figure 9.1. Each of these sinusoidal waveforms has a different frequency, amplitude and phase relationship with the others. Illustrated in Figure 9.3 is an amplitude spectrum. It shows

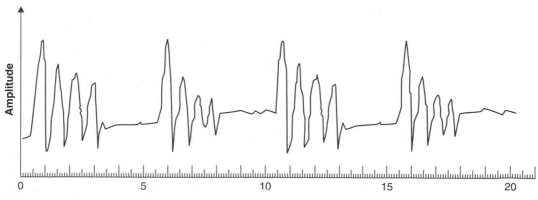

FIGURE 9.1   Four cycles of the waveform /a/.

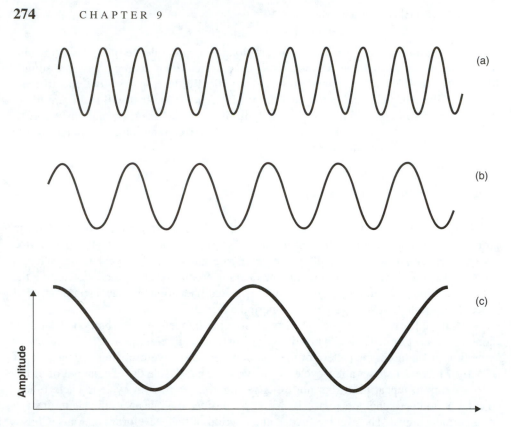

FIGURE 9.2   Components of the quasiperiodic waveform /a/ in Figure 9.1.

the frequency and amplitude of the first three sinusoidal waveforms, or harmonics, of the complex quasiperiodic signal. The amplitude spectrum shown in Figure 9.3 is known as a glottal spectrum because it reveals the amplitude and frequency characteristics of sound produced at the level of the glottis. The first harmonic of the glottal signal has the greatest amplitude and its frequency is equal to the f_o. The amplitude of the higher frequency harmonics will decrease on the order of 6-12 dB per octave. The relative amplitude of the harmonics shown in the glottal spectrum (Figure 9.3) will be modified after the signal has passed through the supralaryngeal vocal tract (pharyngeal and oral cavities). These harmonics that are closest to the resonant frequencies of a particular vocal tract configuration will have the greatest amplitude at the lips. These harmonics whose frequency correspond to valleys in the vocal tract transfer function will be attenuated significantly. The glottal signal, therefore, will be modified after it has passed through the supralaryngeal vocal tract. Its harmonic structure—which is determined at the level of the larynx—will remain essentially unchanged. The relative amplitude of the harmonics, however, will be altered. During vowel production, the acoustic filtering properties of the supralaryngeal vocal tract (the transfer function) are determined by the three-dimensional geometry (cross-sectional area) of the oral and pharyngeal cavities. The waveform shown in Figure 9.1 has passed

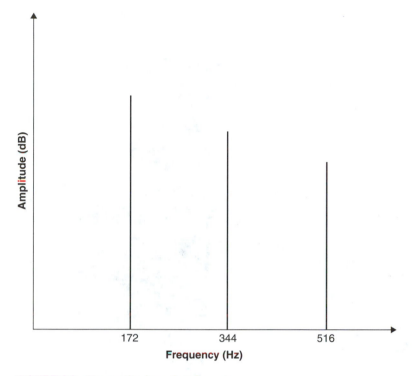

FIGURE 9.3   Harmonics in a glottal spectrum.

through, and has been filtered by, the supralaryngeal vocal tract. Having described the function of the larynx we can now better understand laryngeal-based voice disorders.

Most of laryngeal-based voice disorders are characterized by the presence of noise, which results from inadequate closure of the vocal folds during phonation. In such cases, the line spectrum that should characterize the complex quasiperiodic signal will be replaced, at least in part, by a continuous spectrum (i.e., noise). Figure 9.4a illustrates a power spectrum for a vowel produced with normal voice quality. Note that, as expected, the power spectrum analysis yields a line spectrum. Note also the relative absence of a noise component in the power spectrum of a good quality vowel. Figure 9.4b shows a power spectrum for a vowel produced with a hoarse vocal quality. Note the presence of noise that is characterized by interharmonic and high-frequency energy above 3000 Hz. In effect, a noise component (continuous spectrum) is added to the complex quasiperiodic signal (line spectrum).

An additional consequence of the presence of a mass lesion on the vocal folds is the alteration of vocal fold stiffness and mass (Hirano, 1981; Hirano & Bless, 1993). Such changes in the physical properties of the vocal folds will alter the patient's habitual f_o of vocal fold vibration.

A severe voice disorder can also interfere with the social functions of language. An extreme voice disorder, such as advanced spasmodic dysphonia, usually has severe vocal symptoms associated with it. The ability of an individual with spasmodic dysphonia to

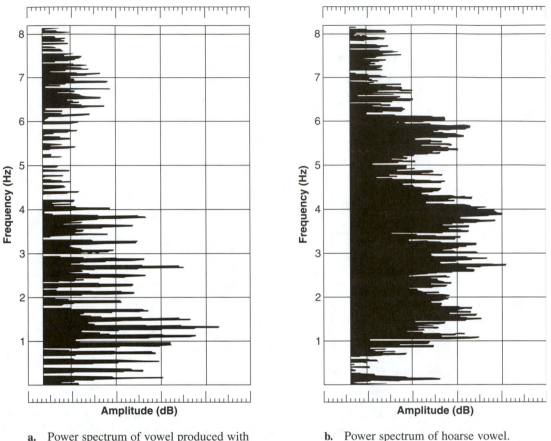

a. Power spectrum of vowel produced with normal vocal quality.

b. Power spectrum of hoarse vowel.

FIGURE 9.4 A, B   Power spectra with a normally produced and hoarse vowel.

function in the world can be compromised considerably. For example, the significant disruption in speech flow associated with untreated spasmodic dysphonia can be so severe that the individual may ultimately cease attempts to communicate verbally. The social and professional consequences of a voice disorder with such severe symptoms can result in dramatic changes in life style, such as the need to change professions or the decision to withdraw from or avoid social contacts. Laryngeal-based voice disorders are characterized by abnormal glottal resistance during phonation. Voice disorders that are marked by reduced glottal resistance (e.g., vocal fold paralysis, vocal nodules, polyps) result in inadequate vocal fold approximation during phonation, which can add a significant amount of noise to the signal. Consequently, the voice is likely to be perceived as hoarse, harsh, breathy, or rough, with varying degrees of severity. Vocal quality and the severity of the dysphonia depend on the size and location of the lesion (or the position of a paralyzed vocal fold) as well as on the clinician's definition of the terms used to designate quality and severity. Other voice disorders are characterized by abnormally high glottal resistance (e.g., adductor spasmodic dysphonia). The voice of an individual with advanced spasmodic dysphonia is often described in the clinical literature as having a strained, strangled quality.

Laryngectomy has severe communication consequences, since the individual has lost one of the primary sound sources for speech. Normal phonation is no longer possible and an alternative sound source must be found. An extrinsic source of vibration (an artificial larynx) or use of an intrinsic vibrating source (use of tissue at the pharyngo-esophageal junction in esophageal speech or following tracheo-esophageal shunt) can serve as the patient's new "voice."

Velopharyngeal dysfunction can alter the normal balance of oral-nasal resonance during speech and phonation, which will result in abnormal vocal quality. Poorly timed and inadequate velopharyngeal closure will result in perceived hypernasality. If velopharyngeal resistance is excessive, a hyponasal quality would be expected. Consequently, resonance-based disorders secondary to velopharyngeal dysfunction are often classified as voice disorders because of the resulting alteration in the quality of speech and voice.

Classifying Voice Disorders

Aronson (1990) advocated classifying voice disorders into two broad categories: organic and psychogenic. According to Aronson, a voice disorder caused by vocal fold tissue changes or neurologic or metabolic disease would be considered an organic voice disorder. Organic voice disorders can result from various congenital conditions (e.g., laryngeal web, laryngomalacia, cysts, stenosis) or viral conditions (e.g., papilloma). In addition, acquired organic voice disorders can be secondary to tumor formation, blunt or inhalation trauma, neurologic disease, or endocrine dysfunction. A psychogenic voice disorder, according to Aronson, is one in which the voice is abnormal in the absence of any significant structural or physiologic abnormalities. Examples include conversion voice disorders, puberphonia, and voice disorders secondary to vocal abuse/misuse or due to excessive musculoskeletal tension. Psychogenic voice disorders may be caused by psychoneurosis (e.g., conversion voice disorders, mutational falsetto) or vocal abuse/misuse (e.g., vocal nodules, polyps, contact ulcers). According to Butcher, Elias, and Raven (1993):

> Factors often associated with psychogenic voice disorder[s] are high levels of anxiety, acute or chronic life stresses, interpersonal relationship or marital difficulties, personal overcommitment or assuming the onus of family responsibilities, difficulties in setting appropriate personal and interpersonal limits, inhibition concerning the expression of thoughts or feelings and associated high levels of helplessness or powerlessness. (pp. 106–107)

Although psychogenic voice disorders are not caused by a structural or physiologic abnormality, organic tissue changes can, and often do, occur. For example, vocal nodules constitute a significant structural change in the vocal folds. However, nodule development is the consequence of faulty habits of voice use. In other words, the cause of the dysphonia is vocal abuse or misuse that results in laryngeal tissue changes. There is some disagreement among voice specialists regarding the classification of abuse-related dysphonias as psychogenic voice disorders. Morrison and Rammage (1994) argued that the diagnosis of a psychogenic voice disorder "should be reserved for those muscle misuse voice disorders that clearly have a primary psycho-emotional etiology, as defined by current standards for psychiatric evaluation" (p. 53).

Sources of Information for Intervention Planning

To develop a comprehensive and well-reasoned intervention plan, the clinician needs to have available critical sources of information. These include:

- knowledge of normal vocal tract structure and function;
- knowledge of maintaining factors;
- baseline data;
- performance demands;
- principles of learning and rehabilitation.

Knowledge of Normal Vocal Tract Structure and Function

A working knowledge of vocal tract structure and function is essential to the development of a rational treatment protocol for patients with voice disorders. A common therapeutic goal for patients who present with dysphonia is the development of "improved breath support." However, before considering the development of long-term, short-term, and session goals to improve breath support, the voice clinician must determine whether it is appropriate to direct intervention efforts to the ventilatory mechanism. Consider the following clinical case:

> M. L., a 26-year-old male (6′ 0″ tall) presented with a dysphonia characterized by severe hoarseness. The clinician, equipped only with a stopwatch and a hand-held spirometer, measured M. L.'s vital capacity (VC) and maximum phonation time (MPT). His measured MPT (the duration of maximum sustained phonation) was 9.4 seconds. Using a spirometer, the clinician determined M. L.'s VC to be 5.4 liters. M. L.'s expected vital capacity based on his age, gender, and body size was 5.34 liters. Given these simple clinical measures, what clinical decision can be made regarding the appropriateness of directing therapy efforts to increasing breath support?

For this patient, the obtained MPT of 9.4 seconds, was excessively low. According to Yanagihara, Koike, and von Leden (1966), an average expected MPT for an adult male is approximately 22.5 s (S.D. = 6.1 s). A reduced MPT can be explained by either a reduced vital capacity or (where the patient's vital capacity is adequate) by a laryngeal valving problem. This voice clinician, having a fundamental understanding of the vocal tract dynamics underlying phonation, recognized she could not interpret the meaningfulness of a 9.4-second MPT without additional diagnostic data. She understood that measurement of the patient's VC was necessary to determine whether the reduced MPT was due to inefficient laryngeal valving during phonation, direct ventilatory system involvement, or both. In this example, M. L.'s reduced MPT was most likely the result of an incompetent laryngeal valve, since his vital capacity was within normal limits for his age, gender, and body size.

The clinician, lacking a basic understanding of the dynamics underlying voice production, might have designed an intervention plan to increase breath support. In this case, rehabilitation efforts directed at an incompetent laryngeal valve would have been more appropriate.

Clearly, an appreciation of ventilatory and phonatory function can assist the clinician in developing appropriate therapeutic goals. Too often, unnecessary work on breath support is undertaken with dysphonic patients because the clinician does not understand normal aspects of voice production. Consider the following two clinical cases in which the clinician developed a long-term therapy goal to improve breath support.

Case Example #1
T. B., a 35-year-old female, presented with a hoarse voice. Monitoring of chest wall movements during speech production revealed that she typically initiated speech of normal conversational loudness at a point between 60% and 65% of her vital capacity. The patient's expiratory limbs typically ended at or slightly below resting expiratory level (REL), that is, around 40% of her vital capacity.

Case Example #2
L. T., a 29-year-old female, presented with a hoarse voice. An examination of her breathing revealed that she typically produced speech of normal conversational loudness at lung volume levels between 30% and 45% of her vital capacity.

The voice clinician who has a basic understanding of normal ventilatory function would be in a position to determine whether a goal to improve breath support was indicated for either patient. The informed voice clinician would recognize that a goal directing intervention efforts on increasing breath support would be appropriate for L. T., but would very likely be contraindicated for T. B. Speech of normal conversational loudness is usually produced within the midvolume range (between approximately 35% and 60% of the vital capacity [Hixon, Goldman, & Mead, 1973]. Within this lung volume range, a speaker can take advantage of the small positive relaxation pressures that exist, thus achieving the subglottal pressures required for speech with minimal muscular effort. Spirometric recordings of T. B.'s speech breathing revealed that she used an appropriate lung volume range (re: REL) during speech production. L. T., on the other hand, appears to have adopted a speech breathing pattern that is highly inefficient. Monitoring of chest wall movements (using variable inductance plethysmography) revealed that L. T. initiated speech at lung volume levels that were inappropriately low, and that she terminated speech at a lung volume level well below REL. Intervention efforts directed at modifying this patient's breathing pattern for speech appear to be worth exploring.

Again, the voice clinician who has a basic appreciation of the physiological factors underlying speech and voice production would be in the enviable position of developing appropriate therapeutic goals. In addition, acoustic and physiologic measures of speech can serve as a means of documenting a patient's progress in therapy, which is an important objective means with which to evaluate therapy efficacy.

The voice clinician who has an adequate background in the basic communication processes should be able to develop appropriate, well-reasoned, therapeutic goals. Objective measures of voice can assist the clinician in making rational clinical decisions.

Consider the following case in which a voice clinician obtained objective measures of the voice and attempted to use those data to guide intervention efforts.

> N. G., a 22-year-old female, presented with a large, nonfibrotic, unilateral sessile polyp. The clinician measured the mean speaking frequency (MSF) and mean f_0 during sustained phonation using a commercially available fundamental frequency analyzer. The clinician noted that MSF and mean f_0 during sustained phonation were unusually low. N. G. presented with a MSF of 168 Hz while reading the "Rainbow Passage," and a mean f_0 during sustained phonation of 171 Hz. Because the patient's f_0 level was too low, the clinician developed the following long-term goal: the patient will increase vocal f_0 to a more appropriate level given the patient's age and sex.

Based on the limited information provided above, does it appear the voice therapist made an appropriate clinical decision?

According to Stoicheff (1981), an expected MSF for a woman N. G.'s age is approximately 224 Hz (normal MSF ranges between 192 Hz and 275 Hz). Therefore, N. G.'s f_0 during reading was lower than expected. Considering that the presence of a nonfibrotic polyp on the vocal fold will result in a decrease in the stiffness and an increase in the mass of the vocal fold cover, a lowered f_0 is not unexpected. For this patient, it is likely that the habitual use of a reduced f_0 is not the cause of the voice disorder, but, rather, a lowered f_0 was the consequence of the changes in the physical properties of the vocal fold, due to the presence of the polyp. Obviously, it would be desirable to have some information regarding the patient's habitual speaking f_0 before the onset of the voice disorder. Since such information is rarely available, patient and family member reports of any changes in f_0 since the onset of the voice disorder often can be helpful in speculating about the premorbid speaking frequency levels. Consequently, a goal directed at increasing vocal f_0 would be contraindicated for this patient. In fact, attempts to increase the patient's MSF may exacerbate the patient's current condition, resulting in additional vocal strain. Rather, therapy directed at eliminating abusive vocal behaviors, if successful, should result in a reduction in the size of the polyp. As the size of the polyp is reduced, the physical properties of the vocal fold will change, and the f_0 of vocal fold vibration should increase to a more appropriate level. Again, knowledge of normal laryngeal structure and function can assist the voice therapist in the clinical decision-making process.

The case example of N. G. illustrates the need to introduce an important caveat regarding instrumental assessment. If the clinician lacks adequate theoretical foundations or is unfamiliar with the capabilities and limitations of the instrumentation, objective measures of vocal function can be misinterpreted. In the case of N. G., the acoustic data were probably valid, but because of the clinician's naivete, they served as the basis for the development of inappropriate intervention goals. The mere acquisition of objective data—which can be invalid, unreliable, or misinterpreted—does not necessarily result in better patient care.

Maintaining Factors

Ideally, voice therapy is initiated only after the etiology of the voice disorder is determined. A desirable, yet sometimes unattainable, goal of the diagnostic voice evaluation is the determination of the specific etiology of the dysphonia. Unfortunately, some voice evaluations include little more than a subjective description of vocal quality. A statement such as "the patient presented with severe hoarseness" provides the clinician with little useful information regarding the etiology, nature, or severity of the voice disorder. Further, such perceptual descriptions do not provide useful information to the voice clinician who must answer critical questions related to clinical management, such as: What is the basis for this patient's dysphonia; What intervention strategies might be indicated or contraindicated; Is voice therapy indicated, and, if so, what should be the initial focus of therapy; What is the prognosis for improvement; What are reasonable expectations for voice production following intervention? Perceptual descriptions of the voice alone are imprecise and are of little diagnostic value to the voice clinician.

Knowledge of the etiology of a voice disorder can assist the clinician in developing an appropriate therapy plan. For example, treatment for a psychogenic voice disorder should be initiated only after the possibility of an organic etiology has been systematically ruled out. Of course, the identification of an organic etiology of a voice disorder does not rule out the possibility, however remote, of a concomitant psychogenic component.

Even when it has been determined that the etiology of a voice disorder is psychogenic (e.g., a voice disorder secondary to vocal abuse or misuse), structural changes in vocal fold tissues can, and usually do, occur. If a voice disorder secondary to vocal abuse or misuse is diagnosed, the clinician must identify the factors that are likely to have contributed to the development of the voice disorder, as well as any behaviors that maintain vocal dysfunction. Aronson (1990) provided a comprehensive discussion on the contribution of stress, which can originate from both internal and external sources, to the development of musculoskeletal tension disorders. He argued that the presence of such tension may lead to the development of a voice disorder in some individuals. According to Aronson, citing Luchsinger and Arnold (1965), these sources of tension may be exogenous (e.g., if the patient works in an environment in which there are great vocal demands in the presence of excessive and intense ambient noise). Endogenous factors such as idiosyncrasies of the patient's personality can serve as the basis of dysphonia as well.

Successful intervention planning for adults with voice disorders requires that the clinician identify variables that can maintain the voice disorder. Among the maintaining factors that need to be considered by the clinician working with the dysphonic patient are sensorimotor and psychosocial factors. In some cases, a patient's dysphonia may be maintained by a significant cognitive impairment.

Sensorimotor Factors.   Voice disorders can result from isolated instances of abuse (for example, screaming at a football game) or from chronic vocal misuse or abuse. Dysphonia can also be a symptom of neurological disease. In the case of an isolated peripheral lesion of the recurrent laryngeal nerve, for example, dysphonia may be the only significant clinical symptom. With more extensive lesions of the nervous system, dysphonia may constitute merely one of many symptoms observed throughout the speech mechanism. In addition, voice disorders can result from benign and malignant tumors, tissue changes due to trauma, the inhalation of caustic materials, viral conditions, metabolic disease, and endocrine dysfunction.

Vocal Abuse or Misuse.   Colton and Casper (1996) provided a comprehensive review of the effects of vocal abuse and misuse on the laryngeal mechanism. The broad category of vocal misuse can include behaviors that result in excessive laryngeal strain or tension (e.g., excessive use of hard attack, chronic maintenance of a high vertical position of the larynx in the neck), habitual use of an inappropriate pitch level, and excessive voice use and singing without proper vocal technique. The definition of vocal abuse, as adopted by Colton and Casper (1996), includes behaviors such as habituated use of an excessively loud voice, excessive throat clearing and coughing, and screaming or cheering. Continued misuse and abuse of the voice will often lead to the development of structural and physiological changes in the larynx and, subsequently, the development of dysphonia. Some examples of tissue changes that are the consequence of abuse or misuse of the voice include vocal nodules, polyps, polypoid degeneration (edema), and contact ulcers. Morrison and Rammage (1994) provided suggestions for maintaining good vocal hygiene. They identified specific vocal behaviors and environmental factors to avoid and those to adopt to promote efficient voice production.

Neurogenic Conditions. Upper motor neuron lesions, resulting from CVA (cerebrovascular accident), traumatic brain injury, or diseases such as multiple sclerosis, will have wide-ranging consequences. The symptoms associated with such global neuropathology are not confined to the phonatory mechanism, but are observed throughout the entire speech mechanism. Although neurological disease and traumatic brain injury (TBI) can occur at any age, the human nervous system is particularly susceptible to insult, injury, and disease with advancing age. As a person ages, expected changes in the structure and function of the nervous system occur, such as neuronal loss, reduced arterial blood flow, and altered neurotransmitter function. These, and other age-related changes that are not associated with any disease process, will compromise nervous system function. In addition to the normal deterioration of nervous system function that accompanies the aging process, various diseases and disorders can afflict the nervous system. The range of symptoms produced by neurological disease depends, in large part, on the site of lesion and the onset and evolution of the disorder. Lesions of the peripheral nervous system are usually focal. Damage to the central nervous system characteristically results in more diffuse manifestations. Some disorders, such as degenerative and metabolic diseases, typically have a diffuse effect on the nervous system. The effect of neoplasms, unless distant metastasis has occurred, is usually focal. Inflammatory diseases can be either diffuse (encephalitis) or focal (abscess) in nature. Similarly, vascular disease can be focal (infarct) or diffuse (subarachnoid hemorrhage) in its distribution. The symptoms associated with global neuropathology are not confined to the phonatory mechanism, but are observed throughout the entire speech mechanism. As Aronson (1990) pointed out:

> [N]eurologic voice disorders, technically, are dysarthrias; although they occur in isolation, most often they are imbedded in a more widespread complex of respiratory, resonatory and articulatory dysarthric signs. (p. 77)

Some examples of neurogenic disorders that present with significant vocal symptoms include pseudobulbar palsy, Parkinson's disease, Huntington's disease, myoclonus, cerebellar ataxia, myasthenia gravis, essential tremor, multiple sclerosis, laryngeal dystonia (spasmodic dysphonia), amyotrophic lateral sclerosis, and peripheral lesions of the vagus (X cranial) nerve. Injury to the vagus nerve, depending on the site of lesion, tends to have a more specific effect on the voice. For example, a unilateral lesion of the recurrent laryngeal nerve has a more focal influence. Specifically, innervation to four intrinsic laryngeal muscles of one vocal fold (posterior cricoarytenoid, lateral cricoarytenoid, thyroarytenoid, and interarytenoid) is interrupted. Consequently, the function of one vocal fold is affected. The consequences of high vagal lesions—those above the level of the pharyngeal branch of the vagus nerve—are more widespread. Such a lesion interferes with speech intelligibility to a greater extent since, in addition to the intrinsic laryngeal muscles, the muscles of the pharynx are affected ipsilaterally. Consequently, in addition to vocal symptoms due to paralysis of all five intrinsic laryngeal muscles, resonance and articulation problems are also expected because of involvement of the muscles of the velopharynx.

Motor speech disorders, such as dysarthria, apraxia and ataxia, are the consequence of neurological disease. Laryngeal and ventilatory motor control problems are commonly associated with neuromotor disorders. Laryngeal and ventilatory dysfunction has a direct effect on a patient's ability to produce voice. The disturbances in motor control that accompany neurological disease are likely to affect the function of the supralaryngeal vocal tract as well, resulting in disorders of articulation and resonance.

Ramig, in Minifie (1994), presented a rational and clinically useful approach to the classification of neurologically based voice disorders. Dysphonia secondary to diseases of or damage to the nervous system can result in any one or a combination of the following: vocal fold hypofunction, vocal fold hyperfunction, and vocal fold instability. Examples of conditions that result in vocal fold hypofunction include cerebellar ataxia, Parkinson's disease, and myasthenia gravis, all of which have a broad effect throughout the entire peripheral speech mechanism. Peripheral damage to the vagus nerve affecting either the recurrent laryngeal nerve alone or both the recurrent and superior laryngeal nerves has a more specific influence on the larynx, resulting in vocal fold hypotonia. Other disorders of the nervous system, such as pseudobulbar palsy, spasmodic dysphonia, and Huntington's disease, result in vocal fold hyperadduction. In the case of amyotrophic lateral sclerosis (ALS), either vocal fold hyperadduction or hypoadduction, can predominate. Hyperadduction of the vocal folds would be expected if the disorder is characterized by spasticity, and hypoadduction would be expected if the disorder is characterized by flaccidity. Laryngeal instability is a prominant feature of essential tremor and cerebellar ataxia.

Organic Disease/Laryngeal Trauma.   Many voice disorders are the result of organic disease or trauma (including exposure to noxious environmental stimuli). Some examples are benign neoplasms, hyperkeratosis, leukoplakia, granuloma and hyperacidic contact ulcer, papilloma, laryngeal carcinoma, cricoarytenoid ankylosis, and a variety of voice disorders secondary to endocrine dysfunction (e.g., hypothyroidism, hyperthyroidism, Addison's disease).

Peripheral Nervous System.   A comprehensive assessment of the peripheral speech mechanism is critical to the planning and implementation of an efficacious intervention plan. This is particularly true for patients with neurogenic voice disorders. For example, patients who present with dysphonia secondary to peripheral lesions of the vagus nerve require a thorough assessment of cranial nerve function. This evaluation can assist the voice clinician in planning appropriate intervention strategies. Consider the following case example:

> R. O. presented with a hoarse voice and hypernasal speech. An examination of the oropharynx revealed asymmetrical movement of the velum during phonation. During vowel production, extensive movement of the velum upward and back was observed only on the right side. The ENT report stated that the left vocal fold was paralyzed between the intermediate and gentle abduction positions.

Based on this information, it is reasonable to conclude that the lesion of the X cranial nerve was high, above the level of the pharyngeal nerve. What are the implications of this information for the planning of therapy? Since R. O.'s vocal fold paralysis was idiopathic and there was some possibility of spontaneous recovery, a trial period of voice therapy was undertaken. However, because the vocal fold was paralyzed such a significant distance from midline (since both the recurrent laryngeal nerve [RLN] and superior laryngeal nerve [SLN] were affected on the left side), the prognosis for improvement with voice therapy was guarded. In addition, resonance problems could be expected for R. O., since motor function to the velum was affected because of the involvement of the pharyngeal branch of the vagus nerve on the left side. Since R. O. presented with two incompetent articulatory valves (velopharyngeal and laryngeal valves), it would not be unreasonable to anticipate difficulties in R. O.'s ability to manage subglottal pressure. His ability to generate and maintain adequate subglottal pressure would be impaired as a consequence of excessive airflow and the premature expenditure of lung volume due to reduced velopharyngeal and laryngeal resistance during speech production. A patient with an isolated lesion of the RLN, resulting in a paralysis of the vocal fold in the paramedian position (closer to midline than for R. O.), would have a more favorable prognosis for improved vocal function with voice therapy.

Hearing Impairment.   The voice can be adversely affected by the presence of a hearing impairment. The effects of a hearing impairment on the voice depend on the degree and time of the onset of the hearing loss. For example, the consequences on voice, as well as speech and language, would be greatest for an individual with a profound, congenital hearing loss. Individuals who present with an organic condition, such as hearing impairment, may be unable to monitor their voice effectively because of impaired auditory feedback. As a result, hearing-impaired individuals will have difficulty controlling pitch, loudness, flexibility, and vocal quality, particularly if the hearing loss is congenital or its onset is prelingual. Resonance problems have been identified with the hearing-impaired population, most likely due to the maintenance of a posterior tongue position (Subtelny, Li, Whitehead, & Subtelny, 1989). Differences in f_o level and f_o variability have been reported between speakers with hearing impairments and speakers with normal hearing (Horii, 1982). Significant problems in ventilatory behavior among hearing-impaired speakers have been reported as well (Forner & Hixon, 1977).

Psychosocial Factors.   The voice has long been considered a barometer of the human psyche. The larynx is extremely sensitive to an individual's physical, psychological, and emotional health. Vocal function is affected by a person's attitudes, emotions, and personality. Anxiety, fear, anger, depression, personality disorders, psychosexual conflict, low self-esteem, disturbed interpersonal relationships, and unresolved conflicts may contribute to the development and maintenance of a voice disorder. The tension and stress associated with everyday life can contribute to vocal dysfunction, particularly in individuals who respond to anxiety by maintaining increased muscle tension in the larynx and perilaryngeal area, pharynx, jaw, tongue, and throughout the ventilatory system. The laryngeal structures appear to be particularly susceptible to emotional stress. Individuals who habitually maintain excessive musculoskeletal tension in response to the psychological stress and tension associated with modern life are at risk for the development of a variety of inflammatory vocal fold tissue changes. Such a response to stress may manifest as nodules, polyps, polypoid degeneration, contact ulcers, or chronic laryngitis. Common sources of anxiety include family problems and disturbed interpersonal relationships. The case histories of patients who present with psychogenic voice disorders may reveal an unfulfilled or disturbed relationship with a parent, child, spouse, or significant person in their lives. In addition, a patient's conversion dysphonia may be related to his or her difficulty expressing feelings of anger, resentment, frustration, or hopelessness.

Many patients who present with psychogenic voice disorders, such as conversion dysphonia, do not require intensive psychological counseling or psychotherapy. Aronson (1990) stressed the need for clinicians who treat patients with psychogenic voice disorders to understand psychological and psychiatric aspects of voice disorders. He argued that voice clinicians should develop improved skills in psychosocial interviewing and psychological therapy. Butcher et al. (1993) provided thorough discussion of the psychological aspects of psychogenic voice disorders. The voice therapist should be sensitive, however, to the need to refer for psychological counseling patients who are unable to deal with the stresses of life on their own or who present with emotional and psychological issues that are beyond the scope of practice for the speech-language pathologist.

An individual's occupation, job responsibilities, work and home environments, family constellation, and life style are important factors in the development and maintenance of a voice disorder. Certain occupations place greater vocal demands on an individual. For example, teachers, clergy, salespersons, professional users of the voice (singers and actors), stockbrokers, and telemarketers all engage in daily activities that require extensive use of the voice. In addition to a person's occupation, the nature of the work environment is another important factor that can contribute to a voice disorder. Does the individual need to use his or her voice under conditions of significant background noise? Does the job require long hours and extended periods of voice use? Do airborne pollutants exist in the workplace? Does the workplace have adequate humidification? In addition, psychosocial issues such as job satisfaction; the quality of relationships with peers, superiors, and subordinates; and the magnitude of job responsibilities are all potential sources of stress and anxiety. For some individuals, their occupation and work environment interact to place them at great risk for the development of voice problems. An extreme example of such an interaction is patient R. L., an untrained aspiring singer in an alternative band. He performed nightly in a smoke-filled room without adequate amplification, and smoked cigarettes and consumed alcohol between sets while mingling with members of the audience.

The dynamics of a person's home environment is also an important consideration for patients with dysphonia. It is not uncommon for adults with several young children or pets to signal them or gain their attention by yelling. In such active home environments, it is not unusual for family members to abuse their voices regularly as they attempt to communicate under conditions of excessive ambient noise. Some examples include a parent who attempts to communicate with a teenage child who is playing music at high intensity or a parent who attempts to mediate a dispute between fighting siblings. If a member of the family has a hearing impairment, it is not uncommon for other family members to speak habitually at excessively high vocal intensities. Extraordinary vocal demands, such as speaking in a noisy environment, reduce the availability of auditory feedback, which can lead to poor monitoring of vocal intensity and unchecked vocal abuse.

Cognitive Factors.   In cases of isolated laryngeal pathology, with no central nervous system involvement, concerns regarding a significant cognitive disability generally do not exist. However, when treating a neurologically based voice disorder with central nervous system involvement, dysphonia may be only one, and often a minor, component of a more global neuropathology. Such patients present with multiple disabilities. For the patient who presents with disorders in cognition, language, resonance, articulation, and ventilatory and laryngeal function, vocal rehabilitation may constitute only one aspect of a larger intervention program. For example, a patient with severe, untreated hypothyroidism may present with myxedema with concomitant lingual edema resulting in dysphonia and articulatory imprecision. If the central nervous system is affected, impairments in language and cognitive function and changes in personality may exist as well. Patients with multiple disabilities who have a severe intellectual disability may present with a voice disorder secondary to laryngeal or velopharyngeal dysfunction. Given the significant deficits in language and cognition, intervention to address the dysphonia or a resonance imbalance is likely to be among the lowest priorities in the treatment program.

Whenever a patient presents with limited cognitive abilities, the clinician should expect the patient to experience difficulty understanding instructions, monitoring the various parameters of the voice and implementing behavioral changes required for improved vocal function.

Baseline Data

Current Vocal Function.   To develop and implement a rational intervention plan for adults who present with voice disorders, it is essential that the clinician have available current and comprehensive diagnostic data. Even for patients who have received a recent voice evaluation, a brief period of diagnostic therapy should not be ruled out. Ongoing assessment is desirable for the following reasons: (a) to confirm initial diagnostic impressions and (b) to evaluate relevant issues related to vocal function that either had not been addressed or were not resolved at the time of the initial voice evaluation. Comprehensive diagnostic data are essential to the development of appropriate rehabilitation techniques and to the formulation of reasonable prognoses. Consider the following clinical example:

> M. H., a 56-year-old female, was seen by an otolaryngologist because of concerns about her voice. The patient complained that her voice was hoarse and that it became "tired" with

continued use. Indirect laryngoscopy revealed small, newly formed, bilateral vocal nodules. M. H. was referred to a local university speech and hearing clinic for voice therapy. During the initial therapy session with M. H., the student clinician initiated a vocal hygiene program. At one point during the session she responded to the patient's expressed concern that her voice might not improve with the comment "Don't worry, we'll fix you right up."

In this example, the student clinician was implementing an intervention strategy based entirely on the otolaryngologist's impressions from a visualization of the larynx. In addition, she attempted, properly, to convey to the patient reasonable expectations regarding her voice following vocal rehabilitation efforts. Unfortunately, in this case, the prognosis offered to the patient was based on the fallacious assumption that the presenting problem was simply the presence of vocal nodules. As a result, the student clinician offered a prognosis that proved to be both premature and inaccurate. Additional perceptual vocal symptoms existed that were overlooked by the clinician, perhaps because she failed to look beyond the otolaryngologist's diagnosis of vocal nodules. These symptoms, which became more severe over several weeks, included intermittent phonation breaks and a strained, strangled vocal quality. Subsequently, airflow and electroglottographic data obtained during diagnostic therapy confirmed instances of intermittent glottal closure during phonation, which resulted in the cessation of phonation for brief periods. Ultimately, adductor spasmodic dysphonia was diagnosed.

This example illustrates the dangers inherent in planning intervention on the basis of a single diagnostic measure. Unfortunately, the speech clinician's a priori acceptance of an otolaryngologist's diagnosis is far too common. Contrary to popular myth, physicians are not omniscient beings. In fact, otolaryngologists, who are specifically trained to identify and differentiate among different forms of tissue pathology, often have little understanding of vocal fold vibratory behavior. Speech clinicians need to assume an active role in the evaluation of vocal function and contribute to the decision-making process, given their unique expertise and knowledge regarding vocal fold vibratory behavior. Appropriate treatment decisions are more likely to occur only after the clinician has completed an independent comprehensive assessment of the patient's vocal function. Such an evaluation includes, in addition to a direct examination of the larynx, the acquisition and interpretation of ongoing perceptual, acoustic, and physiologic data. Appropriate and efficacious treatment techniques cannot be developed and implemented until a comprehensive evaluation of the voice has been conducted.

The importance of maintaining ongoing assessment throughout voice therapy cannot be overemphasized. The acquisition of noninvasive acoustic and physiologic measures of vocal function can be incorporated into the therapeutic process. Such objective measures are sensitive to changes in the status of the larynx and can provide the clinician with indirect objective evidence of the effects of therapeutic intervention. Since it is neither feasible nor desirable to refer patients to the otolaryngologist for frequent visualizations of the larynx, ongoing objective assessment of laryngeal function should be carried out by the voice clinician. Ongoing assessment is an activity that can be reasonably implemented in therapy. The result will be the availability of information that is critical to the evaluation of therapy efficacy.

Baseline Data on Maintaining Factors

The characteristics and capabilities of the dysphonic patient can influence the course and outcome of therapy. Two major determining factors in the success of intervention with abuse-related voice disorders are: (a) the ability of the patient to identify and monitor abusive behaviors and (b) the ability to adopt and habituate new, nonabusive behaviors. Objective voice analysis (i.e., acoustic and physiologic assessment) is a useful means of evaluating the efficacy of voice therapy or medicosurgical intervention.

Patients who possess good auditory discrimination skills and mental representation abilities, for example, can often quickly achieve the behavioral changes necessary to discard poor vocal habits and adopt new behaviors that promote improved vocal function. The degree to which the adult dysphonic possesses these abilities may have important implications for intervention planning. The use of imagery can be an effective technique for modifying vocal behaviors. Although the descriptions provided to the patient using this method may have little or no relationship to underlying physiological processes, imagery has a long history of use in vocal pedagogy and has proven highly successful in the training of professional users of the voice. Voice therapists should not overlook this technique, which can often result in desired changes in vocal function, where physiologically accurate descriptions of voice production or the use of more traditional intervention techniques have failed. For example, traditional symptom modification therapy with Parkinson's patients has not been terribly successful. Ramig (1997) described the effect of providing the simple cue "think loud" to a patient with Parkinson's disease, "Typically, the patient automatically takes a deeper breath, improves vocal fold adduction, opens her mouth more, and uses larger articulator movements (p. 34).

Since most patients with voice disorders need to learn new motor patterns, their ability to use auditory, visual, and tactile and kinesthetic cues are important factors in the outcome of therapy. Patients' ability to identify and discriminate among different voice qualities, intensities, frequencies, and types of vocal attack, and their ability to use such sensory information to effect changes in motor function, will determine, in part, the success of therapy. Patients' intra- and interpersonal discrimination abilities are critical to their adoption and use of new vocal behaviors that are consistent with good vocal hygiene and improved vocal function. Ramig (1997) reported that patients with Parkinson's disease are typically unaware of the extraordinary low vocal intensity of their voices. When the voice of normal conversational loudness is elicited in therapy, it is not uncommon for a patient to respond "I feel like I am shouting." Ramig evaluated the effects of an intensive therapy program for patients with Parkinson's disease, the Lee Silverman Voice Treatment (LSVT). An important focus of the LSVT program is on the sensory self-perception problems characteristic of this population.

The patient's level of motivation to change the voice has important implications for the success or failure of therapy. As a general rule, patients for whom the onset of the voice disorder is sudden and the symptoms are severe will be very concerned about the voice. Patients who are concerned about their voices are usually highly motivated to undertake the often difficult task of modifying habituated behaviors that are inconsistent with good vocal hygiene. On the other hand, patients who enter therapy with a longstanding, chronic dysphonia are generally less concerned about their voices. Consequently, these patients may be less motivated to eliminate habituated patterns of voice use and adopt new behaviors that promote improved vocal function. In some instances, patients with psychogenic voice disorders receive secondary gain from their voice problems. That is, they may derive added benefits from having a voice disorder, such as receiving support and attention from others or using the voice disorder as an excuse not to participate in certain activities. In such instances, the patient may lack sufficient motivation to make the changes necessary to promote improved vocal hygiene and can present a formidable obstacle to vocal rehabilitation. The clinician may find these patients to be both unmotivated and uncooperative.

The clinician should also be aware of the difficulty some patients may experience in carry-over. A patient may be successful in modifying vocal behaviors in the therapeutic milieu and can produce a new, more efficient voice. However, since a person's voice is so intimately related to his or her image of self, it is not uncommon for some patients with chronic dysphonia to reject even an improved voice and resist adopting it. The rejection of a new, more acceptable voice is sometimes reported for patients with a nonorganic mutational falsetto whose vocal fundamental frequency has failed to adjust downward during puberty. Although a more appropriate fundamental frequency may be facilitated quickly in therapy, it is not uncommon for the patient to reject the more appropriate voice because "it doesn't sound like me."

Performance Demands

There are several contextual variables within the therapy session the clinician systematically manipulates to increase or decrease performance demands as intervention progresses. The selection of which variables to manipulate—that is, which performance demands to alter—is usually determined by the skills and abilities of the patient, the parameters of the voice targeted for change, and the nature of the dysphonia. Some examples of the need to reduce complexity based on patient characteristics follow.

Reducing Performance Demands. If a patient has difficulty charting several abusive behaviors simultaneously, the clinician may decide to make the initial performance demands less complex by requiring that the patient initially record only one or two behaviors. The charting of the frequency of occurrence of additional abusive behaviors can be delayed until the patient's monitoring skills have improved. Similarly, the clinician will routinely need to alter the complexity of the linguistic context at various points throughout therapy. Whenever a patient learns a new motor task—for example, learning to produce voice with an easy, soft attack—the clinician may develop an early session goal that requires use of the soft attack only during the production of sustained vowels. As the patient's ability to produce a soft attack improves, new goals requiring the patient to produce this type of attack in more complex linguistic contexts, such as single words, short phrases and ultimately, discourse, may be developed.

Increasing Performance Demands. Alternatively, there may come a point in the rehabilitation program at which the clinician will manipulate contextual variables to increase performance demands. If, for example, a therapy objective is to produce speech with increased vocal intensity, the clinician may, during a later stage in therapy, require the patient to maintain vocal intensity in the presence of increasing amounts of background noise. For a patient who produces speech at an inappropriately low lung volume level, the clinician would work on altering the patient's ventilatory behavior first during speech of normal conversational loudness. Speech production at greater intensity levels, a more difficult task and one that requires the patient to achieve and maintain higher subglottal pressure levels, would be postponed until a later point in the therapy program.

Principles of Learning and Rehabilitation

Throughout this volume several theories of learning and rehabilitation have been identified to guide intervention planning. In the area of voice, treatment programs have been developed around operant (e.g., Butcher et al., 1993) and biofeedback (e.g., Netsell & Daniel, 1979) paradigms. Additionally, there are several general approaches to vocal rehabilitation that have incorporated principles from several theories (see Chapter 4 in this volume). These include auditory training, vocal hygiene, counseling, and the direct modification of faulty or inefficient vocal behaviors. All of these approaches have widespread applicability, irrespective of etiology.

Treatment Programs Based on Specific Theories.
Operant Conditioning. Operant conditioning has a long history among speech-language pathologists as a method of treatment for many speech and language disorders. A therapy program that incorporates operant conditioning techniques typically shapes the behavioral responses of a patient by providing or withholding reinforcement. It is presumed that behaviors will increase in frequency when reinforcement is provided. Conversely, behaviors that are not reinforced should decrease in frequency. Operant conditioning techniques are applied with successful results for patients with nonorganic voice disorders. Butcher et al., (1993) described how cognitive-behavioral treatments, of which operant conditioning is one example, can be applied to patients presenting with psychogenic voice disorders. The rationale underlying cognitive-behavioral treatment is that by improving patients' self-confidence and feelings of control, their level of anxiety or depression will decrease. As stress, anxiety, or depression decreases, it is presumed that patients' vocal symptoms will subside as well.

Biofeedback-Based Therapy.   Historically, voice clinicians have made liberal use of auditory feedback in therapy by evaluating the voices of the patient and others using audio tape recorders and by providing the patient with immediate auditory feedback. Commercial instruments have long been available to permit patient monitoring of vocal intensity level outside of the therapy setting. A variety of visual displays (the Visipitch and Vocal Loudness Indicator, for example) have also been used in therapy to help patients monitor vocal intensity. With the increased availability of more sophisticated, commercially available instrumentation systems, clinicians have increased opportunities to incorporate biofeedback paradigms into vocal rehabilitation programs. For example, many f_0 analyzers, such as the Kay Elemetrics Visipitch, provide real-time visual records of f_0 and relative intensity waveforms. Instruments such as these are noninvasive, menu-driven systems making them "user friendly" and well suited for clinical use. Patients can be provided with immediate visual feedback of f_o and intensity, which can assist the patient in modifying vocal parameters such as pitch and loudness as well as suprasegmental features of speech.

If a voice therapist has access to sophisticated instrumentation arrays that transduce relevant physiological events, these visual signals can be used in a biofeedback-based therapy program. Some physiological signals that might be of interest to the voice clinician for use in therapy include airflow, air pressure, medial contact area of the vocal folds, and chest wall kinematic data. The clinician can provide the patient with immediate visual feedback of these signals. Visual biofeedback, although not routinely embraced by speech-language pathologists, can serve as a valuable clinical adjunct. Netsell and Daniel (1979) provided an example of the successful use of a visual biofeedback paradigm with a dysarthric patient who successfully modified speech behaviors when provided with visual signals of physiologic adjustments. A caveat should be introduced to the clinician considering the use of visual biofeedback in therapy. The clinician must be certain that the signal used in a biofeedback paradigm is reliable, particularly if the patient is required to duplicate or match visual data. Further, the use of biofeedback as a therapeutic tool demands that the clinician has a thorough understanding of the dynamics underlying speech and voice production.

General Approaches.

Auditory Training. Auditory training is a critical component of therapy with the dysphonic patient. Patients who can identify and discriminate among a variety of vocal qualities—normal voices and those representing varying degrees of dysphonia—are more likely to effect changes in voice production and successfully carry over new vocal behaviors outside of the therapeutic setting. Initially, patients need to heighten their awareness of the features of the voice in need of remediation, whether they be quality, flexibility, pitch, or loudness. In addition, the patient needs to have a model of a target voice. As behavioral therapy approaches are introduced, the clinician needs to point out those instances in which the patient produces voice that approximates the target that has been agreed upon by both the patient and clinician. Eventually, the patients serve as their own clinicians, having learned to monitor and evaluate various aspects of their voice production. Fawcus (1986) highlighted the importance of auditory training as a priority in therapy:

> The patient must become a critical and discriminating listener, and this is probably the single most important therapeutic goal. Unfortunately, concentration on breathing in the early stages of treatment—which is normally part of a more traditional approach—inevitably distracts the patient from the more important task of listening to his own voice. (p. 162)

The focus on self-monitoring and evaluation central to auditory training derives from social cognitive theory. Self-monitoring and evaluation may be viewed as metalinguistic or metacognitive strategies taught to the patient by the clinician to facilitate appropriate voice production (see Chapter 4).

Vocal Hygiene. Improved vocal hygiene should be a goal in therapy for all patients presenting with dysphonia. For patients in which laryngeal tissue change has occurred as a result of vocal abuse or misuse, a vocal hygiene program should be a central component of therapy. A thorough examination of environmental and psychosocial factors that are likely to have contributed to the voice disorder should guide the development of the vocal hygiene program. Together, the clinician and patient should identify abusive vocal behaviors and develop strategies for their elimination. At the same time, alternative behaviors that promote good laryngeal health should be identified and substituted for abusive behaviors that have been discarded. It is not enough to simply eliminate bad vocal habits. Given the limitations of the patient's vocal mechanism, the clinician and patient need to search for the most efficient voice the patient can produce. As a general rule, the goal is to produce voice with minimal effort and strain. In addition, environmental factors that contribute to vocal abuse, such as speaking under conditions of excessive environmental noise, need to be identified and modified. Additional examples of environmental control that promote improved vocal hygiene include increasing humidity in the environment, increasing fluid intake and removing airborne pollutants and irritants from the environment, and identifying and eliminating dehydrating drugs and chemicals. Colton and Casper (1996) described some essential components of a vocal hygiene program that include reducing the amount of talking, reducing loudness (which may involve not speaking under conditions of high ambient noise), adopting nonvocal and nonverbal means of signaling others, and learning and adopting a variety of vocal techniques that reduce vocal effort and strain. Strategy training, again, in this program is influenced by principles from social-cognitive theory.

Counseling.   The voice clinician's role as counselor is an important one. All intervention programs should include an explanation of the problem and a discussion of the course, expectations, and objectives of therapy. For most adults with voice disorders, counseling will serve as an important component of intervention. In other cases, when working with patients who present with spasmodic dysphonia, for example, counseling will constitute a major role of the voice therapist. Since the prognosis for improvement with behavioral voice therapy techniques is poor with spasmodic dysphonia, a critical role of the voice clinician is to explore and evaluate with the patient the various treatment options. The advantages and disadvantages of surgical intervention (recurrent laryngeal nerve section, recurrent laryngeal nerve crush) or medical treatment (such as botulinum toxin injection) need to be carefully considered. In the case of advanced laryngeal carcinoma requiring laryngectomy, it is desirable to consult with the patient pre- and postoperatively. Preoperatively, the consequences of a laryngectomy on speech and voice production is often not a major concern of these patients who are, appropriately, more concerned with the issue of their survival. Following surgery, however, the patient may be more responsive to the services of the speech-language pathologist as the realities of alaryngeal communication emerge.

Voice therapy with the adult dysphonic represents a cooperative venture. The prognosis and objectives of therapy should be discussed and agreed upon by the patient and clinician. If, following a phase of treatment, satisfactory improvement has not been achieved, the client and clinician need to evaluate the reasons for the lack of progress. Possible explanations for the failure to achieve success could be the administration of inappropriate behavioral techniques, lack of adequate motivation or cooperation on the part of the patient, inability of the patient to carry out the behaviors specified in the management plan, a mismatch in the objectives of the clinician and patient, or the concomitant existence of an unresolved medical or psychological condition. In any case, the clinician needs to either perform additional tests, design and implement a new treatment protocol, or refer to other health professionals for counseling or medical management, as appropriate. The emphasis on a cooperative venture between patient and clinician may be seen to incorporate principles of collaboration derived from social-cognitive learning theories.

Direct Modification of Speech and Phonatory Behaviors. For a variety of voice disorders, it may be necessary to change specific speech and vocal behaviors. This may require direct intervention to modify faulty habits of voice use or learned behaviors that either are inefficient or maintain vocal dysfunction. For example, if vocal pathology results from chronic and excessive use of a hard vocal attack, patients first must learn to reliably discriminate among various types of vocal attack. Then, patients need to learn to consistently identify their use of hard attack. Once patients can intrapersonally scan for their use of hard attack, they need to modify their vocal attack, substituting a more efficient, less traumatic form of vocal initiation such as the soft attack. Another example is the rare instances in which patients have learned and habituated an aberrant speech breathing pattern. Assuming an intact and competent set of ventilatory structures, any atypical chest wall movement patterns or lung volume expenditures will require modification. Imagery and visual biofeedback paradigms can be effective therapeutic methods for eliminating undesirable learned speech behaviors and substituting more appropriate ones. In the case of mutational falsetto, patients are taught specific techniques to modify habituated speech and phonatory and ventilatory patterns that are presumed to maintain the disorder. According to Aronson (1990), "Therapy for mutational falsetto is based on learning to inhale with increased air volume and to exhale with increased force simultaneous with a sharp glottal attack" (p. 345).

Specialized Treatment Approaches.

Intervention with Psychogenic Voice Disorders. Boone and McFarlane (1994) described conversion aphonia as a somatoform disorder

> in which symptoms suggesting physical etiology occur
> for which no identifiable organicity can be demonstrated, no
> physiological basis is inferred, and symptoms are linked
> through positive evidence or strong presumption to
> psychological disturbance or conflict. (pp. 227–229)

When a conversion voice disorder is suspected, it is important to get clearance from an otolaryngologist, to wit, confirmation of the absence of organic disease. Therapy should begin, as always, with a brief period of patient education. Patients need to understand the etiology of the voice disorder. The negative ENT findings should be revealed and their significance explained. Specifically, patients need to understand there is no physiological or anatomical explanation for their inability to adduct the vocal folds. The clinician must also explain to the patients that the larynx is a common site for the expression of emotional problems and stress. Patients presenting with a conversion voice disorder need to be convinced they are capable of producing normal voice. Therefore, instances of vegetative phonation (e.g., cough, sigh, yawn, laughter) need to be pointed out immediately. These vegetative vocalizations can then be shaped into phonation and speech. In the search for the voice the patient has lost, symptomatic voice therapy, using various facilitating techniques, may result in the patient's rediscovery of volitional phonation. Aronson (1990) pointed out:

> Conversion aphonia and dysphonia are treated according to the principle of re-establishment of the patient's conscious awareness of greater phonatory capability and discussing the emotional conflicts that have generated the voice disorder. (p. 345)

Butcher et al. (1993) described the application of cognitive-behavior treatment to psychogenic voice disorders. According to these authors, the clinician chooses:

> an appropriate combination of strategies from the following possibilities: anxiety or stress-management training . . .; target setting; record keeping; guided evaluation or analysis of dysfunctional or negative thinking; guidance in challenging unhealthy thinking and finding healthy alternatives, sometimes employing cue cards which summarise positive thoughts; giving information about the nature of stressful life events; giving advice; marital therapy focused on improving communication and rewards in relationships; role playing and assertiveness training . . .; and behaviour modification techniques such as prescribing a half-hour worry period and programmes employing operant conditioning principles. (p. 107)

Intervention with Neurogenic Voice Disorders. The dysphonia secondary to neurological disease often represents only one aspect of more global speech system dysfunction. The voice problems associated with central nervous system lesions, for example, may be minor relative to the more severe symptoms present, such as dysarthria, ataxia, apraxia, dysphagia, and aphasia. On the other hand, changes in vocal function may be among the earliest symptoms to appear in patients with neurologically based dysphonia. Typically, lower motor neuron lesions, depending on their location, have a more specific influence on the voice. Patients with voice disorders associated with central nervous system diseases are generally resistant to voice therapy. Lesions of the peripheral nervous system are, as a general rule, more responsive to vocal rehabilitation techniques. A peripheral lesion of the vagus nerve, for example, will have more localized effects. The primary symptom of a unilateral lesion of the recurrent laryngeal nerve will be dysphonia. A vagal lesion above the level of the pharyngeal nerve, however, will result in resonance problems in addition to dysphonia.

For patients with neurological disorders that affect vocal function, Ramig and Scherer (1992) advocated a treatment approach that focuses on the underlying laryngeal pathophysiology. The diagnosis of specific neurologic disorder is less important to management than the nature of laryngeal dysfunction. Common problems in laryngeal function accompanying neurologic disorders identified by Ramig and Scherer (1992) include: "problems in adducting the vocal folds (hypoadduction, hyperadduction), producing a stable voice (phonatory instability), and coordinating movements (phonatory incoordination)" (p. 163).

If a voice disorder is associated with a degenerative neurological disease, or if normal laryngeal function is not a reasonable expectation, the goal of voice therapy may be to maintain the current level of vocal function. In such cases, voice improvement may not be a therapeutic objective. Rather, maintaining current vocal function or delaying further deterioration of the voice may be realistic therapeutic expectations. In many cases of dysphonia associated with degenerative neurological disease, augmentative communication

devices need to be considered when functional speech and phonation are no longer reasonable objectives. Realistic expectations of voice production need to be conveyed to the
patient early in the therapeutic process.

Decisions Regarding Surgical Intervention.   Often, management of a voice disorder
requires a combination of medical, surgical, and behavioral intervention. In cases of laryngeal trauma in which the cartilaginous framework of the larynx is crushed, compromising
the patency of the airway, or the vocal folds are lacerated, surgical intervention may be
required immediately. It is possible that voice therapy may be helpful, after surgery and
healing have taken place, to reestablish the best possible voice given the vocal capabilities
possible with the reconstructed larynx.

In the case of recurrent laryngeal nerve paralysis of idiopathic etiology, voice therapy may be the initial choice for intervention. If voice therapy proves unsuccessful or if
spontaneous recovery of the recurrent laryngeal nerve is not observed after 6 to 12 months,
phonosurgery (vocal-fold medialization) or injection of an inert substance into the affected
vocal fold may be considered.

For cases of vocal misuse or abuse in which large lesions were surgically removed,
voice therapy is an essential postsurgical procedure. Obviously, simply removing large
vocal nodules or polyps will not resolve the underlying cause of the tissue pathology: vocal
abuse/misuse. A period of voice therapy focusing on vocal reeducation, if successful, will
reduce the probability that the lesion will recur, thus eliminating the need for additional
surgery.

Symptomatic Voice Therapy.   As Boone and McFarlane (1994) pointed out, "the abusive vocal behaviors of adults are likely to be more difficult to isolate than those of children. It is the relatively rare adult voice patient whose vocal abuses are bound only to particular situations" (p. 150).

These authors advocated the use of various "facilitating approaches" as therapy
"probes" in the search for the patient's best voice. Such a voice, they asserted, "allows
an individual to produce voice with less effort and strain" (Boone & McFarlane, 1994,
pp. 151–152).

Table 9.1 summarizes 25 facilitating approaches, which, when appropriately applied
to patients with dysphonia, can be used effectively to modify vocal parameters such as
pitch, loudness, and quality.

The focus of symptomatic voice therapy is on vocal symptoms, which, when eliminated, should result in more efficient voice production. Morrison and Rammage (1994,
p. 81) stressed the importance of the "auditory, visual and tactile-kinesthetic processing
systems" to the success of symptomatic voice therapy. It is important that the clinician who
incorporates symptomatic voice therapy as part of a vocal rehabilitation program not arbi-
trarily select a particular facilitating technique. Rather, the choice of a facilitating technique should be based on the clinician's understanding of the nature of the disorder and
should be selected only after an appropriate rationale for its use has been developed.

Boone and McFarlane (1994) pointed out, "The selection of a particular approach
[facilitating technique] should not be an arbitrary, trial-and-error decision. Rather, the possible effects on the parameters of pitch, loudness and quality must be considered" (p. 152).

TABLE 9.1 Twenty-Five Facilitating Approaches in Voice Therapy

Facilitating Approach	Parameter of Voice Affected		
	Pitch	Loudness	Quality
1. Altering tongue position			x
2. Change of loudness	x	x	x
3. Chant talk		x	x
4. Counseling (explanation of problem)	x	x	x
5. Digital manipulation	x		x
6. Ear training	x	x	x
7. Elimination of abuses		x	x
8. Elimination of hard glottal attack		x	x
9. Establishing a new pitch		x	x
10. Feedback	x	x	x
11. Focus	x		x
12. Glottal fry		x	x
13. Half-swallow, boom		x	x
14. Head positioning	x		x
15. Hierarchy analysis	x	x	x
16. Inhalation phonation	x	x	
17. Masking	x	x	x
18. Nasal/glide stimulation			x
19. Open-mouth approach		x	x
20. Pitch inflections	x		
21. Relaxation	x	x	x
22. Respiration training		x	x
23. Tongue protrusion	x		x
24. Warble	x		x
25. Yawn-sigh	x	x	x

Source: Boone, D. & McFarlane, S. C. (1994). *The Voice and Voice Therapy.*

In addition, the voice therapist engaged in direct symptom management should, as a general rule, focus on one vocal parameter at a time. Bless (1988) point out, "A shotgun approach that provides several therapeutic strategies simultaneously may be both confusing and counterproductive" (p.140).

Additional Considerations for Intervention Planning

Collaboration with Allied Professionals. Management of a voice disorder, depending on its nature and etiology, may require voice therapy, medical-surgical intervention, or some combination of rehabilitation strategies. Input from various disciplines may be necessary before an appropriate, comprehensive, and efficacious therapy plan can be developed. Ideally, adults with voice problems should be treated in a comprehensive manner by a team of specialists. Such a team might include a speech-language pathologist and otolaryngologist. Depending on the nature and etiology of the voice disorder, additional team members could include a psychiatrist, psychologist, endocrinologist, neurologist, gastroenterologist, or oncologist. Unfortunately, the team approach to the management of voice disorders is not routine. This is the case even in many medical settings in which potential interdisciplinary team members are on staff but do not subscribe to a model of joint data collection and interpretation. For the vast majority of practicing speech-language pathologists, a team approach, however appealing a concept, cannot be realistically achieved in clinical practice. It is therefore essential for the speech-language pathologist to initiate communication and seek consultation with appropriate allied medical personnel when treating patients with voice disorders.

Voice therapy may be undertaken in each of the following instances: (a) when medical-surgical management is contraindicated; (b) when medical or surgical intervention has been postponed to evaluate the effects of voice therapy; or (c) following medical or surgical intervention of a voice disorder secondary to vocal abuse, misuse, or excessive musculoskeletal tension. Remember that when surgical intervention is undertaken for an abuse-related voice disorder, it must be followed up with a period of voice therapy. The failure to introduce vocal retraining as a postsurgical adjunct will most likely result in the recurrence of tissue pathology. Unless abusive vocal behaviors are eliminated, the long-term success of surgical intervention is unlikely. For voice disorders not responsive to voice therapy, the clinician's primary responsibility, if he or she is the first professional to consult with a patient, is to make an appropriate medical referral. For example, if an examination of phonatory function and review of a comprehensive case history suggest a dysphonia secondary to endocrine dysfunction, a referral to an endocrinologist for medical management would be indicated.

Medical clearance, minimally in the form of a recent visualization of the larynx, is essential before initiating any form of intervention with the dysphonic patient. For some forms of laryngeal pathology, more detailed assessment (such as stroboscopic endoscopy) can provide detailed information about the nature of vocal fold vibratory behavior and can yield more accurate and precise diagnoses. Such objective diagnostic data can assist the clinician in the development of appropriate intervention strategies as well.

In general, voice therapy with patients whose dysphonia is secondary to vocal abuse (e.g., vocal nodules) should be guided by a search for any contributing or maintaining factors. A primary goal of intervention is the identification of any behaviors or factors that have contributed to the development of vocal nodules. In addition, any factors that maintain the voice disorder must also be identified. Once identified, a major focus of therapy is the implementation of a vocal hygiene program. The vocal hygiene program involves the systematic reduction, or ideally, elimination of abusive behaviors. As abusive factors are reduced or eliminated, the effect on the voice should be evaluated both subjectively and objectively. In addition to identifying and eliminating abusive vocal behaviors and misuse of the voice, the patient should be provided with alternative behaviors that promote good vocal hygiene. For example, if screaming has been identified as an abusive factor, in addition to eliminating screaming, the patient will need to adopt nonverbal/nonvocal means of gaining the attention of others and disciplining children.

Patient Education. An important component of all vocal rehabilitation programs for adult dysphonics is a brief period of instruction regarding normal vocal fold structure and function. In addition, it is advisable to demonstrate to the patient the adverse effects of specific vocal or verbal behaviors in which they engage that are likely to have an adverse effect on vocal function. The use of graphic illustrations, functional models of the larynx, and high-speed films or stroboscopic images contrasting normal and abnormal vocal fold vibration (in slow or apparent slow motion) can be effective adjuncts to patient education. Plausible explanations for the patient's condition should be discussed and acknowledged. If, for example, it has been determined that a patient has a conversion aphonia, the patient needs to be presented with evidence of their ability to achieve vocal fold approximation. The clinician should provide the patient with immediate feedback of any instances of voicing (e.g. coughing, laughing). Obviously, all clinical instruction must be individualized so that descriptions are appropriate to a particular patient's background. The clinician needs to be sensitive to differences in socioeconomic and educational level, cognitive function, age, gender, and culture when counseling or providing instruction to patients.

Case Study

Background Information

Marsha, a 36-year-old female, was referred to an otolaryngologist by her internist because of a hoarse voice. Indirect laryngoscopy revealed "good mobility of the vocal cords; however, at the junction of the anterior and mid-third of the cords there are small nodules which are seen at rest." Visualization of the larynx by the ENT, resulted in the medical diagnosis of bilateral vocal nodules. The patient was subsequently referred for voice therapy. During a telephone consult with the otolaryngologist, it was reported that the nodules were newly formed with no evidence of fibrosis at the time of the examination. The initial responsibility of the voice clinician was to determine whether voice therapy alone was indicated. Because the vocal nodules were small and newly formed, the ENT's recommendation of an initial period of voice therapy alone was appropriate. The voice clinician should also confirm the ENT's diagnosis of isolated vocal nodules, ruling out the possibility, however remote, of the existence of other laryngeal or speech system pathology. Such confirmation can be accomplished during a brief period of diagnostic therapy.

Summary of Evaluation Results

Marsha's initial therapy sessions were diagnostic in nature. In addition to the perceptual and objective assessment of the voice, a comprehensive case history was obtained. A thorough case history was obtained to identify any potential precipitating and maintaining factors. Since vocal nodules had already been confirmed visually, the focus of initial intervention efforts was to review Marsha's daily activities to identify any sources of vocal abuse or misuse. Once abusive factors were identified, a major thrust of therapy was to systematically eliminate them while evaluating the effect of their elimination on the voice. An additional objective of diagnostic therapy for this patient was to obtain objective data regarding vocal function before the initiation of the vocal rehabilitation program. Several acoustic and physiologic measures of the voice were obtained during the initial diagnostic therapy sessions.

These measures later served as baseline data with which subsequent measures of vocal function were compared. The acquisition of repeated measures of vocal function every few weeks during therapy permitted an objective evaluation of therapy efficacy.

Based on information obtained from the case history, physical examination, and the objective evaluation of Marsha's voice during two sessions of diagnostic therapy, the following significant factors were identified.

Maintaining Factors Identified Through the Case History.

- Marsha's occupation as a part-time physical education teacher and summer camp counselor and the extraordinary vocal demands associated with these professional roles placed her at high risk for maintaining vocal nodules.
- Marsha engaged in excessive throat clearing.
- Marsha reported excessive instances of "raising" her voice and "yelling," particularly when at home fulfilling her role as the primary caretaker of her three young children.
- Marsha had adopted an habitually "explosive" speech pattern, which was characterized by high vocal intensity and a hard vocal attack.
- Marsha operated a small business out of her home that required extended hours of daily telephone use.

The patient's history was negative with regard to: (a) the use of any prescription or over the counter drugs; (b) food or airborne allergies; and (c) any significant medical or health problems.

Maintaining Factors Identified Through Objective Measures of Voice Production Physiologic Assessment.

- Lung volume change, estimated from chest wall movements, revealed Marsha's habitual use of an inappropriate lung volume range during speech production. Marsha's conversational speech typically took place between 25% and 50% of her vital capacity.
- Marsha's measured VC was 2.6 liters, which represents 83% of her expected VC, based on her height, age, and gender.
- For maximum sustained phonation tasks, Marsha used oppositional prephonatory chest wall movements (that is, rib cage expansion was accompanied by abdominal contraction throughout the prephonatory inhalation).
- Mean airflow during sustained phonation at a comfortable pitch and loudness level was on the order of 280 ml/s.
- The patient's average laryngeal airway resistance (Smitheran & Hixon, 1981) was calculated to be 25 cm H_2O/LPS.
- Marsha's MPT was 8.7 seconds.

Acoustic Analysis.

- Acoustic analysis during sustained phonation at comfortable pitch and loudness yielded relative average perturbation (RAP) values that were consistently in excess of 3%.

- Spectrographic analysis revealed excessive noise above 3000 Hz and the presence of significant levels of interharmonic energy.
- Marsha's MSF during reading of the "Rainbow Passage" was 179 Hz.
- Acoustic analysis during sustained phonation and speech production revealed an average rise time of the amplitude envelope on the order of 28 ms.

Results of the Physical Examination.   Physical examination and manipulation of laryngeal structures, which consisted of digital manipulation of the hyoid bone and thyroid cartilage, revealed no evidence of excessive musculoskeletal tension in the perilaryngeal area. In addition, no observable tension was noted upon palpation of the suprahyoid muscles in the region of the submandibular arch during phonation at various pitches.

Assessment of Laryngeal Valving.   The physiologic assessment of vocal function obtained before the initiation of therapy included measures of mean airflow during sustained phonation. Marsha's mean airflow during phonation was approximately 280 ml/s. According to Koike and Hirano (1968), average airflow during phonation for an adult female is on the order of 93.7 ml/s (S.D. = 31.6 ml/s). At therapy onset, Marsha's average airflow of 280 ml/s during phonation was too high.

The acquisition of simultaneous airflow and air pressure measures permitted the calculation of an estimate of laryngeal resistance during phonation. Marsha's estimated average laryngeal airway resistance during phonation was on the order of 25 cm H_2O/LPS. An average laryngeal resistance of 25 cm H_2O/LPS during phonation is too low. Smitheran and Hixon (1981) reported average values of glottal resistance on the order of 35.7 cm H_2O/LPS (S.D. = 3.3 cm H_2O/LPS).

Marsha's high mean airflow values and reduced glottal resistance during phonation are consistent with bilateral vocal nodules. The high airflow levels and reduced glottal resistance during phonation are expected as a result of inadequate vocal fold closure due to the presence of the nodules (Yanagihara, 1970; Yanagihara & von Leden, 1967).

Additional evidence of inefficient laryngeal valving during phonation was obtained from pretherapy measures of VC and MPT. Marsha's VC was grossly within normal limits for her age, sex, and body size (Kory, Callahan, & Boren, 1961). Consequently, Marsha's reduced MPT appeared to be the result of incomplete glottal closure during phonation, instead of the result of inadequate ventilatory support.

The acquisition of physiologic data during speech and phonation served two important functions. First, they represented objective measures of vocal function, which described the status of the ventilatory and phonatory mechanisms before the initiation of therapy. Second, they served as a useful yardstick for the ongoing assessment of therapy progress.

Acoustic Measures.   Spectrographic analysis of sustained vowels revealed the presence of acoustic energy above 3000 Hz and excessive interharmonic energy. In addition, measures of RAP, an index of vocal jitter, consistently exceeded 3%. These acoustic features of Marsha's vowel production are consistent with vocal roughness (Deal & Emanuel, 1978; Emanuel & Sansone, 1969; Emanuel &Whitehead, 1979; Koike, 1973; Takahashi & Koike, 1975; Yanagihara, 1967). Spectral analysis of normal vowel production resulted in a line spectrum with most of the acoustic energy between 0 and 3000 Hz. In other words, a vowel produced with good vocal quality has little energy above 3000 Hz. Vowels, after all, are low-frequency speech sounds. However, because of the presence of vocal nodules, excessive glottal airflow and turbulence occur during phonation as a result of inadequate vocal fold closure (Isshiki, Yanagihara & Morimoto, 1966). Incomplete glottal closure during phonation results in the addition of a noise component to the complex quasiperiodic signal. In essence, a hoarse voice involves the addition of a noise component (which can be seen as a continuous spectrum) to the complex quasiperiodic signal that characterizes normal phonation. Figure 9.4a, b introduced above compares the power spectra for a normal quality vowel /a/ with that of a vowel produced with a hoarse vocal quality /b/. The presence of interharmonic and high-frequency energy are both characteristic of a hoarse voice. These acoustic features quantified the noise component in Marsha's vocal signal. As Marsha's therapy progressed, spectrographic analysis of sustained phonation documented changes in the status of the vocal folds. Specifically, as the size of the nodules reduced, a concomitant reduction in the noise component would be expected. Thus, noninvasive objective acoustic measures of vocal function, rather than a more invasive endoscopic procedure, could be used to evaluate therapy efficacy.

A pretherapy assessment of vocal f_0 revealed a MSF of 179 Hz during reading. Although f_0 was low for a woman of Marsha's age, it was within the expected range given that bilateral vocal nodules were present. A lowered MSF was expected since the vocal nodules increased the mass of the vocal folds. Direct intervention to alter f_0 would therefore be an inappropriate therapeutic goal and an attempt to modify f_0 was contraindicated.

Table 9.2 summarizes areas assessed and baseline data for intervention planning.

Long-Term Planning Phase

Long-Term Goals. The development of Marsha's long-term (LTGs) goals was guided by: (a) the medical diagnosis of vocal nodules, (b) objective baseline acoustic and physiologic data obtained during diagnostic therapy that quantified the effect of vocal nodules on vocal function, and (c) the clinician's ability to identify relevant maintaining factors from an evaluation of case history information, diagnostic therapy findings, and the clinician's experience and knowledge base.

As a general rule, the initial focus of therapy with vocal nodules should center on the identification of abusive vocal behaviors. Once these behaviors have been identified, a vocal hygiene program should be developed by the voice clinician in consultation with the patient. The primary objective of a vocal hygiene program is to systematically reduce, or ideally eliminate, all of the abusive vocal behaviors identified. Given the nature of Marsha's voice disorder, it was expected that voice therapy would yield significant positive changes in the status of the larynx within approximately eight to twelve weeks. Consequently, LTG achievement for this patient was expected within three months of the initiation of voice therapy. At this time — if voice therapy was successful — the vocal nodules should be eliminated or significantly reduced in size.

One LTG was established a priori.

LTG 1: Marsha will demonstrate an understanding of: (a) normal laryngeal structure and function and (b) the effect of vocal abuse on the vocal fold tissues and on her ability to produce good quality voice.

TABLE 9.2 Areas Assessed and Summary of Baseline Data for Intervention Planning

Name: Marsha B.   Age: 36   Primary Disorder: Vocal Nodules
Area Assessed (include sources and results)

I. Language
    A. Content-form   Informal assessment   WNLs
    B. Use   Informal assessment   WNLs
    C. Phonology
        1. Phonetic   Informal assessment   WNLs
        2. Phonological   Informal assessment   WNLs
    D. Fluency   Informal assessment   WNLs
    E. Voice
        1. Physiological assessment

Area	Description / Result
Vital capacity (VC)	To screen overall cardiopulmonary health: the maximum volume of air the patient can exchange. Result: 2.6 liters (WNLs)
Maximum phonation time (MPT)	To assess the integrity of the laryngeal valve during phonation. Result: 8.7s; the patient's MPT was abnormally short. Given the patient's normal VC, the reduced MPT supports the conclusion of inefficient laryngeal valving during phonation (reduced glottal resistance).
Mean airflow during phonation	To assess the integrity of the laryngeal valve during phonation. Result: 280 ml/s; the high airflow during phonation is consistent with reduced glottal resistance.
Estimated average laryngeal airway resistance during phonation	To assess the integrity of the laryngeal valve for phonation. Result: 25 cm H_2O/LPS; the excessively low laryngeal resistance value reveals reduced glottal resistance during phonation.
Lung volume expenditures during speech	To assess ventilatory support for speech. Result: Speech was typically produced within 25–50% of the patient's VC. This represents an inappropriate lung volume range for speech production.
Chest wall kinematics	To assess breathing pattern during phonatory and speech tasks. Result: The patient consistently used an aberrant oppositional chest wall movement pattern before maximum sustained phonation tasks and occasionally before speech produced at greater loudness levels.

        2. Acoustic analysis

Area	Description / Result
Perturbation analysis	To evaluate the stability of phonation. Result: Relative average perturbation (RAP) values during phonation at a comfortable loudness and pitch consistently exceeded 3%, which reveals considerable

	laryngeal instability and is consistent with vocal roughness.
Spectrographic analysis	To objectively evaluate degree of vocal roughness. Result: Excessive noise above 3000 Hz and significant levels of inter-harmonic energy are consistent with the perception of this patient's hoarse voice.
Average rise time of the amplitude	To objectively evaluate the type of vocal attack used most often by the patient.
Envelope	Result: An average rise time on the order of 28 ms is consistent with the patient's use of a hard vocal attack.
Mean speaking frequency (MSF)	To assess indirectly the physical properties of the vocal folds. Result: The patient's MSF during reading of 179 Hz is low. A low MSF is consistent with the presence of vocal nodules that alter the mass and stiffness of the vocal fold cover.

II. Maintaining Factors
- A. Cognitive   Informal assessment   No abnormalities identified
- B. Sensorimotor
  - 1. Peripheral speech mechanism
    - A. Physiologic assessment revealed:
      - 1. Poor breath support as evidenced by:
        - a. habitual use of an inappropriate lung volume range during speech production;
        - b. inappropriate chest wall posturing for maximum sustained phonation and loud speech.
      - 2. Reduced (inefficient) glottal resistance during phonation as evidenced by:
        - a. excessive airflow during phonation;
        - b. reduced glottal resistance during phonation;
        - c. reduced MPT with a VC that was within normal limits.
    - B. Acoustic analysis revealed:
      - 1. Excessive noise during phonation, which was due to inefficient glottal closure during phonation as evidenced by:
        - a. excessive RAP values;
        - b. excessive noise in the vocal signal.
      - 2. Loading of the vocal folds due to the presence of vocal nodules as evidenced by:
        - a. reduced MSF during reading.
      - 3. The patient's use of a hard vocal attack as evidenced by:
        - a. an average rise time of the amplitude envelope on the order of 28 ms.
  - 2. Body stability   Informal assessment   No problems noted
- C. Psychosocial

The case history revealed the following psychosocial maintaining factors:
1. vocal demands of the patient's occupation as a part-time physical education teacher and as a small business operator, which required extensive hours of telephone use;
2. patient's use of a hard vocal attack;
3. patient engaged in excessive throat clearing;
4. patient reported that she frequently raised her voice and yelled when disciplining her children.

Procedural Approach: LTG 1.   All voice therapy should begin with a period of instruction in which the patient has an opportunity to visualize the structure and function of normal vocal folds and compare these images with those characteristic of the patient's specific laryngeal pathology. In the case of Marsha, she received instruction, in terms that she could understand, regarding the anatomy and physiology of the vocal mechanism. This instruction was replete with still photographs and videotapes of high-speed cinematography showing vocal fold vibration in slow motion. In addition, based on information obtained from the case history, potential abusive factors were identified and their effect on vocal fold structure and function was discussed. Based on this instruction, Marsha was required to identify common etiological factors associated with vocal nodule development and describe to the clinician the effect of vocal nodules on vocal fold vibration. Following a brief tutorial regarding good vocal hygiene, the patient was asked to identify desirable vocal behaviors that are not harmful to the laryngeal mechanism and that would most likely facilitate a reduction in the size of her vocal nodules.

As part of an extensive case history, the patient described, in great detail, her daily routines. With the guidance of the clinician, Marsha's vocal habits were examined within the context of the daily demands placed on her voice. Any potential instances of vocal abuse or misuse were identified and discussed.

Decision-Making Regarding LTG 2.   The finding of an average rise time of the amplitude envelope of 28 ms is consistent with the use of a hard vocal attack (Koike, 1967, 1973). The decision to establish an LTG to promote use of a soft vocal attack was made after objective acoustic evaluation confirmed the clinician's perception of Marsha's frequent use of a hard vocal attack during conversational speech. The following LTG was established:

> **LTG 2:**   Marsha will adopt and habituate use of a soft vocal attack in discourse.

Procedural Approach: LTG 2.   The same instrumentation used to evaluate the rise time of the amplitude envelope was incorporated into a visual biofeedback paradigm. Marsha was instructed in the use of a "confidential voice" (Colton & Casper, 1996). Real-time visual records of her phonatory rise time were monitored during the production of carefully prepared phrases. Negative practice was used in which the patient contrasted different types of vocal attack while evaluating simultaneously the quality and visual representation of the type of vocal attack used. During therapy sessions, Marsha used this visual feedback to help establish an awareness of auditory and tactile and kinesthetic cues associated with the more efficient soft vocal attack that characterized the "confidential voice."

Decision Making Regarding LTG 3.   Marsha's VC, although low given her age, gender, and body size, was grossly within normal limits (83% of her expected VC). The patient's VC served as a gross screening measure that ruled out the possibility of significant ventilatory system pathology. During a maximum-effort task, Marsha was able to exchange 2.6 liters of air, which suggested that she had adequate breath support for speech production. However, further assessment of ventilatory function revealed that Marsha habitually adopted an inefficient breathing pattern for speech. It should be emphasized that most patients who present

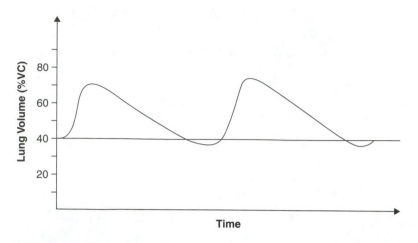

FIGURE 9.5 Typical lung volume excursions during speech at normal conversation levels.

with vocal nodules generally do not require intervention directed at the ventilatory system. In Marsha's case, diagnostic therapy revealed the need to modify her speech breathing pattern.

A brief review of normal speech breathing behavior should help the reader understand the nature of Marsha's problems in ventilatory support. During quiet tidal breathing (at rest breathing), a person begins and ends each ventilatory cycle around REL. In the upright posture, REL corresponds to a lung volume level of approximately 37–40% of a person's VC. During vegetative breathing, the size of the chest wall is increased only slightly beyond its resting size at REL. Specifically, lung volume level increases on the order of 400–500 ml of air beyond REL. For most speech of normal conversational loudness, a person only needs to increase lung volume an additional 250–350 ml of air beyond the level required for quiet tidal breathing. Thus, most speech of normal conversational loudness begins at around 60% of a person's VC (which represents an increase in lung volume to approximately 10–20% of VC above REL [Cavallo, 1988]). Most speakers terminate speech of normal conversational loudness at or slightly below REL (that is, around 35–40% of the VC). Figure 9.5 shows typical lung volume excursions during speech at normal conversational loudness for a normal speaker. Marsha typically initiated speech around 50% of her VC. In effect, she did not take in enough air to support speech. In addition, Marsha frequently terminated speech at a lung volume level well below REL (to approximately 25% of her VC). Figure 9.6 illustrates the lung volume change regarding REL that characterized Marsha's pretherapy speech breathing behavior. As a consequence of using an inappropriate lung volume range, Marsha's ability to generate and maintain the required subglottal pressures for speech was compromised. By not initiating speech at an appropriate lung volume level, Marsha failed to take advantage of the recoil forces that provide relatively small, positive relaxation pressures. Invariably, Marsha's adoption of an inefficient speech breathing pattern added strain on the vocal mechanism during speech production.

Another problem identified during diagnostic therapy was Marsha's use of oppositional rib cage and abdominal movements throughout inhalation before performing

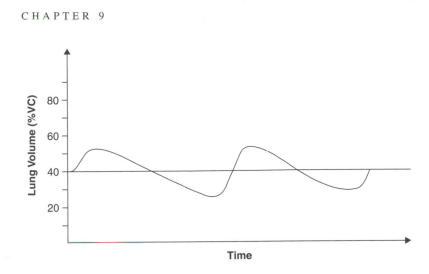

FIGURE 9.6   Lung volume excursions for Marsha.

maximum-effort tasks, such as the maximum sustained phonation (MSP). Normal pre-speech inspirations involve cooperative movements of the rib cage and abdomen, with the exception of a brief oppositional movement of the chest wall components that may occur just before phonatory onset. Specifically, the size of both the rib cage and abdomen increase to approximately 100 ms before phonation, at which time a sudden and small gesture of the chest wall characterized by rib cage expansion and abdominal contraction may occur (Baken & Cavallo, 1981; Baken, Cavallo, & Weissman, 1979). For maximum-effort tasks, Marsha consistently increased the size of the rib cage (an inspiratory gesture) and decreased the size of the abdomen (an expiratory gesture) throughout the entire prephonatory inspiration. This represents an idiosyncratic breathing pattern that proves to be highly inefficient. Marsha did not typically use this abnormal breathing pattern during speech and reading tasks, although she occasionally demonstrated oppositional movements of the two chest wall components when taking a deeper breath to support louder speech utterances.

To summarize, physiologic assessment of Marsha's breathing for speech revealed an abnormal and inefficient breathing pattern. Consequently, direct intervention in the form of breathing exercises was appropriate for this patient. Two additional LTGs were developed.

> ***LTG 3:***   Marsha will consistently produce speech of normal conversational loudness within an appropriate lung volume range (approximately 35–60% of the vital capacity).

Procedural Approach: LTG 3.   A visual biofeedback paradigm was introduced to monitor and modify Marsha's speech breathing pattern. Using variable inductance plethysmography, a real-time lung volume estimate was derived from chest wall movements and displayed on a cathode ray oscilloscope. REL was determined at the beginning of the therapy session while the patient was engaged in quiet tidal breathing. This level was marked on the oscilloscope, providing the patient with a record of lung volume change regarding REL. An estimate of the

midvolume range was marked on the oscilloscope screen and the patient was directed to produce speech within that range. The effect of this modification of breathing on voice quality and the patient's "feeling" of reduced laryngeal effort and tension were evaluated by the patient and discussed with the clinician. Eventually, after several therapy sessions, the patient was required to speak using an appropriate lung volume range without visual cues.

Since the diagnostic evaluation revealed that Marsha used an aberrant chest wall movement pattern before maximum sustained phonation tasks and speech produced at high intensity levels, the following LTG was established.

> *LTG 4:*   Marsha will demonstrate cooperative rib cage and abdominal movements before maximum sustained phonation and before speech produced at comfortable and greater than comfortable loudness levels.

Short-Term Planning Phase

The format for planning short-term goals (STGs) for voice disorders differs from the disorder areas presented in earlier chapters. Given that voice disorders in adults often stem from faulty vocal habits, a set of interactive STGs may be designed: (a) prevocal goals designed to eliminate vocal abuse (e.g., eliminate throat clearing, learn about vocal abuse and optimal voice production), and (b) goals aimed at facilitating the coordination of the vocal system (phonation, ventilation, resonance, and articulation).

In developing STGs, the clinician manipulated linguistic complexity and vocal intensity. For STG 2, linguistic complexity was manipulated as a performance demand. Marsha was initially required to monitor instances of vocal abuse to develop a heightened sense of awareness regarding their existence and frequency of occurrence. Session goals designed to reduce the frequency of abusive behaviors, a more complex task, were not initiated until after Marsha demonstrated the ability to consistently identify instances in which she engaged in vocal abuse. For STG 3, intensity was manipulated as a performance demand. Marsha was required to produce speech within an appropriate lung volume range at a normal conversational loudness level (STG 3) before initiating goals designed to produce speech within an appropriate lung volume range at a louder level (STG 4b).

Short-Term Goals.   The STG developed to achieve LTG 1 was:

> *STG 1 (prevocal):*   Marsha will demonstrate the ability to identify common etiologic and maintaining factors of vocal nodules and describe their effect on the vocal fold tissues and on voice production.

Delimited Procedural Approach: STG 1.   Early in the therapeutic process, considerable time was devoted to improving the patient's understanding of the factors that caused and maintained the nodules, and the effect of vocal nodules on the quality of her voice. In addition to providing the patient with critical information about the nature of her dysphonia, activities such as contrasting normal and dysphonic voices and observing visual images that illustrated differences in the vibratory behavior of normal and pathologic vocal folds increased the patient's motivation to eliminate the nodules. Marsha's initial reaction to seeing vocal nodules was "My God, is that what mine [vocal folds] look like?" After a few sessions reviewing normal and abnormal vocal fold structure and function, and comparing normal and dysphonic voices, Marsha was highly motivated to make the behavioral changes required for a successful therapeutic outcome.

Decision Making Regarding STGs 2a–2f.   Following extensive discussion and consultation with Marsha, several behaviors were identified as likely maintaining factors. Marsha's position as a physical education teacher placed considerable demands on the voice as did her role as primary caretaker of her three children. Marsha reported great chaos in the home, which resulted in "having to raise my voice from the moment I get home, until the children are asleep." From the case history information, specific behaviors were identified that were inconsistent with good vocal hygiene. In addition to routinely raising her voice and shouting at home and at work, Marsha reported that she used the telephone frequently, often in a noisy home environment, as a function of a private, home-based business. Clinical observation revealed excessive throat clearing that was not associated with an upper respiratory infection or allergy and frequent use of a hard vocal attack. Shouting, telephone use, throat clearing, and use of a hard attack were targeted as abusive vocal behaviors in need of elimination. As a substitute for these behaviors, Marsha was instructed in the use of a soft attack and the confidential voice.

STGs established to achieve LTG 2 were:

STG 2a (prevocal):   Throughout the week, Marsha will identify instances of vocal abuse (specifically, instances of raising her voice, throat clearing, and the frequency and duration of telephone use).

STG 2b: Marsha will produce conversational speech without raising her voice and yelling, both at home with her children and in the work environment.

STG 2c (prevocal):   Marsha will eliminate nonproductive throat clearing.

STG 2d (prevocal):   Marsha will reduce telephone use and engage in telephone conversations only under conditions of low background noise.

STG 2e: Marsha will use a soft vocal attack during the production of short, prepared phrases.

STG 2f: Marsha will adopt and use a confidential voice throughout the therapy session and on a daily basis when engaged in discourse on a one-to-one basis with others.

Delimited Procedural Approach: STGs 2a–2f.   Initial session objectives toward the achievement of the LTG to adopt healthy vocal behaviors and eliminate vocal abuse were designed to increase Marsha's awareness of the degree to which she engaged in abusive vocal behaviors. Increased awareness of vocal abuse was achieved by requiring the patient to identify and chart all instances of these behaviors. Instances of throat clearing were monitored both in and out of the therapy milieu. Instances of telephone use and "raising her voice" were tracked outside of the therapeutic setting by the patient. In the case of telephone use, Marsha was required to record the duration of each telephone call and describe the level of ambient noise in the immediate environment during telephone use. Self-monitoring of her voice, consistent with social-cognitive principles of rehabilitation, remained an integral goal throughout therapy.

After several weeks of charting, Marsha had increased her sensitivity to the abusive vocal behaviors identified jointly by the patient and clinician. At this point in therapy, an additional session goal was introduced that required that, in addition to charting these behaviors, Marsha would reduce their frequency and duration.

Instruction in the production and adoption of the confidential voice was introduced early in therapy. The clinician trained Marsha to produce a less forceful form of phonation during speech production. Although Marsha was initially resistant to carrying over this voice outside of the therapy situation, she did succeed in using the confidential voice more consistently during her activities of daily living. When engaged in activities in which Marsha believed she could not use the confidential voice, she was provided with other alternatives to raising her voice or shouting. For example, when leading her physical education classes, she would use nonverbal signals whenever possible. When instructing the students regarding the activities for each gym class, she would instruct one student using the confidential voice and designate that student as class leader who would then provide instruction to the class. In addition, she had her school district purchase a megaphone, which she used during physical education classes and school sports events. Another set of goals that received direct attention during therapy sessions was implemented to improve Marsha's ability to differentiate between an abusive, hard vocal attack and a more efficient soft vocal attack. This goal was accomplished quickly, since Marsha was provided with immediate, real-time visual feedback of the type of vocal attack she had used. Over several weeks she was able to consistently produce spontaneous speech using a soft vocal attack without the aid of a visual signal.

Decision Making Regarding STGs 3–4b. Objective assessment of Marsha's ventilatory behavior during speech revealed that she had an adequate lung volume reserve. However, she habitually used a lung volume range that was inappropriately low both for speech of normal conversational loudness and for speech at increased loudness levels. She also used an inefficient ventilatory pattern that was characterized by oppositional chest wall movements during maximum-effort phonatory tasks.

An STG designed to accomplish LTG 3 was:

STG 3:   Marsha will consistently produce conversational speech (at a normal loudness level) within the midvolume range.

STGs developed to achieve LTG 4 were:

STG 4a: During a MSP task, Marsha will consistently accomplish prespeech inspiration using cooperative movements of the rib cage and abdomen.

STG 4b: During conversational speech production at high vocal intensity level, Marsha will consistently accomplish prespeech inspiration using cooperative movements of the rib cage and abdomen.

Delimited Procedural Approach: STGs 3–4a and 4b.   Marsha's breathing problems were addressed within the context of a visual biofeedback paradigm. Using variable inductance plethysmography, records of real-time rib cage and abdominal movements, as well as an estimate of lung volume change, were available. To accomplish STG 3b, rib cage and abdominal movements were monitored on an oscilloscope screen. An estimate of lung volume change was monitored by the patient on the oscilloscope during speech production in session activities devoted to the achievement of STG 3.

Again, the availability of visual records of chest wall movements and lung volume change resulted in Marsha's ability to modify her breathing pattern within a few therapy sessions. Her ability to consistently produce speech within the midvolume range in the absence of visual cues was achieved more slowly, over several weeks.

Session-Planning Phase

Session Goals.   In the development of the session goal (SG) sequence, the following variables were manipulated to alter performance demands: task complexity, linguistic complexity, biofeedback, and intensity level of speech or phonation. Marsha was required to identify the existence of vocal nodules and differentiate vocal folds with and without nodules from visual images before undertaking the more complex tasks: identifying etiologic and maintaining factors, describing the effect of vocal nodules on the voice, and identifying vocal behaviors that are consistent with good vocal hygiene (addressing LTG 1 and STG 1).

In the development of SG 2, Marsha was first required to monitor the frequency of occurrence of abusive behaviors. When she was unable to do so reliably, the number of behaviors she was required to monitor was reduced.

Before Marsha was required to alter the type of vocal attack used, she was first required to master less complex tasks: interpersonal discrimination between hard and soft attack, intrapersonal discrimination between hard and soft attacks with visual cues, intrapersonal discrimination between hard and soft attacks without the benefit of visual cues, production of soft attack in short phrases, and production of soft attack in discourse.

Linguistic complexity and the presence or absence of biofeedback (visual record of lung volume change) were manipulated by the clinician in the development of SGs 3a–c. Marsha was required to produce short phrases, and then conversational speech within the midvolume range with the benefit of visual biofeedback (SGs 3a and 3b). After successful achievement of these session goals, Marsha was required to produce spontaneous speech in the midvolume range without the benefit of visual biofeedback (SG 3c).

The following SGs were developed to achieve LTG 1 and STG 1:

SG 1a: Following clinician instruction, Marsha will identify vocal nodules and will contrast vocal folds with and without nodules from still and videotape images with 100% accuracy.

SG 1b: Following clinician instruction, Marsha will identify etiologic and maintaining factors associated with nodule development.

SG 1c: Following clinician instruction, Marsha will describe accurately the effect of vocal nodules on voice production.

SG 1d: Following clinician instruction, Marsha will identify vocal behaviors that promote a reduction in the size of vocal nodules.

Session Procedures: SGs 1a–1d. A significant portion of the initial therapy sessions was devoted to educating the patient about the nature of her disorder by contrasting visual representations of vocal fold vibration and auditory recordings of phonation for individuals with and without vocal nodules. Following a brief period of instruction from the clinician, Marsha achieved the criterion of identifying and contrasting normal and disordered phonation with 100% accuracy.

The following session goals were established to achieve LTG 2 and STGs 2a– 2f:

SG 2a: On a daily basis (a minimum of three times per day for 30-minute periods), Marsha will monitor and maintain a frequency count of the following vocal behaviors: incidents of throat clearing, number and duration of telephone calls, and incidents in which the voice was used with excessive loudness.

SG 2b: Marsha will reduce, by at least 25%, the number of instances in which the following behaviors occur during the week: nonproductive throat clearing, use of an excessively loud voice and the frequency and duration of telephone calls.

SG 2c: Marsha will discriminate between the clinician's use of hard and soft vocal attacks during conversational speech with 90% accuracy.

SG 2d: With the assistance of visual biofeedback, Marsha will demonstrate the ability to discriminate between her use of hard and soft vocal attacks with 90% accuracy.

SG 2e: Without the assistance of visual cues, Marsha will demonstrate the ability to discriminate between her use of hard and soft vocal attacks while reading short phrases with 90% accuracy.

SG 2f: Without visual cues, Marsha will produce a soft vocal attack while reading short phrases with 90% accuracy.

SG 2g: Marsha will produce a soft vocal attack during spontaneous speech production throughout the therapy session with greater than 80% accuracy.

SG 2h: Marsha's spontaneous speech during the therapy session will be characterized by the confidential voice greater than 90% of the time.

Session Procedures: SGs 2a–2h. Initially, Marsha was required to monitor, outside of therapy, the frequency of abusive behaviors identified during assessment. After one week, it became apparent that Marsha was having difficulty charting behaviors on a consistent basis and, specifically, monitoring instances of throat clearing. In an attempt to simplify the task for the patient, she was provided with a preprinted charting pocket notebook prepared by the clinician. In addition, she was not required to monitor throat clearing outside the therapy setting until she could consistently identify the behavior in therapy. Consequently, an additional session goal was developed:

> *SG 2a₁:*   Marsha will identify instances of throat clearing during the therapy session with
> 90% accuracy.

The clinician was less concerned with the accuracy and reliability of Marsha's charting than with the heightened awareness she would gain regarding these abusive behaviors as a result of this activity.

Marsha was not required to reduce the number of instances of abusive vocal behaviors (SG 2b) until she had charted the frequency of the behaviors for a few weeks.

With regard to replacing the hard vocal attack with a soft vocal attack, Marsha was first required to discriminate between the two types of vocal attack in the clinician's speech (interpersonal discrimination). Goals directed at intrapersonal discrimination between hard and soft vocal attacks were not attempted until SG 2b was achieved. Intrapersonal discrimination and production of hard and soft vocal attacks were addressed within therapy sequentially in the following contexts: intrapersonal discrimination between hard and soft vocal attacks while reading short phrases first with and then without visual feedback, production of soft vocal attack while reading short phrases with visual cues, and production of soft vocal attack during discourse.

A session goal was also introduced requiring Marsha to use a confidential voice in therapy 90% of the time. Although not a formal goal, Marsha was encouraged to use this voice outside of therapy whenever communicating on a one-to-one basis with others.

The following session goals (SGs 3a–3c) were developed to achieve the goals designed to facilitate speech production within an appropriate lung volume range (LTG 3 and STG 3).

> *SG 3a:*   Within a visual biofeedback paradigm, Marsha will consistently produce short
> phrases between 35% and 60% of her VC (within the midvolume range) with
> 90% accuracy.

> *SG 3b:*   With the assistance of visual cues, Marsha will produce speech at a normal con-
> versational loudness level between 35% and 60% of her VC (within the mid-
> volume range) with 90% accuracy.

> *SG 3c:*   Without the assistance of visual cues, Marsha will produce spontaneous speech
> at a normal conversational loudness level between 35% and 60% of her VC
> (within the midvolume range) with 80% accuracy.

The following session goals (SGs 4a–4f) were generated to achieve the goals designed to promote appropriate chest wall movements before sustained phonation and conversational speech. These SGs were prioritized according to task complexity and subglottal pressure requirements. SGs 4a–4c required the patient to use cooperative chest wall movements first before phonation, then before short phrases, and finally during discourse. SGs 4d–4f required the patient to use cooperative rib cage and abdominal movements through the same sequence of task complexity, but at an increased subglottal pressure level (loud phonation, loud phrases, loud speech).

> *SG 4a:* During prephonatory inspirations, Marsha will consistently use a cooperative breathing pattern (rib cage and abdominal expansion) in preparation for phonation at a comfortable loudness level with 90% accuracy.

> *SG 4b:* During prespeech inspirations, Marsha will consistently use a cooperative breathing pattern (rib cage and abdominal expansion) in preparation for short phrases produced at a comfortable loudness level with 90% accuracy.

> *SG 4c:* During prespeech inspirations, Marsha will consistently use a cooperative breathing pattern (rib cage and abdominal expansion) during conversational speech produced at a comfortable loudness level with 90% accuracy.

Therapy activities that required the patient to produce speech and phonation at high intensity levels were postponed until the later stages of therapy at a time when the size of the vocal nodules had been reduced significantly.

> *SG 4d:* During prephonatory inspirations, Marsha will consistently use a cooperative breathing pattern (rib cage and abdominal expansion) in preparation for loud phonation with 90% accuracy.

> *SG 4e:* During prespeech inspirations, Marsha will consistently use a cooperative breathing pattern (rib cage and abdominal expansion) in preparation for short phrases produced at greater than normal loudness level with 90% accuracy.

> *SG 4f:* During prespeech inspirations, Marsha will consistently use a cooperative breathing pattern (rib cage and abdominal expansion) during conversational speech at greater than normal loudness level with 90% accuracy.

Additional Comments Concerning Treatment

Biofeedback-Based Intervention

Progress in therapy was facilitated, in part, by the availability of biofeedback procedures to assist Marsha in changing behaviors. The instrumentation used to evaluate Marsha's ventilatory support for speech and the type of vocal attack were well suited for a biofeedback paradigm. Marsha was provided with real-time visual representations of lung volume change and the type of vocal attack used. Consequently, changes in the lung volume range used for speech and the type of vocal attack used were accomplished quickly. Once an appropriate lung volume range within the vital capacity was used consistently by the patient and a soft vocal attack had been consistently adopted, visual feedback was gradually withdrawn. The integration of a biofeedback paradigm into the vocal rehabilitation program maximized the efficiency with which new, nonabusive vocal behaviors were taught and adopted.

Monitoring Therapy Efficiency

The following measures of vocal function were obtained weekly throughout therapy to evaluate therapy efficacy: f_0 and RAP during three-second midsegment samples of phonation at high, low, and comfortable loudness levels. Throughout therapy, mean f_0 level during sustained phonation increased steadily from approximately 175 Hz to 194 Hz at the conclusion of voice therapy three months later. RAP values decreased from 3% and greater at therapy onset to approximately 0.23% at the time therapy was terminated. Marsha's MPT increased from 8.7s at therapy onset to 15.8 s at the time of discharge. In addition, spectral analysis of vowels at the conclusion of therapy revealed substantially lower levels of interharmonic and high-frequency energy. These objective measures of vocal function were consistent with a reduction in the size of the nodules. This conclusion was confirmed by indirect laryngoscopy three months after the initiation of therapy. According to the otolaryngologist's report, "The left vocal cord has minimal thickening at the junction of the anterior and mid-third of the cord. There is no evidence of a nodule on the right vocal cord. The cords approximate well."

Although complete resolution of tissue pathology was not accomplished, Marsha was asymptomatic and pleased with her voice. Consequently, she opted to terminate therapy. During the final few therapy sessions, the importance of maintaining good vocal habits was stressed to minimize the possibility of a recurrence of tissue pathology.

Summary

The clinical case described in this chapter is representative of the decision-making process the voice clinician engages in when working with an adult who presents with abuse-related dysphonia. It should be stressed that every patient presents with their own circumstances. Every individual has a unique set of laryngeal structures and presents with different problems, abilities, and motivation levels. Adult dysphonics, depending on their personalities and life style, place different demands on their voices. Consequently, although certain general principles may apply to all patients, each voice case should be approached on an individual basis, taking into account the different characteristics and circumstances each patient presents.

The initial decision the clinician needs to make is whether voice therapy alone is indicated. To make this decision in an informed manner, the voice therapist needs to have comprehensive evaluation data available. It is simply not enough to receive a report from an otolaryngologist in which a specific tissue pathology is identified and voice therapy is recommended. Additional diagnostic data and consultation with the otolaryngologist are required if the voice clinician is to be in a position to generate appropriate therapeutic goals. In this case, well-informed clinical decisions could not have been made without the acquisition of objective physiologic measures. This required access to and a working knowledge of a fairly sophisticated instrumentation array. For example, if the voice clinician limited the evaluation of Marsha's ventilatory function to the acquisition of a VC, or if ventilatory behavior had not been assessed at all, important target goals would not have been identified. In Marsha's case, the VC obtained was grossly within normal limits. In the absence of other objective data, the voice clinician might have been tempted to conclude that ventilatory function for speech was adequate and decide not to direct intervention efforts toward the ventilatory system. Although a VC that is significantly below an expected value usually suggests some form of ventilatory dysfunction, it does not reveal how a patient manages the lung volume reserve for speech production. A more precise examination of Marsha's ability to manage lung volume during speech production revealed an abnormal speech-breathing pattern. Consequently, specific goals to modify speech-breathing behavior were established.

The integration of acoustic and physiologic measures of phonation and speech into voice therapy provided objective measures of vocal function that the clinician and patient were able to use to monitor progress in therapy. For Marsha, the availability of quantitative data regarding the status of her vocal nodules proved highly motivating. She received instruction regarding the relationship between the objective measures of vocal function and the presumed status of her vocal nodules. Once Marsha saw the RAP values drop and visualized the reduction of signal noise in the power spectra of her vowels, she became motivated to continue making positive changes regarding her vocal behaviors. In addition, several instrumentation systems were used in therapy to provide Marsha with visual biofeedback of several speech behaviors that needed modification. The availability of these visual signals helped facilitate positive changes in the patient's breathing pattern and the type of vocal attack used.

Lack of Access to Laboratory Instrumentation: A Clinical Reality

The intervention plan designed to manage Marsha's dysphonia relied heavily on the availability of a sophisticated instrumentation array. The effective implementation of this management plan also required that the clinician have a basic appreciation of physiological assessment and acoustic analysis techniques. It is reasonable to expect that such an intervention strategy can be carried out in a hospital setting, vocal dynamics laboratory, or at a well-equipped university clinic laboratory. Unfortunately, most practicing speech clinicians do not have direct access to the resources required to conduct instrumental voice assessment or to implement biofeedback-based therapy. One might argue that, since most clinical settings do not support the physiologic and acoustic measurement of speech and voice, the information presented in this chapter has limited application and is therefore irrelevant to most speech clinicians. One could argue, on the other hand, that the principles of clinical voice measurement are relevant to all clinicians who treat patients with voice disorders, irrespective of their clinical setting. Let's examine some possible clinical scenarios. Consider the clinician who practices in a school setting and does not have the resources with which to conduct an objective voice evaluation. Patients, on a select basis, can be referred to a local university or vocal dynamics laboratory. Of course, this would require that the clinician have some knowledge of vocal tract structure and function as well as an awareness of available tests of vocal function. Consider an analogous situation in medicine. Physicians need extensive blood testing to assist in reaching a diagnosis, yet they are not equipped to conduct such testing in their office. It is unlikely they would yield to such a constraint, since failure to obtain such critical diagnostic data would be tantamount to nonfeasance. Rather, competent and knowledgeable physicians would determine which blood tests were needed and refer their patients to an appropriately equipped laboratory. Physicians would then interpret the laboratory results, incorporate them into the larger diagnostic database, and explain their meaning to patients. Similarly, voice clinicians can, for cases in which the acquisition of objective voice data are important, make appropriate referrals to a vocal dynamics laboratory.

For clinicians who seek to obtain clinical measures of vocal function themselves, but do not practice in a setting that can support the acquisition of expensive instrumentation, several measurement alternatives exist. Simple objective clinical measures of vocal function, which do not require a sophisticated instrumentation array, have been described for decades in the clinical speech pathology literature for clinicians who have limited access to laboratory instrumentation. For example, a patient's forced VC can be obtained using an inexpensive hand-held dry spirometer. The availability of a VC measure, as discussed earlier in the chapter, is essential to the interpretation of the MPT. In addition, the phonation quotient (PQ), defined as the patient's VC divided by the patient's MPT, appears to be a reasonable clinical substitute for measures of mean airflow during sustained phonation. Direct measurement of mean airflow requires the use of expensive and sophisticated instrumentation, such as a pneumotachograph measurement system. Hirano, Koike, and von Leden (1968) demonstrated the strong relationship between PQ and mean airflow in normal subjects. Iwata and von Leden (1970) also demonstrated a positive relationship between PQ and mean airflow for patients with laryngeal pathology. Additional noninvasive methods have been described in the periodical literature for obtaining an estimate of a patient's ability to generate and maintain adequate subglottal pressure for speech (Hixon, Hawley, & Wilson, 1982; Netsell & Hixon, 1978;). The instrumentation required for each of these techniques, although simple and inexpensive, can provide the clinician with important screening data regarding a patient's ability to generate and maintain vocal tract pressures necessary to support speech and phonation. Netsell and Daniel (1979) described a case study in which such instrumentation was successfully incorporated into the intervention plan of a patient with dysarthria.

Attempts to objectively evaluate laryngeal and velopharyngeal function using simple and inexpensive equipment have a long history in clinical speech pathology. Although not without significant limitations, use of the oral breath pressure ratio (which requires the use of an oral manometer) to evaluate velopharyngeal function in patients with cleft palate was described in the clinical speech pathology literature (Pitzner & Morris, 1966; Spriestersbach & Powers 1959). A method similar to the oral breath pressure ratio, in which oral air volume is measured instead (vis-a-vis VC), was described by Kantner (1947) and evaluated by Spriestersbach and Powers (1959). The s/z ratio, also not without its limitations, was introduced by Eckel and Boone (1981) to quantify the integrity of the laryngeal valve during phonation. Today, given the increased availability of relatively affordable, computer-based instrumentation systems, the possibility of incorporating objective measures into the voice evaluation has become a clinical reality. Apparently, even some school districts have made a financial commitment to upgrade laboratory resources to assess speech and voice.

Boone and McFarlane (1994) reported:

> There is a trend for larger school districts to set up a central voice clinic in which voice equipment . . . can be housed, rather than in each particular school. Children are evaluated in the central clinic, and findings (such as videoendoscopic recordings) are then sent to the referring SLP for use with children in therapy in their particular schools. (p. 275)

Will voice clinicians continue to rely heavily, if not entirely, on perceptual data when evaluating and treating voice disorders? Or, will clinicians and their patients demand more rigorous and objective diagnostic and therapeutic methods? Given the increased availability of commercial instrumentation and the successful integration of the microcomputer into clinical practice, objective measures of voice, for so long confined to the speech science laboratory, have now become a clinical reality. However, given the profession's reluctance to embrace objective measurement techniques to date, it seems unlikely that speech-language pathologists will insist on the routine acquisition of objective measures of vocal function in the near future. Even so, movement toward greater precision in the evaluation and treatment of the voice would be an admirable goal for the discipline as we approach the next millennium.

REFERENCES

Aronson, A. E. (1990). *Clinical voice disorders.* New York: Thieme, Inc.

Atkinson, J. E. (1978). Correlation analysis of the physiological factors controlling fundamental voice frequency. *Journal of Acoustic Society of America 63,* 211–222.

Baken, R. J., & Cavallo, S. A. (1981). Prephonatory chest wall posturing. *Folia Phoniatrica, 33,* 193–203.

Baken, R. J., Cavallo, S. A., & Weissman, K. L. (1979). Chest wall movements prior to phonation. *Journal of Speech and Hearing Research, 22,* 862–872.

Bless, D. M. (1988). Voice disorders in the adult: Treatment. In P. Yoder & R. D. Kent (Eds.), *Decision making in speech-language pathology* (pp. 140–143). Toronto, BC: Decker.

Boone, D. R., & McFarlane, S. C. (1994). *The voice and voice therapy.* Englewood Cliffs, NJ: Prentice-Hall.

Butcher, P., Elias, A., & Raven, R. (1993). *Psychogenic voice disorders and cognitive-behavior therapy.* San Diego, CA: Singular.

Case, J. L. (1994). *Clinical management of voice disorders.* Austin, TX: Pro-Ed.

Cavallo, S. A. (1988). Respiratory function. In P. Yoder and R. D. Kent (Eds.), *Decision making in speech-language pathology* (pp. 126–127). Toronto, BC: Decker.

Colton, R., & Casper, J. K. (1996). *Understanding voice problems: A physiological perspective for diagnosis and treatment.* Baltimore: Williams & Wilkins.

Deal, R. E., & Emanuel, F. W. (1978). Some waveform and spectral features of vowel roughness. *Journal of Speech and Hearing Research, 21,* 250–264.

Eckel, F. C., and Boone, D. R. (1981). The s/z ratio as an indicator of laryngeal pathology. *Journal of Speech and Hearing Disorders, 46,* 147–150.

Emanuel, F. W. & Sansone, F. E. (1969). Some spectral features of "normal" and simulated "rough" vowels. *Folia phoniatrica, 21,* 401–415.

Emanuel, F. W., & Whitehead, R. L. (1979). Harmonic levels and vowel roughness. *Journal of Speech and Hearing Research, 22,* 829–840.

Fawcus, M. (1986). Hyperfunctional voice: The misuse and abuse syndrome. In M. Fawcus (Ed.), *Voice disorders and their management* (pp. 158–192). London: Croom Helm.

Forner, L., & Hixon, T. J. (1977). Respiratory kinematics in profoundly hearing impaired speakers. *Journal of Speech and Hearing Research, 20,* 373–408.

Hirano, M. (1981). Structure of the vocal fold in normal and disease states: Anatomical and physical studies. *Proceedings of the Conference on the Assessment of Vocal Pathology; ASHA Reports, 11,* 11–27.

Hirano, M., Koike, Y., & von Leden, H. (1968). Maximum phonation time and air usage during phonation. *Folia phoniatrica, 20,* 185–201.

Hixon, T. J., Goldman, M. D., & Mead, J. (1973). Kinematics of the chest wall during speech production: Volume displacements of the rib cage, abdomen, and lung. *Journal of Speech and Hearing Research, 16,* 78–115.

Hixon, T. J., Hawley, J. L., & Wilson, K. J. (1982). An around-the-house device for the clinical determination of respiratory driving pressure: A note on making simple even simpler. *Journal of Speech and Hearing Disorders, 47,* 413–415.

Horii, Y. (1982). Some voice fundamental frequency characteristics of oral reading and spontaneous speech by hard-of-hearing young women. *Journal of Speech and Hearing Research, 25,* 608–610.

Isshiki, N., Yanagihara, N. & Morimoto, M. (1966). Approach to the objective diagnosis of hoarseness. *Folia phoniatrica, 13,* 393–400.

Iwata, S., & von Leden, H. (1970). Phonation quotient in patients with laryngeal diseases. *Folia Phoniatrica, 22,* 117–128.

Kantner, C. E. (1947). The rationale of blowing exercises for patients with repaired cleft palates. *Journal of Speech Disorders, 12,* 281–286.

Koike, Y. (1967). Experimental studies on vocal attack. *Practica Otologica Kyoto, 60,* 663–688.

Koike, Y. (1973). Application of some acoustic measures for the evaluation of laryngeal dysfunction. *Studia Phonologica, 7,* 17–23.

Koike, Y., & Hirano, M. (1968). Significance of the vocal velocity index. *Folia Phoniatrica, 20,* 285–296.

Kory, R. C., Callahan, R., & Boren, H. G. (1961). The Veterans Administration-Army cooperative study of pulmonary function, I. Clinical spirometry in normal men. *American Journal of Medicine, 30,* 243–258.

Minifie, F. D. 1994. *Introduction to communication sciences and disorders.* San Diego, CA: Singular.

Morrison, M., & Rammage, L. (1994). *The management of voice disorders.* San Diego, CA: Singular.

Netsell, R., & Daniel, B. (1979). Dysarthria in adults: Physiologic approach to rehabilitation. *Archives of Physical Medicine and Rehabilitation, 60,* 502–508.

Netsell, R., & Hixon, T. J. (1978). A noninvasive method for clinically estimating subglottal air pressure. *Journal of Speech and Hearing Disorders, 43,* 326–330.

Pitzner, J. C., & Morris, H. L. (1966). Articulation skills and adequacy of breath pressure ratios of children with cleft palate. *Journal of Speech and Hearing Disorders, 31,* 26–40.

Ramig, L. O. (1997). How effective is the Lee Silverman Voice Treatment? *ASHA, 39,* 34–35.

Ramig, L. O., & Scherer, R. C. (1992). Speech therapy for neurologic disorders of the larynx. In A. Blitzer, M. F. Brin, C. T. Sasaki, S. Fahn, & K. S. Harris (Eds.), *Neurologic disorders of the larynx* (pp. 163–181). New York: Thieme.

Smitheran, J. R., & Hixon, T. J. (1981). A clinical method for estimating laryngeal airway resistance during vowel production. *Journal of Speech and Hearing Disorders, 46,* 138–146.

Spriestersbach, D. C., and Powers, G. R. (1959). Articulation skills, velopharyngeal closure, and oral breath pressure of children with cleft palates. *Journal of Speech and Hearing Research, 2,* 318–325.

Stoicheff, M. (1981). Speaking fundamental frequency characteristics of nonsmoking female adults. *Journal of Speech and Hearing Research, 24,* 437–441.

Subtelny, J., Li, W., Whitehead, R. L., & Subtelny, J. D. (1989). Cephalometric and cineradiographic study of deviant resonance in hearing-impaired speakers. *Journal of Speech and Hearing Disorders, 54,* 249–263.

Takahashi, H., & Koike, Y. (1975). Some perceptual dimensions and acoustical correlates of pathologic voices. *Acta Otolaryngologica, Suppl 338,* 1–24.

Yanagihara, N. (1967). Significance of harmonic changes and noise components in hoarseness. *Journal of Speech and Hearing Research, 10,* 515–530.

Yanagihara, N. (1970). Aerodynamic examination of laryngeal function. *Studia Phonologica, 5,* 45–51.

Yanagihara, N., Koike, Y., & von Leden, H. (1966). Phonation and respiration: Function study in normal subjects. *Folia Phoniatrica, 18,* 323–340.

Yanagihara, N., & von Leden, H. (1967). Respiration and phonation: The functional examination of laryngeal disease. *Folia Phoniatrica, 19,* 153–166.

10 Intervention Planning with Adults Who Stutter

DAVID A. SHAPIRO
(Western Carolina University)

CHAPTER OUTCOMES

The reader will:

1. identify differential diagnostic characteristics of stuttering;
2. identify factors that increase, reduce, or eliminate stuttering;
3. become familiar with factors that may maintain dysfluency;
4. recognize how maintaining factors may be viewed differently from the perspective of different theories;
5. identify assumptions about stuttering from the perspective of personal construct, family systems, and stuttering modification/fluency shaping theories;
6. be able to apply all of these sources of information to the derivation of a management plan for an adult who stutters.

Introduction

This chapter is about adults who stutter. People who stutter have stories to tell. The stories shared between people who stutter and their clinicians provide a web, a network, a system of communication that connects the participants in the clinical process to each other in a shared focus that transcends time and place. The stories, some of which are yearning to be told, also provide a basis of commonality and dialogue between clients and clinicians. Stories convey a message or a lesson. Stories told within the clinical context are no exception. However, no less significant within the clinical context is the actual telling of the story. Telling, sharing, and exchanging stories express hope, trust, courage, and faith. These entities are not given. They are earned and nurtured by the clinician. They express the client's developing belief that the world of communication can improve, that good things can happen to good people, and that good things can become even better.

For years, student clinicians and practicing speech-language pathologists have told me that when I am engaged in treatment with people who stutter, it looks like we are just talking. Indeed we are, with a shared focus and mission and bond. Stories and dialogue provide a real (i.e., not artificial) and meaningful (i.e., ecologically valid) context for human interaction that promotes through modeling the very communication skills we are trying to establish with adults who stutter. As will be seen, such a forum results in communication confidence and competence that is characterized by both speech and language fluency.

This book tells the story of how to plan intervention with adults who demonstrate communication disorders and helps us understand the foundation upon which such goals and procedures are based. Of particular significance is the section on narratives and their relevance to the clinical context. A description of universal narratives involving problems and resolutions that developmentally take the forms of additive, temporal, and causal chains is presented in Chapter 3. Action stories and more affectively loaded narratives are distinguished from one another. The former involves an actor who commits an action toward a goal with the use of some instrument in a particular scene resulting in trouble or a problem to be resolved. The latter emphasizes state verbs (e.g., thinks, feels, believes, etc.) to convey how the world is perceived by the characters in the story. Both are important to and have implications for the clinical process. Johnson, Sickels, and Sayers (1970) noted that the adults' and children's stories differ more on the basis of subject matter than in the depth of feeling or inherent quality. I noted earlier that people who stutter have stories to tell. The clinical process between a clinician and client is an unfolding story in itself. What follows is yet another story, the lesson of which is how to enable adults who stutter to gain strength and confidence.

There are four purposes to be addressed in this chapter. First, I will review some of what is known about stuttering and adults who stutter. To do so, I will look at several definitions of terms (i.e., fluency, disfluency, and stuttering) and differential diagnostic characteristics of stuttering (i.e., factors that reduce stuttering, others that increase stuttering, and the reciprocal relationship between stuttering and language). Second, I will address etiological considerations (i.e., predisposing, precipitating, and perpetuating/maintaining factors) and theoretical explanations (i.e., stuttering as a neurotic response, communicative failure and anticipatory struggle, learned behavior, physiological deficit, disturbed feedback, demands and capacities, and metatheory). Third, I will consider performance demands (i.e., cognitive, psychosocial, and behavioral/sensorimotor) and guiding intervention assumptions (i.e., involving personal constructs, family systems, and stuttering modification/fluency shaping considerations). Finally, I will integrate these factors with the model presented in Chapters 1 and 2 in a case example for intervention planning. I will design long-term, short-term, and session goals within procedural contexts for a man of 55 years who stutters.

Definition of Terms

In certain ways, speech behavior is like other human behavior. It is produced by all speakers with hesitations, interruptions, prolongations, and repetitions (Conture, 1990). These disruptions in the ongoing, forward flow of speech are called disfluencies and, as will be seen, vary across people and situations. Listeners tend to judge within-word disruptions (e.g., sound or syllable repetitions, prolongations, broken words) as "stuttered speech" and between-word disruptions (e.g., revisions, phrase repetitions, interjections) as "normal disfluency" (Bloodstein, 1995; Conture, 1990; Van Riper, 1982). Furthermore, listeners demonstrate remarkable agreement when distinguishing different speakers as belonging to categories of stutterers or nonstutterers (Bloodstein, 1995). This agreement breaks down, however, when defining stuttering and when identifying individual instances of stuttering. Before characterizing stuttering, I first describe the elements of fluency and disfluency, both of which are continuous rather than dichotomous variables and are related to stuttering.

Fluency

Speech Fluency.   Because of listeners' agreement in categorizing speech on the basis of fluency noted earlier, Starkweather (1984) indicated that we have inadvertently assumed, albeit incorrectly, a definition of fluency as the absence of stuttering. While such a definition is tempting, in part because of its simplicity, it presents several significant problems. First, this definition fails to acknowledge that stuttering behaviors vary in how fluent they are. This fluency varies across time and situations for people who stutter and when different people who stutter are compared with each other. Furthermore, the treatment goal referred to as fluent stuttering (Van Riper, 1973) is a less effortful, less disruptive, and more gentle form of disfluency. Defining fluency as the absence of stuttering, therefore, is counterintuitive. Second, people who stutter do not stutter all the time. Indeed, most of their speech is free of stuttering. Their nonstuttered speech varies in its degree of fluency. People who stutter tend to have the same normal disfluencies as people who do not stutter, but they tend to speak more slowly than people of the same age and sex who do not stutter (Starkweather, 1984). The nonstuttered speech of people who stutter also is less fluent because of the effort and time expended to avoid stuttering. Third, people who do not stutter demonstrate times of varying fluency as well, for reasons of health, fatigue, stress, conviction, and such. Their nonfluency might be characterized by filled pauses, hesitations, false starts, and sound, word, and phrase repetitions. These observations should illustrate that defining fluency as the absence of stuttering is insufficient, and that fluency should be viewed as a continuous rather than dichotomous variable. The speech of all people, including those who do and those who do not stutter, demonstrates varying fluency reflective of differences in relative effort or ease of production.

Language Fluency.   We gauge our own speech fluency by the ease and rapidity with which it is produced, and disfluency when production is slowed by unusual effort. In the speech of others, however, we can only infer the relative ease of speech production since we cannot perceive it directly. We do this from observable events including rate (i.e., units per time) of speech production and continuity (i.e., smoothness) of its output. Both speech rate and continuity are influenced by the information load (i.e., propositional value, or level of uncertainty) of the utterance. Because of the influence of information load on speech fluency and the influence of syntactic and word frequency on information load, Starkweather (1984, 1986, 1987) recommended a distinction between speech fluency (i.e., motor speech production) and language fluency (i.e., word finding and sentence production).

Aspects of language fluency include semantic, syntactic, pragmatic, and phonologic fluency. Semantic fluency refers to the ease of retrieving from a large pool of lexical items for reference to varied concepts. Syntactic fluency is the ease of constructing sentences containing linguistically complex structures. Pragmatic fluency is both knowing and demonstrating what one wants to say within and in response to different situational constraints. Phonologic fluency refers to the ease of producing long and complex strings of sounds within meaningful and complex language units. These definitions and distinctions illustrate that speech fluency and language fluency are different. In fact, most people who stutter demonstrate language fluency.

Disfluency

We noted earlier that disfluency refers to breaks or disruptions in the gentle, forward flow of speech. Some have distinguished between *dis*fluency and *dys*fluency. In such instances, disfluency has referred to the nonfluent speech of people who do not stutter, and the nonstuttered yet nonfluent speech of people who do stutter. Dysfluency has been reserved for the stuttered speech of people who stutter and the stuttered speech of people who do not usually stutter (Ham, 1990). However, such a distinction has proven more problematic than practical (Cooper, 1993). For the purposes here, the term disfluency will be used to refer to breaks in the continuity (i.e., smoothness), effort, and/or rate of speech (Starkweather, 1987) and will be described in as molecular (Van Riper, 1982) a fashion as possible.

Stuttering

Although stuttering is a universal phenomenon, its definition defies universal agreement. Bloodstein (1990) noted that three alternative types of definitions have included the observer's perceptual definition (i.e., what the conversational partner hears or sees it to be), dictionary definitions (i.e., defining stuttering by other words, e.g., prolongation, struggle, etc., each of which is defined by other words), and perceptual definitions of people who stutter (i.e., stuttering is whatever people who stutter feel it to be). My review of the literature on fluency and fluency disorders indeed has confirmed this finding. I found that definitions of stuttering tend to be descriptive, explanatory, or most frequently some descriptive/explanatory combination (Shapiro, 1998). Descriptive definitions address what people do when they stutter. For example, "stuttering can be defined as a higher frequency of sound, syllable, and one-syllable word disfluency (more irregular in rhythm and averaging two to four repetitions per instance) and prolonged sounds or postures of the speech mechanism" (Gregory, 1986, p. 5). Explanatory definitions address why a person stutters. For example, Glauber (1958) argued that "stuttering is a symptom in a psychopathological condition classified as a pregenital conversion neurosis" (p. 78). Finally, most definitions combine descriptive and explanatory elements. For example, Van Riper's (1982) definition, which is frequently quoted, noted that "stuttering occurs when the forward flow of speech is interrupted by a motorically disrupted sound, syllable, or word or by the speaker's reactions thereto" (p. 15).

My own notion of stuttering (Shapiro, 1999) is both explanatory and descriptive and builds upon the work of others, particularly Cooper (1993) and Peters and Guitar (1991).

Stuttering is a diagnostic label referring to a complex, multidimensional composite of behaviors, thoughts, and feelings of people who stutter. Stuttering refers to the individualized and involuntary interruptions in the forward flow of speech and the learned reactions thereto interacting with and generating associated thoughts and feelings about one's speech, oneself as a communicator, and one's communication world (Shapiro, 1999). Stuttering often is distinguished into core behaviors or secondary behaviors (Van Riper, 1982). Core behaviors are the basic, involuntary, observable behaviors of stuttering including part-word and whole-word repetitions, prolongations, and stoppages of air. Reacting to the core behaviors, the person who stutters learns secondary behaviors including escape behaviors (i.e., attempts to exit the stutter and finish the word, e.g., eye blinks, head nods, and interjection of sounds) and avoidance behaviors (i.e., attempts to prevent stuttering, e.g., pauses, word changes, and hand movements). These behaviors often generate negative and internalized feelings of shame and embarrassment. The etiology of stuttering is not known, yet it is conceptualized to relate to the interaction of physiological, psychological/psychosocial, psycholinguistic, and environmental factors (Shapiro, 1999). Whether for clinical or research purposes, stuttering should not be studied and cannot be understood without consideration of the person who stutters, the social contexts within which the person communicates, and the interaction of environmentally generated communicative demands and the speaker's individualized capacities for speech fluency.

Stuttering in adults, as discussed in this chapter, refers to an advanced form of developmental (also called idiopathic) stuttering (Andrews et al., 1983). To distinguish this developmental pattern of stuttering from others and from other disorders of fluency, I offer a brief overview. This is the most common form of stuttering (i.e., Track 1; Van Riper, 1982), which begins gradually in childhood roughly between ages 2.5 and 4.0 years, a period of great speech and language development (hence, "developmental" stuttering). These children begin speech development with normal sounding and integrated speech fluency, rate, and articulation. The disfluency begins gradually with behavioral characteristics including frequent gentle syllabic repetitions (i.e., without schwa, averaging three to five per word) on initial and function words. In the early stages, the child may show a characteristic of the most advanced form of stuttering one day, only to return to gentle syllabic repetitions or normal disfluency the next. At first, the child will experience no speech-related tension, frustration, or fears and will experience long periods of remissions. Therefore, the child talks without any perceived interference. As the stuttering develops, syllable repetitions increase in rate and frequency and their rhythmic pattern becomes less regular. Prolongations begin to appear at the end of the repetitions, as do tension, tremor, and struggle. Vowels within the syllables being repeated begin to be prolonged. Pitch increases indicative of laryngeal tension during prolongation are observed. Prolongations move forward, from the final repeated syllable of a series to the initial syllable. Frustration, concern, and tension become evident with a general overflow of tension indicated by facial contortion, retrials, and decreased speech output. As this pattern develops, word fears and avoidance occur, leading to sound fears, then situation fears. Repetitions and prolongations increase in frequency and complexity, becoming silent fixations with associated struggle. Breathing is interrupted and speech rate falls. Eye contact is impaired and avoidance tactics become evident as a consequence of fear. Embarrassment leads to communication reticence. Ultimately, patterns of stuttering behavior, both overt and covert, become stabilized and stereotyped, entering the child's self-concept, affecting personality factors, and establishing defenses.

While other developmental patterns exist (Bloodstein, 1995; Van Riper, 1982), the one just described provides a shared focus and point of departure. It is important to note that a person can begin to stutter at any age. Stuttering begins in adulthood only in rare cases. When it does, its onset typically is sudden and represents a distinct subtype of the disorder (Haynes, Pindzola, & Emerick, 1992). Furthermore, the pattern of stuttering described as developmental is distinct from other fluency disorders including cluttering, neurogenic disfluency, psychogenic disfluency, acquired disfluency following laryngectomy, among others (Culatta & Goldberg, 1995; Shapiro, 1998; Silverman, 1996).

Differential Diagnostic Characteristics of Stuttering

Adults who stutter know that stuttering varies by time, situation, and language factors. Indeed, stuttering is variable (i.e., changing based on special conditions), individualized (i.e., nonidentical, no two people demonstrate the same stuttering), and intermittent (i.e., not consistent) yet predictable (i.e., people who stutter report knowing when and on which word they are going to stutter, Shapiro, 1999). The factors that relate to stuttering and its variability are important in differential diagnosis and may be useful in building successful and motivating experiences in treatment.

Factors That Eliminate or Reduce Stuttering

There are special conditions that immediately eliminate or at least significantly reduce stuttering (Andrews et al., 1983; Shapiro, 1999; Williams, 1978). They include, among others, the following:

- choral reading (i.e., reading the same text at the same time with a speaker who is fluent);
- lipped speech (i.e., speaking without voicing);
- whispered speech (i.e., speaking with greatly reduced volume);
- prolonged speech with or without delayed auditory feedback (i.e., speaking with an increase in segment duration);
- rhythmic speech (i.e., speaking with increased segment duration in response to a stimulus including timing each syllable with the beat of a metronome or rhythmic finger tapping);
- shadowing (i.e., repeating immediately what someone else is saying but not in chorus);
- singing (i.e., replacing the suprasegmentals—pitch, juncture, intonation, etc.—of speech with that of song);
- slowed speech (i.e., reducing rate by increasing pause time);
- speaking in the presence of a loud bilateral masking noise (i.e., 90 dB), with altered pitch (i.e., increased or decreased fundamental frequency), or alone or with a nonhuman listener.

Factors That Increase Stuttering

A corollary of fluency-inducing conditions is fluency-inhibiting conditions. With some variation, the following situations commonly correlate with an increase in stuttering behavior (Shapiro, 1999; Silverman, 1996; Van Riper, 1982):

- speaking on the telephone;
- saying one's name;
- telling jokes;
- repeating a message that was not understood;
- waiting to respond;
- speaking to authority figures;
- speaking to large audiences;
- attempting to conceal stuttering.

Stuttering and Language

A reciprocal relationship exists between stuttering and language. We know that people who stutter have a tendency to predict the words on which they will and will not stutter. This leads to a subsequent tendency for word substitution or circumlocution (i.e., using a lesser feared word for a greater feared word). Van Riper (1982) noted that because of word fears leading to a need for synonyms, people who stutter develop remarkably large vocabularies. This is an influence of stuttering on language. Language also influences stuttering. Starkweather (1987), Williams (1978), and others noted that stuttering occurs more often in the following language contexts:

- at the beginnings of sentences;
- on words positioned earlier in a sentence than on words positioned later;
- on nouns, verbs, adjectives, and adverbs (i.e., lexical words) than on articles, prepositions, pronouns, and conjunctions (i.e., function words) for adults;
- on longer than shorter words;
- on the first syllable of the word than on later syllables;
- on less frequently used words but only when the sentences are syntactically more simple;
- on stressed than on unstressed syllables;
- at points of high information load (i.e., propositional value);
- on words toward the beginning of long sentences than on the same word when they are at the beginning of short sentences;
- on emotionally loaded material than on emotionally neutral material;
- at locations where language formulation is occurring.

These observations illustrate that stuttering affects language and language affects stuttering.

Attempts to define in more molecular terms the relationship between stuttering and language, however, fall short because of the complex interaction within and between the many variables that constitute communication. For example, I noted that stuttering typically occurs more frequently at the beginning of sentences. Some might explain this observation as the influence of language structure or form on stuttering (i.e., relative position of the word in the sentence). This explanation proves inadequate when the potential influence of other maintaining factors (i.e., both linguistic and nonlinguistic) is considered. Linguistic maintaining factors might include the relative complexity of the message being transmitted (i.e., content or semantics) or the function of the utterance (i.e., use or pragmatics). Nonlinguistic maintaining factors, such as cognitive, psychosocial, and sensorimotor influences, might also explain the frequency and location of stuttering within and between words and sentences.

Other Patterns of Variability and Predictability

People who stutter predict with accuracy the words on which they will stutter (i.e., anticipation). Upon repeated readings of the same passage, people who stutter tend to do so on the same words each time (i.e., consistency) yet demonstrate a decrease in the overall frequency of stuttering across the passage (i.e., adaptation).

Etiology and Conceptualizations of Stuttering

Etiology, or causality, implies an ongoing concept that is developmental in nature and therefore assumes a time frame that must be specified. That time frame is implied by three etiological considerations: predisposing, precipitating, and perpetuating (i.e., maintaining) factors (Shapiro, 1998; Silverman, 1996).

Predisposing and Precipitating Factors

Predisposing factors are the agents that incline a person to stutter and address why one person may be at greater risk to stutter than another person. These might include gender (i.e., boys are more inclined to stutter), age (i.e., most begin to stutter between 2 and 5 years), family history of stuttering, and bilingualism (i.e., bilingual children are at greater risk than unilingual children). Precipitating factors are those that are thought to have made the stuttering surface or brought it to its present state. These include developmental factors (e.g., physical development, cognitive development, social and emotional development, speech-language development, etc.) or environmental factors (e.g., unrealistic speech-related expectations, time pressure, life events generating uncertainty and/or insecurity, etc.) that are thought to present significantly competing demands on the production of fluent speech. Often, determining the predisposing and precipitating factors, particularly their causal connection to each other and to the literal beginning of stuttering, is an estimate at best. Nevertheless, although clinicians cannot alter predisposing factors in a person who stutters, they can work with clients and their families to reduce the potential influence of the precipitating factors.

Perpetuating or Maintaining Factors

Perpetuating factors are those that continue or maintain (hence, "maintaining factors") the stuttering at the present time and address why stuttering continues after it has begun. Klein and Moses (in this volume, Chapter 5) underscored the importance of identifying the maintaining factors for planning and conducting effective intervention with adults who have communication impairments. Although it might not be possible to know the predisposing and precipitating causes of stuttering, it indeed is possible and essential to determine with people who stutter the maintaining factors. Sometimes, however, people who stutter and their families are sincerely unaware of the maintaining factors that might or might not be clear to the insightful and empathic clinician (Shapiro, 1999).

In this book, maintaining factors are categorized into three areas: cognitive, psychosocial, and sensorimotor. This taxonomy may not be directly applicable to the maintaining factors associated with stuttering. A more efficient approach is to conceive of each maintaining factor as embodying all three dimensions. For example, the way people who stutter view themselves involves cognition (i.e., the way they think about and represent themselves as people and communicators), psychosocial factors (i.e., how they feel about themselves as people and communicators), and sensorimotor factors (i.e., how they adjust their pattern of speaking in response to proprioceptive/multisensory feedback and listener reactions). However, the existence of concomitant factors (e.g., mental retardation, cognitive dimension; clinical depression, psychosocial dimension; and right hemiplegia, sensorimotor dimension) affects assessment, prognosis, and intervention planning.

To illustrate the influence of maintaining factors, look at habit strength that is a prime maintaining factor (Haynes et al., 1992). People who stutter and their families have made compensations in cognitive, psychosocial, and sensorimotor factors, in addition to factors more linguistically oriented. Whatever the adjustments might have been, the clinician must help clients decipher the sequence of events that has coincided with the onset and development of stuttering and the potential ongoing effect of such maintaining factors. Sometimes, doing so is a tender and potentially emotional journey for the adult who stutters. The experience of stuttering may have influenced one's educational plans, career ambitions, selection of significant friends and spouses, and other aspects of life. It likely has influenced if not shaped the way people who stutter think about talking and about themselves as people and communicators. Sometimes, precipitating factors, when still present, maintain the stuttering. For example, environmental influences such as criticism of speech, unrealistic expectations, conversational time pressure, and experienced fluency failure might exacerbate the problem and maintain its existence. The negative feelings, thoughts, and attitudes that result from repeated frustration and embarrassment with stuttering often are the most resistant maintaining factors to alter. The accommodations made by people who stutter and others within their communication network (i.e., family, friends, classmates, instructors, colleagues, employers, etc.) influence the dynamics of communication including how they perceive themselves and others as communicators and conversational partners. These dynamics once established are resistant to change because of their predictability and therefore maintain the disorder. The anticipation of fluency failure so often experienced by people who stutter, particularly in situations and with people perceived to be important (e.g., asking someone out for a date, speaking to one's employer, saying one's own name, etc.), maintains the stuttering behavior. The spouse who continues to order in restaurants for her husband during their 40-year marriage is preventing him frustration, yet maintaining the likelihood that he will be unable to be fluent in this setting (Shapiro, 1999).

As noted, identifying the perpetuating or maintaining causes of stuttering tends to be more promising in terms of intervention planning than identifying the predisposing or precipitating factors. Once stuttering has been predisposed and precipitated, any of the following factors maintain the disorder and resist change:

- habituated cognitive, linguistic, and motor adjustments;
- maladaptive environmental conditions;
- interpersonal dynamics within communication systems;
- personal construct (i.e., self-definition) of a stutterer.

Before addressing how the factors reviewed to this point influence the intervention process, I will look now at four remaining foci: maintaining factors from the perspective of stuttering theories, the universality of performance demands, assumptions that are central to and guide intervention planning, and additional considerations.

A Look at Theory: Maintaining Factors (Re)Defined

While efforts to understand the causes of stuttering continue, the bottom line is that at present we do not and possibly cannot know such causes. As tempting as it seems at times to be drawn into the simplicity of unidimensional conceptualizations of etiology, it is most likely that the etiology of stuttering is multidimensional and might vary across people who stutter. What follows is a series of theoretical annotations, and for each the factors that potentially maintain the disorder of stuttering are noted. Being aware of such theory and the relevant maintaining factors is essential for intervention planning. A thorough review of theoretical explanations is beyond the scope of this chapter but may be found in Shapiro (1999).

Stuttering as a Neurotic Response. More than half a century ago, psychoanalytic explanations of stuttering were being developed that stuttering satisfies oral or anal erotic needs or represents repressed hostility. While this explanation is woefully weak on the basis of empirical support, stuttering within this framework is viewed as an attempt to suppress speech and as a symptom of deep neurotic conflict. Such a conception of stuttering implies the following maintaining factors: psychosocial (i.e., people's feelings about themselves as people and communicators are affected by the assumed neurosis and the resulting stuttering), cognitive (i.e., similarly, people's thoughts about themselves and their communicative world are influenced by the psychoemotional pathology, the consequences of which affect both psychological and social functioning), and behavioral/sensorimotor (i.e., the observable symptoms of disfluency are assumed to be caused by and reflective of psychoemotional pathology).

Stuttering as Communicative Failure and Anticipatory Struggle. At least three theories explain stuttering as a communicative failure and/or anticipatory struggle, meaning that people who stutter disrupt the way they speak because they believe that speech is difficult or that they will fail at speaking. The diagnosogenic, or semantic, theory holds that stuttering is caused by parents' or care providers' misdiagnosis of and inappropriate reaction to normal disfluencies in a child's speech, followed by the child's attempts to avoid the disfluencies that are mistakenly assumed to render the child's speech as normal. The continuity hypothesis/theory suggests that stuttering develops from normal disfluency, which becomes tense and fragmented as the child experiences frustration and failure in attempts to talk, namely because of criticism of normal disfluencies, delay in speech and language development, communication disorders, and reminders to "slow down." The primary stuttering theory holds that stuttering emerges gradually from a child's normal hesitations and repetitions, namely from learning (environmental), constitutional (organic), or neurotic (emotional) sources. As a whole, the communicative failure/anticipatory struggle theories present the following maintaining factors: cognitive (e.g., "Speaking is so hard and I just know that I can't say it right. I know I am going to stutter."), psychosocial (e.g., "I feel so badly about myself when I talk with others. Speaking is so much harder for me than it is for others."), and behavioral/sensorimotor (e.g., "My mouth gets stuck because I speak too fast. That's why I always am told to slow down.").

Stuttering as a Learned Behavior.   Within the context of the behavioral sciences, theories of stuttering as a learned behavior define the processes by which stuttering is originally learned and maintained and postulate motivational factors, stimulus variables, and reinforcing conditions. Such theories distinguish between those that view stuttering as an avoidance response (e.g., conflict theory and avoidance reduction, operant conditioning, instrumental avoidance act theory, etc.) and those that view stuttering as an interaction of at least two behavioral phenomena (i.e., two-factor learning theory, e.g., classical conditioning, instrumental conditioning, etc.). The maintaining factors that are observed across the broad spectrum of learning theories include: cognitive (internal thoughts and self-representations change because of avoidance, interactions, and/or association and accommodation to environmental events), psychosocial (i.e., internal feelings similarly change by interaction and accommodation to one's environment), and behavioral/sensorimotor (i.e., visible manifestations of disfluency are reactions to one's environment or learned responses thereto).

Stuttering as a Physiological Deficit.   Theories of stuttering as a physiological deficit assume the moment of stuttering to be an indication of failure or breakdown in the complex coordination required for fluent speech. These theories assume that a person who stutters has a constitutional predisposition toward stuttering that is precipitated by psychosocial or environmental stress and a reduced physiological capacity to coordinate speech. The precise nature of the organic predisposition and the role of heredity varies across the theories. For example, the incomplete cerebral dominance theory holds that ambidexterity or a change in handedness caused a conflict between the two hemispheres resulting in neuromotor disorganization and mistiming resulting in stuttering. Dysphemia and biochemical theory states that stuttering is a manifestation of an internal condition triggered by illness, emotional or environmental stress (i.e., dysphemia), or biochemical imbalance. Perseveration theory implies that a person who stutters has an organic predisposition to motor and sensory perseveration, of which stuttering is an outward manifestation. Finally, brain lesion theory postulates that stuttering involves organically based changes in the interaction of laryngeal, supralaryngeal, and respiratory reflexes, and suggests that stuttering is the consequence of disruption of motor organization, timing, and control. Taken together, physiological deficit theories imply that stuttering, once predisposed and precipitated, is maintained primarily by behavioral/sensorimotor factors, in addition to cognitive and psychosocial factors.

Stuttering as the Result of Disturbed Feedback.   For stuttering to be viewed as the result of disturbed feedback, speaking is viewed as a servomechanism in which the ear is the sensor, the vocal organs and motor innervations are the effector, and the brain is the controller. People who stutter are assumed to possess a defective monitoring mechanism for speech, causing distortion, interference, and overload within the feedback loop. To remain error free, ongoing fluent speech movements require feedback and sensory information. When errors occur, the system corrects itself by searching for the appropriate output until it is achieved. Stuttering is viewed as a consequence of this corrective process, the absence of a correct standard pattern for production of a syllable or word, or a perceptual error on the input side of sensory information processing. Similar to physiological deficit theories, disturbed feedback theories imply that stuttering is maintained primarily by behavioral/sensorimotor factors, in addition to cognitive and psychosocial influences.

Demands and Capacities Theory.   This theory holds that the speaker's capacity for fluent speech and the demands for fluent speech imposed on the speaker by listeners and the speaker are dynamic and typically increasing. When the demands exceed the speaker's capacities for fluent speech, stuttering occurs. If the demands are reduced or increased slowly and/or the speaker's capacities develop sufficiently, stuttering remits. If the demands continue to outpace a child's capacity for fluent speech, stuttering continues. Explaining stuttering as the consequence of demands (e.g., environmental, constitutional, psychoemotional, etc.) exceeding one's capacities for fluent speech implies that stuttering is maintained by behavioral/sensorimotor factors, in addition to cognitive and psychosocial factors.

Metatheory.   Several critical assumptions about stuttering emerge from theories reviewed here, among others. In Shapiro (1999), I reviewed such assumptions to ground my assertion of theoretical truth as I see it (i.e., what predisposes, precipitates, and perpetuates stuttering). I will review these assumptions here, however, to extrapolate the maintaining factors of stuttering. These assumptions are:

- Stuttering is a multidimensional neuromotor disruption in the timing and control of speech-related motor movements.
- Stuttering is caused by the interaction of individually determined yet unknown predisposing (i.e., constitutional) factors with precipitating (i.e., developmental and/or environmental) factors.
- Stuttering is maintained by perpetuating (i.e., maintaining) factors that can and must be identified and systematically eliminated in the treatment process.

- The phenomenology of stuttering can best be explained and conceptualized from the delicate and dynamic balance between multiple demands upon the person and an individually defined capacity for fluent speech.

These assumptions imply that stuttering is maintained by a composite of maintaining factors including behavioral/sensorimotor (i.e., how speakers adjust their pattern of speaking in response to incoming proprioceptive feedback), cognitive (i.e., how speakers think about and represent themselves as people and communicators), and psychosocial (i.e., how speakers feel about themselves as people and communicators, and the relationships they form as a consequence of such thoughts and feelings). I now turn to the clinical implications of performance demands and related intervention assumptions that are central to and guide intervention planning.

Performance Demands: In Search of Universal Truth

Performance demands. Indeed it does! Just as cognitive, psychosocial, and sensorimotor factors have been seen to maintain stuttering, such factors also can be said to affect the relative demand placed upon the individual's capacity to remain fluent. An awareness of such performance demands is critical for intervention planning. Specifically, the clinician initially helps the client to minimize the demands to maximize speech fluency, only to reintroduce the demands deliberately as treatment continues to transfer the successful effect of treatment into extraclinical settings. This transfer process, while a significant challenge to all forms of treatment, is critical to effective, ecologically valid intervention. Consider the following.

Cognitive Performance Demands

People tend to be more successful when they internalize, visualize, and thereby predict successful performance (i.e., fluent speech, in this case). Such success often is reflected in feelings of self-confidence, internalized thoughts and feelings about oneself as able and in control, and self-reminders of previous successes. These are cognitive factors (i.e., thoughts about oneself as successful, able, and in control) that are critical for effective intervention planning with adults who stutter. At the outset of treatment, the clinician creates with and for the person who stutters opportunities to experience such conditions. The clinician provides feedback to the client regarding the aspects of the client's communication performance that are successful. As fluency improves throughout intervention, the client becomes increasingly responsible for creating and maintaining such conditions (i.e., internalizing thoughts and feelings/feedback of fluency success and control) while the clinician deliberately reintroduces counterconditions of an increasingly challenging nature (i.e., "barbs," verbal "put downs" and reprimands for the client to withstand while maintaining fluency success). The clinician might say, "Watch it! Sounds like you're messing up again." Or she might say, "Do you really think you can say that word right? You just forgot your fluency facilitating control in the last sentence." The client will have been pre-pared to counter such claims (e.g., "I did not forget my control. I just used a pull-out on the word girl."), all the while internalizing and verbalizing his fluency success and control. This is one way of minimizing cognitive demands placed upon the client at the beginning of treatment, only to increase such demands as they become more able to withstand their potential effect. In so doing, fluency success is internalized, habituated, and transferred.

Psychosocial Performance Demands

Similarly, the effect of psychosocial performance demands must be accounted for through-out the intervention process. People who stutter often report feeling different degrees of performance demand with variation in conversational partners, audience sizes, conversa-tional settings, and other factors. For example, people who stutter typically report the fol-lowing speaking contexts to be of increasing difficulty: speaking alone, speaking to one's pet, speaking to an infant, speaking to a close friend, speaking to a significant other (e.g., wife, girlfriend, parent), speaking with a casual work colleague, speaking with a formal work colleague (e.g., supervisor, employer). For some, however, speaking with someone who is more familiar may be harder because the performance demand/perceived expecta-tion may feel greater. Some report feeling increasing degrees of challenge as audience size increases (i.e., from one, to two, to three, and so on up to a crowd of people), or as audi-ence visibility decreases (i.e., speaking directly with a person typically is reported less difficult than speaking on the phone; however, each person reports different degrees of fluency challenge with different phone partners). Similarly, variations in the conversational context may alter the degree of fluency challenge. People who stutter often report the following speaking contexts in order of increasing degree of difficulty: speaking casually with one person without interruption, speaking with more than one person without inter-ruption, speaking with interruption/topic shifts/linguistic ambiguity and contradictions/pragmatic violations. Each of these contexts, however, can become increasingly com-plex as conversational partners who are perceived by the speaker to be of greater impor-tance/significance/intimidation are introduced and audience size increases. Psychosocial performance demands must be controlled for at the outset of intervention and then rein-troduced deliberately as intervention continues, thus facilitating fluency success and inter-nalized control.

Sensorimotor Performance Demands

Typically, conversation is the context for my clinical interactions with adults who stutter. Such a context is recommended because of its naturalness, degree of transfer, likeness to real conversation, and ecological validity. However, there are occasions when the speech fluency of a person who stutters is so impaired that the sensorimotor performance demand must be concretely reduced. To do so, the client may be directed in how to generate fluent speech within monosyllables (e.g., vowels, consonants, vowel and consonant combina-tions), multisyllable single words (e.g., reciting numbers, days of the week, months of the year, names of family members), and eventually multiword combinations (e.g., word pairs, antonyms, synonyms, compound words). From such structured interaction, the client may move toward more conversation-like interaction including phrases, responses to questions that require short responses (e.g., "Do you like baseball? What's your favorite sport? How old are you?"), responses that require longer responses (e.g., "Why do you like soccer? How did you decide to buy the Ford over the Chevy? How do you get here from your house?").

"What is your name?"—a simple question—is one of the hardest questions for people who stutter to answer. The question requires a one- or two-word response. However, for reasons we still do not understand, the question and the anticipated response elicit terror in the heart of many adults who stutter. Perhaps the question is so distinctly personal that its response cannot be altered (i.e., if one's name is David, he cannot respond with Susan or Seth or any other name.). Other aspects such as emotionality or propositionality may interfere with a sensorimotor performance demand that otherwise may seem simple. For example, there are questions that may have simple surface structures requiring simple responses, yet may have emotional loading, causing interference at a deeper structure. Consider questions such as the following as examples: "Did you vote Republican or Democrat? Are you faithful to your wife? How often do you like to have sex?" Similarly, linguistic loading may interfere with an otherwise simple sensorimotor performance demand. Consider the potential for fluency reduction resulting from pragmatic rule violations (i.e., deliberately disrupting the rules of intra- or interutterance cohesion; e.g., Question: "How are you today?" Response: "We stop at stop signs."), linguistic complexity or propositional loading (i.e., people who stutter tend to be more disfluent on words and sentences of greater length and complexity), and linguistic ambiguity and contradictions (i.e., utterances that are not semantically joined to previous utterances; e.g., Statement: "My wife Sandy is a schoolteacher." Follow-up question: "You were saying earlier that your wife Joan works outside of your home. How does she like the hair salon business?").

As I discussed earlier for cognitive and psychosocial performance demands, intervention planning must account for the level of sensorimotor performance demand. Initially, opportunities are created to minimize the sensorimotor demand so as to maximize speech fluency and the experience and feeling of fluency control. Where the adult's speech fluency is severely impaired, the response expectation might be a fluent sound or word rather than a fluent turn within an interactive conversation. Later, the response expectation may increase (e.g., a fluent sentence or turn within an interactive conversation) while reintroducing systematically other such demands into the intervention process (e.g., emotionality, propositionality, etc.) to help the client develop a buffer to the potential disruption that was previously experienced. Then, with improved fluency and fluency control, both the clinician and client seek opportunities for the client to encounter such increased sensorimotor performance demands while experiencing improved speech fluency, thus facilitating transfer of speech fluency and fluency facilitating control.

Guiding Intervention Assumptions

I have reviewed the importance of cognitive, psychosocial, and sensorimotor elements in the maintaining factors for stuttering and in the performance demands for people who stutter. I now turn to three guiding intervention assumptions that build upon this foundation.[1] To discuss intervention planning with adults who stutter, these selected assumptions are highlighted within the context of a brief discussion of the respective grounding theory. Each imprints the intervention planning process in unique ways. The assumptions address personal constructs (i.e., cognitive maintaining factors and performance demands), family systems (i.e., psychosocial maintaining factors and performance demands), and stuttering modification/fluency shaping considerations (i.e., cognitive, psychosocial, and sensorimotor maintaining factors and performance demands).

Personal Construct Theory

As a personal construct, stuttering (i.e., thoughts, feelings, and behavior) reflects in part the consequence of active and alternative choices (Shapiro, 1999). The central premise to personal construct theory (Kelly, 1955a, 1955b) is that all people have alternative choices to make. To me, this statement is particularly relevant to planning and conducting intervention activities with adults who stutter. The philosophical assumption to personal construct theory is "constructive alternativism." Discussing this assumption, Kelly (1955a) expressed, "We assume that all of our present interpretations of the universe are subject to revision or replacement. . . . We take the stand that there are always some alternative constructions available to choose among in dealing with the world" (p. 15). Extended to people who stutter, this view holds that each possesses the potential if not the ability to change every aspect of feelings, thoughts, and behavior. People are adaptable because they have individually created an interwoven network of personal constructs, viewpoints of reality based upon past experience in life situations. Because life and its experiences are so varied and individualized, typically people bring many personal constructs to bear on their interpretations of the world. In fact, all of their behaviors including the way they dress, what they eat, how and what they drive, where and how they live, how and with whom they interact, and all of their personal and unique habits reflect their personal constructs. More directly related to this discussion, how speech-language pathologists design the clinical process and interact with their clients reflect our personal constructs about such processes as learning, development, and change, and about the respective roles of the client and clinician within these processes. The importance of clinicians being aware of their own personal constructs has been addressed elsewhere (Shapiro, 1987, 1999; Shapiro & Moses, 1989).

Of particular significance are the points of view developed by people who stutter about talking, about themselves as people, and about communication within a social milieu. In this respect, the internal experience of people who stutter and the experience of stuttering itself become an individualized metacognitive and psychodynamic reality. It is not only interesting but clinically significant that often the most critical feelings and personal constructs escape the awareness of the person holding them (Shapiro, 1999). Bringing about this awareness within an empathic context of ongoing support and positive regard is within the domain of the clinician. I say this based on the conviction that none of

---

[1]In Chapter 6 a set of principles were abstracted from several learning theories. Although the theories presented here are different from those in Chapter 6, the concept of using theory to guide practice is maintained.

Principles Fluency is facilitated by:	Theoretic Derivation	Maintaining Factors Addressed	Implications for Procedures
8. Deliberately revisiting the past	Personal construct	Cognitive Psychosocial	Review with the client video tapes of pretreatment communication Celebrate the client's achievements While viewing the video tapes, encourage the client to discuss previous thoughts and feelings of himself as a communicator and how these have evolved
9. Reexamining one's personal construct	Personal construct	Cognitive Psychosocial	Help client understand the nature of fluency possessed Involve the client and family actively in the treatment process and related decisions Help the client to think of himself in ways other than a person who stutters
10. Integrating treatment changes within the communication system	Family systems Fluency shaping	Psychosocial Cognitive	Encourage conversational partners (family, friends, coworkers, teachers, employers) to adjust and thereby support the changes that have taken place

aFor complete treatment of these issues see Shapiro (1999).

he does not let his communication skills hold him back. He indicated that he could only predict fluency when he speaks alone and when talking to the family's dog. Fred is a long-time factory employee and has no other family history of communication disorders.

An analysis of Fred's conversational speech indicated a rate of 41 words per minute, significantly below the average of 160, reflecting the severity of Fred's disfluency. Disfluencies included rapid initial and medial syllable repetitions for periods of 1 to 16 seconds; part-word, whole-word, and phrase repetition varying from 1 to 9 units of repetition; and syllable, word, and phrase interjections of 1 to 10 units of interjection/repetition. A randomly selected sentence of 13 words lasted 55 seconds and contained 50 distinct units of disfluency. Associated characteristics included facial tension, pitch increase indicative of laryngeal tension, and rapid and vertical jaw movements during syllable repetitions. Islands of complete fluency lasted up to 16 words. Reading proved to be a more disfluent context. When reading "My Grandfather," Fred's rate of speech was 12 words per minute. Types of disfluency were similar to those noted in conversation; however, the severity and intensity were more pronounced. For example, syllable repetition (e.g., guhguhguh . . . grandfather) was extremely rapid and lasted up to 90 seconds in duration. Word interjection lasted up to 20 seconds in duration. All other parameters of articulation, language, and voice (i.e., during fluent, nonstuttered speech) were within normal limits. Trial management combining

us can change behaviors about which we remain unaware. For example, an adult who stutters and has experienced repeated speech attempts and failures might internalize feelings of negativity, worthlessness, and pessimism. It is not hard to visualize how such feelings could affect all aspects of one's life. In contrast, imagine the potential for positive change when a clinician discusses with a person who stutters realistic options through sensitive and strategic intervention planning. When adults who stutter become explicitly aware of their personal constructs, they (and their clinicians) can use this awareness to effect positive changes in the way they view themselves as communicators and in the control they exercise over their own speech fluency. A central tenet here is that when adults who stutter become aware that their interpretation of past events and thereby anticipation of future events was incorrect or undesirable, they may revise their construct system to achieve outcomes that were not or did not seem possible (e.g., speaking with greater fluency, using self-corrections more often, using fluency facilitating controls outside settings, etc.) (Shapiro, 1999). This is the role of the clinician: to make what seems impossible, possible; to help people imagine and realize their own communication dreams.

Family Systems Theory

Because stuttering and people who stutter exist within a family context, both must be addressed within this context to be understood. Furthermore, experiences and change of a person who stutters trigger compensatory changes in family members and significant others (Shapiro, 1999). One part of the family cannot be understood in isolation from the other members of the system (Epstein & Bishop, 1981; Luterman, 1996). Efforts to involve family members in the intervention process often inadvertently continue to center on the person who stutters, an individual, as the center of the treatment. While family members might be directed to participate in activities outside of the clinical setting, they still are not valued and involved as active and equal members of the treatment team. Under this arrangement, the most significant changes are viewed as occurring in the treatment session, which might be enhanced by family cooperation and understanding. In contrast, treating a person who stutters within the context of a family system requires the entire family to be involved in all aspects of assessment and treatment. Such involvement requires understanding by the clinician of the nature and dynamics of the individual family. Within this context, counseling becomes the medium for discussing aspects of family interactive patterns that facilitate or inhibit the goals and procedures that are jointly determined. What this means is that clinicians must assess and understand the strengths, needs, and level of functioning not only of the adult who stutters, but of the family as factors in the intervention process.

Stuttering Modification/Fluency Shaping Considerations

Stuttering modification and fluency shaping are bipolar theoretical endpoints along a clinical continuum. Understanding these two elements and the continuum that lies between them is useful for intervention planning (Guitar & Peters, 1980; Peters & Guitar, 1991; Shapiro, 1999). Stuttering modification therapy assumes that stuttering results from avoiding or struggling with disfluency, avoiding feared words and/or feared situations, and from negative attitudes toward speaking. The intervention seeks to reduce these behaviors, fears, and negative attitudes while modifying the form of stuttering. This is accomplished by reducing the struggle behavior, smoothing out the stuttering into a more gentle form, and reducing the tension and rate of stuttering. On the other hand, fluency shaping assumes that stuttering is learned, and treatment is based upon the principles of behavior modification (i.e., operant conditioning and programming). Fluency is first established in a controlled stimulus environment, and fluent responses are then reinforced and stuttered responses are punished. Both approaches first attempt to achieve spontaneous fluency, with controlled fluency as an acceptable but less preferred goal. If these cannot be achieved, stuttering modification seeks to achieve a level of acceptable stuttering. Any noticeable stuttering, however, would be seen as evidence of program failure to a fluency shaping clinician. Stuttering modification emphasizes the importance of studying and understanding feelings and attitudes and thereby reducing speech-related fears and negative emotions. This is done within a counseling framework where the clinician and client actively discuss and participate in all aspects of the treatment process. In contrast, fluency shaping does not attempt to reduce communication-related fears and avoidances. Rather, fluency shaping is conducted within a structured context where stimuli, responses, and subsequent events are preprogrammed. In reality, most treatment falls somewhere along the continuum. Typically, an intervention oriented more toward stuttering modification is indicated when the person who stutters hides the stuttering, avoids speaking, feels penalized by stuttering, and feels poorly as a communicator. Fluency shaping is indicated when the person who stutters does so openly, does not avoid speaking, does not feel penalized by stuttering, and feels positive as a communicator. The way these and other factors combine guides the clinician toward stuttering modification or fluency shaping in intervention planning.

Summary of Procedural Principles Derived from the Various Theoretic Perspectives

Having reviewed maintaining factors from different theoretical perspectives, I identify a set of procedural principles. These principles may be used to develop a procedural approach for specific clients. Box 10.1 lists these principles, their derivation source, and their applications to procedure planning.

Case Example: Initial Clinical Portrait

Mr. Frederick (Fred) Johnson was a man of 55 years when he was referred by his family physician for a communication assessment because of his severe stuttering. Both Fred and his wife, Mary, attended the scheduled evaluation. Fred's stuttering reportedly began early in childhood and has remained constant in degree and type as long as both Fred and Mary can recall. While Fred has not had treatment in the last 30 years, he did experience two brief periods of treatment before that time involving oral elocution and neuropharmacology (i.e., medication by prescription). Fred reported that he is typically disfluent but that

---

BOX 10.1

Selected Procedural Principles, Their Derivation Source, and Their Application to Intervention Planning[a]

Principles Fluency is facilitated by:	Theoretic Derivation	Maintaining Factors Addressed	Implications for Procedures
1. The client's experience of fluency	Personal construct Fluency shaping	Psychosocial Sensorimotor	Design treatment activities as to ensure fluency
2. The client's heightened awareness of fluency	Personal construct	Cognitive	Help client identify behaviors, thoughts, and feelings that characterize fluency Shift responsibility for identifying fluency from self to client
3. The use of fluency facilitating techniques during instances of stuttering	Personal construct Fluency shaping	Cognitive Sensorimotor	Help the client decide on one or two behaviors or techniques that can facilitate fluency (e.g., slow and gentle, cancellation)
4. Addressing thoughts, feelings, and attitudes directly	Personal construct Family systems	Psychosocial	Involve clients in direct discussions of positive and negative feelings (e.g., "What do you feel when you discipline your children and you find yourself stuttering?" Or "What was it like when you ordered for your wife in a restaurant for the first time in your 35-year marriage?")
5. Transferring fluency facilitating techniques to extra clinical settings.	Fluency shaping	Cognitive Psychosocial	Extend clinical assignments beyond the treatment room
6. Preparing for relapse	Personal construct Family systems	Cognitive Psychosocial	Help the clients and families understand the nature of relapse and prepare them for the likelihood of its occurrence (i.e., "Relapse Happens!")
7. Becoming one's own clinician	Personal construct Family systems	Cognitive Psychosocial	Resist the temptation to enable the client to become dependent on the clinician Discuss the changing roles and responsibilities of each participant Jointly establish goals and design procedures

(continued)

TABLE 10.1 **Areas of Assessment for Intervention Planning with an Adult Who Stutters**

Name: Fred Johnson	Age: 55	Primary Disorder: Stuttering
Necessary Information	**Source**	**Maintaining Factors Assessed (C, Cognitive; P, Psychosocial; S, Sensorimotor)**

I. Language and Speech
  Fluency
	Diagnostic interview (C, P, S)
	Speech-language sample/conversation (C, P, S)
	Structured activities without communicative pressure
	  Reading (S)
	  Recalling/describing events (S)
	  Word and sentence repetition (S)
	  Questions and answers (C, P, S)
	Structured activities with communicative pressure
	Oral mechanism examination (S)
	Hearing examination (S)
	Trial management
	  Fluency shaping (S)
	  Stuttering modification (C, P, S)
	Speech (i.e., overt and covert) analysis (C, P, S)
	Debriefing and recommendations (C, P, S)	

stuttering modification and fluency shaping during the evaluation resulted in a positive behavioral (i.e., 120 words per minute in conversation, 89 words per minute in reading) and attitudinal response. Tables 10.1 and 10.2 summarize the areas assessed during Fred's evaluation and the baseline data resulting from this evaluation.

Long-Term Goals and Procedural Approach

Long-Term Goals

Long-term goals for Fred to accomplish by the end of scheduled direct treatment, tentatively projected from one to two years, include a primary communication goal and two supportive goals. These are as follows:

Communication goal:

- Fred will produce fluent speech in conversational contexts through the use of specific fluency facilitating controls and self-monitoring skills.

  Supportive goals:

- Fred will understand and discuss his communication-related feelings.
- Fred will participate actively in all aspects of treatment planning, execution, follow-up, and evaluation.

TABLE 10.2 Baseline Data for Intervention Planning with an Adult Who Stutters

---

Name: Fred Johnson   **Age: 55**   **Primary Disorder: Stuttering**

Area Assessed and Results

I. Language and Speech
   Fluency

Diagnostic Interview/Conversation:
- Stuttering began in early childhood.
- Has not had treatment over the last 30 years. Prior treatment included oral elocution and neuropharmacology.
- Only predictable fluent context is talking to family dog.
- Generally disfluent, but does not let stuttering hold him back.

Speech in Conversation:
- 41 words spoken per minute (i.e., significantly below the average of 160 wpm).
- Rapid initial and medial syllable repetitions for periods of 1 to 16 seconds.
- Part word, whole word, and phrase repetitions varying from 1 to 9 units of repetition.
- Syllable, word, and phrase interjections of 1 to 10 units of interjection/repetition.
- Random sentence containing 13 words lasted 55 seconds and contained 50 distinct units of disfluency.
- Secondary characteristics included facial tension, pitch increase indicative of laryngeal tension, and rapid and vertical jaw movements during syllable repetitions.
- Islands of complete fluency lasted up to 16 words.

Speech in Reading (My Grandfather):
- 12 words spoken per minute (i.e., significantly below the average of 160 wpm).
- Disfluency types were the same as those in conversation.
- Severity and intensity of disfluency were more pronounced in reading than in conversation.
- Syllable repetition (e.g., guhguhguh . . . grandfather) was extremely rapid and lasted up to 90 seconds in duration.
- Word interjection lasted up to 20 seconds in duration.

Articulation, Language, Voice:
- All parameters of articulation, language, and voice (i.e., during fluent, nonstuttered speech) were within normal limits.

Oral Mechanism and Hearing Evaluation:
- All parameters of oral structure and function and peripheral hearing were within normal limits.

Trial Management:
- Trial management combining stuttering modification and fluency shaping resulted in a positive behavioral (i.e., 120 words per minute in conversation, 89 words per minute in reading) and attitudinal response (i.e., positive expressions; e.g., "I didn't know this was possible; I can't believe this!").

These goals were determined to be appropriate for Fred on the bases of his baseline data (see Tables 10.1 and 10.2), status of fluency at the time the goals were designed, success in trial management during and after the diagnostic evaluation, and after dialogue/negotiation with Fred and his family members. Furthermore, they resulted from an understanding of Fred's views toward himself as a person and as a communicator within a social world and the cognitive, behavioral, and emotional dynamics that operate within Fred's family.

Long-Term Procedural Approach

The long-term procedural approach for Fred's fluency intervention will take the form of a combined stuttering modification and fluency shaping approach within a family systems context. The combined intervention approach will provide an opportunity to help Fred experience more fluent speech and gain a better understanding of the nature of his fluent as compared with his disfluent speech. Furthermore, this approach will provide an opportunity for Fred to experience controlled, volitional fluency (i.e., to get a glimpse of "fluency freedom"), an experience he reported having never had previously; for Fred to come to identify, discuss, understand, and gain control of his communication-related feelings and attitudes; and for all members of Fred's family, particularly his wife Mary, to participate actively and regularly in all aspects of the intervention process. The approach will be interactive and collaborative. This design resulted from an awareness of both the maintaining factors that tend to perpetuate Fred's stuttering and the concepts reviewed earlier that are among those considered central to the intervention planning process. The maintaining factors include the following:

- Cognitive: When asked how improvement in communication skills would affect his life, Fred indicated that he could not respond because he has always stuttered and could not imagine what it would be like not to stutter. Providing Fred an opportunity to experience fluency success seemed essential to enable him to begin to visualize, internalize, and personalize the goals to which he is striving.
- Sensorimotor: Fred reported being utterly unable to control his disfluency and being unaware that his articulatory postures during fixations were frequently inappropriate compared with his target sound. Providing Fred an opportunity to heighten his understanding of his fluency and disfluency in addition to gain control was essential to break the habit strength that has persisted for so many years.
- Psychosocial/Emotional: Fred's family, particularly his wife, shared Fred's commitment toward a brighter fluency future and expressed a willingness to do all they could in active pursuit of shared goals. However, their life was so busy, so chaotic, that there was at best minimal time for real communicative dialogue, and what did exist was rushed and fractured. As will be seen, this maintaining factor not only contributed to the design of the long-term goals, but will imprint the short-term goals as well.

As noted earlier, three basic assumptions guided the design of the long-term goals and procedures. In capsule form now, the implications of that conceptual framework are as follows:

- Personal Construct: Fred viewed himself as a stutterer. He could not imagine any other alternative interpretation. Providing him those alternatives, not by word, but by systematic intervention planning, is the clinician's responsibility. In other words, the clinician cannot persuade Fred to believe differently. However, the clinician can and must create the necessary opportunities for him to experience success from which Fred will draw alternative conclusions.
- Family Systems: Fred and his wife have been married a long time. His development of fluency control is a change that potentially will alter the communication dynamics that have been established over time. Just because he changes through improved speech fluency and communication independence does not mean that his wife and other family members will necessarily know how to change with him. Without attending to the needs and feelings of the other family members, it is possible and understandable that they could come to feel less needed as Fred comes to speak more for himself.
- Stuttering Modification/Fluency Shaping Considerations: Fred's treatment initially will emphasize fluency shaping to develop a measure of functional, albeit controlled, fluency and heightened motivation. Thereafter, the combined approach will favor stuttering modification to reduce the severity of Fred's stuttering and to develop increased communication independence while providing him an opportunity to identify and understand his feelings about himself as a communicator. Treatment will emphasize the fluency already contained within Fred's speech and the importance of transfer activities conducted on a daily basis between scheduled sessions to facilitate fluency control and self-monitoring skills.

Short-Term Goals and Procedural Approach

Short-Term Goals

The short-term goals for Fred to accomplish within a two-month period include the following:

Communication goal:
- Fred will begin to "cancel" (Van Riper, 1973) instances of disfluency in conversational contexts.

This means that he will finish uttering the word that contains an instance of stuttering. Before going on, he will return to the beginning of that word and not before to institute a slow, gentle, yet natural sounding posture to replace the instance of stuttering. In this way, Fred will begin to gain control over this speech after an instance of stuttering has occurred.

Supportive goals:
- Fred will determine with his family a regular, predictable time for quality, uninterrupted family interaction.

- Fred will heighten his awareness of the nature of his fluent speech.
- Fred will discuss specifically what he does when he is fluent and compare that with what he does differently when he stutters.
- Fred will compare the feelings associated with fluency and those associated with stuttering.

These goals were determined from an awareness that they are elemental to the long-term goals described earlier. Fred must gain an understanding of the nature of his fluent speech. In the speech of most people who stutter, even among those who stutter severely, fluency is observed more often than disfluency. However, disfluency draws more attention to itself and therefore fluency often is not as noticeable as stuttered speech. Fred must be able to understand and describe what he does when he is fluent to be able to do it more often. This is highly motivating and a necessary step before beginning to control his stuttered speech and ultimately replacing it with fluency facilitating controls. Also, Fred and his family must be able to find time to communicate, discuss the intervention process, and share responsibility for it. For these reasons, intervention must help Fred and his family develop a communication context that is more conducive to meaningful, less frenetic interaction. This can only happen through involvement with and understanding of the family leading to communicative restructuring.

Short-Term Procedural Approach:

Fred and Mary live a distance from the clinician. While working with them in their home would provide a more natural and ecologically valid setting for conversational interaction, the university Speech and Hearing Center provides a more practical setting because of the distance and scheduling constraints. The room itself will be arranged to encourage informal dialogue and sharing of ideas. Typically this is achieved by the clinician's supportive, professional manner of encouragement, active listening, positive facial expressions and eye contact, and unconditional positive regard. While appropriate furniture for casual, focused interaction combined with appropriate lighting is important, all the furniture in the world cannot replace the significance of the clinician's manner, sincerity, and attitude toward the family and the client's potential for fluency success. In fact, I have become convinced that the clinician's attitude is one of the key elements related directly to and predictive of client's and family's communication success. Again, a supportive, collaborative, engaged interaction provides a procedural context based upon an understanding of the maintaining factors and the principles reviewed earlier. A highlight of the maintaining factors follows:

- Cognitive: The goals and procedures are designed to provide Fred with experiences that will enable him to consider alternative and expanded perceptions of himself (i.e., moving from "I cannot succeed. I am a stutterer." to "I am able and since I know I have achieved some fluency success, I know I can achieve more."). It is significant to track the client's comments about himself over time. Typically they move from expressions of inability (e.g., "I can't speak fluently. I never could do that.") to ability (e.g., "I just used a gentle slide. I know I can do this."), and from being out of control (e.g., "Why is this happening to me?") to being in control (e.g., "I just self-corrected. I know I can get those blocks before they get me. Yeah!").

- Sensorimotor: Recall that Fred initially demonstrated a lack of fluency control and inappropriate articulatory postures. The setting, goals, and procedures provide a supportive context encouraging Fred's active participation, systematic approximations for success, and heightened auditory, visual, and proprioceptive feedback, all of which are prerequisite to fluency control.
- Psychosocial/Emotional: The ongoing involvement of Mary and other family members in Fred's fluency treatment will provide both an opportunity for and model of meaningful conversational interaction that will be carried over into the home and other settings outside the clinic.

These goals and procedures again are generated from the principles discussed earlier. They are highlighted here as follows:

- Personal Construct: This is directly related to the cognitively based maintaining factors discussed earlier. Fred will be given clinical and extraclinical opportunities for fluency success, from which he can revise his personal construct of himself as a stutterer.
- Family Systems: This is directly related to the psychosocial/emotional maintaining factors discussed earlier. Mary and the other family members will be involved regularly both inside and outside of the clinical setting to help them adjust to the altered communication dynamics as Fred achieves increased fluency control. Ultimately, others within Fred's communication system will be involved in transfer activities. These may include Fred's work colleagues, friends, and personal and professional associates.
- Stuttering Modification/Fluency Shaping Considerations: This is directly related to the behavioral/sensorimotor maintaining factors discussed earlier. This procedural approach emphasizes Fred's active role in his achievement of fluency success, heightening his understanding and thereby acceptance of himself as an effective communicator, and transferring of fluency facilitating control and self-monitoring skills to outside settings.

Session Goals and Procedures

Session Goals

Recall that among the short-term goals for Fred were heightening his awareness of the nature of his fluent speech and distinguishing between what he literally does when he is fluent and disfluent. For illustration purposes, an early session goal and one at approximately the end of the two-month period are presented and justified.

Early Session Goal: Fred will identify instances of fluent speech and subsequently describe, following the clinician's model, the location of his articulators and the proprioceptive feedback received from them.

Derivation:

Maintaining Factors Addressed: Sensorimotor and cognitive.

Anchoring Principles: Stuttering modification/fluency shaping (i.e., reducing severity of disfluency by building the feedback mechanism and building motivation through sequential tasks designed for success).

Performance Demands Controlled by: Perceptual support (modeling rather than spontaneous) and response mode (identification before production, clinician identification before client identification).

Session Procedure: The clinician will identify for Fred when Fred demonstrates an instance of fluent speech (i.e., gentle onset with light articulatory contact), describe what he did specifically (e.g., "You really had a light contact on the b in boy. You barely touched your lips together and that was great!"), and offer visual and verbal feedback for the success (i.e., clinician will have a positive facial expression and say something like "Yes!" in a bold voice).

Later Session Goal: Fred will identify and describe an instance of his fluency and offer himself a positive self-comment (i.e., praise) for having done so.

Derivation:

Maintaining Factors Addressed: Sensorimotor, cognitive, and psychosocial/emotional.

Anchoring Principle: Personal construct (i.e., providing opportunities to experience success) and stuttering modification/fluency shaping (i.e., shifting responsibility to Fred to build fluency control and communicative independence).

Performance Demands Controlled by: Response mode (i.e., identification before production) and self-identification after clinician identification (i.e., heightening Fred's awareness of what he already is doing that facilitates fluent speech).

Session Procedure: The clinician will identify for Fred an instance of Fred's fluency and direct Fred to describe what he did to accomplish it. This will lead to the clinician's directing Fred to identify and describe his instances of fluency and offer himself the praise he deserves. The clinician will discuss with Mary how better understanding the nature of fluent speech increases the likelihood that Fred will be able to demonstrate what he is already doing more often. The clinician will have Fred talk to Mary in and out of the clinic setting to tell her what he is doing in treatment and the rationale behind it.

Summary

In this chapter I have discussed some of what is known about stuttering and people who stutter. Specifically, I reviewed several critical definitions, differential diagnostic characteristics, etiological considerations, theories/maintaining factors, performance demands, and guiding intervention assumptions. I then integrated these factors with the model presented by Klein and Moses in this text, and applied both to designing long-term, short-term, and session goals within procedural contexts for a man of 55 years who stutters.

Every good story keeps us wanting to hear more and offers a moral. This one is no exception. At the time I am writing this (i.e., after 24 treatment meetings), Fred has achieved a rate of speech in conversation and reading of 130 words per minute with only occasional disfluencies that are both gentle and self-corrected. Both Fred and Mary feel that they are achieving a shared success and appreciate each other's support and commitment. They enjoy the positive comments that continue to be received from friends and family regarding Fred's improved fluency and appreciate the ongoing support from all involved. About the fluency journal he keeps, Fred commented recently, "I've got so much fluency, I don't have the time to write it all down." Mary remarked how much she is enjoying that Fred now is making his own phone calls and that it is hard to recall how Fred's speech used to be.

So what is the moral? Part of it is that good things usually take a long time and a lot of hard work to accomplish, and those things that might seem impossible usually take a bit more time and work. Acknowledging that there are limits to fluency success, I believe that much of the battle is won on three fronts: the positive and optimistic attitude with which our clients, their families, and we approach fluency intervention as a shared challenge (i.e., personal constructs, e.g., cognitive maintaining factors and performance demands); our commitment to understanding and working and learning with families (i.e., family systems, e.g., psychosocial/emotional maintaining factors and performance demands); and the tailoring of intervention and its planning on the unique strengths and needs of people who stutter and their families (i.e., stuttering modification/fluency shaping, e.g., behavioral/sensorimotor maintaining factors and performance demands). Klein and Moses have provided a valuable model that serves as a template for intervention planning.

REFERENCES

Andrews, G., Craig, A., Feyer, A., Hoddinott, S., Howie, P., & Neilson, M. (1983). Stuttering: A review of research findings and theories circa 1982. *Journal of Speech and Hearing Disorders, 48,* 226–246.

Bloodstein, O. (1990). On pluttering, skivering, and floggering: A commentary. *Journal of Speech and Hearing Disorders, 55,* 392–393.

Bloodstein, O. (1995). *A handbook on stuttering* (5th ed.). San Diego, CA: Singular.

Conture, E. G. (1990). Childhood stuttering: What is it and who does it? In J. A. Cooper (Ed.), *Research needs in stuttering: Roadblocks and future directions* (ASHA Reports 18, pp. 2–14). Rockville, MD: American Speech-Language-Hearing Association.

Cooper, E. B. (1993). Red herrings, dead horses, straw men, and blind alleys: Escaping the stuttering conundrum. *Journal of Fluency Disorders, 18,* 375–387.

Culatta, R., & Goldberg, S. A. (1995). *Stuttering therapy: An integrated approach to theory and practice.* Boston: Allyn & Bacon.

Epstein, N., & Bishop, D. (1981). Problem centered systems therapy of the family. In A. S. Gurman & D. P. Kniskern (Eds.), *Handbook of family therapy* (pp. 444–482). New York: Brunner/Mazel.

Glauber, P. (1958). The psychoanalysis of stuttering. In J. Eisenson (Ed.), *Stuttering: A symposium* (pp. 71–119). New York: Harper & Row.

Gregory, H. H. (1986). *Stuttering: Differential evaluation and therapy.* Austin, TX: Pro-Ed.

Guitar, B., & Peters, T. J. (1980). *Stuttering: An integration of contemporary therapies.* (Publication 16). Memphis, TN: Stuttering Foundation of America.

Haley, G. E. (1970). *A story, a story.* New York: Aladdin Books/Macmillan.

Ham, R. E. (1990). *Therapy of stuttering: Preschool through adolescence.* Englewood Cliffs, NJ: Prentice-Hall.

Haynes, W. O., Pindzola, R. H., & Emerick, L. L. (1992). *Diagnosis and evaluation in speech pathology* (4th ed.). Englewood Cliffs, NJ: Prentice-Hall.

Johnson, E., Sickels, E. R., & Sayers, F. C. (1970). *Anthology of children's literature* (4th ed.). Boston: Houghton Mifflin.

Kelly, G. A. (1955a). *The psychology of personal constructs. Volume One: A theory of personality.* New York: Norton.

Kelly, G. A. (1955b). *The psychology of personal constructs. Volume Two: Clinical diagnosis and psychotherapy.* New York: Norton.

Luterman, D. M. (1996). *Counseling persons with communication disorders and their families* (3d ed.). Austin, TX: Pro-Ed.

Peters, T. J., & Guitar, B. (1991). *Stuttering: An integrated approach to its nature and treatment.* Baltimore, MD: Williams & Wilkins.

Shapiro, D. A. (1987). Myths in the method to the madness of supervision. *Hearsay, Fall,* 78–83.

Shapiro, D. A. (1999). *Stuttering intervention: A collaborative journey to fluency freedom.* Austin, TX: Pro-Ed.

Shapiro, D. A., & Moses, N. (1989). Creative problem solving in public school supervision. *Language, Speech, and Hearing Services in Schools, 20,* 320–332.

Silverman, F. H. (1996). *Stuttering and other fluency disorders* (2d ed.). Boston: Allyn & Bacon.

Starkweather, C. W. (1984). On fluency. *National Student Speech Language Hearing Association Journal, 12,* 30–37.

Starkweather, C. W. (1986). The development of fluency in normal children. In H. H. Gregory (Ed.), *Stuttering therapy: Prevention and intervention with children* (Publication 20, pp. 67–100). Memphis, TN: Speech Foundation of America.

Starkweather, C. W. (1987). *Fluency and stuttering.* Englewood Cliffs, NJ: Prentice-Hall.

Van Riper, C. (1973). *The treatment of stuttering.* Englewood Cliffs, NJ: Prentice-Hall.

Van Riper, C. (1982). *The nature of stuttering* (2d ed.). Englewood Cliffs, NJ: Prentice-Hall.

Williams, D. E. (1978). Differential diagnosis of disorders of fluency. In F. L. Darley & D. C. Spriestersbach (Eds.), *Diagnostic methods in speech pathology* (2d ed., pp. 409–438). New York: Harper & Row.

11 Intervention Planning for Second Language Phonology

CHAPTER OUTCOMES

The reader will:

1. become aware of the "interlanguage" and its relationship to the acquisition of second language (L2) phonology;

2. identify the content/form/use/interactions that affect the learning of L2 phonology;

3. identify the factors that maintain inauthentic L2 productions;

4. be able to apply principles of learning to the acquisition of L2 phonology;

5. observe the derivation of a management plan for an adult learning the phonology of a second language.

Nature of the Problem

An acquaintance recently told us that of the five languages he speaks fluently (Rumanian, German, French, Hebrew, English), none are produced without an accent (R. G. Stern, personal communication, September 28, 1996). Dr. Stern may be unusual with respect to the many languages he speaks fluently but not with respect to the difficulty he encounters with their phonologies. Learning the phonology of more than one language is a complex, challenging process, involving many interacting variables. We are becoming more aware of these variables and their interactions as studies in second language (L2) phonology emerge with greater abundance. Recently described as "a relatively neglected area in the study of second language learning" (Leather & James, 1991, p. 305), L2 speech is receiving renewed attention. Over the past decade research studies from several related disciplines (phonetics, phonology, psychology, speech-language pathology, L2 acquisition, etc.) have converged, yielding new insights into the acquisition of L2 speech. Much of this research focuses on the nature of the "interlanguage" (derived from the interaction between first language [L1] and L2, e.g., Dickerson, 1987; Selinker, 1992); constraints on the acquisition of L2, which may also be viewed as variable factors maintaining a foreign accent (e.g., Flege, 1992, 1995b; Leather & James, 1991; Long, 1990; Major, 1994); and predictions about hierarchies of difficulty for the L2 learner (e.g., Carlisle, 1991, 1994;

Eckman, 1981, 1985, 1987, 1991; Eckman & Iverson, 1994; Edge, 1991; Major, 1986; Yavas, 1994). Results of these studies, accordingly, provide an important theoretical foundation for intervention planning with L2 adults.

Although clinicians have long been involved with the remediation of "foreign accents," assessment and remediation procedures have generally not been driven by L2 acquisition theory or based on research findings with L2 populations (see "speech correction" texts as far back as Raubicheck, 1952). Even current texts in articulation/phonology, while beginning to recognize the need to address pronunciation differences associated with particular dialectal or cultural backgrounds, omit any theoretical foundation for planning remediation for this population (e.g., Bernthal & Bankson, 1998; Lowe, 1994).

The major focus of this chapter is on intervention planning for individuals learning to pronounce a nonnative language. An ancillary focus is to present some of the findings from L2 research, especially from related disciplines outside of speech-language pathology, and to demonstrate how this material may be foundational for formulating goals and procedures at the three phases of intervention planning.

The content of this chapter is different from that of Chapters 7 through 10; it does not deal with disorders. Yet, it deals with adults who may desire assistance with learning the pronunciation of a non-native language. According to the American Speech-Language Association, "accent reduction" is within our scope of practice (ASHA, 1996). "The speech-language pathologist may also be available to provide *elective* clinical services to nonstandard English speakers who do not present a disorder" (ASHA, 1983, p. 24). Given that there are many L2 speakers from a great diversity of language backgrounds who visit speech-language pathologists yearly, this chapter will follow the others in our approach to intervention planning.

Sources of Information for Intervention Planning

Content/Form/Use Interactions

As with normally developing and impaired L1 systems, the acquisition of an L2 involves the interaction of three linguistic components, form, content, and use. Although this chapter focuses on L2 speech (the form of language), other aspects of form (i.e., lexical items), content (meaning to be communicated), and use (conditions under which the speaker pronounces) interact with the accuracy of his/her productions. First we will examine the object of our discussion, L2 phonology.

What Is L2 phonology?   Most current researchers of L2 phonology ascribe the phonetic/phonemic patterns of the L2 speaker to a rule system that is distinct from that of the L1 and the L2. These patterns comprise some sounds directly resulting from L1 interference (substitutions by L1 sounds) and other sounds from hybrid changes resulting from attempts to target phonetic units of L2 (modifications found in neither language). These new pronunciation patterns that derive from the interaction between any two languages along with other related interacting factors are referred to as "interlanguage (IL)" (Selinker, 1969, 1992). During the past decade several publications have been directed toward the elucidation of the interlanguage phenomenon—its characteristics and derivational bases.

In his seminal writings on interlanguage, Selinker (1969) stated,

> An interlanguage may be linguistically described using as data the observable output resulting from a speaker's attempt to produce a foreign, norm, i.e., both his errors and non-errors. It is assumed that such behavior is highly structured. It must be dealt with as a system not an isolated collection of errors (fn 5).

More than 20 years later Selinker (1992) concluded that "the IL *Hypothesis* is [still] a reasonable theoretical story" (p. 246). The IL hypothesis is currently stated as follows:

> In attempting to express meanings in an L2 and in attempting to interact verbally with native, as well as other non-native, speakers of that L2, at least the following occur.
> (1) People create a (partly) separate linguistic system.
> (2) In that system interlingual identifications and language transfer are central.
> (3) One selectively uses the NL [native language] by context.
> (4) One fossilizes [keeps from changing] at least parts of the IL.
> (5) One selectively fossilizes differentially according to linguistic level and discourse domain.
> (6) The IL one is creating is susceptible to the force of several types of language universals, as well as interlanguage universals.
> (7) The IL one is creating is susceptible to the training and learning strategies that are adopted.
> (8) The IL one is creating is susceptible to simplification and complexification strategies. (p. 247)

This description suggests that interlanguage is viewed as an independent rule system derived from the interrelationship of at least two languages. These rules may be considered variable (see also Dickerson, 1975) given the range of fluctuation in pronunciation observed with a variety of alternating factors. These include the nonlinguistic and linguistic contexts (e.g., function of utterance, formality level, interlocutors, phonotactic constraints), linguistic universals (e.g., developmental schedules, markedness phenomena, phonological processes), individual strategies (e.g., production and perception processes, monitoring ability), training approaches, and learning styles. Other researchers (e.g., Leather & James, 1991; Major, 1994) supported the viability of these variables and others in recent comprehensive reviews. Some of the variables affecting the acquisition of L2 speech (i.e., maintenance of an interlanguage) will be examined in the sections on maintaining factors and performance demands appearing later in this chapter.

Interactions with Content and Use.

Form/Content.   Lexical factors may affect L2 learning and pronunciation accuracy. Mack, Tierney, and Boyle (as cited by Flege 1992), found that L2 speakers recognized frequently occurring words better than infrequent ones; this was especially true when words were computer generated. The converse, however, was found with reference to production. Less familiar words were produced with greater accuracy than more familiar words. Flege suggested that this comprehension/production learning discrepancy pattern would be expected if L2 speakers tended to mispronounce some of the earlier words they learned, before the establishment of stable phonetic categories; they then have difficulty in modifying these productions once categories have been established for the L2 sounds.

Pronunciation of L2 words may also be negatively affected if a given L2 word has a cognate (related L1 word). Flege and Munro (1994) found that voice onset time values in English /t/ were less accurate in an English word with a Spanish cognate (i.e., *taco*) than in words without cognates. Similarly, we found, in our clinical practice that a Haitian French speaker produced English words with /r/ (e.g., *republic*) less authetically when these words had Haitian cognates.

Form/Use. The discourse context and function of the speech event has been reported to affect the type and degree of sound transfer from L1 (i.e., the frequency with which L1 for L2 substitutions are made). Leather & James (1991) reviewed several studies, generally concluding that more formal contexts (e.g., word list reading, reading of minimal pairs) are more facilitating of target attainment than an intermediate formal context (e.g., dialogue reading), which in turn is more facilitating than the least formal context (i.e., free speaking). Dickerson (1987) reported similar findings and he attributes this variability within the interlanguage to the amount of attention paid to speech (i.e., the monitoring of one's speech). He suggests that L2 learners be taught formal pronunciation rules in addition to oral work to help them monitor their own utterances. By way of contrast, Leather and James (1991) showed that the "vernacular" style of the developing interlanguage when compared with the "formal" style is more robust to withstanding the influence of L1. This suggests that the stylistic variants of language in use may also affect the type and degree of influence of L1 on L2 in any acquisition context.

Related to the formality of the context is the background of the interlocutor. Beebe (1977) reported that speakers will often accommodate their pronunciation (use language specific variants of L2) when aware of the listener's native language. Beebe showed that Chinese Thai bilingual speakers more readily used a Thai accent when speaking to Thai listeners and a Chinese accent when speaking to Chinese listeners even when the Chinese listeners spoke authentic Thai.

Form/Content/Use. The form of an utterance may also be affected by the requirement to communicate *meaning,* to avoid *communication breakdown.* In this instance an interaction among all three components becomes obvious.

Weinberger (1994) emphasized the difference between functional and phonetic constraints on L2 phonology. He argued that the L2 learner has two goals: (a) a phonetic goal—to learn speech sounds that approximate the target language—and (b) a functional goal—to keep words and sentences intelligible. It is this second goal that relates to language content and use, particularly the awareness of listener knowledge and communication breakdown. Weinberger explained that this functional goal influences the types of processes an L2 learner may adopt. For example, it has been shown that in an effort to simplify an L2 syllable structure (e.g., facilitate the production of the second C of a CVC) an adult L2 speaker will use the process of epenthesis rather than final consonant deletion (typical of a child). An example taken from Weinberger to illustrate the result of application of alternative processes is as follows: If the word *seed* is pronounced with epenthesis (insertion of a vowel) as [sidə], it may be confused with a limited number of English words: *seed* and *cedar.* If, however, the process of final consonant deletion is used, the number of words that would be possible candidates would be significantly greater (e.g. seed, seat, seep, seek, seize, siege, etc). Thus, the motivation to maximize lexical contrasts to maintain meaning in communication (content/use) interacts with the form component of language.

Implication for Intervention Planning.   Knowledge about the nature of the interlanguage and the way it interacts with the other language components guides the clinician in decision making about goals and procedures across the three phases of intervention planning. A summary of the application of knowledge about content\form\use interactions to intervention planning appears in Box 11.1.

BOX **11.1**

Content/Form/Use Interactions and Intervention Planning

Language Component	Application to Intervention Planning
Form: Phonology—The Interlanguage	Affects long-term and short-term goal planning. Clinician can differentiate between L1/L2 substitutions and new sounds (present in neither language). 1. Affects long-term prognosis. 2. Influences short-term priority planning.
Form/Content	Affects short-term goal planning. 1. Influences choice of lexicon according to frequency of use. 2. Influences choice of lexicon according to the availability of cognates across languages.
Form/Use	Affects short-term procedural approach. One would consider: 1. formal (word lists) vs. informal context (conversation); 2. formal (highly monitored) vs. colloquial style; 3. choice of interlocutor (dialect background of L2 speaker).
Form/Content/Use	Affects session goals and procedures. In a client using epenthesis or final consonant deletion, communication breakdown may be promoted by obligating the use of words that are vulnerable to homonomy (e.g. seed vs. cedar; made vs. may).

Maintaining Factors

As noted earlier, efforts to explain variability within the interlanguage have invoked a wide range of nonlinguistic and linguistic factors affecting pronunciation. To be consistent with the model presented in this book, a number of these factors will be organized within the categories of maintaining factors introduced in Chapter 1 and elucidated in Chapter 5: psychosocial, cognitive, and sensorimotor. An additional factor will be added—the phonological system itself. The segments themselves and their interactions (i.e., markedness values) contain inherent relative difficulty (e.g., Eckman, 1977, 1985, 1991; Greenberg, 1965) that contribute to the maintenence of a nonnative dialect.

Psychosocial. Psychosocial factors may influence communication performance (see Chapter 5 in this volume). Current research in interlanguage phonology has highlighted several factors affecting the developing L2 that may be categorized as psychosocial. Those that may affect intervention planning for the acquisition of a second phonological system are (a) age (Long, 1990; Major, 1994; Patkowski, 1994); (b) amount of native language use (Flege, Frieda, & Nozawa, 1997); (c) motivation (Leather & James, 1991), and (d) gender (Leather & James, 1991).

Age. After a careful study of three recent texts, a review article, and three studies, Patkowski (1994) made the following claim about age-related differences in the ability to learn the phonology of an L2.

> There is a period ending around the time of puberty (operationally defined to mean somewhere between the ages of 12 and 15 years), during which it is possible, but not inevitable, for learners to acquire, as an end-product of a naturalistic L2 acquisition process, full native-like fluency in the phonological system of a second language, and after which such a possibility does not exist anymore. Thus a comparison between older and younger learners of their long-term achievement (operationally defined to mean that naturalistic exposure has occurred for at least 5 years or so under "advantaged" sociological, cultural, psychological, and affective circumstances) should reveal (a) that only younger learners can sometimes be shown to attain full native-like phonological L2 competence, and (b) that overall, there is a strong statistical difference in the long-term achievement of younger and older learners. (p. 206)

Long (1990), who reported a growing preference for the term "sensitive" period, supported an age-related constraint on the acquisition of authentic L2 phonology, but suggested that this constraint may set in as early as age 6. Long's position is stated as follows:

> There are sensitive periods governing the ultimate level of first or second language attainment possible in different linguistic domains, not just phonolgy, with cumulative declines in learning capacity, not a catastrophic one-time loss, and beginning as early as age 6 in many individuals, not at puberty as is often claimed. (p. 255)

While there appears to be little dispute regarding the "critical period" (or sensitive period) view, there continues to be conflicting explanations of this phenomenon. Those in the tradition of Lenneberg (1967) have supported a biological view of the sensitive period. For example, Long (1990) asserted that with maturation there is loss of the brain's plasticity because of the myelinization of neural pathways. Contrastively, Flege (1992) opposed the notion of a biological or neurological basis to the sensitive period. According to Flege, the maintenance of a foreign accent is more likely in an older learner because of different perceptual processing and representational mechanisms from L1 learners. Flege suggested, in addition, that adults may not receive phonetic input as rich as the input directed to children learning an L1. It may also be that adults do not maintain attention to words as long as children since adults learn to recognize words more rapidly.

Amount of Native Language Use.   It is likely that many of us know someone who began to learn a second language as a child (below age 10) and still maintains an accented L2, as an adult. Empirical research was recently undertaken by Flege et al. (1997) to investigate this issue. As part of another study, Flege, Munro, and MacKay (1995) observed that some Italian adults, who immigrated to Canada before the age of 10 (some at 3 years of age) continued to exhibit a foreign accent despite many years of experience with English. This appeared to contradict the critical period hypothesis or at least to indicate that other factors may also be constraining authentic L2. This finding prompted further investigation. One factor considered by Flege et al. (1997) was the continued influence of L1 on L2. Flege et al. (1997) were guided by a hypothesis designated as the "single system hypothesis," according to this hypothesis, bilinguals cannot completely separate the L1 and L2 phonetic systems, which interact with one another. According to Flege et al., this hypothesis predicts that the less L1 is used, the less L2 will be affected. To test this prediction, therefore, Flege et al. studied the relationship between the amount of L1 use and degree of accent in L2 of Italian L1 subjects (the authors believe that this is the first study to assess this relationship); the subjects were matched for age of introduction to L2 and experiences in learning English as an L2. The researchers found that in their "HiUse" subjects (self-reported using L1 36% of the time on a daily basis) accents were significantly stronger than in "LoUse" subjects (L1 used 3% of the time on average). Flege et al. asserted that these results challenge the critical period hypothesis as a sufficient explanation of non-nativeness in second language speech.

Motivation.   Another psychosocial factor affecting the acquisition of L2 phonology is the individual's motivation for accurate L2 pronunciation. Leather and James (1991) suggested that various factors may be responsible for motivating individuals to attempt "native-like" authenticity in their speech. Factors for aspiring to authentic L2 speech include (a) the degree of concern felt by the learner about sounding like a native speaker (based on prevailing attitude of L1 culture), (b) the need to produce native-like speech for employment reasons (e.g., using telephone, holding interviews, lecturing), and (c) the attitude toward the culture and society of the L2 (e.g., how much cultural identification is desired). As an example of (c), a multilingual acquaintance of ours has often noted that Americans do not pronounce their words clearly enough. Motivated by this notion, her attempts at English are heavily based on orthographic representations (aspiring to pronounce every consonant in the printed word, especially final stops). This approach results in an overarticulated, inaccurate version of American English devoid of appropriate allophonic variations (including the absence of flaps within and between words).

Gender.   Leather and James (1991) proposed that the gender of the speaker may also affect the variety of L2 pronunciation used. They cite of work of Gussenhoven (as cited in Leather & James 1991) who found that female speakers were more favorably oriented toward the use of "prestige" forms than males. A gender difference in the use of prestige forms was also illustrated by the work of Adamson and Regan (1991) who examined the pronunciation of the '-ing' morpheme by Cambodian immigrants. They found that the [Iŋ] variant (generally considered more prestigious than the [In]) was used more frequently by the females than the males. In addition, the females produced the [In] more frequently as the context became more formal. An interesting finding was that with males the use of [Iŋ] decreased as style became more formal. Adamson and Regan were uncertain about why this should be the case. They suggested that it may reflect the desire of the males to accommodate to a male speaker (which they probably perceived to be [In]) rather than an overall norm.

To summarize, psychosocial factors such as age of acquisition, frequency of L1 use, motivation, and gender should be considered in planning intervention. These factors are likely to affect planning of goals and procedures, especially at the long-term phase, when expectations for outcome and predictions about time duration must be made.

Sensorimotor.   As indicated in Chapter 1, we characterize variables as sensorimotor that involve movement, and reception through the senses of information from movement and from the environment. For the L2 learner we are most concerned with sensorimotor functioning as it affects the perception and production of speech sounds. Related to peripheral perception and production processes are the processes involved with discrimination, evaluation of similarities and differences, and construction of an underlying representation based on perceptual cues and nemonic factors, a representation that forms the basis for production attempts. While the higher level processes may be more cognitive in nature, they emanate from sensorimotor processes and therefore will be addressed here.

Production and Perception.   It is probably safe to assume that every speech-language pathologist has been well oriented toward a consideration of both perceptual and production factors in treating L1 clients with articulatory/phonological difficulties. Most texts on articulatory/phonological disorders focusing on L1 phonology describe procedures for assessing and remediating deficient perceptual and production skills (e.g., Bernthal & Bankson, 1998). This consideration of perceptual and production mechanisms underlying the phonetic change implies an assumption that speech errors result from deficiencies in either or both of these variables (e.g., Bernthal & Bankson, 1998; Fey, 1992).

How production and perception factors affect the acquisition and maintenance of speech sounds has also received some attention in L2 research. Though it is still difficult to determine precisely the contribution of each factor to the speaker's interlanguage (e.g., Flege, 1992, 1995a; Leather & James, 1991; Major, 1994), some points of view regarding the roles of perception, production, and their relationship have been expressed.

1. *Production.*   With reference to *production* capacities. Leather and James (1991) wrote,

> Learners receiving explicit training in L2 articulation must adjust the configurations and movements of their articulators according to verbally formulated instructions, and the accuracy with

which they are able to do this will ultimately be limited by tactile and proprioceptive feedback. Even naturalistic learners who receive no formal instruction must effect some match between target sounds and articulatory configurations during the production of an L2. (p. 311)

Flege (1992) expressed a similar point of view based on his research with Japanese speakers' /r/ and /l/, Spanish learners' word-final fricative production, and Chinese speakers' difficulty in producing a contrast between plosive cognates (+ or – voicing) in word-final position. According to Flege, "Difficulties in L2 production could arise from an inability to *modify* previously established patterns of segmental production or to develop *new ones*" (p. 567). He pointed out that while Japanese speakers have more difficulty in producing /r/ and /l/ in word-final singletons than in word-initial singletons and in word-initial clusters, the opposite pattern obtains for perception. This would suggest that the errors cannot be due only to faulty perception. Flege also pointed out that Spanish learners have more difficulty with the production of /s/ in final than initial position, which may be attributed to the paucity of word-final consonants in Spanish. The presence of final consonants, therefore, creates a more complex syllable structure, possibly posing a greater motoric challenge. For Chinese speakers attempting English plosives, Flege suggested that the inability to produce an effective contrast in final position (while it is possible in initial position) may be due to the difficulty in sustaining closure voicing in word-final consonants to the same extent as speakers of English. This type of articulatory/voicing synchrony has been reported to be difficult for young L1 learners and generally results in consonant devoicing, vowel epenthesis (Klein, 1978), or nasal epenthesis (Fey & Gandour, 1982). When such processes are employed in L1 they are generally attributed to motoric difficulty since it is assumed they are attempts to preserve surface contrast (apparently perceived, e.g., Fey & Gandour, 1982).

Motoric difficulty may also exist for the production of vowels. Flege (1989) found that Spanish speakers use a narrower vertical range of tongue positions to produce Spanish /i, a, u/ than English speakers in producing English /i, ɑ, u/. It is reasonable to hypothesize that given only 5 vowels in Spanish as compared with 14 in English that there would be some difficulty in making the subtle articulatory changes even when perception of these distinctions is possible.

2. Perception   Many researchers have viewed the role of perception as more influential than that of motor ability in the pronunciation patterns of L2 (of the interlanguage). It has been argued that differences in pronunciation between native and nonnative speakers are probably due to underlying perceptual differences. These differences are generally described with reference to the nature of the sound categories established for the L2. (For reviews of this area see Flege, 1992, 1995b; Leather & James, 1991.) Flege asserted that correct production of an L2 sound depends to a great extent on how similar the speaker perceives this sound to be to an L1 phoneme. If the L2 sound is "identical" to or "so similar" to an L1 sound that differences are unnoticeable, the sound is said to be "equated with" or "equivalent" to the L1 sound, and likely to be produced authentically. In such case there is no reason for the L2 learner to establish a new L2 sound category. If the L2 sound differs substantially from the L1 sound the L2 sound is again expected to be produced authentically; in this case, however, the significant difference is anticipated to generate the formation of a new sound category. The situation that is seen as most challenging is when an L2 sound is different enough from any L1 (perhaps only in minor details such as timing, amplitude, or placement) so that the substitution of L1 for L2 would be noticed but not different enough to motivate the formation of a new category. Flege (1992) used the word "sound" to refer "to a class of phones that can be used to contrast meaning" (p. 566). He postulated the concept of class even at a "position-sensitive allophonic level, rather than at a more abstract phonemic level" (1995b, p. 239). Many of the conceptualizations of Flege and his associates regarding the role of perception in L2 learning are captured in the speech-learning model (Flege, 1995b) found in Table 11.1. Flege reminded the reader that this is still a working model and may be revised as new findings suggest.

We now illustrate some of Flege's (1992, 1995b) conceptualizations regarding sound categorization with reference to a native Spanish learner of English. The /i/s of Spanish and English are close enough for the individual to produce English /i/ authentically. The /æ/ of English has no close counterpart in Spanish so that it is likely that the formulation of a new category be triggered. Since Spanish /i/ has been described as lower than English /i/, closer to /I/ (Flege, 1988), it is likely that both English /i/ and /I/ will be attempted with the Spanish /i/ and no new category be formed for /I/. This will result in an i/I substitution, contributing to a listener's perception of an accent. These alternate possibilities are encapsulated by Flege (1992) in the following statement, "Perhaps an L2 vowel will be treated as "new" [forming a separate phone category] only if it is found in a portion of the acoustic phonetic vowel space that is unoccupied by an allophone of an L1 vowel category. Such may be the case of English /æ/ but not English /I/, which is located in a portion of the space occupied by Spanish /i/ (especially the realizations of Spanish /i/ in closed syllables)" (p. 583).

L2 research has also addressed equivalence and nonequivalence in consonants (see the work of Flege and his colleagues, reported in Flege, 1992, 1995b). The consonants receiving most research interest have been /r/ and /l/ produced by Japanese learners and /p, t, k/ by native French and Spanish learners of English. In general, the research has shown that although a sound may be identified as new for a learner, distinct from the consonants in his/her language, it may not be produced correctly by the adult learner. For example /l/ and /r/ could be viewed as new for Japanese (there is no /l/ in Japanese and the /r/ is produced as as a voiced tip-alveolar flap (Price, 1981). This situation would predict the formation of new sound categories for the production of /r/ and /l/ and authentic production would be expected. Research evidence, to date, has not consistently supported this prediction (Flege, 1992, 1995b). The situation is different for the production of English /p, t, k/ by French and Spanish speakers. In this case the difference in L1 and L2 consonants is more subtle; the French and Spanish voiceless stops differ from English only in voice onset time, (with longer voice onset time for English. Because of this subtle difference it would expected that the L1 versions would be perceived as equivalent to the L2 and not produced authentically. Research evidence has supported these predictions for adult learners (Flege, 1992).

Because it is often difficult to evaluate the extent to which perception and production separately, or interactively contribute to phonological performance, both are often considered to be maintaining factors of error productions in L1 (Fey, 1992; Hodson & Paden, 1991). A similar case may be made for the influence of these variables on learning the phonology of L2. When L2 sounds are found in the L1 repertoire or are similar, the intended target is usually an authentic L2 sound and the articulatory plan to achieve the target is known. If, however, a new sound must be learned, "the speaker presumably refers to some less well formed perceptual target and enacts a motor program based on less well

---

TABLE 11.1   Postulates and Hypotheses Forming a Speech Learning Model (SLM) of Second Language Sound Acquisition (Flege, 1995b)

Postulates

P1   The mechanisms and processes used in learning the L1 sound system, including category formation, remain intact over the life span, and can be applied to L2 learning.

P2   Language-specific aspects of speech sounds are specified in long-term memory representations called *phonetic categories.*

P3   Phonetic categories established in childhood for L1 sounds evolve over the life span to reflect the properties of all L1 or L2 phones identified as a realization of each category.

P4   Bilinguals strive to maintain contrast between L1 and L2 phonetic categories, which exist in a common phonological space.

Hypotheses

H1   Sounds in the L1 and L2 are related perceptually to one another at a position-sensitive allophonic level, rather than at a more abstract phonemic level.

H2   A new phonetic category can be established for an L2 sound that differs phonetically from the closest L1 sound if bilinguals discern at least some of the phonetic differences between the L1 and L2 sounds.

H3   The greater the perceived phonetic dissimilarity between an L2 sound and the closest L1 sound, the more likely it is that phonetic differences between the sounds will be discerned.

H4   The likelihood of phonetic differences between L1 and L2 sounds, and between L2 sounds that are noncontrastive in the L1, being discerned decreases as AOL [age of learner] increases.

H5   Category formation for an L2 sound may be blocked by the mechanism of equivalence classification. When this happens, a single phonetic category will be used to process perceptually linked L1 and L2 sounds (diaphones). Eventually, the diaphones will resemble one another in production.

H6   The phonetic category established for L2 sounds by a bilingual may differ from a monolingual's if: 1) the bilingual's category is "deflected" away from an L1 category to maintain phonetic contrast between categories in a common L1-L2 phonological space; or 2) the bilingual's representation is based on different features, or feature weights, than a monolingual's.

H7   The production of a sound eventually corresponds to the properties represented in its phonetic category representation.

Printed with permission.

known production rules. . . . Success in the production of L2 sounds would thus be limited . . . by inadequate knowledge of (a) the phonetic target and/or (b) the means of attaining it." (Leather & James, 1991, p. 314)

In the learning of L1 or L2 one confounding aspect in specifying the influence of perception or production is the intermediating variable of representation. What is perceived may not always be accurately represented mentally (i.e., the target sound may have been perceived but not remembered accurately in context of the target word). Thus, whether addressing new or equivalent sounds still another variable must be considered—one related to perception and production—the L2 speaker's mental representation of the target (i.e, what the speaker intends to say).

Underlying Representation. The speaker's intended target is also referred to as the speaker's mental representation or underlying representation (UR) in the phonological literature involving normally developing L1 learners, speech-impaired L1 learners, and L2 learners. There is some controversy regarding the nature of the UR during the developmental period.

Maxwell (1984) discussed two contrasting views regarding the relationship between the UR and the child's surface production. One view assumes the child's UR is the same as the adult surface form, whether or not the form is produced correctly; the other assumes the child's UR is the same for some surface productions and different for others. Most approaches using phonological processes assume the adult model as the intended target (e.g., Bleile, 1995; Stoel-Gammon & Dunn, 1985). Approaches using generative phonology principles adhere to the second view (Elbert & Gierut, 1986).

Operating under the second premise, if a client produces a sound incorrectly several alternative conclusions are possible: (a) the client perceived the sound correctly, represented it correctly, but the difficulty lies in the production (production problem); (b) the sound is perceived correctly, represented incorrectly, and produced as it was represented (representational problem), or (c) the sound is perceived incorrectly, the incorrect perception is represented mentally, and produced faithfully to the initial perception (perception problem). The possibility of alternative URs has more recently been addressed in phonological assessment procedures (Locke, 1980) and management approaches (Shriberg & Kwiatkowski, 1982). For example, Shriberg and Kwaitkowski's conceptual framework for management provided for the evaluation of perceptual, motor, and representational data as a basis for decision making about intervention points in treatment. Thus, treatment procedures are designed selectively, to address the areas of deficiency. According to Shriberg & Kwiatkowski, points of deficiency (determining specific intervention points) may be (a) the mental representation of the target (the client's mental image of the target), (b) the production of the target, and (c) the comparison between the target and the individual's productions. In a similar vein, Bernthal and Bankson (1998) cautioned the clinician to focus on the perceptual variable only when there is ample evidence to suggest a weakness in this area.

In the case of L2, however, the specification of a UR becomes even more unclear (Major, 1994). This is because there are a greater number of alternatives to consider. According to Major, the UR and processes (which act on the UR to produce surface forms) may be "identical to the learner's native language (NL) or target language (TL), or something intermediate" (p. 192). The pronunciation processes may, likewise, be the same as the NL, the same as the TL or different from the NL and TL. An example from Major, illustrating the lack of clarity that may ensue from the possible permutations and combinations of URs and processes, is the following: A Spanish speaker may represent an English /ð/ as /d/ (an L1 transfer) and pronounce it as /d/ in prevocalic position (*them* [dɛm]). In postvocalic position the speaker would pronounce the sound as [ð]. In this example, the UR of the sound is still an L1 sound [d]; an L1 process (spirantization), however, is applied to the sound in postvocalic position (/d/ → [ð] as in *mother* [mʌðɚ]). Although it appears the postvocalic target is an L2 /ð/, it is actually an allophone of the L1 /d/. Major suggested that the three possibilities for the URs and the processes (noted earlier) yield nine potential production scenarios for L2 speakers. These alternative possibilities reveal the complexity inherent in specifying the roles of perception and production in determining L2 phonetic/phonemic patterns.

Cognition   Cognition is viewed as another possible maintaining factor for the maintenance of inauthentic L2 productions. There are several cognitive processes implicated in the acquisition of L2 phonology that must be engaged to achieve authentic speech patterns. Some of these processes are conceptualized within Piagetian constructivist and Karmiloff-Smith's (1986) modular theories, elucidated in Chapter 6.

Learning Involves Mental Organization or Reorganization.   Based on several studies by Flege and Flege with his associates (reported in comprehensive reviews, Flege, 1992, 1995b), a compelling argument is made for the process of phonetic system reorganization as a basis for authentic L2 pronunciation. This concept was broached in the last section on perception and production processes, and will be reexamined here because of its cognitive implications.

A powerful theme emerging from Flege's (1992) review is that the primary task of the L2 learner is to perceptually differentiate L1 and L2 sounds (i.e., to distinguish between new and similar sounds), and to *formulate new phonetic categories.* It is well known that older children (beyond the age of 6 or 7) and adults have greater difficulty in learning L2 sounds than younger children (see section on critical period, above). This difficulty has been described as a diminished ability to establish additional phonetic categories for new L2 sounds (Flege, 1992). Flege attributed this reduced ability to a "phonetic system shift," which occurs between the ages of 5 and 7, and is characterized by the development and stabilization of the phonetic system. The "5 to 7" shift is seen as reflecting general cognitive changes related to an increase in metalinguistic awareness. As a result there is greater focus on specific aspects of stimuli, such as segment-sized rather than syllable-sized units in speech processing. This is shown in studies of reading readiness (Nesdale, Herriman, & Tunmer, 1984) and studies of metaphonological abilities (e.g., Klein, Lederer, & Cortese, 1991).

Flege (1992) characterized the phonetic system shift as affecting the existing phonetic categories in two major ways: (a) the primary acoustic features of prototypes of each phonetic category and the relative saliency of these features will become better defined, and (b) the range of exemplars representing each category will increase. The first change is believed to stabilize the category center, while the second defines the boundaries between categories. For the L2 learner the shift increases the number of possible variants permitted within a category, thereby reducing "uncommitted" vowel space not occupied by any L1 category. For example, an L1 has an [o] sound with [ɔ] and [ɑ] as acceptable variants. This L1 [o] phoneme will be used in the place of an L2 [ɔ] or [ɑ]; thus, it will not be perceived as different enough to trigger a "new" reaction. An example from an L1 Spanish speaker may further clarify this issue. For a native Spanish learner of English, the /æ/ (which is not a separate phone category in L1 or a variant of any other phone) would be likely to find a location in uncommitted space (not overlapping with any other L1 phonetic category, perhaps, requiring a different tongue posture).

The cognitive process of recognizing equivalence between or among phonemes is considered to be an adaptive process for L1 learners but nonadaptive for older children and adults (Flege, 1992). Young children must learn to regard variations on a phoneme as belonging to the same phoneme to find perceptual constancy and acquire necessary phoneme contrasts. The same process appears to hinder L2 learning because the overextension of perceptual boundaries may cause a new sound to be included in an existing boundary (perceived as equivalent) and produced as the L1 sound (contributing to an accent).

Within the framework of phonetic reorganization, it has also been hypothesized that as new phonetic categories are established in L2, other already established categories may demonstrate some regression (i.e., become more L1 like, Nathan, 1990). The establishment of new L2 categories may even lead to the loss of L2 sounds that are similar to L1 (Major, 1990). Major (1994) pointed out that the reciprocity between L1 and L2 may also contribute to the attrition in L1 (from the modification of sounds to complete loss). This phenomenon may help explain the difficulty in maintaining authentic pronunciation in any one of the five languages spoken by Dr. Stern (referenced at the beginning of this chapter).

Individuals May Pass Through the Same Phases of Cognition in a Cyclic Fashion Each Time They Find Themselves in Complex, Novel, Problem-Solving Situation. This cyclical concept from cognitive theory applies to L2 phonology because it has been observed that L2 learners often approach difficult pronunciation targets as would L1 learners (e.g., Major, 1987, 1994). Guided by principles from natural phonology (reflecting the innate capacity of the human organism, Stampe, 1969), Major indicated that the acquisition process for L2 learners is similar in many ways to children learning an L1. First, acquisition in both cases proceeds via the elimination of processes that do not conform with the language standard production. The process of elimination is different, however, between L1 and L2 learners. At the earliest stage the child's pronunciation is constrained by a full set of universal processes (found in all the world's languages). As these processes are modified or suppressed, sounds of the ambient language are permitted to emerge (Stampe, 1969). For the adult the initial array of universal processes have been reduced by those already mastered with L1. The adult learner, however, must eliminate two sets of processes: developmental and interference ("due to *interference* or transfer of processes, patterns, and structures of one's first language to the second language [e.g., a French speaker's substitution of [R] for English [r]," Major, 1987, p. 208]).

Second, in both L1 and L2 similar sounds are substituted for similar targets. For example, L2 learners modify final voiced stops very much as would children, by devoicing, deleting, or adding schwa to the final stop (even if the L1 had no final voiced stops). This pattern will be discussed later in the section on performance demands. Other processes occurring in L2 English, reminiscent of L1, are consonant-cluster reduction and preference for open rather than closed syllables. Contrastively, some L1 processes never appear in L2—those that have already been suppressed in L1 (e.g., fronting of velars or stopping of fricatives in English) and those that do not appear in any adult language (e.g., assimilation or reduplication, diminutive).

With reference to his *ontogeny* model, Major (1986) made predictions about the relationship between interference processes and developmental processes during the L2 acquisition period. This model claims that "chronologically, errors due to transfer processes decrease, but errors due to developmental processes increase and then decrease" (Major, 1986, p. 455). On the basis of his own research with L2 Spanish and L2 English learners, Major argued against the common notion that all error types will decrease as one gains more experience with the target language. His research demonstrated that transfer processes that predominate at the early stages of learning a language prevent developmental processes from surfacing. As transfer processes are suppressed, developmental processes become more obvious before they too are eventually eliminated and authentic pronunciation may be accomplished. An illustrative example from Major (1987) comes from a speaker of Brazilian Portuguese learning English prevocalic /r/. The acquisition of /r/ occurs in five stages. In stage 1 the speaker attempts to substitute the /r/ with a sound from L1 [x] in Portuguese. In stage 2 [ø] (a form of /r/, which is considered a developmental substitution) alternates with [x]. Stage 3 exhibits three variant forms for the target ([x], [ø], and [r]). In stage 4 these variants are reduced to two ([ø] and [r]). In stage 5 [r] is produced authentically. It is interesting to note that the variation (during stage 3) was observed to emerge after a more stable first two attempts.

Increased variability on the way to learning a target sound has also been documented in L1 development (e.g., Klein, 1981). This variability between the two process types and within the developmental processes supports a constructivist-cognitive orientation, incorporating behavioral variation and self-monitoring as facilitative learning mechanisms. It is the learner's task to unconsciously or consciously (metalinguistically) overcome both process types. As with children the application of phonological processes maintains productions that are different from the adult standard.

In summary, when working with an adult client one must consider the systemic nature of L2 acquisition and the cognitive (organizational) difficulties inherent in acquiring a language late.

The Phonological System As a Source of a Nonnative Accent.
To speak of the phonological system itself, learning an L2 is really to speak of at least three phonetic/phonemic systems (L1 and L2) and their interactions (their developing interlanguage). Some of the challenges confronting the L2 learner in differentiating L1 and L2 have been discussed above within the categories of psychosocial, sensorimotor, and cognitive maintaining factors. Additional challenges inherent in the characteristics of phonological systems will now be addressed.

Different Languages Have Different Phonological Features.   Because the phoneme categories and allophone distributions differ among languages, the learning of one language is expected to affect the learning of another. One of most important influences, therefore, on L2 acquisition is L1 transfer to L2 pronunciation (Major, 1994). A knowledge of this potential transfer motivated the formulation of the contrastive analysis hypothesis. In its strongest form this hypothesis states that "one can predict the errors a language learner will make on the basis of a comparison of the descriptions of the native and target language" (Eckman, 1977, p. 316). This statement suggests that the L2 learner will experience greater difficulty with some sounds than with others because of feature similarities and differences between both languages. Guided by this hypothesis, linguists attempted to explain all nonnative substitutions as motivated by the transfer process. Some substitutions could actually be explained in this manner, for example, the L1 Spanish speaker's use of /d/ for English initial [ð], the German speaker's production of English final voiced stops as voiceless, and the Chinese speaker's substitution of /r/ for English /r/ and /l/—the English targets (L2) comprising features absent from the L1. Linguists, however, soon became aware that some substitutions could not be explained through transfer processes (e.g., sound productions not found in either language). In addition, some predicted errors occurred where others did not. Where the contrastive analysis hypothesis was found to be most lacking, however, was in its inability to predict why certain phonemes were acquired before others. Thus, the contrastive analysis hypothesis was useful to a point. It helped identify areas of contrast between languages (similar and different features) to begin to speculate about relative difficulty and predicted order of acquisition.[3]

Segments Are Universally Marked.   As a reaction to the inadequacies of the contrastive analysis hypothesis, Eckman (1977) introduced the markedness differential hypothesis. This hypothesis was intended to extend the earlier hypothesis by introducing a measure of "universal" (independent of any given language) relative difficulty among segments identified as having the potential for difficulty (not present in L1).

Markedness has been defined in several ways. The term *marked* or *more marked* is used to express the idea that some segments are "less natural" or "less basic" to the capacities of the human speech and hearing mechanism. Least marked structures are acquired first by children and are more likely to occur in all language inventories (e.g., Schane, 1973). For Eckman (1977), " 'degree of difficulty' corresponds to the notion 'typologically marked' " (p. 520). We first look at Eckman's definition of markedness. Eckman stated, "A phenomenon A in some language is more marked than B if the presence of A in a language implies the presence of B; but the presence of B does not imply the presence of A" (p. 320). With this definition of markedness, Eckman proposed the following hypothesis:

> The areas of difficulty that a language learner will have can be predicted on the basis of systematic comparison of the grammars of the native language, the target language and the markedness relations stated in universal grammar, such that, (a) Those areas of the target language which differ from the native language and are more marked than the native language will be difficult. (b) The relative degree of difficulty of the areas of the target language which are more marked than the native language will correspond to the relative degree of markedness. (c) Those areas of the target language which are different from the native language, but are not more marked than the native language will not be difficult (p. 321).

Eckman (1977) argued that if typological markedness is incorporated into the contrastive analysis hypothesis, the degree of difficulty, not only the areas of difficulty, may be predicted. The following example from Eckman illustrates his position. The phoneme /ʒ/ occurs in intitial, medial, and final positions in French; in English it occurs only in

[3]The concept of contrastive analysis in the form of model replica charts has been adapted for studies of phonological acquisition in normally developing children (see Ferguson, 1968; Klein, 1978) and for the assessment of phonological disorders (e.g., Ingram, 1981; Klein, 1984). These charts provide a graphic comparison or "contrast" between the adult phonological system and the emerging child system. These forms will be applied with the L2 learner later in this chapter to contrast L1 and L2 sounds.

medial and final positions. According to the contrastive analysis hypothesis, one would predict that English speakers would have difficulty learning initial /ʒ/. This, however, is not the case. If, on the other hand, universal markedness relations are referenced (these markedness relations come from studies on language universals, e.g., Dinnsen & Eckman, 1978; Greenberg, 1965), the reason that /ʒ/ is, in fact, not difficult becomes clearer.

Based on the work of Dinnsen & Eckman (1978), Eckman (1977) proposed that languages may be typed (or typologized) according to whether a voice contrast is maintained (see Table 11.2 from Eckman, 1977). This table suggests a hierarchy with reference to difficulty or markedness of voicing contrast in various positions. The table shows that languages that have a voicing contrast finally also have the contrast medially and initially. Those with a contrast medially do not necessarily have one finally, and those with a contrast initially do not necessarily have this contrast medially. Thus, an "implicational relationship" exists among these positional sound contrasts: a contrast in final position implies a contrast in medial and initial positions, and a contrast in medial position implies one in initial position. The hierarchy is based on the distribution of features across the world's languages. Moreover, features that occur in most languages are considered to be learned with less difficulty than those that are rarer. With reference to this hierarchy, an English L1 speaker learning French should find the initial /ʒ/ unchallenging. Given that English maintains a voicing contrast in medial and final positions (ʒ vs ʃ), the L2 initial position is implied. Other markedness relationships that have been derived from descriptive studies on language universals deal with clusters (Greenberg, 1965) and segments permitted in final position (Eckman, 1985). A final stop + stop is more marked that a final fricative + stop, C1C2C3# is more marked than C1C2#, C2C3# (Greenberg, 1965). In final position the most marked segment is a voiced obstruent (e.g., /d/), followed by voiceless obstruent (e.g., /t/), sonorant consonants, and vowels (Eckman, 1985).

In a more recent publication, Eckman (1991) further delineated his views on markedness. He introduced the interlanguage structural conformity hypothesis, which states, "The universal generalizations that hold for the primary languages hold also for

TABLE 11.2 How languages may be typologized

Type	Description	Examples
A	Those which maintain a superficial voice contrast in initial, medial and final positions.	English, Arabic Swedish
B	Those which maintain a superficial voice contrast in initial and medial positions, but fail to maintain this contrast in final position.	German, Polish, Greek, Japanese, Catalan
C	Those which maintain a superficial voice contrast in initial position but fail to maintain this contrast in medial and final positions.	Corsican, Sardinian
D	Those which maintain no voice contrast in initial, medial, or final positions.	Korean

From Eckman, 1977. Printed with permission.

interlanguages" (Eckman, 1991, p. 24). Eckman argued that this is a stronger hypothesis than the markedness differential hypothesis because it makes predictions based only on implicational universals in the absence of a difference between L1 and L2 (as required for the markedness differential hypothesis). Because of this difference it would be possible to explain an L2 learner's difficulties with certain features, as evidenced in the interlanguage on the basis of implicational universals within the L2 itself. Eckman (1991) illustrated this point with evidence from adult native Hungarian speakers learning English (Altenberg & Vago as cited by Eckman, 1991). These L2 learners devoiced word-final obstruents of English targets. This situation cannot be explained by the markedness differential hypothesis because it cannot apply (make any predictions) unless there is a difference between the L1 and L2 with reference to this feature. As it happens, both languages contain a voice contrast in final position. According to the structural conformity hypothesis, however, systematic difficulty with voicing in final position would be predicted based on implicational universals (within the L2 itself); voicing in this position is most marked universally.

Several recent studies in L2 acquisition further specified universal hierarchies of difficulty for the production of final stops and consonant clusters. These studies focused on the interactions between structures known to be most marked universally (voicing contrasts in final stops and clusters of increasing numbers of segments) and the phonetic environments in which they are produced. These interactions will be discussed in the following section on performance demands.

One may ask how this information on markedness informs us about maintaining factors. We believe that any deterrent to learning helps maintain a problem. That two languages differ in their phoneme categories and allophonic variants makes learning the L2 difficult. Using the contrastive analysis hypothesis (identifying differences between and among languages) gives us a starting point to make predictions about potentially difficult areas. Certain sounds, sound combinations, and production contexts are intrinsically more difficult than others regardless of the language spoken. Increased difficulty (or markedness), in addition, deters authentic productions. A consideration of any available hierarchy addressing relative complexity of linguistic features may be used (as suggested by the markedness differential and structural conformity hypotheses). This knowledge would be informative for planning short-term and session goals, in which cases it is necessary to determine treatment priorities.

Prosody Influences Segment Production. Another phonological deterrent to authentic pronunciation may be the difference in prosodic characteristics of the contrasting languages. Major (1987) stated "Prosodic processes also affect the acquisition of a second language because to a large extent the prosody of a language governs the segmental processes" (p. 218). He explained there is a difference in syllable reduction in stress-timed languages when compared with syllable-timed languages. This is because degree of stress governs certain processes, as exemplified in the production of the flap (e.g., 'atom [ærəm] vs. a'tomic [ətamɪk]. (In stress-timed languages "syllables recur at regular intervals of time, regardless of the number of intervening unstressed syllables, as in English" [Crystal, 1991, p. 329]; in syllable-timed languages "the syllables are said to occur at regular intervals of time as in French" [Crystal, pp. 339–340]). Because prosodic processes represent differences between L1 and L2, Major considered these *interference* processes (see section on cognition), which take precedence at early learning phases. These processes are believed to interfere with the production of segments. English speakers, accustomed to stress-timed productions, reduce unstressed syllables in Spanish to /ə/; Spanish speakers, who use syllable-timed speech, fail to reduce unstressed syllables to /ə/ and instead produce a full vowel (e.g., *America* [amerika]). As the rhythm of the new language is mastered these segemental differences are expected to decease.

Summary.   Several conditions affect the successful acquisition of authentic L2 (or the maintenance of accented speech). These may be categorized as (a) psychosocial (age of acquisition, motivation level, and gender of the learner), (b) sensorimotor (the perception—differentiating new and equivalent sounds—production, and mental representation of speech sounds, (c) cognitive (the organization of new phoneme categories and the elimination of interference and developmental processes), and (d) phonological (the segmental and prosodic differences inherent in two languages and the universal relative difficulty of features—markedness of segments, segment combinations, and contexts). Clinicians working with adults learning L2 phonology need to be aware of conditions contributing to the maintenance of a foreign accent. It is only with this knowledge that the clinician will be able to plan procedures to facilitate target pronunciation. Maintaining factors of foreign accent are summarized in Box 11.2. The information appearing in this section revealed several diverse points of view as to the primary source of a foreign accent. Not all of these view points will be applicable to each client or appeal to every clinician. Knowledge of these potential maintaining factors, nevertheless, should aid the clinican in the decision making necessary in intervention planning.

Theories of Learning

If we consider the maintaining factors of foreign accent presented in the last section we can see that there are two major tasks for the L2 speaker: the phonetic task of differentiating and producing accurate L2 replicas, and the phonological (organizational) task of recognizing new sound categories and boundaries. If these are the learner's tasks, how may these best be facilitated? To answer this question, we turn to theories of learning presented in Chapter 6. Principles from four of these theories (operant, constructivist, social-cognitive, and motor theory) appear most appropriate in providing guiding principles for procedure planning with individuals learning L2 phonology.

Operant Theory.   As was noted in Chapter 6, principles from operant theory apply to observable behaviors and may be applied to learning across the life span. In addition, behavioral principles apply to the strengthening of behaviors already in the individual's repertoire or the establishment of new behaviors that reflect already established developmental/organizational parameters. This description makes operant principles applicable to the modification of similar sounds and the establishment of new sounds (in conjunction with constructivist-cognitive principles). Treatment tasks guided by operant principles such as the rapid production of stimulus words were found to be highly successful in learning accurate sound productions in L1 (Shriberg & Kwiatkowski, 1982).

A behavioristic orientation to treatment of foreign accent was reviewed by Leather and James (1991). The authors explain that this theoretical position was most prevalent in

BOX **11.2**

The Relationship Between Maintaining Factors and Intervention Planning

Accent Maintaining Factors	Effect on Goal Planning	Effect on Procedure Planning
Psychosocial aspects: 1. age; 2. use of L1; 3. motivation; 4. gender.	▪ Numbers 1–3 may limit long-term goal achievement of authentic targets. ▪ Number 4 may affect formal speech targets.	Procedures may target modification of: ▪ L1 use; ▪ motivation.
Sensorimotor achievements: 1. perception; 2. production of L2 targets.	▪ May limit long-term goal achievement. ▪ Will become target behaviors in session goals.	Procedures may target the modification of: ▪ perception skills; ▪ production skills.
Failure to achieve cognitive milestones: 1. Organization of phonetic categories (accommodation to new sounds). 2. Elimination of developmental and interference processes (viewed as a metalinguistic process).	▪ Targeted as long- and short-term goals	Procedures will include: ▪ opportunity for variations in production; ▪ personal and environmental feedback; ▪ self-evaluation.
The intrinsic difficulty of the phonological system itself: 1. L1 transfer; 2. markedness differentials; 3. prosodic features.	Will affect goal planning at all three phases	

the 1960s, consonant with the contrastive analysis hypothesis framework in vogue. At that time the focus was on teaching the L2 learner "a new set of 'habit structures' namely, S-R pairings" (Leather & James, 1991, p. 325). This approach was weakened as a cognitive interpretation to learning new sound patterns became more popular. The cognitive orientation was influenced by the mentalism of generative grammar and Selinker's (1969) conception of interlanguage as language transfer, implying the learning of new structures rather than habit patterns (Leather & James, 1991). More will be said about the cognitive orientation in the next section.

Application to Goal Planning. As described in Chapter 6, goal planning from a behavioristic perspective includes systematic task selection and analysis. This type of procedural orientation may be illustrated with planning for the acquisition of speech sounds by an L2 learner of English. The derivation of session goals may be facilitated through a task analysis such as the following: (a) identification of a target phoneme and phonetic/syllabic context, (b) production of nonsense monosyllabic syllables with the target sound in desired context following a model, (c) production of the sound in monosyllabic lexical items following a model, (d) production of the target in bisyllabic words following a model, and (e) production of target in CVC or bisyllabic words when identifying pictures. This type of task analysis will be discussed again in the section on performance demands below when the determination of a hierarchy of context difficulty is discussed.

Application to Procedure Planning. If a clinician follows a behavioristic model, procedure planning will center on the identification of an effective reward system. For an adult L2 client awards may be either external to the client (e.g., social praise) or intrinsic to the client (the achievement of a personally set goal: achieving the accurate sound).

Constructivist. While constructivist principles may be most directly applicable to cases of adult language disorders, higher levels of cognitive organization may be present in other problem-solving situations such as defining new speech-sound categories (e.g., Karmiloff-Smith, 1986). Linguists have begun to explain L1 transfers to L2 in cognitive terms. For example, Hammerberg (1990) showed that the transfer of L1 Swedish to L2 German may be viewed as an "inferencing"-type strategy in which "the learner makes use of prior linguistic knowledge to interpret L2 intake" (p. 199). Hammerberg described three levels of analysis involved with transfer:

> (a) at the level of *strategy,* with regard to the learner's plan of action to solve a particular problem in acquiring some phonological regularity in L2; (b) at the level of *execution,* with regard to the event, or process of carrying out the strategy; and (c) at the level of *solution,* with regard to the product of the applied strategy. (pp. 198–199)

Actual treatment data based on these notions are not yet available. A knowledge of constructivist principles, still, may be useful in designing treatment contexts for the facilitation of phonemic representations.

Application to Goal Setting. Constructivist theories allow for the development of organizational parameters of behavior throughout life. These theories, therefore, are applicable to the promotion of phonological reorganization in the adult L2 learner. Long- and short-term goals, therefore, are formulated to target changes in organizational patterns (e.g., phonetic/phonemic categories). Leather & James (1991) described the "best fit" model of L2, the speech-learning process, as one that makes primary the "construction of phonetic prototypes to which processes of both perception and production may be geared" (p. 320). These prototypes (i.e., target phonemes) are believed to be the basis for guiding perception and monitoring articulation attempts (tokens) of the target.

Application to Procedure Planning.   Based on cognitive principles, procedure planning may include the following:

1. the creation of tasks that are appropriate to the adult learner and challenging enough to provoke developmental changes (category boundaries and allophonic variations);
2. the creation of tasks that involve concrete execution of sensorimotor procedures to achieve the task or solve the problem (production and perception tasks); and
3. provoking reflection, specifically on perception/production relationships, and causal mechanisms related to nonauthentic productions or successes.

Social Cognitive Theory.   According to social-cognitive principles, learning target language sounds would be facilitated by (a) noticing similarities and distinctions among actions and events mediated by those who set the standards, (b) imitation, and (c) practice. Ellis (1994) summarized several cognitive theories of L2 learning. These theories and models of L2 acquisition (e.g., the monitor theory [Krashen, 1981], Bialystok's theory of L2 learning [1978]) view "L2 acquisition as a mental process involving gradual mastery of items and structures through the application of general strategies of perception and production" (p. 392). While models such as these focus on syntax, they, too, have the potential for application to the acquisition of phonology. These principles will affect both the planning of goals and procedures of intervention.

Application to Goal Planning.   Much of what we have said about the tasks of the adult L2 learner involves the enhancement of both perceptual and productive skills. These principles support the selection of the session objective, as either perceptual identification or production of a model. The client will be expected to either identify similarities and distinctions among target sounds (based on clinician directed strategies), talk about these distinctions (using metacognitive strategies), and/or produce these targets.

Application to Procedures.   Following social-cognitive principles the clinician will design the clinical context to provide effective "scaffolding" devices (i.e., demonstrations, directions, models of procedures, and strategies—see Chapter 6 for suggestions about interpersonal interactions and linguistic and nonlinguistic contexts in which these devices may be applied). Several Teaching English as a Second Language (TESOL) publications focus on the development of social, metacognitive, and cognitive strategies in establishing control over selected pronunciation features (see Bailey & Savage, 1994; Celce-Muria, 1987; and Morley, 1987, 1994).

Motor Theory.   As discussed in Chapter 6, motor learning theories are concerned with the learning of sensorimotor schemes, which are patterns of behavior—not conscious ideas or cognitive processes. Learning mechanisms cited in these theories include the exercise of motor patterns, self correction in response to problematic feedback, and the differentiation, integration, and coordination of different and often conflicting behavioral patterns.

It has been suggested at various points in this chapter that one of the major tasks of the L2 learner is the mastery of articulatory gestures (the phonetic aspect). As noted in Chapter 6, articulatory gestures promote the development of a motor representation based on various types and levels of feedback: first, peripheral feedback from air and bone-conducted pressure changes and from the joints, tendons, and muscles (auditory, tactile, proprioceptive/kinesthetic)—"closed loop"; second, central feedback from within the brain, which is responsible for monitoring of muscular activity—"open loop" (Leather & James, 1991). Since open-loop feedback relies on matching a current production with a known motor plan or perceptual signal, it would not be appropriate for learning new sounds; thus, it is predicted to be used less by new L2 speakers.

Application to Goal Planning.   Motor theories most directly affect goal planning at the session phase. Operating from a motor theory approach a clinician would include a sensorimotor activity as a session goal (i.e., the execution of an utterance). Examples of such activities are and can be found in some TESOL approaches to pronunciation practice (e.g., Catford, 1987; Temperley, 1987).

Application to Procedure Planning.   The clinician's role would be to:

1. engage the client in activities that require the production of utterances (i.e., producing sounds, syllables, words, sentences, etc., imitatively or spontaneously);
2. model or physically shape the sensorimotor act.

Summary.   This section examined the way theories of learning may be a useful source in making decisions about intervention planning. Box 11.3 lists the principles derived from each theory and the way they may be used to guide the clinician in the formulation of goals and procedures. It is expected that every theoretical model will not appeal to the belief system of every clinician; similarly, every model will not be applicable to each client. Part of the challenge of intervention planning is to choose the learning principles that appear most useful to goal and procedure planning with each client, with each session, and even within sessions. As stated in Klein and Moses (1999), "Thus, it is our position that procedural planning does not involve committing to any single theory to the exclusion of others. Procedure planning requires selecting principles from theories relevant to a particular client's . . . problem and differentially applying these principles to design comprehensive therapeutic contexts" (p. 37).

Performance Demands

Until this point, three bodies of knowledge believed to be useful in intervention planning have been presented: (a) content/form/use interactions, (b) maintaining factors, and (c) theories of learning. The fourth and last source of information for intervention planning is knowledge about factors that increase or decrease the complexity of a task involved with learning to produce the sounds of an L2. The demands made on a client's performance at any time during the intervention process have been referred to as "performance demands"

BOX 11.3

Application of Learning Theories to Intervention Planning for Accented Second Language Speech

Learning Theory	Derived Principles	Application to Goal Planning	Application to Procedure Planning
Operant (O)	Target-sound production is facilitated by: 1. the ability to discriminate stimuli associated with the target sound; 2. events following a behavior that can reinforce or extinguish a behavior.	Guides in the formulation and sequencing of sessions goals.	Supports a consideration of: ■ motivational events; ■ behavioral reenforcers.
Constructivist Cognitive (CC)	Target-sound production is facilitated by: 1. tasks that are complex enough to pose developmental challenges; 2. the execution of sensorimotor procedures to achieve tasks or solve problems; 3. the act of reflecting specifically on task demands.	Influences the conceptualization of Phase 1 and Phase 2 goals as the acquisition of L2 phonetic categories (involving awareness of allophonic variation and category boundaries).	Supports the encouragement of: ■ variations in production attempts; ■ self-reflection on performance.
Social Cognitive (SC)	Target-sound production is facilitated by: 1. noticing similarities and distinctions among speech sounds produced by a standard model; 2. imitation of target sounds; 3. practice of target sounds.	Guides in the formulation of session goals that include discrimination and production activities.	Supports the clinician's role as one who: ■ models target sounds; ■ suggests metalinguistic strategies for differentiating new from similar sounds.
Motor (M)	Learning speech sounds is facilitated by peripheral (sensory) and central feedback from movement involved in the act of articulation.	Influences the performance of a production activity within a session goal.	The clinician is encouraged to: ■ engage the client in activities that require the production of utterances (i.e., producing sounds, syllables, words, and sentences imitatively or spontaneously); ■ model or physically shape the sensorimotor act

(see Klein & Moses, 1999; Chapter 1 of this book). Information about performance demands most directly affects the planning of session goals. It is at this point in intervention planning that three important questions need to be answered: (a) What sound, sound groups, or features should be targeted first? (b) In what linguistic context should this target be embedded? (c) What constitutes a sequence of hierarchically organized steps through which the client will generalize this sound (i.e., reach the short-term goal)? The answers to these questions may be found in a review of those variables contributing to performance demands in learning to pronounce an L2.

Klein and Moses (1999) presented a comprehensive review of several variables believed to contribute to the demands made on a client's performance of session goals in L1 articulation/phonology. They showed that the production of a target segment may be affected by (a) the position of the target sound in a given syllable (e.g., initial/onset or final/coda), (b) the phonetic environment (vowels and consonants surrounding target sound), (c) the prosodic contour of word (specifically, the stress of the syllable in which the sound occurs), (d) the response mode (described by Klein and Moses, 1999, as a way of differentiating between responses that require production of target with those that do not require production of target [i.e., the targeting of discrimination rather than production of sounds]), and (e) the presence or absence of perceptual support (is the response expected after a model [i.e., imitative] or without a model [spontaneous]).

Recent research in L2 acquisition suggests that these performance demands may be equally valid for planning session goals for the adult L2 client. This is especially true for markedness relationships and their interactions with other segments (Carlisle, 1994) and syllable positions (Eckman & Iverson, 1994; Yavas, 1994). This section, therefore, will be organized with reference to the variables listed above; two additional factors often discussed in L2 phonology—"intrinsic complexity" of segment and "formality of task"—will also be examined.

Intrinsic Complexity of Segment.   Whether a clinician is targeting the elimination of a phonological process or the acquisition of a class of sounds, one of the first considerations generally is which sound to target first (e.g., Gierut, Morrisette, Hughes, & Rowland, 1996; Powell, 1991). How does one identify this representative sound or "target" sound? Some of the most common criteria for selecting a target sound in cases of L1 phonological disorders are the following: presence in the child's repertoire, stimulability, generalizability, and developmental schedule (see Edwards, 1992; Elbert & Gierut, 1986; Hodson & Paden, 1991 who suggest distinct criteria for choosing an initial target). Although not stated explicitly, all these criteria reflect a consideration of relative complexity (difficulty in production) as compared with other segments. For example, sounds already present in a child's repertoire are probably earlier in the developmental hierarchy (see commonly referenced schedules such as Prather, Hedrick, & Kern, 1975; Sander, 1972; Templin, 1957); thus, they are presumably less complex than those not produced. These sounds would likely be more stimulable. These earlier developing, more stimulable sounds are currently thought to develop even without intervention, while less stimulable sounds (those more complex) should be targeted first for wider generalizability (e.g., Elbert & Gierut, 1986; Gierut et al., 1996).

More explicit specifications about target complexity as a clinical measure have been made with reference to (a) markedness criteria (Cairns, Cairns, & Williams, 1974; McReynolds, Engmann, & Dimmitt, 1974), (b) implicational laws (e.g., Dinnsen, Chin, Elbert, & Powell, 1991), and most recently (c) consonant specifications (Bernhardt & Stoel-Gammon, 1994).

Markedness of Segments. The concept of markedness (defined above), which developed within the Prague School of Linguistics, was subsequently elaborated and applied to generative phonology by Chomsky and Halle (1968). The markedness framework provides for the differentiation of phonemes on the basis of being "marked" or "unmarked" for a particular feature; the unmarked state represents the less complex or natural. For example, linguistic theory views an optimal consonant as one made in the extreme forward part of the mouth. Consonants that are labials and dentals [+ anterior] will be unmarked for this feature [U for anterior]; consonants that are palatals and velars (which are [– anterior]) will be marked [M] for the feature anterior. The total complexity of the phoneme is indicated by the number of marked features or Ms. In an effort to verify this theory, Cairns et al. (1974) developed an inventory of markedness values (see Table 11.3) that they used as a basis for a research study. As illustrated in this table the least marked sound (receiving a complexity score of 0) would be a /t/ unmarked for vocalic, anterior, coronal, continuant, strident, voiced, lateral, nasal. When viewing Table 11.3, note that both the presence of a feature [+] and the absence of a feature [–] may be designated as unmarked (i.e., more natural in the production of a consonant). The most complex segment (with a score of 4) is the /ð/, marked for coronal, continuant, strident, and voiced. Cairns et al. (1974) used these values to analyze articulation errors of three dialect groups of elementary school children (Standard American English, Black American English, and Mexican American English). The results of this study demonstrated that "markedness theory can predict a substantial portion of the substitutions not due to dialectal or L2 influences" (Cairns et al., 1974, p. 166). Some attempts to use Cairns et al. markedness values to predict substitution patterns in children with articulation disorders (McReynolds et al., 1974), or for children learning to pronounce polysyllabic words (Klein, 1978) did not support Cairns et al.'s findings. Toombs, Singh & Hayden (1981), however, using a different markedness matrix, found that markedness theory could explain the substitutions of their subjects. This discrepancy may be explained by the distinctive features evaluated (Cairns et al. focused on different features from Toombs et al.). In addition, factors such as the syllable position in which segment occurs and surrounding sounds significantly complicate segment markedness (Edwards & Shriberg, 1983). Intrinsic segment complexity, measured by markedness, has not yet been been sufficiently supported as an independent predictor of difficulty in L1 or L2 learners. Word position and phonetic environment must be considered in conjunction.

Implicational Laws. Related to markedness are implicational laws that also predict which sounds or sound classes are more complex than others. Sloat, Taylor, and Hoard (1978) identified the existence of an implicational law between two sounds when the presence of one sound generally implies the presence of the other. To illustrate this phenomenon they compared /t/ and /d/. Since there are languages that have a /t/ and not a /d/ but not the reverse, the presence of /d/ implies the presence of /t/ but not the reverse. The segment

TABLE 11.3   Feature Content Markedness Values and Complexity Index for Relevant Phonemes (Cairns, Cairns, & Williams, 1974)

Features	Phonemes																	
	z	s	ð	θ	d	t	v	f	b	p	ʃ	dʒ	tʃ	g	k	w	l	r
Consonantal	+	+	+	+	+	+	+	+	+	+	+	+	+	+	+	−	+	+
Vocalic	U	U	U	U	U	U	U	U	U	U	U	U	U	U	U	M	M	M
Anterior	+	+	+	+	+	+	+	+	+	+	U	U	U	U	U	U	U	U
Coronal	+	+	+	+	+	+	U	U	U	U	+	+	+	U	U	U	+	+
Continuant	M	M	M	M	−	−	M	M	−	−	M	−	−	−	−	U	U	U
Strident	+	+	−	−	+	−	−	−	−	−	+	+	+	−	−	U	U	U
Voiced	M	U	M	M	M	−	M	−	M	−	U	M	U	M	−	U	+	U
Lateral	U	U	U	U	−	−	U	−	−	−	U	−	−	U	U	−	M	U
Complexity	2	1	4	3	1	0	3	2	2	1	3	3	2	2	1	1	2	1

Note that /f/ is listed as -strident; this is a departure from standard feature charts. We consider it -strident here because /f/ is significantly less "noisy" than any of the sounds indicated as + strident here. Of course, the features are all relative; if English had bilabial fricatives, then we would be forced to list /f/ as strident and the bilabial fricatives as -strident. No M/U values are given for consonantal because these values are dependent on the position within the word. Thus, consonants are unmarked in word-initial position, vowels are unmarked in position after a consonant, and so on.

that implies the presence of another, in this case the /d/, is considered to be the more marked (i.e., more complex and less natural). Other markedness relationships cited by Sloat et al. (1978) are as follows:

1. voiced obstruents are more marked than voiceless;
2. liquids are more marked than obstruents;
3. fricatives are more marked than stops;
4. affricates are more marked than fricatives;
5. [n] is the least marked nasal;
6. [s] and [h] are the least marked fricatives;
7. low vowels are the least marked vowels;
8. high vowels are more marked than mid vowels;
9. high back vowels are more marked than high front vowels;
10. CV syllable is the least marked followed by CVC.

Implicational hierarchies have been used to describe error patterns and suggest remediation hierarchies for children with phonological disorders (Dinnsen et al., 1991). These hierarchies have also been used to explain relative difficulty in the production of clusters in L2 phonology (e.g., Carlisle, 1994; Eckman & Iverson, 1994).

Feature Specification. A third framework for hypothesizing about the relative complexity of consonants is underspecification theory. This theory, an aspect of nonlinear phonology, proports that underlying representations of segments are minimal, containing information only about the distinctive properties of the segment (Bernhardt & Stoel-Gammon, 1994), distinctive properties comprising the unpredictable values for features. The features that remain unspecified are the predictable values for a class of sounds. For example, a segment that is sonorant is expected to be voiced; [+ voice], therefore, does not need to be specified. To distinguish two sonorants (/j/ and /w/) from one another, further specification is necessary. Since coronal place is the least specified place (most natural) universally, it need not be specified for /j/. To distinguish the two sonorants, /w/ receives further specification—labial or [+ round]. Table 11.4 from Bernhardt and Stoel-Gammon provides a list of English segments and their specifications. This table shows that voiced fricatives and /r/ have the greatest number of specifications; consonants with the fewest specifications are /t/ and /j/.

Like markedness values, these different degrees of specification among segments suggest a hierarchy of relative complexity among segments. This hierarchy again must be considered with caution because segments are known to be influenced by their phonetic and syllabic environments.

Phonetic Environment. After decisions about a target segment or group of segments are made, the next important consideration is the context in which the target will be embedded. L1 treatment approaches to target facilitation have long recognized the effect of the phonetic environment (e.g., Hodson & Paden, 1991; Kent, 1982). Current researchers of L2 acquisition have also shown that the phonetic environment affects the production of certain segments, especially those found to be most problematic for L2 learners of English: final consonants and clusters.

TABLE 11.4   Proposed Consonant Specifications for Adult English[a]. (Bernhardt & Stoel-Gammon, 1994)

Segment	Root node	Laryngeal node	Place node
/m/	[+consonantal], [+nasal]		Labial
/n/	[+cons], [+nasal]		
/ŋ/	[+cons], [+nasal]		Dorsal
/p/[b]	[+cons]		Labial
/b/	[+cons]	[+voice]	Labial
/t/[b]	[+cons]		
/d/	[+cons]	[+voice]	
/k/[b]	[+cons]		Dorsal
/g/	[+cons]	[+voice]	Dorsal
/f/	[+cons], [+continuant]		Labial
/v/	[+cons], [+cont]	[+voice]	Labial
/θ/	[+cons], [+cont]		Coronal: [+distributed][a]
/ð/	[+cons], [+cont]	[+voice]	Cor: [+distributed]
/s/	[+cons], [+cont]		
/z/	[+cons], [+cont]	[+voice]	
/ʃ/	[+cons], [+cont]		Cor: [−anterior]
/ʒ/	[+cons], [+cont]	[+voice]	Cor: [−anterior]
/tʃ/	[+cons], Branching [continuant][c]		Cor: [−anterior]
/dʒ/	[+cons], Branching [continuant][c]	[+voice]	Cor: [−anterior]
/w/	[+sonorant]		Labial: [+round]
/h/	[+cons][+cont]	Laryngeal Node	
/j/	[+son]		
/l/	[+cons], [+son]		
/r/	[+cons], [+son]		Lab + Cor Place, or [−anterior][a]

[a]Only featurees presumed to be specified in underlying representation are indicated. The above encodings are derived from McCarthy (1988). In addition, [+distributed] is used for /θ/ and /ð/. To distinguish /r/ from /l/, we use both Labial and Coronal Place for /r/, or, alternatively, [anterior].

[b]Allophonic specification of [+/spread glottis] is assumed for word-initial voiceless stops.

[c]The branching structure of the affricates is assumed to be [−continuant][+continuant].

Printed with permission.

Greenberg's (1965) classic study, based on approximately 104 languages, established implicational universals for the length of codas (final consonants) and onsets (initial consonants) and for the segments coexisting within codas and onsets. In general, the longer the onset and coda, the greater the likelihood that cluster reductions will occur. This reduction results in less marked clusters (Carlisle, 1994). Greenberg also proposed that certain cluster combinations were more marked than others (if length of cluster was kept constant); therefore, the presence of certain combinations implies the presence of others. For example, if a language has a two-consonant coda with a stop-stop ("backed" [bækt]), it will also have one with a fricative-stop ("laughed" [læft]). If a language has a word-final coda of fricative-fricative ("laughs" [læfs]), it will also have stop-fricative ("looks" [lʊks]) or fricative-stop. Stop-stop and fricative-fricative, therefore, are viewed as the more marked sequences. Greenberg also proposed universals for syllable onsets. One of these universals is that if a language has an obstruent-nasal ("snow") onset, it will have an obstruent-liquid onset ("sleep"). The presence of the former implies the presence of the latter, indicating the first is more marked than the second. Based on Greenberg's (1965) summary of findings (p. 29), the following markedness (complexity) relationships (appropriate to English) are proposed:

1. Shorter clusters are less complex than longer clusters.
2. Clusters that are analyzable into subclusters are less complex than unanalyzable clusters. For example, [skw] may be reduced to a subcluster /sk/.
3. Homorganic nasals + obstruents (nd, mb, ŋg) are less complex than heterorganic nasals + obstruents (ng).
4. Clusters in which sonorants are closer to the peak of the syllable (vowel) are favored over clusters in which obstruents are closer to the peak (e.g., in English, initial clusters with two or three consonants must begin with an obstruent and end with a liquid, nasal, or glide—"slow," "splash," "swim," "squeeze"). Codas, similarly, are guided by the requirement to maintain sonority close to the syllable peak. This is illustrated by the reverse order of consonant sonority relationships in "else," "elf," and "dance."

Recent studies by Carlisle (1988) addressing onsets and Eckman (1991) addressing codas supported these proposed universals.

Carlisle (1994) summarized a number of his studies (1988, 1991) that involved variability in the use of vowel epenthesis by native Spanish speakers learning English. Vowel epenthesis (the insertion of a vowel between two consonants within a cluster [e.g., class → kəlæs], or epenthesis at the end of a syllable [e.g., seed → sidə]) has been described as a strategy used more frequently by L2 than L1 learners in an effort to simplify complex syllable structures (Weinberger, 1994). Carlisle also examined the occurrence of vowel epenthesis before specific cluster combinations to specify markedness relationships of the interactions between the preceding segment and the cluster composition (e.g., /sl/ the less marked vs. /st/ the more marked; /sl/ the less marked vs. /sN (collapsed category of /sn/ and /sm/) the more marked. A consistent finding from all Carlisle's studies (reported in Carlisle, 1994) has been that nonepenthesis (the target variant) occurs significantly more frequently after vowels (the less marked) than after consonants, and before the less marked of the cluster combinations. Carlisle concluded that cluster environments can be in a markedness relationship just as the clusters themselves can, and the less marked environment will induce a higher frequency of target variants than will more marked environments. Based on his findings, Carlisle proposed a hierarchy of difficulty that may be useful in planning goals for L2 learners. The following hierarchy, organized in increasing order of difficulty, is consonant with Carlisle's (1994) suggestions for an instructional approach:

1. two-member onsets before three-member onsets (/sp/ before /spl/);
2. two-member onsets with initial onsets should be approached in the following order: /sl/, /s+nasal/, /s+stop/);
3. two-member onset interactions (with different preceding sounds):
   "vocalic environment with /sl/
   vocalic environment with /sm/ and /sn/
   vocalic environment with /st/, /sp/, and /sk/

> consonantal environment with /sl/
> consonantal environment with /sm/ and /sn
> consonantal environment with /st/, /sp/, and /sk/" (Carlisle, 1994, p. 245);

4. three-member onsets.

In contrast to Carlisle (1994) who studied syllable onsets, Eckman & Iverson's (1994) research focused on syllable codas (final consonants). These researchers were interested in describing production patterns affecting syllable final single consonants from different feature classes. Coda consonant errors (affecting obstruents, nasals, liquids, and glides) made by Cantonese, Korean, and Japanese were analyzed. Findings in general indicated that relatively marked coda obstruents of English are generally more difficult for speakers of each of the L1 backgrounds studied than are English sonorants. This was even true for the subjects whose L1 had rich coda structures (including both nasals and stops). Eckman and Inverson discussed pedagogical implications based on their findings. Unlike Carlisle (1994), who proceeded from less to more complex, Eckman and Inverson argued for structuring treatment hierarchies that follow implicational principles. These principles would suggest that final consonants that are found to be more problematic should be targeted first. Mastery of a consonant in a final position implies mastery in an initial position, while the converse is not true. Eckman and Iverson also noted that pronunciation problems with coda consonants may not always be predicted by the presence of these consonant types in the L1.

Position in Syllable.   Final syllable position, especially for the production of stops, was the focus of several studies in L2 phonology (e.g., Eckman, 1981; Edge, 1991; Weinberger, 1994; Yavas, 1994). Although stops occur in all languages, many languages do not include stops in final position and some languages only permit voiceless stops. A restriction on voiced stops appears to be the most common condition (Yavas, 1994). L2 learners whose L1 systems do not permit voiced stops have been observed to have difficulties when learning English. When encountering a voiced stop in final position an L2 learner of English will most likely use any of the following processes: terminal devoicing (Eckman, 1981), final consonant deletion, and vowel epenthesis (Weinberger, 1994). According to Weinberger, vowel epenthesis is used more frequently than final consonant deletion because it is more likely to preserve lexical contrasts (see p. 351 earlier in this chapter). Several current studies attempted to further specify difficulties with the production of final voiceless stops by examining the environment of the final segment. For example, Edge (1991) examined the segments following word-final voiced obstruents. Various environments included those before a pause, before a vowel, before a voiced consonant, and before a voiceless consonant. Edge found differential effects for different environments. Most cases of devoicing occurred before a pause; the next most frequent context was before a voiceless consonant; the next most frequent was before a voiced consonant; and the least frequent was before a vowel. Yavas (1993, cited in Yavas 1994) extended Edge's (1991) consideration of the environment by the place of articulation of the stop and the height of the vowel preceding the stop. Yavas found that subjects devoiced more frequently as the point of articulation went from bilabial, to alveolar, and then to velar. Although changing the vowel from low to high did not affect the bilabial stop it made a significant difference with the alveolar and velar stops.

These studies by Edge (1991) and Yavas (1994) have important implications for planning of session goals. Based on Edge's study, a clinician targeting final stops would be wise to consider the environment following the stop. Edge's findings suggested the following hierarchy (of increasing difficulty) of environmental conditions:

1. before a vowel;
2. before a voiced consonant;
3. before a voiceless consonant;
4. before a pause.

Yavas (1994) discussed implications for targeting voiced stops in final position based on his findings. His suggestions may also be organized within a complexity hierarchy of increasing difficulty:

1. bilabial stops preceded by low vowels (e.g., tub, rob, cab);
2. bilabial stops preceded by high vowels (e.g., bib);
3. alveolar stops preceded by a low vowel (e.g., bed, bad, red);
4. alveolar stops preceded by a high vowel (e.g., bead, food, kid);
5. velar stops preceded by a low vowel (e.g., bag, dog, egg);
6. velar stops preceded by a high vowel (e.g., big, pig);
7. bisyllablic words and words with initial clusters may become appropriate contexts for final voiced contexts next.

The Prosodic Contour of Word. (Specifically the stress of the syllable in which the sound occurs) As noted earlier, prosodic processes also affect acquisition of L2 consonants and vowels (Major, 1987). Vowel reduction and the production of certain consonant allophones (e.g., the intervocalic /t/ produced as a flap) appear problematic to L2 learners of English. Based on these tendencies one would conclude that target sounds should first be introduced in most salient contexts (stressed) before reduced-stress contexts. In addition, when targeting word stress patterns it would wise to consider sounds already in the learner's repertoire. These principles conform with those currently expressed in nonlinear phonology. Within the non-linear framework it is suggested that segmental and prosodic aspects not be targeted simultaneously (i.e., follow the principle of using old forms to express new functions and new forms for expressing old functions, Bernhardt and Stoel-Gammon, 1994).

Response Mode. In the section on maintaining factors it was demonstrated that both perception and production factors are involved in the learning of L2 sounds. The clinician must decide which modality to target first when formulating session goals. These decisions are often based on points of view expressed in published procedural approaches on the correction of foreign accents (e.g., Catford, 1987; Morley, 1994; Wong, 1987). Clinicians can also be guided by results of research in articulation treatment when making decisions about which modality to target first.

Perception. Leather & James (1991) reviewed several studies designed to improve the phonetic ability of L2 speakers. These studies were designed to determine which modality should be trained first, perception or production, to effect the most efficient carryover to the other. Of the nine studies noted, training perception first revealed a slight advantage. The authors, however, concluded that the inconsistent and inconclusive findings were probably due to the differences in methodology and conceptualizations of perceptual and production knowledge.

The "perception first" explanation, nevertheless, continues to gain support. Leather & James (1991) pointed out that one of the reasons the adult L2 learner rarely attains native-like pronunciation is that attempts to communicate occur before much prior perceptual exposure to the target language sound pattern (unlike L1 learners). In a similar vein, Neufeld (1980) hypothesized (based on research data) that if L2 learners begin to pronounce before sufficient exposure to standard productions they will misshape their developing phonetic "templates" that will then continue to guide inauthentic productions. In addition, the work of Flege (reviewed in Flege, 1992) argued for a perceptual basis outlined in his equivalence hypothesis discussed elsewhere in this chapter. Although many researchers agree that perceptual training facilitates the learning of nonnative speech contrasts, there is some controversy as to what constitutes the best training procedure. Identification tasks (presenting a single stimulus on each trial in a two-alternative, forced-choice procedure) and same/different discrimination tasks (presenting two stimuli at each) have been used to train L2 subjects in some recent investigations. For example, Logan, Lively, and Pisoni (1991) found that native speakers of Japanese learning English improved in their perception of /r/ and /l/ with the use of an identification task. Perception, however, was found to be affected by phonetic environment and talker variables. In a follow-up study, Lively, Pisoni, Yamada, Tohikura, & Yamada, (1994), using Logan et al. (1991) procedures, found that gains in perception made after three weeks posttest were maintained above pretest levels even after six months posttest. These gains were attributed to the high-variability identification paradigm (different phonetic contexts and different speakers presenting stimulus words). In another training study (Mandarin speakers learning /t/ and /d/ in word-final position), Flege (1995a) evaluated identification and same/different tasks in learning a categorical contrast. Flege found that both types of training yielded comparable results but that the subjects preferred identification training.

Perception and Production.   Offering another point of view regarding the relationship between perception and production, Leather & James (1991) suggested that the speech-learning mechanism has the capacity to interrelate perceptual and productive knowledge that is conditioned by particular contexts and circumstances. In support of this position, they submitted research findings from one of the authors (i.e., Leather, 1990) on the learning of Chinese tones by Dutch and English speakers. Using computerized techniques some subjects were trained first in perception while others were trained in production. These findings indicated that neither perception nor production training appeared to be prerequisite. Rather, training in either modality facilitated performance in the other.

Perceptual Support.   Klein and Moses (1999) described perceptual support in two major forms: the clinician's model and the orthographic symbols. Each of these support devices is used by clinician's to decrease the performance demand on individuals learning to pronounce. A recent model of a target sound or word facilitates articulatory attempts and, thus, often becomes an early step in treatment (e.g., Bernthal and Bankson, 1998; Schmidt, 1997). Adult L2 speakers may also be guided by the support of the printed word. This form of support would also lessen the demand made on production.

Box 11.4 summarizes the way performance demands affect the planning of session goals.

Summary. The first part of this chapter explored four bodies of information believed to be basic to the intervention-planning process. Each may be referenced at various phases of intervention planning and for specific aspects of the process (i.e., goals and/or procedures). The first, knowledge of content/form/use interactions in L2 learning, helps the clinican understand the nature of the L2 sound system (and the concept of an interlanguage). This knowledge is essential in formulating realistic long- and short-term phonology goals. The second, a knowledge of maintaining factors, orients the clinician to the linguistic and non-linguistic sources of variability in learning the L2. This should be useful knowledge for (a) identifying areas requiring modification as a basis for the achievement of L2 targets, and (b) predicting the time necessary for goal accomplishment. The third, a knowledge of learning theories, is expected to guide the clinician in determining the most appropriate procedural approach for a given client (i.e., how best to facilitate the production of L2 targets). The fourth, performance demands, directs the clinician to these linguistic and non-linguistic factors that affect the ability of a client to carryout a given task. Information about factors influencing performance is most important for envisioning a series of session goals. See Box 11.5 for a summary of the relationship between sources of information and intervention planning.

The next section will introduce an L1 Spanish adult learning English. His case history, including results from testing, will be followed by a plan for treatment management.

BOX 11.4

Performance Demands That Influence the Formulation of Session Goals

Areas of Performance Demand	Aspect of Goal Affected
Intrinsic complexity of segments or sound classes	Selection of target sound or sound group
Syllable position (onset or coda)	Syllable context in which target is embedded
Phonetic environment	Phonetic environment of target sound (surrounding segments and/or cluster compositions)
Prosodic contour of word	Stress of syllable in which target is embedded
Response mode	The response expected of client: verbal or nonverbal
Perceptual support	The presence or absence of a model as a basis of the client's performance
Task formality	Degree of propositionality of task: read minimal word pairs versus conversation

BOX **11.5**

Sources of Information and Intervention Planning

Source	Aspect of Planning Affected	Phase of Planning Affected
The concept of L2 phonology as related to other components of language	Goal planning	All phases
Factors maintaining unauthentic productions	Goal and procedure planning	All phases
Theories of learning and stabilizing speech sounds	Procedure planning	All phases
Performance demands on the production and maintenance of new speech sounds	Goal and procedure planning	Phase 3

Case History Information on José

José, a 30-year-old male, was seen at the University Speech-Language and Hearing Center for an evaluation of his language and phonology. As an L2 speaker of English, he was concerned about his production of vowel and consonant sounds. In the nine years since he arrived from Peru, he had sought assistance with his pronunciation from several sources. He took a course in English at an ESL institute, took a summer university course in voice and diction, and attempted to see a private speech-language pathologist, but was discouraged by the fees. He reports some overall improvement in his vocabulary and his level of confidence in speaking English over the last few years. He still, however, reveals feelings of frustration and anxiety when trying to express himself in English; this occurs primarily at work. He feels most uncomfortable using L2 when speaking to strangers and addressing a group or class. Married to a Spanish speaker, and having mostly Spanish-speaking friends, José spends the greater proportion of speaking time using L1.

While generally experiencing good health, José has suffered from bouts of anxiety and depression, which have contributed to difficulties concentrating. He has been under the care of a psychiatrist who has prescribed various medications.

José recently completed a BA degree in economic science and is entering an MBA program. He believes that improvement in speaking English will enhance his career potential. Box 11.6 presents a listing of the areas of evaluation and the types of procedures used with José. Box 11.7 shows the results of these procedures.

BOX **11.6**

Areas of Assessment for Intervention Planning

Name: José P   Age 31   Communication Problem: Second Language Phonology

Necessary Information	Source	Utility of Procedure
II. Language	Conversational speech sample	To assess client's content/form and use patterns in a naturalistic setting
A. Content/Form/Use	Test of Language Compentence (TLC) Figurative Language Subtest (Wiig & Secord, 1989)	To assess client's understanding of figurative language
B. Phonology	Conversational speech sample	To assess client's speech productions in a naturalistic setting subject to the variables imposed by style and content of interviewers statements and questions
1. Phonetic	Compton Phonological Assessment of Foreign Accent (1983) Sentence Subtest from Fischer-Longemann Test of Articulation Competence (1971)	To assess phonetic repertoire in the context of spontaneous production of single words, phrases, and reading of phonetically balanced sentences and paragraph
2. Phonological	Analysis of deviation patterns (Patterns of difference from L2 productions)	To assess types of consonant, vowel, and prosodic deviations from L2 targets
D. Fluency	Observations across all evaluation tasks	
E. Voice	Observations across all evaluation tasks	
II. Maintaining Factors	Background information on client's academic and vocational status	
A. Cognitive		
B. Sensorimotor 1. Peripheral Speech Mechanism	Oral Speech Mechanism Screening Examination-Revised (OSMSE-R; St. Louis & Ruscello, 1987).	To determine the structural and functional adequacy of the articulators
2. Speech sound stimulability	Informal stimulability task	To determine whether the client can modify a prior production mismatch when presented with a model
3. Speech sound discrimination	Discrimination task for consonants (Proctor, 1994) Discrimination task for vowels (informal assessment)	To determine whether the client can differentiate consonants and vowels
C. Psychosocial	Background information Interview	To determine the nature of the client's psychosocial status

BOX 11.7

Summary of Baseline Date for Intervention Planning

Name: José P_____   **Age:** ___31___   **Primary Disorder:** Second Language Phonology

Area Assessed (include sources and results)
I. Language

    A. Content/Form

Oral language: Mismatches affecting auxilliary "do" ("How _ you phrase it?), plurals ("many kinds of works"); the kind of works, prepositions ("I got my MBA on January"; "at the first five years"), word order ("There are reasons why is that"), third person singular ("My voice change_ when"; "My word order get_ mixed up"), gerund ("It would be like give_ up"), regular past tense ("I haven't respond_"), articles ("I don't like the snakes"; I have a new shoes"), semantics ("The leaves are coming off the trees"; "She's doing a lot of splashed while she's swimming").

Written language:
All of the above errors with the addition of mismatches in subject/verb agreement ("My nervousness *do* not let me control myself"; "Talking with people that *is* close to me").
TLC (Figurative Language): Received 15 of a possible 36 points (mean and standard deviation for adults (18+) = 30.7 (S.D. 4.9). He was unable to match the expression for 25% of the items and was unable to interpret the expression for 50% of the items.

    B. Use: Exhibited a full range of expected language functions and appropriate conversational conventions (e.g., turn taking, topic maintenance)

    C. Phonology

        1. Phonetic: All L2 consonants except for those not sampled (/ʒ/within word, and word final) were within phonetic repertoire though not observed in all L2 positions (e.g., /z/→ [s] word final). Great deal of variability with vowel production, especially for /I/, /æ/, /ɔ/, /ʌ/, /ə/, /ɝ/.

        2. Phonological (See Figure 11.1, contrastive Analysis Chart)
Consonant patterns:
Devoicing of final consonants
Stopping of /θ and /ð/
Interchanges: /dʒ/ → [j]; /j/ → [dʒ]
                /d/ → [ð]; /ð/ → [d]
Individual substitutions: /dʒ/ → [d] or [ʒ], trilled r [r̃]
Clusters are reduced within words and in word final position; some examples are:

Within word			Word Final		
/bj/ → [b]	*vocabulary*	[vokæbulɛri]	/st/ → [s]	*against*	[gens]
/gw/→ [w]	*LaGuardia*	[lawar̃dia]	/lt/ → [l]	*difficult*	[difikʌl]
/gz/ → [z]	*example*	[ezampul]	/dz/ → [s]	*rewards*	[riwɔs]
/nʃ/ → [ʃ]	*internship*	[intɛr̃ʃip]	/gz/ → [s]	*eggs*	[e:s]
	financial	[faɪnæʃul]	/kst/ → [st]	*mixed*	[mɪst]
/ksp/ → [sp]	*explain*	[esplen]	/nst/ → [ns]	*advanced*	[advans]

B O X 11.7   **Continued**

Summary of Baseline Date for Intervention Planning

Name: <u>José P</u>   **Age:** <u>31</u>   **Primary Disorder:** <u>Second Language Phonology</u>

Vowel patterns:
  tensing: $I \rightarrow i;\ \upsilon \rightarrow u;$
  raising: $\varepsilon \rightarrow e;\ a \rightarrow o;$
  lowering: $\mathfrak{O} \rightarrow a;\ \Lambda \rightarrow a$
  backing: $\ae \rightarrow a\ or\ a;\ \Lambda \rightarrow o\ or\ u;\ \vartheta \rightarrow \upsilon\vartheta^{\cdot}\ or\ \varepsilon\vartheta^{\cdot}$
  fronting: $o \rightarrow a\ or\ \Lambda;\ \mathfrak{O} \rightarrow a;\ a \rightarrow ,\ae;$

Prosody: Unstressed L2 syllables of multisyllabic words are not reduced, which gives full vowel value to these syllables rendering a range of full vowels in the place of schwa (e.g., *education* [edukeshon], *immigrant* [imigrΛnt], *institute* [institut], *composition* [kaposiʃon], *united* [djunaItɛd], *characteristic* [karitaristik]

D. Fluency: Normal rate and rhythm

E. Voice: Normal vocal parameters

II. Maintaining Factors

  A. Cognitive: High achieving academically

  B. Sensorimotor
    1. Peripheral speech mechanism
       Missing premolars bilaterally; all other structures appear to be normal.
       Diadochokinetic rates for all syllables were within one standard deviation of the mean for his age.

    2. Body Stability: Within normal limits
    3. Screening revealed a 55DB loss at 4000hz in the left ear; all other frequencies screened bilaterally were within normal limits.
    4. Auditory discrimination testing resulted in 6 errors of 35 pairs of consonant contrasts; 4 errors of 22 pairs of vowel contrasts. The consonants in the following syllable pairs were judged to be the same: bale-vale, tin-sin, doze-those, so-though, mat-pat, bat-pat; the vowels in the following pairs were judged to be the same: set-sat, ball-bull, bet-bat. fit-fit was judged to be different.

  C. Psychosocial
    1. Began to learn English at 21 years of age
    2. Very motivated to improve English syntax and pronunciation
    3. Speaks Spanish primarily at home and with friends; speaks English only at work
    4. Tends to be depressed, unfocused, and anxious generally, and particularly tense when required to express himself in English

The Management Plan

The Long-Term Phase

Long-Term Goals.   As an L2 learner, José's functional communication will be enhanced by improvement in content/form interactions (i.e., vocabulary, written and oral syntax, figurative language) and phonological knowledge and performance. Baseline data (Box 11.7) indicate that José presents with numerous syntactic mismatches (in written and oral language), inappropriate word use, and difficulty in the comprehension and interpretation of figurative expressions. The phonological analysis reveals several interlanguage patterns affecting consonants, clusters, vowels, and prosody, all typical of an L1 Spanish speaker (see Contrastive Analysis Charts, Figures 11.1 and 11.2 and Box 11.7). In light of these baseline data the following long-term goals are planned for José. These goals appear in Box 11.8, Phase 1 of the Management Plan, Long-Term Goals.

The goals for José have been written with differentiated expectations. For example, goals 1 and 2, addressing phonological aspects, target reduction of given patterns, not elimination. This decision is made because of several factors operating against the prospect of long-term unaccented speech. Primary among these is the age at which José started to learn English—21 years of age. Research indicates that phonological learning after the age of 6 is generally marked by some accent (Flege, 1992; Long, 1990; Patkowski, 1994). Another deterrent of unaccented speech is the amount of time José spends speaking his L1. It has been shown that speakers who use their L2 the greater proportion of the time make more progress than those who use the L2 less (Flege et al., 1997). José also has a history of depression, inability to concentrate, and anxiety, which may impede his achievement of authentic pronunciation. Personality factors have also been shown to play a part in the acquistion of authentic L2 speech (Major, 1994). The achievement of content/form interactions expressed in new vocabulary and accurate syntax as well as figurative language may be achieved more completely than phonology (goals 3 and 4). José reports already making strides in vocabulary acquisition and the ability to express himself. In addition, the literature is less consistent with reference to as early a critical period as with phonology (e.g., Major, 1994).

It is anticipated that José will be a good candidate for treatment and will achieve our long-term goals in approximately three years. The client presents with several characteristics operating for linguistic improvement. He is highly motivated to improve (e.g., Leather & James, 1991); he voices serious concern about his inability to express himself in groups and when addressing a class. He is eager to improve his use of English as a means toward academic and professional achievement. In addition, he appears to be a committed, conscientious, intelligent student.

The Procedural Approach.   As outlined in Chapter 1, the procedural approach addresses the modification of maintaining factors and the use of principles from relevant theories of learning. As suggested in the baseline data presented above, José's accented speech may be maintained by both psychosocial and sensorimotor factors. While we cannot modify his late onset of L2, we can encourage him to increase the percentage of time L2 is currently used. As an adult L2 learner, José must learn to expand his categories of L2 sounds, especially vowels (e.g., Flege, 1995b) and learn new articulatory gestures (e.g.,

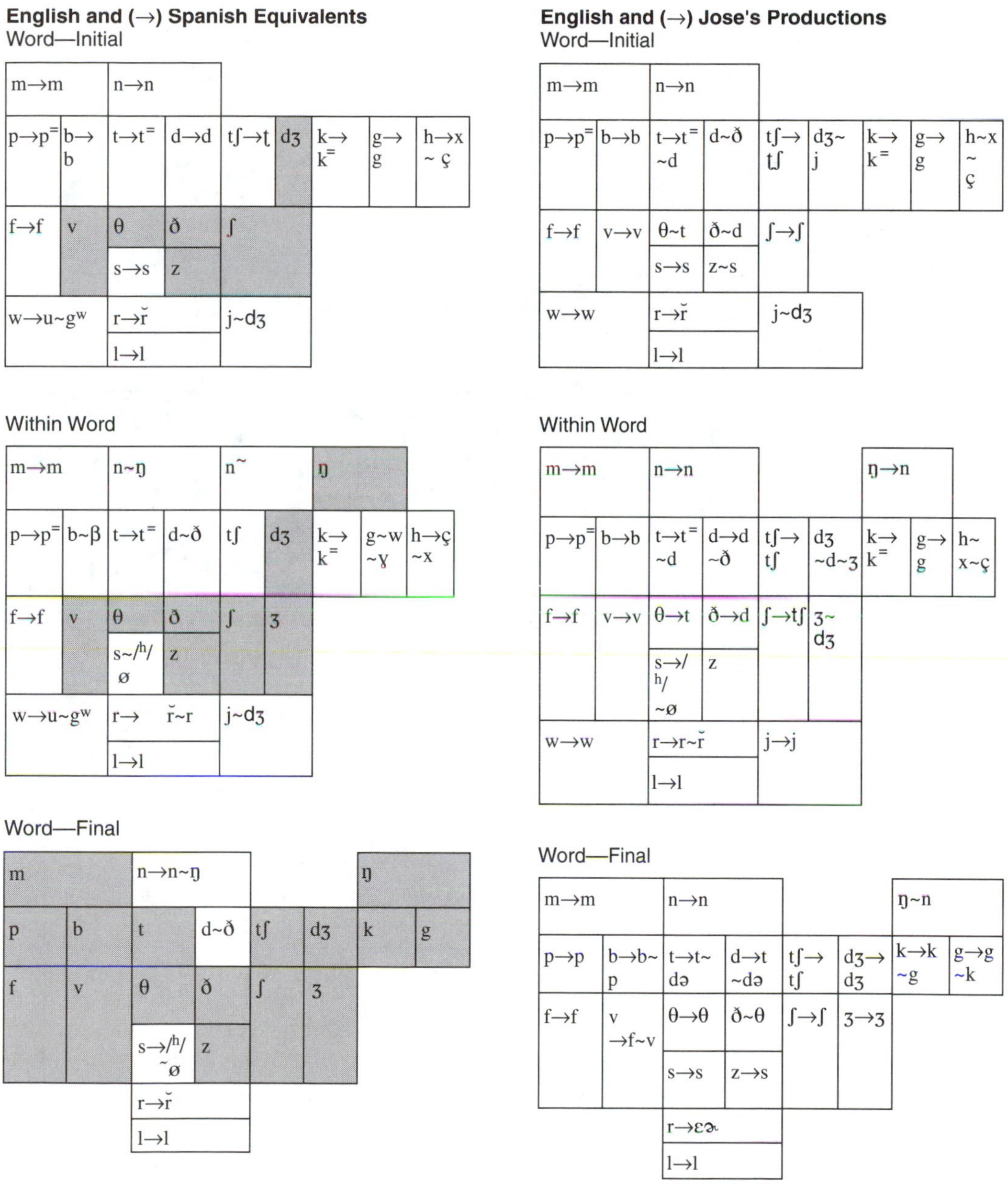

English and (→) Spanish Equivalents
Word—Initial

m→m	n→n					
p→p= b→b	t→t=	d→d	tʃ→t̪	dʒ	k→k=	g→g	h→x ~ ç
f→f	v	θ	ð	ʃ
		s→s	z	
w→u~gʷ	r→ř	j~dʒ
	l→l	

Within Word

m→m	n~ŋ	n̰		ŋ		
p→p= b~β	t→t=	d~ð	tʃ	dʒ	k→k=	g~w ~ɣ	h→ç ~x
f→f	v	θ	ð	ʃ	ʒ
		s~/ʰ/ ø	z	
w→u~gʷ	r→ ř~r	j~dʒ
	l→l	

Word—Final

m	n→n~ŋ			ŋ
p	b	t	d~ð	tʃ	dʒ	k	g
f	v	θ	ð	ʃ	ʒ
		s→/ʰ/ ~ø	z	
	r→ř	
	l→l	

English and (→) Jose's Productions
Word—Initial

m→m	n→n					
p→p= b→b	t→t= ~d	d~ð	tʃ→ tʃ	dʒ~ j	k→k=	g→g	h~x ~ç
f→f	v→v	θ~t	ð~d	ʃ→ʃ
		s→s	z~s	
w→w	r→ř	j~dʒ
	l→l	

Within Word

m→m	n→n			ŋ→n	
p→p= b→b	t→t= ~d	d→d ~ð	tʃ→ tʃ	dʒ	k→k=	g→g	h~ x~ç
f→f	v→v	θ→t	ð→d	ʃ→tʃ	ʒ~ dʒ
		s→/ ʰ/ ~ø	z	
w→w	r→r~ř	j→j
	l→l	

Word—Final

m→m	n→n			ŋ~n	
p→p	b→b~ p	t→t~ də	d→t ~də	tʃ→ tʃ	dʒ→ dʒ	k→k ~g	g→g ~k
f→f	v →f~v	θ→θ	ð~θ	ʃ→ʃ	ʒ→ʒ
		s→s	z→s	
	r→ɛɚ	
	l→l	

FIGURE 11.1 Contrastive analysis charts.
Note: darkened boxes indicate absence of sound;
(~) = alternates with; [ř] = trilled r; [r] = tap.

Vowel Sounds of English and Spanish

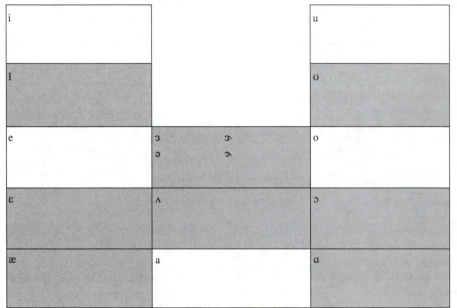

Note: dark boxes = sounds absent in Spanish

Jose's Productions

i→i		u→ʊ~ʌ
I→i~I		ʊ→u
e→e	ɜ ɝ→ɛɚ~ɔ ə ɚ→ʊɚ~ ɛɚ	o→a~ʌ
ɛ→ɛ~e	ʌ→a~o~u~ɔ~æ	ɔ→ɔɚ~o~a
æ→a~ɑ	a→a~æ~o	ɑ→a

FIGURE 11.2
Contrastive analysis of vowel sounds.
Note: (~) = alternates with

BOX **11.8**

Phase 1 of the Management Plan

The Long-Term Phase

Long-Term Goals and Expected Duration:
1. José will reduce the use of dialectal patterns affecting consonants, consonant clusters, and vowels in all pragmatic contexts.
2. José will reduce the tendency to stress unstressed syllables of multisyllabic words.
3. José will eliminate mismatches in syntax and word use in written and oral expression.
4. José will appropriately use a variety of figurative expressions.

All these goals should be achieved in approximately three years.

Rationales with Reference to:
> *Baseline data* (how current linguistic performance motivates goals):
> Dialectal patterns affect vowels, consonants, clusters, prosody, syntax, vocabulary, and figurative language.
>
> *Maintaining factors* (justification of long-term expectation): Psychosocial, sensorimotor
> Pattern reduced rather than eliminated because of:
> - late onset of L2;
> - more frequent use of L1;
> - must learn to discriminate and produce new sound categories.
>
> A three-year period appears reasonable because of his:
> - motivation;
> - intelligence;
> - acquisition level to this point;
> - upward academic and professional strivings;
> - differentiation among most sound pairs; is stimulable for most of his error sounds

Procedural Approach
> *Maintaining factors addressed:* sensorimotor, psychosocial

Guiding principles from learning theories:
Learning is facilitated by:
- the ability to discriminate stimuli associated with the target sound;
- tasks that are complex enough to pose developmental challenges;
- the execution of sensorimotor procedures to achieve tasks or solve problems;
- the act of reflecting, specifically on phonetic categories (involving awareness of allophonic variation and category boundaries);
- efforts to match models presented by clinician;
- peripheral (sensory) and central feedback from movement involved in the act of articulation.

Leather & James, 1991). A focus on modifying these maintaining factors is expected to facilitate the acquisition of authentic productions.

A procedural approach for José will be guided primarily by principles from each of the three theories presented in Box 11.3: constructivist-cognitive, social-cognitive, and motor. (The fourth theory, operant, guides in making incremental changes in goal complexity.) The principles from the three theories appear in Box 11.8, under procedural approach. The way these principles guide decision making about procedures of treatment will be discussed in the next section on short-term goal planning.

The Short-Term Phase

Short-Term Goals.   As suggested in Chapter 1, the short-term phase of intervention planning is one of making decisions about priorities. We must decide on which of the long-term goals to address and how to address each (i.e., what sequence of steps do we take to reach the long-term goal?). A set of priority goals has been added to the management plan as Phase 2 of the management plan in Box 11.9. Both phonology long-term goals 1 and 2 have been addressed. This is because segmental and prosodic features interact in the pronunciation of words (e.g., Major, 1977). Goals 1 and 2, however, involve several dialectal patterns that must also be prioritized, and have been, as represented in short-term goals 1–4. If this chapter covered all aspects of learning an L2, we would have also listed a short-term goal to address goal 3. It is often efficient and useful to target both phonology and syntactic goals during the same period of treatment (see Klein & Moses, 1999, for examples of such multicomponent targets). Goal 4 would not have been addressed at this time with the view that as vocabulary and syntax improved figurative language would be more accessible. Now we examine the derivation of the short-term goals.

The first decision made was to work on goals 1 and 2 simultaneously—the reduction of stress in polysyllabic words and the acquisition of specific segments. Because Spanish is a syllable-timed language, José gives substantial stress to each syllable. This results in full vowel nuclei rather than L2 expected schwa in certain syllable positions. The listener, therefore, perceives the schwa as being replaced by any number of other identifiable vowels (e.g., I, a, ɛ, ʌ). It appears necessary to work on word prosody early in the treatment process since it influences segment production (Major, 1987). Next, we considered which vowels, consonants, and clusters to target during this first period.

Making priority decisions within sound categories required several considerations. First, we wanted to address a pattern that affects a substantial number of phonemes rather than an individual substitution or phonetic difference (e.g., trilled /r/) affecting a single sound. Second, we wanted to recognize contrasts between L1 and L2. As we discussed above in the section on perception and production, L2 sounds that are most problematic for adult learners are those that are absent from the L1 repertoire but are close enough to L1 sounds not to trigger the spontaneous creation of a new category (see pp. 359–360, in this chapter). Our third consideration was that we would be guided by available universal patterns affecting vowels, consonants, and clusters. Short-term goals 2–4 were derived with reference to these considerations.

Goal 2 targets the elimination of the pattern of tensing of lax vowels. This pattern affects several vowels, most consistently the production of I and ʊ, which are differenti-

B O X **11.9**

Phase 2 of the Management Plan: The Short-Term Phase

Short-Term Goals	Long-Term Goals Addressed	Prioritization Source
Client will:		Univeral and markedness hierarchies
1. reduce unstressed syllables in polysyllabic words;	2	
2. eliminate the pattern of tensing lax vowels in words and phrases;	1	
3. eliminate the pattern of final consonant devoicing and epenthesis in words and phrases;	1	
4. eliminate the pattern of cluster reduction in final position of words.	1	

Procedural Contexts	Learning Principles	Maintaining Factors Addressed
Nonlinguistic context will involve:		Psychosocial; sensorimotor; cognitive
1. word lists, minimal pairs, dialogues, newspaper, and magazine articles that are interesting and challenging to client (i.e., about finance, economics, business, etc.);		
2. tape recorder and individual amplification system.		
Linguistic context		
The clinician will:		
1. present contrasting sounds for identification or judgment of same/difference;	SC1; O1	
2. model target sounds in words or phrases for imitation;	SC2,3; M	
3. help client to reflect on kinesthetic and auditory cues;	CC3; M	
4. desensitize client to situations perceived to be anxiety producing;	O2	
5. encourage client to engage in greater use of L2 and monitor this behavior.	SC3; M; CC3	

ated primarily on the basis of tense/lax. It also affects /ɛ/, /ʌ/, and /ɔ/, other lax vowels that engage in more variable substitutions. Although Spanish does not contain any of these vowels, each is close enough to a Spanish vowel to deter the development of a new category (i/I; u/ʌ/; e/ɛ; o/ʌ, ɔ); thus, targeting the tense lax distinction is supported by the number of sounds affected and by the improbabality of spontaneous improvement (Flege, 1992, 1995b).

Goal 3 targets the elimination of final devoicing and epenthesis. This goal is supported with reference to several different sources. First, a glance at the contrastive analysis charts in Figure 9.1, shows that Spanish has few final consonant sounds and no opportunity for voicing contrasts. Voicing contrasts, especially among final stops, are among the most marked universally (e.g., Eckman, 1977) and, therefore, predicted to be problematic for L2 learners. Adding to the difficulty is the subtle quality of the voicing feature as the only difference; a feature, as with subtle vowel differences, is not striking enough to signal the development of a new category. Final devoicing and epenthesis are generally alternative strategies to maintain a word-final consonant (Weinberger, 1994) and are therefore appropriate to target together. Other consonant mismatches affect fewer sounds and have received less attention in terms of universal patterns.

Goal 4 addresses the elimination of cluster reduction in the word-final position. As noted in baseline data, José presents with several mismatches in producing L2 final- and within-word clusters. A decision was made to target final clusters because we are also working with final consonants. These clusters involving final voiced consonants are expected to interact well with final singleton voicing. Final clusters also have a more predictable pattern than within-word clusters; most prominent were those ending in /t/ (lt, st, kst, nst) or /z/ (gz, dz).

The Delineated Procedural Context.   At this point in management planning for José we must make decisions about the nonlinguistic and linguistic contexts that will best facilitate the goals we have targeted. In planning the nonlinguistic context we need to consider the nature of goals targeted and the age, abilities, and interests of the client. Treatment procedures for L2 phonology learners closely resemble procedures of intervention for disordered L1 phonology (Schmidt, 1997). The client will need materials that are appropriate to and facilitative of the targets he is expected to produce, those that will maintain his interest, and those that he perceives as academically and professionally useful. Box 11.9 lists materials that are expected to facilitate attainment of target goals for José. This section also shows the learning theories that have been referenced in the decision-making process.

Next we turn to the *linguistic* context. Here, decisions are made about the role of the clinician in the treatment context and are guided by the principles from learning theories stated in the long-term goals section. The selected principles of learning direct the clinician to enhance José's phonological productions by presenting contrasting sounds for discrimination, modeling specific targets for imitation, and helping José reflect on his articulatory movements (see Box 11.3). These actions on the part of the clinician are also expected to reduce the sensorimotor maintaining factors identified at the long-term phase. In addition to, and perhaps compounding his phonological difficulties, are several psychosocial factors. The role of the clinician with reference to these factors appears in numbers 4 and 5 of the linguistic context (Box 11.9).

The Session Phase

Session Goals and Procedures.   We are now at the phase of intervention planning that is most visible. It is during the session with the client that we have the opportunity to apply what we planned during Phases 1 and 2 and observe the accomplishment of "an act of learning." As discussed in Chapter 1, this act of learning is both observable and measurable and is expected to be one step in a series of steps leading to the short-term goal.

Deciding on a Goal Approach Strategy.   At the final stage in intervention planning we bring to bare all our prior sources of information on the formulation of session goals and procedures. In planning goals at this point, therefore, we reference the client's baseline data, maintaining factors, our decisions about principles from learning theories, and information about performance demands relative to phonological change. Referencing these sources of information helps us decide on a goal approach strategy. This involves answering at least the following three questions: (1.) Do we wish to target all short-term goals within the first few sessions? (2.) Would it be more efficient to target certain goals before others? (3.) How do we approach the achievement of each short-term goal we target?

With reference to questions 1 and 2, we review the short-term goals we have selected for José (Box 11.9). These goals target vowels, final singleton consonants, clusters, and prosody. Of these four areas the two that are most directly related are final consonants and clusters. Recall that José has difficulty with the production of final voiced stops and clusters containing these stops. Some of this difficulty may be explained by the inability to terminate the articulatory gesture simultaneously with the cessation of voicing (since he does not have L1 experience with this feature). When voicing ceases before the articulatory gesture is completed a voiceless final consonant is produced; if voicing continues beyond the completion of the articulatory gestures, epenthesis of a schwa occurs. There is, however, another strategy for maintaining voice in a final stop consonant—the addition of a voiced continuant (as demonstrated for child language by Fey & Gandour, 1982). For José this would mean the production of final voiced stop followed by voiced fricatives (bz, dz, gz). It is reasonable to predict that the production of voiced final singletons would be facilitated by the introduction of final voiced clusters; thus, goal 4 should precede goal 3 by several sessions. Of the other goals, there are no obvious priority needs and they will be addressed in cycle fashion during the first short-term goal period (Hodson & Paden, 1991). The introduction of several separate deviation patterns within a contracted period (e.g., a semester) has been found to be efficient for the remediation of developmental phonological disorders; it is this interference with habitual patterns that generates greater reorganization of the individual's phonological system (Hodson & Paden, 1991). It is likely that the same rationale is appropriate for an adult who exhibits an interlanguage system, constituting several patterns that require reorganization.

Now we turn to question 3. Based on our decision making at earlier phases of intervention planning, we have already established some guidelines for approaching session planning across the various goals. First, we know that we must begin to modify these factors hypothesized to maintain José's accented speech. For José we have determined that these are sensorimotor and psychosocial. As an adult L2 learner, José can be expected to have difficulties with both the discrimination and the production of L2 speech sounds and prosody. In addition, the frequent use of his L1 and his anxiety about certain speaking situations adds a psychosocial deterrent to his progress with L2. These maintaining factors will be targeted now, at the session phase, by incorporating a discrimination or production task at each session. Attempts will also be made, when appropriate, to modify his use of L2 and his sensitivity to new speaking situations.

Session goals are also shaped by our knowledge of learning theories. At the second phase of intervention planning we selected principles from learning theories most suitable for this client (see Box 11.9). We now use these principles to guide us in the development of session procedures. For example, principle SC1 suggests that the clinician present items for discrimination, while principle SC2 suggests that the clinician model desired utterances. Finally, the approach to goal formulation is greatly influenced by our knowledge of the variables that contribute to increasing or decreasing demands on a client's performance. Earlier in this chapter we outlined several variables known to influence the performance of a phonological task; these appear in Box 11.4 and include intrinsic complexity of segments or sound classes, syllable position, phonetic environment, prosodic contour of word, perceptual support, and task formality. These variables will be addressed as a systematic means of modifying complexity and difficulty as a series of session goals is projected.

At this point we are prepared to plan the session goals that should lead to each short-term goal. It is generally not possible to plan ahead the full number of session goals for each short-term goal. We can never be sure how any client will react to our plans and how much progress he or she will make. Moreover, it is not necessary to plan for more than one goal at a time. With the information outlined above to guide us, we continue to modify our targets and procedures for reaching them as we monitor the client's performance. To illustrate the way the above sources of information contribute to (a) the formulation of session goals and (b) the modification of goals via an increase or decrease in task complexity and/or difficulty, two session goals will be formulated for each short-term goal: an early session goal and a late session goal. Each goal may be found in Box 11.10, Phase 3 of the Management Plan. The words italicized in each goal statement highlight the aspects of the goal that have been derived through a consideration of maintaining factors, learning principles, and performance demands. The derivations that are summarized beneath each goal and related procedure statement will now be discussed.

Short-term goal 1: *José will reduce unstressed syllables in polysyllabic words.* José demonstrates the lack of stress reduction in most polysyllabic words, especially with three or more syllables. Because José's L1 was a syllable-timed language, he has little experience with the various stress contours possible in English. It has been shown that English has eight primary stress (or intonation) patterns affecting words of two to four syllables (Sikorski, 1991). Thus, José must learn to differentiate and produce a range of stress contours in polysyllabic words. How to proceed within a series of sessions leading to the achievement of this goal requires, first, hypotheses about these variables contributing to gradations of difficulty and/or complexity with reference to learing L2 stress contours. One factor often associated with increased demands on performance is increased syllable number (Bernthal & Bankson, 1998; Bleile, 1995; Lowe, 1994). As syllable number increases from two to three and four, the number of alternative intonation patterns increases. Thus, greater complexity is present in the patterns possible for three- and four-syllable words. Since José will also be

B O X **11.10**

Phase 3 of the Management Plan

Session Goals and Procedures
Client: <u>José</u>   Clinician: _____
Supervisor: _____ Semester: _____

Short-Term Goal Addressed:
1. José will reduce unstressed syllables in polysyllabic words.

_____

_____

Early Session Goal: José will *produce trochaic* (strong-weak) and *iambic* (weak-strong) word patterns in *two-syllable* words *after the clinician's model* in *18/20* items from a *list* of *novel* words.

Session Procedure: Clinician will:
- provide a list of novel words with trochaic and iambic patterns;
- model correct stress pattern and request imitation;
- tape clinician and client productions;
- ask client to judge accuracy of his production as compared with model;
- encourage client to reflect on any cues differentiating stress levels.

Derivation: Maintaining factor(s) addressed: sensorimotor
                    Principles from learning theory referenced: (SC) 2, 3; (CC) 3; (M)
                    Performance demands controlled:

- Syllable number: two-syllable words before three-syllable words;
- Perceptual support: imitation before spontaneous;
- Stimulus novelty: novel words before words with established patterns;
- Formality of task: lists before less formal tasks.

Later Session Goal: José will *read words* from a prepared *list* of stress patterns, from *five* categories of randomly presented three-syllable word stress contours, with 80% accuracy, and then *categorize* these words according to their stress contours, with 80% accuracy.

Session Procedure: Clinician will:
- provide word list;
- tape client's productions;
- ask José to judge the accuracy of his productions;
- help José to reflect on characteristics of stress contours and points of discrepancy between model and inaccurate renditions.

Derivation: Maintaining factor(s) addressed: sensorimotor
                   Principles from learning theory referenced (SC) 3; (CC) 1, 3; (M)
                   Performance demands controlled:
                   Syllable number: three-syllable words before four-syllable words;

(continued)

BOX **11.10** Continued

Phase 3 of the Management Plan

Perceptual support: reading words before single-word spontaneous responses;
Formality of task: word lists before continuous speech.

Short-Term Goal Addressed:
2. José will eliminate the pattern of tensing lax vowels in words and phrases.

Early session goal: José will *identify* tense and lax vowels comprising the following pairs /i/, /I/ and /u/, /ʊ/ by *pointing* to the phonetic symbol representing each sound *after hearing the clinician's* productions of *monosyllabic words* containing these sounds with *80%* accuracy.

Session procedure: The clinician will:
■ provide lists of monosyllabic minimal pairs;
■ ask client to point to the symbol representing the vowel contained in each word heard;
■ encourage client to reflect on auditory and kinesthetic differences between model and error choices.

Derivation: Maintaining factors addressed: sensorimotor
Principles from learning theories: (SC) 1; (CC) 1, 3
Performance demands controlled:
Response mode: discrimination before production;
Response mode: identification before same/difference judgment;
Syllable number: monosyllabic before multisyllabic;
Familiarity with speaker: production by a familiar speaker before an unfamiliar speaker.

Later session goal: José will *formulate phrases* containing words with *contrasting minimal pairs* of tense/lax vowels (e.g., a bit of beets; look at Luke) with *90%* accuracy.

Session procedure: The clinician will:
■ provide José with minimal word pairs;
■ encourage him to formulate an original phrase;
■ tape his productions;
■ help him to reflect on the accuracy of his productions;
■ help him to reflect on the kinesthetic and auditory cues distinguishing the tense and lax differences.

Derivation: Maintaining factors addressed: sensorimotor
Principles from learning theories: (SC) 1; (CC) 1, 3 (M)
Performances demands controlled:
Perceptual support: spontaneous self-formulation after reading words;
Linguistic context: phrases with contrasting sounds after sounds established individually.

Short-term Goal Addressed:
3. José will eliminate the pattern of final consonant devoicing and epentheis in words and phrases.

Early session goal: José will produce *bilabial stops followed by low front vowels* after *model* with 80% accuracy.

Session procedure: Clinician will:
- provide client with a list of words such as tub, rob, cab;
- tape his productions;
- request a judgment of accuracy of match with L2 targets;
- help client reflect on cues differentiating voiced and voiceless sounds.

Derivation: Maintaining factors addressed: sensorimotor
Principles from learning theories: (SC) 2, 3; (CC) 3; M
Performance demands controlled:
Phonetic context: bilabial position;
Phonetic context: low front vowels;
Task formality: word lists before spontaneous productions.

Later session goal: José will *read short phrases* containing final voiced *stops followed* by a word beginning with a *vowel or a voiced consonant,* with 80% accuracy.

Session procedure: The clinician will:
- provide the phrases;
- tape client's responses;
- ask client to judge responses for target match;
- suggest modifications of productions.

Derivation: Maintaining factors addressed: sensorimotor
Principles from learning theories: (SC) 2, 3; (CC) 3; M
Performance demands controlled:
Phonetic context: followed by initial vowels and voiced consonants before voiceless and pause;
Linguistic context: phrases after single-word productions;
Perceptual: reading after clinician's model.

Short-Term Goal Addressed:
4. José will eliminate the pattern of cluster reduction in final position of words.

Early session goal: José will *read single words* with final clusters *constituting two consonants—stop + fricative* (e.g., eggs; words) with 80% accuracy.

Session procedure: Clinician will:
- prepare list of words with final stop + fricative;
- record client's productions;
- ask client to reflect on match with intended target;
- help client to modify inaccurate productions with attention to disparate features.

(continued)

BOX 11.10 **Continued**

Phase 3 of the Management Plan

Derivation: Maintaining factors addressed: sensorimotor
Principles from learning theories: (M); (CC) 3
Performance demands controlled:
Linguistic context: single words before continuous speech;
Perceptual support: reading before spontaneous speech;
Phonetic complexity: two-element clusters before three-element clusters;
Phonetic complexity: stop + fricative before two stops.

Later session goal: José will produce two- and three-element clusters in words while answering questions posed by his wife with 70% accuracy.

Session procedure: Clinician will:
- provide client with dialogues to use at home;
- encourage client to tape short interchanges with wife;
- help client reflect on accuracy of productions and strategies for modifying productions.

Derivation: Maintaining factors: sensorimotor; psychosocial
Principles from learning theories: (M); (CC) 1, 3; (O) 2
Performance demands controlled:
Phonetic context: three-element clusters after two-element clusters;
Linguistic context: short dialogues after single-word productions;
Perceptual support: spontaneous after modeled;
Interlocutors: extending range of interlocutors after practicing sounds with clinician.

---

introduced to new vowel and consonant targets during this phase of treatment, it is probably wise to start with only two-syllable words including the two basic patterns: trochaic (strong-weak) and iambic (weak-strong). Performance demands, therefore, may be increased by targeting an increase in syllable number and introducing other stress patterns. Other factors that are likely to promote gradations in performance demands are the linguistic and nonlinguistic contexts in which these words will be produced.

A nonlinear approach to phonological change suggests that new segmental and prosodic targets be targeted separately during early stages of treatment (e.g., Bernhardt & Stoel-Gammon, 1994). It is suggested that when a new prosodic structure is introduced the segmental content should be selected among established sounds. This approach suggests that performance demands would also be controlled by modifying the segmental content of two-syllable words by increasing the intrinsic complexity of segments or sound classes (with reference to José's L2 phoneme repertoire or universal specification patterns, e.g., Table 11.4). Perceptual support and task formality are two nonlinguistic areas that may be modified in increasing performance in the development of session goals leading to short-term goal 1. Articulatory treatment for adults or children prescribes the use of a clinician's model to facilitate the attainment of a target response. Imitation of a model is generally an expected step before spontaneous production (e.g., Bernthal & Bankson, 1998). Moving in the direction of reduced perceptual support, therefore, is a move in the direction of increased demand on performance. Task formality has also been shown to be related to accuracy of target achievement (e.g., Dickerson, 1987; Leather & James, 1991). The more formal tasks (i.e., word lists, minimal pairs) have been found to produce a greater proportion of L2 targets than less formal tasks (dialogue, conversation). These research findings suggest that short-term goals may be made more challenging by altering the formality of the task.

The two session goals directed to the achievement of short-term goal 1 appears in Box 11.10. Several items are italicized in the statement of the goal. These italicized items represent decisions that have been made based on a consideration of the sources of information discussed above. We will examine each of these items to understand the basis for their selection.

The word *produce* is italicized because the hypothesized maintaining factors suggest that José should have the opportunity to practice an act of discrimination or production at each session. José has already demonstrated that he can identify the difference between two contrastive two-syllable word stress patterns. Both *trochaic* and *iambic* word patterns have been differentiated receptively, and production of this contrast, as with segments in minimal pairs, may support the distinction. *After the clinician's model* is stipulated because this is an early goal and José has not yet produced structures of this type accurately. The choice of *18/20* items appears a reasonable basis for any advance to more difficult prosodic contours. *List* and *novel* are highlighted because it has been shown that L2 speakers are more likely to achieve the L2 target in words that are not known (for which they have no preexisting representations) and in more formal tasks.

The clinician uses principles from social-cognitive theory by modeling and comparing the client's productions with model; motor theory, by requesting imitation; and constructivist cognitive, by helping the client reflect on his productions. A later session goal is derived by modifying syllable number and the nature of perceptual support (written material rather than a clinician's model) and by adding the cognitive task of categorization. Principles from learning theories and maintaining factors remain essentially the same.

Short-term goal 2. *José will eliminate the pattern of tensing lax vowels in words and phrases.* It has been shown in Box 9.7 that a tense-lax distinction affects primarily the high front and high back vowels. The substitution pattern for these vowel pairs is consistent and related primarily to the absence of lax vowels in Spanish (see Figure 10.2). Thus, it is necessary for José to learn to receptively differentiate these vowels before he can produce them accurately. Consequently, *identification*, rather than production, becomes the target of the early goal. Identification was also the choice over an alternative approach, "same-different." This is because the literature has shown that some clients make greater progress with the identification approach (Logan et al., 1991; Lively et al., 1994) and actually prefer it (Flege, 1995a). *Pointing* is italicized to make the act of learning observable and measurable to the clinician. *After hearing the clinician's productions* incorporates the use of a familiar model before an unfamiliar model. It has been shown that listening to various models in the process of phoneme identification facilitates learning distinctions (Lively et al., 1994). As pointed out in the derivation of the first session goal, syllable number is viewed as an important variable contributing to performance demands. To minimize task difficulty we select *monosyllabic words.* Again, *80%* accuracy gives us minimal assurance that we can proceed with additional goal complexity. The sensorimotor maintaining factor is addressed in act of discrimination, which requires modification. Finally, referencing principles SC#1, SC#1, from social-cognitive theory by providing José with the opportunity to compare speech sounds, and from principle CC#3 constructivist-cognitive theory by requiring José to reflect on auditory and kinesthetic differences.

The later session goal listed in Box 11.10 illustrates a goal occurring later in the sequence with the expected additional complexity. At this time José is asked to *formulate phrases.* This task has the added complexity of an expressive response, the inclusion of both vowels in the same phrase, and the spontaneous nature of the expression. As this goal is closer to the end of the first short-term period, a 90% accuracy criterion is reasonable. With this session goal we attempt to modify the motor aspect of the sensorimotor maintaining factor by practicing the production of the /ɪ/ and /ʊ/ phonemes in a phrase context. In addition to the learning principles applied for the early goal we add the principle from motor-learning theory.

Short-term goal 3. *José will eliminate the pattern of final consonant devoicing and epenthesis in words and phrases.* To choose an early target for this short-term goal we referenced a hierarchy based on Yavas' (1994) research. This research indicated that consonant placement and prior vowel contributed to an L2 speaker's ability to produce final stop consonants. Among these combinations, bilabial position with low vowel appeared to be most facilitative of final voiced consonant. For this reason the *production* of *bilabial stops* preceded by *low vowels* (e.g., tub, rob, cab) were selected to be an early session goal. Later goals will follow the remainder of this hierarchy (see p. 379 in this chapter). As was noted before, when a new sound is introduced it is generally *modeled* by the clinician for the client to imitate. Maintaining factors addressed are sensorimotor, by focusing on production of words. The clinician's actions are guided by principles from social-cognitive theory, prescribing modeling, and constructivist-cognitive, requiring reflection on behavior.

A later session goal directed to the achievement of short-term goal 3 increases performance demands in several ways. Now, José will be asked to *read short phrases* containing final voiced *stops.* These italicized elements indicate that José will be using the printed material as perceptual support rather than the clinician's model. The linguistic context will also be more of a challenge in progressing form single words to phrases. All voiced stops /b/, /d/, and /g/ will now be included. The construction of the phrases will be controlled with reference to the words following the stop. In this session, the point at which phrases are introduced, the words following the stop, will be words beginning with a *vowel or a voiced consonant.* This selection is based on Edge's (1991) hierarchy of phonetic contexts for facilitating production of final voiced stops. Performance demands will be increased in future sessions by introducing contexts that are more challenging for the production of a final voiced stop: a voiceless consonant and a pause. There is no change in the maintaining factors or principles from learning addressed.

Short-term goal 4. *José will eliminate the pattern of cluster reduction in final position of words.* As an early goal José will be expected to *read* rather than spontaneously produce words. *Single words* are typically first in the hierarchy of linguistic contexts for generalization. The reading of words is also found to be among the most formal contexts, associated with greater accuracy. Final clusters *constituting two consonants—stop + frica-*

tive—(e.g., eggs, words) are described as universally less marked than three-consonant cluster combinations; thus, they are the basis of one approach to the achievement of clusters. (Some researchers advocate starting with more marked targets early in treatment, e.g., Eckman, 1977). Last, stop + fricative are considered to be less marked than two stop clusters (Greenberg, 1965) and follow the approach of less marked first in treatment. (Even less marked is fricative stop cluster (/st/) or sonorant + stop clusters (lt), but stop + fricative combinations were also chosen to facilitate the production of final voiced stops, as explained on p. 377). Sensorimotor factors are targeted in the *production* of words. Principles from motor theory and cognitive-constructivist theory are followed.

In a later goal directed toward the achievement of goal 4, José is expected to *produce two-* and *three-element clusters* in *phrases* while answering questions posed by *his wife,* with *70%* accuracy. This goal illustrates the way performance demands have increased. We have progressed from two- to three-element clusters, from words to phrases, and from perceptual support in the form of reading material to spontaneous productions. In addition, the interlocutor has changed. The construction of this goal makes attempts to address the psychosocial maintaining factor in addition to the sensorimotor by incorporating the client's wife. She represents a novel English conversational partner since they usually speak Spanish at home. Principles from learning theories include that guide the clinician in having the client produce phrases and helping the client reflect on his productions.

For this later session goal, as well as for the other examples of later goals, all of the modifications in complexity do not necessarily occur at once. That is, the modifications illustrated between the first and second goal examples may, in reality, occur over several intervening sessions.

Summary

This chapter presented an approach to intervention with individuals learning the phonology of an L2. The approach followed the basic tenets of intervention planning for speech-language disorders. This is because in planning goals and procedures to facilitate the acquisition of L2 phonology, consideration must be given to the same categories of information as with disorder types. In preparing for treatment with an L2 client one must consider (a) the nature of the problem, (b) factors maintaining the problem, (c) theories of learning new sounds, and (d) the factors that contribute to increased demand on performance. It is knowledge of these categories of information relative to each client that makes goal and procedure planning a systematic and accountable endeavor.

REFERENCES

Adamson, H. D. & Regan, V. (1991). The acquisition of community speech norms by Asian immigrants. *Studies in Second Language Acquisition, 13,* 1–22.

American Speech-Language Hearing Association. (1983). Position paper: Social dialects and implications of the position of social dialects. *ASHA, 25,* 23–27.

American Speech-Language Hearing Association (1996). Scope of practice in speech-language pathology. *ASHA, 38* (Suppl. 16).

Bailey, K. M., & Savage, L. (1994). *New ways in teaching speaking.* Alexandria, VA: TESOL.

Beebe, L. M. (1977). The influence of the listener on code-switching. *Language Learning, 27,* 332–339.

Bernhard, B., & Stoel-Gammon, C. (1994). Nonlinear phonology: Introduction and clinical application. *Journal Speech and Hearing Research, 37,* 123–143.

Bernthal, J. E. & Bankson, N. W. (1998). *Articulation and phonological disorders* (4th ed.). Englewood Cliffs, NJ: Prentice-Hall.

Bialystok, E. (1978). A theoretical model of second language learning. *Language Learning, 28,* 69–84.

Bleile, K. M. (1995). *Manual of articulation and phonological disorders.* San Diego, CA: Singular.

Cairns, H. S., Cairns, C. E., & Williams, F. (1974). Some theoretical considerations of articulation substitution phenomena. *Language and Speech, 17,* 160–173.

Carlisle, R. S. (1988). The effect of markedness on epenthesis in Spanish/English interlanguage phonology and syntax. *Issues and Developments in English and Applied Linguistics, 3,* 15–23.

Carlisle, R. S. (1991). The influence of environment on vowel epenthesis in Spanish/English interphonology. *Applied Linguistics, 12,* 76–95.

Carlisle, R. S. (1994). Markedness and environment as internal constraints on the variability of interlanguage phonology. In M. Yavas (Ed.), *First and second language acquisition* (pp. 233–249). San Diego, CA: Singular.

Catford, J. C. (1987). Phonetics and the teaching of pronunciation: A systemic description of English phonology. In J. Morley (Ed.), *Current perspectives on pronunciation* (pp. 83–100). Washington, DC: TESOL.

Celce-Muria, M. (1987). Teaching pronunciation as communication. In J. Morley (Ed.), *Current perspectives on pronunciation* (pp. 1–12). Washington, DC: TESOL.

Chomsky, N., & Halle, M. (1968). *The sound pattern of English.* New York: Harper & Row.

Chrystal, D. (1991). A dictionary of linguistics and phonetics (3rd. ed.). Cambridge, MA: Blackwell Publishers.

Compton, A. J. (1983). *Compton phonological assessment of foreign accent.* San Francisco, CA: Carousel House.

Dickerson, L. J. (1975). Learning interlanguage as a system of variable rules. *TESOL Quarterly, 9,* 401–407.

Dickerson, W. (1987). Explicit rules & the developing interlanguage phonology. In A. James & J. Leather (Eds.), *Sound patterns in second language acquisition.* (pp. 121–140). Dordrecht: Foris.

Dinnsen, D. A., Chin, S., Elbert, M., & Powell, T. (1990). Some constraints on functionally disordered phonologies: Phonetic inventories and phonotactics. *Journal of Speech and Hearing Research, 33,* 28–37.

Dinnsen, D. A. & Eckman, F. R. (1978). Some substantive universals in atomic phonology. *Lingua, 45,* 1–14.

Eckman, F. R. (1977). Markedness and the contrastive analyses hypotheses. *Language Learning, 27,* 315–330.

Eckman, F. R. (1981). On predicting difficulty in second language acquisition. *Studies in Second Language Acquisition, 4,* 18–30.

Eckman, F. R. (1985). Some theoretical and pedagogical implications of the markedness differential hypothesis. *Studies in Second Language Acquisition, 7,* 289–307.

Eckman, F. R. (1987). The reduction of word-final consonants in interlanguage. In A. James & J. Leather (Eds.), *Sound patterns in second language acquisition* (pp. 143–162). Dordrecht: Foris.

Eckman, F. R. (1991). The structural conformity hypothesis and the acquisition of consonant clusters in the interlanguage of ESL learners. *Studies in Second Language Acquisition, 13,* 23–41.

Eckman, F. R., & Iverson, G. K. (1994). Pronunciation difficulties in ESL: Coda consonants in English interlanguge. In M. Yavas (Ed.), *First and second language acquisition* (pp. 251–265). San Diego, CA: Singular.

Edge, B. A. (1991). The production of word-final obstruents in English by L1 speakers of Japanese and Cantonese. *Studies in Second Language Acquisition, 13,* 377–393.

Edwards, M. (1992). In support of phonological process. *Language, Speech and Hearing Services in Schools, 23,* 233–240.

Edwards, M. L., & Shriberg, L. D. (1983). Phonology: Applications in communicative disorders. San Diego, CA: College-Hill.

Elbert, M., & Gierut, J. (1986). *Handbook of clinical phonology: Approaches to assessment and treatment.* San Diego CA: College-Hill Press.

Ellis, R. (1994). *The study of second language acquisition.* New York: Oxford University Press.

Ferguson, C. A. (1968). Contrastive analysis and language development. In C. A. Ferguson (Ed.), *Language structure and language use* (pp. 233–248). Stanford, CA: Stanford University Press.

Fey, M. E. (1992). Clinical forum: Phonological assessment and treatment: Articulation and phonology: Inextricable constructs in speech pathology. *Language Speech and Hearing Services in Schools, 23,* 225–232.

Fey, M. E., & Gandour, J. (1982). Rule discovery in phonological acquisition. *Journal of Child Language, 9,* 70–82.

Fisher, H. B., & Logemann, J. A. (1971). The Fisher-Logemann Test of Articulation Competence. Chicago: Riverside Publishing Company.

Flege, J. E. (1987). Effects of equivalence classification on the production of foreign language speech sounds. In A. James & J. Leather (Eds.), *Sound patterns in second language acquisition* (pp. 9–39). Providence: Foris.

Flege, J. E. (1988). The production and perception of speech-sounds in foreign languages. In H. Winitz (Ed.). *Human communication and its disorders,* A review 1988. Norward, NJ: Albex.

Flege, J. E. (1989). Differences in inventory size affect the location but not the precision of tongue positioning in vowel production. *Language & Speech, 32,* 123–147.

Flege, J. E. (1991). Age of learning affects the authenticity of voice-onset tine (VOT) in stop consonants produced in a second language. *Journal of Acoustic Society of America, 89,* 395–411.

Flege, J. E. (1992). Speech learning in a second language. In C. H. Ferguson, L. Menn, & C. Stoel-Gammon (Eds.), *Phonological development, models, research, implications* (pp. 506–604). Timonium, MD: York Press.

Flege, J. E. (1995a). Two procedures for training a second language phonetic context. *Applied Psycholinguistics, 16,* 425–442.

Flege, J. E. (1995b). Second language speech learning theory, findings, and problems. In W. Strange (Ed.), *Speech perception and linguistic experience* (pp. 233–277). Timonium, MD: York Press.

Flege, J. E. (in press). Assessing non-native perception of English vowels: A categorical discrimination test. *Applied Linguistics.*

Flege, J. E., Frieda, E. M., & Nozawa, T. (1997). Amount of native language (L1) use affects the pronunciations of an L2. *Journal of Phonetics, 25,* 169–186.

Flege, J. E., & Munro, M. J. (1994). The word unit in L2 speech production and perception. *Studies in Second Language Acquisition, 16,* 381–411.

Fledge, J. E., Munro, M. J., & MacKay, I. (1995). Factors affecting degree of perceived foreign accent in a second langue. *Journal of the Acoustical Society of America, 97,* 3623–3641.

Flege, J. E., Munro, M. J., & Skelton, L. (1992). Production of word-final English /t/-/d/ contrast by native speakers of English, Mandarin, and Spanish. *Journal of Acoustic Society of America, 92,* 128–143.

Flege, J. E., Schmidt, A. M., & Wharton, G. W. (1996). Age of learning affects rate-dependent processing of stops in second language. *Phonetica, 53,* 143–161.

Flege, J. E., Takagi, N., & Mann, V. (1995). Japanese adults can learn to produce English /r/ and /l/ accurately. *Language & Speech, 38,* 25–55.

Gierut, J. A., Morrisette, M. L., Hughes, M. T., & Rowland, S. (1996). Phonological treatment efficacy and developmental norms. *Language Speech and Hearing Services in Schools, 27,* 215–230.

Greenberg, J. H. (1965). Some generalizations concerning initial and final consonant clusters. *Linguistics, 18,* 5–34.

Hammerberg, B. (1990). Conditions on transfer in phonology. In Leather, J. & James, A. (Eds.), *New Sounds 90.* (pp. 198–215). Amsterdam: University of Amsterdam.

Hodson, B. W., & Paden, E. P. (1991). *Targeting intelligible speech* (2nd ed.). Austin, TX: Pro-ed.

Ingram, D. (1981). Procedures for the phonological analysis of children's language. Baltimore: University Park Press.

Karmiloff-Smith, A. (1986). From meta-processes to conscious access: Evidence from children's met-alinguistic and repair data. *Cognition, 23,* 95–147. Norwood, NJ: Ablex.

Kent, R. D. (1982). Contextual facilitation of correct sound production. *Language Speech and Hearing Services in Schools, 13,* 66–76.

Klein, H. B. (1978). *The relationship between perceptual strategies and productive strategies in learning the phonology of early lexical items.* Unpublished doctoral dissertation, Columbia University.

Klein, H. B. (1981). Productive strategies for the pronunciation of early polysyllabic lexical items. *Journal of Speech and Hearing Research, 24,* 389–405.

Klein, H. B. (1984). A procedure for maximizing phonological information from single-word responses. *Language, Speech, and Hearing Services in Schools, 15,* 267–274.

Klein, H. B., Lederer, S. H., & Cortese, E. E. (1991). Children's knowledge of auditory/articulatory correspondences: Phonologic and metaphonologic. *Journal of Speech and Hearing Research, 34,* 559–564.

Klein, H. B., & Moses, N. (1999). *Intervention planning for children with communication disorders.* (2nd Ed.). Boston: Allyn & Bacon.

Krashen, S. (1981). *Second language acquisition and second language learning.* Oxford: Pergamon.

Leather, J. (1990). Perceptual and productive learning of Chinese lexical tone by Dutch and English speakers. In J. Leather & A. James (Eds.), *New Sounds, 90,* 72–97.

Leather, J., & James, A. (1991). The acquisition of second language speech. *Studies in Second Language Acquisition, 13,* 305–341.

Lenneberg, E. H. (1967). *Biological foundations of language.* New York: Wiley.

Lively, S. E., & Pisone, D. B. (1994). Training Japanese listeners to identify English /r/ and /l/ III. Long-term retention of new phonetic categories. *Journal of the Acoustical Society of America, 96,* 2076–2087.

Lively, S. E., Pisoni, D. B., Yamada, R. A., Tohikura, Y., & Yamada, T. (1994). Training Japanese listeners to identify English /r/, and /l/: Long-term retention of new phonetic categories. *Journal of the Acoustical Society of America, 96,* 2076–2087.

Locke, J. L. (1980). The inference of speech perception in the phonologically disordered child, Part II: Some clinically novel procedures, their use, some findings. *Journal of Speech and Hearing Disorders. 4,* 445–468.

Logan, J. S., Lively, S., & Pisoni, D. B. (1991). Training Japanese listeners to identify English /r/ and /l/: A first report. *Journal of the Acoustical Society of America, 89,* 874–883.

Long, M. H. (1990). Maturational constraints and language development. *Studies in Second Language Acquisition, 16,* 251–285.

Lowe, R. J. (1994). *Phonology.* Baltimore, MD: Williams & Wilkins.

Major, R. C. (1986). The ontogeny model: Evidence from L2 acquisition of Spanish. *Language Learning, 36,* 453–504.

Major, R. C. (1987). The natural phonology of second language acquisition. In A. James & J. Leather (Eds.), *Sound patterns in second language acquisition* (pp. 207–224). Providence: Foris.

Major, R. C. (1990). L2 acquisition, L1 loss, and the critical period hypothesis. In J. Leather and A. James (Eds.), *New sounds 90 (pp. 14–25).* Amsterdam: University of Amsterdam.

Major, R. C. (1994). Current trends in interlanguage phonology. In M. Yavas (Ed.), *First and second language acquisition (pp. 181–204).* San Diego, CA: Singular.

Maxwell, E. M. (1984). On determining underlying phonological representations of children: A critique of the current theories. In M. Elbert, D. A. Dinnsen, & G. Weismer (Eds.), *Phonological theory and the misarticulating child* (ASHA Monograph No. 22). Rockville, MD: American Speech-Language-Hearing Association.

McReynolds, L. V., Engmann, D., & Dimmitt, K. (1974). Markedness theory and articulation errors. *Journal of Speech and Hearing Disorders, 39,* 93–103.

Morley, J. (1987). *Current perspectives on pronunciation.* Washington, DC: TESOL.

Morley, J. (Ed.). (1994). *Pronunciation pedagogy and theory.* Alexandria, VA: TESOL.

Nathan, G. (1990). On the non-acquisition of an English sound system. In J. Leather and A. James (Eds.), *New sounds 90* (pp. 294–299). Amsterdam: University of Amsterdam.

Nesdale, A. R., Herriman, M. L., & Tunmer, W. E. (1984). Phonological awareness in children. In W. E. Tunmer, C. Pratt, & M. L. Herriman (Eds.), *Metalinguistic awareness in children* (pp. 56–72). New York: Springer-Verlag.

Neufeld, G. G. (1980). On the adult's ability to acquire phonology. *TESOL Quarterly, 14,* 285–298.

Patkowski, M. S. (1994). The critical age hypothesis and interlanguage phonology. In M. Yavas (Ed.), *First and second language acquisition* (pp. 204–221). San Diego, CA: Singular.

Powell, T. W. (1991). Planning for phonological generalization. An approach to treatment target selection. *American Journal Speech Language Pathology, 1,* 21–27.

Prather, E., Hedrick, D., & Kern, C. (1975). Articulation development in children ages two to four years. *Journal of Speech and Hearing Research, 40,* 179–191.

Price, P. J. (1981). *A cross linguistic study of flaps in Japanese and American English.* Unpublished doctoral dissertation, University of Pennsylvania.

Raubicheck, L. (1952). *Speech improvement* (pp. 103–131). Englewood Cliffs, NJ: Prentice-Hall.

Sander, E. (1972). When are speech sounds learned? *Journal of Speech and Hearing Disorders, 37,* 55–63.

Schane, H. (1973). *Generative phonology.* Englewood Cliffs, NJ: Prentice-Hall.

Schmidt, A. M. (1997). Working with adult foreign accent: Strategies for intervention. *Contemporary Issues in Communication Science and Disorders, 24,* 53–62.

Schmidt, A. M., & Flege, J. E. (1996). Speaking rate effects and stops produced by Spanish & English monolinguals and Spanish/English bilinguals. *Phonetica, 53,* 162–179.

Selinker, L. (1969). Language transfer. *General Linguistics, 9,* 67–92.

Selinker, L. (1992). *Interlanguage.* New York: Longman.

Shriberg, L., & Kwiatkowski, J. (1982). Phonological disorders II: A conceptual framework for management. *Journal of Speech and Hearing Disorders, 47,* 256–270.

Sikorski, L. D. (1991). *Mastering effective English communication.* (2nd. Ed.). Santa Ana, CA: LDS.

Sloat, C., Taylor, S. H., & Hoard, J. (1978). *Introduction to phonology.* Englewood Cliffs, NJ: Prentice-Hall.

Stampe, D. (1969). *The acquisition of phonetic representation.* Paper presented at the fifth regional meeting of the Chicago Linguistic Society, Chicago, IL.

St. Louis, K. O., & Ruscello, D. M., (1987). Oral Speech Mechanism Screening Examination-Revised. Austin, TX: Pro-Ed.

Stoel-Gammon, C. & Dunn, C. (1985). *Normal and disordered phonology in children.* Baltimore: University Park Press.

Temperley, M. S. (1987). Linking and deletion of final consonant clusters. In J. Morley (Ed.), *Current perspectives on pronunciation* (pp. 59–82). Washington, DC: TESOL.

Templin, M. (1957). *Certain language skills in children: Their development and interrelationships.* (Institute of Child Welfare Monograph 26). Minneapolis: The University of Minnesota Press.

Toombs, M., Singh, S., & Hayden, M. (1981). Markedness of features in the articulatory substitutions of children. *Journal of Speech and Hearing Disorders. 46,* 184–191.

Weinberger, S. H. (1994). Functional and phonetic constraints on second language phonology. In M. Yavas (Ed.), *First and second language phonology* (283–302). San Diego, CA: Singular.

Wiig, E. H., & Secord, W. (1989). Test of Language Competence-Expanded Edition. San Antonio: Psychological Corporation, Harcourt-Brace Jovanovich, Inc.

Wode, H. (1994). L1 and L2 phonology: Looking ahead. In M. Yavas (Ed.), *First and second language phonology* (pp. 175–179), San Diego, CA: Singular.

Wong, R. (1987). Learner variables and prepronunciation considerations in teaching pronunciation. In J. Morley (Ed.), *Current perspectives on pronunciation* (pp. 13–28). Washington, DC: TESOL.

Yavas, M. (1994). Final stop devoicing in interlanguage. In M. Yavas (Ed.), *First and second language phonology* (pp. 267–282). San Diego, CA: Singular.

INDEX